Norway

Graeme Cornwallis
Andrew Bender
Deanna Swaney

D0961718

LONELY PLANET PUBLICATIONS
Melbourne • Oakland • London • Paris

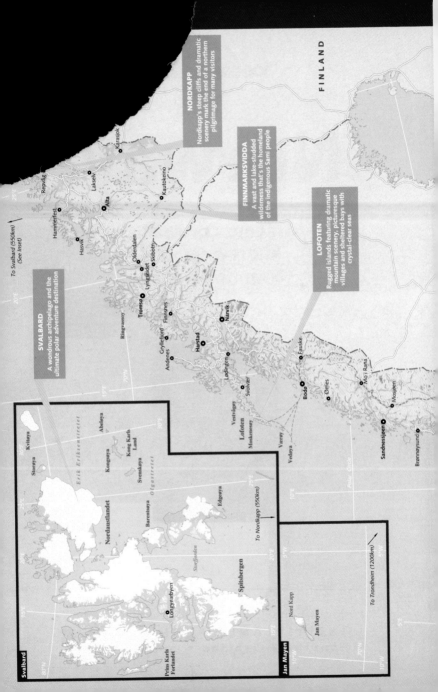

SVALBARD
A wondrous archipelago and the ultimate polar adventure destination

NORDKAPP
Nordkapp's steep cliffs and dramatic scenery mark the end of a northern pilgrimage for many visitors

FINNMARKSVIDDA
A vast and lake-studded wilderness that's the homeland of the indigenous Sami people

LOFOTEN
Rugged islands featuring dramatic mountain scenery, picturesque villages and sheltered bays with crystal-clear seas

FINLAND

To Svalbard (550km)
(See inset)

Repvåg
Karasjok
Hammerfest
Lakselv
Hasvik
Alta
Olderdalen
Skibotn
Lyngseidet
Tromsø
Finnsnes
Ringvassøy
Gryllefjord
Andenes
Harstad
Narvik
Lødingen
Vesterålen
Svolvær
Lofoten
Fauske
Moskenesøy
Værøy
Bodø
Ofnes
Værdøy
Moi Rana
Mosjøen
Brønnøysund
Sandnessjøen

Arctic Circle

To Nordkapp (550km)

To Trondheim (1200km)

Svalbard

Kvitøya
Storøya
Abeløya
Erik Eriksenstretet
Kongsøya
Kong Karls Land
Svenskøya
Olgastretet
Nordaustlandet
Barentsøya
Edgeøya
Storfjorden
Prins Karls Forlandet
Spitsbergen
Longyearbyen

Jan Mayen

Nord Kapp
Jan Mayen

NORWAY

ELEVATION

1800 m
1500 m
1200 m
900 m
600 m
300 m
0

100km
60mi
0 30
0 50

SWEDEN

RØROS
A unique old copper-mining town – so well preserved it's now listed as a Unesco World Heritage Site

JOTUNHEIMEN NATIONAL PARK
Norway's most popular national park with wonderful hiking possibilities

BERGEN
The gateway to the fjords and Norway's best loved and most visited town, full of colour, culture and history

OSLO-BERGEN RAILWAY
One of the world's most spectacular train journeys, with 470km of fabulous scenery including mountains, glaciers, lakes and rivers

STOCKHOLM

OSLO
Parks, museums, restaurants and all the attractions of a capital city but with ready access to the great outdoors

SOUTH COAST
A favourite with boaters and holiday-makers for its islands, bays and coves plus lovely seaside villages

Gulf of Bothnia

Baltic Sea

Norwegian Sea

To Jan Mayen (1200km) (See Inset)

WESTERN FJORDS
Breathtaking coastal scenery whether viewed from the water or from land

Rørvik
Namsos
Grong
Steinkjer
Verdalsøra
Levanger
Trondheim
Orkanger
Stjørdal
Heimdal
Røros
Tynset
Koppang
Rena
Elverum
Trysil
Kongsvinger
Hamar
Lillehammer
Gjøvik
Moelv
Røros
Dombås
(Glittertind 2465m)
Øvre Årdal
Sogndal
Gol
Geilo
Rjukan
Notodden
Kongsberg
Drammen
Ski
Mysen
Sarpsborg
Halden
Fredrikstad
Moss
Horten
Tønsberg
Sandefjord
Larvik
OSLO
Hønefoss
Nesbyen
Råholt
Lillestrøm
Hokksund
Skien
Porsgrunn
Kragerø
Risør
Arendal
Grimstad
Kristiansand
Lillesand
Mandal
Vennesla
Evje
Lyngdal
Flekkefjord
Egersund
Bryne
Sandnes
Stavanger
Jørpeland
Sauda
Odda
Voss
Bergen
Førde
Florø
Måløy
Lågvik
Haugesund
Kopervik
Skudeneshavn
Kristiansund
Molde
Åndalsnes
Sunndalsøra
Spjelkavik
Ålesund
Ørsta
Volda
Stranda

Skagerrak

North Sea

SWEDEN

Norway
2nd edition – May 2002
First published – August 1999

Published by
Lonely Planet Publications Pty Ltd ABN 36 005 607 983
90 Maribyrnong St, Footscray, Victoria 3011, Australia

Lonely Planet offices
Australia Locked Bag 1, Footscray, Victoria 3011
USA 150 Linden St, Oakland, CA 94607
UK 10a Spring Place, London NW5 3BH
France 1 rue du Dahomey, 75011 Paris

Photographs
Many of the images in this guide are available for licensing from
Lonely Planet Images.
email: lpi@lonelyplanet.com.au
Web site: www.lonelyplanetimages.com

Front cover photograph
Icy signpost near Narvik, Nordland (Christian Aslund)

ISBN 1 74059 200 X

text & maps © Lonely Planet Publications Pty Ltd 2002
photos © photographers as indicated 2002

Printed by The Bookmaker International Ltd
Printed in China

All rights reserved. No part of this publication may be reproduced, stored in a retrieval system or transmitted in any form by any means, electronic, mechanical, photocopying, recording or otherwise, except brief extracts for the purpose of review, without the written permission of the publisher.

Lonely Planet, the Lonely Planet logo, Lonely Planet Images, CitySync and eKno are trade marks of Lonely Planet Publications Pty Ltd. Other trade marks are the property of their respective owners.

Although the authors and Lonely Planet try to make the information as accurate as possible, we accept no responsibility for any loss, injury or inconvenience sustained by anyone using this book.

Contents – Text

1

NORDLAND 323

THE FAR NORTH 369

SVALBARD & JAN MAYEN 406

LANGUAGE 423

GLOSSARY 427

INDEX 442

METRIC CONVERSION inside back page

Contents – Maps

SVALBARD & JAN MAYEN

MAP LEGEND   back page

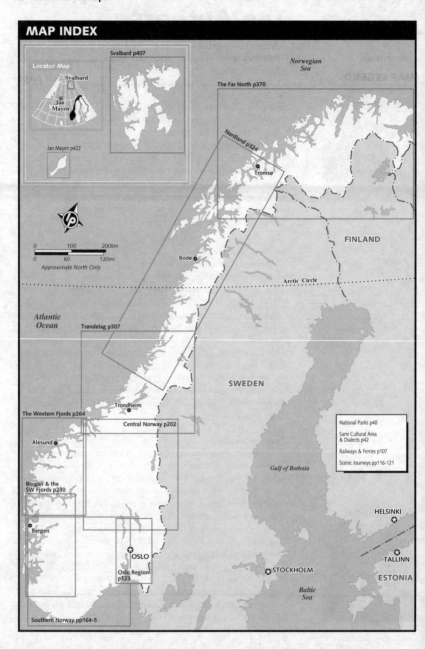

MAP INDEX

Svalbard

Jan Mayen

Norwegian Sea

Tromsø

FINLAND

Bodø

Arctic Circle

Atlantic Ocean

0   100   200km
0   60   120mi
Approximate North Only

SWEDEN

Trondheim

Ålesund

Gulf of Bothnia

HELSINKI

Bergen

TALLINN

OSLO

ESTONIA

STOCKHOLM

Baltic Sea

The Authors

Graeme Cornwallis

Born and raised in Edinburgh, Graeme later wandered around Scotland before coming to rest in Glasgow. While studying astronomy at Glasgow University, he developed a passion for peaks – particularly the Scottish Munros – and eventually bagged all 284 summits over 3000 feet in Scotland at least once. Graeme has travelled extensively throughout Scandinavia since the 1980s and he has a thorough background knowledge of Norway and its culture. He has also travelled extensively in Asia, North & South America and Australasia. Mountaineering successes include trips to the Bolivian Andes, arctic Greenland and Norway. When he's not hiking, climbing, travelling, or writing for Lonely Planet, Graeme teaches mathematics and physics at home in Glasgow.

Andrew Bender

Yet another LP author with an MBA, Los Angeles-based Andrew Bender worked with companies in Japan and America for years but leapt to write full time after selling a short article to *Condé Nast Traveler*. His articles have since appeared in *Travel & Leisure, Fortune,* the *Los Angeles Times,* the *Philadelphia Inquirer, Lifestyle & Travel for Physicians* and in-flight magazines, and he is managing editor of the *Kyoto Diary,* a journal of Japanese culture. He also reviews films for several outlets and restaurants around LA (hence no photo, but trust us: he's cute), and he covered eastern Germany for LP's 3rd edition of *Germany* (2002). At home, he rollerblades at the beach, eats Asian food, sleeps with Elvis the cat and thinks of ways to spoil his nephews, Ethan and Matthew.

Deanna Swaney

After her university studies, Deanna made a shoestring tour of Europe – including a jaunt through Norway – and has been addicted to travel ever since. Despite an erstwhile career in computer programming, she avoided encroaching yuppiedom in midtown Anchorage by making a break for South America, where she wrote Lonely Planet's *Bolivia* guide. Subsequent works include Lonely Planet guides to *Tonga; Samoa; Iceland, Greenland & the Faroe Islands; Zimbabwe, Botswana & Namibia; The Arctic;* and the 1st edition of this book. She has also updated LP titles from *Brazil* and *Madagascar* to *Russia* and the *Seychelles*.

Her time is now divided between travelling, trekking, writing and working on various construction projects around her home base in Alaska's Susitna Valley.

FROM THE AUTHORS

Graeme Cornwallis Thanks to Deanna Swaney for her excellent work on the 1st edition and thanks to everyone who assisted with the new edition, including tireless staff at tourist offices around the country. Andrew Bender was fun to work with and James Pringle and staff kept the car running.

I am particularly grateful to Jens Riisnæs of NRK; Børre Berglund, Kristin Bennick and Elisabeth Rytterager at Norges Turistråd; Mona Lindgren in Bergen; Gisela Endresen and Ståle Brandshaug in Stavanger; Eli Haaland in Egersund; Ronny Andersen in Kristiansand; Monica Ellingsen and Rolf Erik Nilsen in Grimstad; Rune Guttormsen and the museum in Risør; Arvid Lyngås and Ragnhild Munthe-Kaas in Kongsberg; Richard Thorsrud in Rjukan; Geir Kollstrøm in Lillehammer; Torgeir and Svein Garmo in Lom; Kari Kluge in Røros; Karin Stormo in Kristiansund; Marit Giske in Ålesund; Hilde Mari Haugen of Norske Vandrerhjem; Beate Louise Vik Hauge in Stryn; Jonn and Synnøve Beinnes in Stryn; Sissel Merete Vamråk in Florø; Marit Mauritzen in Fjærland; Guri Våge in Balestrand; Laila Immel in Aurland; Bjørn Sandnes in Voss; Sigrun Uppheim in Ulvik; Hildegunn Lund in Norheimsund; and Richard Webb in Wolverhampton.

Cheery Hanne Sundbø joined the hike to Preikestolen and helped with Ryfylke info. Egil Fjellhaug helped enormously at the busy Oslo tourist office and Merete Habberstad provided lots of detail on the DNT. Jonas Blixt rustled up a phenomenal seafood meal at Engelsviken Brygge and Svein Erik Moe took me there! Jon and Helena Siemensen are due special thanks for hospitality and the Hamar bunad experience. Elin Ulateig stayed up very late in Dombås and Torunn Dyrkorn in Molde showed me around town. Ingrid Loftesnes in Sogndal spent lots of time on the update. Ole Drægni and the staff at Turtagrø are due a big thanks for their friendly welcome and allowing me to defeat them at Risk! Special thanks to Olav Hylland for staying upbeat despite the power cut at Gudvangen. Finally, thanks to Siri Giil, Catharine Olsen and Christian Foss for a great time and lots of help with Bergen and Fjord Norway.

Andrew Bender It warms me just to write the names of those friendly folks who made me feel at home in Norway's vast north. Thanks first of all to Harald Hansen of the NTO in New York for pre-departure assistance, and special thanks to Nina Smedseng of Finnmark Reiseliv, Chris Kardoley of Grenseland AS in Kirkenes, Anja Jenssen of Destinasjon Tromsø, Ketil Singstad and Orjan Jensen of Narvik Aktiv, Asbjørn Gabrielsen of Destination Lofoten, Tare Steiro of Polarsirkelen Reiseliv in Mo i Rana, Sigrid Haaberg of Turistinformasjonen Sandnessjøen, Jens Fredrik von der Lippe and Joar Eie of Trondheim Aktivum, Ann-Kristin Irgens of Svalbard

Tourism, and Katrin Josepit for her Russian skills. Vital assistance also came from Riitta Leinonen of Hexeria AS in Vardø, Trine Halvorsen and Kristine of Hammerfest Turist, Camilla Nielsen of Destinasjon Alta, Ingrid Sondenå and Lill Kristin of Vesterålen Reiseliv, Kjersti Karijord Smørvik of Harstad og Omland Arrangement, Steinar Larsen in Å, Tor Arnesen in Værøy, Anniken Vidge of Destinasjon Bodø, Lisa Grimstad of Salten Reiseliv in Fauske, and Frode Lindberg of Kystriksveien Reiseliv in Steinkjer. Finally, my sincere appreciation to Graeme Cornwallis for having a great accent and a good soul and for being such fun to work with, and to Chris Wyness for the opportunity.

This Book

The 1st edition of *Norway* was written by Deanna Swaney using material from the Norway chapter of *Scandinavian & Baltic Europe on a shoestring* (3rd edition), originally researched by Glenda Bendure and Ned Friary. This 2nd edition of *Norway* was written by Graeme Cornwallis and Andrew Bender.

This 2nd edition of *Norway* was produced in Lonely Planet's Melbourne office by Susannah Farfor (editorial) and Csanád Csutoros (mapping and design). They were ably assisted by a talented horde of berserkers, including Darren O'Connell (editing and proofing), Shelley Muir (editing, layout and indexing) and Katie Butterworth, Karen Fry, Cris Gibcus, Birgit Jordan, Lachlan Ross, Amanda Sierp and Ray Thomson (cartography).

Special thanks to Birgit Jordan for the climate charts, and to Celia Wood for the map legend.

Quentin Frayne produced the language chapter – ya! Matt King organised the illustrations, drawn by Martin Harris and Mick Weldon, and LPI provided the images. The cover was designed by Jennifer Jones. Mark Germanchis provided Quark support in layout.

Kieran Grogan and Chris Wyness oversaw the project; and Rachel Imeson and Mark Griffiths put the artwork under a microscope.

Thanks

Many thanks to the travellers who used the last edition and wrote to us with helpful hints, useful advice and interesting anecdotes:

Husain Akbar, Morten Anderson-Gott, Glenn Ashenden, M Basti, Marjorie Begeman, Christopher Bentley, Koos Berkhout, Jean Bernot, Sverre Bjorstad Graff, Abe Brouwer, Chris Burin, Stuart Cameron, Olga Cernohorska, Janus Chan Pui Man, Eunice Chang, Ed cornfield, Christian Cueni, Sander de Vries, Fabian Dollbaum, Sophie Dyson, Louisa Fagan, Bob Franke, Vidar Fyllingsnes, Catalin Garbea, Kate Greenwood, Nicky Griffin, Oyvind Grimstad, Anne-Katrin Grube, David Gyger, Brian Aslak Gylte, Edgar Hee, James Hemingway, Andrea Hemmerich, Jan Hermans, Matt Hoover, Kristin Hussein, Jan Christian Igelkjoen, Trygve Jackson, Elizabeth Jogee, Mika & Eliah Jordan, Yngvar Larsen, Adam Levy, Inger Liberg, Hanne Lorimer, Barbara Lund, Mary Machin, Patrick McMorris, Rob Meier, Gina Messenger, Szabolcs Mosonyi, Fiona Murray, Nancy Ottis, John Paulsen, Tronaune per, Bridget Pereira, Kieth Porteous Wood, Bard Reian, Benjamin Richter, Dale C Rielage, Carl & Michelle Roe, Guy Ron, Bjorn Ronnekliev, Frode Ronning, Caroline Rosen, Gry Schultz, Robert Schwandt, Eyal Shaham, Jason Shumate, Matthew Smith, Kevin Stanes, Melanie Surry, William Swanson, Terence Tam, Kenneth Tangnes, Silje Figenschou Thoresen, Danielle Treacy, Juliette Turner, Aletta & Ruud van Uden, Stefan vanwildemeersch, Patrizia Vernole, Louise Walters, Jo Wang, Alex Wardle, Erik Wegge Bergvik, Joan Weisberg, Froy Lode Wiig, Mark Wilkinson.

Foreword

ABOUT LONELY PLANET GUIDEBOOKS

The story begins with a classic travel adventure: Tony and Maureen Wheeler's 1972 journey across Europe and Asia to Australia. There was no useful information about the overland trail then, so Tony and Maureen published the first Lonely Planet guidebook to meet a growing need.

From a kitchen table, Lonely Planet has grown to become the largest independent travel publisher in the world, with offices in Melbourne (Australia), Oakland (USA), London (UK) and Paris (France).

Today Lonely Planet guidebooks cover the globe. There is an ever-growing list of books and information in a variety of media. Some things haven't changed. The main aim is still to make it possible for adventurous travellers to get out there – to explore and better understand the world.

At Lonely Planet we believe travellers can make a positive contribution to the countries they visit – if they respect their host communities and spend their money wisely. Since 1986 a percentage of the income from each book has been donated to aid projects and human rights campaigns, and, more recently, to wildlife conservation.

> Although inclusion in a guidebook usually implies a recommendation we cannot list every good place. Exclusion does not necessarily imply criticism. In fact there are a number of reasons why we might exclude a place – sometimes it is simply inappropriate to encourage an influx of travellers.

UPDATES & READER FEEDBACK

Things change – prices go up, schedules change, good places go bad and bad places go bankrupt. Nothing stays the same. So, if you find things better or worse, recently opened or long-since closed, please tell us and help make the next edition even more accurate and useful.

Lonely Planet thoroughly updates each guidebook as often as possible – usually every two years, although for some destinations the gap can be longer. Between editions, up-to-date information is available in our free, quarterly *Planet Talk* newsletter and monthly email bulletin *Comet*. The *Upgrades* section of our website (**w** www.lonelyplanet.com) is also regularly updated by Lonely Planet authors, and the site's *Scoop* section covers news and current affairs relevant to travellers. Lastly, the *Thorn Tree* bulletin board and *Postcards* section carry unverified, but fascinating, reports from travellers.

Tell us about it! We genuinely value your feedback. A well-travelled team at Lonely Planet reads and acknowledges every email and letter we receive and ensures that every morsel of information finds its way to the relevant authors, editors and cartographers.

Everyone who writes to us will find their name listed in the next edition of the appropriate guidebook, and will receive the latest issue of *Comet* or *Planet Talk*. The very best contributions will be rewarded with a free guidebook.

We may edit, reproduce and incorporate your comments in Lonely Planet products such as guidebooks, websites and digital products, so let us know if you don't want your comments reproduced or your name acknowledged.

How to contact Lonely Planet:
Online: **e** talk2us@lonelyplanet.com.au, **w** www.lonelyplanet.com
Australia: Locked Bag 1, Footscray, Victoria 3011
UK: 10a Spring Place, London NW5 3BH
USA: 150 Linden St, Oakland, CA 94607

Introduction

Norway (Norge) stretches nearly 3000km from the balmy beach towns of the south to the treeless Arctic archipelago of Svalbard in the north, taking in vast forests, rugged peaks, haunting fjords, dramatic glaciers, expansive icefields and wild Arctic tundra. The country also boasts pleasantly low-key modern cities, rustic fishing villages, hundreds of worthwhile museums and rich historic sites ranging from restored Viking ships to medieval stave churches.

Compared with most of Europe, Norway retains something of a frontier character, and Norwegians value their easy access to wild outdoor country, including the forested green belts that surround even the largest cities. For outdoor enthusiasts, this translates into excellent wilderness hiking, mountaineering and nordic skiing, while the less active can sit back and enjoy some of the most scenic ferry, bus and train rides imaginable.

Most visitors to Norway are struck by its incredible beauty, and nearly every part of the country has inspired poets, artists, composers, photographers and dreamers (well, maybe not the Oslo railyards...). In the south, this beauty is exemplified by the rolling farmlands of Østfold, the rocky coasts of Rogaland, the enchanting forests of Telemark, the sunny Skagerrak beaches, the bleak alpine plateaus of the Interior, the cold coniferous forests along the Swedish border and the dramatic world-renowned landscapes of the Western Fjords.

As one moves north, the population thins and the horizons grow wider. From Trondheim northwards there is a 1500km stretch

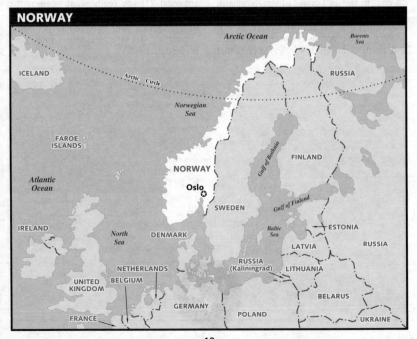

NORWAY

of vast and varied landscapes, most of which lie within the Arctic Circle. Here the terrain ranges from soaring coastal peaks and tiny fishing villages beside turquoise seas to the vast boreal forests of the Sami country and the barren treeless peninsulas of the Arctic Ocean coast. In addition, Norway also extends to two high Arctic possessions. The small volcanic island of Jan Mayen lies well off the beaten track (or any track) and the indescribable Svalbard archipelago, quite literally one of the planet's most breathtaking places, attract adventurers who don't mind paying well for exceptional quality.

Summer visitors are treated to a special high-latitude phenomenon, for Norway is the proverbial 'Land of the Midnight Sun'. Between mid-May and early August, the twilight lingers through the night in southern Norway but, in the counties of Nordland, Troms and Finnmark, as well as Svalbard and Jan Mayen, the sun doesn't set for weeks on end. In fact in Longyearbyen, Svalbard, the sun doesn't set between 19 April and 23 August! The down side, of course, is that winters can be oppressively cold and dark and, north of the Arctic Circle, the perpetual

summer daylight rapidly gives way to the polar night. In Tromsø, the sun doesn't rise at all between 25 November and 17 January, and Longyearbyen is gripped by darkness for nearly four months from 26 October to 15 February! Despite the gloom, however, a winter visit to Norway allows several wonderful opportunities, including the chance to ski some of the world's best alpine and nordic venues, to take an adventurous wilderness trip by dog-sled or to gaze up in wonder at the mesmerising spectacle of the aurora borealis.

There is, however, a fly in the ointment. Thanks to its official policies, extremely high taxes and relative remoteness, Norway is outrageously expensive, and budget travel requires effort. Fortunately, wild camping is free, most hostels aren't much dearer than elsewhere in Western Europe, rail passes allow relatively inexpensive travel in the southern part of the country, and self-catering is far cheaper than restaurant meals. If you really want to enjoy the magic of Norway, however, budget generously, tighten your belt and forget about converting local expenditure into your home currency!

Facts about Norway

HISTORY
Prehistory

Near the end of the last Ice Age around 11,000 years ago, the first humans arrived in the area of modern-day Norway from Siberia. It's thought that this ancient hunting culture – known as the Komsa – was the forerunner of the modern Sami peoples. Regarding the Sami, however, all that's known is that they occupied northern Scandinavia prior to the Christian era. Also evident in prehistoric times, the coastal Fosna culture pursued a hunting, fishing and herding lifestyle around the site of Trondheim and the northern end of the Western Fjords.

After the ice had receded from northern Europe, people also began migrating northwards from central Europe and settling in southern Scandinavia, including along the southern Norwegian coast. These early inhabitants, who belonged to the Nøstvet-Økser culture, didn't have access to flint, which meant that most of their tools had to be made from bone. Initially these people followed a nomadic hunter-gatherer lifestyle, and it was several thousand years before they began establishing more permanent settlements. Although Stone Age peoples in southern Norway would have been of mixed European background, it's likely that the predominant type was tall, blonde, blue-eyed and spoke a Germanic language which was the predecessor of modern Scandinavian languages.

Around 2500 BC, the Battle-Axe, Boat-Axe and Funnel-Beaker cultures (named for the various stone tools they used) entered Southern Norway from what is present-day Sweden. Thanks to the paucity of naturally occurring metals, relatively few of their tools were made from bronze or other metals, and the most significant Bronze Age relics are rock carvings which portray ships and religious symbols. This indicates that travel and trade at this time were increasing in importance, and that trade links had probably been developed with lands to the south and west. The Scandinavians traded amber for metals, particularly bronze, from mainland Europe.

Rock carvings from the era prior to 500 BC depict agricultural and maritime scenes and indicate improvements in farming and shipbuilding methods, as well as other technological advances. In addition, the burial customs of this day, which involved mounds, suggest spiritual and temporal leadership by powerful chieftains. Until around 500 BC, the climate in this region remained relatively warm and amenable to agriculture, but then came a cooling trend and people had to refine their agricultural methods to accommodate the changes, as indicated by the ruins of stone and turf dwellings, farms and furnaces from this period.

During the latter days of the Roman Empire, Rome provided Norway with such items as fabric, iron implements and pottery. The use of iron tools allowed more land to be cleared of trees, and larger boats were built with the aid of iron axes. By the 5th century, the Norwegians had learned how to smelt their own iron from ore found in the southern Norwegian bogs. The runic alphabet also arrived, probably from a Germanic source and, over the following centuries, it became a medium of communication, as evidenced by inscriptions found in stone slabs throughout the region. The fall of the Roman Empire, however, saw a 200-year period of migration and fighting between several regions of the country.

Around AD 700, thanks to its difficult geography, much of Norway was divided into small, independent, non-confederated kingdoms ruled by *jarls* (earls). At this time, the only mainland European awareness of Norway was of the road known as the Norovegr (North Way), the trade route which led from Oslofjord westward along the southern coast.

Norse Seafaring

Realising the vast distances covered by the early voyagers through difficult seas, one can only wonder what sort of ships and technology the Norse people used to travel so far through uncharted territory. Archaeological evidence suggests that Viking longboats, low vessels over 30m long which could travel at up to 12 knots (24km/h), were used primarily in war and raiding. The majority of the settlers travelled in smaller cargo boats called *knerrir* (singular *knörr*). These sturdy little craft, scarcely 18m in length with little freeboard, were designed to carry great loads. Journeys in them must have been crowded, uncomfortable and often frightening.

Perhaps the most interesting aspect of these early voyages, however, is the method of navigation employed. The sagas mention a mysterious device known as a *solarsteinn*, or 'sunstone', which allowed navigation even when the sky was overcast or the sun was below the horizon and celestial navigation was impossible.

It is now generally agreed that the solarsteinn was a crystal of cordierite, which is found around Scandinavia and has natural polarising qualities. When observed from below and rotated, light passing through the crystal is polarised blue when the long axis is pointed toward the source of the sunlight.

This same principle is used today. Jet planes flying over the polar regions, where magnetic compasses are unsuitable and celestial navigation is difficult, use a sky compass which determines the position of the sun by filtering sunlight through an artificial polarising lens.

The Viking Era

Norway's greatest impact on world history probably occurred during the Viking Age, when the prospect of trade, political stress and an increasingly dense agricultural population inspired many Norwegians to seek out greener pastures abroad. The word 'Viking' is derived from *vik*, which now means 'creek' in Norwegian, but in Old Norse referred to a bay or cove (and still does in Icelandic). The connection probably referred to their anchorages during raids.

The catalyst for the Viking movement was probably overpopulation in western Norway, where polygamy led to an excess of male heirs and too little land to go around. The division of land into ever-smaller plots became intolerable for many, causing young men to migrate abroad to seek their fortunes.

The *Anglo Saxon Chronicle* for 787 quotes that three ships came to Britain from Hordaland (Heredalande), piloted by sailors who were described as Northmen, but there's no indication that they were involved in any sort of warfare. Around this time, Nordic shipbuilders developed a relatively fast and manoeuvrable sailing vessel which had a heavy keel, up to 16 pairs of oars and a large square sail, and was sturdy enough for ocean crossings. It's suspected that Norwegian farmers had peacefully settled in Orkney and Shetland as early as the 780s, but it's generally accepted that the Viking Age didn't begin until 793 with the plundering of St Cuthbert's monastery on the island of Lindisfarne, off the coast of Northumberland, Britain.

This initial attack was followed a year later by the plundering of Jarrow, also in Northumberland, but the movement really took off the following year, when a contingency of 100 Viking ships set their sights on south Wales. However, they were successfully resisted by King Maredydd and they next concentrated their efforts on Ireland, where the monasteries presented easy targets and yielded a great deal of loot.

They apparently had no reservations about sacking religious communities and, indeed, many Vikings believed that the Christian monasteries they encountered were a threat to their pantheist traditions. Mainly in the more lawless regions of Britain and Ireland, they destroyed Christian communities and slaughtered monks, who could only wonder what sin they had committed to invite the heathen hordes.

Despite this apparent predilection for warfare, the Vikings' considerable barbarism was probably no greater than the standard of the day, and the colonisation of the Western Isles of Scotland appears to have involved a relatively peaceful coexistence between the Vikings and Celts (although the Northmen did sack monasteries at both Applecross and Iona).

As a result of these initial raids, Viking military forces managed to bring Scandinavia to the attention of the rest of Europe. After the initial raids, they attacked Britain, Ireland and the continent in great fleets, terrorising, murdering, enslaving, assimilating or displacing many local populations and capturing many coastal regions of Britain, Ireland, France (Normandy was named for these Northmen), Russia (as far east as the river Volga), Moorish Spain (Seville was raided in 844), and the Middle East (they even reached Baghdad). Constantinople (present-day Istanbul) was attacked six times but never yielded and, ultimately, Vikings actually served as mercenaries with the forces of the Holy Roman Empire. Perhaps lesser known is the Viking presence in northern Norway, which exploited the hunting and fishing communities there.

Viking activities resulted in an increased standard of living at home. Not only did Norway benefit from the emigration, which freed up farmland, but it also fostered the emergence of a new merchant class and an influx of slaves which were captured abroad and brought back to provide farm labour. According to western Norway's *wergild* system of compensation for murder, a slave was worth only half the value of a peasant, who was worth half that of a landlord. A landlord was valued at 25% of the value of a chieftain and one-eighth that of a king.

During the 9th and 10th centuries, Norwegian farmers also crossed the Atlantic to settle the Faroes, Iceland and Greenland. By the year 1000, according to the Icelandic sagas, Leifur Eiríksson, the son of Eiríkur Rauðe (Eric the Red), had explored the coast of North America, which he named Vinland, or the 'land of wine'.

Partially due to a decisive civil war sea-battle in 872, at Hafrsfjord near Stavanger, as many as 20,000 people emigrated from Norway to Iceland to escape the victorious

king Harald Hårfagre (Fair-Hair), son of Svarta-Halvdan (Halvdan the Black), who went on to confederate several separate realms into the Kingdom of Norway. In 997, Trondheim was founded at the mouth of the river Nid and soon thereafter became the first capital of the new kingdom.

The reign of Harald Hårfagre was such an odd and entertaining time that it was recorded for posterity in the *Heimskringla*, the Norwegian Kings Saga, by the Icelander, Snorre Sturluson.

According to Snorre, the first unification of Norway was said to have been inspired by a woman who taunted the king by refusing to have relations with a man whose kingdom wasn't even as large as tiny Denmark. Through a series of confederations and trade agreements, he was able to extend his rule as far north as Trondheim. His foreign policies were equally canny, and he even sent one of his sons, Håkon, to be reared in the court of King Athelstan of England.

After going through 10 wives, the king had fathered countless heirs, and naturally this presented a succession problem. This was solved by his last child, Erik, who was his only son with Ragnhild the Mighty, daughter of the Danish King Erik of Jutland. The ruthless Erik managed to rise to power by murdering all of his legitimate brothers except Håkon (who was safe in England), then together with a host of squabbling illegitimate brothers, proceeded to destroy his father's hard-won Norwegian confederation in what can only be described as a reign of considerable ineptitude. When Håkon returned from England to sort out the mess as King Håkon den Gode (Håkon the Good), Erik was forced to flee to Britain where he took over the throne of York as King Erik Blood-Axe.

The Battle of Stamford Bridge in 1066, when Harald Hardråda (Hard-Ruler; see the discussion of Medieval Norway) was killed by King Harold of England, is generally regarded as the end of the Viking Age and expansionism. However, Viking power abroad didn't begin to wane significantly until the 13th century, with the death of King Haakon

IV after the Battle of Largs (Scotland) in 1263. In 1261 and 1262, respectively, Greenland and Iceland voluntarily joined the Kingdom of Norway. The dispute with Scotland was resolved in 1266 when the Western Isles and the Isle of Man were sold to the Scots, marking the beginning of the loss of Norwegian territory.

Medieval Norway

King Håkon the Good, who had been baptised a Christian during his English upbringing, brought the new faith back to Norway and attempted to introduce it in his realm by importing missionaries from Britain, as well as an English bishop. However, he met with limited success, particularly in Trondheim, where the subjects appeared to be utterly preoccupied with drinking and toasting Þór (Thor), Oðinn (Odin) and Freyr. Although these missionaries were eventually able to replace the names of the gods with those of Catholic saints, they failed to control the pagan practice of blood sacrifice and when Håkon the Good was defeated and killed in 960, Norwegian Christianity all but disappeared.

It was revived, however, during the reign of King Olav Tryggvason, or Olav I, a Viking who had been converted to Christianity in England and, being a good Viking, decided that only force would work to convert his countrymen to the truth. His downfall came at the hands of his intended wife, Queen Sigrid of Sweden. When she refused to convert to Christianity, Olav cancelled the marriage contract. Sigrid eventually married the pagan king Svein Forkbeard of Denmark and together they managed to orchestrate Olav's death in a great Baltic seabattle, then take over the rule of Norway.

Christianity was finally cemented in Norway by King Olav Haraldsson, Olav II, who was also converted to the faith in England. There, he and his Vikings allied themselves with King Ethelred and managed to save London from a Danish attack under King Svein Forkbeard by destroying London Bridge (from whence we derive the song 'London Bridge is Falling Down'). He was involved in the construction of Norway's first Christian church, at Mosterhamn on the island of Bømlo, Hardanger, in 995. (The foundations of this church were later incorporated into a 12th-century stone church, and the 1000th anniversary of Norwegian Christianity was celebrated here in 1995.) Olav founded the Church of Norway in 1024, and even managed to bring Christianity to recalcitrant Trondheim.

However, King Canute (Knut) of Denmark was eyeing Norway for possible annexation and, in 1028, he invaded the country, forcing King Olav to flee. Although Olav returned after the death of Canute's appointed governor, a popular farmers' uprising in Trøndelag led to his death at the decisive Battle of Stiklestad in 1030. For Christians, this amounted to martyrdom and the king was thereafter canonised as a saint. Indeed, the great Nidaros Cathedral in Trondheim stands as a memorial to Olav and, until the Protestant reformation, it served as a destination for pilgrims from all over Europe (see the boxed text 'Along the Pilgrims' Way' in the Trøndelag chapter). Olav had also provided a lasting identity for Norway as an independent kingdom.

Canute's brief reign was followed, after his death, by four generations of kings who ruled Norway as a semi-autonomous nation. One of these, Harald III (Harald Hardråda, or Harald 'Hard-Ruler'), half-brother of St Olav, raided throughout the Mediterranean region before mounting a disastrous invasion of England in 1066 and falling at the Battle of Stamford Bridge (interestingly, William the Conqueror, who was descended from a Viking *jarl* of Møre, succeeded in a similar attempt only months later). During this period, three cities were founded: Oslo by Harald Hardråda in 1043 and Bergen and Stavanger by King Olav Kyrre (Olav the Peaceful) around 1070.

The 12th century also saw increased power among the clergy and both stone and stave churches were constructed throughout the land. (Of the few buildings which are still extant, the oldest is at Urnes, on Lustrafjorden, which dates from around 1130 to 1150.) In 1107, the Viking king, Sigurd I (the Crusader), who had converted to Christianity, led an expedition of 60 ships to the Holy Land and was involved in the capture of Sidon three years later. Sigurd died in 1130 and much of the rest of the century was fraught with brutal civil wars regarding succession to the throne. These disputes culminated in a crucial naval battle (1184) at Fimreite, on Sognefjord, where a host of wealthy and influential citizens were slaughtered. The victorious King Sverre, a churchman turned warrior, paved the way for medieval Norway's so-called 'Golden Age', which was characterised by a general decline in civil unrest.

Shortly thereafter, Bergen became the national capital and for a while Norway experienced a period of relative peace and prosperity resulting from trade between coastal towns – particularly the capital Bergen – and the Hanseatic League, which was based in Germany. Unfortunately, the increasing power of the Hanseatic traders eventually began to erode Norwegian power and control over the region. (For more on the Hanseatic League, see the boxed text 'Bryggen & the Hanseatic League' in the Bergen & the South-Western Fjords chapter).

Haakon V built brick and stone forts, one at Vardø to protect the north from the Russians, and another at Akershus in 1308 to defend Oslo harbour. The transfer of the national capital from Bergen to Christiania (Oslo) soon followed. Haakon V's successor was his grandson Magnus, son of Haakon's daughter and a Swedish duke. In addition, Magnus was elected to the Swedish crown in 1319; the two kingdoms united that year and the royal line of Harald Hårfagre came to an end. At this stage, Norway's status began a decline which would last for 200 years and result in it becoming just another province of Denmark.

In August 1349, Norway's social fabric was torn by the Black Death, a bubonic plague which arrived on an English ship via the trading port at Bergen. (The disease eventually killed one-third of the population of Europe.) During this tragic period, land fell out of cultivation, towns were ruined,

the church suffered, trading activities faltered and the national coffers decreased by 65%. In Norway, as much as 80% of the nobility perished and, because their peasant workforce had also been decimated, the survivors were forced to return to the land, forever changing the Norwegian power base.

By 1387, Norway had lost both its independence and control of Iceland and, 10 years later, Queen Margaret of Denmark formed the Kalmar Union of Sweden, Denmark and Norway, with Eric of Pomerania as king. Margaret's neglect of Norway continued into the 15th century, when trade links with Iceland were broken and the Greenland colonies mysteriously disappeared without trace.

Around this time, the North Atlantic climate entered a distinct cooling phase, presenting agricultural difficulties. Increasingly powerful Hanseatic traders created a very lopsided trade situation in favour of the Germans, but they did import vital commodities for Norwegian use, and the port of Bergen was largely sustained by the export of dried cod from Nordland. In 1427, the Hanseatic traders in Bergen got word of an impending pirate raid on the port and cleared out; when the attack came, the Norwegian defences were overwhelmed and it was eight years before the Germans returned to re-establish their trade.

In 1469, Orkney and Shetland were pawned to the Scottish Crown by the Danish-Norwegian King Christian I, who had to raise money for his daughter's dowry. This was meant only as a temporary measure but, just three years later, the Scots annexed both island groups. In 1523, the Swedes seceded from the Union, installing the first Vasa king and setting the stage for a prolonged period of war.

Reformation, War & Political Union

During the 16th century, the Danes attempted to make Danish the official language of all Scandinavia, which by this time had been thoroughly converted to Christianity. In 1537, however, the Reformation replaced the incumbent Catholic faith with Lutheran Protestantism. In 1559, Christian III broke the Hanseatic grip on trade in Bergen, which spawned a diversification in the mercantile population as Dutch, Danish and Scottish traders brought wealth and expertise to the city and created a comfortable Norwegian middle class.

In the late 16th century, a series of disputes began between the Danish Union and Sweden, including the Seven Years War between 1563 and 1570, and the Kalmar War between 1611 and 1614, both of which affected Norway. Trondheim was repeatedly captured and re-captured by both sides. During the Kalmar War, a two-pronged invasion of Norway was mounted from Scotland. In Gudbrandsdalen, a grass-roots effort by local farmers succeeded in defeating one of these expeditions (for more details see the boxed text 'Guri Saves the Day' in the Central Norway chapter).

Meanwhile, the Arctic region was undergoing both exploration and exploitation by whalers, sealers and walrus hunters from various nations, followed closely by trappers in search of fox pelts. Uninhabited Svalbard, which offered rich whaling and sealing grounds, had been 'rediscovered' by the Dutch explorer Willem Barents in 1596, as he searched for a north-east passage to China via the Arctic Ocean.

In two further wars during the mid-17th century, Norway lost a good portion of its territory to Sweden. The Great Nordic War with the expanding Swedish Empire was fought in the early 18th century and, in 1716, the Swedes occupied Christiania (formerly Oslo, which was renamed by Christian IV in honour of himself). Trondheim was besieged by the Swedes in the winter of 1718–19, but the effort was abandoned after the death of the Swedish emperor, Karl XII. The Swedes were finally defeated in 1720, ending over 150 years of war.

Also in 1720, a company was formed in Bergen to re-establish the Greenland trade and increase profits from whaling and commerce. A Lofoten missionary, Hans Egede, spent 15 years in Greenland bringing Christianity to the Inuit and in the process he founded the Greenlandic capital, Godthåb (Nuuk). However, the Bergen enterprise was soon abandoned and the missions and trade were taken over by Denmark, which proceeded to impose trade restrictions on the Norwegians. Although they were later loosened – especially on the timber trade – a period of famine at the height of the so-called 'Little Ice Age', from 1738 to 1742, resulted in the failure of crops and the death of one-third of the cattle and thousands of people.

Yet another period of hardship came during the Napoleonic wars when Britain blockaded Norway. After the Danes surrendered on 14 January 1814, the Treaty of Kiel presented Norway to Sweden in a 'Union of the Crowns'. However, the Norwegians didn't take kindly to Swedish rule and a contingent of farmers, businesspeople and politicians gathered at Eidsvoll Verk in April 1814 to draft a new constitution and elect a new Norwegian king. The business was completed on 17 May 1814 (and despite the problems that followed, 17 May is still celebrated as Norway's national day). Sweden would have none of this, and the new king, Christian Frederik, had to give in to Sweden and accept their choice of monarch, Karl Johan. Fortunately, war was averted by a compromise which provided for devolved Swedish power. Disputes between Norway and Denmark ensued over joint debts incurred during their union and over ownership of the colonies of Iceland, Greenland and the Faroe Islands (this issue wasn't resolved until 1931, when the World Court settled in favour of Denmark).

The 19th century saw a national cultural revival, including a flowering of musical and artistic expression led by poet and playwright Henrik Ibsen, composer Edvard Grieg and artist Edvard Munch, and the development of a unique Norwegian dialect known as *landsmål* (or *Nynorsk*). Norway's first railway, from Oslo (King Karl Johan changed the name back from Christiania in order to wipe off that vestige of the Danish union) to Eidsvoll, was completed in 1854, and Norway began looking at increased international trade, particularly of fish and whale products.

A rapidly increasing population combined with an increasingly moneyed populace also brought about a period of mass emigration to North America and, between 1825 and 1925, over 750,000 Norwegians re-settled in the USA and Canada. Technological advances included the early introduction of a telephone exchange in Oslo and electric street lighting in Hammerfest.

In 1905, a constitutional referendum was held and, as expected, virtually no-one in the country favoured continued union with Sweden. The Swedish king Oskar II was forced to recognise Norwegian sovereignty, abdicate and re-instate a Norwegian constitutional monarchy, with Haakon VII on the throne. The hereditary royal succession remains under the authority of the Storting (parliament). Oslo was declared the national capital of the new and independent Kingdom of Norway.

The first three decades of the 20th century brought a flurry of innovation and technological advances. In 1911, the Norwegian explorer Roald Amundsen reached the South Pole. In 1913, Norwegian women became among the first in Europe to be given the vote. Prior to 1914, hydroelectric projects sprang up all around the country and prosperous new industries emerged to drive the increasingly healthy export economy. By the start of WWI, Norway's merchant navy had largely converted from sail to steam. Despite Norway's neutrality during WWI, the German forces sank quite a few Norwegian merchant ships.

Norway's odd attitude toward alcohol was well illustrated in 1919, when prohibition was introduced by referendum. It remained in force until 1927, by which time half the Norwegian population was involved either in smuggling or illegally distilling home brew. At that stage, the state monopoly system emerged as an alternative method of restricting alcohol (but even today, that seems to have little effect on the amount of illegal distilling).

In 1920, Norwegian territory was extended for the first time in several centuries with the signing of the Svalbard Treaty, which took effect in 1925. It granted Norwegian sovereignty over the islands with the provision that mineral residency rights be open to all signatories of the treaty, which included Australia, Canada, China, all EU countries (except Ireland and Luxembourg), India, Japan, New Zealand, South Africa, the USSR (now Russia and the former Soviet republics) and the USA. The 1920s brought new innovations, including the development of factory ships which allowed efficient processing of whales at sea and caused an increase in whaling activities, especially around Svalbard and in the Antarctic.

Also in 1920, the Storting voted to join the newly formed League of Nations, a move which was opposed only by the communist-inspired Labour Party, which advocated central planning and was a growing force in Norwegian politics. By 1927, this increasingly militant and revolutionary party dominated the Storting. In the late 1920s and through the 1930s, the effects of the Great Depression in the USA reverberated around the world and brought economic hardship to Norway. By December 1932, the trade unions were experiencing 42% unemployment and farmers were hit especially hard by the economic downturn.

WWII

Although wages and both industrial and agricultural output generally improved from 1933, Norway continued to be plagued by strikes and industrial disputes. At the same time, the doctrine of fascism began to spread throughout Europe. In 1933, the former Norwegian defence minister Vidkun Quisling formed a Norwegian fascist party, the Nasjonal Samling.

After the Germans invaded Norway on 9 April 1940, King Håkon and the royal family fled to Britain and thence to the US capital, Washington DC (where they stayed for the duration of the war), leaving behind British, French, Polish and Norwegian forces to fight a desperate rear-guard action.

Six southern towns were burnt out and, in fact, the first Allied victory of WWII didn't occur until late May, when a British naval force re-took Narvik and won control over

Those Generous Germans

Shortly following the German invasion of Norway in 1940, the commander-in-chief of the occupying forces, General von Falkenhorst, issued the following declaration:

Announcement

I have been given the task of protecting the land of Norway against attack from the Western powers. The Norwegian government has refused several offers of co-operation. The Norwegian people must now themselves decide over the destiny of their country. If this announcement is complied with, such as it was with great understanding by the Danish people in the same situation, Norway will be spared from the horrors of war.

If resistance should be offered and the hand offered in peaceful intention should be refused, I shall be forced to proceed with the sharpest and most ruthless means to break the resistance.

Anyone who supports the issued mobilisation order of the fled former government or spreads false rumours will be court-martialled.

Every civilian caught with weapon in hand will be SHOT.

Anyone destroying constructions serving the traffic and military intelligence or municipal devices will be SHOT.

Anyone using weapons contrary to international law will be SHOT.

The German army, victorious in many battles, the great and powerful air force and navy will see to it that my announcement will be carried through.

The German Commander-in-Chief von Falkenhorst – Infantry General

this strategic iron ore port. However, the British were out on a limb and they were ordered to abandon Arctic Norway to its fate. On 9 June, Narvik again fell to the Germans.

In Oslo, the Germans established a puppet government under Vidkun Quisling but, over the next five years, a resistance network fomented sabotage against the German military regime.

Among the most memorable acts of defiance was the famous commando assault of February 1943 on the heavy water plant at Vemork (near Rjukan in Telemark), which was involved in the German development of an atomic bomb (see the boxed text 'The Heroes of Telemark' in the Southern Norway chapter). Arms were smuggled by sea from Shetland to western Norway and Shetland fishermen were involved in various daring acts to aid the resistance. British commandos also prevailed over the Germans in battles at Måløy and Svolvær.

The Germans exacted bitter revenge on the local populace and 1500 Norwegians died during the period of occupation. Among the civilian casualties were 630 Norwegian Jews who were sent to central European concentration camps.

On an even larger scale, Serbian and Russian prisoners of war were coerced into slave labour on construction projects, and many perished from the cold and an inadequate diet. In fact, the high number of worker fatalities during the construction of the Arctic Highway through the Saltfjellet inspired its nickname, the *blodveien* (blood road).

Finnmark suffered heavy destruction and casualties during the war. The Germans constructed submarine bases in Altafjorden and elsewhere, which were used to attack convoys headed for Murmansk and Arkhangelsk in Russia, hoping to disrupt the supply of armaments to the Russians.

In early 1945, the Germans faced an escalating two-front war and Hitler went missing. In an attempt to delay the Russian advance into Finnmark, the German forces adopted a scorched-earth policy and utterly devastated northern Norway, burning fields, forests, towns and villages. Shortly after the German surrender of Norway, Quisling was executed by firing squad, other collaborators were packed off to prison and on 7 May, the Russian army withdrew from Arctic Norway.

Although the communist party did well in post-war elections, they never took over the Norwegian government and the Iron Curtain remained in place at the Russian border. Severe wartime rationing ended in 1952, and the late 1940s and early 1950s saw much reconstruction in war-ravaged Arctic Norway. Throughout the country, parts of towns and cities burnt out in 1940 or prior to the German surrender were also rebuilt. In addition, the merchant navy and whaling fleet bounced back.

In 1946, Norway became a founding member of the United Nations. Ever conscious of its proximity to Russia, the country also joined NATO in 1949. Closer links with other Scandinavian countries developed after the formation of the Nordic Council in 1952.

Modern Norway

Oil was discovered in the North Sea in the late 1960s and the economy boomed, bringing greater prosperity and increasingly comfortable living standards. Since then, two decades of socialist Labour government have fostered increased central planning, economic controls, socialised medicine, state-sponsored higher education, and what the government has liked to represent as the 'most egalitarian social democracy in western Europe'.

Having said that, modern Norway is not a classic socialist state, as taxes outstrip individual benefits and users' fees are levied on most services and infrastructure. Although home ownership is still considered a luxury and is taxed accordingly, nearly 80% of Norwegians own their own homes.

In 1960, Norway joined the European Free Trade Association (EFTA) but, in 1972, Norwegians narrowly voted against joining the European Economic Community (EEC). Through the 1980s, a strong Norwegian economy prevented increased unemployment and social decay, and the results of 1972 were repeated in 1994 with a vote against joining the EEC's successor, the European Union (EU). The 'no' vote was due especially to the concerns of traditional family farms and fishing interests which hoped to avoid competition with their larger and more technologically advanced EU counterparts.

Despite Norway's strong economy, in 1995 the unemployment rate increased to 5.2% (not including people involved in 'retraining' programs), and the recent trend has been towards increased urbanisation, especially in the north.

Although modern Norway enjoys an EU concession which grants it trading privileges as a member of the EFTA (along with other European non-EU members Iceland, Switzerland and Liechtenstein), it continues to remain outside the EU and has so far refused to compromise its position on fishing, whaling and other economic issues.

While a majority of Norwegian voters remain adverse to taking directives from Brussels and hope to maintain their internal controls and subsidies, many folks – particularly urban-dwellers and people in the southern part of the country – recognise that Norway cannot remain forever isolated from the larger world economy.

CLIMATE

The typically rainy climate of mainland Norway is surprisingly mild for its latitude and, thanks to the Gulf Stream, all its coastal ports remain ice-free throughout the year. The coastal mountain ranges block the moisture-laden prevailing south-westerly winds, and precipitation can reach 5000mm annually. Bergen, on the south-west coast, is the wettest city, with 2250mm of annual precipitation.

The continental influences and their corresponding high pressure zones are most prevalent in the south-east, in central Norway and in the far north. Rondane and Gudbrandsdal are among the driest districts of Norway, with less than 500mm of precipitation annually.

In summer, the average maximum temperatures for July are 16°C in the south and around 13°C in the north. However, summer temperature extremes are also possible, even in the Arctic region; in July 1998, the temperature in Narvik rose to over 30°C and in August of the same year, even Svalbard saw temperatures over 20°C.

In winter, heavy snowfalls are common, which makes for superb skiing, and snow up to 10m deep can accumulate in the mountains. However, accumulations of 2m to 3m are more usual in the lower areas. In January, the average maximum temperature

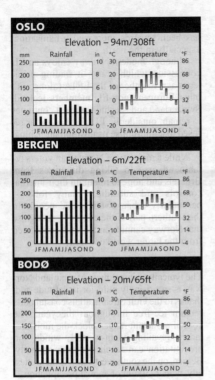

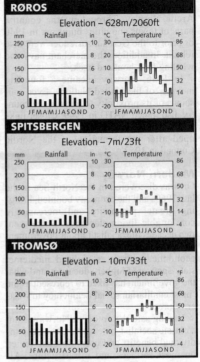

is 1°C in the south and -3°C in the north. It can get much colder, however; in January 1999, the temperature in Kirkenes dropped for a short time to a decidedly chilly -56°C.

Climate details and weather forecasts can be found on the Internet at W www.dnmi.no.

GEOGRAPHY

With a land area of 385,155 sq km, Norway occupies the western part of the Scandinavian peninsula and shares borders with Sweden, Finland and Russia. The country is long and narrow, with a coastline deeply cut by fjords – long, narrow inlets of the sea bordered by high, steep cliffs. The total length of coastline, including islands, is around 57,000km. Mountain ranges, some capped with Europe's largest glaciers and icefields, cover more than half of the land mass. Only 3% of the country is arable.

With a combination of mountains and a wet climate, it's hardly surprising that Norway has many spectacular waterfalls. Waterfall heights vary depending on which list you're looking at. Some authorities place the glacial stream Utigårdsfossen, which flows into Nesdalen and Lovatnet from Jostedalsbreen (not readily accessible to tourists) as the second or third highest in the world at 800m, with a greatest vertical drop of 600m. However, most listings agree on around five Norwegian waterfalls among the 10 highest in the world, including Mongefossen in Romsdal (774m; now dry due to hydroelectric developments); Mardalsfossen in Eikesdal (655m; see Around Molde in the Western Fjords chapter for details); and Tyssestrengene near Tyssedal in Hardanger (646m in multiple cascades; see Odda in the Bergen & South-Western Fjords chapter).

The moniker 'Land of the Midnight Sun' is more than just a promotional slogan for the country, as nearly a third of Norway lies north of the Arctic Circle, which links places at which there is at least one full day when the sun never sets and one day when it never rises. For more information on this, see the boxed text 'Arctic Phenomena'.

GEOLOGY

The pre-Cambrian rocks in Southern Norway were a late addition to the Baltic Shield (the core of the European continent), and date back no more than 1.8 billion years. In the far north, the islands of Lofoten and Vesterålen are largely comprised of granite and gneiss. Interestingly, it's thought that these regions were once attached to the North American crustal plate, as their makeup resembles that of eastern Greenland. When tectonic spreading along the mid-Atlantic ridge separated the European and North American plates, these ancient rocks were left behind. The Caledonian Mountain Range which ran along the length of Norway around 450 million years ago was as high as the present-day Himalayas but, with time, ice and water eroded them down to their current altitude.

In the North Sea lie two rift valleys which contain upper Jurassic shale bearing the rich deposits of oil and gas that are now being exploited. Norway is now the world's second-largest exporter of petroleum products.

During the glacial periods of the past 1.8 million years, the elevated highland plateaux subsided at least 700m due to an ice sheet up to 2000m thick. The movement of this ice, which was driven by gravity down former river courses, gouged out the fjords and valleys and created the surrounding mountains by sharpening peaks and exposing high cliffs of bare rock (just a glance at any map of Southern Norway will reveal a radiating pattern of slender lakes and fjords). The bulk of the ice melted about 8800 years ago, with the end of the last Ice Age, and Norway is currently experiencing an interglacial period. As a result, only a few remnant icecaps and valley glaciers remain on the mainland.

Svalbard, which is geologically independent of the rest of Europe, sits on the Barents continental plate deep in the polar region and currently experiences dramatic glaciation. Sedimentary rock layers in Svalbard include fossils and coal.

ECOLOGY & ENVIRONMENT

Norwegians appreciate their fresh air, clean water and ample elbow room and, among European nations, Norway has one of the better records when it comes to environmental policies. Industrial waste is highly regulated, recycling is popular, there's little rubbish along the roadsides and general tidiness takes a high priority in both urban and rural environments. On the other hand, loss of habitat has placed around 900 species of plants and animals on the endangered or threatened species lists; sport hunting and fishing are more popular here than in most of Europe; the past sin of over-fishing has come back to haunt the economy; and Norway's internationally unpopular stance on whaling and sealing has raised international ire and resulted in boycotts on Norwegian products.

Wilderness Areas

Norway may have one of the lowest population densities in Europe but, thanks to its settlement pattern, which is unique in Europe and favoured scattered farms over villages, even the most remote areas of the country are inhabited and a large proportion of the population is rural. This factor, combined with a national appreciation of fresh air and outdoor recreation, has ensured that most Norwegians have kept some contact with nature.

It has also meant that the natural world has been greatly altered by human activities. The landscape is crisscrossed by roads which connect remote homes, farmsteads and logging areas to the highway system; all but a couple of major rivers have been dammed for hydroelectric power; most Norwegian families own holiday homes beside lakes, around ski slopes or in areas of natural beauty; and even the wild-looking expanses of Finnmarksvidda and the huge peninsulas that jut into the Arctic Ocean serve as vast reindeer pastures. As a result, apart from the upland icefields and the national parks, real wilderness in Norway is limited to a few forested mountain areas along the Swedish border, scattered parts of Hardangervidda and most of Svalbard.

Recycling

Recycling is popular and Norwegians strongly support sorting of household waste – paper, glass, plastics, tyres, car batteries and organic matter – for collection. A deposit scheme for glass bottles has been a success and about 96% of glass beer and soft drink bottles are now

Arctic Phenomena

The Aurora Borealis

There are few sights as mesmerising as an undulating aurora. Although these appear in many forms – pillars, streaks, wisps and haloes of vibrating light – they're most memorable when they appear as pale curtains wafting on a gentle breeze. Most often, the Arctic aurora appears as a faint green or light rose but, in periods of extreme activity, can change to yellow or crimson.

The visible aurora borealis, or northern lights (in the southern hemisphere, the corresponding phenomenon is called the aurora australis), are caused by streams of charged particles from the sun, the solar wind, which are directed by the Earth's magnetic field towards the polar regions. Because the field curves downward in a halo surrounding the magnetic poles, the charged particles are drawn earthward. Their inter-action with electrons in nitrogen and oxygen atoms in the upper atmosphere (about 160km above the surface) releases the energy creating the visible aurora. During periods of high activity, a single auroral storm can produce a trillion watts of electricity with a current of one million amps.

The Inuit (Eskimos) call the lights *arsarnerit* ('to play with a ball'), as they were thought to be ancestors playing ball with a walrus skull. It was believed that the lights could be attracted by whistling or repelled by barking like a dog! The Inuit also attach spiritual significance to the lights, and some believe that they represent the capering of unborn children; some consider them gifts from the dead to light the long polar nights and others see them as a storehouse of events, past and future.

Although science dismisses it as imagination, some people report that the aurora is accompanied by a crackling or whirring sound. However, although it's the sort of sound you'd *expect* to hear from such a dramatic display, I've never heard anything associated with an auroral display.

The best time of year to catch the northern lights in Norway is from October to March, although you may also see them as early as August. Oddly enough, Svalbard is actually too far north to catch the greatest activity.

Midnight Sun & Polar Night

Because the Earth is tilted on its axis, the polar regions are constantly facing the sun at their respective summer solstices and are tilted away from it in the winter. The Arctic and Antarctic circles, at 66° 33' north and south latitude respectively, are the southern and northern limits of constant daylight on the longest day of the year.

The northern half of mainland Norway, as well as Svalbard and Jan Mayan, lie north of the Arctic Circle but, even in southern Norway, the summer sun is never far below the horizon. Between late May and mid-August, nowhere in the country experiences true darkness and in Trondheim, for example, the first stars aren't visible until mid-August. Although many visitors initially find it difficult to sleep while the sun is shining, most people quickly get used to it, even if that simply means joining the locals in their summer nocturnal hyperactivity.

Conversely, winters here are dark and dreary, with only a few hours of twilight to break the long polar nights. In Svalbard, not even a twilight glow can be seen for over a month, and most northern

returned. Supermarkets give money back for returned aluminium cans and plastic bottles (usually Nkr1 to Nkr1.50). There is also a pre-paid recycling charge on automobiles sold in Norway, which ensures that they're turned into scrap metal rather than roadside eyesores when their life is over.

Forestry

Although no forestry operation can be entirely environmentally sound, overall, Norway has one of the world's most sustainable forestry policies and much of the current visible damage to the forests is due to agricultural clearing and timber overexploitation between the 17th and 20th centuries.

Arctic Phenomena

communities make a ritual of welcoming the sun the first time it peeks above the southern horizon. During this period of darkness, many people suffer from SAD syndrome, or 'seasonal affective disorder', but the root cause isn't yet clear. Its effects may be minimised by using special solar spectrum light bulbs for up to 45 minutes after waking up.

Town	Latitude	Midnight Sun	Polar Night
Bodø	67° 18'	4 June to 8 July	15 December to 28 December
Svolvær	68° 15'	28 May to 14 July	5 December to 7 January
Narvik	68° 26'	27 May to 15 July	4 December to 8 January
Tromsø	69° 42'	20 May to 22 July	25 November to 17 January
Alta	70° 00'	16 May to 26 July	24 November to 18 January
Hammerfest	70° 40'	16 May to 27 July	21 November to 21 January
Nordkapp	71° 11'	13 May to 29 July	18 November to 24 January
Longyearbyen	78° 12'	20 April to 21 August	26 October to 16 February
Ny Ålesund	78° 55'	16 April to 25 August	22 October to 20 February

Fata Morgana

If the aurora inspires wonder, the Fata Morgana and related phenomena common in the polar regions may inspire a visit to a psychiatrist. The clear and pure Arctic air doesn't cause distant features to appear out of focus. As a result, depth perception becomes impossible and the world takes on a strangely two-dimensional aspect where distances are indeterminable. An amusing example of distance distortion is described in the enigmatic book *Arctic Dreams*, by Barry Lopez:

> A Swedish explorer had all but completed a written description in his notebook of a craggy headland with two unusually symmetrical valley glaciers, the whole of it a part of a large island, when he discovered what he was looking at was a walrus.

Fata Morgana, a special type of mirage, is also common in the vast expanses of sand, ice and tundra found in the Arctic. Early explorers laid down on maps and charts careful documentation of islands, headlands and mountain ranges that were never seen again.

Fata Morganas are apparently caused by reflections off water, ice and snow, and when combined with temperature inversions, create the illusion of solid, well defined features where there are none. On clear days off the outermost coasts of Lofoten, Vesterålen, northern Finnmark and Svalbard, you may well observe inverted mountains or non-existent archipelagos of craggy islands resting on the horizon. It's difficult indeed to convince yourself, even with an accurate map, that they're not really there!

Also unsettling are the sightings of ships, large cities and forests, where there could clearly be none. Normal visibility at sea is just under 18km but, in the Arctic, sightings of islands and features hundreds of kilometres distant are frequently reported.

Today, Norway's productive forests cover a total of 70,361 sq km, or 23% of the national area. Currently, numerous small forestry operations, mostly in eastern Norway, cut about 8.4 million cubic metres annually. Clear-cutting is practised in some areas but it's thankfully both rare and on a small scale. In general, operations employ selective cutting to prevent soil erosion and unsightly landscape degradation. In addition, companies immediately re-seed the cuts, planting a total of around 50 million seedlings annually.

Fishing & Marine Resources

It's a safe bet that Norway's most controversial environmental issues – among both Norwegians and international conservationists – involve marine mammal hunting,

fishing rights and declining fish stocks, as well as international opinions and the resulting regulations.

Commercial Fishing Throughout recorded history, the seas off the Norwegian coast have provided bountiful fishing opportunities and, until about 25 years ago, deep-sea fishing in the area was pretty much a free-for-all. During the 1960s, the Norwegian fishing community enjoyed particularly high catches, thanks mainly to the development of sonar which located schools of herring and other commercially valuable fish. As a result of the decreasing stock, the herring fishery declined in productivity and, by the late 1970s, herring stocks were nearly wiped out. Over-fishing also depleted stocks of cod all across the North

Glacier & Ice Glossary

Glaciers have forged much of the Norwegian landscape, and even today the country is dotted with remnants of icecaps and valley glaciers, particularly in Svalbard. The following is a list of terms relating to these icy phenomena:

Arête – a sharp ridge between two valley glaciers.
Bergschrund – the crevasse at the top of a valley glacier separating the moving ice from the parent icefield.
Bergy bits – icebergs rising less than 5m above the surface of the sea.
Calving – breaking off of icebergs from tidewater glaciers.
Cirque – an amphitheatre scoured out by a glacier.
Crevasse – a fissure in moving ice, which may be hidden under snow, caused by various strains as the ice flows downhill.
Dead glacier – a valley glacier that stops short of the sea.
Erratic – a stone or boulder which clearly was transported from elsewhere, possibly by a glacier.
Fast ice – a solid sheet of pack ice frozen to some land.
Firn limit – the highest level on a glacier to which the snow melts each year. The snow that remains above this limit is called *firn*.
Frazil – needle-shaped ice crystals which form a slush in the sea.
Glacial flour – the fine, talcum-like silt which flows in glacial streams and is deposited in glacial river valleys. It is formed by abrasion of ice on rock.
Growler – small icebergs, difficult to see and floating just on the surface, thereby hazardous to boats.
Hanging valley – a valley formed when a tributary valley glacier flows into a larger valley glacier.
Horn – the sharp peak that remains after glaciers have scoured all faces of a mountain.
Hummock – a place where ice floes have piled atop one another.
Icecap or **icefield** – a stable zone of accumulation and compression of snow and ice, and a source of valley glaciers. An icecap generally covers a larger area than an icefield. When the entire interior of a landmass is covered by an icecap (as in Greenland or Antarctica), it's known as a *continental glacier*.

Atlantic, from Newfoundland's Grand Banks (Canada) to northern Norway.

On 1 January 1977, Norway established a 200 nautical mile offshore economic zone, which was extended to Svalbard later that year and to Jan Mayen in 1980. The country now has agreements with the EU, Russia, the Faroe Islands, Iceland, Greenland and Poland to set quotas. It took 20 years of intensive conservation measures, including strict quotas, before the herring fishery bounced back. Although cod fishing regulations are now in place, it will be many years before the numbers return.

Another major factor in the success of Norwegian offshore fisheries is the amount of warm Gulf Stream water entering the northern seas, which varies from year to year. The larger the volume of warm water, the greater the growth of plankton in the far north and the greater the amounts of food available to fish and marine mammals. Regulations and quotas also take into account these natural fluctuations.

Today, fishing and aquaculture (fish farming) are the backbone of the coastal economy, providing work for 21,274 people in the fishing fleet, and also providing work in the shipbuilding, fish feed and fishing gear industries and the packaging, processing and transport of fish products. With an annual catch of 2.682 million tonnes (2000), Norway is the 10th largest fishing nation in the world. Fish was the second largest net export earner for the Norwegian economy.

The aquaculture industry, which has thrived for at least two decades, concentrates mainly on Atlantic salmon and trout,

Glacier & Ice Glossary

Ice floe – a flat chunk of floating sea ice, normally pack ice, but it may also refer to a small iceberg.

Jökulhlaup – Icelandic word meaning 'glacial burst'; refers to a sudden and often catastrophic release of water from a glacier, caused by a broken ice dam or by glacial lifting due to volcanic activity beneath the ice.

Moraine – deposit of material transported by a glacier. Rock and silt pushed ahead of the glacier is called a *terminal moraine,* that deposited along the sides is a *lateral moraine,* and down the centre of a glacier, it's called a *medial moraine.*

Moulin – French word meaning 'mill'; refers to a pond or stream inside a glacier, often evidenced by a deep round hole in the ice.

Névé – hard granular snow on the upper part of a glacier that hasn't yet turned to ice.

Nilas – thin crust of sea ice that moves up and down with wave action but doesn't break.

Nunatak – Greenlandic word referring to a mountain peak that protrudes through a glacier or ice-cap.

Pack ice – floating ice formed by frozen seawater, often creating an impenetrable barrier to navigation.

Piedmont glacier – a slumped glacier at the foot of a steep slope, which is fed from above.

Polynya – Russian word referring to an area of open water surrounded by pack ice.

Postholing – what hikers do when crossing fields of rotten or melting snow, sinking up to their thighs at every step.

Roche moutonée – French word for 'sheep rock'; a glacier-scoured boulder. They often resemble sheep grazing on the mountainsides.

Sastrugi – Russian word referring to wind-blown furrows in snow.

Suncup – mushroom-shaped snow formation caused by irregular melting on sunny slopes.

Tarn – Gaelic word referring to a lake in a cirque.

Tide crack – a crack separating sea ice from the shore, caused by the rise and fall of tides.

Tidewater glacier – a valley glacier that flows into the sea and calves icebergs.

Valley glacier – a river of ice which flows downward through a valley from an icefield or icecap.

but there has also been experimentation with Arctic char, halibut, catfish and scallops. Currently, fish farming amounts to 456,000 tonnes of fish per annum, but the export of pen-raised salmon and trout constitutes 54.3% of the value of Norway's fish exports. The main drawback is that diseases in captive stock are spread to wild stock whenever fish escape from the pens, but escapes have been reduced in recent years. That, plus the perceived need for more government regulation, has brought about restrictions in the growth of this industry, but it still promises to be a major force in the Norwegian economy – and environmental concerns – in coming years.

Whaling No Norwegian environmental issue inspires more international fervour and emotion than that of renewed whaling in the North Atlantic. In 1993, Norway resumed commercial whaling of minke whales in defiance of an international whaling ban. While Norway supports the protection of threatened species, the government contends that minke whales, with a North-East Atlantic population of anything between 70,000 and 186,000, can sustain a limited harvest. In 1992, Norwegian hunters harpooned a total of 92 minke whales. The total leapt to 625 in 1998, but it decreased to 487 in 2000. International political circles have reacted apathetically, but conservation groups, especially Greenpeace, have expressed vociferous opposition, spearheaded protest campaigns and physically challenged whaling ships.

While history indicates that whalers in this region have had no qualms about hunting their prey to the verge of extinction, Norwegians claim that modern whalers have a better and more informed perspective, and that they adhere to a more sensible quota system. Most of the pro-whaling ranks feel that conservationists are mainly city folk who have a sentimental relationship with animals and are out of touch with reality. Similarly, they feel that most European and North American city folk have no contact with the land and sea, and that their objections to whaling,

according to the government, are irrational and reflect a 'quasi-religious fervour which projects human relationships and emotions onto wild sea creatures'.

Norwegian whalers work only part time and spend the rest of the year working in the traditional fisheries. To be eligible for whaling, they must own their own boats and be recognised as part of the professional fishing community. They may not use sonar to locate whales and, for the kill, they're required to use 50mm or 60mm grenade-powered harpoon guns to ensure that the whale dies as quickly as possible, but rifles may be used as secondary weapons. Each boat is required to carry a trained veterinarian to ensure that all regulations are followed. When a whale is harpooned, it is hauled onto the deck of the boat and flensed (stripped of its blubber), then the meat and blubber are delivered to coastal packing plants. The Norwegians claim that they support only traditional, family-owned operations and have no intention or desire to return to industrial whaling.

In addition to hunting, a major threat to Norwegian whales comes from chemical pollution, particularly the PCBs which are suspected of damaging cetacean reproductive and immune systems. This damage has already been observed in baleen whales and, in the early 1990s, led to numerous deaths from viral infections.

For further information on whales and marine conservation, contact Greenpeace UK (☎ 020-7865 8100, ⓦ www.greenpeace .org.uk); or the more radical Whale and Dolphin Conservation Society (☎ 0870 870 0027, ⓦ www.wdcs.org). The northern Norwegian perspective is available from High North Alliance (ⓦ www.highnorth .no). For the Norwegian government's take on the issue, see the Ministry of Fisheries' Web site at ⓦ www.odin.dep.no.

Sealing In Norway, seal hunting is restricted to two species, the harp seal and hooded seal, and the purpose is ostensibly to cull a growing population. This is mainly because the fishing community wishes to restrict the competition between fishing boats and marine mammals who depend on fish and eat up to 2.5kg per day. Sealing also provides a livelihood for people in Norway and several other North Atlantic countries.

Sealing occurs only on a very small scale, mainly for fur and meat, but it may successfully be argued that it's a cruel business. To mitigate protests, regulations limit seal hunters to only two tools: a rifle and a *hakapik*, or gaff; the former is for adult seals and the latter for pups (which may not be hunted while still suckling). Hunters are also required to take courses and shooting tests before each sealing season.

In late 2001, plans for tourist seal hunting trips caused worldwide consternation.

FLORA & FAUNA

Although Norway's wildlife populations are fairly sparse compared with those of neighbouring Sweden and Finland, its diverse landscapes and altitude ranges mean that it does harbour many different plant communities and a wider variety of species.

In the UK, an excellent source of natural history books and field guides, including some titles on Scandinavia, is Subbuteo Natural History Books Ltd (☎ 01743-709420, W www.wildlifebooks.com); international orders are welcome. In the USA, try the Adventurous Traveler Bookstore (☎ 800 282 3963, W www.adventuroustravele.com). In Melbourne, Australia, check out Andrew Isles Natural History Books (☎ 03-9510 5750, W www.andrewisles.com).

Flora

In general, Norwegian flora is typical of that in temperate climates, and includes around 250 species of flowering plants. Alpine and Arctic flowers dominate in the highlands and northern areas. Mountain avens, large white flowers with eight petals, commonly grow on limey soils. Other attractive mountain species include the long stalked mountain sorrel, which is an unusual source of vitamin C; glacier crowfoot; various saxifrages (livelong, mossy, purple, pyramidal and starry); alpine milk-vetch, trailing azalea, diapensia; alpine gentian; forget-me-nots (myosotis); bearded bellflower; wood anemone; alpine fleabane;

and alpine aster. Heather grows mainly in low-lying areas around the coast.

Fertile areas at low elevation have well-mixed woodland, where the tree species include conifers, ash, elm, lime, oak, beech, Norway maple and alder. Fruit trees, such as apple and plum, are cultivated in sheltered coastal areas, particularly around Hardangerfjord. In mountainous areas of western Norway, the conifer and birch dominated woodlands climb to between 900m and 1200m. Offshore islands are less wooded and, in northern Nordland, Troms and southern Finnmark, the tree line may be as low as 200m to 300m.

Around the periphery of the high plateaux and around Southern Norway, the forests include Scots pine, Norway spruce, aspen, silver birch, hazel, black alder, mountain ash and, in the higher altitudes, dwarf birch, willow and juniper.

Between the dwarf trees and the snow line, the main vegetation types are mosses, fungi and lichens, such as reindeer moss. Mountain grasses, including sedges, deer grass and Arctic cotton, grow mainly in boggy areas and high in the mountains, near the summer snow line, you'll find saxifrage and a range of smaller tundra plants.

Despite the harsh Arctic conditions, short growing season, severe winters, low precipitation, poor soils and prevailing permafrost, Svalbard has around 165 species of tiny ground-loving plants, including dwarf willow and polar birch and a variety of tundra flowers and lichens.

Hikers will find a profusion of berries, most of which grow low to the ground and ripen between mid-July and early September. The most popular edible varieties are blueberries (huckleberries), which grow on open uplands; blue swamp-loving bilberries; red high-bush and low-bush cranberries; muskeg crowberries; and the lovely amber-coloured cloudberries. The last, which are considered a delicacy, are known locally as *moltebær*, and grow one per stalk on open swampy ground. In the Arctic regions of neighbouring Sweden and Finland, nearly everyone takes to the outdoors in droves to pick this delicious bounty but, in Norway,

The Truth about Lemmings

If you know anything about lemmings, it's about their penchant for mass suicide, right? Well, we've all heard tales of hundreds of thousands of lemmings diving off cliffs to their deaths. Some people also maintain that their bite is fatal and that they spread disease among the human population. Well, those notions may be a bit exaggerated.

Firstly, although lemmings can behave aggressively and ferociously (sometimes even when neither threatened nor cornered), there's no evidence that their bite is any more dangerous than that of other rodents, nor are they particularly prone to spreading any sort of disease.

As for their self-destructive behaviour, things may not be exactly as they seem. Lemmings are known for their periodic mass movements every five to 20 years, when a particularly productive breeding season results in overpopulation (the last lemming swarm was in 2001). Thanks to the increased numbers, the vegetation is decimated and food sources grow scarce. As a result, large numbers descend from the high country in a usually futile attempt to find other, less crowded high ground, only to be squashed on roads or eaten by predators and domestic animals. In fact, for a couple of years following a lemming population surge, there will also be an increase in the population of such predators as foxes, buzzards and owls.

Quite often, however, the swarms head for the sea, and often do face high cliffs. When the press of their numbers builds up near the back of the ranks, the leaders may be forced over the edge. Also, inclement weather when crossing fjords or lakes (note, however, that some brighter individuals refuse to enter the water at all) is likely to result in mass drownings. Neither situation is particularly pleasant for either the lemmings or any observers, but it's generally believed that suicide is not the motive!

The good news is that survival of the fittest is busy at work in the high country. The more aggressive individuals who remain in the hills to guard their territories grow fat and happy. They'll live through the winter under the snow and breed the following year. Females as young as 15 days can become pregnant and most individuals give birth to at least two litters of five each year, so the population again increases rapidly.

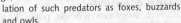

some cloudberry patches are zealously guarded. For rules on picking cloudberries, see Food in the Facts for the Visitor chapter.

Fauna

Land Mammals Although Norway does have a variety of European mammal species, as well as many boreal species, Norway's unique settlement pattern, which spreads the human population thinly throughout the country, limits wildlife habitat and restricts numbers.

Rabbits *(kanin)* live in the south and southwest of the country, where they have probably escaped from captivity. Arctic hares *(hare)* are found throughout the country, typically on moors or mountain grassland and sometimes in woodland. Hedgehogs *(pinnsvin)* are found south of Trøndelag. In Southern Norway, forested and lake-studded areas support a good sized beaver *(bever)* population. Badgers *(grevling)* are found in the river valleys and woods of Southern Norway and otters *(oter)* are found by wooded watercourses and in the sea (except in north Finnmark).

Weasels *(vesel)* and stoats *(røyskatt)* are widespread in all counties; northern varieties turn white in winter, when they're known as ermine and are trapped for their fur. The more solitary wolverine *(jerv)*, a larger cousin of the weasel, inhabits high mountain forests and low alpine areas, mainly near marshes and lakes in Nordland, eastern and Central Norway. Pine martens *(skogmår)* are found in many damp forested areas south of Finnmark. Mink also like water and inhabit forested areas as far north as Tromsø.

Red squirrels *(ekorn)* are ubiquitous in coniferous forests throughout Norway, shrews *(spissmus)* are common, and rodents such as the house mouse *(husmus)*, brown rat *(rotte)*, and voles *(markmus)* are prolific in all counties. Although the Latin name for the brown rat is *Rattus norvegicus*, or 'Norwegian rat', it hails not from Norway (although it has been carried worldwide by Norwegian ships), but from Asia. Some voles, including bank voles, mountain rats and northern water voles, are found as high as 1300m.

Lemmings *(lemen)*, which occupy mountain areas through 30% of the country, stay mainly around 800m altitude in the south and lower in the north. They measure up to 10cm and have soft orange-brown and black fur, beady eyes, a short tail and prominent upper incisors. If you encounter a lemming in the mountains, it may become enraged, hissing, squeaking and attempting to attack! There's also a forest-dwelling version *(skoglemen)* which is found near the Swedish border between Hedmark and Finnmark. Most Norwegian bat species *(flaggermus)* favour the south of Norway, but the northern bat flits around throughout the country.

Red deer *(kronhjort)* range as far north as the Arctic Circle and roe deer inhabit the southern and eastern forests. In the forests from the far south to southern Finnmark, elk (moose in the USA; *elg*) are fairly common, although they wisely tend to stay clear of people and roads. Wild reindeer *(reinsdyr)* exist in large herds, usually above the tree line and sometimes as high up as 2000m, especially on Hardangervidda, but also in Jotunheimen, Dovrefjell and inland areas of Trøndelag. The reindeer of Finnmark are owned by the Sami and most are driven to the coast at the start of summer, then back to the interior in winter. The smaller Svalbard caribou *(svalbardrein)* is native only to Svalbard.

In the late 1940s, musk oxen *(moskusokse)* were re-introduced into Dovrefjell National Park from Greenland (for more information, see the boxed text 'Musk Ox' in the Central Norway chapter).

As in most places, wolves *(ulv)* aren't popular with farmers or reindeer herders and hunters, and only a few still exist in the country – some around Hamar, and a few more in Finnmark. They occasionally wander in from Russia and are normally shot due to a perceived risk of rabies. The red fox *(rødrev)* is found in most places although numbers are reducing due to sarcoptic mange, while Arctic foxes *(fjellrev)* are found north of the Oslo-Bergen rail line, mainly above the tree line, and also in Svalbard. A rare forest-dweller is the solitary lynx *(gaupe)*, Europe's only large cat.

Brown bears *(bjørn)* have been persecuted for centuries, and while some remain in forested valleys along the Swedish border between Hedmark and Finnmark, Norway's only permanent population is in Øvre Pasvik National Park in eastern Finnmark.

Polar bears *(isbjørn)* are found only in Svalbard, but they aren't strictly land animals and spend much of their time on pack ice or drift ice. Since the ban on hunting came into force in 1973, their numbers have increased to over 5000. They're the world's largest land carnivore, weighing up to 720kg and measuring up to 2.5m long. Despite their size, however, they're swift and manoeuvrable, thanks to the hair on the soles of their feet which facilitates movement over ice and snow and provides additional insulation. A polar bear's diet consists mostly of seals, beached whales, fish and birds, and only rarely do they eat reindeer or other land mammals (including – ugh – humans). Polar bear milk contains 30% fat (the richest of any carnivorous land mammal), which allows newborn cubs to grow quickly and survive extremely cold temperatures. Thanks to this rich diet, one polar bear's liver contains enough Vitamin D to kill a human who might eat it.

Marine Mammals The seas around Norway are rich fishing grounds, due to the ideal summer conditions for the growth of plankton. This wealth of nutrients also attracts baleen whales, which feed on the plankton, as well as toothed whales and seals, who feed mainly on the fish that eat the plankton. Sadly, many years of whaling in the North Atlantic and Arctic oceans have brought several whale species to the verge of extinction. Apart from the minke whale, there's no sign that the numbers will ever recover in this area.

Minke whales *(minkehval)* measure around 7m to 10m long and weigh between five and 10 tonnes. They're baleen whales, which means that they have plates of whalebone baleen rather than teeth, and migrate between the Azores area and Svalbard.

The endangered sei whale *(seihval)*, which is also a baleen whale, is found off the coast of Finnmark and is named because its arrival corresponds with that of the *sei* (pollack), which also comes to feast on the seasonal plankton. They measure up to 18m and weigh up to 30 tonnes. The annual migration takes the sei from the seas off northwest Africa and Portugal (winter), up to the Norwegian Sea and southern Barents Sea in summer.

The fin whale *(finhval)* measures 24m and can weigh up to 80 tonnes. These whales were a prime target after the Norwegian Svend Føyn developed the exploding harpoon in 1864 and unregulated whalers left only a few thousand in the North Atlantic. Fin whales are also migratory, wintering between Spain and southern Norway and spending summer in northern Norway, Jan Mayen and Svalbard.

The largest animal on earth, the blue whale *(blåhval)*, measures up to 28m and weighs in at a staggering 110 tonnes. Heavily hunted for its oil, the species finally received protection from the International Whaling Commission in 1967 (far too late!). Prior to 1864, there were between 6000 and 9000, but only a few hundred remain in the world's oceans. There has recently been some evidence that a few hardy blue whales are making a comeback in the north-east Atlantic.

Sperm whales *(spermsetthval)*, which measure up to 19m and can weigh up to 50 tonnes, are characterised by their odd squarish profile. They subsist mainly on fish and squid and usually live in pods of 15 to 20. Their numbers were depleted by whalers after whale oil and the valuable spermaceti wax from their heads. Fortunately, the fish-rich shoals off Vesterålen attract quite a few sperm whales and they're predictably observed on boat tours.

Between Ålesund and Varangerhalvøya, it's possible to see humpback whales *(knolhval)*, toothed whales which measure up to 15m and weigh up to 30 tonnes. These are among the most acrobatic whales and often leap about and flap their flukes before sounding. They're also among the most vocal of whales, producing deep songs that can be heard and recorded hundreds of kilometres away.

The bowhead whale *(grønlandshval)*, or Greenland right whale, was virtually annihilated by the end of the 19th century for its baleen, which was used in corsets, fans and whips. In 1679, Svalbard had around 25,000 bowheads, but only a handful remain.

Killer whales *(spekkhogger)*, or orcas, are the top sea predators and measure up to 7m and weigh 5 tonnes. There are around 1500 off the coast of Norway, swimming in pods of two or three. They eat fish, seals, dolphins, porpoise and whales (such as minke), which may be larger than themselves. The long-finned pilot whale *(grindhval)*, about 6m long, may swim in pods of up to several hundred and range as far north as Nordkapp. Belugas *(hvithval)*, which are up to 4m long, are found mainly in the Arctic Ocean and travel in pods of five to 10 or more.

The grey and white narwhal *(narhval)*, which grows up to 3.5m long, is best recognised by the peculiar 2.7m spiral ivory tusk which projects from the upper lip of the males. This tusk is in fact one of the whale's two teeth and was prized in medieval times. Narwhal live mainly in the Arctic Ocean and occasionally head upstream into freshwater. They live in pods of 15 to 20.

Norway also has bottlenose, white-beaked, Atlantic white-sided and common dolphins.

Seals are often seen near the seashore throughout Norway. The main species include harbour seals *(steinkobbe)*, grey seals *(havert)*, ringed seals *(ringsel)*, harp seals *(grønlandssel)*, hooded seals *(klappmyss)* and bearded seals *(blåsel)*. The much larger walrus *(hvalross)*, which in Norway lives only in Svalbard, measures up to nearly 4m and weighs up to 1300kg. They're best identified by their ivory tusks, which are elongated canine teeth and can measure up to 1m long in the males. Although they were once heavily hunted for their ivory and blubber, since they became a protected species in 1952, their Svalbard population increased to around 1000.

Fish The variety of fish found in the seas around Norway is quite extensive and some are economically important. The most common are the cod *(torsk)*, sprat *(brisling)*, haddock *(kolje)*, mackerel *(makrell)*, capelin *(lodde)*, sandeel *(storsil)*, ling *(lange)*, redfish (or ocean perch; *uer*) and coalfish (or pollock – *sei*). The ugly but rather lovable catfish *(steinbit)* is delicious, as is the blenny *(ålekvabbe)*. Herring *(sild)*, halibut *(hellefisk)* and hake *(lysing)* have all been overfished and are no longer abundant.

Shrimp *(reker)*, crab *(krabbe)* and lobster *(hummer)* are the main edible crustaceans and mussels *(blåskjell)* are also good to eat.

Among freshwater fish, salmon *(laks)* are the most widespread and a large sport angling community ensures that the stocks are kept as healthy as possible. However, diseases are now spreading from farmed fish to the wild stocks, creating major problems in some areas (see Environment & Ecology, earlier in this chapter). The brown trout *(ørret)* is also popular with anglers, but it's found only in the south. Other common and edible freshwater species include perch *(åbor)*, Arctic char *(røye)*, Arctic grayling *(harr)*, bream *(brasme)*, tench *(suter)* and eel *(ål)*.

Birds Norway makes an excellent venue for ornithologists, but the country attracts so many nesting species and permanent residents that it would be quite impossible to discuss them all in detail.

The best birdwatching sites include Revtangen (coastal Rogaland), Utsira (off the Rogaland coast), Fokstumyra (in Dovrefjell), Femundsmarka National Park (Hedmark), Runde (near Ålesund, with over 350,000 nesting pairs of seabirds), the islands of Nordland (especially Lovund, Træna, Røst, Værøy and Bleiksøya), Øvre Pasvik National Park (eastern Finnmark) and Svalbard (for visiting migratory species in summer).

The greatest bird populations in Norway are along the coastline, where millions of sea birds nest in coastal cliff faces and feed on fish and other sea life. The most prolific species include a number of gulls *(måke)*, common tern *(makrellterne)*, Arctic tern *(rødnebbterne)*, oystercatcher *(tjeld)*, cormorant *(skarv)*, gannet *(havsule)*, razorbill *(alke)*, puffin *(lundefugl)*, guillemot *(lomvi)*, black guillemot *(teist)*, shag *(toppskarv)*, fulmar *(havhest)*, kittiwake *(krykkje)*, skuas *(tjuvjo* and *fjelljo)*, little auk *(alkekonge)* and European storm-petrel *(storm petrel)*.

Among Norway's raptors, the most dramatic and rewarding to see and watch is the lovely white-tailed eagle *(havørn)*, of which there are now at least 500 nesting pairs along the Nordland coast, as well as in parts of Troms and Finnmark. The rough-legged buzzard *(fjellvåk)* lives by hunting lemmings and voles in Arctic and alpine tundra areas. There are also about 500 pairs of golden eagle *(kongeørn)* in higher mountain areas. The rare osprey *(fiskeørn)* has a maximum population of 30 pairs and is seen only in heavily forested areas; your best chances of seeing one is in Stabbursdalen and Øvre Pasvik National Parks. You may also see sparrowhawks *(spurvehauk)*, merlins *(dvergfalk)*, gyrfalcons *(jaktfalk)*, peregrine falcons *(vandrefalk)*, hen harriers *(myrhauk)*, kestrels *(tørnfalk)* and goshawks *(hønsehauk)*. All but the last two are rarely observed.

There are also at least four species of owls: short-eared owls *(jordugle)*, found on marshy moors; pygmy owls *(spurveugle)*, which like coniferous forests; snowy owls *(snøugle)*, which like alpine tundra; and eagle owls *(hubro)*, which prefer northern and mountain forests.

Especially in Southern Norway, you'll also find the usual European variety of woodland birds, including wood pigeons *(rindue)*, woodpeckers *(hakkespett)*, woodcocks *(rugde)*, bullfinches *(dompap)*, chaffinches *(bokfink)*, cuckoos *(gjøk)*, jays *(jayskrike)* and a whole range of tits (chickadees; *meis)*. Very few of the spectacular waxwings *(sidensvans)* breed in Norway, but in winter they arrive from Russia in large numbers and may be observed in woods, parks and gardens.

Among the largest woodland birds are the ptarmigan *(fjellrype)* and two other equally tasty species of grouse *(orrfugl* and *jerpe)*.

The red grouse *(skotsk lirype)* prefers treeless moors and tundra and the bizarre capercaillie *(tiur)*, which resembles a wild turkey or a modest peacock, struts around in coniferous forests. Other garden variety birds – crows *(kråke)*, blackbirds *(svarttrost)*, martins *(taksvale)*, ravens *(ravn)*, magpies *(skjære)*, robins *(rødstrupe)*, sparrows *(spurv)* and so on – are quite common.

Norway's host of wading and water birds includes grey herons *(gråhegre)* and numerous sandpiper species – snipe, curlew, ruff, whimbrel, redshanks and so on – as well as godwits *(spove)*, plovers *(lo)*, turnstone *(steinvender)* and dotterels *(boltit)*.

The most prominent ducks are mallard *(stokkand)*, eider *(ærfugl)* and red-breasted merganser *(siland)*. In marshes, lakes and ponds, you may also observe wildfowl, such as whooper swans *(sangsvane)*, bean geese *(sås)*, lesser white-fronted geese *(dverggås)*, greylag geese *(grågås)* and Canada geese *(canadagås)*. Only the greylag is present in large numbers.

Other lovely water birds include the incredible black-throated and red-throated diver *(storlom* and *smålom*, respectively), called 'loons' in North America, and horned grebes *(horndykker)*, cranes *(trane)*, coots

The white-tailed eagle (Haliaeetus albicilla) is the largest northern European raptor, with a wingspan of up to 2.5m

MH

(sothøne) and corncrakes *(åkerrikse)*. The last two are species of rail. Norway's national bird, the dipper *(fossekall)*, lives near and makes its living by diving into mountain streams.

Endangered Species

Threatened and endangered species in Norway include wolves, bears, several species of hawk (especially merlins, gyrfalcons and peregrine falcons) and several species of whale. See the earlier Fauna – Marine Mammals section for details of endangered or near-extinct whale species.

National Parks

Norway's 21 national parks (see the boxed text and map 'Norwegian National Parks') have been established to preserve wilderness areas and to protect wildlife and distinctive natural features of the landscape. In many cases, they don't protect any specific features, but rather, attempt to prevent development of remaining wild areas. As a result, park boundaries don't necessarily coincide with the incidence of spectacular natural features or ecosystem boundaries, but simply follow contour lines around uninhabited areas.

Compared to their counterparts in the USA, Britain and elsewhere, Norwegian national parks are very low profile and pleasantly lack the traffic and overdeveloped tourist facilities which have turned parks in many countries into little more than transplanted (or seasonal) urban areas. Some parks, particularly Jotunheimen and Rondane, are increasingly suffering from overuse but, in most parks, erosion, pollution and distress to wildlife are kept to a minimum.

Nature reserves enjoy an even lower profile, and most are rarely visited, mainly because they're usually closed during wildlife breeding seasons, which normally correspond with the high tourist season between May and July. Fortunately, Norway also enjoys plenty of worthwhile wild areas outside the national parks and reserves, so don't limit your outdoor plans to just the designated areas.

Regulations governing national parks, nature reserves and other protected areas are – not surprisingly in Norway – quite strict. In general, there are no restrictions on entry to the national parks, nor are there any fees, but drivers must nearly always pay a toll to use roads leading into the parks. Dumping rubbish, removing plant, mineral, or fossil specimens, hunting or disturbing wildlife, and using motorised off-road vehicles are all prohibited.

Further national park and reserve information is available at local tourist offices and also from the Directorate for Nature Management (☎ 73 58 05 00, fax 73 58 05 01, ⓔ skjalg.woldstad@dirnat.no, ⓦ www .dirnat.no), N-7485 Trondheim.

GOVERNMENT & POLITICS

Norway is officially a constitutional monarchy under King Harald V and Queen Sonja, but it also enjoys a parliamentary democratic form of government. Although the monarchy has no real political power, it provides a sense of national identity and is widely respected throughout the country and much of the world. General democratic elections are held every four years for the 165 seats in the Storting (ⓦ www.stortinget .no), which serves as a national assembly or parliament, and all citizens over the age of 18 are eligible to vote in both local and national elections.

Traditionally, there were few extremes in Norwegian politics. The Conservative Party *(Høyre)* is fairly moderate by European standards and there are no right-wing neofascist movements. Recently, however, the far right wing Progress Party *(Fremskrittspartiet)* and the far-left Socialist Left Party *(Sosialistisk Venstreparti)* have been gaining support.

From 1986 to 1995, the Labour Party *(Det Norske Arbeiderparti)*, which promotes social-democratic ideals and high taxation to support extensive social programs, was led by Norway's first woman prime minister, Gro Harlem Brundtland. She was succeeded by Labour party chairman Torbjørn Jagland, who stepped down after just a year due to waning support.

Norwegian National Parks

There are currently 21 national parks in Norway, but the Folgefonn and National Park may be created by the time you read this. Skrymtheimen National Park is planned for the central region, in order to protect the Dovrefjell highlands. Here's a quick rundown of the current national parks, with descriptions of what you can expect to find in each:

Børgefjell (1007 sq km; Nord Trøndelag & Nordland)
The boulder-strewn slopes of the Børgefjell massif harbour alpine vegetation in the heights and forested slopes and bogs in lower areas. It's known as a popular birdwatching venue.

Dovrefjell (256 sq km; Oppland, Sør Trøndelag & Møre og Romsdal)
For most Norwegians, Dovrefjell is synonymous with musk oxen, and the hairy beasts attract lots of wildlife buffs. It's also popular with hikers and climbers wanting to tackle Snøhetta (2286m).

Femundsmarka (390 sq km; Hedmark & Sør Trøndelag)
This park, dominated by the lake Femunden, preserves a glaciated highland landscape along the Swedish border.

Forlandet (640 sq km; Svalbard)
This park takes in the 86km-long island, Prins Karls Forlandet, off the west coast of Spitsbergen. It exists mainly to protect breeding grounds for eider ducks, geese and pinnipeds (seals and walruses).

Gressåmoen (182 sq km; Nord Trøndelag)
This park was established to protect one of the country's largest areas of first growth spruce forest. It's also known for boggy areas that attract lots of water-loving birds.

Gutulia (19 sq km; Hedmark)
Tiny Gutulia park preserves an expanse of primeval old growth forest and is home to numerous bird species.

Hardangervidda (3422 sq km; Oppland, Telemark & Hordaland)
Hardangervidda is a vast expanse of upland alpine plateau which dominates the central portion of Southern Norway. It's home to the largest herd of wild reindeer in Europe and is one of Norway's most popular nordic skiing venues.

Jostedalsbreen (1230 sq km; Sogn og Fjordane)
This park takes in the 487 sq km Jostedalsbreen icecap, and its many scenic and impressive valley glaciers provide insight into the natural powers that originally carved out Norway's fjords.

Jotunheimen (1145 sq km; Oppland)
Norway's most popular national park attracts throngs of hikers to its numerous ranges of sharp, scenic and challenging peaks and valleys.

Nordvest Spitsbergen (3560 sq km; Svalbard)
This wild corner of Spitsbergen Island takes in not only the fabulous Kongsbreen icefield but also lovely Magdalenefjord, a number of archaeological sites and some of the world's finest breeding grounds for sea birds, caribou and marine mammals.

Norwegian National Parks

Ormtjernkampen (9 sq km; Oppland)
Norway's smallest national park protects a slice of old growth pine forest, as well as small areas of birch forest and alpine vegetation.

Rago (167 sq km; Nordland)
Lonely and dramatic Rago National Park is characterised by high mountain peaks divided by plunging valleys and waterfalls. It abuts the Padjelanta, Sarek and Stora Sjöfallet National Parks in Sweden, forming a combined protected area of 5700 sq km.

Reisa (803 sq km; Troms)
The most prominent feature of this park is the dramatic Reisa Gorge, its lovely waterfalls, varied wildlife and interesting hiking.

Rondane (580 sq km; Oppland)
Norway's first national park, shelters herds of wild reindeer and also large areas of stark and inspiring alpine peaks and meadows. It also protects the archaeological remains of ancient hunting cultures.

Saltfjellet-Svartisen (2105 sq km; Nordland)
The two-part Saltfjellet-Svartisen National Park, which straddles the Arctic Circle, combines the upland moors of Saltfjellet with the two vast Svartisen icecaps. It also includes a number of Sami archaeological relics and sacred sites.

Stabbursdalen (98 sq km; Finnmark)
The main reason for preserving Stabbursdalen is its pine forest – the world's most northerly. In addition, it offers excellent wild hiking and broad vistas well off the trodden track.

Sør Spitsbergen (5300 sq km; Svalbard)
By far Norway's largest national park, Sør Spitsbergen takes in Spitsbergen's entire southern peninsula. About 65% is covered in ice, but there are several nesting sites for barnacle geese and eider ducks, and the coastal cliffs attract millions of nesting sea birds.

Øvre Anarjåkka (1399 sq km; Finnmark)
This little-known park adjoins Finland's wild Lemmenjoki National Park and protects a vast expanse of birch and pine forests, bogs and lakelands.

Øvre Dividal (743 sq km; Troms)
This lovely, wild park, known for the Arctic rhododendron and heather, and home to the rare wolverine, lies at the heart of a complex network of trekking routes in northern Norway, Sweden and Finland.

Øvre Pasvik (67 sq km; Finnmark)
This park, tucked between Finland and Russia, protects a lovely area of boreal forest as well as large areas of muskeg and the last habitat of the brown bear in Norway.

Ånderdalen (69 sq km; Troms)
This tiny park on the island of Senja protects the bogs and the coastal pine and birch forests typical of Troms county. Some of the trees are over 500 years old.

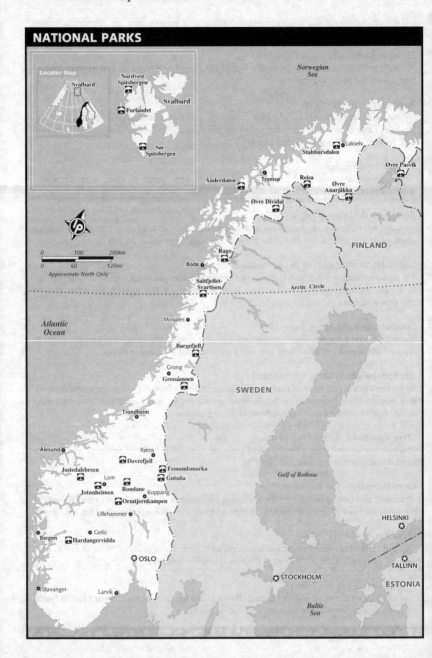

NATIONAL PARKS

Locator Map

Svalbard

Nordvest
Spitsbergen

Forlandet

Svalbard

Sør
Spitsbergen

*Norwegian
Sea*

Lakselv

Stabbursdalen

Øvre Pasvik

Ånderdalen

Tromsø

Reisa

Øvre
Anarjåkka

Øvre Dividal

FINLAND

0   100   200km
0   60   120mi
Approximate North Only

Rago

Bodø

Saltfjellet-
Svartisen

*Atlantic
Ocean*

Arctic Circle

Mosjøen

Børgefjell

Grong

Gressåmoen

SWEDEN

Trondheim

Røros

Dovrefjell

Femundsmarka

Jostedalsbreen

Lom

Gutulia

Jotunheimen

Rondane

Koppang

Ormtjernkampen

Gulf of Bothnia

Lillehammer

HELSINKI

Geilo

Bergen

Hardangervidda

OSLO

Stavanger

Larvik

STOCKHOLM

TALLINN

ESTONIA

*Baltic
Sea*

The 1997 election resulted in a win for a coalition of the Christian Democrat *(Kristelig Folkeparti)*, Liberal *(Venstre)* and Centre *(Senterparti)* parties, with Christian Democrat Prime Minister Kjell Magne Bondevik at the helm, but Bondevik resigned in March 2000 and was replaced by the unpopular Labour government of Jens Stoltenberg.

In September 2001, the Labour Party suffered its greatest election defeat in 75 years, mainly due to its policies of iniquitous taxation and banking Norway's oil wealth while allowing schools and hospitals to disintegrate due to lack of funds. However, with 43 seats, it's still the largest of the six major parties represented in the Storting.

A new government took office in October 2001, with Prime Minister Kjell Magne Bondevik leading a coalition of Christian Democrats, Conservatives and Liberals. The direction this government will take is far from clear, as it will have to rely on support from the far-right Progress Party. Government information can be found on the Internet at W www.odin.dep.no.

The Norwegian prime minister is assisted by 18 government ministers who are responsible for various facets of the government. In addition to the national government, each of the 19 counties and 435 municipalities has its own local government which is responsible for building and maintaining schools, hospitals, roads and other local infrastructure.

As for foreign relations, Norway was a founding member of the League of Nations in 1920 and the United Nations in 1946. In 1949, it also became a member of NATO and joined the OECD. It is currently affiliated with the European Free Trade Association, but has resisted joining the EU (see History earlier in this chapter).

ECONOMY

Norway's current prosperity is largely due to the North Sea oil fields, which were discovered on the Norwegian continental shelf in the 1960s. Today, petroleum accounts for Nkr206 billion (or 29.7%) of Norway's gross domestic product (GDP). In 1999, the Norwegian GDP was US$134 billion, or US$30,100 per capita.

Other economic mainstays include fishing, fish farming, forestry, shipping and shipbuilding, and abundant hydroelectric power provides the basis for a number of industries including aluminium, steel and paper production.

In the late 20th century, tourism began to contribute significantly to the economy and, despite its lofty prices, Norway has experienced a steady increase in visitor numbers. Thanks to convenient summer ferry routes, lots of motorists arrive from Britain and continental Europe, cruise ships call in at coastal ports and many Europeans take day or weekend trips to Oslo, Bergen and Stavanger. In winter, skiers head for the mountains and plateaux. Meanwhile, generous funding and substantial user tolls ensure that the transport infrastructure – new roads, tunnels, bridges and ferries – continues to improve.

While Norwegians enjoy among the world's highest per capita incomes and one of the most developed infrastructures, they must also pay some of the world's highest prices – and among the world's highest taxes. This is thanks mainly to the country's restrictions on imports, labour costs and the comprehensive cradle-to-grave social welfare system which entitles citizens to a government-sponsored university education, generous holiday leave, socialised medical care and a guaranteed pension, among other things.

In many parts of the country, the number of well-compensated government employees exceeds the number employed by the private sector. When you consider that private enterprise must still carry the entire economy, it's easy to work out that entrepreneurial initiative is currently strained to its limit. In fact, it's feared that any liberalisation of trade restrictions – particularly membership of the EU – may well cause the entire system to collapse.

In 2000, inflation was 3.1% (curiously, inflation in the tourist industry is nearer 10%). Unemployment stood at 3.6% in September 2001.

POPULATION

Norway's population of 4,513,000 (July 2001) represents among the lowest population densities in Europe, at 11.7 people per square kilometre. Despite the high taxation, the majority of modern Norwegians sit comfortably in the middle class. To preserve the country's living standard and low population density, immigration is strictly controlled and only *bona fide* refugees (as opposed to nominal 'asylum seekers') are admitted. Most of these refugees have come from Somalia, Bosnia, Kosovo, Sri Lanka and other seriously troubled areas, but the Norwegian government is keen to repatriate them as soon as possible.

The largest cities are Oslo with 508,726 residents, Bergen with 230,829, Trondheim with 135,879 and Stavanger with 106,000. The life expectancy for men is 76.0 years (the fourth highest in Europe) and for women, 81.4 years. Families have an average of two children each and, combined with the negligible immigration, this results in fairly static population numbers. The infant mortality rate of 3.8 per 1000 live births is one of the lowest in Europe.

PEOPLE
Nordic

Most of Norway's population is considered to be of Nordic stock; these people are thought to have descended from central and northern European tribes who migrated northward around 8000 years ago, and modern Nordic peoples are in fact the indigenous peoples of southern and central Scandinavia. The 'Nordic type' is generally characterised by a tall sturdy frame, light hair and blue eyes. Nearly 70% of Norwegians have blue eyes, although many do have darker features.

Sami

Norway's 40,000 indigenous Sami people (formerly known as Lapps) make up the country's largest ethnic minority. This hardy, formerly nomadic people has for centuries occupied northern Scandinavia and north-western Russia, living mainly by

SAMI CULTURAL AREA & DIALECTS

DIALECTS
1 South
2 Ume
3 Pite
4 Lule
5 North
6 Inari
7 Skolt
8 Kildin
9 Ter

herding domestic reindeer. The total population of around 60,000 Sami still forms an ethnic minority in four countries – Norway, Sweden, Finland and Russia.

In Norway, the Sami mainly occupy the far northern county of Finnmark, but there are also scattered groups in Nordland, Trøndelag and Hedmark. The Sami themselves refer to their area as Sápmi, or Samiland.

In 1988, the government passed a constitutional amendment stating: 'It is the responsibility of the authorities of the State to create conditions enabling the Sami people to preserve and develop its language, culture and way of life.' It also provided for the creation of an elected Sami parliament, or Sameting (W www.samediggi.no), to serve as an advisory body to bring Sami issues to the national parliament (similar bodies also exist in Finland and Sweden).

In order to be considered a member of the Sami community, a person must meet one of three criteria: speak Sami as their first language; consider themselves a member of the Sami community and live in accordance with that society; or have a parent who satisfies either of those conditions.

History The oldest written reference to the Sami was written by the Roman historian Tacitus in AD 98 and, in AD 555, the Greek Procopius referred to Scandinavia as Thule, the furthest north, and its peoples as *skridfinns*, who hunted, herded reindeer and travelled about on skis. The medieval Icelandic sagas confirm trading between Nordic peoples and the Sami, and the trader Ottar, who 'lived further north than any other Norseman', served in the court of English King Alfred the Great and wrote extensively about his native country and its indigenous peoples. Sami traditions are also highlighted in the 1673 book *Lapponia*, by Johannes Schefferus.

During this era, the Sami lived by hunting and trapping in small communities or bands known as *siida*. Each community occupied their own designated territory. While 17th- and 18th-century colonisation of the north by Nordic farmers presented conflicts with this system, many of the newcomers found that the Sami way of life was better suited to the local conditions and adopted their dress, diet, customs and traditions.

Most early writings about the Sami tended to characterise them as pagans and, although churches were established in their lands as early as the 12th century, the first real mission was founded by Thomas von Westen in 1716. His efforts concentrated mainly on eradicating the practice of shamanism and discouraging the use of the Sami language. Subsequent missionary efforts, however, reversed this policy and concentrated on translating the Bible into their language. The Lutheran catechism was available in the Fell Sami language as early as 1728, due to the efforts of missionary Morten Lund.

Around 1850, reforms were introduced which restricted the use of the Sami language in schools. From 1902, it became illegal to sell land to any person who couldn't speak Norwegian, and this policy was practised zealously, particularly in the early 20th century. However, there was an about-face after WWII when official policy began promoting internal multiculturalism and, by the 1960s, the Sami's right to preserve and develop their own cultural values and language were enshrined across all government spectra. Increasingly, official policy viewed the Sami as Norwegian subjects but also an ethnic minority and separate people. Their legal status improved considerably and the government formed two committees: the Samekulturutvalget to deal with Sami cultural issues, and the Samerettsutvalget to determine the legal aspects of the Sami status and resource ownership. In early 1990, the government passed the Sami Language Act, which gave both the Sami language and Norwegian equal status and, later the same year, Norway ratified the International Labour Organisation proposition No 169, which guaranteed the rights of indigenous and tribal peoples.

Reindeer herding, was successfully modernised in the 1980s and 1990s, and is now a major capital earner. In addition to reindeer herding, modern Sami engage in fishing, agriculture, trade, small industry and the production of handicrafts, in addition to most other trades and professions in Norwegian society as a whole.

Political Organisations In addition to the Sami parliament, which convenes in Karasjok and is elected by direct ballot every four years, the Norwegian Sami people also belong to the Saami Council (W www.saamicouncil.org), which was founded in 1956 to fosters cooperation between political organisations in Norway, Sweden, Finland and Russia. The Norwegian Sami also participate in the Arctic Council (W www.arctic-council.org) and the World Council of Indigenous Peoples (WCIP), which encourages solidarity and promotes information exchange between indigenous peoples in the various member countries. The Nordic Sami Institute (W www.nsi.no) at Kautokeino was established in 1974 and seeks to promote Sami language, culture and education, as well as promote research, economic activities and environmental protection. It's funded by the Nordic Council of Ministers.

In Tromsø in 1980, the Saami Council's political program adopted the following principles:

We, the Sami, are one people, whose fellowship must not be divided by national boundaries.
We have our own history, tradition, culture and language. We have inherited from our forebears a right to territories, water and our own economic activities.
We have an inalienable right to preserve and develop our own economic activities and our communities, in accordance with our own circumstances and we will together safeguard our territories, natural resources and national heritage for future generations.

Other

Apart from the small Jewish community, most members of ethnic minorities in Norway are either married to Norwegians or are refugees from trouble spots. They comprise only a tiny proportion of the population and, while most live in Oslo, many smaller communities have also accepted limited numbers of refugees.

EDUCATION

Compulsory education was instituted in Norway in 1889, requiring a minimum of seven years' instruction; this was extended to nine years in 1969 and to 10 years in 1997. Currently, about 6.8% of the national budget is spent on education (this has fallen from 7.6% in recent years) and 20% of the Norwegian population is involved in

Russing Around

An unusual tradition for students graduating from high school is called *russ*. When a student becomes russ, or *rødruss*, he or she dons red overalls and a red beret and, by virtue of this status, is permitted for a time to raise all sorts of holy hell. Although the line is drawn at actual property damage, other sorts of mischief – unrestrained noise, partying, removable graffiti and general obnoxiousness – are permitted and encouraged. This may go on for several weeks around the end of the school year.

educational programs. Private school attendance is discouraged unless it's in addition to instruction at state-sponsored schools. About 83% of residents between the ages of 25 and 64 has completed education beyond secondary level and 26% hold higher degrees. High school students select their own curriculum, including apprenticeship and vocational programs, and many choose to attend school away from their home towns.

In an effort to assist in maintaining the Sami culture, education of Sami students includes Sami cultural studies and some course work in the Sami language. Foreign language instruction for non-Norwegian speakers, special education programs and after-school day care are also subsidised.

Norway has four universities: the University of Oslo, which is the oldest; the University of Bergen; the Norwegian University of Science & Technology in Trondheim; and the University of Tromsø. There are also 26 regional colleges and eight speciality colleges teaching veterinary medicine, sport, music, architecture, the arts, agriculture, theology and business/economics. For more details, see [W] www.odin.dep.no/kuf/engelsk.

ARTS

For detailed arts information in Norway, access the English pages at [W] www.odin.dep .no, click on 'About Norway', then select 'History, Culture, Geography, Recreation'.

Music

The earliest recorded Norwegian musical compositions date back to the early 18th century, when town musicians and travelling performers composed music for dances and chamber music performances. After the union with Sweden in 1814, Oslo saw a boom in musical interest whenever the royal court was in town, and officials, landowners and the wealthier classes sponsored musical events at private gatherings.

By the middle of the 18th century, Norway had produced its first virtuoso, violinist Ole Bull (see the boxed text 'Ole Bull' in the Bergen & South-Western Fjords chapter), who came to be known throughout Europe as the 'Nordic Paganini'. His promotion of Hardanger-area folk fiddlers in Bergen concert halls and the collection of Norwegian folk music by Ludvig Mathias Lindeman brought Norwegian folk music traditions to European attention. Also, Bull's mentoring efforts among aspiring Bergen musicians paved the way for composer Edvard Grieg (see the boxed text 'Edvard Grieg' in the Bergen & South-Western Fjords chapter).

Thanks to Grieg's musical genius and the considerable talent of his contemporaries Halfdan Kierulf and Johan Svendsen, the 1870s and 1880s have been called the 'Golden Age' of Norwegian music. By 1905, when the union between Norway and Sweden was dissolved, Norway had this body of work to put forward as part of its national identity and, in the same spirit, Norwegian composers also cast back to the medieval traditions that had preceded the country's political unions with both Denmark and Sweden. David Monrad Johansen, Geirr Tveitt, Fartein Valen and Pauline Hall based their works on the late German romantics and French impressionists. While Johansen and Tveitt concentrated more on monumentalism, Valen and Hall embraced a lighter, more impressionistic style. During this period, most serious musicians were employed by cinemas and cafes, while composers were relegated to earning a living as teachers and music critics.

After WWII, however, any former ties with German culture were necessarily broken and the new generation of composers opted to study in Paris or the USA rather than Leipzig. Among the newcomers were Kvandal, Hovland, Nystedt and Hagerup Bull, who no longer sought a national musical identity, but rather, to achieve a more international voice. This was realised through the technological revolutions of the 1950s and 1960s, much to the dismay of traditionalists. Novel experimental and avant-garde music, involving electronics and sound effects, made its debut and was mostly met with consternation by the bemused public. In fact, churches refused to hire themselves out for such performances, lest their equipment be damaged or their

sanctity profaned! As a result, the avant-garde era in Norway was mercifully quite brief.

During the last quarter of the 20th century, things grew less surreal. There was a brief period of politicism, in which composers identified with various causes; Alfred Hanson dedicated a violin concerto to Chilean president Salvador Allende and the *Trauermusik*, by Søderlind, was inspired by both the war in Biafra and the Soviet invasion of Czechoslovakia. More recent trends, however, have retreated to a long-standing interest in Norwegian folk music and insistence on cultural preservation, which has dominated most modern works while still integrating computer technology.

Classical music is still alive, however, as evidenced by the popular philharmonic orchestras of Oslo, Bergen (which dates from 1765), Trondheim and Stavanger and the Norwegian Opera Company (established in 1958). A new opera house is planned for Oslo, but construction will take years. Both jazz and pop music have also taken hold in Norway, and Norwegian musicians such as saxophonist Jan Garbarek and Sami singer Mari Boine have attracted international attention (and who could forget A-ha, the big Norwegian band of the 80s?).

The increasing enthusiasm for music in Norway is reflected especially in a growing number of local music festivals springing up throughout the country. The best known is the Bergen International Festival, held in May, followed by the internationally acclaimed jazz festivals in Molde and Kongsberg. Other significant music festivals are held annually in Bodø, Trondheim (during the St Olavs-dagene festival), Al, Bø i Telemark, Risør, Kristiansand, Oslo and around 40 other locations, so it's safe to say that nearly every weekend you can find a worthwhile musical bash somewhere in Norway. Details of many music festivals are posted on the Internet at W www.norwayfestivals.com.

The haunting music of the Sami people of northern Norway is also enjoying interest among aficionados of more esoteric musical styles. Recent Sami artists such as Aulu Gaup, Mari Boine Persen and Nils

Aslak Valkeapääs have performed, recorded and popularised traditional and modern versions of the traditional *joik*, or personal songs (see the later discussion of Religion, and the boxed text 'Sami Culture & Traditions' in The Far North chapter).

Literature

As a country, Norway is fairly young, but its literature goes back over a thousand years. Around the turn of the previous millennium, the Vikings were producing sagas reflecting their lives and experiences, long before the time of Norway's best-known modern writers, Ibsen and Hamsun.

There are two large groups of medieval Norse literature: skaldic poetry and eddic poetry. The *skalds* were the Norwegian court poets of the 9th and 10th centuries; they produced songs organised according to a loose rhyme scheme and used a technique of metaphoric descriptions known as *kenning*, as well as complex alliterative structures. These works, with titles such as *Harald's Song* and *Lack of Gold*, served as celebrations of Norwegian kings and their courts.

Eddic poetry is named after the Edda, the most important collection of medieval Icelandic literature, which means that it's culturally Norwegian. The Edda, which combines Christian with pre-Christian elements, is the most extensive source of information on Norse mythology, but it wasn't written down until Snorre Sturluson recorded it in the 13th century, long after the Christianisation of both Norway and Iceland. Its subject matter includes the story of the origin, history and end of the world, instructions on writing poetry, a series of disconnected aphorisms attributed to the god Oðinn, and an anthology of tales similar to the Germanic *Nibelungenlied*.

Apart from the Edda itself, there are three forms of eddic poetry: legendary sagas, heroes' sagas, and didactic poetry. Titles include the *Hymiskviða* (Hymir-Song), which recounts Þór's legendary battle with the Midgård serpent, the *Volsunga Saga*, in which the heroes coincide with those in the Nibelungenlied, and the *Runatal* (Rune-Song), which tells of Oðinn's sacrifice on the world tree *yggdrasil*.

Around the middle of the 14th century, after half the Norwegian population had succumbed to the Black Death, the Norse literary tradition began to wane, and for several centuries following the union with Denmark in 1380, Norway's language, cultural and literary traditions fell into disuse. An indigenous Norwegian literature wasn't resurrected until the late 17th century, with the emergence of writers Petter Dass (1647–1707) and Dorothe Engelbretsdatter (1634–1716). Although Dass was Dano-Norwegian (and actually of Scottish stock), he celebrated northern Norway in his *Nordlands Trompet* (Trumpet of the Northland), and his rhythmic poetry spread around the country in the form of folk songs. Engelbretsdatter's complex baroque poetry was extremely popular in her time but, perhaps because of its overtly Christian content, it has been largely ignored by modern anthologists and literary historians.

Romanticism hit Norway in the works of Henrik Wergeland (1808–45) who, in his short life, wrote large quantities of ecstatic love poetry, mystical religious works, novellas and non-fiction. Wergeland championed his country's cultural independence from Denmark, and also fought for social justice toward the lower classes, especially farmers and the poor.

Near the end of the 19th century, Norwegian literature gained international prominence with the work of 'four great ones': Henrik Ibsen (1828–1906), Bjørnstjerne Bjørnson (1832–1910), Alexander Kjelland (1849–1906) and Jonas Lie (1833–1908). Ibsen was the quintessential Norwegian dramatist, but spent over 30 years of his life travelling and living in Europe. While he started out writing and directing Bergen theatre pieces, his breakthrough came with the German and Italian-influenced plays *A Doll's House* (1880) and *Ghosts* (1881), both of which created a stir all over Europe for their treatment of the role of women and the tensions of family life. In his subsequent plays, including *The Wild Duck* and *Hedda Gabler* (both 1890), Ibsen shifted his emphasis from social to individual psychology. In addition to creating absorbing dramas with interesting subject matter, Ibsen also initiated a new dramatic tradition by abandoning verse in favour of prose.

Less well known today, Bjørnson became hugely popular with his story *Trust and Trial* in 1857. Following in Ibsen's footsteps in Bergen, Bjørnson went on to write short stories, drama, journalism, and around 30,000(!) letters. In his early career, his work concentrated on descriptions of rural life in contemporary Norway, and he was (falsely) accused of romanticising the lot of the rural folk. Later, he focused his attentions on social problems in the hope of promoting industrialisation in Norway. In 1903, he was the first Norwegian writer to be awarded the Nobel Prize in Literature.

Realist and satirist Kjelland, who wrote novels, short stories and dramas, was at the heart of one of Norway's biggest literary controversies in 1885. Recommended to parliament for a government stipend, he was rebuffed for alleged immorality. In his *Gift* trilogy – *Garman & Worse* (1880), *Skipper Worse* (1882) and *Gift* (1883) – Kjelland depicted the transition of a patrician family to modern capitalist entrepreneurs.

A generation after these writers, Knut Hamsun (1859–1952) and Sigrid Undset (1882–1949) both received Nobel Prizes in 1928 and 1920, respectively. Frequently characterised as the most significant female writer in Norwegian literature, Undset began her career with a series of books on the plight of poor and middle-class women. Between 1920 and 1922, she published the *Kristin Lavransdottir* trilogy, a historical novel set in 14th-century Scandinavia. Though much more optimistic than her earlier work, Undset continued to criticise the fact that women must subject their will and sexuality to social and religious standards. *Kristin Lavransdottir* was followed by the *Master of Hestviken* series, which was also set in medieval times.

The work of Hamsun can be divided into three periods. Most of his early work, including his great novels *Hunger* (1890) and *Mysteries* (1892), features romantic heroes,

tragic love stories and psychological examination. Later, Hamsun wrote a number of social novels which praised rural life and criticised industrialisation and urbanisation. A product of this period was *The Growth of the Soil* (1917), for which Hamsun received the Nobel Prize. His last work, the *Vagabond Trilogy* (1927–34), centred around a less romanticised and more human hero. Because of his elitism, his appreciation of Germanic values and his support of rural life, it's no surprise that Hamsun sided with the Nazis in WWII. Unfortunately, his controversial politics have clouded modern appreciation of his literary work, which stands in the tradition of Dostoevsky and Joyce as a significant contribution to literary modernism.

Contemporary Norwegian literature takes on a variety of forms and genres, but little of it has been translated into English. The works of Dag Solstad espouse ironic socialist realism on documentary topics and attack capitalism. In a similar vein, but akin to the Latin American magic realism of Vargas Llosa and García Márquez, Kjartan Flogstad's *Dollar Road* portrays the changes in a small Norwegian town with the advent of industrialism. More traditionally mainstream, Knud Faldbakken writes dystopian novels. *Twilight Country* and its sequel *Sweetwater* are set in an unnamed country in the near future, where society has collapsed and characters eke out a living in the face of apocalyptic chaos. Fladbakken's *The Sleeping Prince* retells the fairy tale *Sleeping Beauty* from a woman's perspective, and explores male/female relationships and sexuality.

Herrbjørg Wassmo, one of several prominent modern female writers, received the Nordic Prize for Literature in 1987. Her books centre around the plight of women and damaged children in Norwegian society. *Dina's Book* tells the eponymous heroine's story in 1840s Norway, while *The House with the Blind Glass Windows* is set in and after WWII.

Finally, the most famous contemporary Norwegian author is Jostein Gaarder. Gaarder's first bestseller *Sophie's World*

(1991) is typical of all of his books: it addresses serious philosophical and religious issues through the eyes of a young adult, employing the narrative technique of a story within a story. In *Sophie's World*, while learning about the history of Western philosophy through a correspondence course she never entered, young Sophie finds out that she is no more than a character in a novel. *Sophie's World* has been published in over 40 languages and has sold over 15 million copies! In *The Solitaire Mystery*, the analogous literary device is a deck of cards, and in *The Christmas Mystery* it's an advent calendar, but in both cases, a child protagonist must solve some riddle or puzzle which will determine their destiny. *Hello, Is Anybody There?* addresses the problem of dealing with the arrival of a younger sibling by making use of an alien figure. More recently, *That Same Flower* is somewhat different, purporting to be the translation of a letter from Floria Æmilia to her lover Saint Augustine. In this feminist guise – giving Augustine's asceticism and ideals a distinctly unusual twist – Gaarder raises familiar issues such as the existence of God and the point of human life. Gaarder's latest work, *Maya* also addresses life, the universe and everything, but not entirely successfully.

Architecture

Due to Norway's vast timber resources, the use of wood has been a major factor in the country's architectural designs. Working in wood required less labour (and less expense) than cutting, shaping and building in stone, so the peasants, farmers, hunters and fishing communities enjoyed cosy wooden homes while the wealthier folks displayed their means by constructing palatial but cold and draughty stone dwellings. In the far north, where both wood and stone were in short supply, the early nomadic Sami ingeniously built their homes of turf, which was in ample supply and provided excellent insulation against the cold.

Most larger religious buildings were also constructed in stone and employed strong Anglo-Saxon influences (notable exceptions include the Gothic-style Nidaros Cathedral in Trondheim and the Romanesque Stavanger Cathedral), which isn't surprising when you consider that Norwegian Christianity was actually imported from England. However, many late Viking Age and early medieval churches were built of ornately worked wood and, although those that survive have been heavily restored, these unique stave churches are some of the oldest surviving wooden buildings on Earth (see the boxed text 'Stave Churches' in the Western Fjords chapter). Named for their vertical supporting posts, these churches are distinguished by detailed carved designs, dragon-headed gables resembling the prows of classic Viking ships and by their undeniably beautiful, almost Oriental forms. Of the 500 to 600 which were originally built, only about 20 of the remaining ones retain many of their original components.

After the Black Death, the country fell into Danish hands. For nearly four centuries, architectural styles reflected the European Renaissance and baroque traditions which predominated in Denmark and Germany at the time, and they continued to prevail even after the 1814 dissolution of the Danish union. After the largely wooden town of Oslo burned in 1624, King Christian IV determined that the town be rebuilt in brick masonry with broad streets to reduce fire hazards in the future. During the 19th century, however, the need for larger public buildings in the capital – the Royal Palace, the university, the Oslo Stock Exchange, the Norges Bank, the Christiania Theatre and other public structures – coincided with the embracing of the new and trendy neoclassical (Empire) architectural tradition.

Around the middle of the 19th century, Norwegian architects habitually travelled to Italy to gain inspiration and en route they discovered the 'gingerbread' wooden architecture which was characteristic of the Alps. Realising that this style would work readily in timber-rich Norway, they inspired a flurry of wooden spa hotels adorned with Norwegian motifs which eventually came to be known as the Norwegian 'dragon style'. Although many examples have since burned down, this tradition is reflected in a number of historic hotels around the country.

In the early 20th century, architect Henrik Bull introduced the German *Jugendstil* (youthful style) or Art Nouveau architecture. This whimsical style is best reflected in the Ministry of Finance, the National Theatre and the Historical Museum, all in Oslo, as well as the entire town of Ålesund, which was completely rebuilt after a devastating fire in 1904.

After all the destruction of WWII, Norway was faced with the task of major reconstruction in most towns. Thanks to the predominant Labour party, Norwegian architecture took a dramatic turn which could best be summed up by the slogan of the day, 'a roof over our heads'. Reflecting the Soviet notion that housing should be functional but equivalent for everyone and not ostentatious, practical high-density housing and bland commercial and public structures sprang up around the country, leaving such towns as Mo i Rana and Honningsvåg with no charm at all. Fortunately, post-modernism took root in the 1980s and most new structures enjoy a bit more originality.

Visual Arts

Although folk art has been part of Norwegian life since the ancient hunters told their stories in carved stone, the stylised Bronze Age artefacts uncovered with the *Oseberg* ship, and the works of the medieval craftspeople who instilled their distinctive religious devotions into their ornate stave churches, it wasn't until the 19th century that painting and sculpture for its own sake entered the Norwegian artistic consciousness. This is partially due to the country's peripheral location, and the fact that Norwegian artists had to go abroad for their training. The result was the late development of a unique Norwegian artistic voice.

Norway's first acclaimed painter was probably the mid to late 19th-century artist JC Dahl who, by superimposing European romanticism on his interpretations of the naturally romantic Norwegian landscapes, came to be known as the father of Norwegian painting. During this period, most

Norwegian artists reflected the ideals of schools in Düsseldorf and Munich but, by the late 19th century, thanks to the Paris realist movements, a Norwegian artistic identity had begun to emerge. Fortunately, most romanticists of this era managed to avoid the cliched 'tourist views' of the country, and preferred to see the magnificent Norwegian landscape from the inhabitants' viewpoint.

During this period, Norway's two best known artists, painter Edvard Munch (1863–1944) and sculptor Gustav Vigeland (1869–1943), produced the body of their work (for more information on these artists, see the boxed texts 'Edvard Munch' and 'Gustav Vigeland' in the Oslo chapter). However, they were better received abroad than at home and their unique works had little effect on future Norwegian artistic directions.

During the early 20th century, the impressionist Henri Matisse inspired several ardently decorative Norwegian artists, Axel Revold, Per Krohg and Alf Rolfsen, who soon came to be known as the 'fresco brothers'. Another pupil of Matisse, Henrik Sørensen, whose nationalistic tendencies placed him in the same league, served unofficially as the 'club's' fourth member.

Between the world wars, the cubist and constructivist genres were exhibited by Ragnhild Keyser and Charlotte Wankel, as well as Thorvald Hellesen, who chose to work in France rather than at home. During the 1930s, the surrealist idiom emerged in the works of Sigurd Winge and Erik Johannessen. At the same time, the socialist Arne Ekeland produced monumental frescoes, but with little effect because of his then unorthodox political leanings.

During the post-war years, the brooding forests of Jakob Weidemann, the constructivist paintings of Gunnar S Gundersen, and the literal (non-figurative) sculptures of Arnold Haukeland and Åse Texmon Rygh dominated the visual arts scene.

Through the 1980s, international interest in Norwegian art grew and the government began funding art programs not only in Oslo, but also in Bergen and Trondheim. As in much of the developed world, the art of this modern era departed dramatically from the protest work of the 1960s and 70s. Throughout the decade and into the 1990s, the artistic community tended toward naive depictions and random displays of colour; the most remarkable progenitor of this period was probably Tore Hansen, but Bjørn Carlsen represented a growing consciousness of the worldwide ecological imbalance. Many down-to-earth Norwegians have dismissed this genre as the 'work of children' or likened it to folk art, but the international community has more generously called it 'subtly humorous'.

The 1990s in Norway were best exemplified by the work of sculptor Bård Breivik, who studied the relationships between humans and their tools, and Per Inge Bjørlo, whose woodcuts and linotype prints primitively depicted both people and animals, as well as a host of high-tech artists who used computers to develop postmodernist images. Odd Nerdrum's provocative paintings have brought him to the attention of many people, both home and abroad. However, Norway's long-standing artistic relationship with nature continues unabated, and it's likely that the wild open spaces will continue to inspire artists for many years to come.

Cinema

Thanks mainly to Norwegian actress Liv Ullman and Swedish director Ingmar Bergman, Norway's first major film success was the screen version of Sigrid Undset's *Kristin Lavransdottir*, the first volume of a medieval tragedy set in Norway. Of Norway's three Nobel Prize-winning authors, Knut Hamsun has been the most appealing to filmmakers. They have brought to the screen such novels as *Hunger*, *Pan* and *The Telegraphist*, while two films by other authors, *The Case Against Hamsun* and a three-hour biographical documentary of his life, reveal a fascination with this controversial author who supported Hitler during WWII.

The modern Oscar-winning film *Babette's Feast* also has a Norwegian connection; in her novel, author Karen Blixen set the story

in northern Norway, but oddly, director Gabriel Axel set the film in much flatter Danish Jutland. On the other hand, the film *Black Eyes*, by Russian director Nikita Michalkhov, was filmed in the spectacular landscapes around Kjerringøy in Nordland.

An Oscar nomination was given to Nils Gaup's *The Pathfinder*, which is based on a medieval legend and presented in the Sami language. So acclaimed was this film that the Disney Corporation invested in Gaup's next film, *Håkon Håkonsson*, about a Norwegian Robinson Crusoe who set off for the South Seas last century. Also nominated was *Nine Lives* by the prolific Arne Skouen, a *Dagbladet* newspaper columnist who made 17 films between 1948 and 1968. The story is set during the German occupation and follows a soldier put ashore on the stormy northern coast of Norway as he attempts to reach neutral Sweden.

Children's films have also featured in Norwegian filmmaking. Erik Gustavson directed a children's comedy entitled *Herman*, about an Oslo 10-year-old with hair problems, and Marius Holst made the 1995 Berlin Festival winner, *Blue Angel*, which also features childhood conflicts in Oslo. Adolescence is explored in Berit Nesheim's *Frida* and Eva Isaksen has made several films in the *Pelle & Proffen* series, about the adventures of two teenage detectives. Ivo Caprino, who specialises in animation and Norwegian fairy tales, created the humorous and acclaimed cartoon film entitled *Pinchcliff Grand Prix*.

The concerns of Norwegian women are probably best explored in the work of Anja Breien, who launched her successful career in the mid-1970s with *Jostedalsrypa*, about a young 14th-century girl who was the only survivor of the Black Death in the western Norwegian valley, Jostedalen. Over the past 20 years, Breien has also made a trilogy of films, *Wives*, *Wives 10 Years After* and *Wives III*, about a trio of women who return to their school reunions and discuss their lives. A fourth instalment, which hopes to continue tracing Norwegian women's issues into the new millennium, is planned for sometime around 2005.

Breien's most acclaimed films, however, are probably *Next of Kin*, which was featured at the Cannes Film Festival in 1979, and *Witch Hunt*, which took awards at the Venice Film Festival in 1982.

Perhaps the film about Norway that's most familiar to international audiences is the rather trite *Song of Norway*, which is a popularised biographical treatment of the lives and work of Edvard and Nina Grieg. While the landscapes and music are monumental, the film itself is dedicated more to its potential entertainment value than to historical fact.

SOCIETY & CONDUCT

In general, Norwegians are both independent and outdoor-oriented, and on summer weekends they head for the hills and lakes to partake in the country's excellent hiking, fishing and boating opportunities. In winter, they take to the slopes and forests for downhill or cross-country skiing. Thanks to the age-old law known as *Allemansretten* or 'every man's right', public access to wild areas is guaranteed and 'No Trespassing' or 'Keep Out' signs are virtually unknown. For details on wild camping and hiking, see Activities in the Facts for the Visitor chapter.

Norwegians tend to have an easy-going attitude towards their neighbours, although negative remarks are sometimes made about Sweden, which was the last foreign Scandinavian power to control Norwegian affairs. Although minority groups are currently fairly well treated (or tolerated) by the authorities, this is a relatively recent phenomenon (see the disturbing book *Eugenics & the Welfare State* by Gunnar Broberg and Nils Roll-Hansen for details). Ordinary people are no more or less xenophobic than anywhere else, but government thinking is moving towards repatriation of refugees.

Traditional Culture

Of all Norway's cultural traditions, one of the most evident elements is the *bunad*, the elaborate regional folk costumes. Each district has developed their own unique designs which exhibit varying degrees of colour and originality. In such traditional regions as Hallingdal, Hordaland, Setesdal

A Prairie Home Companion

The unofficial voice of Norwegian-American culture is the radio show *A Prairie Home Companion*. First broadcast in 1974 in the heavily ethnic-Norwegian state of Minnesota, it's now one of the most popular shows on the US National Public Radio network, a Saturday evening ritual for some three million listeners, equal to two-thirds the population of Norway!

It consists of two hours of sprightly radio. Comedic sound effects and interludes of old-time and folk music frame skits with characters like Guy Noir Private Eye and the cultured cowboys Dusty and Lefty; faux advertisements pitch Bertha's Kitty Boutique (for persons who care about cats) and the Ketchup Advisory Board. The annual joke show teems with titters about Norwegians (and other ethnicities, which would be politically incorrect without Public Radio's upscale imprimatur), and *PHC* is not above occasional excretory humour.

The show's Norwegian heart is the weekly news from Lake Wobegon, a tiny, fictional town in Minnesota's wind- and snow-swept north, where 'all the women are strong, all the men are good looking, and all the children are above average'. Taciturn Norwegian bachelor farmers observe the world from the Chatterbox Café, and locals ice-fish, eat *lutefisk* and fill the Church of Our Lady of Perpetual Responsibility. The town's best-known landmark is the Tomb of the Unknown Norwegian, and its leading civic organisation is the Sons of Knute.

PHC's Norwegian-ness is all the more remarkable given that its host, originator and chief writer, Garrison Keillor, is of Scottish descent. Keillor has also gained fame as an author, with best-selling books including *Lake Wobegon Days; the Book of Guys;* and the most recent (2001), *Lake Wobegon, Summer 1956*. He also contributes to the *New Yorker* and *Time* magazines.

Proof that you don't have to be Norwegian to appreciate *A Prairie Home Companion:* the rabbi of one of your authors counts Keillor among his heroes. If you're not lucky enough to be near a radio playing the show some Saturday, you can hear excerpts and get more information at **w** www.prairiehome.org.

and parts of Telemark, they remained in everyday use until after WWII, but they're currently used mainly for weddings and other festive events.

Traditionally, the intricate embroidery work on these lovely creations was performed by shepherdesses and milkmaids while tending their livestock. Nowadays, these elaborate costumes are produced only by a few serious seamstresses and embroiderers but, because modern folk don't have so much time on their hands, today the purchase of a bunad represents a major financial commitment. The folk museum on the Bygdøy peninsula in Oslo features displays of these memorable costumes, but the best place to observe them is in Oslo during the 17 May National Day celebrations, when men and women from all over the country turn up in the traditional dress of their heritage areas.

Traditional folk dancing and singing is also enjoying a resurgence in popularity and numerous annual music festivals feature these elements. Ring dances such as roundels, pols, reinlenders, polkas and mazurkas fell into disuse in the 18th century, but they re-emerged around the time of independence in 1905, when the country was seeking a distinctive national identity. Today, troupes of *leikarringer* (folk dancers) practise all over the country and compete in *kappleiker* (dance competitions), which attract large audiences. These festivities are often accompanied by traditional instruments such as the unique Hardanger fiddle, which derives its distinctive sound from four or five sympathetic strings stretched out beneath the usual four strings.

Storytelling is another centuries-old tradition, and trolls figure prominently in Norwegian folklore. Although they're best known in the outside world as habitual harrassers of billy goats, in Norway they form the basis for the custom of fireside storytelling that historically helped to pass the dark winter months. These relatively antisocial folks were normally associated with mountainous areas and, while some were considered friendly, most were pesky and cosmetically-challenged creatures who lived underground beneath houses and barns and were a convenient target of blame for the average peasant's woes. Trolls live on in Norway's place names, as mascots, as carved figurines and in scores of folk tales.

Dos & Don'ts

Most Norwegians are straightforward and easy-going, with few customs that differ from those of other Europeans, or of North Americans or Australasians. The traditional handshake is used liberally in both business and social circles when greeting friends or meeting strangers. In the latter case, customary introductions will usually include your full name. A ubiquitous greeting uttered constantly in Norway, is *Vær så god* (pronounced roughly 'var sho GOOT'), which carries all sorts of expressions of goodwill: 'Hello', 'Greetings', 'Goodbye', 'Welcome', 'Pleased to meet you', 'I'm happy to serve you', 'Thanks', 'You're welcome,' and a host of other things. There's no equivalent in English, but it roughly approximates the all-purpose *bitte* in German or *aloha* in Hawaiian.

If you're a guest in a Norwegian home, be sure to remove your shoes before entering the living area. It's customary to present your host with a small gift of sweets or flowers and avoid sipping your drink before he or she makes the toast, *Skål*, which you should answer in return. This traditional ritual is most frequently accompanied by direct eye contact with your host, which symbolises respect and the absence of guile.

RELIGION
Christianity

Olav Tryggvason is credited with the introduction of Catholic Christianity to Norway around the turn of the last millennium, and Olav Haraldsson became the country's first saint, but modern Norwegian religion has been most influenced by the German reformer Martin Luther, who viewed the Scriptures as the sole authority of God and advocated that only by grace can humankind be saved from its savage nature. His doctrines were adopted in Norway in 1537.

Today, 86.3% of Norwegians belong to the Church of Norway, which is the national denomination of Protestant Evangelical Lutheranism. The Norwegian constitution states: 'All inhabitants of the Realm shall have the right to free exercise of their religion. The Evangelical-Lutheran religion shall remain the official religion of the State. The inhabitants professing it are bound to bring up their children in the same.'

Officially, the King of Norway also serves as the head of the Church and has the final say in all controversial decisions. This power was dramatically exercised in 1961, when King Olav V appointed the country's first woman priest and again in 1993, when King Harald V sanctioned the first female bishop. Even more controversial was the occasion in the 1970s when a bishop and quite a few priests quit after the Storting, with royal sanction, passed a liberal abortion law. A good proportion of the populace scarcely noticed the issue, but a few more pious parishioners decided that the Church was Christian in name more than practice and withdrew.

While the average Norwegian attends church about twice a year and the organisation funds missions around the world, as many as 5000 Norwegians leave the official church annually, most of them advocating a separation of Church and State.

Other religious groups represented in Norway include the Humanist & Ethical Union with over 67,900 members, and several Christian denominations: around 45,000 Pentecostals, 42,600 Roman Catholics, the Lutheran Free Church with 21,000 adherents, 15,000 Jehovah's Witnesses, 13,000 Methodists, 10,000 Baptists, over 8000 members of the Missionary Alliance, 6000 Seventh-Day Adventists and 1600 Anglicans. The country also has approximately 50,000 Muslims and over 1000 Jews.

Sami

Historically, the Sami religious traditions were characterised mainly by a relationship to nature and its inherent god-like archetypes. In sites of special power, particularly at prominent rock formations, people made offerings to their gods and ancestors to ensure success in hunting or other endeavours. Intervention and healing were effected by shamanic specialists, who used drums and small figures to launch themselves onto out-of-body journeys to the ends of the Earth in search of answers. Interestingly, as with nearly all indigenous peoples in the northern hemisphere, the bear, as the most powerful creature in nature, was considered a sacred animal.

Historically, another crucial element in the religious tradition was the singing of the *joik* (also spelt *yoik*), or 'song of the plains'. Each person had his or her own melody or song which conveyed not their personality or experiences, but rather their spiritual essence. So powerful and significant was this personal mantra that the early Christian missionaries considered it a threat to their efforts and banned it as sinful.

Although most modern Sami profess Christianity, elements of the old religion have recently made a limited comeback.

LANGUAGE
Norwegian

Norway has two official languages – Bokmål and Nynorsk – which are quite similar and are spoken or understood by all Norwegians. However, rural regional dialects vary tremendously and people from one side of the country may have difficulty understanding people from the other side.

Bokmål (BM), literally 'book-language' (also known as Riksmål, the 'national language') is the modern urbanites' version of the language of the former Danish rulers. As the predominant language in Norwegian cities, it's used by over 80% of the population. It's also the main language of instruction for most school children and the predominant language of the media.

Nynorsk (NN), or 'New Norwegian' (as opposed to Old Norwegian, the language used prior to Danish rule) predominates in the Western Fjords and parts of central Norway; it also serves as a *lingua franca* (common language) in those regions which may have one or more dialects. Prior to WWII, Nynorsk was the first language of nearly one-third of all Norwegian school children; as a result of growing urbanisation this figure has been reduced to about 15% today.

Perhaps the most striking oddity of Norway's linguistic dichotomy is that many words and place names have two or more authorised spellings. Today, Nynorsk is the official administrative language in the counties of Møre og Romsdal and Sogn og Fjordane. Interestingly, the national government has decreed that a certain percentage of television subtitles be translated into Nynorsk.

Fortunately for most visitors, English is also widely spoken in Norway, even in rural areas. However, it's still a good idea to learn a few Norwegian phrases to help you establish contact with people – and if you're having obvious trouble with your Norwegian, most people will be happy to switch to English.

For more information and a list of useful Norwegian words and phrases see the Language chapter at the back of this book. For a more comprehensive guide to the language get a copy of Lonely Planet's *Scandinavian Europe phrasebook*. A number of Norwegian language course books are available internationally – most also come with audio cassettes.

If you're interested in learning Bokmål, the two best Norwegian books are *Ny i Norge* and *Bo i Norge*; both are available locally.

Sami

In northern Norway, a good percentage of the population speaks Sami, a language of the Finno-Ugric group. It's related to Samoyed (among other northern Russian ethnic dialects), Finnish, Estonian and Hungarian.

Sami is spoken by around 20,000 people in Norway (there are also Sami speakers in Finland, Sweden and Russia). Although most of them can also communicate in Norwegian (and some even speak English), visitors who know even a few words of the local language will be able to access this unique culture more readily.

Three distinct Sami dialects exist in Norway – the Fell (also called Eastern or Northern) Sami, Central Sami and South Sami – but a total of 10 different dialects are used within the Sápmi region: Ume, Pite, Lule, Inari, Skolt, Kildin and Ter (see the Sami Cultural Area & Dialects map, earlier). Fell Sami is considered the standard Sami language.

Folklore & Legends

Mythical Creatures

Norwegian folklore includes references to all sorts of supernatural beings. While many people assume that these creatures, common to most cultures, are simply Jungian archetypes, manifestations of the Id, or alien beings, more traditional folk consider them descendants of the children hidden from God by mother Eve.

Perhaps the most Scandinavian of all these beings is the **troll**, which is thought to have emerged in Norway at the close of the last Ice Age. Trolls inhabit gloomy forests, moonlit lakes, deep fjords, snowy peaks and roaring waterfalls, but they're predominantly creatures of shadow and darkness. Any troll who makes the mistake of becoming exposed to direct sunlight will turn to stone.

Trolls come in all shapes and sizes, some large some small, but nearly all have four fingers and toes on each hand and foot, as well as long, crooked noses and bushy tails. Some have multiple heads, with anything from one to three eyes per head, which of course makes them appear frightening. It's believed that trolls can live for several hundred years and are credited with having produced both **Þór's hammer** and **Oðinn's spear**. They also have a penchant for harassing **billy goats** and despising the sound of church bells. They're known to get irritable and may anger easily but they're generally kind to humans.

A larger version of the troll was the giant and, according to the **Edda**, the world was created from the body of the giant **Ymir of Jotunheimen** (home of the giants), after his death at the hand of the Norse god **Oðinn**.

Throughout Europe, a **witch** has long been the personification of evil. Although most modern witches dabble only in 'white' magic, the traditional view is that anyone accused of being a witch or warlock has sold their soul to the devil and is capable of all sorts of heinous behaviour, including the infliction of unpleasant spells. Norwegian witches are no exception and are still considered evil forces, despite the public relations campaign recently mounted by practitioners of Wicca.

Elves, who normally live stream-side in the deepest forests, also come in both good and bad varieties and only emerge at night, when there's no risk of turning to stone. It's said that the sites of their night time festivities and dances are marked by luxuriant rings of grass.

Other elusive creatures include **hulder**, who steal milk from summer pastures; the frightening **draugen**, a headless fisherman who foretells drownings with a haunting wail; and the **vetter** (wights), who serve as the guardian spirits of the wildest coastlines.

Serpents existed in Viking mythology, but at least one is still with us today. The first testimony to the existence of **Selma the Serpent**, in the Telemark lake Seljordvatn, dates back to the summer of 1750, when Gunleik Andersson-Verpe of nearby Bø was 'attacked by a sea horse' while rowing across the lake. In 1880, Bjørn Bjørge and his mother Gunnhild reported killing a bizarre lizard while doing laundry in the lake. Nearly every summer since, witnesses have sighted the fins and humps of this fast-moving lake creature. According to most observers,

Title Page: In Norwegian folklore, trolls, who inhabit dark forests and lakes, are said to crack and turn to stone if exposed to direct sunlight (Photograph by Ned Friary)

the creature measures the size of a large log, or slightly bigger. Some have described it as eel-like while others have likened it to a snail, a lizard or a crocodile and have reported lengths of 25m, 30m and even 50m. Amateur videos filmed in 1988 and 1993 reveal a series of humps in the water but their grainy nature renders the evidence inconclusive. Researchers generally remain open-minded but have suggested that the lake is too small to support creatures more than about 7m long.

As with Scotland's famous Nessie, Selma has fuelled local folklore and drawn tourists to search the surface of the deep pine-rimmed lake Seljordvatn (14km long, 2km wide and 157m deep) for evidence. In 1977, Swedish freelance journalist Jan-Ove Sundberg scanned the lake with sonar equipment and detected several large objects moving in unison, then separating in several directions. In the summer of 1998, he returned with an 11-member team and spent 17 days trawling the lake with imaging equipment and even a mini-submarine outfitted with three underwater cameras, sonar and a gripping arm. Sundberg rejects the sceptics who dismiss the sightings and his own sonar evidence as the movements of moose, otters or beavers. According to him, 'The serpent does not fit any species known to humanity. It has several qualities not seen before, such as travelling on the surface at high speed and moving vertically up and down. It shows a back or a head or a neck or all three for long periods above the surface and travels very fast, maybe up to 25 knots.'

Right: The black depths of Seljordvatn, according to local legend, is the home of Selma the Sea Monster

DEANNA SWANEY

The Seljord Council and the lakeside camp site sponsored Sundberg's search for the beast, hoping that the publicity would result in a boost in tourism – and well it might. The village has already cashed in on its monster by opening a serpent restaurant, setting up a serpent exhibition and changing its coat of arms to depict a yellow Selma on a red background. Appearances are becoming more frequent: the council cultural affairs manager, Bernt Solvoll, reported that he saw the monster in 1998.

Folk Tales

The valleys in western and northern Norway are full of folk tales, sagas and myths, many of them relating to or 'explaining' curious geographic features. In the north, they're an especially rich part of Nordland coastal culture.

In one story, a lonely island-dwelling giantess shouted across the water to a giant named **Blåmann** (blue man) on the mainland, asking him to marry her. He agreed, provided she brought the island along with her but, by the time she'd packed everything up, the sun rose and she turned to stone, as did Blåmann, who'd stayed out too long waiting for her.

The island became known as Gygrøy (giantess island), but local fisherfolk renamed it **Landegode** (the good land), lest the giantess take offence. Landegode's distinctive profile is a familiar landmark on the ferry between Bodø and Kjerringøy. Blåmann is now an icecap (see Sulitjema in the Nordland chapter) and a favourite destination of technical climbers.

Another legend involves **Hestmannen** (the Horseman), who attempted to shoot the princess **Lekamøya** with an arrow when she wouldn't marry him. Her father, the king of Sømna, threw down his hat as a distraction, and the result was **Torghatten**, a hat-shaped peak that looks as if it's been pierced through, on Torget island south of Brønnøysund. Scientific types claim that the hole was the result of aeons of wind and water erosion on weak rock, but this, of course, is balderdash.

Torghatten is a popular trip from Brønnøysund, and is always pointed out as the Hurtigruten Coastal Steamer passes. Hestmannen himself is a knobbed peak on the island of Hestmanna, farther north. It can be seen from the Kilboghamn-Jektvik ferry or it makes a great day hike by private tour from the port of Tonnes (see Mo I Rana in the Nordland chapter).

To delve deeper into Norwegian folk tales and legends, many of which have been translated into English, look for works by Peter Christen Asbjørnsen and Jørgen Moe, in particular.

Facts for the Visitor

HIGHLIGHTS

For most visitors, any list of Norwegian highlights is topped by the clean air and water; the tidiness of the towns; the calm and friendly Norwegians; and of course the magnificent wilderness, which is always readily accessible – even from central Oslo! The following list (in no particular order) includes some of Norway's finest sites and destinations.

The fjords (see all regional chapters except Central Norway) – Nothing typifies Norway more than its fjords, which are the top attraction for visitors. In the popular Western and South-Western Fjords regions, Geirangerfjord has perhaps the most spectacular waterfalls and Fjærland is known for its valley glaciers. Nærøyfjord (an arm of Sognefjord) is the narrowest and perhaps most imposing, while Lysefjord, near Stavanger, is often regarded as the most beautiful and unusual. However, many of the grand fjords of Arctic Norway dwarf anything in the south and present an entirely different dimension. Any fjord is even more dramatic when viewed from a nearby peak or other viewpoint.

The Oslo-Bergen railway (Central Norway, Bergen & the South-Western Fjords, The Western Fjords) – The 470km-long route between Oslo and Bergen is one of the world's finest train journeys, passing between snowy peaks and over the bleak Hardangervidda plateau. Don't miss the side trip on the Flåm line, which hairpins its way down the Flåm valley to Aurlandsfjorden.

Røros (Central Norway) – This well-preserved historic copper-mining town presents some wonderful architecture and hiking opportunities.

Bergen (Bergen & the South-Western Fjords) – Colourful and historic Bergen is Norway's most visited and best-loved town.

Vikingskipshuset (Oslo) – The extraordinary virtually intact 1200-year-old *Oseberg* Viking ship is one of the most interesting museums in the country.

Romsdalen & Trollstigen (The Western Fjords) – The Romsdalen valley and the hairpin road over the Trollstigen pass present some of Norway's most dramatic vertical walls and waterfalls.

Stave churches – Be sure to visit several of Norway's 31 stave churches, most of them medieval. The best-known and most photographed are at Borgund (The Western Fjords), Heddal (Southern Norway) and Urnes (The Western Fjords).

Midnight sun (northern Nordland, The Far North, Svalbard & Jan Mayen) – This is what many travellers come to Norway to see and you'll enjoy it best from a north-facing coastline.

Lofoten (Nordland) – These rugged islands are Norway's premier fishing and whaling ground but they also feature the most dramatic mountain scenery in the country. Don't miss the Viking Museum at Borg or the spectacular peaks of Moskenesøy.

Svalbard (Svalbard & Jan Mayen) – With its walruses, polar bears, whales and icy landscapes, Norway's bit of the high Arctic is the country's ultimate adventure destination.

SUGGESTED ITINERARIES

Depending on your length of stay in Norway, you might like to consider the following suggestions:

Two days
From Oslo, take the 'Norway in a Nutshell' tour that includes a rail trip to Flåm and then a combination of boat and bus to Bergen. After a day in Bergen, catch an overnight train back to Oslo.

One week
Spend two days in Oslo, two days in Bergen and take a three-day jaunt through the Western Fjords, including Fjærland and Geiranger. Alternatively, fly straight to Svalbard and take a cruise up the west coast of Spitsbergen.

Two weeks
As above, plus continue northward through Åndalsnes, Trondheim and Lofoten.

One month
As above, plus hop on the northbound Hurtigruten coastal steamer in Lofoten and break your trip at Tromsø, Nordkapp and Kirkenes.

Two months
Explore the country thoroughly and spend some time skiing or hiking around Jotunheimen, Hardangervidda or the far north. Follow the coastal route north of Nordland, make stops in Tromsø, Alta and Finnmarksvidda (Kautokeino and/or Karasjok). Include a flight to Longyearbyen in Svalbard and take a cruise up the west coast of Spitsbergen.

PLANNING

Some say that Norway is so well developed you don't have to plan a thing before your trip since anything can be arranged on the spot. This is fine if you've decided to blow the massive inheritance sitting in your bank account but, if your finances are more modest, prior knowledge and careful planning can make your hard-earned travel budget stretch further. You'll also want to make sure that the things you plan to see and do will be possible at the particular time of year when you'll be travelling.

When to Go

Although Norway covers the same latitude range as Alaska (and much farther north when you include Svalbard), most of the country enjoys a surprisingly temperate climate. For this you can thank the Gulf Stream, which flows north along the coast. In Bergen, the average monthly temperature in January and February is 1.5°C and in Vardø, in the far north, the average December temperature is only -4°C. In general, the mountainous inland areas experience warmer summers and colder winters than the typically milder coastal areas, and temperatures over 30°C in summer and below -30°C in winter aren't uncommon.

Norway is at its best and brightest from May to September. Late May is particularly pleasant – flowers are blooming and fruit trees blossoming, daylight hours are growing longer and most hostels and tourist sites are open but uncrowded. North of the Arctic Circle, the true midnight sun is visible at least one day a year, and at Nordkapp it stays out from 13 May to 29 July. In Lofoten, it's visible from 28 May to 14 July, but nowhere in the country – even the far south – experiences true darkness between late May and late July.

In addition to climatic factors, visitors should also consider the tourist season, which coincides with European school holidays and runs roughly from mid-June to mid-August. During this period, public transport runs relatively frequently; tourist offices, hostels, summer hotels and tourist sites are open their longest hours; and most upmarket hotels offer better value summer rates. There's also a 'shoulder' season, running from mid-May to mid-June and mid-August to early September, when these places are open shorter hours. At other times of year, public transport runs infrequently; most hostels and camping grounds are closed; and tourist sites, museums and tourist offices are open only very limited hours, if at all. Unless you're an avid skier or hope to glimpse the aurora borealis, Norway's cold dark winters can be trying for visitors.

What Kind of Trip

If you decide to travel with others, bear in mind that travel can strain relationships as few other experiences can. This can be minimised by either pre-planning a rigid itinerary or agreeing to remain flexible about everything. When planning your itinerary, it's wise to consider the costs of moving around in Norway. Unless you have an unlimited rail pass and its validity is ticking away, you may want to just hole up for a while in a place you like and spend some time getting to know it well, observing the local way of life and discovering lesser known sites.

The Getting There & Away chapter has information on organised tours. The young, the elderly and the inexperienced tend to appreciate such tours because they minimise hassles and uncertainties. Longer tours, however, can become experiments in social cohesion and friction can develop. Though often ridiculed, the mad dash that crams an entire country into a one- or two-week holiday does have its merits. If you've never visited Norway before, you won't know which areas you'll like, and a quick 'scouting tour' will provide an overview. If you're short of time, it's probably worth picking up an unlimited rail pass that will allow you to sample the best of the country with the least possible expense.

Maps

The best road maps for drivers are the Cappelens series, which are sold in Norwegian bookshops for Nkr95. There are three maps at 1:325,000 scale: *No1 Sør-Norge Sør*, *No2*

Sør-Norge Nord and *No3 Møre og Trønde-lag*. Northern Norway is covered in two sheets at 1:400,000 scale: *No4 Nordland og Sør-Troms* and *No5 Troms og Finnmark*. The *Veiatlas Norge* (Norwegian Road Atlas), published by Statens Kartverk (the national mapping agency), is revised every two years (Nkr220).

For all travellers, Nortrabooks has produced the colourful and popular *Bilkart over Norge*. This detailed map includes useful topographic shading and depicts the entire country on one sheet at a scale of 1:1,000,000.

Statens Kartverk covers the country in 21 sheets at a scale of 1:250,000, and also produces hiking maps at a scale of 1:50,000 (Nkr70). You'll find the index on the Internet at W showcase.netins.net/web/travelgenie/norbroch.htm.

Most local tourist offices distribute free town plans and hikers can pick up topographic sheets at any DNT office (see Hiking under Activities). General maps are available in bookshops, rural general stores, DNT offices and most large tourist offices.

In the UK, good sources of maps include The Map Shop (☎ 01684-593146, fax 594559), 15 High St, Upton-upon-Severn, Worcester, WR8 0HJ; and Stanfords (☎ 020-7836 1321, fax 7836 0189), 12–14 Long Acre, London, WC2E 9LH. Both can provide detailed listings of available maps and offer mail-order services.

In North America, contact Omni Resources (☎ 336-227 8300, fax 227 3748, W www.omnimap.com), 1004 S Mebane St, PO Box 2096, Burlington, NC 27216-2096.

In Australia, there's Map Land (☎/fax 03-9670 4383), 372 Little Bourke St, Melbourne, VIC 3000, and the Travel Bookshop (☎ 02-9261 8200), Shop 3, 175 Liverpool St, Sydney, NSW 2000.

What to Bring

Norwegians normally dress quite casually (although trendily – especially when it comes to shoes!), so travellers need not pack their finest clothes. However, for cultural events and nights out, it's wise to carry an alternative to jeans and trainers (sneakers).

If you're heading for the great outdoors, remember that the weather can change instantly. You'll be happiest with layers of clothing that can be added or removed as necessary and, even in summer, you won't regret having a jacket or jersey (sweater) handy, or at least an anorak (windbreaker), especially for visits to the high country or for appreciating that 'sea breeze' on fjord cruises and ferries. Good walking shoes are requisite and hikers will need a strong pair of hiking boots, as well as a mountain stove for longer hikes. Budget travellers intending to camp shouldn't be without a tent, a sleeping sheet and a warm sleeping bag. Hostels charge extra for sheets, so pack a sleeping sheet.

For shorter visits, you may also want to cut your food costs by bringing along lightweight food items such as trail mix, peanut butter, Marmite, instant coffee and tea bags. Those staying in hostels will save money by bringing their own sheets, as linen hire adds around Nkr50 per stay.

RESPONSIBLE TOURISM

Avoid adding to the congestion in the larger cities by leaving your car outside the central area and travel in on foot or by public transport.

If the natural environment is to support the growing number of visitors, especially to remote and fragile areas, then human activity needs to be sensitive to that environment. The most important principles to minimising your impact are: leave no trace of your passing (not damaging wildlife, plants or trees); leave no litter (take out what you take in, and that includes no dumping overboard from boats); and stick to the walking trails where they exist. Camper van and caravan users must not stop overnight in lay-bys and waste water must be disposed of at approved locations.

TOURIST OFFICES
Local Tourist Offices

Tourist offices in Norway play an important role for visitors and serve as a one-stop clearing house for general information and bookings for accommodation and activities. Nearly every city and town – even the tiniest places – has its own tourist office and it's most often conveniently located near the train station, docks or town centre. Many offices run their own excursions or have close ties with local companies who fill that gap. Offices in smaller towns may be open only during peak summer months, while in cities they're open year-round but with shorter hours in the off-season.

For general brochures and books on travel in Norway, contact Norges Turistråd (Norwegian Tourist Board, formerly Nortra; ☎ 22 92 52 00, fax 22 56 05 05, e norway@ntr.no, w www.visitnorway.com), PO Box 2893, Solli, Drammensveien 40, N-0230 Oslo.

Tourist Offices Abroad
Australia & New Zealand (☎ 02-6273 3444, fax 6273 3669, e ambassade-canberra@ ud.dep.telemax.no) Royal Norwegian Embassy, 17 Hunter St, Yarralumla, ACT 2600
France (☎ 01 53 23 00 50, fax 01 53 23 00 59, e france@ntr.no) Office National du Tourisme de Norvége, BP 497, F-75366 Paris
Germany (☎ 040-229 4150, fax 229 41588, e germany@ntr.no) Norwegisches Fremdenverkehrsamt, PO Box 113317, D-20433 Hamburg
Japan (☎ 3-5212 1121, fax 5212 1122, e japan@ntr.no) Scandinavian Tourist Board, Izumikan Gobancho 4F, Gobancho 12–11, Chiyoda-ku, Tokyo 102-0076
Netherlands (☎ 0900 899 1170, fax 020-679 8886, e holland@ntr.no) Noors Verkeersbureau, PO Box 75120, NL-1070 AC Amsterdam
UK & Ireland (☎ 020-7839 6255, fax 7839 6014, e greatbritain@ntr.no) Norwegian Tourist Board, Charles House, 5 Lower Regent St, London, SW1Y 4LR
USA & Canada (☎ 212-885 9700, fax 885 9710) Norwegian Tourist Board, 655 Third Ave, Suite 1810, New York, NY 10017

VISAS & DOCUMENTS
Passport
Your most important travel document is your passport, which must be valid at least for the intended length of your trip. Some countries insist that your passport remain valid for a specified minimum period (usually three months but often up to six months) after your intended departure date. If it's about to expire, renew it before you

go, as it can be time consuming to do so on the road. On the trip, carry your passport at all times and guard it carefully.

Visas
Citizens of Denmark, Finland, Iceland and Sweden may enter Norway freely without a passport. Citizens of the USA, Canada, the UK, Ireland, Australia and New Zealand need a valid passport to visit Norway, but do not need a visa for stays of less than three months. The same is true for EU and EEA (European Economic Area) countries, most of Latin America and most Commonwealth countries (except South Africa and several other African and Pacific countries).

Travel Insurance
You should seriously consider taking out travel insurance that covers not only medical expenses and luggage theft or loss but also cancellation or delays in your travel arrangements (due to illness, ticket loss, industrial action etc). It's a good idea to buy insurance as early as possible, as late purchase may preclude coverage of industrial action that may have been in force before you bought the policy. A policy to cover theft, personal liability, loss and medical problems is strongly recommended and often a standard insurer will offer better deals than companies selling only travel insurance. Note that some policies specifically exclude 'dangerous activities' such as motorcycling, skiing, mountaineering, scuba diving or even hiking. Make sure the policy covers ambulances and an emergency flight home.

Paying for airline tickets with a credit card often provides limited travel accident insurance, and you may be able to reclaim the payment if the operator doesn't deliver. A policy that pays doctors or hospitals directly may be preferable to one where you pay on the spot and claim later. If you have to claim later, make sure you keep all documentation.

In Norway, EU citizens may be required to pay a service fee for emergency medical treatment, but presentation of an E111 form will certainly expedite matters and minimise paperwork. Inquire about these at your national health service or travel agent well in advance. Travel insurance is still advisable, however, as long as it allows treatment flexibility and will also cover ambulance and repatriation costs.

Driving Licence & Permits

Short-term visitors may hire a car with only their home country's driving licence. Also ask your automobile association for a Letter of Introduction *(Lettre de Recommendation)*, which entitles you to services offered by affiliated organisations in Norway, usually free of charge. These services may include touring maps and information, help with breakdowns, technical and legal advice etc. See the Getting Around chapter for more details on driving your own vehicle.

Student & Hostel Cards

The most useful student card is the International Student Identity Card (ISIC), a plastic ID-style card with your photograph. It can provide discounts on many forms of transport (including airlines, international ferries and local public transport), reduced or free admission to museums and sights and cheap meals in some student restaurants – a worthwhile way of cutting costs. Children under 16 and seniors normally also receive the same discounts. In addition, a Hostelling International (HI) card will save on hostel rates.

Seniors' Cards

Senior *(honnør)* discounts are the same as those for students and are normally available to those 67 years of age and over for admission to museums, public pools, transport etc. You don't require a special card, but those who look particularly youthful may need proof of their age to qualify, as the ever-proper Norwegian ticket-sellers won't believe you're a day over 39.

Vaccination Certificates

You may need these if you're travelling onwards through parts of Asia, Africa and South America, where yellow fever is prevalent.

Copies

While the risk of theft in Norway is minimal, it's wise to keep photocopies of all your important documents (passport data page, air tickets, insurance policy, travellers cheques serial numbers) in a separate place in case of theft; stash US$100 alongside, just in case. Leave copies of these documents at home, too.

It's also a good idea to store details of your vital travel documents in Lonely Planet's free online Travel Vault in case you lose your photocopies (or can't be bothered with them). Your password-protected Travel Vault is accessible online from anywhere in the world – create it at W www.ekno.lonelyplanet.com.

EMBASSIES & CONSULATES
Norwegian Embassies & Consulates

You'll find an up-to-date listing of Norwegian embassies and consulates on the Internet at W www.embassies.mfa.no.

Australia & New Zealand (☎ 02-6273 3444, fax 6273 3669, e emb.canberra@mfa.no) 17 Hunter St, Yarralumla, ACT 2600
Canada (☎ 613-238 6571, fax 238 2765, e emb.ottawa@mfa.no) Royal Bank Centre, 90 Sparks St, Suite 532, Ottawa, Ontario K1P 5B4
Denmark (☎ 33 14 01 24, fax 33 14 06 24, e emb.copenhagen@mfa.no) Amaliegade 39, DK-1256 Copenhagen K
Finland (☎ 09-171234, fax 657807, e emb.helsingfors@mfa.no) Rehbindervägen 17, FIN-00150 Helsinki/Helsingfors
France (☎ 01 53 67 04 00, fax 01 53 67 04 40, e emb.paris@mfa.no) 28 Rue Bayard, F-75008 Paris
Germany (☎ 030-505050, fax 505055, e emb.berlin@mfa.no) Rauchstrasse 1, D-10787 Berlin
Ireland (☎ 01-662 1800, fax 662 1890, e emb.dublin@mfa.no) 34 Molesworth St, Dublin 2
Japan (☎ 3-3440 2611, fax 3440 2620, e emb.tokyo@mfa.no) Minami Azabu 5-12-2, Minato-ku, Tokyo 106-0047
Netherlands (☎ 070-311 7611, fax 365 9630, e emb.hague@mfa.no) Lange Vijverberg 11, NL-2513 AC Den Haag
Russia (☎ 0501-421 1220, fax 421 1260, e emb.moscow@mfa.no) Ulitsa Povarskaya

7, RU-131940 Moscow
(☎ 51295 10037, fax 51295 10044,
ⓔ generalkonsulat-murmansk@ud.dep
.telemax.no) Ulitsa Sofji Perovskoj 5, RU-
183038 Murmansk

Sweden (☎ 08-665 6340, fax 782 9899, ⓔ emb
.stockholm@mfa.no) Skarpögatan 4, SE-
11593 Stockholm

UK (☎ 020-7591 5500, fax 7245 6993, ⓔ emb
.london@mfa.no) 25 Belgrave Square, London, SW1X 8QD

USA (☎ 202-333 6000, fax 337 0870, ⓦ www
.norway.org) 2720 34th St NW, Washington
DC 20008

Embassies & Consulates in Norway

Australia (☎ 22 47 91 79, fax 22 42 26 83)
Jernbanetorget 2, N-0106 Oslo
Canada (☎ 22 99 53 00) Wergelandsveien 7,
N-0244 Oslo
Denmark (☎ 22 54 08 00, fax 22 55 46 34)
Olav Kyrres gate 7, N-0244 Oslo
Finland (☎ 22 43 04 00, fax 22 43 06 29)
Thomas Heftyes gate 1, N-0244 Oslo
France (☎ 22 28 46 00, fax 22 43 14 85)
Drammensveien 69, N-0244 Oslo
Germany (☎ 22 27 54 00, fax 22 44 76 72)
Oscars gate 45, N-0244 Oslo
Ireland (☎ 22 12 20 00, fax 22 55 08 10)
Drammensveien 126A, N-0212 Oslo
Japan (☎ 22 55 10 11, fax 22 44 25 05)
Parkveien 33B, N-0244 Oslo
Netherlands (☎ 22 19 71 90, fax 22 56 92 00)
Oscars gate 29, N-0244 Oslo
New Zealand (☎ 66 84 95 30, fax 66 84 89 09)
Billingstadsletta 19B, Postboks 113, N-1361
Billingstad
Russia (☎ 22 55 32 78) Drammensveien 74,
N-0271 Oslo
Sweden (☎ 22 44 35 11, fax 22 43 08 84)
Nobelsgata 16, N-0244 Oslo
UK (☎ 23 13 27 70, fax 23 13 27 38) Thomas
Heftyes gate 8, N-0244 Oslo
USA (☎ 22 44 85 50, fax 22 43 07 77) Dram-
mensveien 18, N-0244 Oslo

Your Own Embassy

It's important to realise what your own
embassy – the embassy of the country of
which you are a citizen – can and can't do
to help you if you get into trouble. Generally speaking, it won't be much help in
emergencies if the trouble you're in is remotely your own fault. Remember that you

are bound by the laws of the country you
are in. Your embassy will not be sympathetic if you end up in jail after committing
a crime locally, even if such actions are
legal in your own country.

In genuine emergencies you might get
some assistance, but only if other channels
have been exhausted. For example, if you
need to get home urgently, a free ticket
home is exceedingly unlikely – the embassy
would expect you to have insurance. If you
have all your money and documents stolen,
it might assist with getting a new passport,
but a loan for onward travel is out of the
question.

Some embassies used to keep letters for
travellers or have a small reading room
with home newspapers, but these days the
mail holding service has usually been
stopped and even newspapers tend to be
out of date.

CUSTOMS

Alcohol is extremely expensive in Norway,
so it's probably worth importing your duty-
free allotment: 1L of spirits and 1L of wine
(or 2L of wine), plus 2L of beer. Even if you
don't drink, it will normally be a welcome
gift for Norwegian friends. European
(EEA)/non-European residents may also
import 200/400 cigarettes duty-free.

Importation of fresh food and controlled
drugs is prohibited.

MONEY
Currency

The Norwegian krone is most often represented as Nkr (preceding the number) in
northern Europe (and in this book), and
NOK (preceding the number) in international money markets but, within Norway, it's often simply kr (following the
amount). One Norwegian krone (Nkr1)
equals 100 øre. Coins come in denominations of 50 øre and Nkr1, 5, 10 and 20, and
notes can be worth Nkr50, 100, 200, 500
and 1000.

Exchange Rates

The following currencies convert at these
approximate rates:

country	unit		krone
Australia	A$1	=	Nkr4.64
Canada	C$1	=	Nkr5.58
Denmark	Dkr1	=	Nkr1.07
Euro	€1	=	Nkr7.94
Japan	¥100	=	Nkr6.74
New Zealand	NZ$1	=	Nkr3.77
Sweden	Skr10	=	Nkr8.68
UK	UK£1	=	Nkr12.91
USA	US$1	=	Nkr8.91

Exchanging Money

Travellers Cheques Post offices and banks exchange major foreign currencies and accept all brands of travellers cheques, which command a better exchange rate than cash by about 2%. Post offices charge a service fee of Nkr10 per travellers cheque (minimum Nkr20, maximum Nkr100) or Nkr30 per cash transaction. Some banks, including Kreditkassen and Den Norske Bank, have slightly higher fees but similar exchange rates. Other banks tend to charge steeper travellers cheque commissions (which means you're better off with higher denomination cheques).

ATMs Norwegian ATMs will allow you to access cash in your home account with an ATM card from your home bank. 'Mini-Banks' (the Norwegian name for ATMs) are found adjacent to many banks and around busy public places such as shopping centres. They accept major credit cards as well as Cirrus and/or Plus format bank cards.

Credit Cards Visa, Eurocard, MasterCard, American Express and Diners Club cards are widely accepted throughout Norway and generally you'll be better off using a credit card as you avoid the fees charged for changing cash or travellers cheques. Credit cards can be used to buy train tickets but are not accepted on domestic ferries (apart from Hurtigruten).

If your card is lost or stolen in Norway, report it to the appropriate agency: American Express (☎ 80 03 32 44); Diners Club (☎ 23 00 10 00); Eurocard/MasterCard (☎ 050 12697); and Visa (☎ 22 01 34 20).

Costs

Norway is expensive and, while you can avoid some of the sting by tightening your belt, you'll run through money very quickly, so it pays to plan your trip carefully. One thing to remember is that you must pay for practically everything from parking and coffee refills to using bridges, tunnels and public toilets. Museum admissions may not include parking outside and information leaflets are always sold separately. Drivers must even pay a toll to enter major cities!

If you only stay in camping grounds and prepare your own meals, you can squeak by on around Nkr180 per person per day. Staying in hostels that include breakfast (or eating breakfast at a bakery), having lunch at an inexpensive restaurant and picking up supermarket items for dinner, you can probably manage on Nkr300 per day. Staying at a 'cheap' hotel that includes a buffet breakfast, eating a snack for lunch and an evening meal at a moderately priced restaurant, you can expect to spend Nkr500 per person per day if you're doubling up and Nkr700 if you're travelling alone. This is still pretty bare-bones, however, and day trips, entertainment, alcohol, and even a couple of soft drinks will blow most careful budgets.

Once your daily needs are met, you need to add transport costs. With a rail pass and an itinerary that sticks to the rail lines – or hitching – this will be relatively inexpensive. However, adding bus or ferry travel, or trips to the far north (unless you're just popping into Narvik from Sweden, beyond Bodø this region is really off the rails), the expenses will mount quickly.

If you're content to hike and simply gaze at Norway's magnificent landscapes, sightseeing won't be a major expense but, otherwise, it must be part of your budget. In fact, Norway is one of only a few countries that charges admission to churches. Fortunately, the tourist offices in Oslo and Bergen sell one to three-day tourist cards including unlimited or discounted admission to most sites of interest, access to local transport, swimming pools, municipal parking and cultural programs. Students, seniors over 67 and children under 16 nearly always receive substantial discounts – sometimes as much as 50% – so it pays to have a student card (or proof of your age).

Tipping & Bargaining

Service charges and tips are included in restaurant bills and taxi fares, and no additional gratuity is expected, but there's no problem if you want to reward exceptional service with a tip. As for bargaining, it's as rare in Norway as bargains themselves. However, if you're spending lots of money at a tourist shop, you can reasonably expect some sort of high-volume discount.

Taxes & Refunds

The 24% MVA (the equivalent of Value-Added Tax in many countries or sales tax in the USA), locally known as MOMS, is normally included in marked prices for goods and services, including meals and accommodation. One exception is car hire, where quoted rates may or may not include MVA.

At shops marked 'Tax Free for Tourists', goods exceeding Nkr308 are eligible for an MVA refund, less a service charge, of 10% to 17% of the purchase price. Ask the shop for a 'Tax-Free Shopping Cheque', which should be presented along with your purchases at your departure point from the country (ferry passengers normally collect their refund from the purser during limited hours once the boat has sailed).

POST & COMMUNICATIONS
Post

Norway has an efficient postal service but postal rates have soared in recent years. Postcards and letters weighing up to 20g cost Nkr5 within Norway, Nkr6.50 to other Nordic countries, Nkr7.50 to elsewhere in Europe and Nkr8.50 to the rest of the world. For sending larger parcels, the good-value Verdenspakke rate (up to 20kg) will provide delivery anywhere in the world within 15 working days. Poste restante services are available at all but a handful of Norwegian post offices.

In most towns, post offices are open from 9am to 4pm or 5pm weekdays and 10am to 2pm Saturday. You need not queue at most post offices; just take a number from the machine and when it appears on the digital readout, go to the indicated window. If there are two buttons on the machine, the upper one is for normal postal services and the lower one for foreign exchange transactions.

Telephone

All Norwegian telephone numbers consist of eight digits and there are no regional area codes. Most pay phones accept Nkr1, Nkr5, Nkr10 and Nkr20 coins and will return unused coins but won't give change, so only insert the minimum amount (Nkr5 for all calls) to ensure a connection. There are no local call rates in Norway – to call anywhere in the country from anywhere else costs a fixed national rate. National calls get 33% discount on standard phone rates between 5pm and 8am on weekdays, and any time on weekends. Directory assistance (☎ 180) is available throughout the country and costs Nkr8 per minute.

Card phones accept Telenor phonecards and most also accept credit cards. Card and coin phones are found at post offices, transport terminals, kiosks and other public places. Telenor phonecards (telekort) are sold in Nkr40, Nkr90 and Nkr140 denominations and work out cheaper and infinitely more convenient than using coins. Cards can be purchased at post offices and Narvesen and MIX kiosks. Beware of 'freephones' which will soak you for Nkr5 every time you access a so-called 800 number from a public telephone.

A peak rate national call costs Nkr5 then Nkr0.55 per minute. A call at any time to the USA costs Nkr5 then Nkr3.39 per minute from a coin-operated public phone, Nkr5 then Nkr2.37/2.73 per minute using a Nkr140/90 phonecard, or Nkr2.37 per minute with a credit card.

To phone Norway from outside the country, preface the telephone number with the country code (47). If you're dialling an outside number from within Norway, preface the number with the international access code (00), followed by the country code, area code and number you're calling.

GSM mobile telephone networks cover 80% of populated areas in Norway. There are two service providers – Telenor Mobil (☎ 22 78 50 00) and NetCom (☎ 22 88 82 00). However, ask your home network for advice before taking your mobile phone abroad. Mobile phone rental isn't possible in Norway but you can buy one from a Telehuset shop (from Nkr299, including charge card) and sell it before departure.

eKno Communication Service

Lonely Planet's eKno global communication service provides low-cost international calls – for local calls you're usually better off with a local phonecard. eKno also offers free messaging services, email, travel information and an online travel vault, where you can securely store all your important documents. You can join online at W www.ekno.lonelyplanet.com, where you will find the local-access numbers for the 24-hour customer-service centre. Once you have joined, always check the eKno Web site for the latest access numbers for each country and updates on new features.

Fax

Faxes can be received and sent from most hotels for a commercially minded charge, and telegrams may be sent by dialling ☎ 138. Alternatively, you can send or receive faxes at post offices.

Email & Internet Access

Email and Internet services have taken off in Norway, and most tourism-oriented businesses now have an email address. However, outside of the big cities, there are few Internet cafes and most people access the Internet and email (with permission) at public libraries. Internet access at public libraries is generally free, but there are usually long queues of locals waiting to get online. Some large hotels have credit-card accessed Internet computers in their lobbies, but they're expensive.

If you're bringing a laptop and hope to access the Internet, you'll need a telephone adaptor. Both old and new telephone jacks are in use, so universal access will require the old and new adaptors, as well as a PBX adaptor (for use in hotels). A good source of information on plugs is Tele-Adapt (W www.teleadapt.com).

AOL (W www.aol.com) and Compuserve (W www.compuserve.com) share two ISDN modem access numbers in Norway: ☎ 73 50 38 00, with a baud rate of 57.6 bits per second and a US$6 surcharge per connection; and ☎ 23 35 83 00, which transfers at 9.6 bits per second but only carries a $2.50 surcharge per connection.

DIGITAL RESOURCES

The World Wide Web is a rich resource for travellers. You can research your trip, hunt down bargain air fares, book hotels, check on weather conditions or chat with locals and other travellers about the best places to visit (or avoid!).

There's no better place to start your Web explorations than the Lonely Planet Web site (W www.lonelyplanet.com). Here you'll find succinct summaries on travelling to most places on earth, postcards from other travellers and the Thorn Tree bulletin board, where you can ask questions before you go or dispense advice when you get back. You can also find travel news and updates to many of our most popular guidebooks, and the subWWWay section links you to the most useful travel resources elsewhere on the Web.

Norwegian-language Web sites usually have a UK flag or some other place to click so you can get information in English. General and tourist information about Norway can be accessed on the Internet at W www.norway.org. Norges Turistråd, the Norwegian Tourist Board, has a particularly useful Web site at W www.visitnorway.com. The most useful tourist-oriented Web site for the western part of Norway is W www.fjordnorway.com.

For tour suggestions, attractions and accommodation throughout the country, check out W www.touristguide.no. There's a reasonable hotel listing at W www.hotell.org. Travel information, shopping, doing business, genealogy and more can be found at W www.norway.com. For information on

Oslo, W www.virtualoslo.com, is an excellent site with 'virtual sightseeing'.

The Norwegian government Web site, W www.odin.dep.no, provides all sorts of general information on the country and governmental issues, as well as daily news updates. For the English-language version, click on 'language' near the top of the page and select English. You'll also find news and government info on the Web site W www.norge.no. A good site for news, travel, culture and genealogy is W www.norwaypost.no. National statistical information can be found at W www.ssb.no.

The Norwegian Yellow Pages lists almost all businesses in Norway and has a helpful site at W www.gulesider.no (info is available in English). A listing of all the museums in the country can be found at W museumsnett.kulturnett.no.

Pan-European rail info is detailed on W www.raileurope.com and airline info and tickets are available on W www.travelocity.com. You'll get the lowdown on the latest currency exchange rates on W www.oanda.com.

Other useful Web addresses are provided throughout the text, where they're most relevant.

BOOKS

Most books are published in different editions by different publishers in different countries. As a result, a book might be a hardcover rarity in one country while it's readily available in paperback in another. Fortunately, bookshops and libraries search by title or author, so your local bookshop or library is best placed to advise you on the availability of these recommendations.

Lonely Planet

If you're planning a big trip around Europe, check out Lonely Planet's *Europe on a Shoestring*. For trips around Northern Europe, look for *Scandinavian Europe*. Lonely Planet also offers individual guides to *Denmark*, *Sweden*, *Finland* and *Iceland, Greenland & the Faroe Islands*. To help with communication throughout the region, pick up LP's *Scandinavian phrasebook*, which includes sections on Norwegian, Swedish, Danish, Finnish and Icelandic.

Guidebooks

For drivers, Erling Welle-Strand has written the concise *Motoring in Norway* and the flashier *Adventure Roads in Norway*, both of which describe a number of the country's most scenic driving routes.

The same author has also written *Mountain Hiking in Norway*, which outlines wilderness trail information including hiking itineraries, sketch maps and details on trail huts. A better choice for avid hikers is probably *Norwegian Mountains on Foot* by the Norwegian Mountain Touring Association (DNT), which is the English edition of the Norwegian classic, *Til Fots i Fjellet*. Other hiking books include *Great Hikes & Treks in Norway* by Graeme Cornwallis (only available on the Internet from W www.ablibris.com) and *Walking in Norway* by Connie Roos. Avid climbers will want to pick up the excellent *Climbing in the Magic Islands*, by Ed Webster – a labour of love covering an exhaustive choice of climbing routes in the Lofoten Islands.

A handsome coffee-table production that describes some of Norway's finest attractions is *Highlights of Norway* by Gro Stangeland, Alison Arderne Olsen and Eva Valebrokk. This worthwhile edition is indeed 'Norway in a Nutshell' and includes all sorts of fascinating background information on sites you probably want to see. A concise overview of Lofoten and Vesterålen is provided in the colourful tourist book *Lofoten & Vesterålen – Mountain Kingdom in the Sea* by Leif Ryvarden.

If you're spending a while in Norway, you'll especially appreciate the cultural direction offered in *Culture Shock! Norway: A Guide to Customs & Etiquette* by Elizabeth Su-Dale.

Travel

The earliest 'intrepid English traveller' account of Norway is *A Short Residence in Sweden, Norway & Denmark*, by Mary

Wollstonecraft (whose daughter Mary Shelley found fame by producing the monstrous bestseller *Frankenstein*). It recounts several emotion-filled months in late-18th-century Scandinavia. Another compilation of boreal experiences is provided in *Letters from High Latitudes* by Lord Dufferin, which details a mid-19th-century sailing trip around Greenland, Iceland, Jan Mayen, Svalbard and mainland Norway, with extensive references to the more romantic aspects of Norwegian history.

Norway has also been a major player in polar exploration, and numerous expeditions have set off from Tromsø, Jan Mayen and Svalbard. Countless works have been written on this subject, including explorers' journals, exposés and histories of success and dashed dreams. An excellent treatment of one of Norway's most intrepid characters is intriguingly covered in *Nansen: The Explorer Hero* by Roland Huntford. Thor Heyerdahl, the slightly quirky modern Norwegian explorer who has postulated ancient sea voyages between the old and new worlds and across the Pacific, is also well represented in print. His most prominent titles include *The Ra Expeditions*, *The Tigris Expedition*, *The Kon-Tiki Expedition* and *Fatu Hiva*.

For an ethereal and haunting treatment of the Arctic regions, which readily applies to Svalbard and includes references to the Sami culture, read Barry Lopez's classic, *Arctic Dreams*.

Andrew Stevenson's affectionate and illuminous account of a walk from Oslo to Bergen, *Summer Light: A Walk across Norway,* reveals the magical appeal of this wonderland.

History & Politics

A Brief History of Norway by John Midgård covers Norwegian history from prehistoric to modern times. Midgård has also written *Norway & the Second World War*, an easily digestible account of the most tumultuous times in modern Norwegian history. Another concise treatment of Norwegian history (at least through its 1972 publication date) is found in the simply titled *Norway* by Ronald G Popperwell. One of WWII's most diabol-

ical characters is examined in the biography *Quisling: A Study in Treason* by Oddvar K Hoidal. One of the finest works on Norway's exotic Arctic wonderland is provided in *No Man's Land* by Martin Conway, which details the history of Svalbard from its discovery to the present day.

There are also a number of works on the Viking era, including *The Vikings*, by Else Roesdahl, and F Donald Logan's *The Vikings in History*. *The Viking World*, by James Graham-Campbell and David M Wilson, traces the history of the Vikings by detailing excavated Viking sites and artefacts.

Biographies

The country's leading cultural figures are revealed in a number of biographies, including *Edvard Munch* by JP Hodin; *Enigma – The Life of Knut Hamsun* and *Ibsen*, both by Robert Ferguson; *Ole Bull: Norway's Romantic Musician & Cosmopolitan Patriot* by Einar Haugen and Camilla Cai; *The Life of Ole Bull* by Mortimer Brewster Smith; *Gustav Vigeland – The Sculptor & His Works*, by Ragna Thus Stang; *Edvard Grieg: The Man & Artist* by Finn Benestad; and *Song of the Waterfall – The Story of Edvard & Nina Grieg* by Elisabeth Kyle.

Fiction & Literature

If you're interested in Norse mythology and folk tales, your best bets are *The Gods & Myths of Northern Europe* by HR Ellis Davidson and the colourful *Norwegian Folk Tales – from the collection of Peter Christen Asbjørnsen and Jørgen Moe*. The same authors have also produced two volumes entitled *East o' the Sun & West o' the Moon*; one includes 21 tales and the other, 59. The classic *Vinland Sagas*, translated by Magnus Magnusson and Hermann Palsson, contains the *Saga of Eric the Red* and the *Saga of the Greenlanders*, two classic medieval literary works that describe the Norse colonisation of Greenland and earliest forays into North America. For a rundown on the modern Norwegian literary effort, see Literature in the Facts about Norway chapter.

NEWSPAPERS & MAGAZINES

Domestic newspapers, including the Oslo dailies *Aftenposten* and the tabloids *Dagbladet* and *Verdens Gang* (better known as just *VG*), are available nationwide, but they're published only in Norwegian. The same goes for Bergen's daily, *Bergens Tidende*. The *International Herald-Tribune*, London dailies, and English-language magazines such as *Time*, *Newsweek* and *The Economist* are sold at major transport terminals and at kiosks in larger towns.

RADIO & TV

Norway's national radio and television network, NRK, has historically struggled to remain informational rather than commercial. However, competition from the commercial TV2 and TV Norge networks, and the satellite broadcasts of TV3, has brought about a change in character and a good number of British and US television programs and films are now creeping in. Most TV broadcasts are in Norwegian, though US and British programs are presented in English with Norwegian sub-titles. Hotels with cable TV often have CNN and English-language sports channels.

The BBC World Service broadcasts to Norway on 9410kHz.

PHOTOGRAPHY & VIDEO
Film & Equipment

Although print and slide film are readily available in major cities, prices are high. A 24-/36-exposure roll of Fuji Superia costs around Nkr45/55 and processing costs Nkr99/119. Fujichrome Sensia/Velvia 36-exposure slide film costs Nkr49/75. The best value by far is offered by the chain Japan Photo, which offers discounts on bulk orders. If you purchase videos in Norway, note that the usual system is PAL, which is incompatible with the North American NTSC system.

As you'd imagine, import duties make photographic equipment extremely expensive in Norway – even second-hand equipment prices reflect the scarcity of inexpensive items. It's therefore wise to bring everything you need from elsewhere. If you have a camera problem, Oslo is by far the best place to have it repaired; they not only have the expertise, but also access to parts (which must be imported).

Technical Tips

Photographers worldwide sing the praises of the magical northern light, and the crystalline air combined with the long, red rays cast by a low sun create excellent effects on film. Add spectacular scenery with a picturesque fishing village and you have a photographer's paradise. Due to the clear northern light and glare from water, ice and snow, photographers may want to use a UV filter or a skylight filter and a lens shade. In winter, you may want to polar oil your camera so the mechanism doesn't freeze up. In temperatures below around -20°C, electronic cameras may fail altogether.

For general advice on taking good pictures, consult Lonely Planet's *Travel Photography*, by Richard I'Anson.

Photographing People

Finding subjects and taking interesting 'people photos' are always a photographer's greatest challenge but, happily, most Norwegians enjoy being photographed and few are camera-shy. However, it's still a courtesy to ask permission before snapping away. This is especially important in the Sami areas, where you may encounter some camera sensitivity, as well as in villages where whaling is a mainstay, as people may be concerned that the photos will be used against them in environmental pieces.

TIME

Time in Norway is one hour ahead of GMT/UTC, the same as Sweden, Denmark and most of Western Europe. When it's noon in Norway, it's 11am in London, 1pm in Finland, 6am in New York and Toronto, 3am in San Francisco, 9pm in Sydney and 11pm in Auckland. Between the last Sundays in March and October, Norway observes daylight-savings time. Timetables and business hours are posted using the 24-hour clock, but dates may be given by week number (1 to 52).

When telling the time, note that in Norwegian the use of 'half' means *half before* rather than half past. Always double check which time is required – otherwise, you may be an hour late!

ELECTRICITY

The electric current in Norway (now including passenger ferries and Hurtigruten coastal steamers) is supplied at 220 volts AC and 50Hz. However, on trains, sleeping cars may use either 110 or 220 volts AC, at 50 Hz. Round continental-style two-pin plugs are used throughout the country and you're recommended to get any suitable adapters in advance.

WEIGHTS & MEASURES

Norway uses the metric system; to convert between metric and imperial units, see the table at the back of the book. At delicatessens, the price may be followed by '/hg'; that is, per 100g. Fruit and other items are commonly sold by the piece (*stykke*, abbreviation *stk*). Another oddity is the frequent use of *mil* (mile) for distance, which is not 1.6km but rather a Norwegian mile, which is 10km.

LAUNDRY

Coin laundries *(myntvaskeri)* are expensive and extremely rare; they don't exist at all outside the big cities or in the north. However, hostels and camping grounds often have coin-operated washers and dryers available to guests. The prices are usually very reasonable. You may want to bring a supply of laundry soap for washing by hand.

TOILETS

Toilets are western style and nearly every town has public facilities. However, at shopping malls, train stations, bus terminals and even some restaurants (!) you may have to pay up to Nkr5.

HEALTH

Norway is a very healthy place and no special precautions are necessary when visiting. The biggest risks are likely to be viral infections in winter, sunburn and insect

Medical Kit Check List

Following is a list of items you should consider including in your medical kit – consult your pharmacist for brands available in your country.

☐ **Aspirin or paracetamol (acetaminophen in the USA)** – for pain or fever

☐ **Antihistamine** – for allergies, eg, hay fever; to ease the itch from insect bites or stings; and to prevent motion sickness

☐ **Cold and flu tablets, throat lozenges and nasal decongestant**

☐ **Multivitamins** – consider for long trips, when dietary vitamin intake may be inadequate

☐ **Antibiotics** – consider including these if you're travelling well off the beaten track; see your doctor, as they must be prescribed, and carry the prescription with you

☐ **Loperamide or diphenoxylate** –'blockers' for diarrhoea

☐ **Prochlorperazine or metaclopramide** – for nausea and vomiting

☐ **Rehydration mixture** – to prevent dehydration, which may occur, for example, during bouts of diarrhoea; particularly important when travelling with children

☐ **Insect repellent, sunscreen, lip balm and eye drops**

☐ **Calamine lotion, sting relief spray or aloe vera** – to ease irritation from sunburn and insect bites or stings

☐ **Antifungal cream or powder** – for fungal skin infections and thrush

☐ **Antiseptic (such as povidone-iodine)** – for cuts and grazes

☐ **Bandages, Band-Aids (plasters) and other wound dressings**

☐ **Water purification tablets or iodine**

☐ **Scissors, tweezers and a thermometer** – note that mercury thermometers are prohibited by airlines

bites in summer, and foot blisters from too much hiking.

For a medical emergency dial ☎ 113; visit a local pharmacy or medical centre if you have a minor medical problem and can explain what it is. Hospital casualty wards will help if the problem is more serious.

Nearly all health professionals in Norway speak English; tourist offices and hotels can make recommendations.

Pre-departure Planning

If you're reasonably fit, the only things you should organise before departure are a visit to your dentist to get your teeth in order, and travel insurance with good medical cover (see Travel Insurance under Visas & Documents earlier in this chapter).

Jabs are not necessary for travel in the region, unless you have been travelling through a part of the world where yellow fever may be prevalent. Ensure that your normal childhood vaccines (against measles, mumps, rubella, diphtheria, tetanus and polio) are up to date and/or you are still showing immunity. You may also want to have a hepatitis vaccine, as exposure can occur anywhere.

If you wear glasses take a spare pair and a copy of your optical prescription. You will have no problem getting new glasses or contact lenses made up quickly and competently in Norway but you will pay for the privilege. If you require a particular medication, don't forget to carry a copy of your prescription, which will be necessary to get a refill. Most medications are available in Norway, but may go by a different name than at home, so be sure to have the generic name as well as the brand name.

Basic Rules

Food Stomach upsets are as possible in Norway as they are at home and the same rules apply. Take great care with fish or shellfish (for instance, cooked mussels that haven't opened properly can be dangerous). As autumn approaches, collecting mushrooms is a favourite pastime in this part of the world but don't eat any mushrooms until they've been positively identified as safe.

Water Tap water is always safe to drink in Norway but it's wise to beware of drinking from streams, as even the clearest and most inviting water may harbour giardia and other parasites. For extended hikes where you must rely on natural water, the simplest way of purifying water is to boil it thoroughly. Vigorous boiling should be satisfactory; however, at high altitude water boils at a lower temperature, so germs are less likely to be killed. Boil it for longer in these environments.

If you cannot boil water it should be treated chemically. Chlorine tablets (Puritabs, Steritabs or other brands) will kill many pathogens but not giardia and amoebic cysts. Iodine is more effective in purifying water and is available in tablet form (such as Potable Aqua). Follow the directions carefully and remember that too much iodine can be harmful.

Environmental Hazards

Hypothermia Hypothermia occurs when the body loses heat faster than it can produce it and the core temperature of the body falls. It's surprisingly easy to progress from very cold to dangerously cold due to a combination of wind, wet clothing, fatigue and hunger, even if the air temperature is above freezing. It's best to dress in layers; silk, wool and artificial fibres like Capilene polyester are all good insulating materials. A hat is important, as a lot of heat is lost through the head. A strong, waterproof outer layer (and a 'space' blanket for emergencies) is essential. Carry basic supplies, including food containing simple sugars to generate heat quickly, and fluids to drink.

Symptoms of hypothermia are exhaustion, numb skin (particularly toes and fingers), shivering, slurred speech, irrational or violent behaviour, lethargy, stumbling, dizzy spells, muscle cramps and violent bursts of energy. Irrationality may take the form of sufferers claiming they are warm and trying to take off their clothes.

To treat mild hypothermia, first get the person out of the wind and/or rain, remove their clothing if it's wet and replace it with dry, warm clothing. Give them hot liquids – not alcohol – and some high-kilojoule, easily digestible food. Do not rub victims: instead, allow them to slowly warm themselves. This should be enough to treat the early stages of hypothermia. The early recognition and treatment of mild hypothermia is the only way to prevent severe hypothermia, which is a critical condition.

Sunburn You can get sunburnt surprisingly quickly, even through cloud. Use a sunscreen, a hat, and a barrier cream for your nose and lips. Calamine lotion or Stingose are good for mild sunburn. Protect your eyes with good-quality sunglasses, particularly if you will be near water, sand or snow.

Infectious Diseases

Diarrhoea Simple things like a change of water, food or climate can all cause a mild bout of diarrhoea, but a few rushed toilet trips with no other symptoms is not indicative of a major problem. Dehydration is the main danger and can occur quite quickly with diarrhoea, particularly in children or the elderly. Under all circumstances fluid replacement (at least equal to the volume being lost) is the most important thing to remember. Stick to a bland diet as you recover.

Giardiasis Another possible concern is the intestinal parasite *Giardia lamblia*, which causes giardiasis, commonly known as giardia. Symptoms include stomach cramps, nausea, a bloated stomach, watery, foul-smelling diarrhoea and frequent gas. Giardiasis can appear several weeks after you have been exposed to the parasite. The symptoms may disappear for a few days and then return; this can go on for several weeks. You should seek medical advice if you think you have giardiasis.

Hepatitis Hepatitis is a general term for inflammation of the liver. Several distinct viruses cause hepatitis, and they differ in the way they're transmitted. All forms of the illness exhibit similar symptoms, including fever, chills, headache, fatigue, feelings of weakness and aches and pains, followed by loss of appetite, nausea, vomiting, abdominal pain, dark urine, light-coloured faeces, jaundiced (yellow) skin and a yellowing of the ocular sclera. After a bout of hepatitis, it's wise to avoid alcohol for several weeks, as the liver needs some time to recover.

Hepatitis A is transmitted by contaminated food and drinking water, but those stricken by this virus can't do much apart from resting, drinking lots of fluids, eating lightly and avoiding fatty foods. Hepatitis B is spread through contact with infected blood, blood products, body fluids or sexual contact, use of unsterilised needles, blood transfusions, or contact with blood through dermal abrasions. It may also be contracted by having a shave, tattoo or body piercing with contaminated equipment. The symptoms of hepatitis B may be more severe than type A and the disease can lead to long-term problems such as chronic liver damage, liver cancer or a chronic infectious status.

Hepatitis A and B may be controlled by vaccine, but following basic sanitation practices will minimise the possibility of contracting hepatitis A and avoiding risky situations will help prevent hepatitis B.

HIV & AIDS Infection with the human immunodeficiency virus (HIV) may lead to acquired immune deficiency syndrome (AIDS), which is fatal. Any exposure to blood, blood products or body fluids may put the individual at risk. It's often transmitted through sexual contact or dirty needles – vaccinations, acupuncture, tattooing and body piercing can be potentially as dangerous as intravenous drug use.

Sexually Transmitted Diseases STD clinics are widespread in Norway, and don't be shy about checking them out if you think you may have contracted something. Gonorrhoea and syphilis are typically treated with antibiotics, but each strain requires a doctor's attention to determine which antibiotic will be most effective. At present, there's no cure for herpes or HIV/AIDS.

Cuts, Bites & Stings

Bee and wasp stings are usually more painful than dangerous, but people who are allergic to stings may experience severe breathing difficulties and will require urgent medical care. Calamine lotion or Stingose spray will give relief and ice packs will reduce the pain and swelling.

In northern Norway, the greatest nuisances are the plagues of blackflies and mosquitoes that swarm out of tundra bogs and lakes in summer. Fortunately, malaria is unknown, but the mental risks can't be underestimated, as people have literally been driven insane by the ravenous hordes. Midsummer is the worst, and regular mosquito coils and repellents are scarcely effective; hikers must cover exposed skin and may even need head nets to keep the little buggers from making kamikaze attacks on eyes, nose, ears and throat. If you're camping, a tent with mosquito netting is essential. Most people get used to the mosquito bites after a few days as their bodies adjust and the itching and swelling become less severe. An antihistamine cream should help alleviate the symptoms.

Rabies Rabies, caused by a bite or scratch by an infected mammal, is found in Svalbard and (occasionally) in eastern Finnmark. Dogs are a noted carrier, but cats, foxes and bats can also be infected. Any bite, scratch or even lick from a warm-blooded, furry animal should be cleaned immediately and thoroughly. Scrub with soap and running water, and then apply alcohol or iodine solution. If you've been infected by a rabid animal, medical help should be sought immediately.

Ticks Check your body after walking through tick-infested areas, as ticks can cause skin infections and other more serious diseases. If a tick is found, press down around the tick's head with tweezers, grab the head and gently pull upwards. Avoid pulling the rear of the body as this may squeeze the tick's gut contents through the attached mouth parts into the skin, increasing the risk of infection and disease.

Snakes Snakes are rarely seen in Norway and adders (the only poisonous variety) don't exist north of Tysfjorden in Nordland. To minimise your chances of being bitten always wear boots, socks and long trousers when walking through undergrowth where snakes may be present. Don't put your hands into holes and crevices, and be careful when collecting firewood.

Adder bites aren't normally fatal and antivenins are available. Immediately wrap the bitten limb tightly, as you would for a sprained ankle, and then attach a splint to immobilise it. Keep the victim still and seek medical help, if possible with the dead snake for identification. Don't attempt to catch the snake if there is a possibility of being bitten again. Tourniquets and sucking out the poison are now comprehensively discredited.

Women's Health
Use of antibiotics, synthetic underwear, sweating and contraceptive pills can lead to fungal vaginal infections, especially when travelling in hot weather. Fungal infections are characterised by a rash, itch and discharge and can be treated with a vinegar or lemon-juice douche, or with yoghurt. Nystatin, miconazole or clotrimazole pessaries or vaginal cream are the usual treatment.

WOMEN TRAVELLERS
Women travellers have few worries in Norway, and sober Norwegian men are normally the very picture of decorum. While alcohol-impaired men may become tiresome or obnoxious, they're still unlikely to press any uncomfortable issues. Norway's main feminist organisation is Kvinnefronten (Women's Front; ☎ 22 37 60 54, e kvinnefronten@online.no), Holsts gate 1, N-0473 Oslo. Women who have been attacked or abused can contact the Krisesenter (☎ 22 37 47 00) in Oslo or dial ☎ 112 nationwide.

Recommended reading for first-time women travellers is the *Handbook for Women Travellers* by Maggie and Gemma Moss, published by Piatkus Books. *Going Solo* by Merrin White (Penguin 1998) is also useful; unfortunately, it's hard to find a copy and it's not available in the USA.

There are some good general Web sites dedicated to women travellers, including w www.journeywoman.com and also w www.passionfruit.com. There is also a women's page on LP's Web site Thorntree (w thorntree.lonelyplanet.com).

GAY & LESBIAN TRAVELLERS

Norwegians are generally tolerant of alternative lifestyles, and Norway, along with several neighbouring countries, allows gay and lesbian couples to form 'registered partnerships' that grant every right of matrimony except access to church weddings, adoption and artificial insemination. However, public displays of affection (regardless of sexual preference) are not common practice.

Gay and lesbian travellers can find gay entertainment spots in larger cities and towns. The Spartacus International Gay Guide, published by Bruno Gmünder Verlag (Berlin), is an excellent international directory of gay entertainment venues, but it's now well out of date and is best used in conjunction with up-to-date listings in local papers, as popular places tend to change quickly.

For local information on gay issues, contact Landsforeningen for Lesbisk og Homofil frigjøring (LLH; ☎ 22 36 19 48, ⓔ llh@c2i.net), St Olavs plass 2, N-0130 Oslo. Alternatively, call the Oslo gay and lesbian helpline on ☎ 22 11 33 60.

DISABLED TRAVELLERS

Although Norway is better than most countries in catering for disabled travellers, it can still be a challenging destination, and anyone with special needs should plan ahead. The Norwegian Tourist Board publishes a list of wheelchair-accessible hotels and hostels. Nearly all street crossings are equipped with either a ramp or a very low kerb (curb), and crossing signals produce an audible signal – longer beeps when it's safe to cross and shorter beeps when the signal is about to change. Most (but not all) trains have carriages with space for wheelchair users.

You may want to contact your national support organisation and try to speak with its 'travel officer', if there is one. They often have complete libraries devoted to travel, and can put you in touch with tour companies who specialise in disabled travel.

Organisations

For information on disabled travel and sites of special interest to disabled travellers in Norway, contact Norges Handikapforbund (☎ 22 17 02 55, ⓔ nhf@nhf.no, ⓦ www.nhf.no), Schweigaards gate 12, Postboks 9217 Grønland, N-0134 Oslo.

The British-based Royal Association for Disability & Rehabilitation (RADAR; ☎ 020-7250 3222), 12 City Forum, 250 City Rd, London, EC1V 8AF, UK, can supply general advice for disabled travellers in Norway.

In the USA, contact the Society for Accessible Travel and Hospitality (☎ 212-447 7284, fax 725 8253, ⓔ sathtravel@aol.com), 347 5th Ave, Suite 610, New York, NY 10016. In Canada, visit the Web site ⓦ www.cta-otc.gc.ca/eng/toc.htm and click on 'Accessible Transportation'.

SENIOR TRAVELLERS

Seniors are normally entitled to discounts on museum admissions, air tickets and other transport. A few hotels, including the Radisson SAS chain, also have senior discount schemes – be sure to inquire when making a booking. See Train in the Getting Around chapter for information on the ScanRail 55+ pass.

In your home country, you may already be entitled to various travel packages and discounts (on car hire, for instance) through organisations and travel agents that cater for senior travellers. Start hunting at your local senior citizens advice bureau or larger seniors' organisations, such as the American Association of Retired Persons (AARP) in the USA (ⓦ www.aarp.org) or Age Concern England (ⓦ www.ace.org.uk) in the UK.

TRAVEL WITH CHILDREN

Successful travel with young children requires planning and effort. Don't try to overdo things; packing too much into the time available causes problems, even for adults. Make sure the activities include the kids as well; if they've helped to work out where you're going, chances are they'll still be interested when you arrive. Lonely Planet's *Travel with Children* by Cathy Lanigan is a useful source of information.

In many ways, Norway is a children's country, and most towns have attractions and museums specifically for the younger set (one of the finest is Dyrepark in Kristiansand, which offers an open-air zoo, pirate ship battles and family accommodation in the fantasy town of Kardamomme By). Domestic tourism is largely organised around children's interests: regional museums invariably have a children's section with toys and activities, and there are also numerous public parks for kids. Most attractions allow free admission for young children up to about six years of age and half-price (or substantially discounted) admission for those up to 16 or so. Family tickets are occasionally available. Hotels, HI hostels, camping grounds, and other accommodation options, often have 'family rooms' or cabins that accommodate up to two adults and two children. In hotels, this may cost little more than the price of a regular double.

Car rental firms hire out children's safety seats at a nominal cost but it's essential that you book them in advance. The same goes for highchairs and cots (cribs); they're standard in many restaurants and hotels but numbers may be limited. Norway offers a relatively wide choice of baby food, infant formulas, soy and cow's milk, disposable nappies (diapers) etc, but remember that supermarket opening hours are generally shorter than they are elsewhere and, after hours, you may have to resort to more expensive convenience stores.

DANGERS & ANNOYANCES

Your person and belongings are safer in Norway than in many people's home countries, and the cities – even east Oslo, which has a relatively poor reputation – are reasonably safe at all hours of the night. However, don't become blasé about security and be careful near the nightclubs in the Rosenkrantz gate area of Oslo. Normally, the greatest nuisance value will come from drug addicts, alcoholics and/or beggars – mainly in Oslo – who can spot a naïve tourist a block away.

Oslo and other larger cities suffer from a growing drug problem, and although dope may be readily available in places, it isn't legal.

BUSINESS HOURS

Business hours are generally from 9am or 10am to 4pm or 5pm weekdays and 10am to 2pm Saturday, though some shops stay open until 7pm or 8pm on Thursday. In summer, banks normally open from 8.15am to 3pm weekdays (until 5pm on Thursday), while post offices operate 9am to 4pm or 5pm on weekdays and 10am to 2pm on Saturday.

Many Rimi supermarkets stay open until 9pm or 10pm on weekdays and 8pm on Saturday, and some larger shopping centres, particularly in Oslo, have extended hours from 10am to 8pm on weekdays and 10am to 6pm on Saturday. Nearly everything closes on Sunday, although shops catering for tourists may be open.

All but the most popular museums have relatively short hours (from 11am to 3pm is common), so museum fiends need to plan their day carefully before setting out.

PUBLIC HOLIDAYS & SPECIAL EVENTS
Public Holidays

The following public holidays are observed in Norway:

New Year's Day *(Nyttårsdag)* 1 January
Maundy Thursday *(Skjærtorsdag)* March/April
Good Friday *(Langfredag)* March/April
Easter Monday *(Annen Påskedag)* March/April
Labour Day *(Første Mai, Arbeidsdag)* 1 May
Constitution Day *(Nasjonaldag)* 17 May
Ascension Day *(Kristi Himmelfartsdag)* 40th day after Easter, May/June
Whit Monday *(Annen Pinsedag)* Eighth Monday after Easter, May/June
Christmas Day *(Første Juledag)* 25 December
Boxing Day *(Annen Juledag)* 26 December

On Norway's Constitution Day national holiday, 17 May, people take to the streets in traditional dress and attend celebratory events throughout the country. The biggest bash is in Oslo, where marching bands and thousands of schoolchildren parade down Karl Johans gate to the Royal Palace, to be greeted by the royal family.

In Karasjok and Kautokeino, the Sami people hold their most colourful celebrations at Easter, with reindeer races, *joik* concerts and other festivities. Midsummer's

Eve, or *Jonsok*, is generally observed on St Hans Day (23 June) and is celebrated with much fanfare and bonfires in every community from Halden to Grense Jakobselv.

On 13 December, Christian children celebrate the feast of Santa Lucia by dressing in white and holding a candlelit procession. Boys generally wear cone-shaped hats and girls put silver tinsel and glitter in their hair.

Special Events

Norway is chock-a-block with special festivals, which take place at all times of year in every city, town and village. Large and popular ones are covered in most regional chapters of this book, but for a listing of 39 recommended events, pick up a copy of the free booklet *Norway Festivals*, which is produced by Norske Festivaler (☎ 22 38 00 66, fax 22 38 11 16, ℮ norfest@online.no, ⓦ www.norwayfestivals.com), Sagveien 23a, N-0459 Oslo.

ACTIVITIES

Much of Norway's appeal to visitors lies in its wilderness areas. The Western Fjords, Lofoten Islands and Lyngen Alps (in northern Troms) attract throngs of mountaineers and rock climbers; glacier hikes and ice-climbing are available on Jostedalsbreen, Svartisen and other smaller icecaps; bird-watchers flock to the prolific bird cliffs, marshes and forests; skiers will find the world's best nordic skiing and some very respectable downhill slopes; and hikers will never exhaust the range of excellent day hikes and long-distance walking routes.

Thanks to Norway's 1000-year-old *allemannsretten* (every man's right; see the 'Minimal Impact Camping' boxed text in this chapter) tradition and the *Friluftsleven* (Outdoor Recreation Act), anyone is legally entitled to hike or ski across wilderness areas, including outlying fields and pastures; camp anywhere for up to two days, as long as it's more than 150m from a dwelling; cycle or ride horseback on all paths and roads; and canoe, kayak, row and sail on all rivers and lakes. However, these freedoms come with some responsibilities: not to light fires between 15 April and

Christmas in Norway

Christmas, or jul, is as much of a holiday in Norway as it is elsewhere in Christendom; the name is derived from joulu or lol, a pagan fertility feast that was celebrated all over Europe in pre-Christian times and synchronised nicely with the holiday to honour the birth of Christ. Currently, most people celebrate between Christmas Eve and Epiphany, or 12th night, although some continue until the Feast of St Canute, which is the 20th day of Christmas.

A Christmas tree is a requisite part of the décor in most homes, and gifts are exchanged on Christmas Eve. In the countryside, sheaves of oats known as julenek are mounted on a pole and left out for the birds. In gratitude for past blessings, a bowl of porridge is also left out for the nisse, the gnome that historically brought good fortune to farmers. This concept has now been merged with the international tradition of Santa Claus in the personage of Jule-nissen, whom Norwegians believe makes his home in Drøbak, south of Oslo (and there's a Santa Crossing road sign there to prove it!).

There are all sorts of special Christmas confections and concoctions. Among them are rømmegrøt, an extremely sweet cream porridge; rupa, ptarmigan or grouse; lutefisk, a glutinous fish dish that's definitely an acquired taste; pinneribbe, mutton ribs steamed over birch or juniper branches; and pork roast, which stems from the Viking tradition of sacrificing a pig at yuletide. Children like to munch raisin buns and a variety of biscuits, including strull, krumkake and goro. And then everyone drinks gløgg, readily translated as 'grog'. Good gløgg blends cinnamon, raisins, almonds, ginger, cloves, cardamom and other spices with juice, which may or may not be fermented. Many people also imbibe julaøl, or 'holiday beer', which dates from the Viking days when it was associated with pagan sacrifices; as with the lutefisk, not all foreigners fully appreciate it. Die-hard alcohol fans celebrate the season with generous quantities of Norway's own potato power brew, aquavit.

15 September; not to litter; to avoid damaging plant or animal life; to leave cultural
sites perfectly intact; and to leave the countryside as pristine as it was found.

Hiking

Norway has some of Europe's best hiking,
including a network of around 20,000km of
marked trails that range from easy strolls
through the green zones around cities to long
treks through national parks and wilderness
areas. Many of these trails are maintained by
DNT and are marked either with cairns or
red 'T's at 100m or 200m intervals.

The hiking season runs roughly from late
May to early October, with a much shorter
season in the higher mountain areas. In the
highlands, the snow often remains until
June and returns in September. The most
popular wilderness hiking areas are the
Jotunheimen and Rondane mountains and
the Hardangervidda plateau. If you're after
a wilder experience, try such national parks
as Øvre Dividal, Stabbursdalen, Rago,
Reisa, D.ovrefjell, or any of the vast number of unprotected areas throughout the
country, such as Trollheimen near Oppdal,
the fabulous Sunnmøresalpane in the Western Fjords or the extensive Sylenefjell range
along the Swedish border. Avid hikers will
never run out of options!

DNT Den Norske Turistforening (DNT;
Norwegian Mountain Touring Club) and its
various chapters maintain a network of over
370 mountain huts and lodges throughout
the country. For details and prices for the
use of these huts, see Accommodation, later
in this chapter.

If you're doing lots of hiking, it's certainly
worth joining DNT; membership for one calendar year will set you back Nkr365/175

Crossing Streams

Fortunately, most large rivers along major Norwegian hiking routes are bridged, but trekkers and
mountaineers are still bound to face the odd swollen stream or unbridged river. In most cases, however, you need not be put off.

Normally, the sun and heat of the day melt the snow and glacial ice in the high country and cause
water levels to rise, so the best time to cross is early in the morning, preferably no sooner than 24
hours after a rainstorm. Remember that constricted rivers passing through narrow passages run
deep, so the widest ford is likely to be the shallowest. The swiftest and strongest current is normally
found near the centre of straight stretches and at the outside of river bends. Observe the character
of the water as it flows and choose a spot with as much slack water as possible.

Never try to cross just above a waterfall and avoid crossing streams in flood – identifiable by dirty,
smooth-running water carrying lots of debris and vegetation. A smooth surface suggests that the
river is too deep to be crossed on foot. Anything over knee-deep shouldn't be considered 'cross-
able' without experience and extra equipment.

Before attempting to cross deep or swift-running streams, be sure that you can jettison your pack
in midstream if necessary. Put anything that mustn't get wet inside sturdy waterproof bags. Unhitch
the waist belt and loosen shoulder straps, remove any bulky clothing that will inhibit swimming, and
remove long trousers. Lone hikers should use a hiking staff to probe the river bottom for the best
route and to steady themselves in the current.

Never try to cross a stream barefoot. While crossing, face upstream and avoid looking down or
you may risk losing your balance. Two hikers can steady each other by resting their arms on each
other's shoulders. More than two hikers should cross forming a wedge pointed upstream, with the
people behind holding the waist and shoulder of the person at the head of the wedge.

If you do fall while crossing, don't try to stand up. Remove your pack (but don't let go of it), roll
over onto your back, and point your feet downstream, then try to work your way to a shallow eddy
or to the shore and attempt to regain your footing.

(Nkr425/235, with yearbook and seven *Fjell og Vidde* magazines) for people over/under 26 years of age; members' families pay Nkr140 per person. For further information, contact Den Norske Turistforening (☎ 22 82 28 22, fax 22 82 28 23, **W** www .turistforeningen.no, Storgaten 3, Postboks 7, Sentrum, N-0101 Oslo. DNT also sells hiking maps and topographic sheets. The latter, which are published by Statens Kartverk, cover the entire country at scales of 1:50,000 and 1:100,000; catalogue maps outlining map titles and sheet numbers are available free of charge.

Rock Climbing & Mountaineering

As one would imagine, a country with the astounding vertical topography of Norway would be a mecca for climbers interested in rock, ice and alpine pursuits. In fact, outside the Alps, Norway is probably Europe's finest climbing venue. However, due to Norway's topographic and climatic extremes, technical climbers face harsher conditions, shorter seasons and many more concerns and restrictions than hikers and backpackers. The most popular alpine venues include the Lyngen Alps, Lofoten and Western Fjords.

For general information on climbing in Norway, contact Norsk Tindeklub (☎ 22 50 54 66, **e** egil.fredriksen@ntk.no, **W** www .ntk.no), c/o Egil Fredriksen, Sorkedalsveien 202b, N0754-Oslo.

In addition to the rock climbers' classic *Climbing in the Magic Islands* by Ed Webster, which describes most of the feasible routes in the Lofoten Islands, prospective climbers may want to look for *Ice Fall in Norway* by Sir Ranulph Feinnes, which describes a 1970 jog around Jostedalsbreen, and the more practical *Scandinavian Mountains* by Peter Lennon, which introduces the country's finest climbing venues.

Skiing

'Ski' is a Norwegian word and thanks to aeons-old rock carvings depicting hunters travelling on skis, Norwegians make a credible claim to having invented the sport. Interest hasn't waned over the years and these days, it's no exaggeration to say it's

The Virtues of Skinny Skis

Not only do nordic skiing, ski jumping and biathlon (skiing and target-shooting) competitions dominate Norwegian Olympic efforts, they also provide a recreational foundation among people for whom winter is the dominant season of the year. Nearly everyone outside the big cities skis and all villages have a floodlit ski track for winter use. Nordic skiing isn't only a great source of exercise but it's also a ticket into the wilderness when few folks are prepared to venture far from the home fires.

The concept sounds easy, but it's actually fairly difficult for adults to learn. Most of the propulsive effort is made by kicking downwards on the stationary ski, so that the waxed under-surface comes into contact with and grips the snow, even on gentle uphill gradients. As the skier kicks with one foot, the weight decreases on the other ski, which arches slightly upwards in the middle, so the waxed section is above the snow and the ski can glide forward. Movement and rhythm is augmented by the ski poles. The process is often made easier in popular areas with pre-laid parallel tracks cut into the snow.

For steeper gradients, you may have to apply skins – strips of brushed nylon which attach to the bottom of the skis and ensure maximum gripping power.

The Telemark region of Norway has lent its name to the graceful turn that has made nordic skiing popular around the world. Nordic ski bindings attach the boot at the toes, allowing free movement of the heel; to turn, one knee is dropped to the surface of the ski while the other leg is kept straight. The skis are positioned one behind the other, allowing the skier to smoothly glide around the turn in the direction of the dropped knee.

the national pastime. Most skiing is of the cross-country (nordic) variety, and Norway has thousands of kilometres of maintained cross-country ski trails. However, visitors should only set off after studying the trails/routes (wilderness trails are identified by colour codes on maps and signposts) and ensuring that they have appropriate clothing, sufficient food and water, and emergency supplies such as matches and a source of warmth. You can either bring your own equipment or rent or purchase skis, poles and boots on site. You'll probably find the best deals on second-hand gear at weekend flea markets.

Most towns and villages provide some illuminated ski trails, but elsewhere it's still worth carrying a good torch, as winter days are very short and in the north there's no daylight at all in December and January. The ski season generally lasts from early December to April. Snow conditions vary greatly from year to year and region to region, but February and March, as well as the Easter holiday period, tend to be the best (and busiest) times.

There are also scores of resorts with downhill runs, but these are quite expensive due to the costs of ski lifts, accommodation and the *aprés-ski* drinking sessions. The spring season lasts longer than in the Alps and the snow is better quality too. Popular spots include the Holmenkollen area near Oslo, Geilo on the Oslo-Bergen railway line, Voss, Lillehammer and the nearby Gudbrandsdalen region. Summer skiers can head for the glaciers near Finse, Stryn, Folgefonn or Jotunheimen National Park. For general information on skiing in Norway, contact DNT.

River Rafting

Norway's steep slopes and icy, scenic rivers create an ideal environment for avid rafters, and a number of reputable operators offer trips. These range from short, Class II doddles to Class III and IV adventures and rollicking Class V punishment. While these trips aren't especially cheap, most are guaranteed to provide an adrenalin thrill, and the rates include all requisite equipment and

waterproofing. Among the finest venues are Evje (Setesdalen), Sjoa (Heidalen) and Oppdal (Drivadalen). Evje is described in the Southern Norway chapter, and Sjoa and Oppdal in the Central Norway chapter.

Norges Padleforbund (☎ 21 02 98 35, ℮ webmaster@padling.no, ⍵ www.padling .no), Service boks 1, Ullevål stadion, N-0840 Oslo, provides a comprehensive list of rafting operators in Norway.

Dog-Sledding

Although dog-sledding isn't an indigenous Norwegian sport, this Inuit means of transport readily transfers to the Norwegian wilds, and several operators can take you on a range of adventures. While many people are content with just a half-day taster of the sport, keen prospective 'mushers' can jump in the deep end and opt for a two-week dogsled safari through Troms, Finnmark or Svalbard.

DNT organises several trips through southern Norway. In the north, you'll want to contact Bjørn Klauer in Innset (see Øvre Dividal Nasjonalpark in The Far North chapter) or Sven Engholm in Karasjok (see The Far North chapter). All Svalbard operators can also arrange Svalbard dog-sled tours (see the Svalbard & Jan Mayen chapter) and Arcturus Expeditions in the UK offers extended dogsledding tours in Norway with operator Odd-Knut Thoresen (see Organised Tours in the Getting There & Away chapter).

Fishing

In the 19th century, Norway was a mecca for wealthy anglers, principally European aristocrats. English lords fished the rivers of western Norway, such as the Lågen (Suldal) and the Rauma (Romsdal). During the 20th century, they were mostly replaced by avid anglers from the USA.

Norway's salmon runs are legendary and, in June and July, you can't beat the rivers of Finnmark. In addition to salmon, 41 other fish species inhabit the country's 200,000 rivers and lakes. In the south, you'll normally find the best fishing from June to September, and in the north, in July and August. In Svalbard, the best fishing holes are well-kept secrets, but Arctic char inhabit some rivers and lakes. The 175-page book *Angling in Norway*, available from tourist offices for Nkr170, details the best salmon and trout-fishing areas, fees and regulations. In the UK, it's available from The Scandinavia Connection (☎ 020-7602 0657, W www.scandinavia-connection.co.uk), 26 Woodsford Square, London, W14 8DP, UK.

Regulations vary between rivers but, generally, from mid-September to November, fish under 20cm must be thrown back. At other times between August and May, you can't keep fish less than 30cm in length.

For sea or fjord fishing, no licence is required. All river and lake fishing in Norway requires an annual licence (Nkr180 for salmon, trout and char and Nkr90 for other fish), which is sold at post offices. A weekly licence is also available for Nkr45. To fish on private land, you must also purchase a local licence (Nkr50 to Nkr300 per day), which is available from sports shops, hotels, camp sites and tourist offices. Some areas require a compulsory equipment disinfection certificate (Nkr100). See also the boxed text 'Commandments for Anglers'.

Tracing Your Ancestors

In the 19th and early 20th centuries, almost 800,000 Norwegians migrated westward to settle in the USA and Canada, especially Wisconsin, Minnesota, North Dakota, Utah and Manitoba, and nowadays many of their descendants are returning to the old country to find their roots. Genealogy buffs should check out the excellent pamphlet *How to trace your ancestors in Norway*, available on the Internet at W www.ide-as.com/fndb/howto.html. Other useful Web sites include W www.norway.com and the National Archives of Norway site (click on the US flag) W digitalarkivet.uib.no.

Other sources of help include the Norwegian Emigrant Museum (☎ 62 57 48 50, fax 62 57 48 51, e knut.djupedal@emigrant.museum.no) in Hamar and the Norwegian Emigration Centre (☎ 51 53 88 60, W www.emigrationcenter.com) located in Stavanger.

Commandments for Anglers

1. Foreigners may fish for free on the Norwegian coast but can't sell their catch.
2. Fishing is prohibited within 100m of fish farms, cables and nets that are anchored or fastened to the shore.
3. Anyone who damages fishing equipment must pay compensation for the damage.
4. Anchoring is prohibited in the vicinity of drift nets or line-fishing sites.
5. It is forbidden to shoot off firearms or make noises that can disturb the fish.
6. Fishing with live bait is prohibited.
7. It's forbidden to abandon fishing tackle or other rubbish that can disturb, delay or damage fish catches or fishing boats.
8. Only Norwegian citizens or permanent residents may catch lobsters.
9. Salmon, trout and char fishing with a rod is permitted year-round. For rivers with fishing bans, you may still fish within 100m of the river mouth. From 1 June to 4 August, between 6pm on Friday and 6pm on Monday, you can fish for salmon, trout and char with a hook and troll. All anglers for these fish must have a national fishing permit, and must also follow other local fishing regulations (which may include compulsory disinfection of fishing equipment).
10. All anglers from boats must wear life-jackets.
11. Don't throw rubbish or pollute the waters in any way.

WORK

Norway has a relatively low unemployment rate, so foreigners can sometimes land a job, particularly in the less desirable service industry. A command of Norwegian is generally required and preference is generally given to Scandinavians.

As a member of the European Economic Area (EEA), Norway grants citizens of other EEA countries (essentially EU countries, plus Switzerland, Liechtenstein, Greenland and the Faroe Islands) the right to look for work for a three-month period without obtaining a permit; those who find work have a right to remain in Norway for the duration of their employment.

Other foreigners must apply for work permits through a Norwegian embassy or consulate in their home country before entering Norway. However, a ban on immigration is in effect until further notice, and exceptions are granted only in the case of extenuating circumstances (such as marriage to a Norwegian or valid refugee status) or in cases where highly skilled workers are in demand in a specialised occupation.

The Directorate of Labour (W www .aetat.no/english/), EURES Dept, PO Box 8127 Dep, N-0032 Oslo, distributes two free booklets, *Looking for Work in Norway* and *Norway – Access to Job Vacancies*. For further information, ask your nearest Norwegian Embassy for information on the labour market (reference UDA166).

ACCOMMODATION
Camping
Norway has around 1000 camping grounds. Tent space generally costs from Nkr50 at basic camping grounds to as much as Nkr180 in popular or expensive areas, such as Oslo and Bergen. Most camping grounds also rent simple cabins with cooking facilities starting at around Nkr250 for a very basic two- or four-bed bunkhouse. Bring a sleeping bag, as linen and blankets are provided only at an extra charge, which is anywhere from Nkr40 to Nkr60 per visit.

Unless you opt for a more expensive deluxe cabin with shower and toilet facilities, which could range from Nkr400 to Nkr1000, you'll normally also have to pay for showers and often for washing water (there are, however, a few enlightened exceptions). Normally, cabin occupants must clean their cabin before leaving or pay an additional cleaning charge, which averages around Nkr100.

Note that although a few complexes remain open year-round, tent and caravan sites are closed in the off-season (normally early September to mid-May).

See the 'Minimum Impact Camping' boxed text for information on free-camping.

Summer Homes & Cabins
Most tourist offices in popular holiday areas keep lists of private huts, cabins and summer homes that are rented out to holiday-makers when the owners aren't using them. The price for a week's rental starts from around Nkr1000 for a simple place in the off-season to about Nkr13,000 for the most elaborate chalet in mid-summer. Most cabins sleep at least four people, and some accommodate as many as 12, so if you have a group and want to spend some time in a certain area, it's a very economical option. Advance booking is normally required, and you'll probably have to pay a deposit of around Nkr500 or 20% of the total fee, whichever is less.

For further information, contact Novasol (☎ 81 54 42 70, W www.novasol.com), Postboks 309 Sentrum, N-0103 Oslo, which publishes an English-language photo catalogue describing nearly 2000 self-catering cabins and chalets in Norway. A similar scheme is offered by the Danish company Dansommer (Denmark ☎ 86 17 61 22, e booking@ dansommer.dk, W www.dansommer.com).

DNT & Other Mountain Huts
DNT (☎ 22 82 28 00, e turinfo@dntoa.no, W www.turistforeningen.no), Postboks 7 Sentrum, N-0101 Oslo, maintains a network of 374 mountain huts a day's hike apart all along the country's 20,000km of well-marked and maintained wilderness hiking routes. These range from unstaffed huts with two beds to large staffed lodges with more than 100 beds and renowned standards of service. All unstaffed huts offer cooking facilities but, in most places, you must also have your own sleeping bag or a hostel-style sleeping sheet; sleeping sheets are often sold or included in the price at staffed huts. Staffed lodges do not normally have cooking facilities for guests, but a self-service section with cooking facilities is available at some lodges when unstaffed.

At staffed huts, which are concentrated in the south, you can simply turn up and pay your fees. In compliance with international mountain courtesies, no one is turned away, even if there's only floor space left (however,

Minimum Impact Camping

Campers taking advantage of the wonderful *allemansretten* (every man's right) in Norway will help to preserve the country's beauty and foster goodwill by heeding the following regulations:

- Camp at least 150m from any hut or house, but preferably much further away and out of sight.
- If it's raining, select a well-drained camp site and use a waterproof groundsheet to prevent having to dig trenches.
- Along popular routes, particularly in the Jotunheimen or Rondane national parks, set up camp on previously used sites.
- Carry out all your rubbish, including cigarette butts. Biodegradable items may be buried but anything with food residue should be carried out, lest it be dug up and scattered by animals.
- Use established toilet facilities if they're available. Otherwise, select a site at least 50m from water sources and bury waste at least 20cm below the surface. Carry out or bury used toilet paper (it's probably wise to carry a sturdy plastic bag for this purpose).
- Use only biodegradable soap products and use natural temperature water if possible. When washing with hot water, avoid damage to vegetation either by letting the water cool before pouring it out or by dumping it in a gravelly, nonvegetated place.
- In times when you're permitted to build a fire (15 September to 15 April), try to select an established site and keep fires as small as possible. Use only fallen, dead wood and, when you're finished, make sure ashes are cool and buried before you leave the site.
- Caravans and camper vans must use signed waste disposal points.

DNT members over 50 years of age are guaranteed a bed, even if it means displacing a younger hiker!) Huts tend to be packed at Easter. Nightly fees for DNT members/nonmembers in a room with one to three beds is Nkr170/220; rooms with four to six beds, Nkr130/180; dormitories Nkr85/145;

and overflow on the floor, Nkr60/110. Lodging and full board (for DNT members only) ranges from Nkr400 to Nkr435 in the low season, Nkr415 to Nkr455 in high summer and Nkr460 to Nkr505 over Easter week.

Members/nonmembers who prefer to camp outside the huts and use their facilities will pay Nkr40/50. (Otherwise, tenters must camp at least 150m from the hut and may not use the facilities.) Breakfasts are Nkr70/90; a thermos of coffee or tea, Nkr20/25; sandwiches are Nkr10/13; light dinners are Nkr105/120; and three-course meals cost Nkr155/185. Dinners, often including local specialities, can be excellent.

For unstaffed huts, you must pick up keys (Nkr100 deposit) in advance from a DNT office or a staffed hut. To pay, fill out a Once-Only Authorisation slip and leave either cash or a valid credit card number in the box provided. There are two classes of unstaffed huts. Self-service chalets are stocked with blankets and pillows and have wood stoves, firewood, gas cookers and a wide range of food supplies for sale (on the honour system). In these, DNT members/nonmembers pay Nkr130/185 for a bed and Nkr50/80 for overflow space on the floor. At other unstaffed huts, users must carry in their own food.

Most DNT huts are closed between 15 October and 15 February. In winter, staffed DNT lodges are open between the Saturday before Palm Sunday and Easter Monday, but huts along the Oslo-Bergen railway and a few others open for the cross-country ski season as early as late February. DNT can provide lists of opening dates for each hut.

There are also numerous private hikers' huts and lodges peppered around most mountain areas, but not all are open to the public. Some places offer DNT members a discount.

Hostels

In Norway, reasonably priced hostels *(vandrerhjem)* offer a bed for the night, plus use of communal facilities that usually include a self-catering kitchen (but you're advised to take your own cooking and eating utensils). Hostels vary widely in character, but increasingly, they're open longer hours and 'wardens' with a sergeant-major mentality are an endangered species. (Note, however, that consumption of alcohol on hostel premises is prohibited.) The trend has also been towards smaller dormitories with just two to six beds. Guests must bring their own sleeping sheet and pillowcase, although most hostels hire sleeping sheets for around Nkr50 for as long as you stay at that hostel.

Several hostel guides are available, including the HI's annually updated Europe guide. The Norwegian Hostelling Association, Norske Vandrerhjem (☎ 23 13 93 00, fax 23 13 93 50, ℮ hostels@online.no, Ⓦ www.vandrerhjem.no), Torggata 1, N-0181 Oslo, also publishes a free 52-page booklet, *Experience Norway with Hostelling International*. This publication lists 75 hostels, which are found in most cities, towns or other places of interest to visitors. There are very few private hostels in Norway.

Some hostels are quite comfortable lodge-style facilities and are open year-round, while others occupy school dorms and are open in summer only. Most have two to six beds per room and cost from Nkr80 to Nkr225. The higher-priced hostels usually include a buffet breakfast, while other places may charge from Nkr40 to Nkr60 for breakfast. Some also provide a good-value evening meal for around Nkr100.

In summer, reservations are recommended, particularly for popular destinations. Most places in Norway accept phone reservations and are normally happy to book beds at your next destination for a small fee (around Nkr20). Note, however, that popular hostels in Oslo and Bergen are often heavily booked in summer.

Prices listed in this book are those for HI members; nonmembers pay an additional Nkr25 per night. Even if you haven't bought a membership in your own country, you can pick up a Welcome Card; after six nights at nonmember prices, you'll qualify for the lower HI member rates. Be sure to request the card on your first night and pick up stamps to fill it on each consecutive night.

Private B&Bs/Pensions

Next to camping and hostels, the cheapest places to sleep are in private rooms booked through tourist offices. These rooms average Nkr225/350 for singles/doubles and breakfast isn't normally included. Many towns also have pensions and guesthouses with singles in the Nkr270 to Nkr400 range, but linen and/or breakfast will only be included at the higher-priced places. A couple of useful listings on the Internet include Ⓦ www.bbnorway.com and Ⓦ www.bedandbreakfast.no.

Along highways, you'll also see some *Rom* signs, indicating inexpensive informal accommodation typically costing from Nkr100 to Nkr250 (without breakfast); those who bring their own sheets or sleeping bags may get a discount. For information on farmhouse accommodation, contact local tourist offices.

Hotels

Although normal hotel prices are high, most hotels offer substantially discounted rates on weekends and in the summer season (usually mid-June to mid-August, but sometimes just July), which are slow periods for business travel. Nationwide chains offering such deals include the Tulip Inn/Rainbow Hotels, Radisson SAS Hotels and Rica Hotels, all of which maintain high standards. A significant consideration in this land of daunting food prices is that hotels, unlike pensions, normally offer an enormous all-you-can-eat breakfast buffet.

If you're travelling with children, ask about family rooms, which accommodate two adults and up to two children for little more than a regular double.

The Norwegian Tourist Board's annually updated accommodation brochure lists most hotels but discount schemes are outlined in its general travel guide. The Fjord Pass (Nkr95) gives accommodation discounts at 225 hotels, guesthouses and cabins around the country. Singles/doubles cost from Nkr395/450 to Nkr675/1010 and the pass is valid for variable periods depending on the establishment. Contact Fjord Tours (☎ 55 55 76 60, fax 55 55 16 40, ℮ fjordpass@rugruppen.no,

W www.fjordpass.com), PO Box 1752 Nordnes, N-5024 Bergen, for details. Rainbow and Norlandia's Scan+ Hotel Pass (☎ 23 08 02 00, W www.scanplus.no) costs Nkr90 and provides discounts at 200 hotels around Scandinavia; doubles start at Nkr295 per person. Best Western's Euro Guestcheque (☎ 22 55 07 60, W www.bestwestern.no) elicits discounts at 30 Best Western Hotels, but overnight rates vary. The Nordic Hotel pass offered by Choice Hotels (☎ 22 40 13 00, W www.choice.no) for Nkr100 allows up to 50% discount on summer and weekend rates. Rica Hotels (☎ 67 85 45 00, e rica@rica.no, W www.rica.no) have a free Feriepass offering discounts on room prices throughout Scandinavia (and the fifth consecutive night is free).

FOOD

The prices of food and drink in Norway may inspire newly arrived visitors to finally begin that diet program they've been planning. The key is to think in krone and avoid converting the Norwegian price into your home currency or you may wind up emaciated. To minimise the sting, you can prepare your own meals, but it's wise to know a few good recipes involving hot dogs and pasta. Most hostels and camping grounds offer cooking facilities but, as an alternative, you may just want to buy a loaf of bread or pack of Ryvita, a slab of Jarlsberg cheese and a tin of smoked fish and enjoy a quiet lunch out in a park somewhere. For other price-conscious ideas, see Budget Options section.

By international standards, Norwegian food is fairly bland and it's often heavy and difficult to digest. Flavourful condiments may be hard to come by, so you may want to carry a supply of your favourite spices from home. However, Norway does have its own culinary tradition, and what Betty Crocker and Julia Child are to the Americans and Delia Smith is to the Brits, Ingrid Espelid is to the Norwegians. For anyone who wants to prepare meals in the local manner, her numerous cookbooks are considered the last word on Norwegian cuisine.

Meals

Breakfast or *frokost* is generally a fairly big production, especially at upmarket hotels where you can choose a gargantuan buffet which includes English, American, Continental and Scandinavian options all on one groaning table. The typical Norwegian breakfast, however, consists of coffee (always!), a boiled egg and some sort of bread or dry crispbread (normally Ryvita) topped with cheese (especially Gudbrandsdalsost!), cucumber, tomato and some sort of pickled herring. A basic breakfast is often served at hostels for Nkr40 to Nkr60 (or included in the overnight price) and, for non-guests, the big hotels offer the huge buffet for around Nkr100.

For lunch, most people opt for a sandwich or piece of cold *smørbrød*, a slice of bread topped with *pålegg*, which rather recursively refers to 'that which goes on top', be it sardines, shrimp, ham, olives, cucumber, egg or whatever. In the mid-afternoon, Norwegians often break for a snack of coffee and waffles with cream and jam.

The main meal is *middag*, which is eaten anywhere from 4pm to 6pm and is usually the only hot meal of the day. This will normally include a meat, seafood or pasta dish, with boiled potatoes, a scoop of vegetables and perhaps even a small salad or green garnish.

Budget Options

There's no such thing as a cheap lunch in Norway, but some supermarkets have reasonably priced delicatessens where you can pick up salads sold by the kilogram, or grilled chickens from Nkr30. At a *konditori*, a bakery with a few tables, you can enjoy relatively inexpensive baked goods, pastries and sandwiches. Cafeterias, which are found everywhere, and university messes (you'll need a student card to qualify for discounts) are marginally more expensive but offer better nutritional value, with simple hot dishes starting at around Nkr50. However, they're more popular for a coffee fix and a waffle or quick snack of smørbrød.

Petrol stations normally sell several types of *varm pølse* (hot dogs), which are the cheapest hot meal you can buy, but note that the plumper versions are invariably more palatable than the flavourless slender ones. A basic hot dog without bread typically costs Nkr15 to Nkr20; with a bun, it ranges from Nkr20 to Nkr25 and with a wrapping of streaky bacon, from Nkr25 to Nkr30. Some places charge extra for a garnish of fresh or deep-fried onions.

Other fairly cheap eats are found at a *gatekjøkken* (food wagon or kiosk), which generally serves hot dogs, burgers, chips, previously frozen pizza slices and the like for Nkr20 to Nkr60. Fast-food chains such as McDonald's and Burger King, offer 'meal deals' (large burger, chips and a drink) from around Nkr50 to Nkr75, but you'll find cheaper and better quality food elsewhere.

Pizzas also feature prominently in the local diet, and it's often cited that *Pizza Grandiosa*, a marginally satisfying brand of frozen pizza, is in fact Norway's national dish. Given its popularity with harried urbanites who lack the time to cook anything elaborate or the money to eat out, that would be difficult to dispute. There are also a couple of pizza chains, notably Peppe's Pizza and Pizza Hut, which sometimes offer good-value lunch time buffets on weekdays. At Peppe's, all-you-can-eat pizza and a soft drink is Nkr93. At restaurants, diners are disappointed to see prices exceeding Nkr200 per pizza, but these gigantic offerings are suitable for at least two hungry people.

Meals at moderately priced restaurants are typically Nkr80 to Nkr120, though some may feature a *dagens rett* (daily special) for as little as Nkr80. The best-value restaurant meals are found around the ethnic areas of Oslo, especially Grønland, which enjoys a range of relatively great value Indian, Bangladeshi and Middle Eastern choices. Open-air markets in the same area offer the country's best deals on fresh produce. Most Chinese restaurants and takeaways are worth avoiding.

It may surprise you to see how much processed and chemical-laden convenience food fills supermarket shelves, and that there's a notable dearth of good, old-fashioned staples (or anything that takes

more than 10 minutes to prepare). In particular, give cooked and fresh meat in supermarkets a wide body swerve. If you can subsist on bread, pasta, cheese, milk, yoghurt and expensive fresh vegetables, you'll have few worries but – otherwise you may want to spend some time reading labels.

Note that supermarkets are open from around 8am or 9am to around 6pm to 8pm on weekdays in smaller towns and 9pm to 11pm in cities. On Saturday, they *normally* close around 4pm in towns and 6pm in cities. Except in very few instances (eg, in tourist areas such as Geiranger), they're closed on Sunday and holidays.

Meat

While many Norwegians eat meat only in the form of hot dogs and reconstituted meat patties, those who can afford it normally prefer beef, lamb, elk or reindeer. Although few Norwegian meat dishes will knock your socks off, most are quite palatable. Wind-dried meat, or *spekemat*, is a leftover from the days before refrigeration and the ubiquitous *lapskaus* (often called *biddus*, or 'wedding stew', in the Sami areas of the far north) is a hearty meat stew with vegetables.

Seafood

Norwegian seafood specialities are thoroughly recommended and include grilled or smoked salmon *(laks)*, boiled shrimp *(reker)*, cod *(torsk)* and catfish *(steinbit)*. In summer, you can often buy *ferske reker*, fresh shrimp, from fishing boats for around Nkr55 to Nkr75/kg, and it's a real treat. Freshly caught fish are also often sold for relatively good prices around harbourside markets; one of the most popular – and pungent – is at Torget in Bergen.

Seafood also turns up in an odd array of special dishes that appeal more to die-hard traditionalists than anyone else. *Fiske-bollur*, or reconstituted cod, mackerel or saithe balls, are a staple for older folk, and *torsketungur*, cod tongues, are enormously popular in Lofoten. Throughout the country, Norwegians rave about *fiskesuppe*, or fish soup, which is more a thin, creamy and slightly fish-flavoured soup than a hearty stew. It may contain a shrimp or two but *we* don't generally recommend it.

Historically, several creative methods were used to preserve fish, resulting in seafood standards that survive to the present day. *Lutefisk*, which is dried cod made almost gelatinous by soaking it in potash lye, is popular around Christmas but it's definitely an acquired taste. *Rakørret* (also called *rakfisk*), or fermented trout, is considered by many to be utterly disgusting. Herring, or *sild*, which was once the fish of the poor masses, is now considerably more expensive and is normally served pickled in onions, mustard or tomato sauce. The excellent *gravat laks* is similarly made, by marinating salmon in sugar, salt, brandy and dill. In the north, *torrfisk* (also called *stokkfisk*), or dried cod remains popular and is exported in large quantities to Italy, Spain and Portugal.

Dairy Products

Milk and dairy products are a staple in Norway, and Norwegians of all ages drink milk daily. There's also a range of cheeses, the most renowned of which is the mild but tasty Jarlsberg, a white cheese that is exported and has gained worldwide popularity. It was first produced in 1860 on the Jarlsberg estate in Tønsberg. A stronger export cheese is an award-winning continental-style offering known as *ridder*.

Traditional cheeses come in several varieties: *gammelost* has always been considered a 'luxury' cheese, which was suitable for export but not for commoners; *mysost*, or 'whey cheese' was eaten by the masses and *pultost* was a simple cheese made from curdled milk and flavoured with caraway. Although these are no longer the standards, one traditional cheese that's still ubiquitous, especially on breakfast buffets and in cafeterias, is the sweet caramel-coloured goat cheese (*geitost*), the most popular brand being *Gudbrandsdalsost*. This unusual confection is unique to Norway and has now become an integral part of the national culture. It was first made by a milkmaid, Anne Hov, in 1863 at Solbråsetra, above Gudbrandsdalen. She took a notion to add fresh cream to some leftover

whey and discovered a new taste treat. Nowadays, it's sliced thinly and eaten on waffles, flatbrød or whole-grain bread, or served as a creamy sweet fondue.

Breads & Pastries

As an accompaniment to cured meats and some hot dishes, many Norwegians like to eat *flatbrød*, a crunchy wafer-like unleavened crispbread that crumbles to the touch. Traditionally it was made from oats and barley and could be stored for many years in a *stabbur* (elevated storage shed). *Lefse*, a light and normally unsweetened griddle cake, which is in fact a leavened version of flatbrød, is often served with sweet condiments. Variations include *lumpe*, which is a potato flour pancake, and *kumpe*, or potato flour dumpling.

In the afternoon, people often eat a delightful snack of waffles, normally with jam and cream. Unlike the firm Belgian waffles, which are better known abroad, Norwegian *vaffler*, which are flower-shaped and divided into four or six heart-shaped bits, are soft and normally strongly flavoured with cardamom. Many of the standard Danish/European pastries are sold in konditori all over the country.

Fruit & Vegetables

Unfortunately, fresh fruit and vegetables are rather expensive in Norway – they are almost literally worth their weight in gold!

Potato features prominently in nearly every Norwegian meal and may be considered a staple in the national diet. Most restaurants serve boiled or roasted potatoes with every dish, and an order of chips is normally twice the size – and three times the price – it would be elsewhere in Europe. Other vegetables that turn up with some regularity are cabbage (*kål*) and turnip (*nepe*). Carrots (*gulrot*), swedes (rutabagas; *kålrot*), cauliflower (*blomkål*) and broccoli also grow fairly well and appear frequently in restaurant meals.

While vegetarianism isn't big in Norway, nearly every restaurant offers some sort of vegetarian dish, even if it's just a cheese and onion omelette or a pasta with cream sauce. Oslo, Bergen and other cities enjoy a choice of trendy but rarely over-priced European-style cafes that will offer a range of creative and inexpensive dishes, normally including several well-conceived vegetarian options. At lunch time, you'll normally find something decent for Nkr60 to Nkr100.

The country's main fruit-growing region is around Hardangerfjord, where strawberries, plums, cherries, apples and other orchard fruits proliferate. Although berries are only rarely cultivated, a range of wild berries grow in the forests, mountains, tundra and bogs. Among them are wild strawberries *(ville jordbær)*, cranberries *(tyttebær)*, black currants *(solbær)*, red currants *(rips)*, blueberries *(blåbær)*, raspberries *(bringebær)* and the most prized, cloudberries *(moltebær)*.

The wild berries, which make excellent snacks and jams, are available to anyone, but there are some restrictions on picking cloudberries, which grow in boggy areas of Nordland, Troms and Finnmark. On private land, they're reserved for the landowners, and on public land in Finnmark, are available only to residents of that county. However, on public land, anyone is welcome to pick them and eat them on the spot. Try warm cloudberry jam with ice cream – it's fantastic!

DRINKS

If Norway has a national drink, it's coffee, and it's drunk in such staggering quantities that one can only wonder how people can remain so calm under the influence of so much caffeine. Coffee first arrived in Norway in the mid-18th century but didn't really take off until a century later, when it was embraced by the upper class. Today its popularity is universal and most Norwegians drink it black and strong, but foreigners requiring milk and/or sugar are normally indulged. In bakeries and cafeterias, a small cup normally costs around Nkr14, and refills cost from Nkr6 to Nkr10.

Teas and infusions are also available all over the country but don't enjoy the same popularity as coffee. The usual range of fizzy drinks *(brus)* and mineral water *(mineralvann)* are available everywhere. Try to buy them at supermarkets rather than kiosks, petrol stations or convenience stores, where they're usually more expensive.

Alcoholic Drinks

Norway's official attitude toward alcohol borders on paranoia. Alcohol sales are strictly controlled and a few towns have implemented virtual prohibition. In some places, including parts of Telemark, drinking beer in public actually calls for a fine of Nkr2000 and/or prison time! The legal drinking age is 18 years for beer *(øl)* and wine *(vin)* and 20 for spirits.

Beer is available in some supermarkets for extortionate prices, but wine and spirits may be purchased only at state monopoly shops known as *Vinmonopolet* (fondly known as just *pole*), which open 9am to 4pm, 5pm or 6pm on weekdays and 9am to 2pm or 3pm on Saturday. Unfortunately, only the largest cities and towns actually have a Vinmonopolet and those that would like to have one must apply to the government and face all sorts of scrutiny before a licence will be granted. Generally, the presence of another monopoly shop within a two-hour drive will disqualify any applicant. Fortunately, most of these places are permitted to have an *ølutsalg*, or 'beer outlet', where a range of beers are available in bulk for the most reasonable prices you'll find.

On the mainland, the best value wine is the Italian red, *Cappella*, which costs just Nkr69 for a 75cL bottle. In Svalbard, alcohol is available duty-free, but it's rationed for residents and visitors must present a valid plane ticket in order to purchase it.

Despite its cost (an average of Nkr47 for 400mL), beer is extremely popular, and in bars it's commonly sold in 400mL or 500mL glasses (about 30% and 15% less than a British pint, respectively). The standard Norwegian beer is pils lager, with an alcohol content of around 4%, and it's still brewed in accordance with the 16th-century German purity law. The most popular brands are the lagers Ringsnes in the south and Mack in the north. *Munkholm* is a fairly pleasant alcohol-free beer. Note that when friends go out drinking, people generally buy their own drinks rather than rounds.

For a powerful dose of Norwegian culture, don't miss the national spirit, *aquavit* (or *akevitt*) – a potent potato and caraway liquor that dates from the early days of Norwegian trade on the high seas. The name is derived from the Latin *aqua vitae*, the 'living waters'. Although caraway is an essential ingredient, various modern distilleries augment the spicy flavour with any combination of orange, coriander (cilantro), anise, fennel, sugar and salt! The confection is aged for three to five years in 500L oak barrels that have previously been used to age sherry.

Perhaps the most esteemed version of this libation is Linje Aquavit, or 'line aquavit', which first referred to stores that had crossed the equator. In the early days, ships carried oak barrels of aquavit abroad to trade, but the unsold barrels were returned to Norway and offered for sale. When it was discovered that the product had improved with age and travel, these leftovers became a highly prized commodity. Today, bottles of Linje Aquavit bear the name of the ship involved, its route and the amount of time the barrels have aged at sea.

Given the prices of beer, wine and spirits, it's probably not surprising that many Norwegians do a great deal of illegal distilling and home-brewing. If you're offered any home-made swill, exercise due caution, as things sometimes go wrong and, even when they don't, the effects can be diabolical!

ENTERTAINMENT

Norway isn't known for its awe-inspiring entertainment scene, but the larger cities do provide some semblance of nightlife. Film admissions vary from Nkr40 to Nkr75 and cover charges in nightclubs average around Nkr70. Most well-known nightspots provide live music performances or dancing on Friday and Saturday night, and may also offer a bit of action on Thursday and Sunday. Norway also has a phenomenal number of music festivals; for more information, see Special Events, earlier in this chapter.

Bars & Clubs

In most bars and nightclubs, a 400mL glass of lager will set you back around Nkr47, but it can be as low as Nkr25 to Nkr35 on the *Børsen* ('stock exchange') system employed in some places, in which the price rises and falls with demand. A glass of house wine is typically Nkr50 and the cheapest 75cL bottle will cost around Nkr130, but you'll more often pay over Nkr170. Inexpensive spirits average around Nkr40 for a 4cL shot.

Other

Most towns have at least one cinema but the offerings are generally about three months behind most of the rest of the world. Oslo, Bergen and other larger towns have theatre, opera and ballet companies, as well as philharmonic orchestras. Classical performances take place in summer in Bergen but elsewhere most are in winter, when outdoor activities are limited, and few visitors are around to enjoy them.

SPECTATOR SPORTS

For thousands of years, skis were the only practical means of winter transport in much of Norway and, as a result, it is in winter sports that Norwegians have excelled. In fact, the people of Telemark invented the graceful Telemark turn and the word slalom is derived from the Norwegian words *sla låm*, or 'slope track', which originally referred to a nordic ski competition that wove over hill and dale, dodging thickets! In 1928, 1932 and 1936, Sonja Henie was the Olympic figure-skating gold medallist; speed-skater Johann Koss won three gold medals at the Lillehammer Winter Olympics in 1994; and, in 1998 in Nagano, Norway finished second on the overall medal table (behind Germany) with 10 gold medals. In winter, big ski-jumping events normally take place at Holmenkollen near Oslo, and other winter events occur at the Olympic venues in Hamar and Lillehammer.

In the 1990s the Norwegian men's national football (soccer) team maintained a top-20 FIFA ranking and a fearsome competitive reputation in world football. The team qualified for the World Cup in 1994 and 1998 and did very well in the 1998 competition, causing a sensation by beating early favourites Brazil in the first round. They were knocked out in the second round by Italy. The bulk of Norway's national team stars play for Premier League teams in the UK, notably Manchester United striker Ole Gunnar Solskjær and his Glasgow Rangers counterpart Tore Andre Flo. Back at home, Trondheim's Rosenberg team usually plays well in European club competitions. But it's the Norwegian women's national team that has strutted the world stage with most success, clinching the second ever Women's World Cup in 1995 (they also did well in 1999) and consistently rating among the best five nations around the globe.

Other sporting successes have been scored by Norwegian women, including long-distance and marathon runners Grete Waitz and Ingrid Kristiansen, and javelin champion Trine Hattestad.

SHOPPING

Given the prices, few people would consider a shopping holiday in Norway. While items in shops are mostly high quality, beware of the cheaper kitsch. Upmarket shop windows can be veritable works of art, but the prices would put off all except the most well-heeled visitors. Specialities include wool sweaters and other hand-knitted clothing, pewter ware, intricate silver jewellery, Sami sheath knives, reindeer-leather products, troll figurines, wooden toys and woodwork adorned with *rosemaling* (painted or carved floral motifs). For the best quality Norwegian handicrafts – at corresponding prices – look for the Husfliden shops, which exist in most large cities and towns.

If you're shipping purchases back home, a good option is the post office's Verdenspakke option (see the earlier Post section in this chapter).

Getting There & Away

The first step for anyone headed for Norway is to get to Europe and, in these days of airline competition, you'll find plenty of deals to European 'gateway' cities, particularly London, Paris, Frankfurt, Berlin or even Copenhagen. Only a handful of travellers approach Norway and Scandinavia from the east, via Russia, although the trans-Siberian and trans-Mongolian routes offer exceptionally adventurous options.

AIR

Remember to reconfirm your onward or return bookings at least 72 hours before departure for international flights. Otherwise there's a real risk that you'll turn up at the airport only to find that you've missed your flight because it was rescheduled, or that you've been reclassified as a 'no-show' and 'bumped' (see the Air Travel Glossary later in this chapter).

Airports & Airlines

SAS, British Airways, KLM-Royal Dutch Airlines, Air France, Lufthansa, Swissair, Alitalia, Finnair and Icelandair link Oslo's Gardermoen airport with major European and North American cities. Bergen, Stavanger and Trondheim also have direct international flights. If you're flying between the UK and Stavanger (a route used mainly by oil businesspeople) you'll get the best non-business fares by staying at least one Saturday night in Norway.

Braathens (Norway: ☎ 81 52 00 00, UK: ☎ 0191-214 0991, W www.braathens.no) has several daily flights between London's Heathrow or Gatwick and Oslo's Gardermoen. There are daily flights between London Gatwick and Bergen, twice daily (except Saturday) services between Newcastle and Stavanger, and once or twice daily flights between Aberdeen and Stavanger. There are also once daily (except Saturday) international services between Billund (Denmark: ☎ 75 35 44 00) and Oslo. The best fares are available on super-Apex tickets purchased at

Warning

The information in this chapter is particularly vulnerable to change: Prices for international travel are volatile, routes are introduced and cancelled, schedules change, special deals come and go, and rules and visa requirements are amended. Airlines and governments seem to take a perverse pleasure in making price structures and regulations as complicated as possible. You should check directly with the airline or a travel agent to make sure you understand how a fare (and ticket you may buy) works. In addition, the travel industry is highly competitive and there are many lurks and perks.

The upshot of this is that you should get opinions, quotes and advice from as many airlines and travel agents as possible before you part with your hard-earned cash. The details given in this chapter should be regarded as pointers and are not a substitute for your own careful, up-to-date research.

least seven days in advance, but you can stay no longer than a month and must spend at least one Saturday night. The tourist class baggage limit is 20kg per person.

Scandinavian Airlines System, or SAS (Norway: ☎ 81 00 33 00, W www.sas.no), flies daily between London's Heathrow, Gardermoen, Bergen and Stavanger. It also connects Manchester and Oslo daily except Saturday and flies twice daily between Aberdeen and Stavanger. Its North American hub is New York's Newark airport, with daily flights to/from Oslo, Copenhagen and Stockholm. SAS also offers numerous daily services between various European capitals and Oslo, most of which are routed via Copenhagen. Its free baggage allowance is 32kg per person.

Currently, the best deal available between the UK and Norway is with Ryanair (Stansted: ☎ 08701 569569; Torp: ☎ 33 42 75 00; W www.ryanair.com), which flies twice daily Sunday to Friday and once on Saturday between Stansted and Torp airport, 112km south of Oslo. Fares start at UK£50 (Nkr650) return, plus tax, and express coaches (Nkr98 one-way) to/from Oslo connect with all flights.

Coast Air (Norway: ☎ 52 84 85 00, fax 52 84 85 01, W www.coastair.no), based in Haugesund, flies daily except Saturday between Bergen, Haugesund and Aberdeen. British Midland Airways has daily flights between London Heathrow and Oslo Gardermoen, with occasional special fares. The Danish airline Maersk (Norway: ☎ 81 50 07 40, fax 38 07 06 03), with its Norwegian offices in Kristiansand, flies one to three times daily between London and Kristiansand, via Copenhagen.

Widerøe (Norway: ☎ 81 00 12 00, fax 67 11 61 95, e internetbooking@wideroe-inter .net, W www.wideroe.no), the Norwegian airline based in Lysaker (near Oslo), has services between Aberdeen and Stavanger (UK£208 including taxes), Copenhagen and Sandefjord, Stockholm and Sandefjord, and Oslo Gardermoen and Gothenburg.

Buying Tickets

Your plane ticket will probably be the single most expensive item in your travel budget, and it's worth taking some time to research the current state of the market. Start early: some of the cheapest tickets must be purchased well in advance, and some popular flights sell out early. Have a talk to recent travellers, look at the ads in newspapers and magazines, and watch for special offers. Don't forget to check any Scandinavian or Norwegian newspapers and magazines published in your country of origin.

Inexpensive tickets are available in two distinct categories: official and unofficial. Official ones have a variety of names including advance purchase tickets, advance purchase excursion (Apex) fares, super-Apex and simply budget fares.

Unofficial tickets are discounted tickets that the airlines release through selected travel agents and are usually not sold by the airline offices themselves. Airlines can, however, supply information on routes and timetables and make bookings; their low-season, student and senior citizens' fares can be competitive. Normal, full-fare airline tickets sometimes include one or more side trips in Europe free of charge, which can make them good value.

Return (round-trip) tickets usually work out cheaper than two one-way fares – often much cheaper. Be aware that immigration officials may ask to see return or onward tickets and, if you can't show either, you might have to provide proof of 'sufficient means of support', which means you have to show a lot of money or, in some cases, valid credit cards.

Round-the-world (RTW) tickets are often real bargains and can work out to be no more expensive or even cheaper than an ordinary return ticket. The official airline RTW tickets are usually put together by a combination of two or more airlines and permit you to fly anywhere you want on their route systems so long as you don't backtrack. Other restrictions are that you (usually) must book the first sector in advance and cancellation penalties then apply. There may be restrictions on how many stops (or kilometres) you are permitted, and usually the tickets are valid for between 90 days and a year. Prices start at around UK£1000/US$1500, depending on the season and length of validity. An alternative type of RTW ticket is one put together by a travel agent using a combination of discounted tickets. These can be much cheaper than the official ones but usually carry a lot of restrictions.

Generally, you can find discounted tickets at prices as low as, or lower than, advance purchase or budget tickets. Phone around the travel agencies for bargains. You may discover that those impossibly cheap flights are 'fully booked, but we have another one that costs a bit more...'. Or that the flight is on an airline notorious for its poor safety standards and leaves you in the world's least favourite airport mid-journey for 14 hours confined to the transit lounge because you don't have a visa. Or the agent claims to have the last two seats available for that country for the whole of August,

Air Travel Glossary

Alliances Many of the world's leading airlines are now intimately involved with each other, sharing everything from reservations systems and check-in to aircraft and frequent-flyer schemes. Opponents say that alliances restrict competition. Whatever the arguments, there is no doubt that big alliances are the way of the future.

Courier Fares Businesses often need to send urgent documents or freight securely and quickly. Courier companies hire people to accompany the package through customs and, in return, offer a discount ticket which is sometimes a bargain. However, you may have to surrender all your baggage allowance and take only carry-on luggage.

Fares Airlines traditionally offer 1st class (coded F), business class (coded J) and economy class (coded Y) tickets. These days there are so many promotional and discounted fares available that few passengers pay full fare.

Lost Tickets If you lose your airline ticket, an airline will usually treat it like a travellers cheque and, after inquiries, issue you with another one. Legally, however, an airline is entitled to treat it like cash and if you lose it then it's gone forever. Take very good care of your tickets.

Onward Tickets An entry requirement for many countries is that you have a ticket out of the country. If you're unsure of your next move, the easiest solution is to buy the cheapest onward ticket to a neighbouring country or a ticket from a reliable airline which can later be refunded if you do not use it.

Open-Jaw Tickets These are return tickets where you fly out to one place but return from another. If available, this can save you backtracking to your arrival point.

Overbooking Since every flight has some passengers who fail to show up, airlines often book more passengers than they have seats. Usually excess passengers make up for the no-shows, but occasionally somebody gets 'bumped' onto the next available flight. Guess who it is most likely to be? The passengers who check in late. If you do get 'bumped', you are normally offered some form of compensation.

Reconfirmation Some airlines require you to reconfirm your flight at least 72 hours prior to departure. Check your travel documents to see if this is the case.

Restrictions Discounted tickets often have various restrictions on them – such as needing to be paid for in advance and incurring a penalty to be altered or cancelled. Others are restrictions on the minimum and maximum period you must be away.

Round-the-World Tickets RTW tickets give you a limited period (usually a year) in which to circumnavigate the globe. You can go anywhere the carrying airlines go, as long as you don't backtrack. The number of stopovers or total number of separate flights is decided before you set off and they usually cost a bit more than a basic return flight.

Ticketless Travel Airlines are gradually waking up to the realisation that paper tickets are unnecessary encumbrances. On simple one-way or return trips, reservations details can be held on computer and the passenger merely shows ID to claim their seat.

Transferred Tickets Airline tickets cannot be transferred from one person to another. Travellers sometimes try to sell the return half of their ticket, but officials can ask you to prove that you are the person named on the ticket. On an international flight, tickets are compared with passports.

which he will hold for you for a maximum of two hours as long as you come in and pay cash. Don't panic – keep ringing around.

If you're coming from the USA, South-East Asia or the UK, you'll probably find the cheapest flights are being advertised by obscure agencies. Many such firms are honest and solvent, but there are a few rogues who will take your money and disappear only to reopen elsewhere a month or two later under a new name.

If you feel suspicious about a firm, don't give them all the money at once – leave a deposit of 20% or so and pay the balance when you get the ticket. If they insist on cash in advance, go somewhere else or be prepared to take a very big risk. Once you have the ticket, ring the airline to confirm that you actually have been booked onto the flight.

You may decide to pay more than the rock-bottom fare by opting for the safety of a better known travel agent. Firms such as STA Travel, which has offices worldwide, Council Travel in the USA and elsewhere or Travel CUTS in Canada offer good prices to most destinations and won't disappear overnight leaving you clutching a receipt for a nonexistent ticket.

A more novel way of finding inexpensive tickets, but only available if you're coming from the USA, is on the Web site **w** www .priceline.com, which allows you to name your own price for airline tickets; within 15 minutes, it'll advise you by email whether your bid has been accepted.

Use the fares quoted in this book as a guide only. They are approximate and based on the rates advertised by travel agents at the time of research. Most are likely to have changed by the time you read this.

Travellers with Special Needs

If you have special needs of any sort – you're vegetarian or require a special diet, you're travelling in a wheelchair, taking the baby, terrified of flying, whatever – let the airline people know as soon as possible so that they can make the necessary arrangements. Remind them when you reconfirm your booking (at least 72 hours before departure) and again when you check in at the airport. It may also be worth ringing around the airlines before you make your booking to find out how they can handle your particular requirements.

Children aged under two travel for 10% of the full fare (or free on some airlines) as long as they don't occupy a seat. They don't get a baggage allowance in this case. 'Skycots', baby food and nappies (diapers) should be provided by the airline if requested in advance. Children aged between two and 12 can usually occupy a seat for half to two-thirds of the full fare and get a standard baggage allowance.

Departure Tax

Norwegian airport departure tax (Nkr213) is always included in the price of the airline ticket.

The USA

The North Atlantic is the world's busiest long-haul air corridor and the flight options are bewildering. Larger newspapers such as *The New York Times*, *Chicago Tribune*, *San Francisco Chronicle* and *Los Angeles Times* all produce weekly travel sections in which you'll find any number of travel agents' ads for air fares to Europe.

Thanks to the high ethnic Norwegian population in Minnesota, Wisconsin and North Dakota, you may find small local agencies specialising in travel to Scandinavia and offering good-value charter flights in those areas. Otherwise, you should be able to fly return from New York or Boston to Oslo, Copenhagen or Stockholm for around US$500 in the low season and US$1000 in the high season. With most tickets you can usually travel 'open jaw', allowing you to land in one city (Copenhagen, for example) and return from another (such as Oslo) at no extra cost.

Many European destinations, including Oslo, Stockholm and Copenhagen, are serviced by Icelandair (**☎** 800 223 5500, **e** america@icelandair.is, **w** www.icelandair .net), via Reykjavík, from New York, Boston, Baltimore-Washington, Minneapolis and Orlando. It offers some of the best deals, and on its transatlantic flights it allows a free three-day stopover in Reykjavík – making it a great way to spend a few days in Iceland. Return fares start at around US$800 (including taxes), but special fares are sometimes available.

On the other hand, if you're planning on flying within Norway (or around Scandinavia), SAS (☎ 800 221 2350, W www .sas.no) has some interesting regional discounts available to passengers who fly on its transatlantic flights (see Air in the Getting Around chapter).

Airhitch (☎ 800 326 2009 or ☎ 310-394 4215, W www.airhitch.org) specialises in stand-by tickets to Europe for US$165/233 plus fees and taxes one-way from the east/west coast, but the destinations are by region (not a specific city or country), so you'll need a flexible schedule.

If you're interested in courier flights (see the Air Travel Glossary), you can join the International Association of Air Travel Couriers (IAATC). The membership fee of US$45 (US$50 outside the USA and Canada) gets members a bimonthly update of air-courier offerings (the Travel Guide newsletter) and access to daily courier updates on the Internet. For more information, contact IAATC (☎ 352-475 1584, fax 475 5326, e iaatc@courier.org, W www .courier .org). However, be aware that joining this organisation doesn't guarantee that you'll get a courier flight.

Discount Travel Agencies Discount travel agents in the USA are known as consolidators. San Francisco is the ticket consolidator capital of America, although some good deals can be found in Los Angeles, New York and other big cities.

Consolidators can be found through the Yellow Pages or the major daily newspapers. The New York Times, the Los Angeles Times, the Chicago Tribune and the San Francisco Examiner all produce weekly travel sections in which you will find a number of travel agency ads.

Council Travel, America's largest student travel organisation, has around 60 offices in the USA; its head office (☎ 800 226 8624,

W www.counciltravel.com) is at 205 E 42nd St, New York, NY 10017. Call for the office nearest you. STA Travel (☎ 800 777 0112, W www.statravelgroup.com) has offices in Boston, Chicago, Los Angeles, Miami, New York, Philadelphia, San Francisco and other major cities. Call for office locations.

Other travel agencies include:

Air-Tech (☎ 212-219 7000, e fly@airtech .com) 588 Broadway, Suite 204, New York, NY 10012-5405
  Web site: W www.airtech.com
Cheap Tickets, Inc (☎ 888 922 8849)
  Web site: W www.cheaptickets.com
Educational Travel Centre (☎ 800 747 5551) 438 N Frances St, Madison, WI 53703-1084
  Web site: W www.edtrav.com
High Adventure Travel (☎ 800 350 0612 or ☎ 415-912 5600, e airtreks@highadv.com) 442 Post St, 4th floor, Suite 400, San Francisco, CA 94102
  Web site: W www.highadv.com
Interworld Travel (☎ 800 468 3796, e sales@ interworldtravel.com) 1701 Ponce de Leon Boulevard, Coral Gables, FL 33134
  Web site: W www.interworldtravel.com

Canada
Travel CUTS (toll free ☎ 866 246 9762, W www.travelcuts.com) is Canada's national student travel agency and has offices in all major cities. Airhitch (see the USA section) has stand-by fares to Europe from Toronto, Montreal and Vancouver. You may also find excellent deals to Norway from smaller agencies in parts of Manitoba, where there's a high ethnic Norwegian population.

In some years, Icelandair (see the USA section) runs low-cost seasonal flights from Halifax in Nova Scotia to Oslo, Stockholm and Copenhagen via Reykjavík.

It's also worthwhile scanning the budget travel agents' ads in the Globe & Mail, Toronto Star and Vancouver Sun. For courier flights, contact FB On Board Courier Services in Montreal (☎ 514-631 7925).

The UK & Ireland
If you're looking for a cheap way into or out of Scandinavia, London is Europe's major centre for discounted fares. You can fly from

London to Oslo for as little as UK£25 one way. Most air fares from London now beat surface alternatives in terms of cost.

Airline ticket discounters are known as bucket shops in the UK. Despite the somewhat disreputable name, there's nothing under-the-counter about them. Discount air travel is big business in London. Advertisements for many travel agents appear in the travel pages of the weekend broadsheets, such as the *Independent* on Saturday and the *Sunday Times*. Look out for the free magazines, such as *TNT*, which are widely available in London – start by looking outside the main railway and underground stations.

STA Travel (☎ 08701 600599, ⓦ www .statravel.co.uk), which has offices at 86 Old Brompton Rd, London, SW7 3LQ, and around the UK, including elsewhere in London, Birmingham, Manchester, Edinburgh and Glasgow is a popular travel agent, particularly for students and travellers under 26.

Charter flights can work out as a cheaper alternative to scheduled flights, especially if you do not qualify for the under-26 and student discounts. British Airways offers courier flights through the Travel Shop (☎ 0845 606 0747), 101 Cheapside, London, EC2V 6DT.

Travellers pay a departure tax of UK£10 when flying from Britain to another EU country, normally quoted in the ticket price.

Other recommended travel agencies include:

Trailfinders (☎ 020-7937 1234) 215 Kensington High St, London, W8 6BD
Web site: ⓦ www.trailfinders.com
Bridge the World (☎ 0870 444 7474, ⓔ sales@bridgetheworld.com) 4 Regent Place, London, W1R 5FB
Flightbookers (☎ 020-7757 2626, 0870 010 7000) 117 Tottenham Court Road, London, W1T 5AL
Web site: ⓦ www.ebookers.com

Continental Europe & Scandinavia

Although London is the travel discount capital of Europe, there are several other cities where you'll find a range of good deals. Generally, there's not much variation

in air fare prices for departures from the main European cities. All the major airlines are usually offering some sort of deal and travel agents generally have a number of special offers, so shop around.

You can fly to Oslo and Bergen (from May to October) with Finnair from Helsinki. SAS (ⓦ www.sas.no) flies directly to a range of other European destinations, including Stockholm, Copenhagen, Amsterdam, Hamburg, Frankfurt and Brussels, respectively.

Many travel agents in Europe have ties with STA Travel, where you'll find inexpensive tickets that may be altered once without charge. STA and other discount outlets in important transport hubs include:

Alternativ Tours (☎ 030-881 2089, ⓔ info@ alternativ-tours.de) Wilmersdorferstrasse 94, D-10629 Berlin
Kilroy Travels (☎ 020-524 5100, ⓔ netherlands.sales@kilroytravels.nl) Singel 413–415, NL-1012 WP Amsterdam
Web site: ⓦ www.kilroytravels.com
NBBS Reiswinkels (☎ 0180-393344) Postbus 281, NL-2910 AG Nieuwerkerk aan den Ijssel
OTU Voyages (☎ 01-44 41 38 50, ⓔ infovente@otu.fr) 39 Ave Georges Bernanos (5e), F-75005 Paris
SSR Travel (☎ 01-297 1111, ⓔ info@statravel .ch) Ankerstrasse 112, 8026 Zürich
Web site: ⓦ www.ssr.ch
STA Travel (☎ 01805 456422, ⓔ frankfurt .uni@statravel.de) Bockenheimer Landstrasse 133, D-60325 Frankfurt
Web site: ⓦ www.statravel.de

Australia & New Zealand

There's a large difference between low and high-season fares and, unlike trans-Atlantic flights, where prices rise and fall gradually on either side of the high season, the change in fares for travel from Australia and NZ fares are more sudden. However, if you shop around, you can still get some good travel deals for travel to Oslo. Start early as some of the cheapest tickets need to be brought well in advance and popular flights can sell out.

STA Travel and Flight Centre are well known for cheap fares in both Australia and New Zealand. STA Travel (☎ 131 776, ⓦ www.statravel.com.au) has offices in all

Oslo's cafe scene

Switchbacks on Rv63 to Geirangerfjord

Dropping in on the Ula River, Rondane NP

They've 'heard' it all in Arctic Norway

Vikingskipshuset, Bygdoy Peninsula, Olso

Cold calling in Troms

Lupin, a common spring wildflower

The breathtaking view of Aurlandsfjord

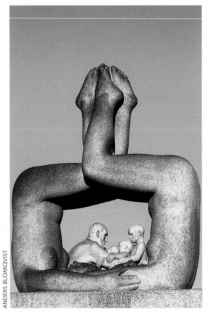

Emotive statues in Vigeland Park, Oslo

Norangsdalen valley near Øye

major Australian cities and on many university campuses. Flight Centre (W www .flightcentre.com.au) has dozens of offices throughout Australia. To find your nearest branch call ☎ 131 600.

In Auckland, Flight Centre (☎ 09-309 6171) has a large central office at National Bank Towers (corner of Queen and Darby Sts) and many branches throughout the country. STA Travel (☎ 09-309 0458, W www .statravel.co.nz) has offices in Auckland, as well as in Hamilton, Palmerston North, Wellington, Christchurch and Dunedin.

From Australia, flights to Oslo require a couple of stopovers on the way, usually Singapore or Bangkok and another European city. In the low season, expect to pay around A$1650 for a return fare with Air France/Qantas or KLM. Air France/Qantas and Cathay Pacific have high season return fares starting from A$2350. From New Zealand, Lufthansa offers some of the best deals for travel to Oslo. Low season return fares start from NZ$2299/2659 in low/high season.

Asia

Singapore and Bangkok are the discount plane-ticket capitals of the region. However, be careful: not all agents are reliable. Ask the advice of other travellers before buying tickets. STA Travel has branches in Tokyo, Singapore, Bangkok, Manila, Seoul, Taipei and Kuala Lumpur. Mumbai and Delhi are India's air transport hubs but tickets are slightly cheaper in Delhi. Aeroflot and LOT offer inexpensive deals from India to Europe. Lauda Air (W www.laudaair.com) flies to Vienna from Bangkok.

Africa

Nairobi and Johannesburg are the best places in Africa to buy tickets to Europe, thanks to the strong competition between their many bucket shops. Several West African countries offer cheap charter flights to France, and charter fares from Morocco can be incredibly cheap if you're lucky enough to find a seat.

Some major airlines have offices in Nairobi, which is a good place to determine

the standard fare before doing the rounds of the travel agencies. Getting several quotes is a good idea since prices always change. Flight Centres (☎ 02-210 024) in Lakhamshi House, Biashara St, Nairobi, has been in business for a number of years.

From South Africa, Air Namibia and South African Airlines offer particularly cheap return youth fares to London. STA Travel (☎ 012-342 5292, e pretoria@ statravel.co.za) are at 1102 Hilda Street, Hatfield, Pretoria 0028. The South African Student's Travel Service (☎ 011-716 3045) has an office at the University of Witwatersrand in Johannesburg.

LAND
Border Crossings

Border crossings between Norway and Sweden or Finland are straightforward; passports are rarely checked and half the time you aren't even aware that you've crossed a border. For Russia, however, everyone needs a visa and travellers will face greater scrutiny.

Note that if you're travelling by rail into Norway, bicycles will be counted as excess baggage and charged accordingly.

Train Passes

Eurail The ScanRail pass is generally a better deal than the Eurail pass.

Eurail passes can only be bought by residents of non-European countries, and are supposed to be purchased before arriving in Europe. However, Eurail passes can be purchased within Europe as long as your passport proves you've been there for less than six months, but the outlets where you can do this are limited, and the passes will be more expensive than getting them outside Europe. Oslo is the only place in Norway where you can buy Eurail passes (at the international ticket counters in the main train stations). In London, try Rail Europe (☎ 0870-584 8848) at 179 Piccadilly.

If you've lived in Europe for more than six months, you're eligible for an Inter-Rail pass, which is a better buy.

Eurail passes are valid for unlimited travel on national railways and some private lines in many European and Scandinavian countries. The passes do not cover the UK or the Baltic countries.

Eurail is also valid for some ferries between Ireland and France (but not between the UK and France), and from Sweden to Finland, Denmark or Germany. Reductions are given on some other ferry routes and on steamer services in various countries.

Eurail passes offer reasonable value to people aged under 26. A Youthpass is valid for unlimited 2nd-class travel for 15 days (US$401), 21 days (US$518), one month (US$644), two months (US$910) or three months (US$1126). The Youth Flexipass, also for 2nd class, is valid for freely chosen days within a two-month period: 10 days for US$473 or 15 days for US$622.

For those aged over 26, a Flexipass (available in 1st class only) costs US$574/756 for 10/15 freely chosen days within two months. The standard Eurail pass has five versions, costing from US$572 for 15 days unlimited travel up to US$1606 for three months. Two to five people travelling together can get good discounts on a Saverpass, which works like the standard Eurail pass. A 15-day Saverpass costs US$486 per person. Eurail passes for children are also available.

The Eurail Select Pass allows you to travel within three bordering countries by rail or sea. In Norway, this includes various combinations for Denmark, Sweden, Finland and Germany. It covers between five and 10 days travel over two months and you must use the pass within six months of purchase. It costs US$346/380/444/502 for 5/6/8/10 days of travel for an adult in first class. There are greater discounts for groups of two to five people under the Eurail Selectpass Saverpass (US$294/322/378/428 in first class) and people under 25 years of age (US$243/266/310/352 in second class). Reservations are required. The pass also offers various discounts on some ferry crossings and for car rental.

Inter-Rail Inter-Rail passes are available to European residents of six-months standing (passport identification is required). Terms and conditions vary from country to country, but in the country of origin there's only a discount of around 50% on normal fares.

Travellers over 26 can get the Inter-Rail 26+, valid for unlimited rail travel in many European and Scandinavian countries. The pass also gives 30% to 50% discounts on various other ferry routes (more than covered by Eurail) and certain river and lake services. A one-zone, 22-day pass costs UK£185 and an all-zone, one-month pass costs UK£319.

The Inter-Rail pass for those under 26 is split into zones. Norway is in Zone B along with Sweden and Finland. The price for any one zone is UK£129 for 22 days. Multizone passes are better value and are valid for one month: two zones is UK£169, three zones is UK£199, and all zones is UK£229.

The Baltics are expected to join the Inter-Rail system at some future date. Check for the latest information if considering buying a pass.

Euro Domino Euro Domino pass for adults (travelling 1st or 2nd class) and youths under 26 travelling within one country on any three to eight days during one month. In Norway, adult/youth prices for 10 days in 2nd class are UK£174/130.

ScanRail This is a flexible rail pass covering travel in Denmark, Norway, Sweden and Finland.

There are three versions. For travel on any five days within a two-month period, the pass costs UK£290/214 for 1st/2nd-class travel (UK£218/190 for travellers under age 26). For travel on any 10 days within a two-month period, the pass costs UK£388/288 for 1st/2nd class (UK£291/216 for those under 26). For a pass allowing unlimited travel during 21 consecutive days, the cost is UK£448/332 for 1st/2nd class (UK£336/249 for those under 26).

If you're aged 55 or over, then you're eligible for the ScanRail 55+ pass, which will allow 1st/2nd-class travel over five days in a two-month period for UK£258/190, 10 days in a two-month period for UK£345/256 and 21 consecutive days for UK£399/295.

To get ScanRail passes at these prices they must be purchased before you arrive in Scandinavia. ScanRail passes can also be purchased in Scandinavia, but they'll cost roughly 10% to 20% more, depending on exchange rates.

The pass also includes free travel on NSB-bus (Trondheim-Storlien).

There's a 50% discount on the following services: Frederikshavn-Oslo (Stena Lines); Hirtshals-Moss, Hirtshals-Larvik, Hirtshals-Oslo and Frederikshavn-Larvik-Moss (Color Line); Bergen-Stavanger (Flaggruten); Sandefjord-Strömstad (Scandi Line); and Hardanger Fjord and southern Hordaland ferries (HSD Snoggbåtene).

There's also a 50% discount on most of Norway's northern express buses (including Bodø-Fauske-Narvik-Tromsø-Alta-Kirkenes); and on some other Norway buses, including the Lofotbus (Narvik-Harstad-Andenes-Svolvær-Leknes-Å). A few other boats offer a discount of 20% or 25%. The Myrdal–Flåm Flåmsbanen offers 30% discount.

Sweden

Bus Nor-Way Bussekspress (Sweden: ☎ 031-100240) runs express buses from Oslo to: Gothenburg (Göteborg; Skr240, 4¼ hours, six daily); and Malmö (Skr377, 8¾ hours, three daily). Three or four daily Swebus Express buses (Sweden: ☎ 0200 218218) run between Stockholm and Oslo (Skr413, eight hours).

There are also buses between Bodø and Skellefteå (Skr480, 8¾ hours, once daily except Saturday) and along the Blå Vägen, or 'Blue Highway', between Mo i Rana and Umeå (Skr244, 7½ hours to 8¾ hours, once daily).

Train There are daily trains from Stockholm to Oslo (Skr648, seven hours) and Narvik (Skr1307, 18¾ hours). Journeys from Trondheim to Sweden via Storlien and Östersund require changing trains at the border. Trains also run between Oslo and Malmö (Skr674, 8¼ hours, twice daily), via Gothenburg (Skr500, four hours, four daily). Note that the Swedish 'X2000' trains, which leave in the morning and cater

to business travellers, tack on a Skr150 surcharge.

Car & Motorcycle The main highways between Sweden and Norway are the E6 from Gothenburg to Oslo, the E18 from Stockholm to Oslo, the E14 from Sundsvall to Trondheim and the E12 from Umeå to Mo i Rana. Many secondary roads also cross the border.

Denmark

Bus To travel by bus from Copenhagen to Oslo (Dkr327, 9½ hours, five daily), take the E6 Ekspressen (Denmark: ☎ 70 10 00 10) via the Øresund bridge and Malmö (see Sweden).

Train Trains run three times daily from Copenhagen to Oslo (Dkr573, from 8¾ hours), including a night route which leaves at 10.12pm (this is currently run by bus, but train tickets are valid). Trains run via the Øresund bridge and Malmö and trips to Oslo require changing in Malmö or Gothenburg.

Finland

Bus The E8 highway runs from Tornio, in Finland, to Tromsø and secondary highways connect Finland with the northern Sami towns of Karasjok and Kautokeino. Regular buses serve all three routes. From 1 June to 16 September, the daily bus run by the Finnish company Eskelisen Lapin Linjat (Finland: ☎ 016-342 2160) runs between Oulu and Tromsø (€77.34, 13½ hours), via Rovaniemi, Karesuvanto and Kilpisjärvi. It leaves at 7.40am southbound and 7.10am northbound. The company also runs buses between Rovaniemi and Tana Bru (€62.25, 8¼ hours, daily 1 June to 5 October, otherwise three per week), via Ivalo and Inari, with a continuation to Vadsø from 1 June to 5 October. There are also runs buses between Oulu and Karasjok (€60.55, 11½ hours), with a connection to Lakselv (€65.60, 12½ hours) and Nordkapp (€100, 15¾ hours). Four times weekly from 2 June to 12 August, buses connect Kautokeino with Enontekiö

(€12.60, 1¼ hours), with connections to Rovaniemi and Oulu.

Germany
Bus Nor-Way Bussekspress (Germany: ☎ 0308-60960) buses connect Berlin with Oslo (€99.70, 14¾ hours), via Rostock, Germany and Gothenburg (Göteborg), Sweden. Southbound they run on Monday and Thursday (plus Tuesday and Saturday, 22 June to 2 September); and northbound on Tuesday and Friday (plus Sunday and Monday, 22 June to 2 September).

Train Hamburg is the central European gateway for Scandinavia, with four or five daily trains to Copenhagen or Malmø; connections for Oslo are available for two of these services. Trains from Hamburg to Copenhagen travel between Puttgarden and Rødby Havn by ferry, which is included in the ticket price. From Denmark to Sweden, trains cross the Øresund bridge.

There's a daily overnight train from Berlin to Oslo (from €149.80 including couchette, 17¾ hours) via the Sassnitz (Germany) to Trelleborg (Sweden) ferry and Malmö. Travelling to/from Oslo always requires changing trains in Malmö (see the earlier Sweden section), and in Gothenburg from 20 August to 16 June. For fares and timetables, see the Web site W www.berlin-night-express.com.

A good train deal to know about in Germany is the Super-Sparpreis fare which allows a 2nd-class, round trip anywhere in Germany within one month for €101.75 (up to four accompanying people pay just €50.60); for more details, see the Deutsche Bahn Web site at W www.bahn.de and click on 'International Guests'. From northern Germany, you can easily make your way to Denmark and the rest of Scandinavia.

The UK
Bus If you like long and arduous journeys, you can bus it between London and Oslo in about 36 hours, but you may have to change buses as often as four times! This year-round service operates three to five times weekly via Amsterdam, Hamburg, Copenhagen and Gothenburg. Reservations are compulsory. Contact National Express (UK: ☎ 08705 808080, W www.gobycoach.com) or Nor-Way Bussekspress in Oslo (see Bus in the Getting Around chapter for contact details). Return fares start at UK£173, so it's usually cheaper to fly!

Train Travelling by train from the UK to Scandinavia can be more expensive than flying. From London, a return 2nd-class train ticket to Oslo, valid for two months, costs around UK£390 including couchettes and a ScanRail Pass valid for any five days in the two months. Note that the lowest equivalent return air fare is UK£50! For tickets, contact Deutsche Bahn UK (London: ☎ 0870 243 5363) or European Rail (London: ☎ 020-7387 0444).

Russia & Asia
Bus & Train Russia has a short border with Norway and buses run three times weekly between Kirkenes and Murmansk. The rail link to/from eastern Asia via Russia can work out at about the same price as flying, depending on how much time and money you spend along the way, and it can be a lot more fun. Russian trains run as far as Murmansk (from St Petersburg), then a short hop by bus takes you to northern Norway (see the previous paragraph).

There are several routes to choose from. For more details on overland travel to/from Russia, see Visiting Russia under Kirkenes in The Far North chapter or check out Lonely Planet's comprehensive *Trans-Siberian Railway* for detailed information on trans-Siberian travel.

SEA
Transatlantic Passenger Ships & Freighters
Regular, long-distance passenger ships disappeared with the advent of cheap air travel and were replaced by a small number of luxury cruise ships. Cunard Line's *QEII* (US: ☎ 800 728 6273; UK: ☎ 0800 052 3840) sails between New York and Southampton around nine times a year each way, taking five nights/six days per trip. The cost of a one-way crossing starts at around US$1800,

but they also offer return and 'fly one-way' deals (including return on Concorde). In July, it does a circuit around the Arctic region, including Nordkapp (North Cape), Tromsø and the Western Fjords. Most travel agents can provide the details.

A more adventurous – but not necessarily cheaper – alternative is as a paying passenger on a freighter. Freighters are far more numerous than cruise ships, and there are many more routes from which to choose. With a bit of homework, you'll be able to sail to Europe from just about anywhere else in the world, with stopovers at exotic little-known ports. The book *Travel by Cargo Ship* (Cadogan, London, 1995) covers this subject.

Passenger freighters typically carry six to 12 passengers (more than 12 would require a ship's doctor aboard) and, although they're less luxurious than dedicated cruise ships, they provide a real taste of life at sea. Schedules tend to be flexible and costs vary, but normally hover around US$100 a day; vehicles can often be included for an additional charge.

Ferry

Ferry connections between Norway and Denmark, Germany, Iceland, the Faroe Islands, Sweden and the UK provide straightforward links, especially for anyone bringing their own vehicle. There may be special deals for people travelling with a car and most lines offer substantial discounts for seniors, students and children, so it pays to ask when booking. Taking a bicycle incurs a small extra fee.

If you're travelling by international ferry, consider picking up your maximum duty-free alcohol allowance on the boat, as alcohol is prohibitively expensive in Norway and, even if you don't drink, it will make a welcome gift for Norwegian friends.

Denmark DFDS Seaways (Denmark: ☎ 33 42 33 42, bookings ☎ 33 42 30 80, W www.dfdsseaways.com) runs daily overnight ferries (16 hours) between Copenhagen and Oslo. Cabin fares start at Dkr525 for Sunday to Thursday in the low season

and the package for two people with a car starts at Dkr1375. All cabin categories are quite comfortable and you can take advantage of an excellent dinner buffet en route. The departure in either direction is at 5pm, arriving at 9am the following day.

Color Line (Norway: ☎ 22 94 44 00, booking ☎ 81 00 08 11; Denmark: ☎ 99 56 19 77; e kundeservice@colorline.no, W www .colorline.no) runs two to five ferries daily between Hirtshals and Kristiansand, which takes from 4½ hours and is the shortest ferry connection between Norway and Denmark. Color Line also has one or two daily ferry services on the M/S *Peter Wessel* between Fredrikshavn and Larvik (from 6¼ hours). M/S *Skagen* sails between Hirtshals and Larvik once or twice daily (but only four sailings per week between 21 September and 4 April) and takes from 5¼ hours. Between Hirtshals and Oslo, M/S *Color Festival* takes from eight hours and sails once daily. Fares are the same for all routes; they range from Dkr160 (between 17 September and 30 April) to Dkr385 (on weekends from 15 June to 19 August). To transport a vehicle costs from Dkr200 to Dkr550, depending on the time of year. At certain times, there are special discount car packages on these routes.

Stena Line (Norway: ☎ 02010; Denmark: ☎ 96 20 02 00; W www2.stenaline.com) operates ferries between Frederikshavn and Oslo daily (except Tuesday between 20 August and 21 June), taking 12½ hours. Passenger fares cost from Dkr90 at mid-week in winter to Dkr290 on summer weekends. A car with driver included costs from Dkr300 to Dkr1120.

Fjord Line (Norway: ☎ 55 54 88 00; Denmark: 97 96 14 01; e booking@ fjordline.com, W www.fjordline.com) sails from Hanstholm to Bergen (from 15¾ hours) once on most days of the year, stopping en route in Egersund. From Hanstholm to Bergen, deck class fares range from Dkr300 (on most weekdays from September to April) to Dkr770 (on some Fridays and Sundays in July). Cabins start at Dkr370 per person (reclining chairs are from Dkr60). For vehicles, you'll pay from Dkr330 to Dkr680.

Germany Color Line (Norway: ☎ 22 94 44 00, bookings ☎ 81 00 08 11; Germany: ☎ 0431-7300 300; e kundeservice@ colorline.no, W www.colorline.no) has a ferry link between Kiel and Oslo (20 hours, daily), departing Kiel at 2pm and Oslo at 1.30pm. From 15 June to 19 August (high season), reclining chairs start at €85.40 and cars are €72.60. The cheapest two-person cabin ranges from €80.30 at midweek in the low season to €107.90 on weekends in the high season. With a car and a basic cabin for four people, you'll pay from €203.50 at mid-week in the low season to €300.15 in high season.

Iceland & the Faroe Islands Smyril Line (Norway: ☎ 55 32 09 70; Faroes: ☎ 345900; W www.smyril-line.fo) runs once weekly from 22 May to 4 September between Bergen and Seyðisfjörður (Iceland), via Lerwick (Shetland; see the UK section) and the Faroe Islands. One-way fares from Bergen begin at Dkr630/870 to Tórshavn in the Faroes and Ikr16,980/24,200 to Seyðisfjörður, Iceland. These fares are for a couchette, with the lower fares for sailings until mid-June, most sailings in August and all sailings in September, and the higher fares for mid-summer travel. The boat leaves Bergen at 3pm on Tuesday. It takes 25 hours from Tórshavn and 46 hours from Seyðisfjörður.

Sweden DFDS Seaways (Sweden: ☎ 042-266000; W www.dfdsseaways.com) runs daily overnight ferries between Helsingborg and Oslo, with fares varying according to the season and day of the week, but usually beginning at about Skr575. Southbound boats leave Oslo at 5pm and northbound from Helsingborg at 7pm; the sailing takes around 14 hours. DFDS Seaways also sails between Gothenburg and Kristiansand at least three days weekly year-round. Passenger/car fares start at Skr110/240 and the journey takes from 6½ hours.

Two to three times daily, Color Line (Sweden: ☎ 0526-62000; W www.colorline.no) does the 2½-hour run between Sandefjord (Norway) and Strömstad (Sweden). From 15 June to 12 August passengers pay Skr150

and a car is Skr210. During the rest of the year, passengers pay Skr110 and cars go for Skr140.

Fjordlink (☎ 69 31 60 56) and M/S Silverpilen (☎ 69 39 65 04, W www.silverpilen .com) sail between Strömstad and Fredrikstad four times daily (Skr80/110 oneway/return) and take about 1¼ hours. The ferry M/S *Sagasund* (mobile ☎ 90 99 81 11) connects Strömstad with Halden. From midMay to mid-August it operates on Wednesday, Friday and Saturday; at other times of year it only sails on Wednesday and Saturday (except January and February, when it doesn't sail at all). The fare is Skr100/150 one-way/return and it takes about 1¼ hours. These services are more like Swedish and Norwegian 'booze cruises' rather than real transport links.

The UK Fjord Line (UK: ☎ 0191-296 1313; Norway: ☎ 55 54 88 00; e booking@ fjordline.com, W www.fjordline.com) sails from Newcastle to Bergen, via Haugesund/ Stavanger, twice weekly in winter and thrice weekly in summer. Summer sailings are on Monday, Wednesday and Saturday from Newcastle and Tuesday, Friday and Sunday from Bergen. The trip from Newcastle to Bergen takes from 21 hours. For a bunk in a basic four-berth cabin below the car deck, fares range from UK£40 for some sailings between January and March to UK£105 on summer weekends. Reclining seats are a cheaper option (available 5 April to 21 September only) and range from UK£42 to UK£88. Fares to transport a car start at UK£46.

Smyril Line (UK: ☎ 01224-572615, W www.smyril-line.fo) sails between Lerwick (Shetland) and Bergen, from 20 May to 2 September, and takes from 10½ hours. Couchette fares in low/high season are UK£42/59 and cars up to 5m long cost UK£34/50. See also the earlier Iceland & the Faroe Islands section.

The popular DFDS Seaways (UK: ☎ 01255-240240; W www.dfdsseaways .com) service between Newcastle and Kristiansand sails twice weekly from midJanuary to mid-November and takes from

16½ hours. Return fares start at UK£109 for pedestrians and UK£364 for four people in a car.

ORGANISED TOURS

Given the expenses involved in Norwegian travel, it may be worth looking into an organised tour. Several reputable operators offer affordable itineraries concentrating either on Scandinavia in general or Norway in particular.

North America

Backroads (☎ 800 462 2848 or ☎ 510-527 1555, fax 510-527 1444) 801 Cedar St, Berkeley, CA 94710-1800. Backroads offers all-inclusive and generally upmarket seven-day hiking, rail and ferry tours between Geilo and Bergen, via the Hardangervidda plateau, Aurlandsdalen, Flåm and Sognefjorden (US$2498).
Web site: **W** www.backroads.com

Borton Overseas (☎ 800 843 0602, fax 612-822 4755) 5412 Lyndale Avenue S, Minneapolis, MN 55419. Borton's forte is adventure outdoor travel. It offers seven to 18-day escorted tours and can arrange independent tours including Hurtigruten and train trips.
Web site: **W** www.bortonoverseas.com

Brekke Tours (☎ 701-772 8999 or ☎ 800 437 5302, fax 701-780 9352, **e** tours@brekketours.com) 802 N 43rd St, Grand Forks, ND 58203. This company caters mainly for North Americans of Norwegian descent, and cobbles together a host of Norwegian and Scandinavian options – with the two-week US holiday period in mind. The 'Ultimate Fjord Adventure', a four-day unescorted tour from Oslo to Bergen (or back to Oslo) via the best of the Western Fjords, costs US$545 excluding flights. It also offers several other options involving Denmark, Finland, Iceland, Sweden and St Petersburg.
Web site: **W** www .brekketours.com

Maupintour (☎ 800 255 4266) Maupintour organises an upmarket 15-day tour which includes Stockholm, Copenhagen, Oslo, the Western Fjords and glaciers, and Bergen for US$3495, excluding flights.
Web site: **W** www.maupintour.com

Scanam World Tours & Cruises (☎ 800 545 2204, fax 609-655 1622) 108 N Main St, Cranbury, NJ 08512. This operator organises cruises and shorter upmarket tours, including a seven-day fjord tour with two nights in Bergen (from US$1369 per person).
Web site: **W** www.scanamtours.com

Scanditours (☎ 800 432 4176, 800 377 9828, fax 416-482 9447, **e** toronto@scanditours.com, vancouver@scanditours.com) 308-191 Eglinton Ave E, Toronto, Ontario M4P 1K1 or 21-1275 W 6th Ave, Vancouver, BC V6H 1A6. The Canadian company Scanditours concentrates on northern Norway and offers a 12-day Norwegian coastal voyage for US$3261 excluding flights.
Web site: **W** www.scanditours.com

Scantours (☎ 800 223 7226, **e** info@scantours.com) Scantours offers an extensive range of short tours in Norway, from one day around Sognefjord (Norway in a Nutshell) to 12 days aboard the Hurtigruten coastal steamer. Its Web site includes details and prices for all its offerings.
Web site: **W** www.scantours.com

The UK

Arctic Experience (☎ 01737-214214, fax 01737-362341, **e** sales@arctic-experience .co.uk) 29 Nork Way, Banstead, Surrey, SM7 1PB. This friendly agency is one of the most popular British tour operators to Scandinavia and the North Atlantic. It offers icebreaker cruises (from around UK£1840), hiking tours, skiing expeditions, snowmobile safaris and short breaks, all in Svalbard.
Web site: **W** www.arctic-experience.co.uk

Arcturus Expeditions (☎/fax 01389-830204, **e** arcturus@btinternet.com) PO Box 850, Gartocharn, Alexandria, Dunbartonshire, G83 8RL. Arcturus Expeditions, one of Britain's most inventive operators, organises hiking, trekking, dog-sledding and cruising tours through the furthest reaches of the polar regions. In Norway, it offers hiking and dog-sledding in Finnmark and Dividalen, visits to Jan Mayen and Bjørnøya, and icebreaker cruises and trekking in and around Svalbard. It's highly recommended.

Discover the World (☎ 01737-218802, fax 01737-362341, **e** sales@discover-the-world.co.uk) 29 Nork Way, Banstead, Surrey, SM7 1PB. This tour operator, associated with Arctic Experience, offers exciting killer whale-watching cruises in Nordland (from UK£719).
Web site: **W** www.discover-the-world.co.uk

Go Fishing Worldwide (☎ 020-8742 1556, **e** info@gofishingworldwide.co.uk) 2 Oxford House, 24 Oxford Rd N, London, W4 4DH. If you're a fish fan, this is the company to go with. It can organise tailor-made fishing trips to Norway on request.
Web site: **W** www.gofishingworldwide.co.uk

Scantours (☎ 020-7839 2927, **e** info@
scantoursuk.com) 47 Whitcomb Street, London,
WC2H 7DH. This company's Web site includes
details and prices for a wide range of options
throughout Norway and Svalbard, lasting from
five to 13 days.
Web site: **W** www.scantoursuk.com

Taber Holidays (☎ 01274-594656, **e** info@
taberhols.co.uk) 30A Bingley Road, Shipley,
West Yorkshire, BD18 4RS. Taber offers a range
of highlight-oriented, all-inclusive tours around
Norway, including cruises, coach tours and self-
drive possibilities.
Web site: **W** www.taberhols.co.uk

Tangent Expeditions International (☎ 01539-
737757) 3 Millbeck, New Hutton, Kendal, Cum-
bria, LA8 0BD. Tangent runs well-organised ski
mountaineering expeditions to Newtontoppen
and Perriertoppen in Svalbard (18 days,
UK£2200).
Web site: **W** www.tangent-expeditions.co.uk

Waymark Holidays (☎ 01753-516477) 44 Wind-
sor Rd, Slough, SL1 2EJ. This company specialises in nordic skiing and hiking holidays in
the Gol and Oslo areas.
Web site: **W** www.waymarkholidays.com

WildWings (☎ 0117-965 8333) 577–579 Fish-
ponds Rd, Bristol, BS16 3AF. WildWings runs
bird watching and adventure tours to Svalbard,
from UK£1749.
Web site: **W** www.wildwings.co.uk

France

Grand Nord Grand Large (☎ 01-40 46 05 14, fax
01-43 26 73 20) 15 rue du Cardinal Lemoine,
F-75005 Paris. As one of the world's most adventurous agencies, GNGL seeks out the locations and activities that are noticed by only a
handful of other companies. In Norway, it offers
cruises and hiking in Svalbard and Lofoten. The
14-day south-west Svalbard tour (€1,448-1,753)
includes visits to Hornsund and Belsund.
Web site: **W** www.gngl.com

Australia

Bentours International (☎ 02-9241 1353, fax
9251 1574, **e** scandinavia@bentours.com.au)
Level 7, 189 Kent St, Sydney. Bentours is the
only Australian travel agency specialising in
Scandinavian travel.
Web site: **W** www.bentours.com.au

Explore Holidays (☎ 02-9857 6200, **e** info@
exploreholidays.com.au) Level 2, Blaxland Rd,
Ryde, NSW 2112. Explore runs outdoor and
adventure-oriented tours in Norway.
Web site : **W** www.exploreholidays.com.au

Wiltrans/Maupintour (☎ 02-9255 0899,
e travel@wiltrans.com.au) Level 10, 189 Kent
St, Sydney. This company offers a range of
pricey luxury tours in Norway and elsewhere in
Scandinavia.

Getting Around

Norway's efficient domestic public transport systems include trains, buses and ferries and they're often timed to link with each other. The handy *NSB Togruter*, available free at train stations, details rail timetables and includes information on connecting buses. Boat and bus departures vary with the season and the day (services on Saturday are particularly sparse), so pick up the latest timetables *(ruteplan)* from regional tourist offices.

Rail lines extend as far north as Bodø (you can also reach Narvik by rail from Sweden); farther north you're limited to buses and ferries. Thanks to the great distances, bus fares can add up, but InterRail and ScanRail holders are entitled to 50% discount on express buses between Bodø and Alta. Some express boats and buses offer 50% discount for the second person when two people travel together, so it pays to ask. A fine alternative to land travel is the Hurtigruten coastal steamer, which calls in at every sizable port between Bergen and Kirkenes and provides stunning views of some of Europe's finest coastal scenery.

AIR
Domestic Air Services

Norway has nearly 50 airports with scheduled commercial flights from Kristiansand in the south to Longyearbyen and Ny Ålesund in the north. Thanks to the time and distances involved in overland travel, even budget travellers may want to consider doing some segments by air.

Typical one-way fares with the main airlines, Braathens (W www.braathens.no) and SAS (W www.scandinavian.net), from Oslo to Trondheim/Tromsø cost Nkr1748/3118, but there are several discount programs that make air travel more accessible (see Discounts & Air Passes). With Widerøe (☎ 81 00 12 00, fax 64 81 72 08, e internetbooking@wideroe-inter.net, W www.wideroe .no), which flies small planes, flights are more like 'flightseeing' trips than mere transport from A to B, and even standard

fares are considerably lower than on the big airlines. Coast Air (☎ 52 84 85 00, fax 52 84 85 01, W www.coastair.no), based in Haugesund, also flies small planes and concentrates on the main airports in Southern Norway.

Discounts & Air Passes

With Braathens and SAS, standard 'minipris' return tickets cost only about 10% more than full-fare one-way tickets and there are sometimes promotional fares that make return tickets even cheaper than one-way tickets. In addition, spouses (including gay partners), children aged two to 15 and senior citizens over 67 years of age are eligible for 50% discounts. There are also special summer fares, valid on return tickets between mid-June and mid-August.

Travellers aged under 26 (and students under 32) can opt for various discounts, including Superhike and stand-by fares. On Braathens, for example, youth stand-by fares from Oslo to Bergen would set you back just Nkr528, and from Oslo to Tromsø, Nkr853. SAS offers its international passengers (who aren't resident in Scandinavia) advance-purchase coupons for Nkr800 to Nkr1100 (excluding tax), which allow travel on direct flights between any two Scandinavian airports it serves, including several in Norway. Coupons are valid on most SAS flights within the region and must be purchased at least seven days in advance. You can buy up to eight coupons, which are good for one segment each. Note that the free baggage limit for economy ticket holders is 20kg (plus 8kg cabin baggage).

There are also some good-value air passes and other tickets. Widerøe offers good-value Summerpass tickets (valid from 1 June to 31 August) which cost Nkr500 for one-way flights within any one of four zones, divided at Trondheim, Bodø and Tromsø (some short flights cost Nkr400). Multi-sector flights cost Nkr1000/1500/2000 for two/three/four zones. These tickets must be purchased outside of Norway. Widerøe's *Minipris* ticket, valid one month, costs 40% less than the normal return fare, but you'll either have to stay at least one Saturday night or complete your return journey on Saturday or Sunday.

Braathens Northern Light Pass, available year-round, divides Norway into northern and southern sectors at Trondheim. Flights between any two points in one sector cost Nkr868 including taxes (excepting flights between Tromsø and Longyearbyen) and less than double that when your travel involves two sectors. You can purchase tickets directly from Braathens after arrival in Norway, but budget seats are limited so, if you're short on time, it's wise to make advance reservations.

Domestic Departure Taxes

Norwegian domestic airport departure taxes totalling Nkr178 are included in ticket prices. There's also a Nkr35 'transfer tax'.

BUS

Buses on Norway's extensive long-distance bus network are quite comfortable. Tickets are sold on the buses and fares are based on the distance travelled, averaging Nkr135 for the first 100km. Many bus companies quote bus fares excluding any ferry costs. However, bus fares given in this book include ferry tickets.

Many bus companies offer student, child, senior and family discounts of 25% to 50%, so it pays to ask. Groups (including two people travelling together) may also be eligible for discounts. In northern Norway, holders of InterRail and ScanRail passes are often eligible for discounts.

Nor-Way Bussekspress (☎ 23 00 24 40, within Norway ☎ 82 05 43 00, fax 23 00 24 49, e ruteinformasjon@nor-way.no, w www .nor-way.no) operates the largest network of express buses in Norway, with routes connecting most towns and cities, from Mandal in the far south to Alta in the far north. There are also a number of independent long-distance companies which provide similar prices and levels of service.

In Nordland, several Togbuss (train-bus) routes offer half price to Eurail, InterRail and ScanRail pass holders. They run between Fauske and Bodø, Narvik, Tromsø, Svolvær and Harstad. To/from the Western Fjords, between Oslo and Åndalsnes, Ålesund, Molde, Måløy, and various other routes in southern Norway, InterRail and ScanRail passes get half-price bus tickets.

There is also a host of local buses, most of which are confined to a single *fylke* (county). Each of these routes has a designated number, but it's rarely marked on the bus, which is identified by its destination. To confuse matters even further, some buses also have a second route number, which is used in the specific area where it circulates. This number normally does appear on the bus.

Travellers are warned that local and even some long distance bus schedules are drastically reduced everywhere in Norway on Saturday. Sunday and off-season (usually mid-August to mid-June) schedules may also be reduced – and non-existent in some cases.

For information on city and town buses, see Local Transport later in this chapter.

TRAIN

Norwegian State Railways (NSB; Norges Statsbaner) operates an excellent, though limited, system of lines connecting Oslo with Stavanger, Bergen, Åndalsnes, Trondheim, Fauske and Bodø; there are also lines between Sweden and Oslo, Trondheim and Narvik. For timetable information and bookings phone NSB (☎ 81 50 08 88). Most train stations offer luggage lockers for Nkr10 to Nkr40 and many also have baggage storage rooms.

Most long-distance day trains have 1st- and 2nd-class seats and a buffet car or refreshment trolley service. Mobile telephones can be found in all express trains and most Inter-City trains. Doors are wide and there's space for bulky luggage such as backpacks or skis.

Train Passes

The Norway Rail Pass, which allows unlimited travel within the country, can be

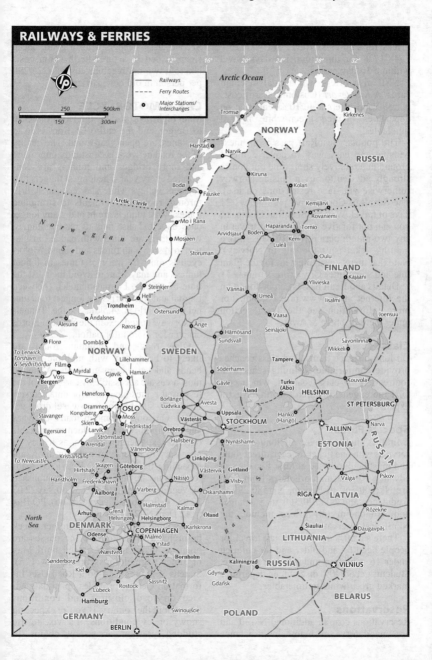

RAILWAYS & FERRIES

Railways
Ferry Routes
Major Stations/Interchanges

0   250   500km
0   150   300mi

Arctic Ocean

NORWAY

RUSSIA

Tromsø
Kirkenes
Harstad
Narvik
Kiruna
Kolari
Bodø
Fauske
Gällivare
Kemijärvi
Rovaniemi
Arctic Circle
Mo i Rana
Haparanda
Tornio
Arvidsjaur
Boden
Kemi
Møsjøen
Luleå
Storuman
Oulu
FINLAND
Steinkjer
Vännäs
Ylivieska
Kajaani
Hell
Umeå
Trondheim
Iisalmi
Østersund
Vaasa
Åndalsnes
Ånge
Seinäjoki
Joensuu
Ålesund
Røros
Härnösand
Sundsvall
Savonlinna
Florø
Dombås
Mikkeli
NORWAY
SWEDEN
Lillehammer
Tampere
Kouvola
Myrdal
Hamar
Söderhamn
Flåm
Gol
Gjøvik
Turku
(Åbo)
Voss
Gävle
Åland
HELSINKI
Bergen
Borlänge
Avesta
ST PETERSBURG
Hønefoss
Ludvika
Uppsala
Hanko
(Hangö)
Drammen
Moss
Västerås
TALLINN
Stavanger
Kongsberg
OSLO
STOCKHOLM
Narva
Skien
Fredrikstad
Örebro
ESTONIA
Egersund
Larvik
Hallsberg
Nynäshamn
Arendal
Strömstad
Vänersborg
Linköping
Kristiansand
Skagen
Göteborg
Västervik
Gotland
Valga
Pskov
Hirtshals
Fredrikshavn
Nässjö
Visby
Hanstholm
RĪGA
LATVIA
Ålborg
Varberg
Oskarshamn
Rēzekne
Halmstad
Kalmar
Öland
Grenå
Daugavpils
Århus
Helsingør
Helsingborg
Karlskrona
Odense
COPENHAGEN
Malmö
LITHUANIA
DENMARK
Næstved
Ystad
Sønderborg
Bornholm
Kiel
Kaliningrad
RUSSIA
VILNIUS
Lübeck
Rostock
Sassnitz
Gdynia
Hamburg
Swinoujscie
Gdańsk
GERMANY
POLAND
BELARUS
BERLIN

To Lerwick,
Tórshavn
& Seyðisfjörður

To Newcastle

North
Sea

Norwegian
Sea

Baltic
Sea

purchased after you arrive in Norway. Prices for 2nd-class travel are Nkr1250/1548/1728 for three/four/five days travel within a 30-day period.

NSB also offers two annual discount cards. A *Kundekort* (Customer Card) costs Nkr390 and offers a 40/10% reduction in departures marked green/white in rail timetables.

The popular ScanRail pass is an inexpensive and easy way to cover a lot of ground in a relatively short time but you're strongly advised to buy it outside Norway (otherwise you face restrictions on use). The ScanRail Consecutive pass allows 21 days of travel. With the ScanRail Flexipass, you can opt for five or 10 days of travel in any two-month period (the 10 days in two months ticket isn't for sale in Norway). Note that there's a supplement for the Flåm line and some Inter-City express trains.

Details about rail passes can be found on the Internet at W www.railpass.com. For more information see the Train section under Getting There & Away.

Classes
On long-distance trains, 2nd-class coaches provide comfortable reclining seats with footrests. First-class coaches, which cost 50% more, generally aren't worth the extra expense.

Special Fares
'Minipris' tickets cover all long-distance services with one ticket for each direct route and must be purchased at least five days in advance. Regular/minipris fares from Oslo are Nkr600/360 to Bergen, Nkr580/290 to Åndalsnes and Nkr700/360 to Stavanger and Trondheim (all prices include the Nkr30 seat reservation).

There's a 50% discount on rail travel for people aged 67 and older and for children under 16. Children under four travel free. Students get 60/40% discount on departures marked green/white in timetables.

Reservations
Reservations cost an additional Nkr30 and are mandatory on many long-distance

routes, including between Oslo and Bergen. Second-class sleepers offer a good, cheap sleep: a bed in a three-berth cabin costs Nkr150; two-berth cabins cost Nkr225/290 per person in old/new carriages.

CAR & MOTORCYCLE
Main highways, such as the E16 from Oslo to Bergen and the entire E6 from Oslo to Kirkenes, are open year-round. The quality of the road network is constantly improving and more bridges and tunnels are constructed every year. The longest tunnels link adjacent valleys while shorter tunnels drill through rocky impediments to straighten routes. Most tunnels are lit and many longer ones have exhaust fans to remove fumes, while others are lined with padded insulation to absorb both fumes and sound. Motorcyclists must be wary of fumes in longer tunnels and may want to avoid them. At the time of writing, Lærdalstunnelen (between Lærdal and Aurland) is the longest road tunnel in the world at 24.5km. See the 'Tunnels in Norway' boxed text in the Western Fjords chapter for more information.

Older roads and mountain routes are likely to be narrow with multiple hairpin bends and very steep gradients. Although most areas are accessible by car, some of the less-used routes have poor or untarred surfaces only suitable for four-wheel drive vehicles. On some mountain roads, caravans and motorhomes are forbidden or advisable only for experienced drivers, as it may be necessary to reverse in order to allow approaching traffic to pass. Restricted roads for caravans are outlined on a map published by Vegdirektoratet (☎ 22 07 35 00, fax 22 07 37 68, e firmapost@vegvesen.no), PO Box 8142 Dep, N-0033 Oslo.

In winter, spring or early summer, check beforehand to make sure the passes are open, as many remain closed until May or June. Vegmeldingssentralen (☎ 175), Statens Vegvesen's 24-hour Road User Information Centre, provides up-to-date advice on road closures and conditions throughout the country. If you're expecting snowy or icy conditions, it's wise to use studded tyres or carry snow chains. In

Road Distances (km)

	Ålesund	Alta	Bergen	Bodø	Florø	Hammerfest	Harstad	Kautokeino	Kirkenes	Kristiansand	Kristiansund	Lillehammer	Narvik	Odda	Oslo	Røros	Stavanger	Tromsø	Trondheim
Ålesund	---																		
Alta	1701	---																	
Bergen	384	2071	---																
Bodø	1008	814	1378	---															
Florø	201	1970	248	1277	---														
Hammerfest	1845	144	2215	959	2114	---													
Harstad	1186	557	1556	300	1455	701	---												
Kautokeino	1827	131	2197	941	2096	276	684	---											
Kirkenes	2215	519	2585	1329	2484	498	1072	451	---										
Kristiansand	811	2226	492	1533	652	2370	1711	2352	2740	---									
Kristiansund	142	1609	517	916	329	1753	1094	1735	2123	867	---								
Lillehammer	382	1756	439	1063	466	1900	1241	1882	2270	473	396	---							
Narvik	1190	511	1560	304	1459	655	119	637	1025	1715	1098	1245	---						
Odda	416	2064	159	1371	320	2208	1549	2190	2578	333	549	362	1553	---					
Oslo	533	1909	478	1216	512	2053	1394	2035	2423	322	562	168	1398	357	---				
Røros	401	1569	635	876	535	1713	1054	1695	2083	704	327	263	1058	624	382	---			
Stavanger	603	2251	179	1558	426	2395	1736	2377	2765	245	736	587	1740	187	453	836	---		
Tromsø	1440	290	1810	554	1709	435	296	417	805	1965	1348	1495	250	1803	1648	1308	1990	---	
Trondheim	287	1414	657	721	556	1558	899	1540	1928	812	195	342	903	650	495	155	837	1153	---

Oslo, snow chains can be hired from Hakres (☎ 35 51 48 57, fax 35 51 52 50) for Nkr950/1250 for one/two weeks, including changing of tyres. Your ordinary tyres are kept as a deposit. Snow chains can also be obtained in the UK from Snowchains Europroducts (☎ 01732-884408, fax 884564).

Vehicle Ferries

Travelling along the scenic but mountainous and fjord-studded west coast may be spectacular, but it also requires numerous ferry crossings, which can prove time-consuming and costly. Reservations aren't usually possible and are rarely needed anyway. For a complete list of ferry schedules, fares and operators' phone numbers, get hold of the Nkr210 *Rutebok for Norge*, a telephone-book-sized transport guide sold in bookshops and larger Narvesen kiosks. Otherwise, order directly from Norsk Reiseinformasjon (☎ 22 47 73 40, fax 22 47 73 69, e nri@reiseinfo.no), Karl Johans gate 12A, N-0154 Oslo.

Tolls

One bugbear of driving around Norway is having to pay tolls at every turn, so keep a stack of coins handy. New segments of highway and recently built tunnels and bridges must be paid off in user tolls and these can be as high as Nkr145 per car. In theory, the tolls are dropped when the construction project is paid off although some privately funded facilities become quite lucrative so this doesn't always happen. Free tunnels on the national road network, such as Lærdalstunnelen, were paid in full by the state.

Oslo, Bergen, Trondheim, Stavanger and Kristiansand impose tolls on drivers every time they cross the city limits – this is just a tax, since no attempt is made to encourage people to switch from cars to buses. You must also pay tolls to help maintain many

Haste Makes Waste

In Norway, speed limits are set relatively low by international standards but they're taken very seriously (particularly around the Nordland town of Fauske, which is known as the speed trap capital of the country!).

The national speed limit is 80km/h on the open road but pass a house or place of business and the limit drops to 70km/h or even 60km/h. Through villages, limits range from 50km/h to 60km/h and, in residential areas, they're 30km/h. If those speeds seem laborious by your home standards, avoid the temptation to crank up the revs. You'll be nabbed for even 5km/h over the limit – there's no leniency, no compromises, and fines range from Nkr1000 to well over Nkr10,000. Norwegian nationals risk losing their driving licence and could even land in jail.

The lethargy-inspiring national speed limit turns many compliant drivers into tranced-out zombies who often drive in the middle of the road. However, you'll see wrecked vehicles and ambulances on the move all too frequently in Norway.

private roads, including roads leading into national parks.

Breakdown Services

By reciprocal agreement, members of AIT-affiliated (Alliance Internationale de Tourisme) national automobile associations are eligible for 24-hour breakdown recovery assistance from the Norges Automobil-Forbund (NAF; ☎ 81 00 05 00). NAF patrols ply the main roads from mid-June to mid-August. Emergency telephones can be found along motorways, in tunnels and at certain mountain passes.

Another recommended company to call if you break down is Falken Redningskorps (☎ 80 03 00 50).

Petrol

Leaded and unleaded petrol is available at most petrol stations. Regular unleaded fuel averages around Nkr9/L in the south but it can be well over Nkr10/L in the north; super premium costs at least Nkr1 more and diesel around Nkr1 less. Credit cards are accepted at most places. In towns, petrol stations may be open until 10pm or midnight, but there are some 24-hour services. In rural areas, many stations close in the early evening and don't open at all on weekends. Some have 24-hour automatic pumps operated with credit cards or cash notes.

Road Rules

In Norway, traffic keeps to the right. On motorways and other main roads the maximum speed is generally 80km/h (a few roads have segments allowing 90km/h and you can drive at 100km/h on part of the E6), while on roads through built-up areas, it's normally 50km/h or 60km/h. The speed limit for caravans (and cars pulling trailers) is usually 10km/h less than for cars. If you're tempted to drive faster, bear in mind that the speed limits are zealously enforced, and mobile police units lurk at the side of the roads. Similarly, watch for signs designating *Automatisk Trafikkontrol*, which means that there's a speed camera ahead; these big and ugly grey boxes have no mercy at all.

The use of seat belts is obligatory at all times and children under the age of four must have their own seat or safety restraint. The use of dipped headlights (including on motorcycles) is required at all times and right-hand drive vehicles must have beam deflectors affixed to their headlights to avoid blinding oncoming traffic. Drivers must carry a red warning triangle to use in the event of a breakdown; motorists must give way to pedestrians at zebra crossings; and vehicles from other countries must bear an oval-shaped nationality sticker on the back. Motorcycles may not be left on the pavement (sidewalk) and are subject to the same parking regulations as cars.

Drunken driving laws are strict in Norway: the maximum permissible blood alcohol content is 0.02% and violators are subject to severe fines and/or imprisonment. Because establishments serving alcohol may legally share liability in the case of an accident, you may not be served even a small glass of beer if the server or bartender knows you're driving a car.

Third-party car insurance (unlimited cover for personal injury and Nkr1,000,000 for property damage) is compulsory and, if you're bringing a vehicle from abroad, you'll have fewer headaches with an insurance company Green Card. Ensure that your vehicle is insured for ferry crossings.

UK-registered vehicles must carry a vehicle registration document (Form V5), or a Certificate of Registration (Form V379, available from the DVLA in the UK). For vehicles not registered in the driver's name, you'll require written permission from the registered owner.

Road Signs

Most road signs are international, but a white M on a blue background indicates a passing place on a single-track road (the 'M' stands for *Møteplass*). *All Stans Forbudt* means 'No Stopping', *Enveiskjøring* is 'One Way'; *Kjøring Forbudt* is 'Driving Prohibited' or 'Do Not Enter'; *Parkering Forbudt* is 'No Parking'; and the bizarre *Rekverk Mangler* is 'Guardrail Missing'.

Car Rental

Norwegian car hire is ludicrously expensive and geared mainly to the expense-account business traveller. Walk-in rates for a compact car with 200km free start are typically over Nkr1000 per day (including VAT but insurance is Nkr40 per day extra). Rent-a-Wreck currently offers better deals. However, it may be advisable to hire your car in Sweden and return it there afterwards. Negotiations for one-way deals have been fruitful, so it's worth trying.

Some major rental agencies offer a 'relatively' good and readily available weekend rate, which allows you to pick up a car after noon on Friday and keep it until 10am on Monday for around Nkr1200 – be sure it includes unlimited kilometres.

All major firms, such as Hertz, Avis, Budget and Europcar, have desks at Oslo's Gardermoen airport, as well as other airports around the country. They're also represented in city centres. If you have hired a car, any speed camera tickets are automatically paid through your credit card. Beware – some Scandinavian car hire companies have been known to charge 'extras' to customers' credit card bills.

The following is a partial list of firms:

Avis (☎ 23 23 92 00) Munkedamsveien 27, Oslo; (☎ 55 55 39 55) Lars Hilles gate 20B, Bergen
Web site: W www.avis.no
Bislet Bilutleie (☎ 22 60 00 00, fax 22 60 01 19) Pilestredet 70, Oslo
Budget (☎ 23 16 32 40, fax 22 17 10 60) Sonja Henies plass 4, Oslo; (☎ 55 90 26 15) Lodin Leppsgate 1, Bergen
Europcar (☎ 22 83 12 42) Haakon VIIs gate 9, Oslo
Hertz (☎ 22 21 00 00, fax 22 11 00 93) SAS Hotel, Holbergs gate 30, Oslo
Web site: W www.hertz.no
Rent-a-Wreck (☎ 23 37 59 49, fax 23 37 59 48) Østre Akersvei 21, Oslo
Web site: W www.rent-a-wreck.no

BICYCLE

Given its great distances, hilly terrain and narrow roads, Norway is not ideally suited for extensive cycle touring, but many people still take the challenge. The long-distance cyclist's biggest headache (sometimes literally) will be tunnels, and there are thousands of them. Many of these, especially in the Western Fjords, are closed to non-motorised traffic due to the danger from hydrocarbon emissions and carbon monoxide fumes. This severely limits where cyclists can go and, even when alternative routes are available, they may involve a couple of days pedalling around a long fjord or over a high mountain pass.

A good Web site with details for cyclists is W www.bike-norway.com. For further information on long-distance cycling routes and tunnels, contact Syklistenes Landsforening (☎ 22 47 30 30, fax 22 47 30 31), Storgata 23C, N-0028 Oslo. The map *Sykkelruter i Norge* (Nkr110), is sold by Syklistenes Landsforening, but it's only available in Norwegian. However, the English text *Sykkelguide* series of booklets with maps is available for Nkr120 each and includes Lofoten, Rallarvegen, the North Sea

Cycleway from the Swedish border at Svinesund to Bergen, and other routes.

The good news is that there are lots of regional cycling venues, and bike hire is available at some tourist offices, hostels and camping grounds. All over the country, regional tourist offices have devised suggested cycling tours and most have produced maps of the best routes. Among the most cycle-friendly communities, providing excellent maps and information, are Larvik in the south; Sandnes, just south of Stavanger; and Røros in central Norway.

Rural buses, express ferries and non-express trains carry bikes for various additional fees (around Nkr100), but express trains don't allow them at all and international trains treat them as excess baggage (Nkr250). Nor-Way Bussekspress charges half the adult fare to transport a bicycle!

HITCHING

Hitching isn't entirely safe and we don't recommend it. Travellers who decide to hitch should understand that they're taking a small but potentially serious risk. People who choose to hitch will be safer if they travel in pairs and let someone know where they're planning to go. What's more, the Norwegian government generally considers car ownership a luxury and sets up its tax structure accordingly, so motorists may look askance at anyone who can't afford a vehicle. For that reason, hitching isn't especially popular.

That said, if you're determined to hitch, you will find Norwegians generally friendly, and they understand that not all foreigners enjoy an expense-account budget. With a measure of luck and patience, most hitchhikers do manage to find lifts, but the chances of success are unpredictable; they are generally somewhat better on main highways such as the E6, but you still may wait for hours in bad weather. Western Norway is generally the most difficult area for hitching, while the more laid-back north is probably the best. One good approach is to ask for rides from truck drivers at ferry terminals and petrol stations; that way, you'll normally have a place to keep warm and dry while you wait.

BOAT

Due to Norway's rugged geography, ferry links are crucial, and an extensive network of reasonably frequent car ferries and express boats links the country's offshore islands, coastal towns and fjord districts. Most ferries along the highway system accommodate motor vehicles, but express coastal services normally take only foot passengers and cyclists, as do the lake steamers. See specific destinations for details.

Highway ferries are subsidised and therefore aren't overly expensive (this is of course relative…), but long queues and delays are possible at popular crossings in summer and reservations are rarely possible. Details on schedules and prices for vehicle ferries and lake steamers are provided in the timetables published by the Norwegian Tourist Board, or *Rutebok for Norge*.

Hurtigruten Coastal Steamer

For more than a century, Norway's legendary Hurtigruten coastal steamer route has served as a lifeline linking coastal towns and villages. One ship heads north from Bergen every night of the year, pulling into 34 ports on its six-day journey to Kirkenes, where it then turns around and heads back south. The return journey takes 11 days and covers a distance of 2500 nautical miles. In agreeable weather the fjord and mountain scenery along the way is nothing short of spectacular. All the ships are modern and have the comforts of a cruise liner.

If you're travelling as a deck-class passenger, there are baggage rooms, a shower room, a 24-hour cafeteria and a coin laundry available. Meals are served in the dining room and you can buy snacks and light meals in the cafeteria. At night, some people roll out a sleeping bag on the floor in one of the lounges, but all-night activity will mean short nights of little sleep, especially in the 24-hour summer daylight. Sample deck-class fares from Bergen are Nkr1404 to Trondheim, Nkr2392 to Stamsund, Nkr2879 to Tromsø, Nkr3629 to Honningsvåg and Nkr4466 to Kirkenes. Cars can also be carried for an extra fee. Children aged four to 16, students, and seniors over the age of 67, all receive 50% discount, as do accompanying spouses and your children aged 16 to 25.

There are also some great off-season deals. From 1 September to 30 April, passengers get 40% discount off basic fares for sailings on any day except Tuesday and receive a further 50% reduction on the return portion of the ticket. Also, between September and April, passengers aged 16 to 26 years may buy a 21-day coastal pass for Nkr1750.

If you prefer an en suite cabin – and most people do – you'll pay an additional Nkr260 to Nkr950 per night from mid-April to mid-September and Nkr120 to Nkr395 in the low season. Basic cabins with shared bathroom start at Nkr80 per night all year. Cabins are extremely popular, so be sure to book well in advance. Contact the operators if you wish to book Hurtigruten as an informal cruise.

You may want to break up the trip with shore excursions, especially if you're travelling the entire route. The possibilities, which are organised by the shipping company, include the following (northbound/southbound excursions are denoted by N/S): an overland tour between Geiranger and Ålesund or Molde (N; three or seven hours); a short tour of Trondheim (S; two hours); a day trip to Svartisen (N; six hours); spins around Lofoten (S; three hours) and Vesterålen (S; four hours); a haul from Honningsvåg up to Nordkapp (N; four hours); an overland tour between Honningsvåg and Hammerfest, via Nordkapp (N; seven hours); and a tour from Kirkenes, at the end of the line, to the Russian border (two hours). These offer fairly good value (contact the operators for prices) but, in some cases, you'll miss segments of the coastal scenery.

There's a toll-free number for information and bookings (☎ 81 03 00 00), or you can contact either Troms Fylkes Dampskibsselskap (☎ 77 64 82 00, fax 77 64 82 40, e booking@tfds.no, W www.hurtigruten .com), N-9291 Tromsø; or Ofotens og Vesterålens Dampskibsselskab (☎ 76 96 76 96, fax 76 96 76 11, e booking@ovds.no), PO Box 43, N-8501 Narvik. In North America, you can book through Leisure Sails

(☎ 800 574 7829, e bergen@leisuresails .com); in the UK, contact Norwegian Coastal Voyage (☎ 020-8846 2666, e sales@ norwegiancoastalvoyage.com, W www .norwegiancoastalvoyage.com); and in Australia, Bentours International (☎ 02-9241 1353, e scandinavia@bentours.com.au).

LOCAL TRANSPORT
Bus, Tram, Underground & Ferry

Nearly every town in Norway supports a network of local buses and ferries, which circulate around the town centre and also connect it with outlying areas. In many smaller towns, the local bus terminal is adjacent to the train station, ferry quay and/or long-distance bus terminal. Fares range from around Nkr15 to Nkr20 per ride, but if you're doing a lot of bus hopping, it's probably worth buying a 24-hour ticket. In Oslo, these cost Nkr50 and are good on all forms of local public transport, including buses, trams, underground trains and ferries; in most other towns, they range from Nkr30 to Nkr55.

Taxi

Taxis are best hailed around taxi ranks, but you can also reserve one by telephone. If you're phoning for a taxi immediately, charges begin at the moment the call is taken. Daytime fares, which apply from 6am to 7pm on weekdays and from 6am to 3pm on Saturday, are Nkr26.80 at flagfall, plus Nkr12 per kilometre. Weekday evening fares are 21% higher and in the early morning, on Saturday afternoon and evening, and on Sunday, they're 28% higher. On holidays, you'll pay 45% more. These fares are good for up to four passengers, but in some places, you may find 'maxi-taxis' which can carry up to eight passengers for about the same price.

ORGANISED TOURS

Numerous local tour companies operate in Norway and in every tourist office you'll find an exhaustive collection of leaflets, folders and brochures outlining their offerings in the immediate area. Typical offerings include bird- or whale-watching cruises, lighthouse cruises, mine tours, city and town tours, glacier-walking tours, mountaineering tours, dog-sledding trips, white-water rafting trips and excursions to hard-to-reach places of interest. Most tourist offices provide a booking service for any tour that may interest you, but many charge a booking fee of around Nkr20. Recommended tours and companies are listed throughout the book.

A very popular option is the so-called 'Norway in a Nutshell' tour, organised through travel agencies, NSB rail services and tourist offices around southern Norway. Itineraries vary, but most involve a one- or two-day excursion taking in the rail line between Oslo and Myrdal, the Flåmbanen line to Flåm, a cruise along Nærøyfjord to Gudvangen, a bus to Voss, and then rail trips to Bergen and back to Oslo (overnight or otherwise). Some versions include a guided tour around Bergen. An alternative to this route involves the rail line between Oslo and Stavanger. For details and prices, see Organised Tours under Oslo, Bergen, Flåm, Voss and Stavanger, in the relevant chapters of this book.

Den Norske Turistforening (DNT, the Norwegian Mountain Touring Club; ☎ 22 82 28 22, 🅆 www.turistforeningen.no), Postboks 7 Sentrum, N-0101 Oslo, organises hundreds of year-round adventure trips in the Norwegian mountains, including fishing, hiking, ski tours, glacier hiking, rock and ice climbing, family activities, hut-to-hut trekking, Svalbard tours, and so on. Five-/eight-day hiking tours cost around Nkr2700/4000.

Most visitors travel to Norway to see the fjords, mountains and glaciers for which the country is rightly famous. Some parts of Norway have extraordinary scenery, sculpted out of solid rock by the great glaciers of the last ice age. Following is a list of five journey suggestions covering some of the best Norway can offer, but there's no shortage of other possibilities.

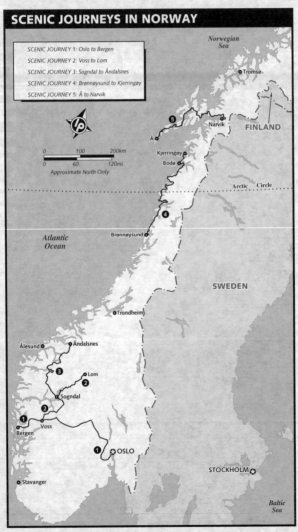

SCENIC JOURNEYS IN NORWAY

SCENIC JOURNEY 1: Oslo to Bergen
SCENIC JOURNEY 2: Voss to Lom
SCENIC JOURNEY 3: Sogndal to Åndalsnes
SCENIC JOURNEY 4: Brønnøysund to Kjerringøy
SCENIC JOURNEY 5: Å to Narvik

Title Page: Bird's eye view of Geirangerfjord & the Geiranger valley from Mt Dalsnibba (Photograph by Anders Blomqvist)

The Oslo-Bergen Railway

Classed as one of the finest train journeys in the world, the Oslo–Bergen railway not only links Norway's two largest cities, but it presents an excellent cross section of Norwegian scenery.

Starting from Oslo, the line passes through the city's suburbs, westwards towards Drammen. Beyond Drammen, travellers will see the forested hills of Buskerud from valleys dotted with small towns. Shortly after Hønefoss, the train follows the eastern bank of Hallingdalselva, beginning its gradual ascent to the central highland plateau. Hallingdal is famous for its waterfalls, which attract daring ice climbers in winter.

In upper Hallingdal, beyond the rhyming villages of Gol, Ål and Hol, and the Geilo ski centre, the line enters the wild mountain and glacier country of Hardangervidda. At Myrdal station, continue to Voss or take the wonderful Flåmsbanen alternative, down steep gradients and past magnificent waterfalls to Flåm, connect to Gudvangen on a fjord cruise and continue to Voss by bus. Beyond Voss, the railway passes through a forested and lake-studded landscape, becoming ever more impressive. Huge walls of rock soar up from the west-coast fjords, which the line hugs for most of the way into Bergen.

Voss to Lom

The E16 highway north of Voss passes waterfalls, lakes and villages, then descends steeply from Stalheim into the amazing Nærøydalen valley. Beyond Gudvangen, with its immense waterfalls, the road continues through tunnels to Flåm, then there are wonderful fjord views most of the way to Aurland. The new Lærdalstunnelen, from Aurland to Lærdal, is the longest road tunnel on Earth (24.5km). Lærdal is an attractive village with old wooden houses and an impressive setting. Another tunnel (Rv5) leads to the Sognefjorden ferry crossing, then the road continues past Kaupanger (with a worthwhile stave church) to Sogndal.

From Sogndal, Rv55 turns north, over low passes to Hafslo and Gaupne. Lots of hamlets and villages dot the shores of the green fjord Lustrafjorden, fed by out-of-sight glaciers up in the mountains. Beyond Skjolden, at the head of the fjord, there's a lovely lake, followed by Fortun village. Hairpin bends lead upwards, beyond the

tree line, to Turtagrø, with a wonderful vista of the Skagastølstindane mountains on your right.

The road climbs to 1440m on Sognefjell, with superb views of mountain lakes, glaciers and snowy peaks. The gradual descent to Lom follows lovely Bøverdalen, with its little lakes, glacial rivers, grass-roofed huts and patches of pine forest.

When the Sognefjell road is clear of snow (from June to October), this route can be completed by bus (change at Gudvangen and Sogndal), requiring an overnight stay in Sogndal.

Sogndal to Åndalsnes

Follow Rv5 through the mountains and long tunnels to beautiful Fjærland, a veritable Shangri-la of fjord, glaciers and peaks. Another tunnel leads to the impressive Jølstravatnet, a lake hemmed in by steep slabby mountainsides. North of Skei, the E39 road passes through a deep valley to Byrkjelo, then Rv60 climbs through forest up to a good viewpoint of Nordfjord. Continue along the fjord to the scenic villages of Olden and Loen; side trips to the Jostedalsbreen glacier from either village are highly recommended.

Continue to Stryn, then take Rv15 west and Rv60 north, passing the extraordinary peak Hornindalsrokken on your left. Just before Hellesylt, a recommended side trip leads down the fantastic chasm of Norangsdalen to lovely Norangsfjorden, dominated by some of the most impressive mountains in Norway.

At Hellesylt, ferries chug to and fro on Geirangerfjord, the ultimate Norwegian fjord, with tiny farms perched on ledges, wispy waterfalls

Left: A small village sitting on the shores of Sognefjord, near Flåm

and towering cliffs. The one-hour boat trip leads to touristy Geiranger village; from there, take Ørnevegen (Rv63) north to the famous viewpoint of the area, then continue over a pass to another ferry across Norddalsfjorden. Rv63 continues north, through Valldal, past impressive mountains then down the Trollstigen road, with steep gradients, waterfalls and hairpin bends, to Romsdal, with 1.5km-high vertical cliffs – the highest in Norway, and the end of the route in Åndalsnes.

This journey is possible in one day by bus and ferry (changing at Skei, Hellesylt and Geiranger) daily except Saturday, mid-June to late August.

Right: The magnificent view over Åndalsnes from Mt Nesaksla in the Western Fjords region

CRAIG PERSHOUSE

SCENIC JOURNEYS

Brønnøysund to Kjerringøy

The best of the spectacular Nordland coastal scenery includes Torghatten (just south of Brønnøysund), the Seven Sisters mountain range at Sandnessjøen, the Engabreen glacier tongue of Svartisen, the Saltstraumen maelstrom, Landegode, Kjerringøy fishing village and the peak Strandåtind. For more details, see the Nordland chapter.

Although public transport exists along this route, including five ferry crossings, schedules are patchy. Most travellers use private cars and take two or three days for the trip. The Kystriksveien coastal road (Rv17) runs north from Brønnøysund to Bodø, then Fv834 continues to Kjerringøy.

CRAIG PERSHOUSE

Left: The picturesque Kabelvåg harbour in Austvågøy, Lofoten Islands

Å to Narvik: Lofoten & Vesterålen

Å is the southernmost village on Moskenesøy, arguably the finest island in Lofoten and a fine example of glacial rock sculpture. Island hopping by bridge leads to Flakstadøy, then by undersea tunnel to the more pastoral Vestvågøy. Sweeping bridges bring you through more wild mountains to Kabelvåg and Svolvær on Austvågøy.

North of Svolvær, an alternative route follows the north coast of Austvågøy, via Laukvik (great for watching the midnight sun), to the Fiskebøl ferry. Otherwise, stick to the faster E10, which passes below the highest peaks on the island.

The Fiskebøl ferry leads to Vesterålen, with more farms and several large towns, including Sortland, where a huge bridge arches over Sortlandssundet to Hinnøya. Much of the rest of the route to Narvik follows pleasant fjord shorelines backed by steep but more rounded mountains, an interesting contrast with the needle-like peaks of Lofoten.

Buses run along the E10 between Å and Narvik, but you'll have to stay overnight in either Svolvær or Sortland.

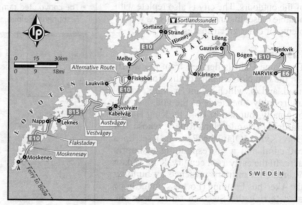

Oslo

OSLO

pop 508,730

Oslo (pronounced with a soft 's'), Norway's capital and largest city, presents a casual, low-key and readily manageable face. Unlike most European cities, it isn't full of architectural wonders, but buildings are neatly kept and some districts, such as Frogner, offer elegant examples of historic architecture.

Oslo sits at the head of the Skagerrak strait inlet known as Oslofjord. The Nordmarka (North Woods) to the north of the city provide a green belt for hiking and skiing, turning Oslo into a very liveable city for lovers of the outdoors. The city is also replete with notable museums and monuments, as well as plenty of other green spaces.

History

The name Oslo is derived from the words *Ás*, the Old Norse name for the Norse Godhead, and *lo*, which meant 'pasture', yielding roughly 'the fields of the gods'. It was originally founded in 1048 by King Harald Hardråda (Harald Hard-Ruler), whose son Olav Kyrre (Olav the Peaceful) set up a cathedral and a corresponding bishopric here. In the early 14th century, King Håkon V created a military presence by building the Akershus Festning (Fortress) in the hope of deterring the Swedish threat from the east. After the mid-14th-century bubonic plague wiped out around half of the country's people, Norway united with Denmark and, from 1397 to 1624, Norwegian politics and defence were handled from Copenhagen. As a result, Oslo slid into obscurity and, in 1624, it burned to the ground. Fortunately, it was resurrected by King Christian IV, who rebuilt it on a more easily defended site and renamed it Christiania, after his humble self.

For three centuries, right through WWII, the city held on as a seat of defence. In 1814, the framers of Norway's first constitution designated it the official capital of the new realm but their efforts were effectively

Highlights

- Inspecting the bizarre and erotic sculptures in Vigeland Park
- Visiting the lovely Bygdøy peninsula, with its several worthwhile museums
- Celebrating National Day on 17 May with the festively clad people of Oslo
- Shopping in the markets and dining at the good-value restaurants in the ethnically diverse Grønland district
- Strolling the quaint streets of Gamlebyen in Fredrikstad
- The convoluted ramparts of Fredriksten Festning in Halden

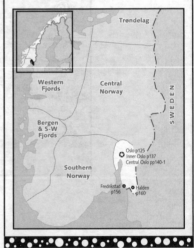

nullified by Sweden, which had other ideas about Norway's future and unified the two countries under Swedish rule. (In history books, you may occasionally see Oslo at that time referred to as Kristiania, the Swedish spelling of Christiania.) In 1905, when that union was dissolved, the stage was set for Christiania to flourish as the capital of modern Norway. It reverted to its

OSLO REGION

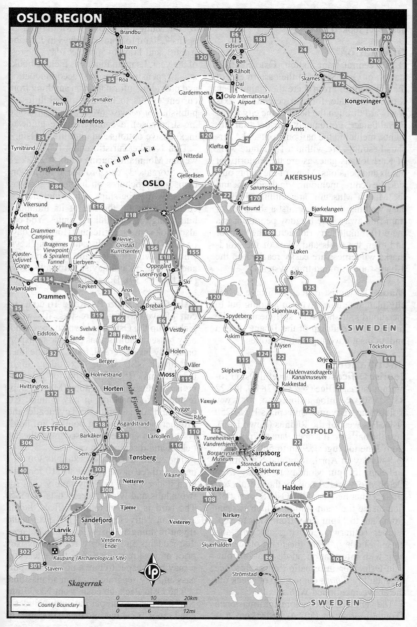

Brandbu
Jaren
245
4
Randsfjorden
Hadelandsvegen
Eidsvoll
181
Bøn
120
Råholt
24
Storsjøen
209
Kirkenær
20
210
35
Roa
Dal
Skarnes
2
175
E16
Hen
Gardermoen
Oslo International
Airport
Kongsvinger
7
241
Jevnaker
2
Hønefoss
Jessheim
Tyristrand
35
E16
4
120
Kløfta
2
Årnes
175
Tyrifjorden
Nittedal
Nordmarka
OSLO
Gjelleråsen
E6
AKERSHUS
21
284
Sørumsand
170
Vikersund
E18
22
Fetsund
Bjørkelangen
Geithus
Åmot
Sylling
285
Henie-
Onstad Kunstsenter
120
Øyeren
169
170
Drammen
Camping
Bragernes
Viewpoint
& Spiralen
Tunnel
156
E18
155
Løken
21
Kjøster-
udjuvet
Gorge
Lierbyen
Oppegård
TusenFryd
22
Bråte
E134
Røyken
23
Åros
Sætre
Ski
115
125
21
Mjøndalen
Drammen
319
Drøbak
Ås
120
E18
Skjønhaug
123
35
166
E6
Spydeberg
SWEDEN
Fiskeren
Eidsfoss
Svelvik
281
Filtvet
Vestby
Askim
E18
Töcksfors
32
Sande
Tofte
Holen
Mysen
E18
40
Berger
Våler
115
124
22
Haldenvassdragets
Kanalmuseum
21
Hvittingfoss
312
35
Holmestrand
Moss
Skiptvet
Rakkestad
Horten
115
Glomma
Oslo Fjorden
Vansjø
111
124
306
E18
Åsgårdstrand
Rygge
OSTFOLD
Barkåker
311
Råde
110
E6
22
Larkollen
Tuneheimen
Vandrerhjem
Ise
40
Sem
305
Tønsberg
116
Borgarsyssel
Museum
Sarpsborg
Stokke
303
Nøtterøy
Vikane
Storedal Cultural Centre
Skjeberg
308
Vikane
Fredrikstad
Halden
Tjøme
108
Sandefjord
Kirkøy
Svinesund
21
Larvik
303
Vesterøy
22
E18
Verdens
Ende
302
Skjærhalden
101
301
Kaupang (Archaeological Site)
Stavern
E6
Ed
Skagerrak
Strömstad
SWEDEN

County Boundary

0   10   20km
0   6   12mi

OSLO

original name, Oslo, in 1925 and the city has never looked back.

Orientation

Oslo's central train station (Oslo Sentralstasjon or Oslo S) sits at the eastern end of the city centre. From there the main street, Karl Johans gate, forms a ceremonial axis westward through the heart of the city to the Royal Palace. Fortunately, most central city sights, including the harbourfront and Akershus Festning, are within a 15-minute walk of Karl Johans gate, as are the majority of hotels and pensions. Many of the sights outside the centre, including Vigeland Park and the Munch Museum, are within relatively easy walking distance or just a short bus or tram ride away. The Bygdøy peninsula is a mere 10-minute ferry ride across the harbour and even the trails and lakes of the Nordmarka wilderness are easily reached on the T-bane (underground train system).

Maps The tourist offices distribute a free city plan and, unless you're heading out to the suburbs, it should be sufficient. On the reverse side is a map of the T-bane system and an inset covering Holmenkollen.

Information

Tourist Offices The resourceful Oslo Promotion tourist office (☎ 23 11 78 80, fax 22 83 81 50, e info@oslopro.no, W www.oslopro.no), Brynjulf Bulls plass 1, N-0250 Oslo, lies west of the Rådhus (Town Hall), near the harbour. It's open 9am to 7pm daily from June to August; 9am to 5pm Monday to Saturday in April, May and September; and 9am to 4pm Monday to Friday from October to March. Look for the useful *Oslo Guide* either here or at the Oslo S tourist office inside the train station, which is open from 8am to 11pm daily from May to September (otherwise closing at 5pm, and closed Sunday). Only the main office can help with information on destinations outside Oslo. For information on events, see the monthly *What's On in Oslo* or check out the above-mentioned Web site.

The very helpful Ungdomsinformasjonen (Youth Information Office), better known as Use-It (☎ 22 41 51 32, fax 22 42 63 71, W www.unginfo.oslo.no), Møllergata 3, opens 7.30am to 5pm weekdays in July and August, and 11am to 5pm weekdays the rest of the year. Its main functions include booking inexpensive or private accommodation and providing information on anything from current events to hitching possibilities. It publishes *Streetwise* (W www.unginfo.oslo .no/streetwise), a comprehensive guide to inexpensive options and nightlife in Oslo.

Den Norske Turistforening (DNT; Norwegian Mountain Touring Club; ☎ 22 82 28 22), Storgata 3, can provide information, maps and brochures on hiking in Norway and sells memberships which include discounted rates on the use of its mountain huts along the main hiking routes. You can also book some specific huts (for three days or more full board only) and pick up keys. Climbers will find information, directions and gear at Skandinavisk Høyfjellsutstyr (☎ 81 50 05 30), Bogstadveien 1.

Oslo Card & Oslo Package To do a circuit of even a few Oslo sites, it's worth picking up the Oslo Card, which covers not only museum admissions but also transport on all city buses, ferries, trams, T-bane lines and local NSB trains (excluding night buses/trams). It's also valid for a 'minicruise' sightseeing boat tour (May to September), free parking in city council car parks and admission to the Tøyenbadet and Frognerbadet swimming pools. Card holders are also entitled to discounted theatre tickets and discounts on car hire.

The card costs Nkr180/290/390 for one/two/three days (Nkr60/80/110 for children under 16). A one-day family card for two adults and two children costs Nkr395. The card is sold at tourist offices, hotels and some Narvesen kiosks. It's great value if you're doing a lot of sightseeing, but note that students and senior travellers pay half price at most museums and other sites, and it may be cheaper to buy a public transport pass and pay separate museum admissions.

The Oslo Package costs from Nkr395 to Nkr1070 per person per day and includes a hotel room, breakfast and the Oslo Card. Up

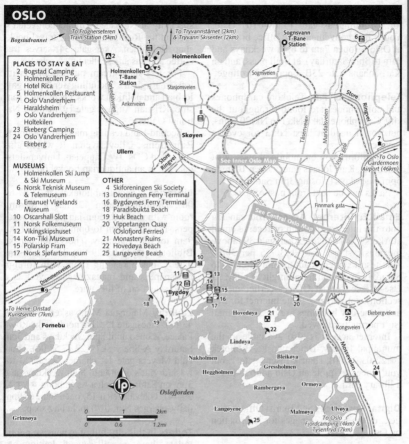

OSLO

Bogstadvannet

To Frognerseteren Train Station (5km)

To Tryvannstårnet (2km) & Tryvann Skisenter (2km)

Sognsvann T-Bane Station

Holmenkollen

Holmenkollen T-Bane Station

Sognsveien

Stasjonsveien

Ankerveien

Sørkedalen

Store Ringvei

Tåsenveien

Maridalsveien

Vogts gate

To Oslo Gardermoen Airport (46km)

PLACES TO STAY & EAT
2 Bogstad Camping
3 Holmenkollen Park Hotel Rica
5 Holmenkollen Restaurant
7 Oslo Vandrerhjem Haraldsheim
9 Oslo Vandrerhjem Holtekilen
23 Ekeberg Camping
24 Oslo Vandrerhjem Ekeberg

Skøyen

Ullern

See Inner Oslo Map

Kirkeveien

Finnmark gata

MUSEUMS
1 Holmenkollen Ski Jump & Ski Museum
6 Norsk Teknisk Museum & Telemuseum
8 Emanuel Vigelands Museum
10 Oscarshall Slott
11 Norsk Folkemuseum
12 Vikingskipshuset
14 Kon-Tiki Museum
15 Polarskip Fram
17 Norsk Sjøfartsmuseum

OTHER
4 Skiforeningen Ski Society
13 Dronningen Ferry Terminal
16 Bygdøynes Ferry Terminal
18 Paradisbukta Beach
19 Huk Beach
20 Vippetangen Quay (Oslofjord Ferries)
21 Monastery Ruins
22 Hovedøya Beach
25 Langøyene Beach

See Central Oslo Map

Drammensveien

To Henie-Onstad Kunstsenter (7km)

Fornebu

Bygdøy

Hovedøya

Lindøya

Nakholmen

Heggholmen

Oslofjorden

Grimsøya

Langøyene

Store Ringvei

Ekebergveien

Kongsveien

Mosseveien

Bleikøya

Gressholmen

Rambergøya

Ormøya

Malmøya

Ulvøya

E18

To Oslo Fjordcamping (4km) & Tysenryd (7km)

0   1   2km
0   0.6   1.2mi

---

to two children are included free. Contact your local travel agent in your home country for details and bookings.

Money The bank in the Gardermoen airport departure hall is open 6am to 6.30pm daily (closing 4pm on Saturday). The Oslo S post office changes money from 7am to 6pm weekdays and 9am to 3pm on Saturday. There's a 24-hour automatic teller near the rail information desk at Oslo S. You'll find banks scattered all over town, but most of the major ones have branches along Karl Johans gate near Oslo S.

The American Express office (☎ 22 98 37 35), Fridtjof Nansens plass 6, offers the best rates with no commission on most brands of travellers cheques. It's open 9am to 4.30pm weekdays, 10am to 3pm Saturday (and 11am to 3pm Sunday in July and early August only).

Outside banking hours, the tourist office changes money (into Norwegian kroner only) at a less advantageous rate.

Post The main post office (☎ 23 14 90 00), Dronningens gate 15, opens 9am to 5pm weekdays only. To receive mail, have it sent to Poste Restante, Oslo Sentrum Postkontor, Dronningens gate 15, N-0107 Oslo. You'll find convenient post office branches at Oslo S (open 7am to 6pm weekdays and 9am to 3pm Saturday), at Solli plass, and on Karl Johans gate 23B, opposite Stortinget.

Telephone & Fax Telekort cardphones and coin phones are found throughout the city. Coin phones take Nkr1 to Nkr20 coins, but you'll need at least Nkr3 for even a local call.

For information on mobile phones, visit Telehuset, Karl Johans gate 3, open 10am to 5pm weekdays (closing 3pm Saturday).

Faxes can be sent from post offices.

Email & Internet Access You can log onto the Internet and send or receive email at Akers Mic Nettcafé, Akersgata 39 (above the music shop), for Nkr30/55 per 30/60 minutes; it's open 10am to 1am Monday to Saturday and noon to midnight Sunday. At Use-It (see Tourist Offices earlier in this section), you can access the Internet for free and same-day bookings are possible; email isn't normally allowed.

Internet access is also available at the municipal library, Deichmanske Bibliotek (☎ 22 03 29 00), Henrik Ibsens gate 1, but you'll need to quote an Oslo address to get a library card.

Digital Resources See Tourist Offices, earlier, for the best Web pages for information on Oslo.

Travel Agencies Kilroy Travels (☎ 02633), Nedre Slottsgate 23, specialises in student and youth travel and offers discounted standby tickets for anyone under 26 and students under 35 with a valid ISIC card. STA Travel (☎ 81 55 99 05) is at Karl Johans gate 33.

Bookshops Tanum Libris at Karl Johans gate 43, Ark Bokhandel on Karl Johans gate, Ark Qvist at Drammensveien 16, and Norli, nearby on Universitetsgata, are large bookshops with comprehensive selections of maps and English-language literature, novels, books on Norway and travel publications.

Travel-oriented books, maps and gear are the speciality at Nomaden, Uranienborgveien 4 (behind the Royal Palace). The travel bookshop Bokkilden, Akersgata 34, serves free coffee and has an excellent map selection.

For less mainstream publications (with lots in English), including feminist, gay, lesbian and political works, check out Tronsmo, Kristian Augusts gate 19, near the National Gallery.

Second-hand reading material is found at Ringstrøms, Ullevålsveien 1, which also sells used CDs. JW Cappelen, Universitetsgata 20, is an antiquarian bookshop.

Libraries Nasjonalbiblioteket (☎ 23 27 60 00), Drammensveien 42, has a reading room with major foreign-language newspapers. It's open 9am to 6pm weekdays and 9am to 2pm Saturday. The Deichmanske Bibliotek (☎ 22 03 29 00), Henrik Ibsens gate 1, has a reading room with foreign newspapers and magazines, as well as a good selection of literature.

Laundry Majorstua Myntvaskeri (☎ 22 69 43 17), Vibes gate 15, 1km north of the Royal Palace, is open until 8pm weekdays and 3pm Saturday. A-Snarvask (☎ 22 37 57 00), Thorvald Meyers gate 18, charges Nkr35/20 for wash/dry; it's open until 8pm weekdays and 3pm on Saturday. Selva As (mobile ☎ 94 22 29 74), Ullevålsveien 15, open 8am to 9pm daily, charges Nkr30/20 including soap.

Toilets In this city full of expensive public toilets, there are still several daytime options for free relief: the 3rd floor of the GlasMagasinet arcade on Stortorvet; upstairs in the Paléet arcade at Karl Johans gate 37-43; and in the Deichmanske Bibliotek, Henrik Ibsens gate 1. Alternatively, visit a museum, pop into the Brynjulf Bulls plass tourist office, or buy a drink or fries at any McDonald's or Burger King and you can use their typically clean facilities. Toilets at Oslo S and the Galleri Oslo bus terminal cost Nkr5.

Left Luggage Oslo S has various sizes of lockers for Nkr10 to Nkr40.

Photography By far the best value for film and processing is Japan Photo, with an outlet at Akersgata 43. You'll get excellent deals on film purchases (three or more films).

Medical Services For after-hours prescription services, visit Jernbanetorget Apotek (☎ 22 41 24 82), the 24-hour pharmacy opposite Oslo S. The Oslo Kommunale Legevakten (☎ 22 11 80 80) casualty medical clinic at Storgata 40 offers 24-hour emergency services. The recommended dental practice is Tannlegesvakten (☎ 22 67 30 00), Tøyen Senter, Kollstadgata 18, open until 10pm daily.

Emergency Dial ☎ 112 for police, ☎ 113 for an ambulance and ☎ 110 to report a fire, accident or serious pollution (such as a chemical leak). The central police station (☎ 22 70 54 00) is at Henrik Ibsens gate 10.

Walking Tour

Many of Oslo's central sights can be combined in a short walking tour. Starting at Oslo S, head west along Karl Johans gate, the main pedestrian street lined with shops, buskers, beggars (panhandlers), fast-food outlets and pavement cafes.

A couple of blocks north-west of the station, you'll reach **Oslo Domkirke** (☎ 22 41 27 93, Stortorget 1; admission free; open 10am-4pm daily), the city cathedral, which dates from 1697. It's worth seeing for its elaborate stained glass by Emanuel Vigeland (brother of Gustav Vigeland) and painted ceiling (completed between 1936 and 1950). The exceptional altarpiece, a 1748 model of the Last Supper and the Crucifixion by Michael Rasch, was an original feature of the church (from 1700), but it was moved all over the country before being returned from Prestnes church in Majorstue in 1950. The organ front and pulpit were both part of the original construction. Occasionally, concerts are held in the church (Nkr60).

The **Basarhallene** (bazaar halls), around the back of the church, date from 1858 and are currently used by summer handicraft sales outlets.

Midway along Karl Johans gate rises the yellow-brick parliament building, **Stortinget** (☎ 23 31 35 96, Karl Johans gate 22; admission free; guided tours 10am, 11.30am & 1pm daily 1 July to 15 Aug, otherwise Sat only). Across the street is the stately **Grand Hotel**, constructed in the 1870s.

Eidsvolls plass, a city square filled with fountains and statues, stretches between Stortinget and **Nationaltheatret** (National Theatre; ☎ 22 00 14 00, Stortingsgata 15; open for shows). The latter, with its lavish rococo hall, was constructed specifically as a venue for the works of Norwegian playwright Henrik Ibsen.

Across Karl Johans gate is the University of Oslo's law and medical campus, and a block north lies the university's **Historisk Museet** (Historical Museum) and **Nasjonalgalleriet** (National Gallery). Karl Johans gate ends at **Det Kongelige Slott** (Royal Palace), which is surrounded by a large public park.

Heading down from the National Theatre, Olav V's gate leads to the **Oslo Rådhus** (Town Hall) and the bustling harbourfront. For a good view, follow Rådhusgata to Akersgata and turn right to **Akershus Slott** and **Akershus Festning**, where the castle and museums merit a couple of hours of exploration.

Det Kongelige Slott

The Royal Palace, on a hill at the end of Karl Johans gate and lying within a public park, is the official residence of the king of Norway. The palace building is open from 17 June to 12 August for guided tours of 15 rooms (in English, once daily at 2pm), but tickets are extremely difficult to obtain; ask the tourist office for details. For a virtual tour, visit the palace Web site at Ⓦ www .kongehuset.no. At 1.30pm, you can watch the changing of the guard, but it's not worth expending much effort to see.

Nasjonalgalleriet

The National Gallery (☎ 22 20 04 04, Universitetsgata 13; admission free; open 10am-6pm Mon, Wed & Fri, 10am-8pm Thur, 10am-4pm Sat, 11am-4pm Sun) houses the nation's largest collection of Norwegian art, including works from the Romantic era and more modern works from 1800 to WWII. Some of Edvard Munch's best known creations are on display, including his most renowned work, *The Scream*, which created quite a stir when it was brazenly stolen (and later recovered) in 1994. There's also a respectable collection of European art, including works by Gauguin, Picasso and many of the impressionists: Manet, Degas, Renoir, Matisse, Cézanne and Monet.

Oslo Rådhus

The twin-towered red brick functionalist Oslo Town Hall (☎ 22 46 16 00, *Fridtjof Nansen's plass; adult/child Nkr25/15, free Sept-May or with Oslo Card; open 9am-5pm daily June-Sept, slightly shorter hours Oct-Apr*), completed in 1950 to commemorate the city's 900th anniversary, houses the city's political administration. Its outside entrance is lined with wooden reliefs from Norse mythology and the interior halls and chambers are decorated with splashy and impressive frescoes and paintings by some of Norway's most renowned artists. It's here that the Nobel Peace Prize is awarded on 10 December each year (see the boxed text 'The Noble Nobels'). You can view the main hall for free from the front corridor. Guided tours (in English) are available at 10am, noon and 2pm daily (no extra charge).

Akershus Slott & Festning

Strategically located on the eastern side of the harbour, dominating the Oslo harbourfront, are the medieval Akershus Castle and Fortress (☎ 23 09 39 17; *admission free; open 6am-9pm daily*). In 1299, after the coronation of King Håkon V Magnusson, Oslo was named the capital of Norway and, the same year, the king ordered the construction of Akershus to protect the city from external threats, such as the one experienced in 1287.

Since it suffered repeated fires and sieges, as well as the 1563 to 1570 War of the North, the fortress was reconstructed to withstand the increased fighting power of the day, including the 1559 addition of the Munk gun tower. Between 1580 and the mid-18th century, it was further fortified with moats and reinforced ramparts.

Oslo was levelled by fire in 1624, but instead of being rebuilt on its original site, the city was renamed Christiania (the name Oslo wasn't re-adopted until 1925) and shifted to the less vulnerable and more defensible site behind the protective fortress walls. In 1818, however, most of the outer rampart was destroyed to accommodate population growth, and much of the castle was subsequently converted into an arsenal and later, a national archive. From 1899 to 1963 it underwent major renovations, and nowadays, the park-like grounds serve as a venue for concerts, dances and theatrical productions. Note, however, that this complex is a military installation and may be closed to the public whenever there's a state function.

Akershus Slott   In the 17th century, Christian IV renovated Akershus Slott (*Akershus Castle;* ☎ 23 09 35 53; *adult/child Nkr30/10; open 10am-4pm Mon-Sat, 12.30pm-4pm Sun May–mid-Sept, Sun afternoon only 16 Sept-31 Oct*) into a Renaissance palace, although the front remains decidedly medieval. In its dungeons you'll find dark cubbyholes where outcast nobles were kept under lock and key (one still holds a rather miserable-looking model wrapped in sackcloth), while the upper floors contained banquet halls and staterooms.

The chapel is still used for army events, and the crypts of King Håkon VII and Olav V lie beneath it. Tours led by university students in period dress provide an entertaining anecdotal history of the place at 11am, 1pm and 3pm, and are included in the admission fee. However, if you prefer, you can wander through on your own.

Akershus Festning   Entry to the fortress (☎ 23 09 39 17; *admission free; open 6am-9pm*) is through a gate at the end of Akersgata or over a drawbridge spanning Kongens gate, which is reached from the southern end of Kirkegata. After 6pm (in winter), use the Kirkegata entrance.

The Akershus Festning Information Centre (☎ 23 09 39 17; *open 9am-5pm Mon-Fri &*

The medieval Akershus Castle & Fortress dominate Oslo's harbour

Oslo's harbour and city centre

ANDERS BLOMQVIST

NED FRIARY

Stave church, Norsk Folkemuseum, Bygdoy

Old sailing ships on the harbour, Oslo

The rooftops of Kardamomme By, Kristiansund

A traditional farm building, Telemark

The Noble Nobels

Each October, in Stockholm, the Nobel Committee announces the winners of its prestigious prizes for physics, chemistry, medicine, literature, peace and economics. One Nobel prize – the lauded Peace Prize – is presented in Oslo, however, and each year on 10 December, the Oslo Rådhus becomes a focus of world attention as it honours individuals who have successfully encouraged or brought peace to tumultuous areas of the world.

Between 1814 and 1905, Norway and Sweden were united as one realm. In his will in 1895, Alfred Nobel, the Swedish founder of the prize (who was also credited with the invention of dynamite), stipulated that the scientific and literary prizes be awarded by Swedish institutions, but that the responsibility for the Peace Prize be delegated to a committee appointed by the Norwegian Storting (Parliament). It's thought that his intentions may have been to foment growing Norwegian agitation against this union, and since 1901, when the first Peace Prize was awarded to Jean Henri Dunant, the Swiss founder of the International Red Cross, the presentation ceremony has been held in Oslo.

Although the Norwegian Storting appoints the five-member committee that determines the winner of the Peace Prize, the parliamentary delegates have no say in the committee's decisions. Instead, nominations are made by such bodies as the executives of the Permanent International Peace Bureau; present and past members of international parliamentary bodies; members of the International Court of Justice in The Hague; university professors of law, political science, history and philosophy; former winners of the Nobel Peace Prize; and the Nobel Committee members themselves. Nominations must be submitted by 1 February each year, and the prize may be awarded to organisations and institutions as well as individuals.

Once the names have been proposed (currently they number around 100 each year) the committee goes to work investigating the merits of each nominee and eventually narrows them down to a shortlist, from which the winner is selected. In recent years, the prize has been awarded to such luminaries as Martin Luther King, Jr (1964); Anwar Sadat and Menachem Begin (1978); Mother Teresa (1979); Lech Walesa (1983); the 14th Dalai Lama, Tenzin Gyatso (1989); Mikhail Gorbachev (1990); Aung San Suu Kyi (1991); Nelson Mandela and FW de Klerk (1993); Yitzhak Rabin, Shimon Perez and Yassir Arafat (1994); the International Campaign to Ban Landmines (1997); Northern Ireland's John Hume and David Trimble (1998); and Kofi Annan and the United Nations (2001).

11am-5pm Sat & Sun mid-June–mid-Aug, otherwise closing an hour earlier), inside the main gate, has an exhibit entitled *New Barricades* which recounts the history of the Akershus complex. At 1.15pm, you can watch the changing of the guard at the fortress. Free guided tours of the fortress grounds, in Norwegian and English, leave from the information centre at 10am (except Saturday and Sunday), noon, 2pm and 4pm daily from mid-June to mid-August.

Prison Museum The small prison museum *(☎ 23 09 39 17; admission free; open on request)*, near the information centre, originally served as a powder magazine, but in 1830 it was converted into a prison which

held up to 60 people. It was expanded in 1853 and 1890, and during WWII the Nazis used it as a holding tank for resistance leaders and supporters who had been sentenced to death. Visits may be arranged through the information centre (ask before 2pm).

Norges Hjemmefront Museet During WWII, the Nazis used Akershus as a prison and execution grounds, and today it's the site of the popular Norwegian Resistance Museum *(☎ 23 09 31 38; adult/child Nkr25/10; open 11am-3pm daily, longer hours in summer)*. This interesting museum graphically recounts the German occupation of Norway, the murder of half of Norway's 1800 Jews, and the local and Allied resistance movements which published clandestine newspapers, ran a grass-roots weapons industry and sabotaged German installations. The museum arouses strong emotions and is recommended to everyone, not just WWII buffs. Don't miss the radio receiver used to listen to the BBC's European services, which was rigged up using the dentures of a senior prisoner of war (POW), or the diary of POW Petter Moen, who used a needle to prick his writing into sheets of toilet paper. (Moen was eventually killed, but his diary was later uncovered beneath the prison floorboards.) An informative guidebook is available for Nkr50.

Forsvarsmuseet The Norwegian Armed Forces Museum (☎ 23 09 35 82; admission free; open 10am-6pm Mon-Fri & 11am-4pm Sat & Sun June-Aug, otherwise 10am-3pm Mon-Fri & 11am-4pm Sat & Sun), at the fortress parade ground, presents models and dioramas of key moments in Norwegian military history from the Viking age, through the 1814 to 1905 Independence wars, to WWII and the present day. Also on display are the weapons that made it all possible. There's also a small cafeteria.

Christiania Bymodell Of interest to history buffs, the Christiania Bymodell (☎ 22 33 31 47; admission free; open 11am-6pm Tues-Sun June-Aug), just outside the northern wall of the fortress, features a 10m by 15m model of old Christiania in 1840, and a multimedia display of its history from its founding in 1624 up until 1900.

Bygdøy

The Bygdøy peninsula holds some of Oslo's top attractions: an open-air folk museum; excavated Viking ships; Thor Heyerdahl's raft, the Kon-Tiki; and the Fram polar exploration ship. You can rush around all the sights in half a day, but allotting a few extra hours will be more enjoyable.

Although only minutes from central Oslo, Bygdøy has a rural character and a couple of good beaches. The royal family maintains a summer home on the peninsula, as do many of Oslo's well-to-do residents.

Ferries operate from 20 April to 30 September, making the 15-minute run to Bygdøy (Nkr20, free with the Oslo Card) every 40 minutes from 7.45am (9.05am on weekend). The last crossing returns from Bygdøy at 6.40pm in April and September, 9.20pm in summer. The ferries leave from Rådhusbrygge 3 (opposite the Rådhus) and stop first at Dronningen ferry terminal, from where it's a 10-minute walk to the folk museum. The ferry continues to Bygdøynes, where the Kon-Tiki, Fram and maritime museums are clustered. You can also take bus No 30 to the folk museum from Jernbanetorget. From the folk museum it's a five-minute walk to the Viking ships (avoid the overpriced tourist train charging Nkr50) and 20 minutes to Bygdøynes. The route is signposted and makes a pleasant walk.

If you're hungry, there's a fruit stand opposite the folk museum entrance and cafes at the folk and maritime museums.

Norsk Folkemuseum Norway's largest open-air museum and one of Oslo's finest attractions is the Norwegian Folk Museum (☎ 22 12 37 00, Museumsveien 10; adult/child Nkr70/20, free with Oslo Card; open 10am-6pm daily 15 June-14 Sept, 11am-3pm Mon-Fri & 11am-4pm Sat-Sun 15 Sept-14 June). More than 140 buildings, mostly from the 17th and 18th centuries, have been gathered from around the country and are clustered according to region of origin. Paths wind past old barns, elevated storehouses (stabbur) and rough-timbered farmhouses with sod roofs sprouting wildflowers. The Gamlebyen (Old Town) section is a reproduction of an early-20th-century Norwegian town and includes a village shop and old petrol station, and in summer (daily except Saturday) you can see weaving and pottery-making demonstrations. Another highlight is the restored stave church, built around 1200 in Gol and shifted to Bygdøy in 1885.

The exhibition hall near the main entrance includes exhaustive displays on Norwegian folk art, historic toys, festive costumes from around the country (including dress for weddings, christenings and burials), the Sami culture of Finnmark, domestic and farming tools and appliances, as well as visiting exhibits. Sunday is a good day to visit, as folk music and dancing is staged at 2pm (in summer). On Tuesday, Wednesday, Friday and Saturday from 3 July to 22 August, there are Norwegian evenings of folk tales (in English) and folk dancing (Nkr195, including museum tour).

Vikingskipshuset The captivating Viking Ship Museum (☎ 22 43 83 79, Huk Aveny 35; adult/child Nkr40/20, free with Oslo Card; open 9am-6pm daily May-Aug, 11am-3pm or later Sept-Apr) houses three Viking ships excavated from the Oslofjord region and has a good general exhibit on Vikings upstairs. The ships had been drawn ashore and used as tombs for nobility, who were buried with all they expected to need in the hereafter: jewels, furniture, food, servants, intricately carved carriages and sleighs, tapestries and fierce-looking figures. Because such burial practices were the exception rather than the rule in Viking society, these graves clearly held nobles of high status. Built of oak in the 9th century, these Viking ships were buried in blue clay, which preserved them amazingly well.

The impressive *Oseberg*, buried in 834, is festooned on prow and stern with elaborate dragon and serpent carvings, measures 22m and required 30 oarsmen. The burial chamber beneath it held the largest collection of Viking-age artefacts ever uncovered in Scandinavia, but had been looted of all jewellery. The sturdier 24m-long *Gokstad*, built around 890, is the finest remaining example of a Viking longship, but when it was unearthed, its corresponding burial chamber had also been looted and only a few artefacts were uncovered. Of the third ship, the *Tune*, only a few boards and fragments remain.

Kon-Tiki Museum The *Kon-Tiki* Museum (☎ 23 08 67 67, Bygdøynes; adult/child Nkr30/15, free with Oslo Card; open 9.30am-5.45pm daily June-Aug, 10.30am-4pm or 5pm Sept-May) dedicated to the balsa raft which Norwegian explorer Thor

Heyerdahl sailed from Peru to Polynesia in 1947. The aim of his journey was to prove that Polynesia's first settlers could have originated in South America. The museum also displays the totora reed boat *Ra II*, built by Aymara people on the Bolivian island of Suriqui in Lake Titicaca. Heyerdahl used it to cross the Atlantic in 1970, to demonstrate the possibility that ancient North Africans and Middle Easterners could have reached the Americas long before the Europeans. There are also interesting displays on Easter Island and the Galapagos Islands.

Polarskip Fram Opposite the *Kon-Tiki* Museum lies the 39m rigged schooner *Fram* (☎ 23 28 29 50; adult/child Nkr25/free, free with Oslo Card; open 9am-6.45pm daily mid-June–31 Aug, shorter off-season hours), launched in 1892. From 1893 to 1896 Fridtjof Nansen's North Pole expedition took *Fram*, meaning 'forward', to Russia's New Siberian Islands, and en route back to Norway the team passed within only a few degrees of the North Pole itself. It was also used by Roald Amundsen in 1911 to land on the Ross Ice Shelf before he struck out on foot for the South Pole, and by Otto Sverdrup who sailed it around southern Greenland to Canada's Ellesmere Island between 1898 and 1902.

You can clamber around inside the boat and imagine how it must have felt to be trapped in the polar ice. The museum also includes an interesting rundown on the history of polar exploration.

Norsk Sjøfartsmuseum The Norwegian Maritime Museum (☎ 22 43 82 40, Bygdøynesveien 37; adult/child Nkr30/20; open 10am-6pm daily mid-May–30 Sept, 10.30am-4pm or 6pm Oct–mid-May) is dedicated to the numerous aspects of Norway's relationship with the sea, including the fishing and whaling industry, the seismic fleet (which searches for oil and gas), shipbuilding and wreck salvaging. Outside the museum there's a seamen's memorial commemorating the 4700 Norwegian sailors killed in WWII, and alongside is Roald Amundsen's ship *Gjøa*, the first ship to completely transit the North-West Passage (from 1903 to 1906). Other features of the museum include Norway's largest collection of maritime art, a dried cod display, a film with scenic footage of the Norwegian coastline and the underwater realm, lots of figureheads and traditional fishing craft, and an abundance of model ships. These models include the ocean liner *Stavangerfjord* (the best model in the museum), the *Gibraltar* (used by Norwegians sailing from Morocco to Gibraltar to escape Vichy forces), and the naval frigate *Kong Sverre*. The top-floor balcony of the larger wing opens onto a view over the islands of Oslofjord.

Oscarshall Slott Oscarshall Castle (☎ 22 56 15 39, Oscarshallsveien; adult/child Nkr20/10, free with Oslo Card; open noon-4pm Tues, Thur & Sun 23 May-16 Sept), designed by Johan Henrik Nebelong to reflect a blend of romantic and English neo-Gothic styles, was constructed as a residence for King Oscar I from 1847 to 1852.

Other Museums

Barnekunstmuseet If you have a particular affinity for your friends' refrigerator art galleries, visit the Children's Art Museum (☎ 22 46 85 73, Lille Frøens vei 4; adult/child Nkr40/20, Oslo card not valid; open 11am-4pm Tues-Thur & Sun 26 June-9 Aug, shorter hours rest of year, closed 10 Aug-14 Sept), near the Frøen T-bane station. Actually, if you're in a certain frame of mind, this collection of children's work from 180 countries – textiles, sculpture, paintings and drawings – can seem pleasantly inspiring.

Sporveismuseet Vognhall 5 The Tramhall No 5 Transport Museum (☎ 22 60 94 09, Gardeveien 15; adult/child Nkr20/10, free with Oslo Card; open noon-3pm Sun & Mon), in the 1913 trolley station No 5, is home to a collection of historic trams and trolleys, including the 1875 horse-drawn *Grønntrikken* tram. Other exhibits deal with 125 years of public transport in Oslo.

Skøytemuseet The Skating Museum (☎ 22 43 49 20, Middelthuns gate 26; adult/child Nkr20/10, free with Oslo Card; open 10am-2pm Tues-Thur, 11am-2pm Sun) is dedicated to speed and figure skating in Norway. Featured are historical skating apparatus and information on such Norwegian champions as speed-skater Johann Olav Koss and figure-skater Sonja Henie.

Vigeland Museum For an in-depth look at Gustav Vigeland's work, visit Vigeland Museum (☎ 22 54 25 30, Nobels gate 32; adult/child Nkr40/20, free with Oslo Card; open 10am-6pm Tues-Sat, noon-6pm Sun May-Sept, noon-4pm Tues-Sun, noon-7pm Thur Oct-Apr), opposite the southern entrance to Frognerparken. It was built by the city in the 1920s as a home and workshop for the sculptor, in exchange for the donation of the bulk of his life's work, and it contains his early statuary and monuments to public figures, as well as plaster moulds, woodblock prints and sketches. When he died in 1943, his ashes were deposited in the tower, and four years later the museum was opened to the public.

Emanuel Vigelands Museum Few visitors realise that Gustav Vigeland's brother Emanuel was also an accomplished artist and many Norwegians feel that he actually produced work superior to that of his better-known sibling. For a taste of his efforts, check out the stained glass in the Oslo Domkirke, then visit the museum (☎ 22 14 57 88, Grimelundsveien 8; T-bane: line 1 to Slemdal stop; adult/child Nkr30/15, free with Oslo Card; open noon-4pm Sun only) dedicated to his work.

Historisk Museet The highly recommended Historical Museum (☎ 22 85 99 64, University of Oslo, Frederiks gate 2; admission free; open 10am-4pm Tues-Sun, 11am-4pm Tues-Sun mid-Sept–mid-May) is actually three museums under one roof. Most interesting is the ground floor Oldsaksamlingen (National Antiquities Collection), with exceptional displays of Viking-era coins, jewellery and ornaments. Look out

Edvard Munch

Edvard Munch (1863–1944) is Norway's most renowned visual artist. The son of a military doctor, he grew up in Christiania (Oslo) in an environment of illness, death and grief that came to dominate his art. His mother died of tuberculosis when Edvard was only five, his elder sister succumbed to the same disease at the age of 15, and his younger sister was diagnosed with mental illness as a young girl.

After studying at the Technical School in Oslo and the Royal School of Drawing, Munch chose art as his life's work. In 1885, he went to Paris where he was influenced by French Realism, and there he produced his first great work, *The Sick Child*, a portrait of his sister Sophie shortly before her death. So provocative was the painting that professional criticism was largely negative, and in his next works he made an effort to lighten up his style, as shown in the holiday scene *Inger on the Beach*.

After returning to Christiania, however, he fell in with a bohemian element whose influence turned him back to his natural tendency for darker themes. In 1889, Munch exhibited his work and was granted a three-year travel study grant which allowed him to return to Paris and study under Léon Bonnat. He learned of the death of his father while in Paris and, in 1890, produced the haunting painting *Night*, which depicts a lonely figure in a dark window. The following year he completed *Melancholy* and began sketches of what would be his best known work, *The Scream*, which unequivocally reveals Munch's own 'inner hell'.

In 1892, Munch exhibited at the Artist's Association of Berlin and was so taken with the city and the welcome it afforded him that he decided to remain there and join the city's vibrant artistic community (which at the time included fellow Norwegian Gustav Vigeland). Here he moved into a cycle of dark atmospheric themes that he would collectively entitle *Frieze of Life – A Poem about Life, Love and Death*, which included *Starry Night, Moonlight, The Storm, Vampire, Ashes, Anxiety* and *Death in the Sickroom*. His obsession with darkness and doom eventually led him to an obsession with alcohol, as well as chronic emotional instability and a tragic love affair that was revealed in the 1907 work *Death of Marat*.

After the death of Henrik Ibsen in 1906, Munch was involved in creating the set for Berlin's Deutsches Theatre production of Ibsen's *Ghosts*. The painting *Self-Portrait with a Bottle of Wine* shows how Munch subsequently identified himself with one of the play's characters, the hopeless Osvald. He then went through a commercial period, painting commissioned portraits of Friedrich Nietzsche and his sister Elizabeth. By 1908, however, he decided to face his personal problems by checking into a Copenhagen mental health clinic for eight months.

After leaving the clinic, Munch returned to Norway, where he settled on the coast at Kragerø. There he enthusiastically embraced and reproduced the stark winter scenes of the coastal landscape, otherwise favoured as a summer holiday spot. He also produced a body of work for the newly constructed Aula auditorium at the University of Christiania. These works clearly represented the forces of life, light and hope, and displayed a more positive outlook than ever before. *Alma Mater* depicts a woman at the shore with a child at her breast, and *History* portrays an elderly man beneath a spreading oak tree, relating the history of humanity to a young child.

In 1916, Munch purchased the Ekely estate near Christiania and began producing bright and sunny works dedicated to humans in harmony with their landscape. Before his death in 1944, he bequeathed his body of works to the City of Oslo, and today much of his life's work is displayed in the National Gallery, the Munch Museum and also the Bergen Art Gallery.

for the 9th-century **Hon treasure**, the largest such find in Scandinavia (2.5kg). A section on medieval religious art includes the doors and richly painted ceiling of the Ål stave church (built around 1300). The 2nd level has an Arctic exhibit and the Myntkabinettet, a numismatic collection with the earliest Norwegian coins from as early as AD 995.

The 2nd level and top floor hold the Ethnographic Museum with changing exhibitions on Asia, Africa and the Americas.

Kunstindustrimuseet The unusual Museum of Applied Art (*☎ 22 03 65 40, St Olavs gate 1; adult/child Nkr25/15, free with Oslo Card; open 11am-3pm Tues-Fri, noon-4pm Sat & Sun*) displays Norwegian and international – mainly East Asian – pictorial tapestries, fashion designs and ceramic, silver and glassware from the 7th century to the present day.

Norsk Teknisk Museum & Telemuseum The Norwegian Science & Technology Museum (*☎ 22 79 60 00, Kjelsåsveien 143; adult/child Nkr50/25, free with Oslo Card; open 10am-6pm daily 20 June-20 Aug, shorter hours rest of year*), near lake Maridal, has an extensive technical library and a hands-on 'Teknoteket' (learning centre) for scientific research and experimentation. Displays include information on modern advances in communications, industry and energy production. The adjacent Norsk Telemuseum (*☎ 22 77 90 00, Kjelsåsveien 143; adult/child Nkr50/25, free with Oslo Card; open 10am-6pm daily 20 June-20 Aug, shorter hours rest of year*), or Telecom Museum, reveals the history of communications in Norway from Viking beacons to modern Internet technology. Take bus No 22, 25 or 37 to Kjelsås station or tram No 12 or 15 to Kjelsås Allé.

Munchmuseet Munch fans who didn't get enough of the work of Edvard Munch (1863–1944) in the National Gallery can visit the Munch Museum (*☎ 23 24 14 00, Tøyengata 53; adult/child Nkr60/30, free with Oslo Card; open 10am-6pm daily 1 June–mid-Sept, shorter hours in winter*), which is dedicated to his life's work. It holds over 5000 drawings and paintings bequeathed to the City of Oslo by Munch himself. Despite the artist's tendency towards tormented visions, all is not grey. Yes, you'll see works like *The Sick Child* and *The Maiden & Death*, but lighter themes, such as *The Sun* and *Spring Ploughing*, are also represented. To get there,

take T-bane: to Tøyen, followed by a five-minute signposted walk.

Post Museum The well-presented Post Museum (*☎ 23 14 80 59, Kirkegata 20; admission free; open 10am-5pm Mon-Fri, 10am-2pm Sat, noon-4pm Sun*) has exhibits on Norway's 350 years of postal history, including a reindeer sledge once used for mail delivery and Norway's largest stamp collection. Ask for a free museum booklet in English.

Teatermuseet The Theatre Museum (*☎ 22 42 65 09, Christiania Torv 1; adult/child Nkr25/15; open 11am-3pm Wed, noon-6pm Thur & noon-4pm Sun*), is housed in the first town hall (rådhus) of old Christiania (1641). The exhibits cover the history of Oslo theatre from 1800 to the present day.

Norsk Arkitekturmuseum The Norwegian Museum of Architecture (*☎ 22 42 40 80, Kongens gate 4, Kvadraturen; admission free; open 11am-4pm Thur-Tues & 11am-6pm Wed*), near the Akershus Fortress, contains a permanent exhibition of 1000 years of Norwegian architecture and construction, as well as temporary exhibits on various aspects of modern Norwegian design.

Astrup Fearnley Museet A block east is the Astrup Fearnley Museum (*☎ 22 93 60 60, Dronningens gate 4; adult/child Nkr50/25, free with Oslo Card; open noon-4pm Tues-Sun, noon-7pm Thur, noon-5pm Sat & Sun*) which presents worthwhile modern Norwegian and international art exhibitions.

Museet for Samtidskunst The National Museum of Contemporary Art (*☎ 22 86 22 10, Bankplassen 4; adult/child Nkr40/free; open 10am-5pm Tues, Wed & Fri, 10am-8pm Thur, 11am-4pm Sat, 11am-5pm Sun*) occupies a building which formerly housed the Central Bank of Norway and features the National Gallery's collections of post-WWII Scandinavian and international art.

Stenersenmuseet The Stenersen Museum (*☎ 22 83 95 60, Munkedamsveien 15;*

adult/child Nkr30/15, free with Oslo Card;
open 11am-5pm Tues-Sun, 11am-7pm Tues
& Thur), contains three formerly private collections of works by Norwegian artists from
1850 to 1970. The museum and much of the
art, which includes works by Munch, were a
gift to the city by Rolf E Stenersen. Other
collections were provided by Oslo residents
Amaldus Nielsen and Ludvig O Ravensberg.

Ibsen-museet The Ibsen Museum *(☎ 22*
55 20 09, Arbins gate 1; adult/child Nkr40/
10, free with Oslo Card; open for guided
tours at noon, 1pm & 2pm Tues-Sun) is
housed in the last residence of Norwegian
playwright Henrik Ibsen. The study remains
exactly as he left it and other rooms have
been restored in the style and colours popular in Ibsen's day.

Parks & Gardens
Frognerparken & Vigeland Park North-
west of the centre is green Frognerparken,
which attracts Oslo locals with its broad
lawns, ponds, stream and rows of shade
trees. On a sunny afternoon it's ideal for
picnics, strolling or lounging on the grass.
Near the southern entrance to the park lies
Oslo Bymuseum *(Oslo City Museum; ☎ 22*
43 06 45, Frognerveien 67; adult/child
Nkr30/15, free with Oslo Card; open 10am-
6pm Tues-Fri & 11am-5pm Sat & Sun Jun-
Aug, shorter hours at other times). Housed
in the historic Frogner Manor (the first
manor was built here during the Viking era,
but the current building was constructed in
the 18th century), it presents paintings and
other exhibits on the city's history.

The main Frognerparken attraction is
Vigeland Park, brimming with nearly 200
granite and bronze works of Norwegian
sculptor Gustav Vigeland (1869–1943). His
highly charged work, which takes in the entire range of human emotional extremes –
from entwined lovers and tranquil elderly
couples to contempt-ridden beggars – also
includes some less obvious artistic expressions involving lizards and other creatures.
His most renowned work, *Sinataggen* (the
'Little Hot-Head'), portrays a London child
in particularly ill humour.

The monolithic granite pillar crowning
the park's highest hill portrays a mass of
writhing human forms, both entwined with
and undermining others in their individual
struggle to reach the top. The circle of steps
around it supports rows of stone figures. It's
a great place to visit in the evening after
other city sites have closed. Take tram No
12 or 15, marked Frogner, from city centre.

If you wish to see more of Gustav Vigeland's work, check out Vigeland Museum
(see Other Museums section), opposite the
southern entrance to Frognerparken.

Botanisk Hage & Museums Oslo's
Botanical Garden *(☎ 22 85 17 00, Sars gate*
1; admission free; open 7am-8pm Mon-Fri,
10am-8pm Sat & Sun Apr-Sept, shorter
hours rest of year) features over 1000 alpine
plants from around the world as well as sections dedicated to vegetation from both
temperate and tropical regions. Specimens
in the aromatic garden are accompanied by
text in both print and braille.

By the gardens, the university's Zoological Museum *(☎ 22 85 17 00, Sars gate 1;*
admission free; open 11am-4pm Tues, Thur-
Sun, 11am-8pm Wed) has well-presented
displays of stuffed wildlife from Norway
and elsewhere, including a special exhibit
on Arctic wildlife. The adjacent Geological-
Paleontological Museum *(☎ 22 85 17 00,*
Sars gate 1; admission free; open 11am-4pm
Tues, Thur-Sun, 11am-8pm Wed) contains
displays on the history of the solar system,
Norwegian geology, and examples of myriad minerals, meteorites and moon rocks.
The paleontological section is full of bones
and fossils, including a 10m-long iguanodon
skeleton and a nest of dinosaur eggs.

Gamle Aker Kirke
This medieval stone church *(☎ 22 69 35*
82, Akersbakken 26; admission free; open
to visitors noon-2pm Mon-Sat), located
north of the centre on Akersbakken, dates
from 1080 and is Oslo's oldest building.
Lutheran services are held at 9am and
11am on Sunday. Take bus No 37 from
Jernbanetorget to Akersbakken then walk
up past the churchyard.

Gustav Vigeland

The Norwegian sculptor Gustav Vigeland (1869–1943) was born to a farming family near Mandal in the far south of the country. As a child he became deeply interested in Protestantism and spirituality and, during his teenage years, he also expressed interests in woodcarving and drawing. At the age of 14, he was enrolled as an apprentice to a master woodcarver in Oslo but, when his father died two years later, Gustav was forced to return home to care for his family. Even so, he never abandoned his hopes of becoming an artist and read all he could on drama and the arts, especially studying the anatomical sculptures of Danish neoclassicist Bertel Thorvaldsen.

In 1888, Vigeland returned to Oslo and, with a great deal of effort, secured an apprenticeship to sculptor Brynjulf Bergslien. The following year he exhibited his first work at the State Exhibition of Art and it wasn't long before his talents were being recognised by the public. In 1891, he travelled to Copenhagen and then to Paris and Italy, where he worked with various masters; he was especially inspired by the work of French sculptor Auguste Rodin. When his public grants ran out he returned to Norway to make a living working on the restoration of the Nidaros Cathedral in Trondheim, producing or revitalising many of its gargoyles and other fantasy figures, and fulfilling commissions to produce portraits of prominent Norwegians.

In 1921, the City of Oslo recognised his talents and built him a spacious studio in which to work; in return, he would bequeath to the city all his subsequent works as well as his original models and sketches. This seemed too good to pass up, and in 1924 Vigeland retired to Oslo and spent the rest of his life producing the sculptures now displayed in the enormously popular Vigeland Park and its adjacent museum.

The highlight of the park is the 14m-high Monolith; this incredible production required three stone carvers working daily from 1929 to 1943. It was carved from a single stone pillar quarried from Iddefjorden in south-eastern Norway and depicts a writhing mass of 121 detailed human figures. The figures, together with the pillar, have been interpreted in many ways: as a phallic representation, the struggle for existence, yearnings for the spiritual spheres and transcendence of cyclic repetition.

Leading down from the plinth bearing this column is a series of steps supporting sculptures depicting people experiencing a range of human emotions and activities, while the numerous sculptures dominating the surrounding park carry the artist's themes from the realist to the ludicrous. The result is truly one of Norway's artistic highlights and, best of all, there are no signs admonishing you to keep off the grass or forbidding picnicking on the lawn, wading in the fountains, feeding the ducks or climbing on the statues!

Damstredet District

The skewed wooden homes of the Damstredet district, some dating back to the early 19th century, add a splash of character amid otherwise ordinary architecture. This rather quirky looking neighbourhood, north of the city centre, provides a pronounced counterpoint to the deprived and dreary suburb of Akerselva, just east across the river.

Grønland District

Oslo's down-to-earth Grønland district, behind the Oslo S train station, has attracted much of the city's immigrant and refugee population and provides a relatively cosmopolitan flavour, as well as a range of inexpensive grocery stores and restaurants. In case you're unsure about the area's politics, check out the enormous rose-clenching fist (the symbol of socialism) which has burst through the pavement at the edge of Grønlandstorg.

Holmenkollen

The Holmenkollen ski jump (☎ 22 92 32 00, Kongeveien 5; admission free; always open) – perched on a hilltop overlooking Oslo – offers a panoramic view of the city and doubles as a concert venue. During

INNER OSLO

PLACES TO EAT
4 Krishna's Cuisine
5 Curry & Ketchup
16 Sult
17 Olympia Lunch-bar
18 Mucho Mas
19 Café Kjøkkenhagen;
Fru Hagen
20 Markveien Mat
& Vinhus

MUSEUMS
1 Barnekunstmuseet
2 Sporveismuseet
Vognhall 5
6 Skøytemuseet
8 Oslo
Bymuseum
9 Vigeland Museum
21 Zoological
Museum

22 Geological-Palaeontological
Museum
25 Munchmuseet

OTHER
3 Vinmonopolet
7 Frognerbadet Swimming
Pool
10 Swedish Embassy
11 British Embassy

12 Majorstua Myntvaskeri
13 Underwater Pub
14 Gamle Aker Kirke
15 A-Snarvask
23 Tøyenbadet Swimming
Pool
24 Botanisk Hage
26 Tannlegevakten
27 Tyrilikollektivet Climbing
Centre

Oslo's annual ski festival, held in March, it draws the world's best ski jumpers.

At the Holmenkollen ski jump, the Ski Museum (☎ 22 92 32 00, Kongeveien 5; adult/child Nkr60/30; open 9am-8pm June-Aug, 10am-5pm May & Sept, 9am-4pm Oct-Apr) leads you through the 4000-year history of nordic and downhill skiing in Norway. Highly worthwhile are the exhibits on the Antarctic expeditions of Amundsen and Scott, and Fridtjof Nansen's slog across the Greenland icecap (you'll see the boat he constructed from his sled and canvas tent to row the final 100km to Nuuk). The remarkable

thing was that these guys did it all without the aid of North Face or Patagonia! You can also see how it feels to win the Olympic downhill in the ski simulator.

Admission to the Ski Museum includes a visit to the ski jump tower. Part of the route to the top of the tower is served by a lift, but you're on your own for the final 114 steep steps. To get to the museum, take T-bane line 1 to Holmenkollen, then follow signs uphill.

Tryvannstårnet

The Tryvannstårnet observation tower (☎ 22 14 67 11, Voksenkollen; adult/child

Nkr35/20; open 10am-6pm daily June-Aug, 10am-5pm daily May & Sept, 10am-4pm daily Oct-Apr), north of the ski jump, sits at 538m and overlooks the suburban wilderness of Nordmarka. A lift zips you to the top and a 20,000-sq-km view as far as snow-capped Mt Gausta to the west, the Oslofjord to the south and the boundless Swedish forests to the east. From the Holmen T-bane station, take the scenic ride to the end of the line at Frognerseteren and look for the signposted walking route to the tower.

Henie-Onstad Kunstsenter

In Høvikodden, west of the centre, lies the low-profile but slightly aristocratic Henie-Onstad Art Centre *(☎ 67 80 48 80, Høvikodden; open 10am-9pm Tues-Thur & 11am-6pm Fri-Mon)*, founded in the 1960s by Norwegian figure skater Sonja Henie and her husband Niels Onstad. The couple actively sought out collectible works of Joan Miró and Pablo Picasso, as well as assorted impressionist, abstract, expressionist and modern Norwegian works. It all comes together pretty well, and when you've seen enough art you can head downstairs for a look at Sonja's various skating medals and trophies. From Jernbanetorget, take any bus towards Sandvika and get off at Høvikodden; the centre lies a few minutes' walk from the stop.

TusenFryd

Parents and children love TusenFryd *(☎ 64 97 66 99, Vinterbro; height over/under 140cm Nkr215/185; open 10.30am-7pm most days 1 June-19 August, 10.30am-7pm Sat & Sun May & 20 August-23 September)*, where there's swimming, carousels, a fantasy farm, an excellent new wooden rollercoaster which creates zero gravity 12 times each circuit, and various other rides. You'll find it 10km south of Oslo, just off the E6. The TusenFryd bus departs from the Galleri Oslo bus terminal nine times daily from 10am to 4pm (Nkr30/20).

Islands & Beaches

If the weather's fine, head to one of Oslo's beaches. Ferries to half a dozen islands in the Oslofjord leave from Vippetangen quay, south-east of Akershus Fortress. Boats to Hovedøya and Langøyene are relatively frequent in summer (running at least hourly), while other islands are served less often.

Hovedøya The south-western shore of otherwise rocky Hovedøya, the nearest island to the mainland, is popular with sunbathers. The island is ringed with walking paths to old cannon emplacements and the ruins of a 12th-century Cistercian monastery, built by monks from Kirkstead in Britain. Boat Nos 92 and 93 to Hovedøya leave from Vippetangen once or twice hourly between 6.17am and midnight from late May to mid-August, with fewer runs the rest of the year.

Langøyene South of Hovedøya lies the undeveloped island of Langøyene, with superb swimming from rocky or sandy beaches (one on the south-eastern shore is designated for nude bathing). Boat No 94 runs hourly to Langøyene from Vippetangen, 9.35am to 8.25pm, 26 May to 19 August.

Bygdøy Peninsula The Bygdøy peninsula also has two popular beaches, Huk and Paradisbukta, which can be reached on bus No 30 from Jernbanetorget to its last stop. While there are some sandy patches, most of Huk comprises grassy lawns and large smooth rocks which are ideal for sunbathing. It's actually separated into two beaches by a small cove; the beach on the north-western side is open to nude bathing. If Huk seems too crowded, a 10-minute walk through the woods north of the bus stop leads to the more secluded Paradisbukta.

Activities

Hiking A network of trails with a total length of around 1200km leads off into Nordmarka from Frognerseteren (at the end of T-bane line 1), including a good trail down to the lake Sognsvann, 6km north-west of the centre at the end of T-bane line 5. There's also an excellent network of hiking trails around the lake itself; the pleasant route around the lake takes less than an hour. On hot days, the eastern shore offers refreshing swimming, while the wilder western shore is a bit better for relative solitude. Other hiking routes radiate out into the hills beyond.

A more urban but mostly green two-hour walk will take you along the Akerselva river from the Kjelsås tram stop to Vaterlands bru (bridge), right in the heart of Grønland. Other city walks are outlined in two maps produced by Park og Idrettsvesenet (☎ 22 08 22 00), at Kingos gate 17, available from the tourist office.

Avid hikers may want to stop by the DNT office (☎ 22 82 28 22), at Storgata 3, which maintains several mountain huts in the Nordmarka region and can provide information on longer-distance hiking routes all over Norway.

Climbing The best local climbing is on the pre-bolted faces of Kolsåstoppen, which is accessible on T-bane line 3 to Kolsås. Otherwise, climbers can head for Oslo's two indoor climbing walls. Villmarkshuset (☎ 22 05 05 22), at Christian Krohgs gate 16, rises above the urban banks of Akerselva and offers a climbing wall, shooting range and pool diving centre. It also sells a range of outdoor books and equipment. There's another indoor climbing wall at Tyrilikollektivet Climbing Centre (☎ 22 67 28 44), Sverres gate 4.

Cycling Glåmdal Cycle Hire (☎ 22 83 39 79), Vestbaneplassen 2, near the harbour and by the tourist office, rents bicycles at extortionate rates – from Nkr265 for 24 hours. Unfortunately, there's no alternative.

One popular outing is to take the weekend bike train (sykkeltoget) to Stryken, 40km north of Oslo, and cycle back through Nordmarka. The train leaves Oslo S at 9.15am on Saturday and Sunday from May to October. For a shorter ride, take the T-bane to Frognerseteren and cycle back.

For cycling information contact the local club, Syklistenes Landsforening (☎ 22 47 30 30, fax 22 47 30 31), Storgata 23C.

Horse Riding At Stall Nordbye (☎ 22 49 91 27), Nordre Solberg Gård, you can horse ride around the farm for Nkr100 per hour.

Take T-bane line 2 to Røa, then bus No 41 to Solberg.

Skiing Oslo's ski season is roughly from December to March, and the area has over 2400km of prepared nordic tracks (1000km in Nordmarka alone), many of them flood-lit. Easy-access tracks begin right at the end of T-bane lines 1 and 5. Tomm Murstad Skiservice (☎ 22 13 95 00), at Voksenkollen station, one T-bane stop before Frogner-seteren, hires out snowboards and nordic skis. The downhill slopes at Tryvann Skisenter (☎ 22 13 64 50) are open in the ski season. Skiforeningen (Ski Society; ☎ 22 92 32 00, e skif@skiforeningen.no), Kongeveien 5, N-0390 Oslo, can provide further information on skiing options, or check out w www.holmenkollen.com.

Ice Skating At the Narvisen outdoor ice rink on Karl Johans gate, you can skate for free whenever it's cold enough to freeze over. Skates may be hired for Nkr35.

Swimming Oslo has two outdoor municipal swimming pools. Frognerbadet (☎ 22 44 74 29), in Frognerparken, is open variable hours from 18 May to 20 August. Tøyenbadet (☎ 22 67 18 87), Helgesens gata 90 near the Munch Museum, is open varying hours. Admission costs adult/child Nkr44/22 and is free with the Oslo Card.

Organised Tours

Oslo is so compact that organised city tours aren't really necessary, but they may be an option for anyone short on time.

Båtservice Sightseeing (☎ 23 35 68 90, fax 23 35 68 99), Pier 3, Rådhusbrygge, does a tidy 7½-hour city tour to the Bygdøy museums, Vigeland Park and the Holmenkollen ski jump, plus a cruise of the Oslofjord for a reasonable Nkr405 (June to August only), or a three-hour version minus the cruise for Nkr210. Their 50-minute 'mini-cruise' on Oslofjord costs Nkr90 (free with the Oslo Card) and a two-hour cruise costs Nkr160, or Nkr290 with evening prawn buffet included.

HM Kristiansen Tours (☎ 23 15 73 00, fax 23 15 73 01), Hegdehaugsveien 4, offers

OSLO

CENTRAL OSLO

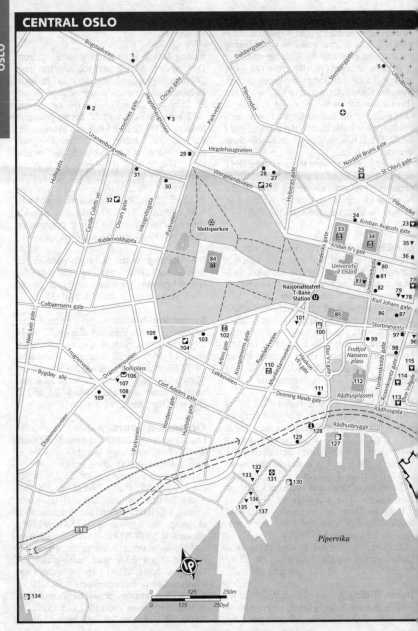

Bogstadveien
Dalsbergstien
Stensberggata
Ullevålsveien
1
5
Oscars gate
Josefines gate
Hegdehaugsveien
Pilestredet
Parkveien
4
2
▼3
Nordahl Bruns gate
St Olavs gate
29
Hegdehaugsveien
25
Uranienborgveien
Wergelandsveien
28 27
Holbergs gate
31
26
Holtegata
30
Pilestredet
32
Camille Colletts vei
Oscars gate
Inkognitogata
Parkveien
24 Kristian Augusts gate
23
Slottsparken
33
34
35 ▼
Riddervoldsgata
Kristian IV's gate
36
Frederiks gate
University of Oslo
80
84
81
83
82
79 ▼78
77
Colbjørnsens gate
Universitetsgata
Karl Johans gate
Nasjonalteatret
T-Bane Station
85
86
87
Niels Juels gate
105
101
Stortingsgata
100
97
99
Frognerveien
102
96
103
104
Fridtjof Nansens plass
98
115
Drammensveien
Solliplass
106
Kronprinsens gate
Abins gate
Ruseløkkveien
Munkedamsveien
Haakon VII's gate
Olav V's gate
Tordenskiolds gate
Rosenkrantz' gate
114
Bygdøy allé
107
108
110
112
113
Øvre Vollgate
109
Cort Adelers gate
Løkkeveien
111
Dronning Mauds gate
Rådhusplassen
Hansteens gate
Huitfelds gate
Rådhusgata
Parkveien
Rådhusbrygge
Drammensveien
129
128
127
132
133
131
130
E18
135
136
137
134
Pipervika

0   125   250m
0   125   250yd

CENTRAL OSLO

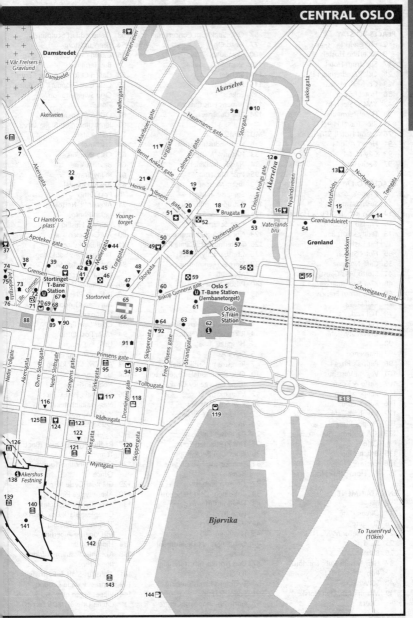

Damstredet

Vår Frelsers
Gravlund

Damstredet

Brenneriveien

8

Akerselva

Akersveien

6

7

Maribos gate

Torggata

Hausmanns gate

Storgata

9 10

Lakkegata

22

Bernt Ankers gate

11

Calmeyers gate

Christian Krohgs gate

Akerselva

Nylandsveien

12

13

Norbygata

Teisegata

Henrik Ibsens gate

21

19

Motzfelts

15

14

Grønlandsleiret

CJ Hambros
plass

Youngs-
torget

20

51

18 Brugata 17

16

Grønland

Apoteker gata

37

Grubbegata

50

49

52

Stenersgata

53 Vaterlands
bru

54

Torggata

58

57

56

Tøyenbekken

55

Schweigaards gate

74
75

38

39

40

43

45

48

Storgata

59

Oslo S
T-Bane Station
(Jernbanetorget)

Grensen

Stortinget
T-Bane
Station

41

46

47

60

Lille Grensen

42

44

Apotergata

73

72 70 69 68

67

Stortorvet

65

66

61

Oslo
S Train
Station

62

76

71

88

89 90

64

63

92

91

Bispo Gunnerus gate

Nedre Vollgate

Akersgata

Øvre Slottsgate

Nedre Slottsgate

Kongens gate

Kirkegata

Prinsens gate

Skippergata

95

94

93

Fred Olsens gate

Strandgata

Tollbugata

116

117

118

E18

125

124

123

122

121

120

Dronningens gate

Rådhusgata

Skippergata

119

126

Kirkegata

Myntgata

138 Akershus
Festning

139

140

141

142

Bjørvika

To TusenFryd
(10km)

143

144

CENTRAL OSLO

PLACES TO STAY
2   Ellingsens Pensjonat
9   Albertine Hostel
17 Spectrum Hotel
28 Oslo Vandrerhjem IMI
29 Cochs Pensjonat
36 Hotel Bristol
42 YMCA Sleep-In
58 Hotel Terminus
73 Rica Travel Hotel
76 Grand Hotel; STA Travel
91 Hotell Astoria
93 City Hotel
97 Cecil Hotel

PLACES TO EAT
3   Peppe's Pizza
11 Sushi Nam King
14 Oslo Kebab & Pizza House
15 Punjab Tandoori
18 Teddy's Soft Bar
19 Far East
35 Hotel Stefan
38 Café Norrøna
41 Stortorvets Gjæstgiveri
48 Kiwi Supermarket
68 A Touch of France
74 Kaffistova
78 TGI Friday's
79 Paléet Complex; Ma'Raja
83 University Café
90 Salsa
92 Flamenco
96 Peppe's Pizza
101 Vegeta Vertshus
107 Kaffe & Krem
108 Peppe's Pizza
116 Kafé Celsius
122 Engebret Café
132 Peppes Pizza
133 ICA Gourmet Supermarket
    Cafe
135 Beach Club
136 Costa
137 Big Horn Steak House

ENTERTAINMENT
8   Blå
13 Oliven Café
16 Stargate
21 Rockefeller Music Hall
23 Jazid
25 Blitz
37 Herr Nilsens Pub; London
    Pub
40 So What
49 Miami Club; Den Norske
    Opera

57 Oslo Spektrum Concert Hall
77 Head On
100 Saga Kino
113 Skansen
114 Smuget
115 Potpurriet
117 Enka
118 Filmens Hus Cinema
124 The Dubliner

MUSEUMS
6   Kunstindustrimuseet
33 Historisk Museet
34 Nasjonalgalleriet
95 Post Museum
102 Ibsen-Museet
110 Stenersenmuseet
120 Astrup Fearnley Museet
121 Museet for Samtidskunst &
    Kafé Sesam
123 Norsk Arkitekturmuseum
125 Teatermuseet; Gamle Rådhus
126 Christiana Bymodell
139 Norges Hjemmefront
    Museum
140 Prison Museum
143 Forsvarsmuseet

OTHER
1   Skandinavisk Høyfjellsutstyr
4   Rikshospitalet (National
    Hospital)
5   Selva As
7   Ringstrøms Antikvariat
10 Oslo Kommunale Legevakten
    (Oslo Emergency Clinic)
12 Villmarkshuset
20 Kiwi Supermarket
22 Deichmanske Bibliotek
24 Tronsmo
26 Canadian Embassy
27 HM Kristiansen Tours
30 Nomaden Bookshop
31 Den Rustne Eike (Bicycle
    Repairs)
32 German Embassy
39 Bokkilden; Oslo Helsekost
43 Ungdomsinformasjonen
    (Use-It)
44 Vinmonopolet
45 Husfliden
46 Glasmagasinet Department
    Store
47 Den Norske Turistforening
    (DNT)
50 Syklistens Landsforening
51 Police Station
52 Gunerius Shopping Centre

53 Clenched Fist Sculpture
54 Grønlandstorg
55 Galleri Oslo Long-Distance
    Bus Terminal
56 Galleri Oslo Shopping Centre
59 Oslo City Shopping Complex
60 Oslo Sweater Shop
61 Finnair
62 Oslo S Østbanehallen
63 Jernbanetorget; Stena Line;
    Trafikanten
64 Telehuset
65 Oslo Domkirke
66 Basarhallene
67 Kilroy Travels
69 Ark Bokhandel
70 Post Office
71 Akers Mic Nettcafé
72 Japan Photo
75 Heimen Husflid
80 JW Cappelen
81 Norli Bookshop
82 Tanum Libris Bookshop
84 Det Kongelige Slott
    (Royal Palace)
85 Nasjonalteatret
86 Eidsvolls Plass
87 Narvisen Outdoor Ice Rink
88 Stortinget
89 Color Line Ferries
94 Main Post Office
98 Unique Design
99 American Express
103 Ark Qvist Bookshop
104 US Embassy
105 Nobel Institute
106 Solli Plass Post Office
109 Nasjonalbiblioteket
111 British Airways
112 Oslo Rådhus
119 Palékaia
127 Rådhusbrygge Quay (Boat
    Terminal)
128 Oslo Promotion Tourist
    Office
129 Glåmdal Cycle Hire
130 Aker Brygge Pier
131 Aker Brygge Shopping
    Complex; Black Box; IMAX
    Theatre; Noodle Bar;
    McDonalds; Albertine
134 Hjortneskaia
138 Akershus Festning Informa-
    tion Office
141 Akershus Slott & Festning
142 Fortress Parade Ground
144 Vippetangen quay No 2
    (Stena Line & DFDS Ferries)

two-hour tours including a spin around the city centre and visits to Vigeland Park and Holmenkollen (adult/child Nkr160/80); and three-hour versions including a couple of Bygdøy museums (Nkr240/120).

Nor-Way Bussekspress (☎ 81 54 44 44) runs a variety of bus tours from Oslo – contact them for details or pick up a leaflet at the tourist office.

The popular 'Norway in a Nutshell' day tours cost Nkr1350, and may be booked through any tourist office or travel agency, or directly through NSB. From Oslo, the typical 'Norway in a Nutshell' route includes a rail trip from Oslo across the Hardangervidda to Myrdal, a rail descent to Flåm along the dramatic Flåmbanen, a cruise along Nærøyfjord to Gudvangen, a bus to Voss, a connecting train to Bergen for a short visit, then an overnight return rail trip to Oslo (including a 2nd-class sleeper compartment).

Special Events

Oslo's most festive annual event is surely the 17 May Constitution Day celebration, when Oslo residents, whose roots spring from all over Norway, descend on the Royal Palace dressed in the finery of their native districts. It's known mainly as a time for celebration of the family and reverence for child-like fun and children's interests.

In March, the Holmenkollen ski festival attracts nordic skiers and ski jumpers from around the world. During the last weekend in July there's the Summer Parade, an indoor and outdoor contemporary music festival. In early August, there's the Offshore Boat race, mainly involving fast and expensive craft; you can watch the fun from Aker Brygge or Akershus Slott. August also sees the Oslo International Jazz Festival and October, the Scandinavia-oriented Ultima Contemporary Music Festival (☎ 22 42 99 99). The former pales in comparison to its counterpart in Molde but, thanks to its capital-city location, it does draw a substantial following.

Places to Stay

Camping *Ekeberg Camping* (☎ 22 19 85 68, fax 22 67 04 36, Ekebergveien 65) Tent

sites for 1-2 people without/with car Nkr120/160, 10% surcharge in early Aug. Open 24 May-2 Sept. Ekeberg Camping occupies a scenic knoll south-east of the city and affords one of the best views over Oslo, but it's seriously overcrowded and the facilities are in poor shape. Take bus No 34 from Jernbanetorget to Ekeberg (10 min).

Bogstad Camping (☎ 22 51 08 00, fax 22 51 08 50, Ankerveien 117) Tent sites Nkr110-170; 4-bed cabins Nkr550-850. Open year-round. This enormous camping ground, situated less than 1km from lake Bogstadvannet, has a reputation for overnight noise and other unpleasantries. There are basic kitchen facilities (but no cooking implements) and food is available at the adjacent petrol station. Take bus No 32 from Jernbanetorget to Bogstad Camping stop (30 min).

Oslo Fjordcamping (☎ 22 75 20 55, fax 22 75 20 56, Ljansbrukveien 1) Tent sites Nkr110-140, static caravan rental Nkr300-400. Open year-round. A good alternative is this family-friendly camping ground by the Oslofjord. There are showers, a kiosk selling simple snacks, and a nearby restaurant. It's 8km south of the city; take bus No 76, 79 or 83.

Those who prefer wild camping can take T-bane line 1 to Frognerseteren at the edge of the Nordmarka or line 5 to Sognsvann. You can't camp at Sognsvann itself, but walk a kilometre or two into the woods and you'll find plenty of natural camp sites.

Hostels Oslo has four HI-affiliated hostels. Rates given here are for members; non-members pay Nkr25 extra. Sleeping bags aren't allowed; you must have HI regulation sheets or hire sheets for Nkr50 per visit.

Oslo Vandrerhjem Haraldsheim (☎ 22 22 29 65, fax 22 22 10 25, Haraldsheimveien 4) Beds in 4-bed dorms Nkr160/180 without/with bath; singles Nkr280/350, doubles Nkr380/460. Open year-round. This hostel is 4km from the city centre. It has 24-hour reception and 270 beds, mostly in four-bed rooms. There are kitchen and laundry facilities. It's a busy place so make advance reservations. Breakfast is included. Take tram No

12, 15 or 17, or bus No 31 or 32 to Sinsenkrysset, then walk five minutes uphill.

Oslo Vandrerhjem Holtekilen (☎ 67 51 80 40, fax 67 59 12 30, Michelets vei 55, Stabekk) Bed in small dorms Nkr165, singles/doubles Nkr265/430. Open year-round. This hostel is 9km west of Oslo. It's fairly good value but you'll also have to factor the bus fare into your costs, as the area is too far out to be included in day cards or the Oslo Card. Breakfast is included. Take bus No 151, 153, 161, 162, 251, 252 or 261 to Kveldroveien, or local train to Stabekk and cross footbridge over the E18.

Oslo Vandrerhjem Ekeberg (☎ 22 74 18 90, fax 22 74 75 05, Kongsveien 82) Dorm beds Nkr175, singles/doubles Nkr280/440. Open 1 June-14 Aug. The third HI hostel is located in an atmospheric old house. Take tram No 18 or 19 towards Ljabru and get off at Holtet; from there, it's about 100m along Kongsveien. Breakfast is included.

Oslo Vandrerhjem IMI (☎ 22 98 62 00, fax 22 98 61 01, Staffelsgata 4) Dorm beds Nkr170, doubles Nkr430. Open 4 June-19 Aug. You'll get decent accommodation at this hostel, which is used for student accommodation the rest of the year. There's a kitchen and laundry facilities. Breakfast is included.

Albertine Hostel (☎ 22 99 72 00, fax 22 99 72 20, Storgata 55) Doubles Nkr370, beds in 4-bed/6-bed dorms Nkr150/125. Open 8 June-23 Aug. This good-value hostel boasts an 'international atmosphere'. Breakfast costs Nkr55, but cooking facilities are available and you can hire towels and linen. Take bus No 30, 31 or 32, or tram No 11, 12, 15 or 17 from Jernbanetorget to Hausmannsgate.

YMCA Sleep-In (☎ 22 20 83 97, Grubbegata 4) Mattresses Nkr100. Open 1 July-25 Aug. Reception open 8am-11am & 5pm-midnight. The YMCA summer hostel, a 10-minute walk from Oslo S, fills up quickly and you need a sleeping bag. Beds consist of mattresses on the floor in large dorms. Basic kitchen facilities are available.

The DNT has lists of around 40 locally owned huts in Nordmarka. Among them are better-known staffed huts, where beds must

be booked in advance. Detailed hiking maps can be obtained from the DNT (see Information for details) in order to get to the following places.

Kikutstua (☎ 22 92 32 00) Beds for members/nonmembers Nkr170/220. Kikutstua is a typical mountain lodge about a 20km walk north from Frognerseteren.

Kobberhaughytta (☎ 22 82 28 22, fax 22 82 28 01) Beds for members/nonmembers Nkr170/220. The DNT lodge Kobberhaughytta is around 10km from Frognerseteren.

Pensions *Ellingsens Pensjonat* (☎ 22 60 03 59, fax 22 60 99 21, Holtegata 25) Singles/doubles from Nkr270/410. This homely pension in a quiet neighbourhood of older houses offers the best value in its class. It has 20 small but adequate rooms, each with a desk, chair and sink; toilets and showers are located off the hall. Reservations are required in summer. Take tram No 19 (towards Majorstuen) from Jernbanetorget.

Cochs Pensjonat (☎ 23 33 24 00, fax 23 33 24 10, Parkveien 25) Singles/doubles from Nkr330/460. Somewhat pricey but nearer the centre, Cochs Pensjonat has 65 comfortable but rather spartan rooms, some of which are en suite with kitchenette.

Private Homes Staff at the tourist office window at Oslo S book rooms in private homes (two nights minimum stay) for around Nkr225/350 for a single/double (plus Nkr35 booking fee), usually excluding breakfast. They also book unfilled hotel rooms at discounted rates.

Use-It (☎ 22 41 51 32, fax 22 42 63 71, Møllergata 3) Doubles Nkr475, with breakfast. Open 7.30am-5pm Mon-Fri July-Aug, 11am-5pm Mon-Fri rest of year. Use-It also books rooms in private homes; there's no minimum stay and bookings are free. If you'll arrive in Oslo outside of the opening hours, phone beforehand and ask for suggestions and phone numbers so you can book directly.

Hotels Lower rates are offered to holders of hotel passes at weekends and during the 'summer period', usually mid-June to mid-August.

City Hotel (☎ 22 41 36 10, fax 22 42 24 29, Skippergata 19) Singles Nkr395-600, doubles Nkr540-795. The older City Hotel has a bit of character, including a front parlour with Victorian furniture. The rooms are mostly straightforward, but some are en suite. Request a courtyard room if you're sensitive to traffic noise.

Rica Travel Hotel (☎ 22 00 33 00, fax 22 33 51 22, Arbeidergata 4) Singles Nkr680-875, doubles Nkr850-1020. This is a good-value business hotel. Rooms are modern and compact yet pleasant, and have private shower, TV, phone and minibar.

Four members of the Tulip Inn/Rainbow chain of hotels offer reasonably good-value weekend and summer rates.

Spectrum Hotel (☎ 23 36 27 00, fax 23 36 27 50, Brugata 7) Singles Nkr480-895, doubles Nkr610-1095. The Spectrum Hotel offers comfortable rooms with private bath, TV & phone, which are on a par with those in many of Oslo's better hotels.

Cecil Hotel (☎ 23 31 48 00, fax 23 31 48 50, Stortingsgata 8) Singles/doubles Nkr545/745 daily May-Sept & weekends year-round, from Nkr1045/1245 at other times. This hotel has a great location just a stone's throw from Stortinget; the entrance is on Rosenkrantz gate. Rooms are modern and quiet with private shower, TV, minibar and the like and there's an excellent breakfast buffet.

Hotell Astoria (☎ 22 42 00 10, fax 22 42 57 65, Dronningens gate 21) Singles Nkr480-750, doubles Nkr595-850. West of Oslo S, this hotel may not be as spiffy as the Cecil, but amenities are similar, rates cheaper and it has been recommended by readers.

Hotel Terminus (☎ 22 05 60 00, fax 22 17 08 98, Stenersgata 10) Singles/doubles Nkr450/650 22 June-30 Sept & weekends year-round, Nkr945/1145 at other times. Tulip Inn/Rainbow's best summer value is Hotel Terminus, just 200m north of Oslo S. The comfortable rooms have full amenities. What's more, the breakfast is above average and complimentary coffee, tea and fruit are available throughout the day.

Hotel Bristol (☎ 22 82 60 00, fax 22 82 60 01, Kristian IV's gate 7) Singles/doubles Nkr1275/1775, weekends Nkr805/995, summer Nkr925/1095. Hotel Bristol is the best value of the city's classic hotels and it has an excellent restaurant. Rooms are pleasant with cable TV, minibar and bathtub, and the halls and lobby are filled with antiques, chandeliers and old-world charm.

Grand Hotel (☎ 23 21 20 00, fax 23 21 21 00, Karl Johans gate 31) Singles/doubles Nkr1755/1885 weekdays, Nkr995/1190 daily 22 June-5 Aug & weekends year-round. The regal Grand Hotel is another place brimming with period character.

Holmenkollen Park Hotel Rica (☎ 22 92 20 00, fax 22 14 61 92, Kongeveien 26) Singles Nkr1545-1895, doubles Nkr1595-1995. For a real splurge, head uphill to this historic hotel, near the Holmenkollen ski jump. In 1891, Dr Ingebrigt Christian Lund Holm opened a castle-like sanatorium here with one of the finest views in Oslo. It subsequently served as a hotel, a military residence and a course centre, but in 1986 it opened under its current name.

Places to Eat

Breakfast Nearly all the hotels set up elaborate breakfast buffets for their guests and most of them are open to non-residents for Nkr80 to Nkr100. This is the best option for anyone who wants to start the day with a good-value feast.

For something lighter, try one of the ubiquitous bakeries or coffee shops, where a cup of coffee and a pastry go for around Nkr50; the tourist office keeps an up-to-date list of places that open around 7am. You'll find some of the best sticky pastries at *Kaffe & Krem* (Drammensveien 30) on Solli plass.

Fast-food places haven't yet taken up the breakfast challenge.

Snacks & Pizza Bakeries are an economical option; they normally sell relatively inexpensive sandwiches as well as bread and pastries. The *Baker Hansen* chain has numerous outlets around Oslo.

Salsa (☎ 22 41 20 60, Nedre Slottsgate 15) Dishes from Nkr29. The Salsa restaurant, with outdoor seating, is a good choice and serves reasonable tapas and bocadillos.

The recommended Norwegian pizzeria chain *Peppe's Pizza* (☎ 22 95 53 51, Hegdehaugsveien 31) offers huge pizzas from Nkr126, lasagne for Nkr96 and lunchtime buffets for Nkr89. Other outlets can be found at Stortingsgata 4, on Observatoriegata and behind Aker Brygge. *Flamenco* (☎ 22 64 64 64, Skippergata 34) offers a weekday pizza and salad buffet (available 11am to 3pm) for Nkr79, as well as dishes like beef stroganof and lasagne for under Nkr100. Other pizzerias include the American chain Pizza Hut, which has several branches around the city.

Around Oslo S & Grønland Oslo S has a small *Kiwi* food mart (open till 9pm on weekdays and 8pm on Saturday), hot-dog stands, a *Subway* sandwich shop, a *Burger King* and a *Pizza Hut*, where two slices and a drink costs Nkr59. The south wing, Østbanehallen, has *McDonald's* and *Tacoland*; the recommended *Rooster Coffee* espresso bar; *Baker Nordby*, with pastries and sandwiches; and a grocery store with fruit and a deli. Fruit stalls operate most days except Sunday in front of Oslo S.

The Oslo City shopping complex, opposite the north side of Oslo S, also has several places to eat: bakeries, a baked potato and grill joint, and Chinese and Mexican restaurants. The complex is open until 9pm weekdays and 6pm on Saturday. At the bus terminal, you'll find a couple of small shops selling fruit and snacks, and a *Baker Nordby* bakery that opens weekdays at 7am.

Teddy's Soft Bar (☎ 22 17 36 00, Brugata 3A) Light meals around Nkr68. The nearby Teddy's Soft Bar has become a local 1950s institution. You can get a light, typically Norwegian meal (until 10.30pm) – try the *pytt i panne*, which is essentially eggs with diced potato and meat.

The Grønland district north and east of Oslo S has several good-value ethnic eating places.

Punjab Tandoori (☎ 22 17 20 86, Grønlandsleiret 24) Lunch special Nkr55. The Punjab Tandoori near the Grønland T-bane station, has simply presented Indian fare – curry, dal, samosas and other meals. The lunch special includes chicken tandoori with rice and nan. A plate of chicken curry costs a bargain Nkr35.

Oslo Kebab & Pizza House (☎ 22 17 11 21, Grønlandsleiret 2) Dishes Nkr30-99. You'll get a kebab for Nkr30, fish and chips lunch for Nkr69, steak and chips for Nkr89 and large pizzas from Nkr99.

Aker Brygge Aker Brygge, the old shipyard turned shopping complex west of the main harbour, has a food court with various eateries including *Noodle Bar*, with Chinese dishes for Nkr70 to Nkr95, a *McDonald's*, a baked-potato stall and other options. At the rear of Aker Brygge, the *ICA Gourmet supermarket cafe* sells filled baguettes (Nkr39), wok dishes (Nkr59), pasta dishes (Nkr69) and seven-bit sushi for Nkr89. You can eat inside, but takeaway works out a bit cheaper.

Costa (☎ 22 83 19 30, Bryggetorget 4) Dishes from Nkr105. Just south of the ICA Gourmet supermarket, this Italian restaurant serves acceptable pizza and pasta dishes.

Albertine (☎ 21 02 36 30, Stranden 3) Snacks Nkr28-75, light lunches Nkr85-128. Inside Aker Brygge, the early-20th-century-style Albertine offers bistro-style food.

Beach Club (☎ 22 83 83 82, Bryggetorget 14) Burgers and other meals Nkr80-130. The American-theme Beach Club has outdoor seating on the pier and is great for a sunny afternoon, but you may need patience to wait for a table. This is one place which serves a full American breakfast (Nkr95). At lunch, burgers range from Nkr80 to Nkr130.

Big Horn Steak House (☎ 22 83 83 63, Fjordaléen 6) Steaks Nkr146-408. The similarly US-style Big Horn Steak House specialises in steaks of various sizes.

The Central Area *University Café* (Universitetsgata) Dinner Nkr35/45 students/others. The University Café, in the basement of the law school, serves basic but good-value meals.

Egon (☎ 22 41 77 90, Paléet complex, Karl Johans gate 37) Dishes Nkr85-199.

Open 10am-6pm daily, to 11pm Sun. Egon does pizza, burgers and kebabs; the best deal is the Nkr89 pizza buffet with a simple salad bar.

Ma'Raja (☎ 22 41 22 63, Paléet complex, Karl Johans gate 37) Starters from Nkr49, mains Nkr149-189. Ma'Raja is a mainstream Indian restaurant with a typically vast menu.

TGI Friday's (☎ 22 33 32 00, Karl Johans gate 35) Mains Nkr115-248. Also on Karl Johans gate, you'll find the American chain TGI Friday's, which sizzles up Oslo's most expensive but good-sized burgers (Nkr115 to Nkr128) with a choice of relishes. TGI's also offer pasta dishes (from Nkr109), steaks (Nkr185 to Nkr248) and US-style Mexican dishes, which range from vegetarian fajitas for Nkr155 to meat-oriented dishes for Nkr205.

Kaffistova (☎ 23 21 42 10, Rosenkrantz gate 8) Mains Nkr79-89. The friendly Kaffistova cafeteria serves traditional Norwegian food, including reindeer carbonades (meat cakes), meatballs and pork chops; salad is always included.

Café Norrøna (☎ 23 31 80 00, Grensen 19) Mains Nkr65-110. Café Norrøna is another place recommended for its traditional filling Norwegian fare.

Sushi Nam Kang (☎ 22 20 19 40, Torggata 24) 2-/13-bit sushi from Nkr32/159. This Japanese-Chinese hybrid is one of Oslo's best places for a sushi fix.

Far East (☎ 22 20 56 28, Bernt Ankers gate 4) Most main dishes Nkr68-78. Far East serves excellent, good-value and filling Vietnamese food in a pleasant modern milieu.

Kafé Celsius (☎ 22 42 45 39, Rådhusgata 19) Main courses Nkr108-149. Open 11am-midnight Mon-Sat, 1pm-1am Sun. The low-key Kafé Celsius, a popular place with art students, has a pleasant courtyard beer garden and salads and pastas are served.

Kafé Sesam (☎ 22 86 22 10, in the Museet for Samtidskunst, Bankplassen 4) Snacks and mains Nkr25-69. Open museum hours. Kafé Sesam has reasonably priced and filling fare, including lasagne for Nkr65.

Hotel Stefan (☎ 23 31 55 80, Rosenkrantz gate 1) Mains Nkr185-225. Lunch buffet Nkr275. The good-value lunch buffet at the Hotel Stefan comes highly recommended and is generally regarded as the best in town; check it out and judge for yourself! Try the evening main courses.

Stortorvets Gjæstgiveri (☎ 23 35 63 60, Grensen 1) Main courses Nkr120-230. If money is no object, you'll find well-prepared traditional Norwegian delicacies at this historic place which also has a bar and jazz performances at 1.30pm on Saturday. Pasta dishes are good value at Nkr120 to Nkr136.

A Touch of France (☎ 23 10 01 60, Øvre Slottsgate 16) Starters Nkr65-95, mains Nkr145-360. A Touch of France serves French-style cuisine and fosters an informal atmosphere with long communal dining tables. The shellfish platter at Nkr360 is particularly recommended.

Engebret Café (☎ 22 82 25 25, Bankplassen 1) Fish dishes Nkr225-318. Open Mon-Sat. This cafe is named after Engebret Christoffersen, who founded the restaurant beside the Christiania Theatre in 1857. It thereby became the city's first 'theatre cafe' and attracted both actors and writers. Today it's an upmarket place serving Norwegian and international cuisine, specialising in fish dishes.

Gamle Rådhus (☎ 22 42 01 07, Nedre Slottsgate 1) Mains Nkr195-275. 3-course meal with fish or meat from Nkr400/person. Housed in an historic 1641 building, this is Oslo's oldest restaurant, and has also served as the town hall (hence the name) and a prison. The dark, cosy atmosphere is enhanced by an English-style pub and roaring fire. If you've always wanted to try the glutinous fish dish *lutefisk*, pop in here in the weeks before Christmas, when they make up big batches of it.

Krishna's Cuisine (☎ 22 60 62 50, Kirkeveien 59B) Buffets Nkr90. Vegetarians will relish this restaurant which offers great value vegetarian buffets; smaller portions are available for Nkr40 to Nkr80.

Curry & Ketchup (☎ 22 69 05 22, Kirkeveien 51) Mains Nkr55-75. You'll get straightforward Indian fare at the recommended Curry & Ketchup, including excellent nan breads and balti and korma dishes.

Vegeta Vertshus (☎ *22 83 42 32, Munkedamsveien 3B)* Small/large plate Nkr85/95, all you can eat Nkr135. Open 11am-11pm daily (buffet to 10pm). The popular Vegeta Vertshus serves hearty vegetarian buffets, including wholegrain pizza, casseroles and salads.

Grünerløkka Better known as just 'Løkka', the formerly downmarket workers' district of Grünerløkka has developed into one of Oslo's trendiest neighbourhoods, and the doctors, lawyers and MBAs are still filtering in to snap up some of its good-value charm. As a result, the restaurant and cafe scene presents several good choices.

Sult (☎ *22 87 04 67, Thorvald Meyers gate 26)* Dishes Nkr75-169. The popular and informal Sult prepares superb fish and pasta dishes, as well as more unusual fare. It's always packed so get there early and wait for a table in the attached bar (appropriately called Tørst), where the draught beer costs a bargain Nkr44 per 500mL.

Olympia Lunch-bar (☎ *22 71 62 30, Thorvald Meyers gate 33)* Dishes around Nkr75-90. At the unassuming Olympia Lunch-bar, opposite Birkelunden Park, you'll find souvlaki for Nkr75, falafel and kebab main courses for Nkr79, as well as lamb curry with rice and salad for Nkr89.

Mucho Mas (☎ *22 37 16 09, Thorvald Meyers gate 36)* Starters Nkr30-77, mains around Nkr100. Open 11am-1am Mon-Sat, 1pm-1am Sun. One of Norway's best Mexican restaurants is the recommended Mucho Mas. Starters include tacos (vegetarian/meat Nkr30/50), chips and salsa (Nkr45) and vegetarian/meat taco salad (Nkr48/77), while vegetarian/meat nachos are Nkr77/95 and burritos Nkr78/108. Beans and rice cost an additional Nkr15 each. The beer is also great value at Nkr42 per 500mL. Note that credit cards aren't accepted.

Café Kjøkkenhagen (☎ *22 35 68 71, Thorvald Meyers gate 40)* Dishes Nkr52-85. This informal continental cafe cum art gallery serves delicious light lunches for moderate prices, including salads (Nkr69 to Nkr85), pizzas (Nkr69 to Nkr75), quiche (Nkr44 to Nkr75), pita sandwiches

(Nkr52 to Nkr56) and tagliatelle (Nkr59 to Nkr65).

Fru Hagen (☎ *22 35 67 87, Thorvald Meyers gate 40)* Mains Nkr75-130. This trendy and arty place serves International-style meals until 9.30pm, then turns into a popular upmarket bar, open nightly until 1.30am (2.30am Friday and Saturday).

Markveien Mat & Vinhus (☎ *22 37 22 97, Torvbakkgata 12)* Starters Nkr70-125, main courses Nkr125-145, 3-course dinner Nkr250. Another popular option, Markveien Mat & Vinhus is not only a gourmet restaurant but also a bohemian hangout. If the food price is too steep for your budget, drop by late in the evening for a drink and relaxed conversation (its entrance is on Markveien).

Holmenkollen *Holmenkollen Restaurant* (☎ *22 13 92 00, Holmenkollveien 119)* Mains Nkr198-278, 3-course summer menu Nkr375. This well-known restaurant, uphill from the Holmenkollen T-bane station (line No 1), offers fine food but prices are as lofty as its altitude. Alternatively, you can enjoy the same view and the lighter meals (including the daily special of Norwegian home-cooking) at the adjacent cafeteria for around Nkr120.

Self-Catering Supermarkets aren't generally open on Sunday due to strict regulations, but small ones class as kiosks and can open for business.

For the best selections in town, try the *ICA Gourmet supermarket* (Holmens gate 7) at Aker Brygge. The various *Rimi* outlets offer the best-value and generally the longest opening hours; there's one in the basement of the Gunerius Shopping Centre on Storgata. Alternatively, try one of the ubiquitous *Kiwi supermarkets* at Storgata 11 and elsewhere around the city centre.

Some of the *7-Eleven* outlets around town are open 24 hours daily and sell light beer, Nkr11 coffee, hot dogs, overpriced confectionery and other light items.

Oslo Helsekost (☎ *22 42 96 00, Akersgata 32)* Next door to the Bokkilden bookshop is a small health-food store which sells organic produce and wholesome snacks.

Fresh shrimp *(reker)* are sold from boats near Aker Brygge. The best-value fresh produce comes from the market stalls around Grønlandstorg; the Grønland district and the back streets west of Storgata are also brimming with inexpensive ethnic supermarkets where you'll find otherwise unavailable items such as fresh herbs and African, Asian and Middle Eastern ingredients.

Alcohol Anyone over 18 can buy beer at Oslo supermarkets until 8pm on weekdays and 6pm on Saturday, but for wine or spirits, you'll have to be at least 20 years old and visit a Vinmonopolet.

Vinmonopolet (Kirkeveien 64, Oslo City Shopping Centre, Møllergata 10 & Elisenbergveien 37) Open 10am-5pm or 6pm Mon-Thur, 9am or 10am-6pm Fri, 9am or 10am-2pm or 3pm Sat. These are the most convenient Vinmonopolet outlets.

Entertainment

The tourist office's free monthly brochure *What's on in Oslo* lists current concerts, theatre and special events, but the best publication for night owls is the free *Streetwise*, published annually in English by Use-It (see Information earlier in this chapter).

Note that many Oslo night spots have an unwritten dress code which expects patrons to be relatively well turned out. Although foreigners may be excused, it's still best not to show up in grubby gear and hiking boots. For most bars and clubs that serve beer and wine, you must be over 18 years of age, but many places – especially those that serve spirits – impose a higher age limit. On weekends, most Oslo night spots remain open until at least 3am.

Pubs, Discos & Nightclubs Some bars serve beer in 400mL glasses, while others still serve 500mL measures. Beer prices typically range from Nkr50 to Nkr65, but some places (usually grim) charge as little as Nkr29 and others as much as Nkr99! Bars and clubs in the centre tend to be pricey, while those east of the centre and north of Oslo S are generally more downmarket. Cover charges of around Nkr60 or

Nkr70 normally apply when DJs or live bands are playing.

Smuget (☎ 22 42 52 62, Rosenkrantz gate 22) Cover charge Nkr60/70 weekdays/ weekends. Smuget is a reliable hot spot with a pounding disco and live jazz, rock and blues.

Jazid (☎ 22 11 02 33, Pilestredet 17) For a mellow atmosphere with jazz and modern dance music, there's the cosy and relaxed Jazid. The minimum age limit is 24.

Underwater Pub (☎ 22 46 05 26, Dalsbergstien 4) The weirdly named and oddly-appointed Underwater Pub is notable on Tuesday and Thursday, when students of the State School of Opera lubricate their vocal chords and treat patrons to their favourite arias. Yes, the ceiling really is the surface of the sea!

Herr Nilsens Pub (☎ 22 33 54 05, CJ Hambros plass 5) Cover charge Nkr70. This is a pleasant hangout for the smoking post-30 crowd. From 11pm to 2am on Saturday, you can gear up for a night on the town with a dose of smooth live jazz.

So What (☎ 22 33 64 66, Grensen 9) Just a stone's throw from the YMCA Sleep-In there's this renowned cafe and club, with alternative music most nights.

Blitz (☎ 22 11 23 49, Pilestredet 30C) You'll find the rebellious bohemian scene at Blitz, in an old house near Slottsparken. It also features a book cafe and live concerts.

Head On (☎ 22 33 99 10, Rosenkrantz gate 11B) Cover charge Nkr60. Head On attracts a wealthier and trendier clientele to its lively dance venue, with funk and a lively dance floor. The minimum age limit is 24.

The Dubliner (☎ 22 33 70 05, Rådhusgata 28) Cover charge Nkr60. There are live Irish folk bands several times weekly in this friendly and authentic Irish pub. A pint of Guinness will set you back Nkr59 and pub food costs Nkr95 to Nkr155.

Skansen (Rådhusgata 25) Open 9pm-3.30am Fri & Sat. Billed by the British magazine *The Face* as one of the three best clubs in the world, Skansen, a former public lavatory now transformed into a club, resounds to the beats of house, funk, jazz and techno.

OSLO

Miami Club (*Storgata 25*) Open 8pm-3.30am Fri & Sat. The Miami Club makes a laudable attempt at Caribbean salsa and other Latin beats.

Oliven Café (☎ *22 17 39 45, Norbygata 15*) On Friday and Saturday nights, this Grønland cafe dishes up inexpensive Middle Eastern meals accompanied by Lebanese belly dancing.

Stargate (*Grønlandsleiveret 2*) If you prefer a down-to-earth drinking-den atmosphere, try Stargate, which offers the best-value beer in town; 500mL of draught costs only Nkr24 to Nkr29.

Blå (☎ *22 20 91 81, Brenneriveien 9C*) At Blå, reputedly the best modern jazz spot in Oslo, you can catch new artistes and bands before they hit the big time.

Enka (*Kirkegata 34*) Pub open 3pm-3.30am daily, disco open 9pm-3.30am Thur-Sun. Enka, the largest gay bar/disco in Oslo, has three dance floors and features chart sounds, techno and house. Beer costs Nkr28/43 before/after 9pm; the minimum age is 20.

Potpurriet (☎ *22 41 14 40, Øvre Vollgate 13*) No cover charge before 11pm. Open 6pm-1am Wed & Thur, 8pm-6am Fri & Sat, 8pm-1am Sun. Potpurriet, especially popular with the lesbian crowd, features techno, latin, salsa and other music on two lively dance floors.

London Pub (☎ *22 70 87 00, CJ Hambros Plass 5*) Cover charge Nkr40. Open 3pm-3.30am daily. This dark but popular gay bar may be a bit too camp for some but it's a varied place with DJs, a disco and a piano bar.

Concerts If you're lucky enough, you might catch a big-name outdoor gig at Vigeland Park.

The city's largest concert halls, *Oslo Spektrum* (☎ *22 05 29 00, Sonja Henies plass 2*) and *Rockefeller Music Hall* (☎ *22 20 32 32, Torggata 16*) host a wide range of artists and events, including internationally known musicians.

Den Norske Opera (☎ *81 54 44 88, Storgata 23*) Tickets from around Nkr300 per performance. Every month except July,

Oslo's opera company stages opera, ballet and classical concerts.

Cinema *Saga Kino* (☎ *82 03 00 00, Stortingsgata 28*) The six-screen Saga Kino cinema shows first-run movies, including Hollywood fare, in their original language; the entrance is on Olav V's gate.

Filmens Hus (☎ *22 47 45 00, Dronningens gate 16*) Almost daily, Filmens Hus screens old classics and international festival winners.

IMAX Film Theatre (☎ *23 11 66 00, Holmens gate 1, Aker Brygge*) For a more thrilling show, you can check out the IMAX Film Theatre, which presents high-tech productions, including 3D films and simulators.

Other Take advantage of summer's long daylight hours and spend mellow evenings outdoors – splash out on a beer at one of the outdoor cafes in Vigeland Park, or ride a ferry out to the islands in Oslofjord. If the weather isn't cooperating, check out the alternative dance and theatre scene at the cafe-style *Black Box* (☎ *22 10 40 20, Stranden 3*), in the Aker Brygge complex.

Shopping
Oslo excels in upmarket shopping and there are many fine shops on Bogstadveien. For art, try the galleries on Frognerveien.

Oslo Sweater Shop (☎ *22 42 42 25, Biskop Gunnerus gate 3*) Traditional Norwegian sweaters are popular purchases and the Oslo Sweater Shop has good prices and selections.

Unique Design (☎ *22 42 97 60, Rosenkrantz gate 13*) This shop is also worth checking out for sweaters.

Husfliden (☎ *22 42 10 75, Møllergata 4*) Husfliden is a larger shop selling quality Norwegian clothing and crafts, with items ranging from carved wooden trolls to elaborate folk costumes.

Heimen Husflid (☎ *23 21 42 00, Rosenkrantz gate 8*) This shop is another place for clothing and crafts.

Vestkanttorget flea market (*Amaldus Nilsens plass*) Open 10am-4pm Sat. If you're happy with pot luck and sifting through heaps of junk, take a chance here. It's at the plaza which intersects Professor Dahls gate, a block east of Vigeland Park.

Getting There & Away

Air Oslo's relatively new international airport (☎ 81 55 02 50) is at Gardermoen, 50km north of Oslo. It opened in October 1998 and has a motorway and high-speed rail link to the city centre.

At Torp, 112km south of town, there is another international airport which is used by the UK-based Ryanair (☎ 33 42 75 00) for its flights to and from London's Stansted airport. An express bus connects it with Oslo S (Nkr98 for Ryanair passengers, two hours).

The SAS ticket office is in the basement at Oslo S. Braathens (☎ 81 52 00 00) has an office just across the hall. Widerøes Flyveselskap (☎ 67 11 60 00, fax 67 11 61 95) is at Vollsveien 6, Postboks 131, N-1324 Lysaker (a suburb out of the town's centre). Other airlines include Air France (☎ 23 50 20 01), Gardermoen; British Airways (☎ 80 03 31 42, fax 22 82 20 49), Dronning Mauds gate 1-3; and Finnair (☎ 81 00 11 00), at Jernbanetorget 4A.

Bus Long-distance buses arrive and depart from Nor-Way Bussekspress (☎ 82 05 43 00, W www.nor-way.no), Schweigaardsgate 8, in Galleri Oslo (east of Oslo S). The train and bus stations are linked via an overhead walkway. Some bus services offer discounts to Eurail, InterRail and ScanRail pass holders, so be sure to ask.

Oslo-Bergen services (Nkr575, 11½ hours) depart at 9.30am daily from Oslo and 7.30am from Bergen. There are also direct services to/from Trondheim (Nkr590, 9½ hours); Stryn (Nkr525, 8½ hours); Florø (Nkr640, 10½ hours); Måløy (Nkr685, 10½ hours); Røros (Nkr450, six hours); Kristiansand (Nkr385, 5½ hours); Stavanger (Nkr550, 9½ hours); and numerous other destinations in Southern Norway.

Train All trains arrive and depart from Oslo S in the city centre. The reservation desks are open from 6am (international from 6.30am) to 11pm daily and an information

desk (☎ 81 50 08 88) provides details on routes and timetables throughout the country.

In addition to the frequent services around Oslofjord (to Drammen, Skien, Moss, Fredrikstad, Halden, etc), trains connect Oslo to Bergen (Nkr570, 6½ to eight hours, five daily); Åndalsnes (Nkr550, 5½ hours, two or three daily) via Dombås; Trondheim (Nkr650, 6½ to eight hours, four or five daily) via Dombås; Trondheim (Nkr668, 7½ hours, once daily except weekends) via Røros (Nkr480, five to 5½ hours, one to three daily); and Stavanger (Nkr670, 7½ to 8¾ hours, one to six daily) via Kristiansand (Nkr440, 4½ to 5¼ hours, one to six daily). All fares are in 2nd-class seats. In addition to daytime trains, all these routes except Stavanger on Saturday night and Trondheim via Røros are conveniently served by overnight trains; 2nd-class sleepers cost an additional Nkr150.

Oslo S has backpack-sized lockers for Nkr10 to Nkr40 per 24 hours (open 4.30am to 1.10am daily).

Car & Motorcycle The main highways into the city are the E6 from the north and south, and the E18 from the east and west. Each time you enter Oslo, you must pass through one of 19 toll stations and pay Nkr13 (there's also an Nkr15 toll for use of the Drammen-Oslo E18 motorway). Note that there's a Nkr313 fine if you use a lane reserved for vehicles with subscription (*abonnement*) passes. Motorcycles aren't subject to the tolls.

If you plan to hire a car, see the Getting Around chapter for a list of car rental companies.

Hitching When leaving Oslo it's generally best to take a train to the outskirts of the city in your direction of travel and start hitching from there.

To hitch to Bergen, take bus No 161 to its final stop and wait beside the E16 towards Hønefoss; from there, follow Rv7 to Hol, Rv50 to Aurland and the E16 to Bergen. For Trondheim, take T-Bane line 5 (direction: Vestli) to Grorud and wait beside Rv4, which connects to the E6 north. For the south coast and Stavanger, take bus No 31 or 32 to the Maritim petrol station or bus No 151, 161, 251, 252 or 261 to Oksenøy-veien, near Lysaker, and hitch from the bus stop. For Göteborg (Sweden) and points south, use bus No 81, 83 or 85 to Bekkelaget or a local train (Ski) to Nordstrand, which both provide access to the E6 south.

Boat Ferries operated by DFDS Seaways (☎ 22 41 90 90), Vippetangen 2, and Stena Line AS (☎ 23 17 90 00), Jernbanetorget 2, connect Oslo with Copenhagen and Frederikshavn (Denmark). The ferries use the Vippetangen quay off Skippergata. Bus No 60 stops within a couple of minutes walk of the terminal.

Color Line ferries (☎ 22 94 44 00), Øvre Slottsgate 12A, to and from Hirtshals (Denmark) and Kiel (Germany) dock at Hjortneskaia, west of the central harbour. Take tram No 10 or 13 from Oslo S, or the Color Line bus which leaves Oslo S one hour before boat departures.

Getting Around

Oslo has an efficient public transport system with an extensive network of buses, trams, underground trains and ferries. A single fare on any of these services costs Nkr20 and includes one transfer within an hour of purchase. An unlimited 24-hour ticket *(dagskort)* costs Nkr50 and a weekly/monthly card is Nkr150/580 (Nkr75/290 for youths under 20 and seniors over 67). The *flexikort* (Nkr125) is valid for up to eight trips and may be shared between two or more people. The single and day tickets are sold on buses and trams while other passes are available from Trafikanten, Narvesen kiosks, post offices and staffed underground stations. Children aged four to 16 and seniors over 67 years of age pay half price on all fares; on weekends, adults using a dagskort or flexikort may travel with up to four children for no extra charge.

The Oslo Card includes all public transport options within the city, with the exception of night buses. Bicycles are carried on trams and trains for an additional Nkr10.

The automatic fine for travelling without a ticket is a rather punitive Nkr750.

Trafikanten (☎ 177 or ☎ 81 50 01 76), below Oslo S tower on Jernbanetorget, provides free schedules and a public transport map, *Sporveiskart Oslo*. It's open 7am to 8pm weekdays and 8am to 6pm weekends.

To/From the Airport The Flybussen (☎ 177 or ☎ 22 17 70 30) airport shuttle to Oslo International Airport at Gardermoen departs from the bus terminal at Galleri Oslo three or four times hourly from 4.15am to 10pm. The trip costs Nkr90 and takes 40 minutes. Flybussekspressen (☎ 177) connects Gardermoen with Majorstua (Nkr100), Bekkestua (Nkr120), Ski (Nkr140), and other places, one to four times hourly.

FlyToget rail services (☎ 81 50 07 77, 🔳 www .flytoget.no) leave Asker station for Gardermoen every 20 minutes between 4.18am and 11.36pm, stopping en route at the National Theatre and Oslo S. From Oslo S to Gardermoen costs Nkr130 and takes 24 minutes. Extra trains run every 10 minutes on this section, from 5.35am to 9.15pm on weekdays. In addition, most northbound NSB intercity and local trains (☎ 81 50 08 88) stop at Gardermoen (Nkr70, from 26 minutes, hourly but fewer on Saturday).

Bus & Tram Bus and tram lines lace the city and extend into the suburbs. There's no central station but most converge at Jernbanetorget in front of Oslo S. Most westbound buses, including those to Bygdøy and Vigeland Park, also stop immediately south of the National Theatre.

The frequency of service drops dramatically at night, but on weekends, night buses N12, N14 and N18 follow the tram routes until 4am or later; there are also weekend night buses – Nos 201 to 218. These services are called Nattlinjer and cost Nkr40 per ride, and no passes are valid. For details, ask Trafikanten for the appropriate timetables.

T-Bane The five-line Tunnelbanen underground system, better known as the T-bane, is faster and extends farther from the city centre than most city bus lines. All lines pass through the Nasjonalteatret, Stortinget and Jernbanetorget stations.

Car & Motorcycle Oslo has its share of one-way streets which can complicate city driving a bit, but the streets are never as congested as in most European cities. A car may be convenient for exploring outlying areas, but the best way to see the central sites of interest is on foot or with local transport.

Metered street parking, identified by a solid blue sign with a white 'P', can be found throughout the city. The hours listed indicate the period in which the meters are in effect, usually from 8am to 5pm, with Saturday hours written in brackets. At other times, parking is free unless otherwise posted. Most meters gobble up Nkr5 to Nkr22 per hour, with the highest rates at busy spots such as post offices. The city centre also has 16 multistorey car parks, including those at Oslo City and Aker Brygge shopping centres; fees range from Nkr70 to Nkr200 per 24-hour period.

Note that the Oslo Card includes parking at all municipal car parks; to use it, fill in your vehicle registration number and the date of validity of your Oslo Card (in ink), tear off the Oslo Card section and display the parking card section in the front window. For further parking information, contact the tourist office.

Taxi Taxis charge Nkr46 to Nkr91.50 at flagfall and from Nkr10 to Nkr16 per kilometre. There are taxi stands at Oslo S, shopping centres and city squares. Any taxi with a lit sign is available for hire. Otherwise, phone Norgestaxi (☎ 08000) or Oslo Taxi (☎ 02323), but note that the meter starts running at the point of dispatch, adding from Nkr46 to Nkr69 to what will become a gigantic bill! Oslo taxis accept major credit cards.

Bicycle Bicycles may be carried on public transport which will get you beyond the edge of town and into the forest before you even begin pedalling. You can hire bikes from Glåmdal Cycle Hire (☎ 22 83 39 79) at Vestbaneplassen 2, beside the main tourist

office. Rates start at an excessive Nkr265 for 24 hours.

Den Rustne Eike (☎ 22 44 18 80), Oscars gate 32, can handle bike repairs.

Boat Ferries to Bygdøy leave from Rådhusbrygge every 40 minutes (for the Bygdøy museums, disembark at the Dronningen pier), while ferries to the Oslofjord islands sail from Vippetangen Quay. The express boat *Princessin* (☎ 81 50 01 76) connects Oslo with Drøbak and other Oslofjord stops en route: Ildjernet, Langåra and Håøya (which is a holiday spot offering fine swimming and camping). It departs from Aker Brygge pier.

Around Oslo

DRØBAK
pop 3000
Drøbak, the capital city's nearest 'charming village', makes a pleasant day trip. The large number of clapboard timber buildings here, as well as the cosy atmosphere, bizarre Christmas-theme shop, and several local attractions, are good for a couple of hours of rambling. There's a small tourist office (☎ 64 93 50 87) by the harbour at Havnegata 4.

Saltvannsakvarium (☎ 64 93 09 74, Havnegata 4; adult/child Nkr20/5; open 11am-7pm daily May-Aug, 11am-4pm daily Sept-Apr), features the denizens of Oslofjord and the world's only lutefisk museum. There's also the small **Drøbak Båtforenings Maritime Samlinger** (☎ 64 93 09 74, Kroketønna 4; adult/child Nkr10/5; open 11am-7pm daily May-Aug, 11am-4pm daily Sept-Apr), a museum of maritime paraphernalia which includes a number of boat engines. The **Oscarsborg fortress**, on an offshore island and built in the 1850s, fired the shots that sank the German warship *Blücher* on 9 April 1940. Boat tours to the island lasting 2½ hours depart from the tourist office at 12.30pm and 4.15pm on weekdays (noon and 2.30pm at weekends) from June to August and cost Nkr50/25.

There are several places to eat on Torget and nearby Storgata.

Getting There & Away

From Jernbanetorget in Oslo, bus No 541 to Drøbak (one hour, Nkr58) leaves approximately hourly. Alternatively, the express boat *Princessin* (☎ 177) does one trip from Oslo's Aker Brygge pier daily Wednesday to Sunday, allowing at least 1½ hours in Drøbak before returning to Oslo. The one-way fare is Nkr58. It's recommended to go by boat one way and by bus the other way.

The new tunnel under Oslofjorden, between Drøbak and Drammen, charges Nkr50 each way for a car.

DRAMMEN
pop 54,852

Primarily known as a dormitory community for Oslo, Drammen is an industrial centre in its own right and most of the cars imported to Norway are offloaded into vast car parks near the fjord. Not only was Drammen the start of the Royal Road to Bergen, it was also the original home of the potato alcohol Aquavit. In late autumn, Drammen holds a national Aquavit competition in which celebrities judge which is the best brand.

Information

Tourist information is available from Drammen Turistinformasjon (☎ 32 80 62 10, fax 32 80 66 31, e turist@drammen.kommune .no) at Bragernes Torg 6.

Things to See & Do

Drammen has several buildings of note: the historic **Stock Exchange** on Bragernes Torg (which now houses a McDonald's); the restored **Rådhus** on Engenes 1 (the city hall, a former courthouse and jail); the **fire station** in Bragernes Torg (now a bank); the old **Free Masonic lodge** in Gamle Kirkeplass (closed to the public); the lovely prize-winning **Drammen Theatre** *(☎ 32 21 31 00, Gamle Kirkeplass; open for events only)*, built in 1870, burned down in 1993 and reopened in 1996; and the Gothic-style **Bragernes church** *(Bragernes Torg)* from 1871. You can also see the house where **Aquavit** was first produced in 1804, on Sommerfrydveien, by merchant Johan Godtfried Schwencke in response to a royal decree that corn not be used

to produce spirits, but it's closed to the public. The district along Øvre Storgate and Mossegården is also prominent in Aquavit history.

The five-part **Drammen Museum** *(☎ 32 20 09 30, Gamle Kirkeplass 7; adult/child Nkr35/20; open noon-4pm Tues-Sun & 6pm-8pm Thur)* has a notable art collection.

Worthwhile hikes will take you up into the **Bragernesåsen** woodlands or up the scenic 50m-deep **Kjøsterudjuvet Gorge**, just over 1km north of town. Pick up hiking maps from the tourist office.

Many people believe Drammen's big highlight is the 1650m-long **Spiralen tunnel** to the 200m-high summit of Bragernes, which affords a fabulous view over the city. The best part, however, is the fact that the tunnel makes six spirals inside the hill en route to the top. If you don't have a car, go on a summer weekend, when bus No 41 does the trip at 10.17am, 12.02pm and 2.32pm from Bragernes Torg (15 minutes, Nkr18).

An interesting day excursion will take you to Åmot, where the **Royal Blåfarveværk** *(☎ 32 78 67 00, W www.blaa.no, Åmot; hourly tours Nkr40; open noon-6pm daily 19 May-23 Sept, noon-6pm Tue-Sun only 20 Aug-23 Sept)* was established by King Christian VII in 1773 to extract cobalt to produce blue pigments for the glass and porcelain industries. You can visit either on your own or with a guided tour. It's also worth looking at the large Haugfoss waterfall, the Mølla shop (which sells cobalt-blue glass work – alas, the pigments weren't mined on site), and the various art exhibitions in the attached **museum** *(☎ 32 78 67 00, Åmot; adult/child Nkr55/free; open 10am-5pm daily 19 May-23 Sept, closes 6pm 23 June-19 Aug)*. Take the relatively frequent Nettbuss express bus No 100 or 101 from Drammen to Åmot (one hour, Nkr59) then change to bus No 105 (seven minutes, Nkr22), or walk 4km north-west.

Places to Stay & Eat

Drammen Vandrerhjem & Davik Troika (☎ 32 26 77 00, fax 32 26 77 01, Fagerlibakken 1) Dorm beds Nkr200, hotel singles/doubles Nkr350/550. The clean and friendly hostel offers high-standard dorms or even better hotel rooms in the attached Davik Troika.

There's a good mix of cafes, restaurants, pubs and nightclubs either in or near Bragernes Torg.

Getting There & Away
Trains run to Oslo every 30 minutes (Nkr62, 35 minutes) and buses depart once or twice every hour (Nkr65, 35 minutes).

Østfold

The Østfold region, the detached slice of Norway to the east of Oslofjord, is a mix of forest, pastoral farmland and small industrial towns which rely on the timber trade.

FREDRIKSTAD
pop 67,415
Fredrikstad was founded by King Fredrik II as a trading centre between mainland Europe and western Scandinavia. The modern city is dominated by the 1880 cathedral, which contains stained glass work by Emanuel Vigeland. Bizarrely, the steeple contains a lighthouse, which is still functioning at night. Another landmark is the delicate silver arch of the 824m-long and 40m-high Glomma bridge. The Konsten fortress and historic Gamlebyen are most emphatically worth a visit, but thanks to the dearth of decent inexpensive accommodation, many travellers make Fredrikstad a day trip from Oslo.

Information
The friendly tourist office (☎ 69 35 76 00) is at Voldgaten 98, in the old town (Gamlebyen). It's open daily June to August, weekdays only during the rest of the year. There's also a smaller office (☎ 69 39 65 00), at the marina on Dampskipsbrygga, open daily from June to August. Both offices may close down or move in 2002.

Gamlebyen
The Fredrikstad Gamlebyen (Old Town), east of the Glomma, was originally constructed in 1663 as a military enclave which could be readily defended against Swedish belligerence with multiple embankments, moats, gates and even a drawbridge. The moats and embankments make for a pleasant stroll – follow the perimeter walls that were once defended by 200 cannons. The narrow cobbled streets have also been preserved and are still lined with picturesque 17th-century buildings, many of which remain occupied. It's by far the best-preserved fortress town in Scandinavia. In Kongens Torv, the central square, you'll find an ATM and a rather ludicrous statue of the pompous town founder, King Fredrik II.

From the train station it's a five-minute walk to the riverfront, where a ferry shuttles across the river Glomma to the main gate of Gamlebyen (Nkr6, two minutes). From 23 June to 17 August, the Gamlebyen tourist office (☎ 69 35 76 00) runs guided tours (Nkr45/35). They leave hourly from the tourist office, 11am to 3pm Monday to Saturday and at 1pm and 3pm Sunday.

Fredrikstad Museum
The three-part Fredrikstad Museum (☎ 69 30 68 75; combined admission adult/child Nkr30/10; open 11am-5pm Mon-Sat & noon-5pm Sun, mid-June-late Aug) preserves the best of this historic fortress town.

Slaveriet Museum The Slaveriet portion of the Fredrikstad Museum, at the southwest end of Gamlebyen, overlooking the river Glomma, occupies a 1731 building on the site of the old guard house. It contains a model of the early city and a collection of relics from three centuries of Fredrikstad's civilian, military and industrial activities.

Kongsten Festning A 15-minute walk beyond the Gamlebyen drawbridge (turn off Tornesveien at Fredrikstad Motell & Camping) lies the flower-festooned Kongsten Fort, which dates from 1685 and once served as a lookout and warning post for the troops at nearby Gamlebyen. Little happens here today, but it's fun to scramble around the turrets, embankments, walls and stockade, or just sit in the sun and soak up the silence of this lonely and appealingly

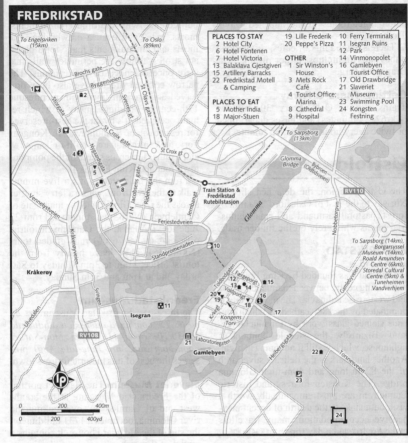

FREDRIKSTAD

PLACES TO STAY
2 Hotel City
6 Hotel Fontenen
7 Hotel Victoria
13 Balaklava Gjestgiveri
15 Artillery Barracks
22 Fredrikstad Motell & Camping

PLACES TO EAT
5 Mother India
18 Major-Stuen

19 Lille Frederik
20 Peppe's Pizza

OTHER
1 Sir Winston's House
3 Mets Rock Café
4 Tourist Office; Marina
8 Cathedral
9 Hospital

10 Ferry Terminals
11 Isegran Ruins
12 Park
14 Vinmonopolet
16 Gamlebyen Tourist Office
17 Old Drawbridge
21 Slaveriet Museum
23 Swimming Pool
24 Kongsten Festning

unkempt spot. It's always open and admission is free.

Isegran The Norse sagas mention the 13th-century fortress on the islet of Isegran, which later became a back-row line of defence against Sweden in the mid-17th century. The ruins remain visible at the eastern end of the island. It's also the site of a boathouse containing a sailing exhibit and the modern history of Fredrikstad (1860–1960), as well as visiting exhibitions. Isegran is 400m west of Gamlebyen but access is from Rv108, about 600m south of Fredrikstad city centre.

Special Events

The Glomma Festival takes place during the second week in July and features one week of very well-attended festivities, including music performances, ritual duels, a 'bathtub regatta' for creative vessels and a veteran sailing ship exhibition. There's also a four-day music festival in late August. Contact the tourist office for details of both events.

Places to Stay

Fredrikstad Motell & Camping (☎ 69 32 05 32, fax 69 32 36 66, Torsnesveien 16) Tent sites without/with car Nkr90/140, caravan

Nkr140-170, 2- to 4-person cabins Nkr260-Nkr360, motel singles/doubles Nkr390/490. This fairly average place, in the grounds of Kongsten Fort, is the only choice for budget accommodation in Fredrikstad. Take bus No 362 towards Torsnes from the centre.

Tuneheimen Vandrerhjem (☎ 69 14 50 01, fax 69 14 22 91, Tuneveien 44) Dorm beds Nkr195, singles/doubles Nkr330/480. Open year-round. The nearest youth hostel is near lake Tunevannet, 1km from Sarpsborg, which is in turn a 10km bus ride from Fredrikstad. Breakfast is included and dinner is available.

Artillery Barracks (☎ 69 32 30 40, Gamlebyen) 4-person room Nkr500. In the renovated former artillery barracks, room rates exclude breakfast and there are no kitchen facilities.

Hotel Victoria (☎ 69 38 58 00, fax 69 38 58 01, Turngaten 3) Singles/doubles from Nkr700/900. Hotel Victoria, opposite the cathedral grounds, offers fine rooms with en suite facilities.

Hotel Fontenen (☎ 69 38 56 00, fax 69 38 56 01, Nygaardsgata) Singles/doubles from Nkr595/795. This economic hotel, beside the cathedral, offers acceptable rooms with an extensive breakfast buffet.

Hotel City (☎ 69 31 77 50, fax 69 31 30 90, Nygaardsgata 44/46) Singles/doubles from Nkr750/950. Hotel City is the upmarket option in town, with modern en suite rooms. There's also a nightclub, plus four places to eat: a pub, a casual pizza place, the a la carte Restaurant Frederik and the finer Bourbon St, serving Creole cuisine.

Balaklava Gjestgiveri (☎ 69 32 30 40, fax 69 32 29 40, Færgeportgata 78, Gamlebyen) Doubles without en suite Nkr800-900, with en suite Nkr900-1000. If you're up for a major splurge, you won't regret a night at this atmospheric hotel.

Places to Eat
By the Gressvikbrygge quay and just off Storgata, there's a host of fairly good ethnic restaurants, including Chinese, sushi, Italian, Spanish and Greek places; lunches are around Nkr80 and dinner mains are around Nkr100.

Mother India (☎ 69 31 22 00, Nygaardsgata 17) Mains Nkr115-180. Open afternoon & evening daily. You'll find reasonable Indian cuisine and ethnic decor at Mother India.

Lille Frederik (Torvgaten) Burgers with salad Nkr49-83. For burgers, snacks and coffee in Gamlebyen, Lille Frederik is just the place.

Peppe's Pizza (☎ 69 32 32 10, Toldbodgaten, Gamlebyen) Pizza from Nkr130. Peppe's Pizza is a good option and a great spot to sit along the cobbled street, drink a beer and gaze at the river. You can also get a decent lasagne for Nkr98.

Major-Stuen (☎ 69 32 15 55, Voldportgata 73) Mains Nkr145-199. Open noon-9pm daily. Another fine place in Gamlebyen, the recommended Major-Stuen has an international menu but specialises in Norwegian whale dishes (Nkr175).

Balaklava Gjestgiveri (☎ 69 32 30 40, Færgeportgata 78) 3-course dinner Nkr450. For a special occasion, you can eat in the outdoor garden at this elegant restaurant located in a historic building in Gamlebyen. It specialises in Norwegian fish and beef dishes, as well as international cuisine.

Engelsviken Brygge (☎ 69 35 18 40, Engelsvikveien 6, Engelsviken) 3-course dinner around Nkr325. One of the best places in the area is this excellent quayside seafood restaurant, 15km north-west of Fredrikstad, where wonderfully prepared foods include crab, mussels, catfish and halibut.

Entertainment
Mets Rock Café (☎ 69 31 78 99, Dampskipsbrygga 12) On the river promenade, this place serves Mexican meals for around Nkr100 and it has a bar with DJ rock music nightly from 10pm. There's no cover charge but you must be over 20 years of age.

Sir Winston's House (☎ 69 31 00 80, Storgata 17) Beside the river, this English-style pub serves meals such as fish and chips for Nkr89, and you can choose between 10 draught beers. On weekends it also offers DJ music (mostly 1960s, but some contemporary) and dancing.

Getting There & Away

Intercity buses arrive and depart from the Fredrikstad Rutebilstasjon (☎ 177) at the train station. Bus Nos 200 and 360 run to/from Sarpsborg (Nkr27, 25 minutes, twice hourly). Nor-Way Bussekspress has one to seven daily services between Oslo and Fredrikstad (Nkr135, 1¼ hours), with most buses continuing to Hvaler; there are also regular Flybussekspressen services (☎ 177) from Fredrikstad to Oslo international airport Gardermoen (Nkr190, 2¼ hours, every hour or two).

Fredrikstad lies on the rail line between Oslo and Göteborg. Trains to/from Oslo (Nkr140, one hour) run about 10 times daily, but note that southbound international trains require a seat reservation.

Fjordlink (☎ 69 31 60 56) and M/S *Silverpilen* (☎ 69 39 65 04) sail to/from Strömstad in Sweden four times daily (Nkr80/110 one-way/return).

Getting Around

For information on city bus routes, phone or visit the Fredrikstad Rutebilstasjon (☎ 177).

To cross the Glomma (the country's longest river) to Gamlebyen, you can either trek over the high and hulking Glomma bridge or take the Nkr6 *Go'vakker Randi* ferry (named for a prominent local dance teacher) from Strandpromenaden. It operates from 5.30am to 11pm on weekdays (to 1am on Friday); from 7am to 1am on Saturday and from 9.30am to 11pm on Sunday.

For a taxi, phone ☎ 69 36 26 00. Bicycle hire is available from either tourist office (your credit card number or driving licence will be required as a deposit).

AROUND FREDRIKSTAD
Hvaler

Norwegian holiday-makers and artists love Hvaler ('the skerries'), an offshore archipelago of 833 forested islands and islets guarding the southern entrance to Oslofjord. The main islands of Vesterøy, Spjærøy, Asmaløy and Kirkøy are connected to the mainland by a toll road (Nkr50) and tunnel. Bus No 365 (Nkr50) runs all the way to Skjærhalden, at the far end of Kirkøy, but the best way to ex-

plore these quiet islands is by bicycle. Nor-Way Busekspress runs from Skjærhalden (on Kirkøy) to Oslo one to seven times daily for Nkr170.

Hvaler tourist office (☎ 69 37 86 76), Skjærhalden, opens daily from June to August.

Above the coastline of Akerøy island, accessible only by ferry (taxi boat), clings a well-preserved 17th-century coastal fortress, renovated in the 1960s. Admission is free and it's open at all times.

The mid-11th-century **stone church** *(Skjærhalden; open to visitors noon-4pm daily in July, noon-4pm Sat only mid-June–mid-Aug)* on the island of Kirkøy is one of the oldest in Norway. The church hosts a week-long music and arts festival in July – for details, contact the tourist office.

Kystmuseet *(☎ 69 37 66 47, Spjærøy; admission free; open 10am-3pm Mon-Sat late June-early Aug & noon-4pm Sun year-round)* explains the relationship between the island people and the sea.

If you wish to find self-catering accommodation in Hvaler, the tourist office has a list of fully-equipped private houses and chalets available for Nkr400 to Nkr700 per day or Nkr2600 to Nkr4200 per week.

Hvaler Kurs & Konferansesenter (☎ 69 37 91 28, fax 69 37 91 32, Skjærhalden, Kirkøy) Apartments Nkr500 per night. The conference centre has excellent apartments for rent.

All year, the M/S *Hollungen* and M/S *Hvalerfergen II* sail roughly every hour from Skjærhalden and through the Hvaler skerries (Nkr40, one hour). Alternatively, you can sail with the scheduled ferry M/S *Vesleø II* between Skjærhalden, Koster (Sweden) and Strömstad (Sweden) from mid-June to mid-August for Nkr105/85 adult/child return.

Roald Amundsen Centre

The renowned polar explorer Roald Amundsen, who in 1911 was the first to reach the South Pole, was born in 1872 at Hvidsten, midway between Fredrikstad and Sarpsborg. Although the family moved to Oslo when Roald was still a small child, the family home in Hvidsten, which was the base for its small shipbuilding and shipping business, is now the Roald Amundsen Centre (☎ 69 34 83 26, Hvidsten; admission free, tours adult/child Nkr30/15; open 10am-4pm daily May-Aug) which is dedicated to the man's life and expeditions. The centre is about 7km from Fredrikstad – follow Rv110 east towards the E6 and Sarpsborg and look out for the sign.

Borgarsyssel Museum

Borgarsyssel (☎ 69 15 50 11, Kirkegata, Sarpsborg; adult/child Nkr40/20; open 10am-5pm Tues-Sat & noon-5pm Sun 18 May-31 Aug), the county museum of Østfold, lies in the town of Sarpsborg (14km north-east of Fredrikstad) and makes an interesting day visit. This open-air display contains 30 period buildings from various parts of the country and includes a vast collection of cultural art and artefacts. There's also a herbal garden, a petting zoo and the ruins of King Øystein's St Nikolas church, constructed in 1115 and destroyed by the Swedes in 1567. From Fredrikstad, trains and buses run frequently to Sarpsborg.

Storedal Cultural Centre

A unique and worthwhile site is the Storedal Cultural Centre (☎ 69 16 92 67, Storedal; admission free; open 10am-5pm daily 20 May-31 Aug), 8km north-east of Fredrikstad. King Magnus the Blind was born here in 1117; he took the throne at 13 years of age and earned his nickname at 18 when he was blinded by an enemy in Bergen. Coincidentally, a later owner of the farm, Erling Stordahl, also lost his sight at an early age and decided to develop a monument to King Magnus as well as a centre dedicated to blind and other disabled people. In 1970, the Crown Prince Harald opened the centre.

In the botanic garden, which is laid out in the shape of a leaf, the locations of the various plants and herbs are identified by raised areas in the footpath, and are described in both script and Braille. The most intriguing feature is the *Ode til Lyset* (Ode to the Light), a 'sound sculpture' by Arnold Haukeland and Arne Nordheim which translates the fluctuations in natural light into ever-changing music. To get there, follow Rv110 east for about 6km

from Fredrikstad – the centre is just north of the main road and is signposted.

Oldtidsveien

People have lived and worked in the Østfold region for thousands of years, and numerous examples of ancient stone works and rock paintings lie along the 'Oldtidsveien' ('Old Times Way', a promotional name for Rv110 – the old sunken road between Fredrikstad and Sarpsborg) lie. At Solberg, there are three panels with around 100 figures dating back 3000 years. At Gunnarstorp are several 30m-wide **Bronze Age burial mounds** and several **Iron Age standing stones**. The site at Begby includes well-preserved renditions of ships, men and animals, while Hunn has several **stone circles** and a series of rich **burial mounds** dating from 500 BC to AD 800; they were found to contain jewellery, bronze and glass treasures. The **rock paintings** at Hornes clearly depict 21 ships complete with oarsmen. Access is easiest by car or bus towards Sarpsborg, but all these sites may also be visited on a long day walk or bike ride from Fredrikstad.

HALDEN
pop 21,121

The soporific border town of Halden, at the end of Iddefjord between steep rocky headlands, has served as a keystone of Norwegian defence through more than two centuries of Swedish aggression. Locals proudly relate that the two occasions (in 1659 and 1716) on which the Halden resistance resorted to fire to drive out the enemy are commemorated in the Norwegian national anthem by Bjørnsterne Bjørnson, who wrote '... we chose to burn our nation, lest we let it fall'. The fortress crowns the hill behind Halden and makes the town a worthwhile day trip from Oslo or a stop along the rail route between Norway and Göteborg, Sweden. Shopping prospects are good and draw even more travellers off the E6 highway.

History

Halden served as a garrison during the Hannibal Wars from 1643 to 1645, and from 1644 it was fortified with a wooden stockade. In

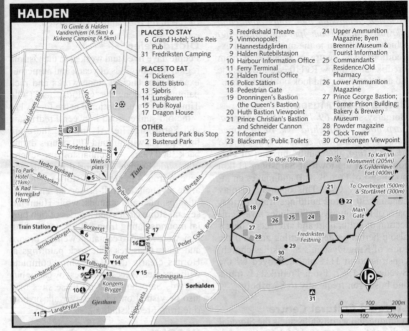

HALDEN

PLACES TO STAY
6 Grand Hotel; Siste Reis Pub
31 Fredriksten Camping

PLACES TO EAT
4 Dickens
8 Butts Bistro
13 Sjøbris
14 Lunsjbaren
15 Pub Royal
17 Dragon House

OTHER
1 Busterud Park Bus Stop
2 Busterud Park
3 Fredrikshald Theatre
5 Vinmonopolet
7 Hannestadgården
9 Halden Rutebilstasjon
10 Harbour Information Office
11 Ferry Terminal
12 Halden Tourist Office
16 Police Station
18 Pedestrian Gate
19 Dronningen's Bastion (the Queen's Bastion)
20 Huth Bastion Viewpoint
21 Prince Christian's Bastion and Schneider Cannon
22 Infosenter
23 Blacksmith; Public Toilets
24 Upper Ammunition Magazine; Byen Brenner Museum & Tourist Information
25 Commandants Residence/Old Pharmacy
26 Lower Ammunition Magazine
27 Prince George Bastion; Former Prison Building; Bakery & Brewery Museum
28 Powder magazine
29 Clock Tower
30 Overkongen Viewpoint

1658, 1659 and 1660, it was attacked by Swedish forces and the need for a better fortification became apparent. In the 1658 Roskilde Treaty between Sweden and Denmark, Norway lost its Bohuslän province (and Bohus fortress), and Halden was left as a border outpost requiring heavy defences. As a result, on 28 July 1660 King Fredrik III of Denmark issued a declaration ordering a stronger fortification on the site.

The pentagonal citadel, as well as the adjoining Gyldenløve fort, Stortårnet and Overberget, was constructed across two parallel hills from 1661 to 1671 (and augmented between 1682 and 1701) from plans drawn up by Dutch architect Willem Coucheron. Between 1716 and 1718, the fort was repeatedly besieged by Swedish forces but the Norwegians managed to resist the onslaught. Its crowning event came on 11 December 1718, when the warmongering Swede King Karl XII was shot dead on the site (a monument now marks the spot).

Further attacks continued into the 19th century. In the first few years of the 20th century, Fredriksten Fortress was armed with increasingly powerful modern cannons, turret guns and howitzers. However, this firepower was removed during the 1906 negotiations for the dissolution of the Swedish-Norwegian union.

Information

The Halden Turist tourist office (☎ 69 19 09 80, fax 69 19 09 81, e info@haldentourist .no), at the bus terminal, is open from 9am to 4.30pm weekdays from June to August (the rest of the year until 3.30pm). The information office (☎ 69 18 14 78) at the harbour is open from 8am to 8pm daily between 1 June and 17 August.

Fredriksten Festning & Museums

Crowning the hilltop behind Halden is the 1661 Fredriksten Fortress (☎ 69 18 54 11;

adult/child Nkr40/10, includes all museums, tours Nkr45/20; open 10am-5pm daily 18 May-20 Aug), which has resisted six Swedish sieges and never been captured. From the top of Festningsgata in Sørhalden (a neighbourhood of 19th-century sea captains' cottages), a half-overgrown cobbled footpath climbs the unkempt lilac-covered slopes to the pedestrian entrance of the fortress.

The museums in the castle grounds cover various facets of the fortress' history. Halden's history is outlined in the **Byen Brenner** ('the town is on fire') exhibition in the upper part of the fortress. Displays in the **old pharmacy** describe the history of pharmacology from early Norwegian folk remedies to early-20th-century apothecaries. It's housed in the former **Commandant's Residence**, constructed between 1754 and 1758 and damaged by fire in 1826. After renovation it was used as a powder laboratory, armoury and barracks. Note the Fredrik V monogram over the doorway.

In the former prison building near the entrance is the military section, displaying artefacts and describing the history of military conflict in Halden from the 17th century to WWII. Perhaps the most interesting sites are the **brewery**, which once produced up to 3000L of beer a day, and the **bakery ovens**, which baked bread for up to 5000 soldiers. There's also a multimedia presentation and shop at the Infosenter, just inside the main entrance of the fortress.

Guided tours in Norwegian or English are given daily at noon, 1.30pm and 3pm (only at noon and 1.30pm on Sunday in September) between 20 June and 20 August. Note that the high bastions are unfenced and not particularly safe for children.

Fredrikshald Teater
The baroque Fredrikshald Theatre, just off Oscars gate, was designed by Balthazar Nicolai Garben, completed in 1838 and restored in 1982, but it's only open to the public during plays and concerts. The Halden Historiske Samlinger (☎ 60 18 54 11) has information on upcoming theatre productions and concerts.

Rød Herregård
Rød Herregård manor (☎ 69 18 54 11, *Herregårdsveien; tours adult/child Nkr40/10; open for tours noon, 1pm & 2pm Tue-Sun, also 3pm Sun, 26 June-19 Aug, noon, 1pm & 2pm Sun 6 May-24 June & 26 Aug-30 Sept)*, dating from 1733, has fine interiors, notable collections of both weapons and art, and one of the best gardens in Norway. It's 1.5km west of the town centre and is well-signposted.

Activities
A relaxing but adventurous way to explore Haldenkanelen (the Halden Canal) and other waterways in the border area is on your own by canoe. Canoe hire is available from Kirkeng Camping (☎ 69 19 92 98), 5km north-east of town in Aremark. You can pick up a boating and recreation map from the tourist office in Halden. For information on canal travel in larger private boats, contact Båt & Motor a/s (☎ 69 17 58 59) at Jernbanebrygga in Halden.

Organised Tours
East and north of Halden, a canal system connects the town with Göteborg, Sweden, but there's a short dry section (1.8km). The highlight is the Brekke Locks, a system of four locks between Femsjøen and Aspern (on the Halden-Strømsfoss run) which raise and lower the boats a total of 26.6m. The region is popular with canoeists and boat owners, but visitors can get a quick taste on the tourist cruise boat M/S *Turisten* (☎ 90 99 81 11), which follows the Haldenkanalen between Tistedal (east of Halden) and Strømsfoss (one-way/return Nkr200/250, 3½ hours) on Wednesday and Friday to Sunday; and, between Strømsfoss and Ørje (Nkr150/200, two hours) on Thursday in July. To reach Tistedal, take bus No 103 or 106 (Nkr27, 18 minutes, twice hourly except late Saturday afternoon and Sunday).

On the Thursday trip, you can visit the Haldenvassdragets Kanalmuseum (Halden Waterways Canal Museum; ☎ 69 81 10 21, Ørje; adult/child Nkr40/15; open 10am-5pm Tues-Sun), beside the canal.

OSLO

Places to Stay

Fredriksten Camping (☎ *69 18 40 32, fax 69 18 75 73, Fredriksten Festning)* Tent & car sites Nkr110, 4-person cabins Nkr275-300. This convenient camping ground located in the fortress grounds offers a quiet green spot to pitch a tent.

Halden Vandrerhjem (☎ *69 21 69 68, fax 69 21 66 03, Brødløs)* Dorm beds Nkr100, singles/doubles Nkr135/255. Open 25 June-8 Aug. The hostel, at the suburban Tosterød school, offers standard rooms in ordinary modern buildings. Take bus Nos 102-104 from Busterud Park (marked Gimle).

Grand Hotel (☎ *69 18 72 00, fax 69 18 79 59, Jernbanetorget 1)* Singles/doubles Nkr490/690 July & weekends. The Grand Hotel, opposite the train station, has rooms with modern en suite facilities, TV and minibar.

Park Hotel (☎ *69 21 15 00, fax 69 21 15 01, Marcus Thranes gate 30)* Singles/doubles from Nkr640/790. The Park Hotel, 1km from the centre, has fairly luxurious rooms with cut-price rates in July and at weekends.

Places to Eat

Around Gjesthavn (Guest Harbour), you'll find several pleasant restaurants with outdoor seating.

Pub Royal (☎ *69 18 00 80, Olav V's gata 1)* Pizzas from Nkr65. This local favourite is near the waterfront, with steaks, pizza and a la carte pasta and chicken dishes.

Dickens (☎ *69 18 35 33, Storgata 9)* Main dishes from Nkr100. Dickens does standard lunches and dinners. You can choose between outdoor seating or the dining room in a 17th-century cellar.

Butts Bistro (☎ *69 17 20 12, Tollbugata 3)* Mains Nkr59-300 (most under Nkr150). The unfortunately named Butts Bistro, behind the tourist office, serves reasonable Indian-style cuisine.

Dragon House (☎ *69 18 44 67, Borgergata 3)* Mains from Nkr70. Dragon House serves a wide range of acceptable Chinese dishes.

Lunsjbaren (☎ *69 17 60 95, Torget)* Sandwiches from Nkr25, snacks & burgers from Nkr48. At Lunsjbaren, you'll get decent sandwiches, ice cream, burgers, lasagne and chips.

Enjoy an ice cream (from Nkr13), coffee or waffles on board the moored boat ***Sjøbris*** *(Kongens Brygge)*.

Entertainment

Siste Reis Pub (☎ *69 17 61 45, Jernbanetorget 1)* At this pub, in the Grand Hotel building, beer costs only Nkr29 for 500mL (before 11pm).

Hannestadgården (☎ *69 19 77 81, Tollbugata 5)* Cover charge Nkr50 after 11pm. Open to 3am weekends. According to locals, the best night spot is this disco, nightclub, and piano bar; there's also a good restaurant here. Cover charges are higher during concerts.

Getting There & Away

Trains run every one or two hours between Oslo and Halden (Nkr175, 1¾ hours), and an average of four daily trains continue on to Göteborg and Malmö, Sweden. The long-distance bus terminal sits right at the harbour.

The ferry M/S Sagasund (☎ 90 99 81 11) connects Halden with Strömstad (Sweden). From mid-May to mid-August it operates on Wednesday, Friday and Saturday; at other times of year it only sails on Wednesday and Saturday (except January and February, when it doesn't sail at all). The one-way/return fare is Nkr100/150; staff are quick to point out that duty-free goods are available on board.

Southern Norway

When the weather turns warm, the rocky, island-studded south coast of Sørlandet, with its many bays and coves, becomes a paradisiacal magnet for Norwegian boaters and holiday-makers. The 586km-long Sørland rail line connecting Stavanger and Oslo (via Kristiansand) keeps mainly inland but buses frequently meet the trains and link the rail line with most south coastal towns. The main highway, the E18/39, runs inland between Stavanger and Mandal but from there to Oslo it follows a winding route through many lovely coastal towns and villages.

The Coast

TØNSBERG
pop 26,620

In the *Saga of Harald Hårfagre*, Snorre Sturluson mentions that the town of Tønsberg existed prior to the Battle of Hafsfjord, which took place in 872. Because of this, as well as the excavation of the medieval St Olav's monastery and the fact that the *Gokstad* and *Oseberg* ships (now in the Viking Ship Museum in Oslo) were discovered nearby, Tønsberg claims to be the oldest town in Norway, and celebrated its 1100-year anniversary in 1971. The name, meaning 'farm hill', probably refers to the farm Haugar (now in the centre of town). At Haugar, there are the graves of King Olav of Vestfold and King Sigrød of Trøndelag, both of whom fell in the Battle of Haugar against their brother, Erik Blodøks.

When King Harald Hårfagre divided the kingdom in the 9th century, he appointed his son, Bjørn Farmann, to rule over Vestfold, and the court of Sæheimr, at Tønsberg, became the royal seat. In the late medieval period it served as one of three Hanseatic trading posts in Norway, with ties to Rostock in northern Germany. By the 17th century the town had developed into a major shipping and commercial centre, dominated by the timber trade with Dutch

Highlights

- Touring the royal silver mines outside the pleasant town of Kongsberg
- Strolling through the narrow streets of the 'white towns' of Risør, Grimstad and Mandal
- Camping, cycling and exploring the beaches and offshore islands of Norway's sunshine coast along the Skagerrak
- Taking a leisurely cruise through the scenic Telemark canal system
- Marvelling at the exquisite roof lines and paintings in the stave church at Heddal
- Scouring the surface of Seljordvatn in search of the monster

Central Norway

Bergen & S-W Fjords

Rjukan pp194-5

Kongsberg p188

Oslo

SWEDEN

Kristiansand p179

and English merchants and by 1850 it had the largest merchant fleet in Norway.

In the mid-19th century, Svend Foyn, the 'father' of Norwegian sealing and whaling, turned Tønsberg into a base of operations and source of expertise for whalers in the Arctic and Antarctic waters. This led to the invention of the exploding harpoon at

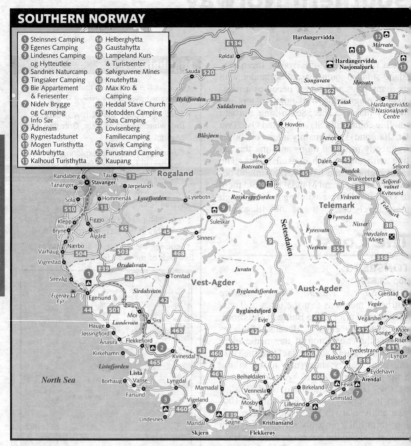

SOUTHERN NORWAY

1 Steinsnes Camping
2 Egenes Camping
3 Lindesnes Camping og Hytteutleie
4 Sandnes Naturcamp
5 Tingsaker Camping
6 Bie Appartement & Feriesenter
7 Nidelv Brygge og Camping
8 Info Sør
9 Ådneram
10 Rygnestadtunet
11 Mogen Turisthytta
12 Mårbuhytta
13 Kalhoud Turisthytta
14 Helberghytta
15 Gaustahytta
16 Lampeland Kurs- & Turistsenter
17 Sølvgruvene Mines
18 Knutehytta
19 Max Kro & Camping
20 Heddal Stave Church
21 Notodden Camping
22 Støa Camping
23 Lovisenberg Familiecamping
24 Vasvik Camping
25 Furustrand Camping
26 Kaupang

Tønsberg's Henriksen Mechanical Works, which changed the stakes in modern whaling. Cheesemaking at the Jarlsberg Estate (formerly Sæheimir) began in 1860 and now Jarlsberg cheese is internationally renowned. The world's first bulk oil tanker was built in Tønsberg in 1878, and, to round off the list, in 1953 Arne Gravdahl furthered the cause of feminine hygiene by inventing the sanitary pad.

In spite of its ample history, modern Tønsberg may not be as exciting as one would expect, as the Jarlsberg Estate is privately owned and not open to the public.

You can easily cover the main sites in a couple of hours.

Information

Tønsberg Turistkonteret (☎ 33 35 02 00, fax 33 35 02 01, e info@tonsberghorisont.no, w www.visittonsberg.com), on the Tønsberg Brygge waterfront, has done an amazing job on its tourist publication detailing the town's history and attractions. The office is open 8.30am to 6.30pm Monday to Saturday mid-June to mid-August; in July the hours are 10am to 8pm daily. The rest of the year it's open 8.30am to 3.30pm weekdays.

you can still see the 700m-long outer wall and poke around the remaining medieval stone foundations, which include King Magnus Lagabøte's Keep, the 1191 Church of St Michael, the hall of King Håkon Håkonsson and various guard towers. The park is always open.

Ruins

Several other interesting ruins are scattered around the town and can be seen on a short walking tour. At Haugar, by the art museum, you'll see the **Viking-age grave mounds** of kings Olav and Sigrød. In the park off Kongsgaten lie the ruins of **Kongs-gården**, the old Royal Court of King Håkon Håkonsson where the kings of Vestfold were elected. From 1987 to 1991, excavations at Storgaten 17 revealed the ruins of the medieval **Church of St Olav**, the largest round church in Scandinavia (possibly based on the round church in Jerusalem), as well as St Olav's monastery and several Viking-age graves.

Historic Buildings

Tønsberg has several interesting old buildings. The most noteworthy include timber homes in **Nordbyen**, and the **Britannia House** (on the waterfront at Tønsberg Brygge, now housing Peppe's Pizza), a 1700 timber building with a Louis XVI facade. Also, take a look at Svend Foyn's 'arbeiderboliger', a self-contained block of 73 flats built by the whaling magnate for his workers.

Castrum Tunsbergis

The 13th-century ruins of Castrum Tunsbergis (☎ 33 31 18 72; admission to ruins park free, tower adult/child Nkr10/5; tower open 11am-6pm daily late June–mid-Aug, shorter hours other times mid-May–mid-Sept) spread across the 63m-high hill behind the town, culminates in the modern, 17m-high Slottsfjellstårnet tower, built in 1888, which provides a good viewpoint. In front of the tower there's a bronze model of how the castle looked in 1500. Little remains of the castle itself, which was destroyed by the Swedes in 1503. However,

Vestfold Fylkesmuseum

The Vestfold County Museum (☎ 33 31 29 19, Formannsveien 30; adult/child Nkr30/5; open 10am-5pm Mon-Sat, noon-5pm Sun mid-May–mid-Sept) is along Grev Wedels gate at the foot of Slottsfjellet (Castle Rock). It presents a large exhibit of model ships, displays on the excavation of the Oseberg Viking ship, a host of medieval artefacts from the local district, a collection of historic period-furnished farm buildings, and a section on Tønsberg's whaling history, including skeletons of both a sperm whale and a blue whale. The latter, at 23m long, is the largest whale skeleton on display in the world.

Organised Tours
In July the historic ship D/S *Kysten I* (☎ 33 31 25 89), built in Trondheim in 1909 and one of the oldest steamships in Norway, operates 3½-hour cruises through the skerries south of Tønsberg. Cruises depart from Honnørbryggen at noon daily and cost Nkr120 (Nkr100 for kids and seniors). Tickets are sold on board.

Ask the tourist office for details of tours to Færder lighthouse.

Places to Stay
Furustrand Camping (☎ 33 32 44 03, fax 33 32 74 03, Tolvsrød) Tent sites Nkr60 plus Nkr30/20 per car/person, cabins Nkr420-950. Campers should head for this beach-front camping ground, 5.5km east of the centre, which has acceptable facilities. Take bus No 111 or 116 to Tolvsrød (Nkr18).

Tønsberg Vandrerhjem (☎ 33 31 21 75, fax 33 31 21 76, e tonsvand@online.no, Dronning Blancasgata 22) Dorm beds Nkr170-195, singles/doubles from Nkr290/395, breakfast included. The well-equipped, clean and tidy hostel is just a five-minute walk from the train station.

Rainbow Hotel Brygga (☎ 33 34 49 00, fax 33 34 49 01, Nedre Langgate 40) Singles Nkr520-1045, doubles Nkr740-1245. This modern hotel offers fine accommodation and excellent breakfasts.

Hotell Maritim (☎ 33 31 71 00, fax 33 31 72 52, Storgaten 17) Singles/doubles from Nkr600/800. Hotell Maritim, beside the Church of St Olav ruins, is a flash place with high standards.

If you prefer to stay in the skerries, south of town, contact the tourist office for a listing of holiday huts, cabins, cottages, guesthouses and private rooms.

Places to Eat
For its size, Tønsberg has an unusually large number of restaurants.

Himmel & Hav (☎ 33 00 49 80, Tønsberg Brygge) Buffet Nkr290, mains Nkr108-267. Himmel & Hav is recommended for its excellent fish and meat buffet, available from 6pm daily in summer. There's also a cheaper lunch-time version or you can order a main course from the a la carte selection.

Brygga (☎ 33 31 12 70, Nedre Langgate 35) Mains Nkr159-179. More upmarket than Himmel & Hav is the rustic Brygga, which has an outdoor terrace and a fine menu with a good range of choices. There's also a reasonable pub here.

Esmeralda (☎ 33 31 91 91, Nedre Langgate 26C) Salads Nkr78-98. Esmeralda serves good-value light meals on the terrace.

Peppe's Pizza (☎ 33 31 70 71, Nedre Langgate 26B) Pizzas from Nkr130. Friendly Peppe's does its usual pizza thing in an excellent old house dating from 1700.

Kong Sverre Pizza (☎ 33 31 29 03, Storgaten 24) Lunch buffet Nkr69 Mon-Fri. The great-value pizza buffet here includes 0.5L of soft drink.

Getting There & Away
The Tønsberg Rutebilstasjon (☎ 33 30 01 00) is on Jernbanegaten, a block south of the train station. Nor-Way Bussekspress buses run once or twice daily (except Saturday) between Tønsberg and Kristiansand (Nkr300, five hours), via most coastal towns en route. For an interesting excursion, head out to Verdens Ende (Nkr38, 45 minutes) on bus No 101 and see the nautically charming 1932 copy of a low-tech 17th-century fire basket 'lighthouse'.

Intercity trains run hourly between Tønsberg station (☎ 81 50 08 88) and Oslo (Nkr150, 1½ hours).

Getting Around
City buses cost Nkr18 per ride.

LARVIK
pop 21,159
When the sun shines, the pleasant little town of Larvik is an inviting place for travellers to stop for a day or so and explore the surrounding holiday areas.

Larvik's favourite son is Thor Heyerdahl, the quirky scientist and explorer who masterminded the *Ra*, *Ra II* and *Kon-Tiki* expeditions. These voyages were made to demonstrate that the Americas and the South Pacific may well have been settled by migrants from the Middle East rather than Asia, as is conventionally believed. On the occasion of Heyerdahl's 75th birthday in 1989, a statue in his honour was unveiled at Tollerodden, east of the town's harbour. It's sculpted in blue larvikite, a beautiful 50 million-year-old type of granite which is quarried locally. Tollerodden also bears a monument to Colin Archer, who built the polar ship *Fram*.

Oddly enough, Heyerdahl's *Ra* isn't Larvik's only renowned Ra. The other is the great Ice-Age Ra moraine which dammed Farris Lake and created the Farris Well; it slips into the sea at Mølen, at the southwestern corner of the Brunlanes Peninsula (for more about moraines, see the boxed text 'Glacier & Ice Glossary' in the Facts about Norway chapter).

Ask the tourist office if tours of the Farris Well have restarted; legend has it that this mineral source was used by King Olav in medieval times but it's now the source for Farris-brand mineral water. The tourist office can also advise about the archaeological dig at the long-abandoned Viking town of Kaupang, 5km east of Larvik, where you may be able to watch work in progress. Plans for a museum are also being mooted.

Information

You'll find Larvik town and kommune information at the helpful Larvik Turistkontor (☎ 33 13 91 00, fax 33 13 91 11, W www .visitlarvik.no), Storgata 48, opposite the ferry dock. It's open 8am to 6pm Monday to Saturday and 1pm to 5pm Sunday from 22 June to 1 August, with shorter hours the rest of the year. Internet access is available for Nkr20 per 15 minutes.

A coin-operated laundry is available at the Guest Harbour.

Larvik Museum

The three-part Larvik Museum (☎ 33 13 04 04; adult/child combined ticket Nkr40/10) includes the Herregården (the main building), as well as the Larvik Maritime Museum, immediately east of the harbour, and the Fritzøe Museum.

The **Herregården manor house** (Herregårdsletta 6; open for tours only noon & 1pm Wed-Sun (also 4pm & 5pm Thur) 24 June-12 Aug; noon & 1pm Sun 10-23 June & 13 Aug-16 Sept) was constructed from 1674 to 1677 as the home of the Norwegian Governor General, Ulrik Frederik Gyldenløve, who also served as the Duke of Larvik. As the illegitimate son of King Fredrik IV of Denmark, Gyldenløve was given a dukedom and an estate and sent off to Norway where he wouldn't cause any problems. In the 19th century, this classic baroque timber structure served in turn as a town theatre, a vicarage, the town hall and a school. It's currently furnished in the 17th- and 18th-century mode. Over the road you can see the inscriptions commemorating royal visits from King Fredrik V of Denmark to King Olav V.

The **Larvik Maritime Museum** (Kirkestredet 5; open 4pm-8pm Tues, noon-4pm Wed-Sun 24 June-31 Aug; noon-4pm Sun 8 May-23 June & 1-16 Sept), housed in a 1730 brick structure, also served as a vicarage and was later used as a Custom House. The main attractions include a collection of maritime art and artefacts, and a number of model ships. There's also an exhibition on the nearby Viking town of Kaupang.

The **Fritzøe Museum** has a collection of tools and implements used in the 17th-century sawmill and ironworks that operated here from 1670 to 1870. At the time of writing, the museum was closed pending relocation, but ask the tourist office regarding reopening.

Bøkeskogen

The 300-hectare Bøkeskogen (Beech Woods) north of the town centre form a pleasant green belt for strolling and they contain 80 ancient and Viking-era grave mounds. The highest point affords a fine view over the forest as well as the lake Farrisvatn. There's a variety of hiking trails in the area north of the graves.

Larvik Kirke

Larvik's Trinity Church (☎ 33 17 30 00, Kirkestredet; admission free; open 11am-1pm & 6pm-8pm Mon-Fri 25 June-10 Aug) was commissioned in 1677 by Duke Gyldenløve for his wedding and was completed in 1763 with the addition of the tower. Note the elegant baptismal font, and Lucas Cranagh's excellent altarpiece painting, *Suffer the Little Children to Come Unto Me*, that was probably commissioned by Duke Gyldenløve. The monument outside, by Arne Vigeland, commemorates Norwegians who died in WWII.

Places to Stay

The tourist office keeps a comprehensive list of accommodation options, including private rooms, cabins and guesthouses.

Hovlandbanen Camping (☎ 33 11 44 22, Hovland) Tent/caravan sites Nkr100/150, cabins Nkr200-220, electricity per person Nkr20. Open June-Sept. Campers are in luck as this camping ground next to a race track lies within easy walking distance of the centre.

Vasvik Camping (☎ 33 18 16 09, Vasvik) Tent sites for 2 without/with car Nkr80/100, caravan sites Nkr125-150, cabins Nkr300-500. The pleasantly located Vasvik Camping is beside the lake Farrisvatn. There aren't any buses currently and it's a 40-minute walk from the town centre.

Lysko Gjestegaard (☎ 33 18 77 79, fax 33 13 03 30, Kirkestredet 10) Singles/doubles with bath from Nkr500/600. This atmospheric guesthouse, opposite the Maritime Museum, has self-catering facilities. Prices don't include breakfast.

Gyldenløve Hotel (☎ 33 18 25 26, fax 33 18 79 70, Storgata 26) Singles/doubles with bath Nkr600/750. Given its charm, this renovated 1903 hotel offers fairly good summer value. There's a piano bar and a bistro on the premises.

Places to Eat

Ferdinands Lillekjøkken (☎ 33 13 05 44, Storgata 32) Nkr128-239. You'll find steak and seafood dinners nightly at this fine, fully licensed restaurant.

Restaurant Hansemann (☎ 33 14 00 01, Kongegata 33) Specials from Nkr89, mains Nkr149-239. Restaurant Hansemann offers decent meals including meat and fish, and caters to a range of budgets.

Café Lilletorget (☎ 33 14 00 01, Kongegata 33) and **PPP** (same address & phone), adjoining Restaurant Hansemann, offer good-value main courses (Nkr72 to Nkr92), plus a range of pizzas, pasta dishes and pancakes.

Jeppe's (☎ 33 18 08 08, Storgata 24) Pizza & Mexican buffet Nkr98, 6pm-9pm Wed, Fri & Sun. Nearer the centre than Café Lilletorget and PPP, Jeppe's offers a rather more exciting buffet.

Larvik Pizza (☎ 33 18 53 10, Oscarsgata 4) Pizza buffet including soft drink Nkr69, Mon & Thur. You'll get good pizza here, from Nkr65 on the a la carte menu.

Bøkekroa restaurant (☎ 33 18 10 53, Bøkeskogen park) On Friday from 6.30pm to 10pm, there are jazz concerts here; on Sunday morning breakfast is served, accompanied by choir music.

For breakfast, you're limited to the hotels or the **Jensens Conditori** (Kongegata 23) bakery, just uphill from Øvre Torggata. Supplies of strong beer, wine and liquor can be obtained from **Vinmonopolet** (Nansetgata 36/38).

Getting There & Away

The train and bus stations are side by side on Storgata. NSB buses (☎ 33 19 29 40) between Larvik and Kongsberg (Nkr134, 2¼ hours) run three times daily (once on Saturday and Sunday). Local trains run up to 20 times daily between Oslo S (Central Station) and Larvik (Nkr210, two hours). Some of these trains continue from Larvik to Skien (Nkr50, 45 minutes), where there are a few daily connections to Nordagutu on the Oslo-Stavanger rail line.

Color Line (☎ 33 12 28 10) operates ferries to Fredrikshavn in Denmark (see the introductory Getting There & Away chapter).

Getting Around

The Vestfold region is fabulous for cycling and bike trails have been meticulously laid out from one end of the county to the other. The tourist office hires bicycles for Nkr100/525 per day/week and sells the indispensable three-part map *Sykkelkart Vestfold* for Nkr90.

AROUND LARVIK

Most visitors to the Larvik area head straight for the Brunlanes Peninsula, which is a major holiday venue with lots of coastal camping grounds that are chock-a-block with permanently moored caravans. Some people, however, charge off up the Numendalslågen for a spot of salmon fishing at Holmfoss or Brufoss, or to the lakes and woods for a quieter escape.

Stavern

The appealing little coastal town of Stavern, just a stone's throw south of Larvik, makes a nice stop to stroll around the mid-18th-century fort, **Fredriksvern Verft**, and visit the exceptionally colourful 1756 **church** (☎ 33 19 99 75, Kommandør Herbsgata 1; admission free; open 11am-1pm Tues-Fri), which was Norway's first naval house of worship.

Stavern is also the start of the popular 33km-long Kyststien coastal walk to Ødegården on the western coast of Brunlanes. From mid-June to mid-August, the Stavern Turistkontor (☎ 33 19 73 00, Havnegata 3) provides free route maps entitled Kyststien i Larvik.

Fredtun Folkehøyskole (☎ 33 19 99 55, fax 33 19 75 15, Route 301) Singles/doubles Nkr265/450. This good mid-range accommodation option is 1km south of town.

Hotel Wassilioff (☎ 33 11 36 00, fax 33 11 36 01, Havnegata 1) Singles/doubles from Nkr720/890. Well-heeled Hotel Wassilioff, on the waterfront, charges Nkr200 extra for sea views.

To get to and from Larvik (Nkr20, 15 minutes, once or twice hourly), use bus No 1.

Helgeroa

The popular and pleasant seaside village of Helgeroa offers little except for some marginal beaches and a sunset view of the sea. Still, in summer it's packed to overflowing with holiday-makers who bet on the odds of fine weather and come looking for a dose of sunshine. There are several camping grounds in the area, but they tend to be hopelessly overcrowded from mid-June to mid-August.

Helgeroa Hotel (☎ 33 18 93 00, fax 33 18 83 50, Krabbegata) Singles/doubles Nkr700/

850. Helgeroa Hotel has fine modern facilities, including a swimming pool.

Vertshuset Syd-Vesten (☎ 33 18 86 50, Helgeroa harbour) Pizzas Nkr150-200, fish specialities from Nkr170. This friendly restaurant serves superb pizzas and fish.

Kristinus Bergman (☎ 33 18 85 33) Starters & mains Nkr58-215. If money is no object, visit the elegant Kristinus Bergman restaurant, which offers steak, seafood and chicken dishes.

You can reach Helgeroa from Larvik (Nkr30, 20 to 40 minutes), via Stavern, on bus No 1, or directly from Larvik on bus No 3.

Mølen

The Mølen Promontory, the end of the Ra moraine which extends from the lake Farrisvatn to the south-western end of Brunlanes, is the only place in this area that experiences big ocean-style waves (and there are postcards to prove it). Most of the time, however, the sea is as flat as a millpond. The 230 stone cairns and heaps of boulders, which are laid out in parallel rows, are Iron Age burial mounds. The larger ones – particularly those in the shape of boats – probably honoured nobles, while the nondescript heaps were for those of lower standing. It makes a nice day walk from Helgeroa, about 4km away along the Kyststien coastal walk.

Damvann

When you've had enough of the coast, head north to beautiful, haunting Damvann, a classic 'lake in the woods' and the home of a legendary witch, Huldra. It's said that any man who looked upon her exquisite beauty was doomed. On Sunday in July, a modern-day version of Huldra (Ellen Dalen, ☎ 33 11 25 17) serves meals here from noon to 4pm (for groups, by arrangement). Access is difficult without a car – the nearest bus stop is at Kvelde (about 6km from the lake), 20km north of Larvik on the Numendalslågen road.

KRAGERØ
pop 5458

The popular seaside resort of Kragerø, with its narrow streets and whitewashed houses, has been a market town since 1666 and has

SOUTHERN NORWAY

long served as a retreat for Norwegian artists. In fact, Edvard Munch spent a few restorative fishing holidays here and (apparently a better painter than author) he wrote 'Many a sleepless night my thoughts and dreams go to Kragerø... Above blasts the wind from the sea, behind are the fragrant pines, and beyond, the waves breaking over the skerries. My regards to Kragerø, the pearl of the coastal towns.' (A statue of Munch has recently been unveiled in the spot where he painted a winter sun over the sea.)

In the early 20th century, Kragerø began attracting Norwegian holiday-makers and today the district boasts around 4000 summer cottages. For a great view over the town and its skerries, climb from Kragerø Stadium to the lookout point on Steinmann Hill.

Information
The exceptionally helpful Kragerø Turistkontor (☎ 35 98 23 88, fax 35 98 31 77), Torggata 1, is the place to go for all you need to know about Kragerø and surrounds. It's open 9am to 8pm weekdays, 9am to 6pm Saturday and 11am to 6pm Sunday mid-June to mid-August (shorter hours at other times of year).

Berg-Kragerø Museum
The Berg-Kragerø Museum (☎ 35 98 14 53, Lovisenbergveien 45; adult/child Nkr40; open noon-6pm daily 9 June–mid-Aug) on the southern shore of Hellefjord, 3km from the centre, occupies a 120-hectare estate with an 1803 country residence, gardens, walking tracks, a cafe and a gallery for visiting art and history exhibits.

Jomfruland
If you're in Kragerø, chances are you're headed for the offshore island of Jomfruland, which is the most popular destination hereabouts. The island measures about 10km long and up to 600m wide and is covered largely in forest and encircled by mostly sandy beaches. The landmark old (1869) and new (1937) lighthouses (☎ 35 99 11 79; adult/child Nkr20/10; open noon-4pm Mon-Sat, noon-6pm Sun mid-June–mid-Aug) can be visited.

Jomfruland Camping (☎ 35 99 12 75, Åsvik brygge) Tent sites per person from Nkr70, caravan sites with electricity Nkr150, 4-bed cabins Nr400. The atmospheric Jomfruland Camping is near the Åsvik brygge ferry terminal.

In summer, ferries between Kragerø and Jomfruland (Nkr29, 50 minutes) are run by Kragerø Fjordbåtselskap (☎ 35 98 58 58) two or three times daily.

Activities
For something totally different, how about a rail-bicycle ride along the 13km railway between Sannidal and Merkebekk. Railbikes (bicycles on bogies, called dressin in Norwegian) rent for Nkr50/200 per hour/day. Book through Støa Camping (see Places to Stay).

Places to Stay
Kragerø Vandrerhjem (☎ 35 98 57 00, fax 35 98 57 01, Lovisenbergveien 20) Dorm beds Nkr210, singles/doubles Nkr365/420. Open 18 June-22 Aug. This fine HI hostel, about 2km from town, includes breakfast. It also serves dinner for Nkr95.

Lovisenberg Familiecamping (☎ 35 98 87 77, fax 35 98 85 27, Lovisenbergveien) Tent & caravan sites from Nkr100 plus Nkr20/person, 4-bed cabins from Nkr650. Open May-Aug. If you don't mind a 5.5km walk each way (there's no bus service yet), you can camp here. Without a vehicle you'd probably do better elsewhere.

Støa Camping (☎ 35 99 02 61, Sannidal) Tent sites with car Nkr100, basic cabins Nkr200-350. Readily accessible, Støa Camping has acceptable standards. Take bus No 607 (Nkr23, 12 minutes).

Victoria Hotel (☎ 35 98 75 25, fax 35 98 29 26, PA Heuchtsgata 31) Singles/doubles Nkr780/1000. Rooms at the attractive Victoria Hotel are particularly well appointed.

Places to Eat
Stim (☎ 35 98 30 00, Storgata 1) 2-course meal Nkr350. Stim is a new and highly recommended fish and fowl restaurant, with a contemporary international menu and fresh local produce.

El Paso Western Saloon (☎ 35 98 15 32, PA Heuchtsgata 31) Lunches Nkr75, mains Nkr89-239. This rather disoriented 'saloon', combining the Norwegian seaside with the badlands of West Texas, is the tourist's choice for steaks, burgers, pizza, attempts at Mexican fare and other non-seafood dishes.

Amadeus Musikk Kafé (☎ 35 98 15 32, PA Heuchtsgata 31) Mains around Nkr100. This cafe, adjoining El Paso, is a long way from Salzburg but it's not bad on a weekend evening, when live performances are staged.

Kafe Edvard (☎ 35 98 15 50, Edvard Munchsvei 2) Lunch specials from Nkr70. You'll find simple Norwegian fare here.

Restaurant Admiralen (☎ 35 98 31 11, Ytre Strandvei 24) Mains Nkr98-149, takeaways from Nkr75. The prominent Admiralen serves reasonable Norwegian and Chinese specialities.

Getting There & Away

Drivers should prepare for headaches in this town of narrow streets, tangled tourist traffic and few parking places. The simplest approach is by rail from Oslo or Kristiansand to Neslandsvatn, where most trains are met by a connecting Drangedal Bilruter bus (☎ 35 99 81 00) to Kragerø. Nor-Way Bussekspress runs two to five buses daily to Oslo from Tangen, by the E18 (Nkr275, 3½ hours), where there are connecting buses to/from Kragerø.

RISØR

pop 4000

Risør, the 'White Town on the Skagerrak', is defined by a cluster of historic white houses (dating from 1650 to 1890) arranged around a busy inner harbour, Indrehavn, which is cluttered with colourful fishing boats and private yachts. In 1861, two thirds of the town burned down.

The fact that it's one of the south coast's most picturesque villages hasn't been lost on Norwegian tourists, and it's also a haunt for artists who make it their summer hangout. You can see what sort of inspiration it has provided at the Risør Kunstpark gallery, at the museum on Prestegata.

Information

Risør's tourist office (☎ 37 15 22 70), at Villvin on Kragsgata, is open 10am to 6pm weekdays, 10am to 4pm Saturday and noon to 6pm Sunday, from 15 June to 5 August. There's also the larger Info Sør complex (☎ 37 11 90 00, fax 37 11 90 01, **W** www.in fosor.no), on the E18 near the Telemark boundary.

Risør Saltvannsakvariet

The interesting Risør Saltwater Aquarium (☎ 37 15 32 82, Dampskipsbrygga; adult/child Nkr40/20; open 11am-7pm daily 25 June-5 Aug, noon-4pm daily 11 June-24 June & 6 Aug-19 Aug, noon-4pm Sat & Sun 20 Aug-10 June), on the quay in front of the Risør Hotel, houses examples of saltwater fish, crustaceans and shellfish common to Norway's south coast. Highlights of the aquarium include baby lobsters and the colourful cuckoo wrasse.

Risør Museum

For the lowdown on the geology, fishing economy and 275-year history of Risør, check out the Risør Museum (☎ 37 15 17 77, Prestegata 9; adult/family Nkr30/50; open 11am-5pm daily mid-June–mid-Aug). Ask for a loan of the explanatory booklet in English.

The museum also includes the WWII **fortification and memorial** (admission Nkr20; open by appointment) at the Urheia viewpoint, north of the centre.

The Skerries

In addition to wandering around the harbour area soaking up the rustic charm, visitors also like to explore the offshore skerries, which are accessed by scheduled ferries and inexpensive water taxis.

The most frequented island, **Stangholmen**, sports the requisite lighthouse; this one dates from 1855 and also contains the pricey *Stangholmen Fyr restaurant and bar* (☎ 37 15 24 50), serving main courses from around Nkr200.

In summer, ferries (☎ 37 15 24 50) leave Tollbubrygga twice hourly from 10am to at least midnight and cost Nkr30 return.

SOUTHERN NORWAY

Inland

Vegårshei, Åmli and Gjerstad are touted by the tourist office as pleasant and relaxing places with lots of rural activities; contact Info Sør for details. These forested areas are most popular with the huntin', shootin' and fishin' brigade.

Special Events

Over one weekend in early August, Risør hosts the Risør International Wooden Boat Festival, that attracts old salts and other boat people from all over Norway. In early September in even-numbered years (2002, 2004 etc) you can catch Risør's annual Shantyfestival, which features three days of – you guessed it – sea shanties. It's unique and people really do get into this sort of thing. For specific dates, contact Info Sør (☎ 37 11 90 00, fax 37 11 90 01).

Places to Stay & Eat

The tourist office can arrange rooms, houses and cabins.

Moen Camping (☎ 92 23 74 75, fax 37 15 17 63, Moen) Tent sites with car/bike Nkr120/80, cabins Nkr400-500. This is the closest camping ground, 11km west of town, and 2km from the E18. Regular buses (Risør to/from Arendal, Kristiansand and Oslo) run past Moen Camping.

Risør Kunstforum (☎ 37 15 63 83, fax 37 15 55 44, Tjenngata 76) Singles/doubles Nkr400/500. Reasonable Risør Kunstforum, 1km west of the harbour, offers do-it-yourself breakfast as well as art and sculpture classes.

Risør Hotel (☎ 37 15 07 00, fax 37 15 20 93, Tangengata 16) Singles Nkr695-995, doubles Nkr995-1495. At the only in-town option, prices are rather steep, but you get a nice sea view.

Around the harbour and along Kragsgata, you'll find several moderately priced cafes and restaurants.

Big Horn/Excellensen (☎ 37 15 30 50, Torvet 1) Dinner & drinks Nkr350. This daytime cafe transforms into a steakhouse in the evening.

Brasserie Krag (☎ 37 15 04 50, Kragsgata 12) Mains Nkr98-186. This recom-

mended restaurant has a fairly diverse selection on the menu.

Ice-cream shops abound and you'll find inexpensive produce at the **harbourside market**. For coffee and sweet snacks from Nkr15, there's the **Stavelin** bakery on Kragsgata.

Getting There & Away

Local buses link Risør with the rail line at Gjerstad (Nkr51, 45 minutes) several times daily. Nor-Way Bussekspress buses between Kristiansand (Nkr140, three hours) and Oslo (Nkr320, 3¾ hours) connect at Vinterkjær with local buses to/from Risør (Nkr26, 20 minutes).

Motorists should note the Nkr15 tolls on the E18 west of Risør.

LYNGØR
pop 100

Tiny Lyngør, consisting of several offshore islets near the ready-made village of Gjeving, isn't shy about the fact that it won the 1991 European competition for the tidiest town on the continent. Even if it weren't for that distinction, this picturesque little settlement would be worth a visit – largely because visitors can't bring their vehicles across on the ferry. Many wealthy Norwegians have houses in Lyngør.

Places to Stay & Eat

Knatten Pensjonat (☎ 37 16 10 19, Odden) Singles/doubles Nkr500/700. If you want to soak up Lyngør's atmosphere after the daytrippers head back to the mainland, you can hole up at the only option on Lyngør, but it's pricey for what's on offer. It's located 300m from Holmen quay.

Norwegians, it seems, regard Lyngør as a place to spend a few hours for a meal.

Den Blå Lanterne (☎ 37 16 64 80, Holmen) Fish soup around Nkr300. The seriously wealthy can ostentatiously burn their cash in here.

Seilmakerfruens Kro (☎ 37 16 60 00, Ytre Lyngør) Pizzas around Nkr150. More reasonably priced than Den Blå Lanterne, Seilmakerfruens Kro dishes up pizza and a la carte specialities.

Getting There & Away

Ferry The Lyngør Båtselskap ferry (☎ 37 16 68 88 or ☎ 41 45 41 45) between Gjeving, Holmen and Lyngør leaves every one or two hours between 7.40am and 9.15pm on weekdays, 9.45am to 7pm on Saturday and 9.45am to 9.15pm on Sunday (Nkr25/10 per adult/child).

For details of the M/S *Patricia* ferry, see the following Arendal section.

Car & Motorcycle You can't drive to Lyngør but if you approach by car from the east, forsake the E18 and follow the slow but lovely coastal route, which winds narrowly over forested peninsulas and past idyllic coves and fishing settlements.

ARENDAL
pop 25,444

Arendal, the administrative centre of Aust-Agder county, climbs steeply up the hillsides that surround its harbour area, better known as Pollen. For swimming and other sorts of communion with the sea, head for the islands of Merdø (accessible by ferry), and Tromøy and Hisøy (both reached by bus and ferry).

Information

From mid-June to mid-August, the Arendal Turistkontor (☎ 37 00 55 44, fax 37 00 55 40), Langbrygga 5, dispenses friendly information. It's open 9am to 7pm Monday to Saturday and noon to 7pm on Sunday from mid-June to mid-August (otherwise 9am to 4pm on weekdays only).

For advice about laundry, ask the tourist office.

There's a week-long jazz and blues festival in late July; tickets cost around Nkr20. For details, contact the tourist office or visit the Internet at W www.canalstreet.no.

Tyholmen

A few minutes' walk south of the bus station brings you to the old harbourside Tyholmen district, with its 17th- to 19th-century timber buildings featuring neoclassical, rococo and baroque influences. In 1992 it was awarded the Europa Nostra prize for its expert restoration. Predictably, the district is also home to some skilled (and often nautically oriented) artists and craftspeople. Originally, Tyholmen was separated from the mainland by a canal which connected Pollen and Kittelsbukt (the industrial harbour west of the town centre), but it was filled in after the great sailing era. Currently, there are plans to restore the canal, so Tyholmen will again be an island.

You may want to check out the unusual **Rådhus** *(☎ 37 01 30 00, Rådhusgata 10; admission free; open 9am-3pm Mon-Fri)*, which is actually a shipowner's home dating from 1815, but became the town hall in 1844. The original star-spangled dome gave way to a flat ceiling and modern tastes in the late 19th century but the elegant original staircase remains. Upstairs hang portraits of 20th-century Norwegian royalty and former mayors of Arendal.

Aust-Agder Museum

Oddly enough, the Aust-Agder Museum *(☎ 37 07 35 00, Parkveien 16; adult/child Nkr20/10; open 9am-5pm Mon-Fri, noon-5pm Sun 25 June-13 Aug; closes 3pm rest of year)* was first conceived in 1832, when the town asked its globetrotting sailors to be on worldwide lookout for items which may be of interest back home. The results of this search are now housed in the county museum, along with relics of Arendal's shipbuilding, timber and import-export trades. There are also decent collections of folk art, furniture, farming implements and sailing paraphernalia.

Offshore Islands

The 260-hectare island of **Merdø** has been inhabited since the 16th century and bears the remnants of vegetable species introduced in the ballast of early sailing vessels. The **Merdøgård Museum** *(☎ 37 07 35 00, Merdø; adult/child Nkr20/10; open noon-4.30pm daily 25 June-12 Aug)*, housed in a historic 1736 sea captain's residence, is decked out in period furnishings. The admission fee includes hourly guided tours.

Ferry access to Merdø and Hove (on the island of **Tromøy**) is on the M/F *Merdø*

(☎ 37 02 64 23), which operates from the end of June to mid-August (Nkr25). You can also get to Merdø on the M/F *Trau* (☎ 37 08 56 09), which runs year-round.

On the islets of **Store** and **Lille Torungene** rise two grand lighthouses which have guided ships into Arendal since 1844. They're visible from the coasts of both Hisøy and Tromøy.

Popular beaches on **Hisøy** include Stølsvigen, Tangen and Vrageviga. But there's no bus access (the bus runs only as far as Sandvigen), so you'll need a car or bicycle to reach them. The favoured bathing sites are on Tromøy, Spornes and Hove. The nearest access to Spornes is on the bus marked Tromøy Vest/Øst but you'll still have to walk for 15 minutes. Alternatively, take a bike on the M/S *Skilsøy* ferry (☎ 37 00 55 44), which sails frequently between Arendal and the western end of Tromøy (Nkr15, six minutes – or Nkr35 after midnight on weekends). Kolbjørnsvik, on Hisøy, may be reached from Arendal (Nkr14, six minutes) on the frequent M/S *Kolbjørn III* (mobile ☎ 94 58 71 72), and Hove is accessed on the Merdø ferry (Nkr25).

Places to Stay
For anything inexpensive, you'll have to head out of town.

Nidelv Brygge og Camping (☎/fax 37 01 14 25, Vesterveien 251, Hisøy) Tent sites Nkr60 plus Nkr15/person, caravan sites Nkr100, cabins Nkr250-500. This place lies on the Nidelv River at Hisøy, 6km west of Arendal. From town, take any bus headed for Kristiansand or Grimstad; they run approximately every half-hour (Nkr22).

Arendal Hytteutleie (☎ 37 04 57 22, fax 37 04 57 26), Postboks 114, N-4889 Fevik, can arrange accommodation in a *private home* or *holiday cabin*; most places are rented only on a weekly basis but there are a few exceptions.

Ting Hai Hotel (☎ 37 02 22 01, fax 37 02 23 25, Østregate 5) Singles/doubles from Nkr580/780. The Ting Hai Hotel incorporates a Chinese restaurant.

Scandic Hotel (☎ 37 02 51 60, fax 37 02 67 07, Friergangen 1) Singles/doubles from

Nkr595/695. The modern Scandic Hotel rises from the Tyholmen historic district.

Clarion Tyholmen Hotel (☎ 37 02 68 00, fax 37 02 68 01, Teaterplassen 2) Singles/doubles summer Nkr695/760. If budget is not an issue, you'll get relatively posh accommodation and the nicest spot here, right on the water. The architecture attempts to emulate Tyholmen's historic theme.

Places to Eat
Pollen boasts several atmospheric open-air restaurants and cafes which double as evening drinking spots.

Sjøloftet (☎ 37 02 46 00, Langebryggen 3) Pizzas for 2 Nkr154-164. At the northern end of Langebryggen, Sjøloftet specialises in pizza.

Madam Reiersen (☎ 37 02 19 00, Nedre Tyholmsvei 3) Mains Nkr125-238. Madame Reiersen offers more sophisticated fare than Sjøloftet, with an emphasis on pasta dishes.

Ting Hai (☎ 37 02 22 01, Østregate 5) Takeaways & mains from around Nkr100. Open for lunch & dinner daily. Away from the shore, this is one of Norway's few recommended Chinese restaurants.

Café Det Lindvedske hus (☎ 37 02 18 38, Nedre Tyholmsvei 7b) Sandwiches, salads & pastas Nkr48-88. There's a good choice of food at this American-run cafe, with atmospheric 200-year-old decor.

If you just want a tasty snack, the waterfront *fish market* sells inexpensive fish cakes. There's a *McDonald's* on the nondescript Torvet (town square).

Café Sam (☎ 37 02 46 63, Havnegaten 8) Snacks from Nkr15. Café Sam, on Torvet, does the usual ice cream and snacks, but it also has an attached bakery.

Entertainment
Bars and discos in Arendal are open until 2am or 2.30am.

Fishermans Pub (☎ 37 02 88 70, Langbryggen 19) Open 8pm-2am daily. The Fisherman's Pub, appropriately on the harbourside, is recommended.

Club Papparazzi (☎ 37 02 40 45, Friergangen 4) There's dancing nightly here from Tuesday to Saturday.

Mammarazzi (☎ 37 02 72 02, Lang-bryggen 15) The comically named Mammarazzi is Arendal's main nightly disco-dancing haunt.

Rubens Danserestaurant (☎ 37 02 51 60, Friergangen 1) Open Fri & Sat. Try this venue for a laid-back experience.

Getting There & Away
The Nor-Way Bussekspress buses between Kristiansand (Nkr97, 1¾ hours) and Oslo (Nkr340, four hours) or Sarpsborg (Nkr360, 5½ hours) call in several times daily at the Arendal Rutebilstasjon, which is in a large square a block west of Pollen harbour. Local buses connect Arendal with Grimstad (Nkr36, 30 minutes, once or twice hourly) and Kristiansand (Nkr93, 1½ hours, hourly).

Arendal is connected with the main rail system by a trunk line from Nelaug, but the station (☎ 37 02 20 03) lies a 10-minute walk through the Fløyheia tunnel (the only vehicles using this tunnel are accessing Arendal's underground car park) from Torvet. If the tunnel still puts you off, you can climb over the hill along Hylleveien and Iuellsklev.

In summer, the Nordic Express sails from Arendal to Strömstad (foot passengers and bicycles only); ask the tourist office for details. M/S *Patricia* (☎ 37 08 55 78) sails from Arendal (Pollen) to Lyngør on Tuesday, Thursday and Sunday in July (Nkr150/250 single/return).

Getting Around
Town buses in Arendal charge Nkr18. Sykkelsport (☎ 37 02 39 60), on the corner of Nygaten and Vestre gate, rents bicycles for Nkr70 to Nkr100 per day. This is a great way to explore the islands and reach the bathing beaches on Hisøy and Tromøy.

GRIMSTAD
pop 8182
The white town of Grimstad is one of the loveliest on the Skagerrak coast and, what it lacks in surrounding scenery, it makes up for in the charm of its narrow pedestrianised centre. It's also renowned as the sunniest spot in Norway, with an average of 266 hours of sunshine per month in June and July.

However, Grimstad's current low-key atmosphere, peacefulness and charm belies its past importance for, between 1865 and 1885, Grimstad was one of the greatest – if not *the* greatest – shipbuilding centres in the world. The oak forests that grew on the hillsides were chopped down and sawn into timbers to supply the booming industry; at one point the town had 40 shipyards, and 90 ships were under construction simultaneously.

During the same period, a land shortage caused many local farmers to turn to fishing. Many of them set about building their own boats, thereby extending the shipbuilding tradition even to inland farmsteads. By 1875, Grimstad had a home fleet of 193 boats and ships.

During WWII, blocks for Hitler's 'Victory Monument' were taken from a quarry 4km north of town (of course, the monument was never built). The quarry now presents theatre productions (☎ 38 12 28 88) six days a week (Nkr300 for a 90-minute event).

Information
Helpful Grimstad Turistkontor (☎ 37 04 40 41, fax 37 04 93 77, W www.grimstad.net), near the waterfront at Smith Petersensgata 3, is open 8.30am to 4pm weekdays, with longer hours from June to August.

There's a coin laundry on the ground floor of the Grimstad Kulturhus (that is, the cinema and bowling alley!), on Storgata.

Free Internet access is available Monday to Saturday at the library, opposite the Kulturhus on Storgata.

Ibsenhuset & Grimstad By Museum
On 3 January 1844 Henrik Ibsen arrived in Grimstad from his home town of Skien on the sailing ship *Lykkens Prøve*. He took a job as an apprentice in the pharmacy of Jens Aarup Riemann, on the corner of Tverrestredet and Vestregata and, when it was sold in 1847, he shifted to the Lars Nielsen pharmacy. Here he lived in a small room, and this was where he cultivated his interest in writing. By the time he left Grimstad for university studies in Christiania (Oslo), he'd qualified as a pharmacist's assistant

Henrik Ibsen

MH

Henrik Johan Ibsen, Norway's most famous playwright, was born in Skien in 1828. His parents had financial difficulties and by the age of 15 Ibsen was forced to make his own way in the world, beginning as a pharmacist's apprentice in Grimstad. He intended to become a doctor, but after failing courses in both Greek and mathematics, he decided that the sciences weren't his lot. He did, however, have a penchant for poetry and drama. The violinist Ole Bull (who was the driving force behind the musical education of Edvard Grieg) was impressed by Ibsen's early poems and sense of drama and steered him in the direction of the theatre.

Early in his career, Ibsen worked for six years with the theatre in Bergen, followed by five years at the theatre in Christiania (Oslo), and he thereby acquired a sharp eye for theatrical technique. His masterpiece during this period, The Pretenders (1863), takes place in 13th-century Norway, with King Håkon Håkonsson expressing anachronistic dreams of national unity.

Between 1864 and 1891 Ibsen lived and studied in Rome, Dresden and Munich, decrying the small-mindedness of the Norwegian society of the day, yet living on an annual pension granted by the Norwegian state (he didn't return home until 1891, at the age of 63). In his later works, notably Brand (1866), the enormously popular Peer Gynt (1867), Emperor and Galilean (1873), Pillars of Society (1877), the highly provocative Ghosts (1881), A Doll's House (1879), An Enemy of the People (1882), The Wild Duck (1884) and Hedda Gabler (1890), he achieved a more realistic dialogue and came to be known as the father of modern Norwegian drama. Most of these works, however, ascribe to their heroes and heroines deeds that are less than universally heroic, at least in the modern sense.

Peer Gynt was Ibsen's most-renowned international success, especially when combined with the music of Edvard Grieg. In this epic, an ageing hero returns to his Norwegian roots after wandering around the world and is forced to face his own soul. As he looks back on a wasted life of travel and his fruitless search for truth, his essence peels away like the skin of an onion, revealing ever deeper facets of his personality. In the end, he discovers that when all the layers are peeled away, there's no core to be found. 'So unspeakably poor, then, a soul can return to nothingness, in the misty grey. You beautiful earth, don't be annoyed that I left no sign when I walked your grass. You beautiful sun, in vain, you've shed your glorious light on an empty house. There was no-one within to cheer and warm. The owner, they tell me, was never at home.'

In his highly acclaimed The Doll's House, he successfully examined the doctrine of critical realism and the experiences of the individual in the face of the majority. As his protagonist Nora puts it, 'I will have to find out who is right, society or myself.' It is a sentiment which echoes loudly in the present day. As a result, Nora has become a symbol for women who sacrifice family life to struggle for equality and liberation.

In his last drama, the semi-autobiographical When We Dead Awaken, Ibsen describes the life of the estranged artist, sculptor Professor Rubek, who returns to Norway in his later years but finds no happiness, having forsaken his only love and his youth to misplaced idealism.

Toward the end of his life, Ibsen summed up his philosophy, quoting to a German friend: 'He who wishes to understand me must know Norway. The magnificent but severe natural environment surrounding people up there in the north forces them to keep to their own. That is why they become introspective and serious, they brood and doubt – and they often lose faith. There, the long, dark winters come with their thick fogs enveloping the houses – oh, how they long for the sun!'

Ibsen became a partial invalid after suffering a heart attack in 1901 and died five years later.

and was on his way to future renown as a writer. His 1861 poem *Terje Vigen* and his 1877 drama *Pillars of Society* take place in the skerries offshore from Grimstad. (Interestingly, another well-known Norwegian author, Knut Hamsun, lived at nearby Norholm from 1918 to 1952.)

The Grimstad Town Museum *(☎ 37 04 46 53, Henrik Ibsens gata 14; adult/child Nkr40/15; open 11am-5pm Mon-Sat, 1pm-5pm Sun 1 May-15 Sept)* includes the Lars Nielsen pharmacy and Ibsenhuset, which contains many of the writer's belongings, some donated by his widow and son after his death in 1906, the rest donated after the death of his wife in 1914.

There are plans to make Grimstad an 'author town' because of its connections with Ibsen and Hamsun.

Sjøfartsmuseet

The Grimstad Maritime Museum *(☎ 37 04 04 90, Hasseldalen; adult/child, including admission to the Grimstad By Museum, Nkr40/15; open 11am-5pm Mon-Sat, 1pm-5pm Sun 1 May-15 Sept)*, in the office of the 1842 Hasseldalen shipyard, provides a glimpse into the history of Grimstad's former economic mainstay. While you're there, it's worth climbing the short track from the end of Batteriveien up the hill Binabben for a view over Grimstad.

Organised Tours

Two-hour sailing trips around the outlying skerries on the M/S *Bibben* (☎ 37 04 31 85, mobile ☎ 90 15 04 60) are offered Sunday to Friday in July. They depart at noon and cost Nkr120/80 per adult/child. Three-hour fishing trips during the same period are offered at 3pm on Tuesday and Thursday for Nkr160/120. Longer three- to four-hour trips are offered on the schooner *Solrik* several times weekly in July for Nkr100/50; contact the tourist office for bookings.

Places to Stay

Grimstad Hytteutleie (☎ 37 25 10 65, fax 37 25 10 64, Grooseveien 103) can book *holiday cabins* in the area for one night (from Nkr350) or one week.

Bie Appartement & Feriesenter (☎ 37 04 03 96, fax 37 04 96 88, Off Arendalsveien) Tent sites for 2 Nkr185, cabins Nkr450-1200. The nearest camping option, this is 800m north-east of the centre along Arendalsveien.

Grimstad Vertshus & Kro (☎ 37 04 25 00, fax 37 04 96 88, Grimstadtunet) Singles/doubles with shower Nkr550/695. The odd but cosy Grimstad Vertshus & Kro is in the upper part of town. The 'Kro' bit refers to an attached restaurant which isn't everyone's favourite.

Norlandia Sørlandet Hotel (☎ 37 09 05 00, fax 37 04 97 70, Televeien 21) Singles/doubles from Nkr520/740. This modern hotel has fine rooms in a quiet woodland setting on the western edge of town.

Helmershus Hotel (☎ 37 04 10 22, fax 37 04 11 03, Vesterled 23) Singles/doubles Nkr705/845. The Helmershus Hotel is at Grømbukt, west of town.

Places to Eat

Apotekergården (☎ 37 04 50 25, Skolegaten 3) Mains from Nkr198. The highly recommended Apotekergården is an excellent gourmet restaurant with outdoor seating.

Helmershus Hotel (☎ 37 04 10 22, Vesterled 23) Mains around Nkr200. The recommended dining room at this hotel serves a well-prepared international menu but it's quite expensive.

Dr Berg (☎ 37 04 44 99, Storgata 2) Dishes around Nkr140. For tasty fish dinners, you can't beat Dr Berg right at the harbour.

You can get good hot dogs for only Nkr10 from the *Dampen kiosk* down at the harbour.

Getting There & Away

The Grimstad Rutebilstasjon (☎ 37 04 05 18) is on Storgata at the harbour. Nor-Way Bussekspress buses between Oslo (Nkr360, five hours) and Kristiansand (Nkr74, one hour) call at Grimstad three to five times daily. Nettbuss buses to/from Arendal run once or twice hourly (Nkr36, 30 minutes).

Motorists have to pay a new and iniquitous Nkr20 toll to use the E18 west of Grimstad.

SOUTHERN NORWAY

SOUTHERN NORWAY

Getting Around

You can hire 21-speed bicycles from the tourist office for Nkr75 per day.

LILLESAND

pop 3000

Between Kristiansand and Arendal you'll pass Lillesand, which has an unspoiled village centre of old whitewashed houses befitting the 'white town' image claimed by so many south-coast towns. Lillesand Turistkontor (☎ 37 26 16 80, fax 37 26 15 99), Rådhuset, is open 9am to 6pm weekdays, 10am to 4pm Saturday and noon to 4pm Sunday mid-June to mid-August.

Places to Stay & Eat

The tourist office can book self-catering cabins, private rooms and apartments from Nkr150.

Tingsaker Camping (☎ 37 27 04 21, fax 37 27 01 47, Lillesand) Tent or caravan sites for 2 with car Nkr150, cabins Nkr690-910. This popular camping ground, on the shore 1km east of the centre, is a typical seaside holiday resort with camping, caravans, cabins and crowds. Unfortunately it's rather expensive. Cabins range from simple four-person huts to plusher affairs.

Lillesand Hotel Norge (☎ 37 27 01 44, fax 37 27 30 70, Strandgata 3) Singles Nkr450-1020, doubles Nkr700-1750. Snacks & mains Nkr75-260. This hotel considers itself a sort of international relic and is certainly Lillesand's most atmospheric option. It dates from 1837 but has undergone several renovations, the latest of which was in 1995. There are rooms dedicated to King Alfonso XIII of Spain and author Knut Hamsun, both of whom stayed here, and the antiquarian library was inspired by a graphic print by local artist Ferdinand Finne. The dining room serves good food, too.

Getting There & Away

The most pleasant way to reach Lillesand is by boat from Kristiansand (see The Skerries, under Kristiansand). Otherwise, the Nor-Way Bussekspress bus serves Lillesand from Kristiansand (Nkr44, 40 minutes) and Arendal (Nkr59, one hour) three or four times daily. There's also an hourly Nettbuss to Kristiansand (Nkr46), Grimstad (Nkr37) and Arendal (Nkr59).

KRISTIANSAND

pop 57,039

Busy Kristiansand, the capital of Sørlandet and the fifth-largest city in Norway, is Norway's closest port to Denmark and offers the first glimpse of the country for many ferry travellers from the south. As a seaside resort, it's a popular venue for Norwegian families with children but many foreign visitors just pile off the ferries and onto the first train out of town.

Kristiansand's grid-like layout of wide streets was conceived by King Christian IV, who founded the city in 1641. Just a few years ago, the city was known for its polluted air, foul coastline and dying salmon stream but, thanks to local ingenuity, industrial effluent is now cleaned in three massive sewage plants before it's dumped into the sea and the air pollutants are now filtered. The previously choking residue is now sold as concrete strengthener used on offshore oil rigs, netting millions of kroner annually. The small boat harbour area has also been nicely spruced up with a fabulous fish market, several upmarket seafood restaurants and a pizza place.

Unfortunately, there's a rip-off system of toll booths on roads around Kristiansand which sponge Nkr10 off passing cars.

Orientation

Central Kristiansand's locally termed *kvadraturen*, the square grid pattern measuring six long blocks by nine shorter blocks, is surrounded on two sides by the sea, one side by the river and on the fourth side by a large city park. The rail, bus and ferry terminals form a cluster west of the city centre. Parking is available here and along most city streets. Pedestrianised Markens gate serves as a focus for the central shopping and restaurant district.

Information

The enthusiastic Destinasjon Sørlandet tourist office (☎ 38 12 13 14, fax 38 02 52 55,

KRISTIANSAND

PLACES TO STAY
1 Villa Frobusdal B&B
4 Tangen Vandrerhjem
5 Tangenbobil-Parkering
8 Norlandia Kristiansand Apartment
22 Hotel Bondeheimen; Kristiansand og Oppland Turistforening
23 Sjøgløtt Hotel
31 Clarion Hotel Ernst; Nightcap
33 Hotel Norge

PLACES TO EAT
3 Snadderkiosken
10 Rimi Supermarket
12 Peppe's Pizza
13 Østens Perle
15 Mega Supermarket & Cafeteria
18 Amigo's; XO Vestre
19 Bakery
27 Sjøhuset
29 McDonald's
35 Fish Market
36 Hastmanns Brygge

OTHER
2 Vinmonopolet
6 Bystrand Beach
7 Swimming Pool
9 Police Station
11 Domkirke
14 Destinasjon Sørlandet Tourist Office; Vinmonopolet
16 Bus Terminal
17 Color Line Ferry Terminal
20 Post Office
21 Library
24 Christiansholm Festning
25 Gjestehavn
26 Nupen Fountain
28 Zanzibar & Kick
30 Markens Pub
32 M/S Maarten & M/S Silius Terminal; M/S Øya to Lillesand
34 Fønix Cinema

SOUTHERN NORWAY

e destinasjon@sørlandet.com, w www.sor landet.com), Vestre Strandgate 2, is handy to the ferry, rail and bus terminals. From 18 June to 19 August, the office is open 8.30am to 6pm weekdays, 10am to 6pm Saturday and noon to 6pm Sunday. The rest of the year, it's open 8.30am to 3.30pm weekdays.

For maps and information on hiking, huts and organised mountain tours in far southern Norway, contact Kristiansand og Oppland Turistforening (☎ 38 02 52 63), Kirkegata 15. It's open 8am to 3.30pm weekdays (closes 6pm Thursday).

You can change money at the post office at Markens gate 19 or at all the major banks (there are several on Markens gate). For Internet access, try the library, Rådhus gate 11, near the cathedral (closed Sunday).

Laundry services are available at the Gjestehavn (Guest Harbour, ☎ 38 02 07 15), where you'll pay Nkr30 to wash a load and the same to dry.

Christiansholm Festning

The most prominent feature along the Strandepromenaden is Christiansholm Fortress (☎ 38 07 51 50; admission free; open

9am-9pm daily 15 May-15 Sept), built by royal decree between 1662 and 1672 to keep watch over the strategic Skagerrak straits and protect the city from pirates and rambunctious Swedes. The construction featured walls up to 5m thick and an armoury buried within a concentric inner wall, and was financed by the 1550 local citizens, who were taxed and coerced into labour. Despite – or because of – its strength, the only action it ever experienced was during the Napoleonic Wars in 1807, when soldiers fired on the English ship *Spencer*, whose captain had demanded a handover of the Danish ship *Prins Christian Fredrik*, moored in Kristiansand harbour. The hint was taken and the *Spencer* left without further ado.

In 1872 the structure was damaged when a town fire burned the roof and caused a massive explosion in the powder room. Then, during WWII, the occupying Germans plastered over the walls with a layer of concrete, which was subsequently removed. More recently, there have been some major changes, including a new roof with glass clerestory windows, but a ring of eight bronze cannons, cast between 1666 and 1788, still menaces the offshore skerries. Guided tours are available at 1pm daily between 15 June and 15 August.

Nupen Fountain

The rather elaborate three-part fountain near the fortress, which was sculpted by Kjell Nupen, represents the four-masted tall ship of town founder Christian IV, the grid pattern of the town centre, and the solidity of the modern city. The curious and enormous ceramic jar standing nearby was a gift to the town from the Hennig Olsen Is ice-cream factory.

Kristiansand Domkirke

The Kristiansand Cathedral (☎ 38 02 11 88, *Kirkegata; tower climb Nkr20; open 9am-2pm daily June-Aug)*, built in neo-Gothic style in 1884, has seating for 1800 people and is Norway's largest church. Guided tours (Nkr20/10) of the cathedral, including the tower, run on request from 11am to 5pm Monday to Saturday between 2 July and

4 August. You might catch some early-morning organ playing on weekdays in July.

Baneheia & Ravnedalen Parks

Baneheia and Ravnedalen, both north of the city centre, offer wild greenery and a network of lakeside hiking and skiing tracks, some of which are lit up during winter. Both parks were created between 1870 and 1880 by Kristiansand's city chairman, General Oscar Wergeland. Over a 30-year period, he oversaw the planting of 150,000 coniferous trees and transformed the area into a recreational green belt. From the centre, Baneheia is readily accessed on foot, and is connected to Ravnedalen by a series of pleasant walking tracks.

Agder Naturmuseum & Botaniske Hage

The winding paths through the 50-hectare park at Gimle Estate (☎ 38 09 23 88, *Gimleveien 23; house adult/child Nkr30/10, house & garden Nkr45/15; open 10am-6pm Tues-Fri, noon-6pm Sat-Mon 20 June-20 Aug; shorter hours rest of year)* will lead you through a botanical garden containing a number of rare (and labelled) trees, shrubs, flowers, rocks, minerals and stuffed animals. The estate house has 19th-century period interiors and there's also a historic rose garden dating from 1850. It lies just over 1km from the centre, over the Oddernes bridge.

Posebyen

The Kristiansand Posebyen, or 'Old Town', takes in most of 14 blocks at the northern end of the town's characteristic kvadraturen. It's worth taking a slow stroll around this enchanting quarter, whose name was given by French soldiers who came to *reposer* (French for relax). Currently, Kristiansand seniors are constructing a scale model of the city as it appeared when it was designed by Christian IV, with buildings around 1m high. When it's completed in 2002, it will be on view at Vest-Agder Fylkesmuseum.

Kristiansand Dyrepark

Over the years, the former Kristiansand zoo (☎ 38 04 98 00; *admission, including all* activities, adult Nkr80-200, child Nkr65-170, depending on time of year; open 10am-7pm daily mid-May–Aug) has gradually expanded into one of Norway's most popular domestic attractions. Off the E18, 9km east of town, it is probably *the* favourite holiday destination for children from around the country and other parts of Scandinavia. Although it can't compare with the Disney parks, it also lacks the tackiness of Blackpool, and makes quite a pleasant day out for children and adults. The funfair portion includes a log ride and pirate ship cruise, and the zoo portion offers a surprising variety of specimens, including the near-extinct golden lion tamarin. If you want to take advantage of the water park, be sure to bring a swimming costume.

The real highlights, however, are the Nordisk Vilmark (Northern Wilderness), where visitors are transported over the habitat of moose, wolves, lynx and wolverines on elevated boardwalks; and Kardamomme By (Cardamom Town, named for a key ingredient in Scandinavian waffles), a fantasy village based on the popular children's stories of Thorbjørn Egner. The town, which vaguely suggests a setting in northern Africa, has been carefully laid out exactly as it appeared in the illustrated book, and the houses are available as self-catering family accommodation. Year-round, up to five persons can stay overnight (☎ 38 04 98 00, fax 38 04 33 67) in the charming fantasy houses for Nkr2390 to Nkr3290, including two days' admission to the park.

To get there, take the Dyreparkbussen or local bus No 1, which operate more or less hourly June to August.

Vest-Agder Fylkesmuseum

The open-air Vest-Agder folk museum (☎ 38 09 02 28, Vigeveien 22B; adult/child Nkr30/10; open 10am-6pm Mon-Sat, noon-6pm Sun 20 June-20 Aug, noon-5pm Sun rest of year), 4km east of town on the E18, is a collection of farmsteads and hamlets from the Setesdalen region. It also includes displays of traditional costumes, art and children's toys. You can see folk dancing at 5.30pm on Wednesday from mid-June to mid-August.

Setesdalsbanen

The 78km-long narrow-gauge railway between Kristiansand and Byglandsfjord was opened in 1896 to link Setesdalen with the coast. It was used to transport nickel from the Evje mines and local timber and barrel staves which were used in the salting and export of herring. Although competition from the normal-gauge state railway forced its closure in 1962, the Setesdalsbanen Railway (☎ 38 15 64 82; adult/child return Nkr70/35) still runs steam-powered locomotives along the last 6km between Grovane (2km north of Vennesla) and Beihøldalen. In July, trains leave Grovane at 6pm Tuesday to Friday; from 17 June to 2 September they run on Sunday at 11.30am and 2pm. NSB trains run three to five times daily from Kristiansand to Vennesla (Nkr28, 12 minutes).

Kristiansand Kanonmuseum

The Kristiansand Cannon Museum (☎ 38 08 50 90, Møvik; adult/child Nkr50/20; open 11am-6pm daily 7 June-2 Sept, 11am-6pm Thur-Sun 1 May-6 June & 3-30 Sept), 8km south of town, preserves the Germans' heavy Vara Battery which, along with an emplacement at Hanstholm in Denmark, ensured marginal German control of the strategic Skagerrak straits. At each end, four 337-tonne, 38cm cannons with a range of 55km (which was covered in two minutes) controlled traffic along either end of the strait, while the unprotected middle zone was heavily mined. In the autumn of 1941, over 1400 workers and 600 soldiers occupied this site.

After the war, the site was renamed Møvik Festning (Møvik Fort) and used by the Norwegian coastal defence forces to keep history from repeating itself. Visitors to the current museum can see the big guns as well as bunkers, barracks, munitions storage (including some daunting 800kg shells), a power generator and all the machinery that accommodated operations there.

The Skerries

In summer, Kristiansand's archipelago of offshore skerries turns into one of the country's greatest sun-and-sea destinations for Norwegian holiday-makers.

SOUTHERN NORWAY

Foreign visitors, who generally spend less time in the area, are normally content with a tourist office cruise either around the islets or a 2½-hour passage along the Blindleia channel to Lillesand. The most popular island, **Bragdøy**, lies almost within spitting distance of the mainland and boasts a coastal museum, cultural centre and preservation workshop for wooden ships, as well as several nice walks and bathing sites. In the distance, notice the beautiful classic lighthouse Grønningen Fyr, which is still attended by a lighthouse keeper. During school holidays, you can sleep in a dorm bed in the lighthouse for Nkr100; for information, phone ☎ 95 10 25 23.

From 25 June to 5 August, the M/S *Maarten* and M/S *Silius* sail from Kristiansand at 11am daily and from Lillesand at 2.30pm (Nkr160/70 adult/child return). From 25 June to 19 August, the M/S *Vilhelm Krag* does 1½-hour cruises to Flekkerøya via Bragdøy (Nkr90/40), at 11am and 3pm daily. (This run can also be used as a ferry service to Bragdøy for Nkr60/30 return; the last return to the mainland is at 4.10pm.)

Activities

Kristiansand is one of Norway's most popular beach-bathing venues, and if the 15°C waters of the Skagerrak don't put you off, you can join the locals on the sandy Bystrand (town beach). Otherwise, head for the nearby Kristiansand Svømmehall (swimming pool; ☎ 38 12 05 90), open Monday to Saturday, for adult/child Nkr38/25 and then return to the sand to dry off. (It's also open Sunday during bad weather.)

Kristiansand also caters to scuba divers. Dykkeren (☎ 38 05 86 20), Kongsgård Allé 53, offers diving excursions (even at night) and information on local marine ecology and biology. The tourist office has a list of other companies offering excursions and equipment rental.

Places to Stay

You can book *holiday cabins* through Agderferie Hytteformidling (☎ 38 06 31 61), Postboks 36, N-4699 Tveit, for Nkr500 to Nkr1200 per day.

Roligheden Camping (☎ 38 09 67 22, fax 38 09 11 17, [e] kherlof@online.no, Framnesveien) Tent sites Nkr100 plus Nkr25/person, 4-person cabins Nkr650-1100. Tent campers have to go to this popular beach site 3km east of the centre. Take bus No 15 from centre.

Tangen Vandrerhjem (☎ 38 02 83 10, fax 38 02 75 05, Skansen 8) Dorm beds Nkr180, singles/doubles Nkr340/390. Open year-round. The huge Kristiansand HI hostel lies in a rather bland warehouse landscape a 10-minute walk north-east of the fortress. Prices include breakfast.

Villa Frobusdal B&B (☎ 38 07 05 15, fax 38 07 01 15, Frobusdalen 2) Singles/doubles Nkr490/690. Open Jan-Nov. For something rather rustic, there's the cosy Villa Frobusdal at the edge of the Baneheia park but within 10 minutes' walk of the centre.

Sjøgløtt Hotel (☎/fax 38 02 21 20, Østre Strand gate 25) Singles/doubles with shared toilet & shower Nkr350/590, with all facilities Nkr590/760. The small and cosy Sjøgløtt Hotel is known as 'det lille hotel' (the little hotel).

Norlandia Kristiansand Apartment (☎ 38 07 98 00, fax 38 07 98 01, Tollbodgata 46) Apartments for 2 per day Nkr450-880. These small self-catering student flats are centrally located.

Hotel Bondeheimen (☎ 38 02 44 40, fax 38 02 73 21, Kirkegata 15) Singles/doubles from Nkr570/820. This modern hotel offers high-standard rooms.

Hotel Norge (☎ 38 17 40 00, fax 38 17 40 01, Dronningens gate 5) Singles/doubles from Nkr630/890. Just off the classy lobby of this fine hotel, you can relax amid the shelves of the antiquarian library.

Clarion Hotel Ernst (☎ 38 12 86 00, fax 38 02 03 07, Rådhus gate 2) Singles Nkr645-1145, doubles Nkr850-1250. At this luxurious hotel, near the post office, you can enjoy an excellent breakfast in the glass-roofed courtyard.

Places to Eat

Hartmanns Brygge (☎ 38 12 07 21, Østre Havn) Mains Nkr230-240. For high-quality beef, duck and fish dishes, join the crowds at this popular, upmarket seafood restaurant at the harbourside.

Sjøhuset (☎ 38 02 62 60, Østre Strandgate 12a) Mains Nkr190-240. You'll pay as much for the setting as for the good food here, which includes fish, shellfish, and some meat and vegetarian dishes.

Østens Perle (☎ 38 09 85 50, Markens gate 35) Lunches Nkr69-79, dinner mains Nkr79-179. You'll get reasonable Asian food at Østens Perle, including a Mongolian buffet for Nkr145.

Amigo's (☎ 38 02 67 60, Vestre Strandgate 22) Lunch mains Nkr69-85, dinner mains Nkr99-210. This is a popular but rather formal Mexican choice, with vegetarian dishes.

Peppe's Pizza (☎ 38 07 20 70, Gyldenløves gate 7) Pizzas for 2 from Nkr130. The popular Peppe's Pizza also serves smaller dishes such as lasagne.

XO Vestre (☎ 38 07 22 56, Vestre Strandgate 24a) Pizzas/pastas from Nkr49/59. Remarkably reasonable and inexpensive dishes are on offer in this basic restaurant.

Snadderkiosken (☎ 38 02 90 29, Østre Strandgate 78a) Dishes Nkr15-50. Copy the locals and go to this kiosk near the town beach for a great meal deal. It has an extensive and great-value menu: hot dogs starting at Nkr15, meatballs and mashed potatoes Nkr47, cod with mashed potatoes and salad for Nkr50 and grilled chicken for Nkr48.

You'll find one of the world's most unusual *McDonald's (Cnr Markens gate & Dronningens gate)* housed in an 1897 bank building here.

The *Mega* supermarket, opposite the train station, has a cheap 2nd-floor cafeteria and there's a good *bakery (Rådhus gate 5)*, near the post office.

Rimi supermarket *(Gyldenløves gate 14)* Open 9am-8pm Mon-Fri, 9am-6pm Sat. This large supermarket offers a wide range of groceries.

For the freshest and best-value seafood around, try the *fish market*, where the vendors will cook up fish soup or salmon, shrimps and fishcakes (Nkr35 to Nkr170) for you to enjoy, with a beer or two, on the outdoor patio.

Entertainment

Zanzibar (☎ 38 02 62 44, Dronningens gate 8) Open year-round. Zanzibar is one of the most popular hang-outs for young people.

Kick (☎ 38 02 62 44, Dronningens gate 8) The outdoor cafe attached to Zanzibar presents DJ music and dancing.

Markens Pub (☎ 38 02 06 99, Tollbodgata 3) Markens Pub has disco music in the evening from Wednesday to Saturday.

Nightcap (☎ 38 12 86 00, Rådhus gate 2) At the Clarion Hotel Ernst, this is a popular night spot for the 25- to 35-year-old crowd.

Fønix cinema (☎ 82 03 01 00, Vestre Strandgate 9) Take in a movie at this large venue.

Getting There & Away

Nor-Way Bussekspress buses head north at 9am daily to Haukeligrend, with connections to Bergen (Nkr570, 12 hours). Buses to/from Oslo (Nkr385, 5½ hours) run three to five times daily. To/from Stavanger (Nkr310, 4½ hours), they run two to four times daily. Regional buses depart hourly to Arendal (Nkr93, 1½ hours) and Flekkefjord (Nkr130 to Nkr180, two hours). To Evje (Nkr80, one hour), buses run four to eight times a day. Express bus fares are half-price for students.

There are three to six trains daily to Oslo (Nkr440, 4½ hours) and Stavanger (Nkr320, three hours).

With a vehicle, access to the E18, north of the centre, is via Vestre Strandgate. The city is surrounded with toll booths – sometimes you'll pay just to do a U-turn.

M/S *Øya* (mobile ☎ 95 93 58 55) sails from/to Lillesand once daily except Sunday, 23 June to 4 August (Nkr150/75 per adult/child one way, Nkr250/125 return). There are also Thursday and Sunday evening trips from 1 July to 6 August.

For information on ferries to Denmark, Sweden and the UK, see the Getting There & Away chapter.

Getting Around

City buses around the centre cost Nkr15 per ride; to the Kristiansand Dyrepark costs Nkr23. For bicycles, you should check out

SOUTHERN NORWAY

the Sykkelsenter (☎ 38 02 68 35), Grim Torv 3, which charges Nkr150/490 per day/week.

MANDAL
pop 12,800

The white town of Mandal, Norway's southernmost town, is best known for Norway's finest bathing beach. The 800m-long Sjøsanden, about 1km from the centre, is Norway's Copacabana and the forest backdrop is as lovely as the sand and sea itself. When the sun isn't cooperating, you can always stroll through the strip of white clapboard buildings of the old town, north of the Mandalselva River. Historically, the town thrived by supplying the timber trade from its ample pine and oak forests.

Information

For queries, Mandal Tourist Information (☎ 38 27 83 00, fax 38 27 83 01, e info@ visitregionmandal.com), Bryggegaten 10, opens 9am to 7pm weekdays, 10am to 3pm Saturday and 11am to 5pm Sunday from mid-June to mid-August (otherwise 9am to 4pm weekdays only).

Mandal Museum

On a rainy day, you may want to have a look around the Mandal Museum (☎ 38 27 30 00, Store Elvegata 5/6; adult/child Nkr10/ free; open 11am-5pm Mon-Fri, 11am-2pm Sat, 2pm-5pm Sun 25 June-15 Aug), which displays a host of historical maritime and fishing artefacts and works by local artists, including Amaldus Nielsen and Adolph Tidemand, and pieces by Mandal's favourite son, Gustav Vigeland.

Places to Stay & Eat

Accommodation in Mandal tends to be rather expensive and the HI hostel has closed.

Sandnes Naturcamp (☎ 38 26 51 51, *Sandnes*) Tent or caravan sites Nkr100. Campers can stay at this pleasant camping ground which lies by the Mandalselva, 2km north of town.

Kjøbmandsgaarden Hotel (☎ 38 26 12 76, fax 38 26 33 02, Store Elvegaten 57) Singles/doubles without bath Nkr450/670,

with bath Nkr680/970. The basic rooms in this atmospheric old building from 1863, formerly a hardware shop, seem a bit overpriced but they are clean.

Sjøsanden Feriesenter (☎ 38 26 14 19, fax 38 26 27 79, Sjøsandveien 1) Doubles Nkr300-550, 2–6-person self-catering apartments Nkr400-800. If you fancy staying by the beach, Sjøsanden Feriesenter is just a few metres away. It also allows you to pitch your tent.

First Hotel Solborg (☎ 38 26 66 66, fax 38 26 48 22, Neseveien 1) Singles/doubles from Nkr645/970. Main courses Nkr172-220. The flash First Hotel Solborg, west of the centre, is only a 10-minute walk from the beach but on those less-than-optimum days, guests can use the indoor pool. Its dining room is probably the best formal restaurant in town and it also has a bar and a Saturday disco called Soldekket. For another nightlife possibility, try the *Grand pub* (☎ 38 26 01 86, Store Elvegate 16).

Biffen (☎ 38 26 52 08, Store Elvegate 47b) Dishes around Nkr100. If you just want a reasonable mid-range meal, French-style Biffen is a good option.

Dr Nielsen's (☎ 38 26 61 00, Store Elvegate 47a) Mains around Nkr70-80. This restaurant serves Greek food including pasta, chicken and some fish dishes.

Getting There & Away

The Mandal Rutebilstasjon lies north of the river, just a short walk from the historic district. Bus No 301 connects Mandal with Oslo-Kristiansand-Stavanger trains at Marnadal Station (Nkr33, 30 minutes) four or five times each weekday. The Nor-Way Bussekspress coastal route between Stavanger (Nkr265, 3½ hours) and Kristiansand (Nkr67, 45 minutes) passes through Mandal two to four times daily.

LINDESNES

As the southernmost point in Norway (latitude 57°58'53"N), Lindesnes (literally 'arching land peninsula') provides an occasional glimpse of the power nature can unleash between the Skagerrak and the North Sea and, as the brochures point out, 'the camera angles are better than at Nordkapp' (2518km away by road). However, it's not only photographers who will be inspired by **Lindesnes Fyr** (☎ 38 26 19 02, Lindesnes; adult/child Nkr30/free; open 10am-9pm daily July & Aug, 10am-8pm daily June & Sept, 10am-6pm daily May), the classic lighthouse which rises above the cape. Inside the tower, there are exhibitions on the history of the lighthouse.

The first lighthouse on the site was fired up in 1655 using coal and tallow candles to warn ships off the rocks. The current one, built in 1915, has been electrified, of course, and is visible up to 19½ nautical miles out to sea.

Also of interest is the **Lindesnes District Museum & Gustav Vigeland Gallery** (☎ 38 25 80 68, Near E39 in Vigeland; adult/child Nkr30/free; open 11am-4pm Mon-Sat, 1pm-5pm Sun 25 June-10 Aug) which reveals the history of the Lindesnes district and the inspiration behind the works of sculptor Gustav Vigeland.

Places to Stay & Eat

Lindesnes Camping og Hytteutleie (☎ 38 25 88 74, fax 38 25 88 92, Lillehavn) Tent sites Nkr100, camper vans Nkr350, cabins Nkr180-600. Open Apr-Oct. You'll find excellent modern facilities at this place, on the shore 3.5km north-east of Lindesnes Fyr.

Lindesnes Gjestehus (☎ 38 25 97 00, fax 38 25 97 65, Spangereid) Bed & breakfast per person Nkr275. About 11km north of the cape lies this simple but cosy guesthouse.

Getting There & Away

Buses from Mandal (one hour, Nkr49) travel to the lighthouse via Spangereid on Monday, Wednesday and Friday.

FLEKKEFJORD

pop 5511

Flekkefjord first emerged as an entity in 1660, but thanks to it competing with royally supported Kristiansand, the Danish king tried to shut it down two years later. Despite that, the fishing industry thrived and, by the time it was granted town status in 1842, Flekkefjord was a significant herring

fishery and later became a major tannery. The town is noted for having virtually no tidal variation (typically less than 10cm between high and low tides).

Information

The Flekkefjord Tourist Office (☎ 38 32 21 31, fax 38 32 21 30), at Elvegaten 15, is open 9am to 6pm weekdays and 10am to 2pm weekends from mid-June to mid-August. At other times, it's open 9am to 4pm weekdays only.

Things to See

For a view over the town, make the short climb to the top of **Lilleheia**, which is accessed from Dr Kraftsgata. You may also want to stroll through the **Hollenderbyen** (Dutch Town) district, with its narrow streets and old timber buildings. Here you'll find the **Flekkefjord Museum** (☎ 38 32 26 59, Dr Kraftsgata 15; adult/child Nkr15/free; open 11am-5pm Mon-Fri, noon-3pm Sat & Sun June-Aug), housed in a home from 1724 but with 19th-century interiors.

Other associated buildings include the **waterfront warehouses** in adjacent Sjøbodene and the **Flekkefjord Elektrisitetsmuseum** (ask at the Flekkefjord Museum regarding admission before 3pm weekdays).

The octagonal log-built **Flekkefjord church** (Kirkegaten; admission free; open 11am-1pm Mon-Sat 1 July-20 Aug), consecrated in 1833, was designed by architect H Linstow, who also designed the Royal Palace in Oslo. Note that the columns, steeple and baptismal font are also octagonal, as are the tower on the Grand Hotel and some other structures around Flekkefjord.

Jøssingfjord, 32km west of Flekkefjord on Rv44, has spectacular perpendicular rock scenery, including a fine waterfall and two 17th-century houses nestling under an overhanging cliff.

Places to Stay & Eat

Egenes Camping (☎ 38 32 01 48, fax 38 32 01 11, e camping@online.no) Tent sites without/with car Nkr70/90 plus Nkr20/person, caravan sites Nkr100, 4-person/6-person cabins from Nkr250/450, self-catering flats Nkr400-600. This spectacularly located camping ground is beside the lake Seluravatnet 1km off the E39, 5km east of Flekkefjord. There's boat and canoe hire and a good-value cafeteria (mains around Nkr70) with outdoor seating. Buses running from Flekkefjord towards Kristiansand pass within 1km of the site (Nkr21, 10 minutes).

Bondeheimen Hotel (☎ 38 32 21 44, fax 38 32 29 79, Elvegata 7-9) Singles/doubles with shared bathroom Nkr345/510. Mains Nkr74-99. This hotel has simple rooms and a reasonable restaurant/cafeteria.

First Hotel Maritim (☎ 38 32 33 33, fax 38 32 43 12, Sundegaten 9) Singles Nkr849-1049, doubles Nkr949-1149. More upmarket than Bondeheimen Hotel, this has an attached restaurant (mains from Nkr100) and the piano bar offers dancing six nights a week.

Getting There & Away

The Nor-Way Bussekspress bus between Kristiansand (Nkr160, two hours) and Stavanger (Nkr170, two hours) passes through Flekkefjord. Buses run to Jøssingfjord once or twice daily except Sunday (Nkr50, 40 minutes). The nearest train station is at Sira, on the Oslo-Stavanger line, which is accessed by bus (Nkr31, 25 minutes, seven to 10 daily).

EGERSUND
pop 8314

Egersund, arranged around an island-dotted cove amid low hills, was named after the sound which divides it from the offshore island of Eigerøy. The identity of the first known settler in the region, Laithigar, was revealed by an ancient rune stone found in nearby Møgedal, and other sources indicate that there has been a church here since at least 1292.

Nearly two-thirds of the original town was gutted by fire in 1843, after which Egersund was reconstructed with wide streets to thwart the spread of future fires. From 1847 to 1979, the local economy was sustained by the pottery and porcelain industry but nowadays most people derive much of their income from fishing and related industries, and the oil and gas industry.

Information

The Egersund Tourist Office (☎ 51 46 82 33, fax 51 46 82 39, e turistinfo@eigersund .kommune.no), Jernbaneveien 2, is open daily from 20 May to 31 August. The rest of the year, on weekdays, it has a desk at Skrivergården, Strangaten 58.

Dalane Folkmuseum & Egersund Fayancemuseum

The two-part Dalane Folk Museum (☎ 51 46 14 10, Slettebø; adult/child Nkr20/10; open 11am-5pm Mon-Sat, 1pm-6pm Sun mid-June–mid-Aug; 1pm-5pm Sun rest of year) features a series of historic timber homes at Slettebø, 4km north of town along the Rv42, and the very worthwhile Egersund Fayance Museum (☎ 51 46 14 10, Eia; adult/child Nkr20/10; open 11am-5pm Mon-Sat, 1pm-6pm Sun mid-May–mid-Aug; 1pm-5pm Sun rest of year), a walkable 1km north-east of town. The latter displays the history and wares of Egersund Fayance, the ceramic and porcelain firm which sustained the entire district from 1847 to 1979. To get there, take the StavangerExpressen bus (three to six buses daily except Sunday).

Historic Buildings

Thanks to a lack of funds for 'modernisation', many historic timber buildings remain. **Strandgaten**, a street of timber houses constructed after the fire of 1843, is worth a stroll. **Skrivergården** (the judicial residence) at Strandgaten 58 was constructed in 1846 as the home of the local magistrate Christian Feyer. The town park opposite served as his private garden. The **Bilstadhuset** at Nygaten 14 still has its original timberwork and includes a sailmaker's loft upstairs, but it's not open to the public.

Also picturesque are the lovely timber homes and warehouses at **Sogndalsstrand**, 2km south of Hauge, 30km south-east of Egersund. Buses run from Egersund to Hauge (Nkr45, 40 minutes) once or twice daily except Sunday.

If you're driving along the Rv42, have a look at **Terland Klopp**, 20km north-east of town. This lovely 60m-long bridge from

1888 is constructed in 21 stone arches and has been proposed for inclusion on Unesco's list of historical monuments.

Egersund Kirke

The earliest parts of the Egersund Church *(Torget; admission free; open 11am-2pm daily 20 June-15 Aug)* date from the 1620s, but some features are older. The carved altarpiece, a depiction of the baptism and crucifixion of Christ by Stavanger carpenter Thomas Christophersen and painted by artist Peter Reimers, dates back to 1607 and the baptismal font is dated 1583.

Varberg

You'll get a fine view over the town centre from the summit of Varberg, the hill with the prominent TV mast. The path to the top will take you about 15 minutes from the centre of town.

Eigerøy Fyr

Eigerøy Fyr *(Midbrødøy; adult/child Nkr20/ 10; open 11am-4pm Sun July)*, the majestic 1855 lighthouse on Midbrødøy, near the south-western tip of Eigerøy island, is accessible from the car park by a 2km footpath. There are great views at any time, but especially on stormy days. Take the Nord Eigerøy bus from the Rutebilstasjon and get off at the sign 'Eigerøy fyr' on the Rv502 (Nkr20, 15 minutes). From there, it's a 30-minute one-way walk down the Fyrvegen road to the lighthouse.

Places to Stay & Eat

Steinsnes Camping (☎ 51 49 41 36, fax 51 49 40 73, Tengs) Tent sites Nkr100 plus Nkr25/person, cabins Nkr250-500. The most convenient camping ground is Steinsnes Camping, 3km north of Egersund. Buses heading for Hellvik will get you there.

Grand Hotell (☎ 51 49 18 11, fax 51 49 36 46, Johan Feyersgate 3) Singles Nkr525-800, doubles Nkr730-800. The Grand Hotell is a lovely old 19th-century building.

Vinstokken (☎ 51 49 06 60, Strandgaten 60) Mains from Nkr150. Vinstokken is a very nice French-style restaurant in the historical district.

Telegrafen (☎ 51 49 80 00, Areneset) Medium pizzas from Nkr107. For a cheap eat, try a pizza at Telegrafen; slices are Nkr25 each.

Getting There & Away

The best way to reach Egersund is by rail. Trains to/from Oslo (Nkr600, eight hours) run via Kristiansand three to six times daily. There are also numerous daily services to/from Stavanger (Nkr115, one hour). Fjord Line (☎ 81 53 35 00) runs an international ferry between Bergen and Hanstholm in Denmark, via Egersund (but it's not available for transport between Bergen and Egersund). For details, see the Getting There & Away chapter.

The Interior

Much of the interior portion of southern Norway lies within the sparsely populated Telemark county (yes, it lends its name to that graceful nordic ski manoeuvre – see the boxed text 'The Virtues of Skinny Skis' in the Facts for the Visitor chapter). This lovely region is characterised by steep forested terrain, high plateaus and countless lakes, and also takes in parts of Buskerud county and the northern portions of Aust-Agder and Vest-Agder.

Apart from routes to Kongsberg, public transport in this region isn't particularly convenient; buses run infrequently and the rail lines cover only the area between Bø and Kongsberg, so sightseeing is best done by car. For Telemark tourist information, contact Telemarkreiser (☎ 35 90 00 20), Postboks 2813 Kjørbekk, N-3702 Skien.

KONGSBERG
pop 15,730

Kongsberg, founded in 1624, owes its existence to the discovery of one of the world's purest silver deposits in the nearby Numedal Valley. In the resulting silver rush, it briefly became the second largest town in Norway, with 8000 inhabitants, including 4000 miners and 2000 farmers. Today, the surrounding hills bear cast-off mining relics

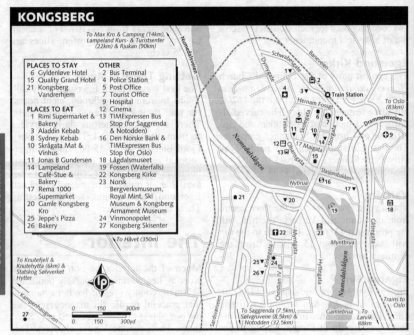

KONGSBERG

To Max Kro & Camping (14km),
Lampeland Kurs- & Turistsenter
(22km) & Rjukan (90km)

To Oslo (83km)

To Håvet (350m)

To Knutefjell &
Knutehytta (6km) &
Statskog Sølvverket
Hytter

To Saggrenda (7.5km),
Sølvgruvene (8.5km) &
Notodden (32.5km)

Trains to
Oslo

To
Larvik
88km

PLACES TO STAY	OTHER
6 Gyldenløve Hotel	2 Bus Terminal
15 Quality Grand Hotel	4 Police Station
21 Kongsberg	5 Post Office
Vandrerhjem	7 Tourist Office
	9 Hospital
PLACES TO EAT	12 Cinema
1 Rimi Supermarket &	13 TIMExpressen Bus
Bakery	Stop (for Saggrenda
3 Aladdin Kebab	& Notodden)
8 Sydney Kebab	16 Den Norske Bank &
10 Skrågata Mat &	TIMExpressen Bus
Vinhus	Stop (for Oslo)
11 Jonas B Gundersen	18 Lågdalsmuseet
14 Lampeland	19 Fossen (Waterfalls)
Café-Stue &	22 Kongsberg Kirke
Bakery	23 Norsk
17 Rema 1000	Bergverksmuseum,
Supermarket	Royal Mint, Ski
20 Gamle Kongsberg	Museum & Kongsberg
Kro	Armament Museum
25 Jeppe's Pizza	24 Vinmonopolet
26 Bakery	27 Kongsberg Skisenter

and the scars of over 300 shafts. The main shaft of the largest mine, the Kongsgruvene (Royal Silver Mine), plunges all of 1070m into the mountain, to a depth of 550m below sea level.

History

The history of Kongsberg begins and ends with silver, which was discovered by two children with an ox in 1623. Their father attempted to sell the windfall but the king's soldiers got wind of it and the family was arrested and forced to disclose the site of their discovery. (It's almost certain that silver was discovered earlier, but by wiser individuals who kept it to themselves, lest the peaceful folk and their lands be subject to government interference, pillage or regulation.) Between 1623 and 1957, a total of 1.35 million kilograms of pure thread-like 'wire' silver was produced for the royal coffers. Kongsberg is still home to the national mint but the last mine – unable to

turn a profit in the modern context – closed in 1957.

Orientation

Kongsberg is neatly split into old and new sections by the falls of the river Numedalslågen. The new eastern section takes in the main shopping district, the tourist office and the rail and bus terminals. In the older section west of the river lie the museum, historic church and HI hostel.

Information

The tourist office (☎ 32 73 50 00, fax 32 73 50 01, ℮ office@kongsberg-turistservice.no, 🆆 www.kongsberg-turistservice.no), conveniently opposite the train station at Storgata 35, is open 9am to 5pm weekdays and 10am to 5pm weekends from 26 June to 16 August. The rest of the year, hours are 9am to 4.30pm weekdays, 10am to 2pm Saturday. Laundry services are available at Kongsberg Renseri, Schwabesgate 1, opposite the train station.

Kongsberg Kirke

Norway's largest baroque church (☎ *32 73 50 00, Kirketorget; open 10am-5pm Mon-Fri, 10am-1pm Sat, 2pm-4pm Sun 18 May-21 Aug; 7pm-8pm Wed rest of year)*, which lies in the Old Town west of the river, was officially opened in 1761. The rococo-style interior features ornate chandeliers and an unusual altar that combines the altarpiece, high pulpit and organ pipes on a single wall. Guided tours cost Nkr30.

Norsk Bergverksmuseum

The worthwhile Norwegian Mining Museum (☎ *32 72 32 00, Hyttegata 3; adult/child Nkr50/10; open 10am-5pm daily 18 May-Aug, noon-4pm daily Sept, noon-4pm Sun-Fri 1 Oct-17 May)*, over the bridge in a 1844 smelter, tells the story of mining in Kongsberg with relics, models and mineral displays, and the old smelting furnaces still survive in the basement. In the same building, other sections include the Royal Mint, which was moved from Akershus Fortress in Oslo to the source of silver in 1686, the Kongsberg armament museum, and a ski museum featuring mainly silver trophies won by Norwegian skiers.

Lågdalsmuseet

The Lågdal folk museum (☎ *32 73 34 68, Tillischbakken 8-10; adult/child Nkr40/10; open 11am-5pm daily (to 7.30pm late mid-July–mid-Aug) 23 June-15 Aug, 11am-5pm Sat & Sun 17 May-22 June & 16-31 Aug, 11am-3.30pm Mon-Fri rest of year)* is a 10-minute walk south-east of the train station. It has a collection of 32 period farmhouses and miners' cottages, an indoor sampling of recreated 19th-century workshops, a local WWII resistance museum and an optics museum. Turn left on Bekkedokk and follow the signposted walkway which parallels the tracks. There are guided tours at 11am, 1.30pm and 5pm.

Sølvgruvene

Kongsberg's *raison d'être* is the profusion of silver mines in the surrounding district, especially those collectively known as Sølvgruvene.

Tours run daily in summer – for information and current times, contact Norsk Bergverksmuseum (see earlier) or the tourist office. The most frequent and popular mine tour leaves from the signposted Kongsgruvene, which lies about 700m from Saggrenda (8km south of Kongsberg). It begins with a 2.3km rail ride along the *stoll*, a tunnel which was painstakingly chipped through the mountain in order to drain water from the mines. Constructed without machinery or dynamite – the rock was removed by heating it with fire, then throwing water on the rock to crack it – the job progressed at the laborious pace of about 7cm per day and took 73 years (1782 to 1855) to complete.

Inside, visitors are guided around some of the equipment used in the extraction of silver, including an ingenious creaking and grinding lift which replaced 300m of the climb between the surface and work area on 65 wet and slippery ladders. Tours run daily in July and early August at 11am, 12.30pm, 2pm and 3.30pm. From mid-May to the end of June and in late August, only the first three tours run. In September, they're at 2pm on Sunday only. Check all details with Norsk Bergverksmuseum before heading out to the mines. Tours cost Nkr55/20 per adult/child. Be sure to bring warm clothing, as the underground temperatures can be rather chilly.

An alternative is a two-hour walk through the Christian VII mine (which operated between 1843 and 1865), which finishes up in the constricted 'North Passage'. This trip also ends with a 2.3km train ride. It runs at 5pm Monday and Thursday from 1 July to 17 August, and costs Nkr200.

If you prefer staying above ground, you can follow the route to work taken by the miners, who left Kongsberg at 4am to begin their 15-hour work day. The route passes the waterworks which powered the underground machinery and lots of abandoned equipment, finishing up at the Saxony mine. This special tour (Nkr45) operates at irregular times in summer, but can be arranged for groups at any time.

The most exciting option is the 'rope and torch' tour, which begins with a 1km walk through Crown Prince Fredrik's tunnel. You must then abseil by torchlight down 112m into the mine (after a crash course in abseiling), where you'll see vast mined areas and lots of historical equipment. These tours cost Nkr800, including abseiling instruction, and run three times over summer; contact the Kongsberg tourist office for specific dates.

Before or after your mine tour, check out the Sakkerhusene (derived from the German *zechenhäuse*, 'mine houses'), three buildings which were constructed between 1867 and 1874 and served as administrative offices, housing for workers, and areas for washing and leisure. They now house a restaurant and a souvenir shop selling rocks and fashion leather goods.

The Oslo-Notodden TIMExpressen bus runs from Kongsberg to Saggrenda (Nkr40, 10 minutes, hourly); you then walk for 15 minutes towards the mines.

Activities

Kongsberg's best hiking and cross-country skiing is found in the green, forested Knutefjell, immediately west of the town, and the Kongsberg tourist office sells the map *Kultur- og Turkart Knutefjell* (Nkr80), which details the maintained hiking and skiing tracks.

From town, the most convenient route heads into the hills from the Kongsberg Skisenter, from where it's a stiff 6km climb to *Knutehytta* hut (☎ 32 73 12 83, phone for details of accommodation), at 695m in the heart of the range. In winter, the steepest part of the climb may be negotiated on the Skisenter's 1700m chairlift. An easier and slightly shorter route to Knutehytta leads north from Meheia, on the Notodden road (accessible on Notodden buses). You can then return to town via the Skisenter. In winter, transport to the Skisenter is by Skitaxi (Nkr25 one way).

Special Events

Kongsberg's best-known annual event is the famed four-day Kongsberg Jazz Festival (☎ 32 73 31 66), which takes place in early July and attracts well-known artists from around the world.

Places to Stay

Max Kro & Camping (☎ 32 76 44 05, fax 32 76 44 72, Jondalen) Tent sites with or without car Nkr80, caravan sites Nkr120-150, 4-bed/6-bed self-catering cabins Nkr320/450. The nearest camping ground to town, this is 14km north-west on Rv37 towards Rjukan. Use the twice-daily Kongsberg-Rjukan Nor-Way Bussekspress bus (Nkr22, 15 minutes).

Kongsberg Vandrerhjem (☎ 32 73 20 24, fax 32 72 05 34, Vinjesgata 1) Dorm beds with breakfast Nkr195, singles/doubles from Nkr395/480, linen Nkr60. Kongsberg Vandrerhjem is probably your best-value accommodation option, bridging the gap between budget and mid-range.

Statskog Sølvverket Hytter (☎ 32 73 50 00, fax 32 73 50 01) Cabins Nkr250-450. Statskog, beyond the Skisenter, offers 14 simple cabins with open fireplaces.

Gyldenløve Hotel (☎ 32 86 58 00, fax 32 86 58 01, Hermann Fossgata 1) Singles Nkr645-1120, doubles Nkr795-1270. Of Kongsberg's two finer hotels, this one offers the lowest rates.

Quality Hotel Grand (☎ 32 77 28 00, fax 32 73 41 29, Christian Augustsgata 2) Singles/doubles from Nkr745/895. The Quality Hotel Grand, near the river, is a comfortable establishment with all modcons. There's a weekend nightclub here in summer (Nkr80 cover charge).

Lampeland Kurs- & Turistsenter (☎ 32 76 20 46, fax 32 76 25 03, Lampeland) Singles/doubles Nkr650/790, 4-bed family rooms with breakfast from Nkr900. About 22km north of town on Rv40 you'll find this outdoor-oriented centre, featuring rustic outdoor barbecues and canoes and bicycles for hire.

Places to Eat

Gamle Kongsberg Kro (☎ 32 73 16 33, Thornesveien 4) Mains Nkr157-243. This popular place, south of the river bridge, offers a varied but rather expensive menu. The outdoor seating allows fine views of the upper river chutes.

Jonas B Gundersen (☎ 32 72 88 00, Nymoens Torg 10) Mains Nkr99-215. At this restaurant, menus look like vinyl records and include pizzas, lasagne and salads.

Skrågata Mat & Vinhus (☎ 32 72 28 22, *Nymoens Skrågate*) Lunch sandwiches Nkr74-79, salads & pastas Nkr74-115, dinner mains Nkr88-235. The dinner menu at this fine restaurant includes beef, fish and pasta dishes.

Jeppe's Pizza (☎ 32 73 15 00, *Kirkegata 6*) Pizzas from Nkr80, other dishes Nkr86-219. In the Old Town, Jeppe's also offers steaks, Mexican-style dishes, spareribs and salads. Good fish and chips costs Nkr86.

Sydney Kebab (☎ 32 76 88 58, *Storgata 1*) Kebabs Nkr47-82, felafel Nkr45. Open to 4am Sat & Sun. The clean but basic Sydney Kebab dishes up Middle Eastern fare.

Aladdin Kebab (*Schwabesgate 3*) Kebabs Nkr49-89. Aladdin, a drive-in with authentic Middle Eastern music, does kebabs and burgers.

For coffee and snacks, try *Lampeland Café-stue* (☎ 32 73 31 30, *Storgata 19*). There's an unnamed *bakery* on Kirkegata and another at the *Rimi supermarket* (*Schwabesgate 5*), west of the train station. A good grocery selection is available at the *Rema 1000* (*Stasjonsbakken 4*), east of the bridge, and *Vinmonopolet* is located just south of the church.

Getting There & Away

By rail, Kongsberg is one to 1½ hours from Oslo (Nkr130); services connect the two cities every two hours.

NSB buses between Kongsberg and Larvik (Nkr134, 2¼ hours) run one to three times daily. Nettbuss Telemark TIMExpressen buses (☎ 35 02 60 00) connect Kongsberg with Oslo (Nkr120, 1½ hours), Saggrenda (Nkr40, 10 minutes), and Notodden (Nkr60, 35 minutes) at least hourly throughout the day and overnight. Oslo-bound ones stop at Den Norske Bank; for Saggrenda and Notodden, they stop in front of the cinema.

Getting Around

The tourist office hires out bicycles for a cost of Nkr150 for the first day, then Nkr100 per day.

THE TELEMARK CANAL

The 105km-long Telemark Canal system, a series of lakes and canals which connect Skien and Dalen (with a branch from Lunde to Notodden), lifts and lowers boats a total of 72m in 18 locks. It was built for the timber trade from 1887 to 1892 by up to 400 workers. Most canal travellers bring their own boats (the return trip from Skien to Dalen costs Nkr600 per boat) but boat-less visitors can choose between popular canal cruises or hiring a canoe and paddling on their own.

Notodden

pop 7998

The centre of industrial Notodden has little to recommend it to tourists but the surrounding area is one of Telemark's most visited places, thanks to the impressive Heddal stave church. This lovely and imposing structure, flanked by a tidy churchyard and gentle agricultural land, lies about 5km west of town on the E134.

For visitor information, contact the Notodden Turistkontor (☎ 35 01 50 00), Teatergate 3. It's closed Sunday from June to August.

Heddal Stave Church Heddal (☎ 35 02 00 93, *Heddal; bus: No 301 from Notodden; adult/child Nkr30/free (except for Sunday services); open 9am-7pm daily 21 June-20 Aug, 10am-5pm daily 20 May-20 June & 21 Aug-10 Sept)*, the largest of Norway's 28 remaining stave churches, possibly dates from 1242 but parts of the chancel date from as early as 1147. In 1952 it was heavily restored.

As with all stave churches, it's constructed around Norwegian pine support pillars – in this case, 12 large ones and six smaller ones, all topped by fearsome visages – and has four carved entrance portals. Of special interest are the lovely 1668 'rose' paintings on the rear wall, a runic inscription in the outer passageway (which suggests that construction was completed on 25 October 1242) and the 'Bishop's chair', which was made of an old pillar in the 17th century. Its ornate carvings relate the pagan tale of the Viking Sigurd the Dragon-slayer, which has been reworked

SOUTHERN NORWAY

SOUTHERN NORWAY

into a Christian parable involving Jesus Christ and the devil. The altarpiece originally dates from 1667 but was restored in 1908, and the exterior bell tower was added in 1850.

The displays in the adjacent building describe the history of the church and its carvings and reveal the finer points of general stave church construction. There's also a cafeteria.

On Saturday, when weddings are held, it may be closed to the public. On Sunday from Easter to November, services are held at 11am (visitors are welcome but to avoid disruption, they must remain for the entire one-hour service); after 1pm the church is again open to the public.

From Notodden, buses heading for Seljord and Bondal stop at Heddal.

Heddal Bygdetun The Heddal Rural Museum (☎ 35 02 08 40, Heddal; adult/child Nkr20/free; open 11am-5pm daily mid-June–mid-Aug), near the stave church, includes a collection of houses from rural Telemark.

Hydro Notodden The historic Hydro Notodden complex (☎ 35 01 71 00, Hydro Notodden Næringspark; adult/child Nkr20/10; open noon-4pm daily mid-June–mid-Aug) is now an interesting museum. In the furnace house of the old 1907 potassium nitrate (saltpetre) factory, it includes historic industrial exhibits and paintings by Norwegian fairy-tale illustrator Theodor Kittelsen.

Special Events In early August, Notodden hosts a well-attended four-day blues festival. For programs and information, contact the organising committee, Notodden Blues Festival (☎ 35 02 76 50, fax 35 02 76 51, e nbf@bluesfest.no, w www.bluesfest.no), PO Box 211, N-3672 Notodden.

Places to Stay Notodden Camping (☎ 35 01 33 10, Reshjemveien) Tent sites without/with car Nkr50/90, caravan sites Nkr115, plus Nkr10/person, cabins Nkr300-400. Notodden Camping is an acceptable site 3km west along the E134, then 200m south on Reshjemveien. Take a bus from the cen-

tre in the direction of Heddal Stavkyrkje or Seljord.

Nordlandia Telemark Hotel (☎ 35 01 20 88, fax 35 01 40 60, Torvet 8) Singles/doubles from Nkr695/895. You'll get a modern hotel room and a reasonable breakfast in this fairly bland building in the town centre.

Getting There & Away Between Kongsberg and Notodden, TIMExpressen buses run once or twice an hour (Nkr60, 35 minutes).

Skien
pop 30,411
Industrial Skien is visited mainly by travellers along the Telemark Canal. For tourist information, contact Skien Turistkontor (☎ 35 90 55 20, fax 35 90 55 30, w www.grenland.no), Nedre Hjellegate 18.

Ibsens Venstøp Author and playwright Henrik Ibsen was born in Skien on 20 March 1828, the son of a local shopkeeper and owner of a spirit distillery. In 1835 the family fell on hard times and moved out to the farm Venstøp, 5km north of Skien, where they stayed for seven years. The 1815 farmhouse, along with the brewery, servants' quarters, storehouse, barn and English-style gardens, has now been converted into a worthwhile museum (☎ 35 52 57 49, Venstøphøyda; adult/child Nkr40/20; open 10am-6pm daily 15 May-30 Aug). Buses from Skien run only twice daily.

Places to Stay Skien Vandrerhjem (☎ 35 50 48 70, fax 35 50 48 79, Moflatveien 65) Dorm beds Nkr130, singles/doubles Nkr280/400. Open year-round. Breakfast costs Nkr50 at this well-equipped hostel.

Hotell Herkules (☎ 35 59 63 11, fax 35 59 65 88, Moflatveien 59) Singles/doubles Nkr525/720. Hotell Herkules is a reasonably good mid-range option.

Getting There & Away Nor-Way Bussekspress buses run to Notodden (Nkr97, 1¾ hours) and Rjukan (Nkr185, 3¼ hours) once or twice daily. NSB trains run every hour or two from Skien to Larvik and Oslo (Nkr220, 1¾ hours).

Dalen

Visitor information for the beautifully located town of Dalen is dispensed by the Dalen/Tokke Turistkontor (☎ 35 07 70 65, fax 35 07 73 41). If you're there for a while, you may want to visit the nearby **Åmdals Verk mines** (☎ 35 07 79 30, Åmdals Verk, Tokke; adult/child Nkr50/15; open 10am-5pm daily 1 June-15 Aug).

Buøy Camping (☎ 35 07 75 87, fax 35 07 77 01) Tent sites Nkr130, singles/triples Nkr200/350, cabins Nkr450-650. This is a reasonable camping ground with hostel-style rooms and cabins.

Dalen Hotell (☎ 35 53 70 00, fax 35 53 70 11, Dalen) Singles/doubles from Nkr850/1170. The ornate Dalen Hotell, first opened in 1894, lies 1km from Dalen Brygge but, for a night soaking up its historic atmosphere you'll pay a rather hefty price.

Organised Tours

Daily from 24 June to 12 August, the ferry M/S *Telemarken* plies the Øst-Telemark Canal system between Akkerhaugen, 24km south of Notodden, and Lunde (Nkr200, 1½ hours). It leaves Akkerhaugen/Lunde at 10am/1.50pm. If you only want to sail one way from Lunde to Akkerhaugen, buses leave from Notodden for Lunde (Nkr88, one hour) at 11.55am (10.55am on weekends) and from Akkerhaugen back to Notodden at 5.10pm (6.10pm on weekends).

Three times weekly between mid-May and early September (daily from 18 June to 11 August), the sightseeing boats M/S *Victoria* (built in 1882) and M/S *Henrik Ibsen* (built in 1907) make the leisurely (if not rather sluggish) 11-hour journey between Skien and Dalen (Nkr300/150). Round trips, including one-way by boat from Skien to Dalen and return to Skien by bus (three hours), cost a total of Nkr500. In the opposite direction, you can take the Telemark Bilruter (☎ 35 06 54 00) bus from Skien back to Dalen (Nkr200, 3¼ hours, daily except Saturday 19 June to 10 August).

For further information, contact Telemarkreiser (☎ 35 90 00 30, fax 35 90 00 21, e info@telemarkreiser.no, w www.visitTelemark.com), or the *Victoria* (mobile ☎ 94 15 25 90) or *Henrik Ibsen* (mobile ☎ 94 58 00 15).

A great way to see the canal is by canoe, kayak or bicycle, and the ferries will transport your own boat/bicycle for Nkr150/100 between Skien and Dalen. Canoe hire at Gåsodden Camping (☎ 35 54 50 77), Fjærekilen, Skien, costs Nkr200/50 per day/hour.

RJUKAN
pop 3732

The 6km-long industrial town of Rjukan, squeezed into the deep Vestfjorddalen, nestles at the foot of Telemark's highest and most-recognisable peak, Gausta (1883m). Thanks to its founders, industrial engineer Sam Eyde and physicist Kristian Birkeland, this hydroelectric company town was aesthetically planned and designed and, in the first 10 years after its founding in 1907, the industry supported 10,000 residents.

In the early days, the administrators' homes occupied the highest slopes, where the sun shone the longest; below them were the homes of office workers and in the valley's dark depths dwelt the labourers. That segregation has now been eliminated but, on the valley floor, direct sunlight remains a premium commodity. Today, tourists can visit local industries and handicrafts outlets, including the Mår Kraftverk hydroelectric plant, with its daunting wooden stairway of 3975 steps (it's the world's longest!).

An ambitious new ski area is planned for nearby Gaustablikk, with 61 new alpine runs (there are currently 15 alpine runs) and accommodation (mostly chalets) options totalling 10,000 beds. The Rjukan area offers some of the best ice climbing in Europe, with around 140 frozen waterfalls when conditions are optimum.

Information

The very helpful Tinn/Rjukan Turistkontor (☎ 35 09 12 90, fax 35 08 15 75, e info@visitrjukan.com), Torget 2, can load you up with brochures, information and inspiration. If you need outdoor gear, you'll find a selection at the Veidemannen shop in the centre, and there's a bookshop on Sam Eydes gate.

SOUTHERN NORWAY

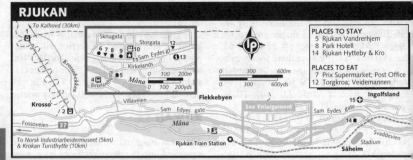

RJUKAN

PLACES TO STAY
5 Rjukan Vandrerhjem
8 Park Hotell
14 Rjukan Hytteby & Kro

PLACES TO EAT
7 Prix Supermarket; Post Office
12 Torgkroa; Veidemannen

Norsk Industriarbeidermuseet

The Norwegian Industrial Workers' Museum (☎ 35 09 90 00, Vemork power plant; adult/child Nkr55/30; open 10am-6pm daily May-Sept), 7km west of Rjukan, honours the Socialist Workers' Party, which reached its height of Norwegian activities in the 1950s. The Soviet-style propaganda may now seem rather ludicrous, but you won't want to miss the 30-minute film If Hitler Had the Bomb describing the events which inspired the 1965 Kirk Douglas film The Heroes of Telemark. It recounts the brave exploits of the Norwegian Resistance movement, which thwarted Hitler's WWII nuclear program with its daring sabotage of the Nazis' heavy-water laboratory in the cellar of the hydroelectric power station (see the boxed text 'The Heroes of Telemark').

There's also an interesting exhibition about the world-wide race in the 1930s and '40s to make an atom bomb. It consists of short films, touch-screen exhibits, photos and dioramas. Look out for the miniature power station in the main hall, which really does make electricity!

The museum is housed in the Vemork power station, which was the largest in the world when it was completed in 1911. If you're driving, you'll have to park at the swinging bridge and either take the summer shuttle up the hill (Nkr20/10 adult/child return) or hoof it, which takes about 15 minutes (only disabled travellers and seniors over 65 are permitted to drive up). By bus, take a westbound Bybuss (Nkr23, five minutes), three of which run on weekdays.

Hardangervidda National Park Centre

Around 21km west of Rjukan, this new visitor centre (☎ 35 09 57 00, Møsvatn; adult/child Nkr55/30; open 10am-6pm daily July-mid-Sept, 10am-6pm Sat & Sun rest of year) features exhibitions on Norwegian reindeer, interactive computer displays, an interesting 3D map, and a video (available in English). The children's room is particularly well presented.

Tinn Museum

This small roadside folk museum (☎ 35 08 15 32, Sam Eydes gate; adult/child Nkr20/10; open 3pm-5pm Tues-Fri, 2pm-4pm Sat & Sun late June-early Aug) is a collection of houses and furnishings from the 16th to the 20th centuries. Guided tours run at 4pm Tuesday to Friday and 3pm at weekends.

Dressin Trips

Ask the tourist office for details about local trips by dressin (rail-bikes, or bicycles on bogies). The 10km-long trips (Nkr250) start at lake Tinnsjø and follow the disused rail line up the valley to Rjukan; maximum one adult and two children per dressin.

Krossobanen

The Krossobanen cable car (☎ 35 09 04 44; one-way/return Nkr35/70, bike Nkr15; operates 10am-6pm daily 2 July-2 Sept, 10am-5pm daily 1 June-1 July & 3-16 Sept) was constructed in 1928 by Norsk Hydro to provide its employees with a bit of access to the sun. It has now been renovated and

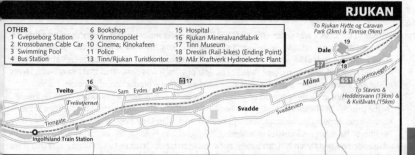

SOUTHERN NORWAY

whisks tourists up to Gvepseborg (886m) for a view over the deep, dark recesses.

Hiking

The popular hiking track up Gausta (1883m) leads to DNT's *Gaustahytta* (☎ 35 09 41 50) at the summit, which it shares with an enormous NATO radio tower that severely disrupts the mountain's profile. The hut was built in 1893 and provides accommodation for hikers. In former times hikers had to struggle up to the peak all the way from Rjukan, but there's now a road link (the Fv651) to Stavsro at lake Heddersvann, at a height of 1173m. There's no public transport on the 16km route from town but taxis (☎ 35 09 14 00) are available for a cost of around Nkr240.

Allow all day for the hike, which leaves plenty of time for exploring the summit. The tourist office distributes a map of the Fv651, but the *Turkart Gausta Området* is better (Nkr40).

From Gvepseborg, the top station on the Krossobanen cable car, good walking or cycling tracks strike out onto the expansive Hardangervidda plateau, which is home to Europe's largest herd of wild reindeer. The main route, which can be used by cyclists, leads 13km north to DNT's *Helberghytta* and the *Kalhovd Turisthytta* (☎ 35 09 05 10). An eight-hour walk takes you from Gvepseborg to Kalhovd – where you can catch a bus out or head on to connect with the ferry (Nkr100) to *Mårbuhytta*. From there it's a two-day hike west to *Mogen Turist-hytta* (☎ 35 07 41 15), where you can catch the Møsvatn ferry (Nkr160) back to Skinnarbu, west of Rjukan on Rv37.

Alternatively you can follow the marked route which begins above Rjukan Fjellstue, just north of the Rv37. This historic track follows the Sabotørruta (Saboteurs' Route), the path taken by the members of the Norwegian Resistance as they approached their target, the heavy-water laboratory at Vemork. Along the way, several information plaques describe their activities in context. Instead of dropping down from Nystaul, however, you can also continue 2½ hours farther east to Gvepseborg.

The best map to use for these hikes is Statens Kartverk's *Hardangervidda Øst*, at a scale of 1:100,000 and available from the tourist office (Nkr118).

Places to Stay

Rjukan Hytte og Caravan Park (☎ 35 09 63 53, fax 35 09 62 30, Near Rv37) Small tent sites Nkr30-40 plus Nkr12-14/person, car or caravan extra Nkr60-70, 2-bed huts Nkr235-270, 3-bed/4-bed/7-bed huts Nkr310/335/450. Acceptable camping is available here about 7km east of the town centre; the huts share toilet facilities. Take the Bybuss (Nkr23, five minutes) to get there.

Rjukan Vandrerhjem (☎ 35 09 05 27, fax 35 09 09 96, Birkelandsgata 2) Dorm beds Nkr115, singles/doubles Nkr220/300. Open year-round. The only hostel in the area, this is well equipped (it's Nkr55 extra from September to April, when breakfast is included).

Rjukan Hytteby & Kro (☎ 35 09 01 22, fax 35 09 01 32, Brogata 9) 2-bed/4-bed

The Heroes of Telemark

In 1933 in the USA it was discovered that 0.02% of all water molecules are 'heavy', meaning that the hydrogen atoms are actually deuterium, an isotope that contains an extra neutron. Although heavy water looks and tastes like water, it weighs 10% more, boils at 1.4°C higher and freezes at 4°C higher than ordinary water. In the nascent stages of nuclear physics, it was discovered that heavy water serves to stabilise nuclear fission reactions, making it invaluable in the production of the atom bomb.

During WWII in Norway the occupying Germans were aware that heavy water could be created by the process of electrolysis and, in the hope of eventually building an atom bomb, they set up a heavy-water production plant at Vemork, near Rjukan. Had they been allowed to continue, they might well have been successful in achieving their goal and building the bomb, and the war might have ended quite differently. Fortunately, between March and October 1942, Allied insurgents were able to gather intelligence and mount Operation Grouse, which turned out to be one of the most daring sabotage missions of the entire war.

The mission was launched in October 1942 when four Norwegians parachuted into Sognadal, west of Rjukan. They were to be joined a month later by 34 specially trained British saboteurs who would arrive in two gliders. The British insurgents had prepared for their landing at Skoland near the lake Møsvatnet, but one tow plane and its glider crashed into a mountain, and the other glider crashed on landing. All the British survivors were shot by the Germans.

Undeterred, the Norwegian group changed its mission name to Swallow and retreated to Hardangervidda, where they subsisted through the worst of the winter. On 16 February 1943 a new British-trained group called Gunnerside landed on Hardangervidda. Unfortunately a blizzard was raging and they wound up a long 30km march from their intended drop site. By the evening of 27 February the saboteurs were all holed up at Fjøsbudalen, north of Vemork, waiting to strike. After descending the steep mountainside along the now-famous Sabotørruta (Saboteurs' Route), they crossed the gorge to the heavy-water plant, wire-clipped the perimeter fence and planted the explosives which largely destroyed the facility. Some of the saboteurs retreated on skis to Hardangervidda then fled, in uniform and fully armed, into neutral Sweden, while the rest remained on the plateau, successfully avoiding capture.

The plant was rebuilt by the Germans, but on 16 November 1943, 140 US planes openly bombed Vemork, killing 20 Norwegians in the process. The Germans abandoned any hopes of producing heavy water in Norway and decided to shift their remaining stocks to Germany. However, the remaining saboteurs realised that this relocation procedure involved a ferry across the lake Tinnsjø and, on 19 February 1944, the night before the ferry was due to sail, they placed a timed charge on the boat. The following night, the entire project was literally blown out of the water.

In 1965 this intriguing story was made into the dramatic (but historically inaccurate) film *The Heroes of Telemark*, starring Kirk Douglas.

cabins Nkr495/740. Rjukan Hytteby & Kro is built to emulate the early-20th-century hydroelectric workers' cabins.

Park Hotell (☎ *35 08 21 88, fax 35 08 21 89, Sam Eydes gate 67*) Singles/doubles Mon-Fri Nkr570/790, Sat & Sun Nkr495/ 645. This rather plush hotel is very central.

A couple of places at the lake Kvitåvatn, off the Rv651 and 15km from town, provide a front-row view of Gausta and easy access to the Skipsfjell/Gaustablikk ski area, but you currently need a car for access.

Gaustablikk Høyfjellshotell (☎ *35 09 14 22, fax 35 09 19 75, Gaustablikk*) Singles/ doubles Nkr705/830. Lunch mains Nkr58-114, 2-course dinner Nkr175. Here you'll find a pleasant mountain lodge with good facilities and meals.

Kvitåvatn Fjellstoge (☎ *35 09 20 40, fax 35 09 20 95, Gaustablikk*) Beds per person

Nkr165, minimum charge Nkr330. The simple accommodation here is either in a cosy pine lodge with six bunks per room, or in smaller annexes or huts.

Krokan Turisthytte (☎ 35 09 51 31, fax 35 09 01 90, Near Rv37) 4-bed cabins Nkr350-450. About 10km west of Rjukan, you can visit this historic place, built in 1869 as DNT's first hut but no longer part of the DNT network. You're housed in museum-like 16th-century log cabins, and traditional meals include meat soup (Nkr45).

Places to Eat

Central Rjukan is a bit short on places to eat.

Park Hotell (☎ 35 08 21 88, Sam Eydes gate 67) Mains Nkr133-233. This fine but expensive restaurant, strangely named 'Ammonia Restaurant', serves meat and fish dishes. There's also a bar and a week-end disco.

Kinokafeen (☎ 40 85 60 48, Storstulgate 1) Mains Nkr150-264. Kinokafeen, at the cinema, offers a range of main courses, but also smaller dishes (Nkr48 to Nkr89) and ciabatta sandwiches (Nkr30).

Torgkroa (☎ 35 09 09 30, Sam Eydes gate 93) Burgers Nkr39-70, mains Nkr85-169, pizzas from Nkr140. This straightfor-ward and popular place on the square serves burgers and a variety of dinners.

Rjukan Hytteby & Kro (☎ 35 09 01 22, Brogata 9) This has a pizza and fast-food hang-out with dishes for around Nkr100.

Self-caterers can get supplies at the *Prix* supermarket, by the post office on Sam Eydes gate.

Entertainment

Park Hotell (☎ 35 08 21 88, Sam Eydes gate 67) The bar clientele here is mostly over 30 and the disco attracts the 18 to 25 crowd.

There is a *swimming pool* across the river, and a *cinema (Storstulgate 1)* which changes films weekly.

Getting There & Away

A daily express bus connects Rjukan to Oslo (Nkr260, 3¾ hours) via Kongsberg (Nkr160, 2¼ hours). If you're driving, there's a summer-only shortcut between Rjukan and Geilo over the Tessungdalen toll road (Nkr25 per car).

Getting Around

Rjukan's linear distances will seem intimi-dating, but fortunately, the convenient local Bybuss runs from Vemork to Rjukan Hytte og Caravan Park. Bike hire at the tourist of-fice costs Nkr130/day, plus Nkr500 deposit.

SELJORD
pop 1500

Scenic little Seljord is known mainly as the home of Selma, the Nessie-type monster that inhabits the depths of the lake Seljordvatn (see the special section Folklore & Legends in Norway). She has been seen on occasion since the early 18th century and still makes an occasional appearance on warm, sunny days. **Sjøormsenteret** *(Lake Serpent Centre; ☎ 35 05 03 55; adult/child Nkr40/free; open noon-6pm daily July)*, by the road through the centre of town, offers the lowdown on Seljord's best-known resident.

Hikers can also seek out the area's other enigmatic residents – the feuding troll women, Ljose-Signe, Glima and Tårån, who inhabit the surrounding peaks. Seljord was also the inspiration for some of Nor-way's best-known folk legends, including Asbjørnsen and Moe's *The Three Billy Goats Gruff*, known the world over.

You may also want to check out the charming 12th-century Romanesque stone *church (admission free; open 11am-5pm daily July)*, built in honour of St Olav and located at the northern end of town. In the grounds, between the church and the churchyard wall, there are two impressions reputedly made by two mountain trolls who were so upset by the encroachment of Chris-tianity that they pummelled the site with boulders, hoping to destroy the structure.

Seljord Turistinformasjon (☎ 35 05 10 06) is open 8am to 7pm weekdays year-round and also 9am to 6pm weekends from mid-June to mid-August.

Special Events

On the second weekend of September, Seljord holds the Dyrsku'n festival, which started in 1866 and is now Norway's largest traditional market and cattle show, attracting 60,000 visitors annually. If you want to experience the full measure of rural Telemark, don't miss it; it's wise to book accommodation in advance.

Places to Stay & Eat

The tourist office keeps lists of rooms, cabins and houses for rent.

Seljord Camping og Badeplass (☎/fax 35 05 04 71) Tent sites Nkr100, cabins Nkr300-650. Open 23 June-20 Aug. This pleasantly situated camping ground beside the lake is the dock for monster cruises on Seljordvatn (fares vary with the number of passengers).

Seljord Hotel (☎ 35 05 10 00, fax 35 05 10 01) Singles/doubles Nkr795/895. This hotel is on the main street in town.

Sjøormkroa (☎ 35 05 05 02, by E134 and the lake) Mains Nkr76-139. You'll get a decent meal in this odd serpent-shaped building.

Getting There & Away

Nor-Way Bussekspress (Haukeliekspressen) buses connect Seljord with Notodden (Nkr97, 1¼ hours) and Oslo (Nkr230, 3¼ hours) up to four times daily.

SETESDALEN

Setesdalen, one of Norway's most traditional and conservative regions, makes a secluded and little-trodden side-trip off the southern coastal route. This forested and lake-filled mountain valley enjoys some of southern Norway's most beautiful landscapes, thanks mainly to its fabulous geology, and is popular with outdoor enthusiasts: rafters, canoers, hikers and climbers. In Valle (90km north of Evje), for example, rock climbers will find granite ascents up to 700m high, and the same area also boasts several DNT mountain huts.

Evje
pop 1400

The heart of the action is the village of Evje, which serves as a gateway to the wilder parts of upper Setesdalen and dishes up heavy doses of outdoor recreation.

It's also a geologist's paradise – the ridge east of town is dotted with mines and mineral deposits.

Information The useful Setesdal Informasjonsenter (☎ 37 93 14 00, fax 37 93 14 55, ⓦ www.setesdal.com) occupies the same building as the bus terminal. For information on mountain hiking and huts in the Setesdalen area, contact the Kristiansand og Oppland Turistforening (☎ 38 02 52 63), Kirkegata 15, in Kristiansand.

Evje og Hornnes Museum Rock fans will enjoy the Evje og Hornnes Museum (☎ 37 93 07 94; adult/child Nkr25/15; open 11am-4pm daily mid-June–mid-Aug), 2km west of town and across the river in Fennefoss, which displays a large collection of minerals found in the surrounding hills, as well as exhibits on local nickel mining and traditional rural life in Setesdalen.

Setesdal Mineral Park For interesting displays of local and worldwide minerals, visit one of Norway's finest collections at the Setesdal Mineral Park (☎ 37 93 13 10, Hornnes; adult/child Nkr70/40; open 10am-5pm daily mid-June–mid-Aug, shorter hours May–mid-June & mid-Aug–Oct), about 10km south of Evje.

Activities The Setesdal Rafting & Activity Centre (☎ 37 93 11 77, fax 37 93 13 34, ⓔ tim@troll-mountain.no, ⓦ www.troll-mountain.no), about 7km north of Evje, and Viking Adventures Norway (☎ 37 93 13 03, fax 37 93 15 63, ⓔ vanevje@online.no, ⓦ www.viking-adventures.no), in town, both organise a range of outdoor adventure activities, from white-water rafting, canoeing, kayaking, canyoning and riverboarding to rock climbing, mountain climbing and abseiling.

If that's too much adrenalin for your tastes, the Setesdal Rafting & Activity Centre also offers hiking and wildlife-viewing safaris in search of beaver, moose and other critters. Horse riding can also be arranged. Alternatively, you can hire a canoe or mountain bike and head off on your own.

On the mountain east of town, a short and easy nature trail for mineral aficionados winds between several mines and mineral deposits. Take the Gautestad road and turn south about 3km from town.

Places to Stay & Eat *Odden Camping (☎ 37 93 06 03, fax 37 93 11 01)* Tent sites without/with car Nkr50/110, plus Nkr10/person, caravan sites per 2 people Nkr120, 4–5-bed huts Nkr350-400. Wonderful Odden Camping is located by the river just 200m south of town.

Viking Adventures B&B (☎ 37 93 13 03, fax 37 93 15 63) B&B per person Nkr295. Located 1km south of central Evje, Viking Adventures offers good quality bed and breakfast with en suite facilities.

Evje Vandrerhjem (☎ 37 93 11 77, fax 37 93 13 34, Surveit) Dorm beds Nkr120, singles & doubles Nkr250, breakfast Nkr60. Evje Vandrerhjem, in Surveit, 7km north Evje, is a modern hostel run and used by the Setesdal Rafting & Activity Centre.

Revsnes Hotell (☎ 37 93 43 00, fax 37 93 41 27, Byglandsfjord) Singles Nkr575-750, doubles Nkr830-940. 3-course dinner Nkr250. The recommended modern Revsnes Hotell, 10 minutes north of town, has a lovely location by the lake Byglandsfjorden.

Stigeren Restaurant (☎ 37 93 08 28; Central Evje) Mains Nkr83-258. Here you'll find a three-course a la carte menu with soup, meat and fish dishes, and desserts.

Pernille Cafeteria (☎ 37 93 00 69; Central Evje) Mains Nkr89-115. The reasonable Pernille Cafeteria serves a good variety of tasty traditional Norwegian offerings, fish dishes and burgers.

Dragon Inn (☎ 37 93 09 19, Near Rv9) Dishes Nkr83-129. The Dragon Inn serves acceptable Chinese specialities and is located just south of the town centre.

Getting There & Away The daily Nor-Way Bussekspress bus between Kristiansand (Nkr80, one hour) and Haukeligrend (Nkr230, three hours) runs via Evje. It provides access to Byglandsfjord, Valle, Bykle and Hovden, and connects with services to Haugesund and Bergen at Haukeligrend.

Getting Around You can hire a mountain bike at Setesdal Rafting & Activity Centre (☎ 37 93 11 77), 7km north of Evje.

Rygnestadtunet
One of the finest Norwegian folk museums in the country is Rygnestadtunet *(☎ 37 93 63 03, Valle; adult/child Nkr40/20; open 10am-6pm daily July, 11am-5pm daily 20-30 June & 1-15 Aug)*, 9km north of Valle by Rv9. At this old farm, with a unique three-storey storehouse (from 1590) and an extraordinary collection of 15th-century painted textiles, staff may be dressed in traditional costume.

Bykle
A nice short stop for drivers through Setesdalen is the distinctive log-built **Bykle Kirkje** *(☎ 37 93 81 01; admission Nkr20; open 11am-7pm daily 23 June-12 Aug)*. This church dates from 1619 and is one of the smallest churches in Norway. The roses on the front of the galleries and traditional rose paintings on the wall were added in the 1820s, after an 1804 restoration.

There's also a lovely signpost-guided **walk** past many historical and cultural sites above the Otra River, 5km south of town. The route, which takes about 30 minutes, dates from at least 1770 and was once the main route through Setesdalen.

Hovden
In a wild, open landscape at the very top of Setesdalen lies the **ski centre** of Hovden *(☎ 37 93 81 80)*. Tourist information about the region is dispensed by Hovdenferie (☎ 37 93 96 30, fax 37 93 97 33, ⒠ hovden@setesdal.com).

In summer, you can reach the viewpoint or start a hiking trip by taking the chairlift to the summit of Mt Nos (1176m), which costs Nkr60. It operates from noon to 2pm daily in July and on Wednesday and Saturday in August. During the ski season, lift tickets cost Nkr230/400/550 for one/two/three days; alpine equipment costs Nkr195/295/365 to rent; nordic equipment rental is Nkr120/170/205; and snowboard rental costs Nkr260/410/540.

SOUTHERN NORWAY

In any season, climbers may want to practise on the 6m-high indoor climbing wall at the **G-Sport shop** *(☎ 37 93 95 66)*. If the weather's bad, visit the adventure swimming pool **Hovden Badeland** *(☎ 37 93 98 00; admission Nkr115 for 3hrs; open June-Apr)*.

The **Hovden Jernvinnermuseum** *(Iron Production Museum; ☎ 37 93 96 30; admission Nkr20; open 11am-5pm daily 23 June-12 Aug)* surrounds a reconstructed ancient smelter and presents methods of medieval iron and coal extraction and processing.

Places to Stay & Eat *Hovden Fjellstoge & Vandrerhjem (☎ 37 93 95 43, fax 37 93 98 18, Lundane)* Dorm rooms Nkr190, singles/doubles Nkr290/450. Lunches/dinners from Nkr65/89. Accommodation at this hostel, a traditional-style wooden building with a grass roof, includes breakfast. It also serves traditional Norwegian meals.

There's also a host of ski huts, flats, chalets and hotels offering good deals in summer. To hire a *holiday home* for five to 12 people, contact Hovden Hytteformidling *(☎ 37 93 97 29, fax 37 93 98 33, ⓦ www .hovden-hytteformidling.no)*.

You'll find a range of meal options at the *Furumo Kafé (☎ 37 93 97 72)* and *Bamse Gatekjøkken (☎ 37 93 91 88)*.

SIRDAL
Sirdal, one of Norway's most important hydroelectric areas, is best known as the access route to the scenic 1000m road descent through 27 hairpin bends to Lysebotn, depicted on dozens of postcards. From the well-appointed DNT hut at *Ådneram*, at the top of Sirdal, hikers can reach Lysebotn in nine hours (you need to follow the road for the last 4km).

For tourist information and details of wilderness tours, horse riding and dog sledging, contact Sirdalsferie *(☎ 38 37 13 90, fax 38 37 13 80, ⓦ www.sirdalsferie .com)* in Tjørhom.

At **Tonstad Kraftverk** *(power station; ☎ 38 37 13 90, Tonstad)*, in the central part of the valley, there's an interesting 17-tonne glass sculpture called *Pure Energy*. There are tours (Nkr120) of the station at 1.30pm weekdays.

Sinnes Fjellstue (☎ 38 37 12 02, fax 38 37 12 05, Sinnes) Singles/doubles from Nkr500/700. This mountain lodge is closed in May.

Bus No 471 *(☎ 38 37 77 77)* runs once daily except Sunday between Tonstad and Ådneram (Nkr59, 1¼ hours), but advance booking is required for pick-up at Ådneram. The Nor-Way Bussekspress Suleskareks-pressen connects Stavanger (Nkr150, two hours) and Oslo (Nkr450, 7½ hours) via Fidjeland, 7km south of Ådneram, daily from 8 June to 30 September.

Central Norway

Stretching northwards from Oslo to the historic mining town of Røros and westwards across the highland plateaus, Central Norway takes in the country's highest mountains and best-known national parks. Not surprisingly, it's also one of the most popular outdoor playgrounds for both Norwegians and visitors. Railways create major arteries through the region. The scenic Oslo-Bergen railway climbs through forests and alpine villages up to Norway's cross-country skiing paradise, the stark Hardangervidda Plateau.

Eastern Central Norway

HAMAR
pop 22,224
The commercial town of Hamar sits beside the immense lake Mjøsa and is the capital of Hedmark county. There's a couple of worthwhile sites and many people stop en route between Oslo, Lillehammer and points north. The tourist office (☎ 62 52 12 17, fax 62 53 35 65), Torggata 1, opens daily from 18 June to 12 August, and weekdays the rest of the year.

Olympic Sites
Hamar boasts proudly of hosting several Olympic events in 1994. The impressive **Northern Lights amphitheatre**, the world's largest wooden hall, was built for figure skating and short-track skating events. The town's landmark, however, is the **sports arena** (☎ 62 51 75 00, Åkersvikaveien; admission Nkr20; open 8am-6pm Mon-Fri, 10am-6pm Sat & Sun 1 June-15 Aug), a graceful structure with the lines of an upturned Viking ship. The building holds 10,000 spectators and has been described as a 'sports cathedral without equal'. Ice skating (Nkr70) is available late July to mid-August.

Highlights

- Exploring the old copper mines and entering a time warp in the Unesco World Heritage List town of Røros
- Trekking along the extensive hiking routes through the spectacular Jotunheimen and Rondane national parks
- White-water rafting on the Driva or in Heidalen
- Visiting the superb Norsk Skogbruksmuseum (Norwegian Forestry Museum) in Elverum
- Looking for musk oxen in Dovrefjell
- Nordic skiing on the vast Hardangervidda Plateau

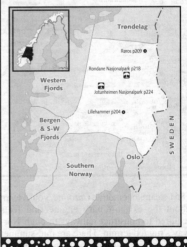

Norsk Jernbanemuseum
The open-air Norwegian Railway Museum (☎ 62 51 31 60, Strandveien; adult/child Nkr30/20; open 10am-4pm daily 27 May-2 Sept, to 6pm July), on the Mjøsa shore, was established in 1896 in honour of Norway's railway history. In addition to lovely historic stations, engine sheds, rail coaches and the

201

CENTRAL NORWAY

CENTRAL NORWAY

1. Vassendsetra Hut
2. Johan Falkberget Museum
3. Røros Hestesportsenter
4. Olavsgruva Mine
5. Henningsgården Turiststasjon
6. Langen Gjestegård
7. Johnsgård Turistsenter
8. Hummelfjellet Ski Area
9. Vingelsgård Gjestgiveri
10. Kongsvold Fjellstue
11. Hjerkin Fjellstue
12. Renheim Hut
13. Snøheim
14. Fokstumyra Naturreservat
15. Bjørkhol Camping
16. Kvitskriuprestene
17. Bøverdalen
18. Spiterstulen
19. Klara Camping

CENTRAL NORWAY

1861 steam locomotive *Caroline*, you'll learn about the extraordinary engineering feats required to construct railways through Norway's rugged terrain. There are mid-summer tours with the *Caroline*; book in advance.

Hedmarkmuseet & Domkirkeodden

The extensive open-air county museum (☎ 62 54 27 00, Strandveien 100; adult/child Nkr60/30; open 10am-4pm daily 18 May-16 June & 20 Aug-9 Sept, to 6pm 17 June-19 Aug), 1.5km west of the town centre, includes 18th- and 19th-century buildings, a local folk

history exhibit featuring the creepy Devil's Finger, the partly re-roofed bishop's house from 1250, the ruins and well of the adjacent castle, and the extraordinary 'glass cathedral'. The cathedral and castle dominated Hamar until 1567, when they were sacked by the Swedes – in 1998 the ruined arches were protected by a huge glass roof. Take bus No 6 from the town library (Nkr20, hourly).

Places to Stay & Eat

Hamar NAF Camping (☎ 62 52 44 90, fax 62 52 23 90, Strandveien 156) Tent sites without/with car Nkr100/130, basic cabins

Nkr250-320. Near the railway museum, you'll find this reasonable camping ground.

Vikingskipet Motell og Vandrerhjem *(☎ 62 52 60 60, fax 62 53 24 60, Åkersvikavegen 24)* Dorm beds Nkr135, singles/doubles Nkr260/360. This place offers good-value accommodation within 100m of the sports arena.

Seiersted Pensjonat *(☎/fax 62 55 22 48, Holsetgata 64)* Singles/doubles Nkr350/695. Centrally located Seiersted Pensjonat offers a homy atmosphere and dinner is available from Nkr55.

Pizza figures prominently in Hamar. ***Pizzaninni*** *(☎ 62 52 49 65, Torggata 24)* is quite reasonable and charges from Nkr80 for pizza, while ***Bykjeller'n*** *(☎ 62 54 31 00, Torggata 82)* serves meat and fish dishes for Nkr185 to Nkr265.

Seaside *(☎ 62 52 62 10, Brygga)* Mains Nkr125-230. This lakeside restaurant offers meat, fish and vegetarian dishes. Baked potatoes start at Nkr71.

Getting There & Away

Nor-Way Bussekspress buses run to/from the Western Fjords several times daily. Frequent trains run between Oslo (Nkr175, 1¼ hours, once or twice hourly) and Hamar; some services continue to Trondheim (Nkr510, five hours, four or five daily) via Lillehammer. Trains also run to Røros (Nkr370, 3¼ hours, one to three daily), with connections for Trondheim.

Skibladner (☎ 62 52 70 85, fax 62 53 39 23, e skibladner@online.no, w www.skibladner.no), the world's oldest paddle steamer, offers relaxing transport around lake Mjøsa. From 26 June to 11 August, it plies the lake between Hamar, Gjøvik and Lillehammer. Most travellers opt for the route between Hamar and Lillehammer (Nkr200, four hours) on Tuesday, Thursday and Saturday, which can be done as a return day trip (from Hamar only). Jazz evenings aboard the steamer cost Nkr380, including food.

LILLEHAMMER
pop 18,560

Lillehammer lies at the northern end of Mjøsa, surrounded by farms, forests and small settlements. The town has long been a popular Norwegian ski resort but became internationally renowned in 1994, when it successfully hosted the Winter Olympics. Lillehammer is architecturally pleasant and has decent restaurants and nightlife.

Orientation & Information

There's no denying that Lillehammer's tunnels, one-way streets and convoluted traffic patterns create a nightmare for motorists. For pedestrians, however, the centre is small and readily negotiated. The main shopping street, Storgata, lies just two blocks east of the Skysstasjon (the bus and train stations). The Lillehammer tourist office (☎ 61 25 92 99, fax 61 25 65 85, e info@lillehammerturist.no, w www.lillehammerturist.no) is at Elvegata 19, with a branch at the Strandtorget shopping centre. Lillehammer og Omland DNT (☎ 61 25 13 06), Storgata 34, sells hiking and skiing maps, dispenses mountain hut information and organises mountain hiking trips.

Olympic Sites

When Lillehammer won its bid for the 1994 Winter Olympics, the Norwegian government ploughed over two billion kroner into the infrastructure. Most of these amenities remain in use and visitors can tour the main Olympic sites, including the Lysgårdsbakkene **ski jump tower** *(☎ 61 25 11 40, Olympiaparken; admission Nkr15; open 9am-8pm daily mid-June–mid-Aug, shorter hours at other times)*. The **ski jump chairlift** ascends to a panoramic view over the town and costs Nkr30/25, including admission to Lysgårdsbakkene.

The **Norwegian Olympic Museum** *(☎ 61 25 21 00, Olympiaparken; adult/child Nkr60/30, or if including Maihaugen Folk Museum Nkr120/55; open 10am-6pm daily mid-May–mid-Sept)*, at the Håkons Hall hockey venue, is a worthwhile effort outlining the history of the Olympics in both ancient and modern times.

At Hunderfossen, 15km north of town, you can career down the **Olympic bobsled run** *(☎ 61 27 75 50, Hunderfossen)* with a

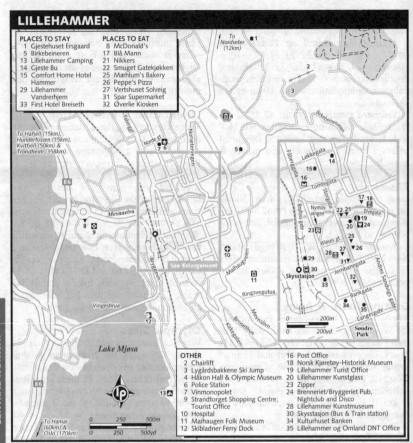

LILLEHAMMER

PLACES TO STAY
1 Gjestehuset Ersgaard
5 Birkebeineren
13 Lillehammer Camping
14 Gjeste Bu
15 Comfort Home Hotel Hammer
29 Lillehammer Vandrerhjem
33 First Hotel Breiseth

PLACES TO EAT
8 McDonald's
17 Blå Mann
21 Nikkers
22 Smuget Gatekjøkken
25 Mæhlum's Bakery
26 Peppe's Pizza
27 Vertshuset Solveig
31 Spar Supermarket
32 Øverlie Kiosken

OTHER
2 Chairlift
3 Lygårdsbakkene Ski Jump
4 Håkon Hall & Olympic Museum
6 Police Station
7 Vinmonopolet
9 Strandtorget Shopping Centre; Tourist Office
10 Hospital
11 Maihaugen Folk Museum
12 Skibladner Ferry Dock
16 Post Office
18 Norsk Kjøretøy-Historisk Museum
19 Lillehammer Turist Office
20 Lillehammer Kunstglass
23 Zipper
24 Brenneriet/Bryggeriet Pub, Nightclub and Disco
28 Lillehammer Kunstmuseum
30 Skysstasjon (Bus & Train station)
34 Kulturhuset Banken
35 Lillehammer og Omland DNT Office

professional bobsled pilot. Taxibobs (the real thing!) take four passengers and cost Nkr700 per person for 70 seconds. Bob rafting, aimed at tourists, takes five passengers and costs Nkr145 per person. Bookings are advised.

Lillehammer's two Olympic ski slopes, the **Hafjell Alpine Centre** (☎ 61 27 47 00, W www.hafjell.no), 15km north of town, and the **Kvitfjell Alpine Facility** (☎ 61 28 36 00), 50km north of town, offer public skiing between late November and late April. Hafjell is accessible on the ski bus (Nkr26, 20 minutes, six or seven daily).

Maihaugen Folk Museum

This open-air museum (☎ 61 28 89 00, Maihaugveien 1; adult/child including Olympic Museum admission Nkr120/55; open 9am-6pm daily 1 June-15 Aug, 10am-5pm daily 16 Aug-30 Sept) is lauded as Norway's finest. The collection of around 180 buildings, including the transplanted Garmo stave church, traditional Gudbrandsdalen homes and shops and 27 buildings from the farm Bjørnstad, is the life work of local dentist Anders Sandvig. There are also a number of exhibits, workshop demonstrations by interpreters in period costumes, and a section featuring Norwegian homes from every decade of the 20th century. Maihaugen is a 20-minute walk from the train station; go up Jernbanegata, right on Anders Sandvigs gate and left up Maihaugvegen.

Norsk Kjøretøy-Historisk Museum
The Norwegian Museum of Historic Vehicles (☎ 61 25 61 65, Lilletorget; adult/child Nkr40/20; open 10am-6pm daily 15 June-19 Aug, shorter hours rest of year) is a must for auto aficionados. It displays all sorts of vehicles, from horse-drawn sleighs and wagons to the stars of Norway's short-lived auto industry. Norwegian production of the odd-looking 'Troll Car', which appears to be a cousin of the Saab, wound up in the 1950s.

Lillehammer Kunstmuseum
The architecturally unique Lillehammer Art Museum (☎ 61 26 94 44, Stortorget 2; adult/child Nkr50/free; open 11am-5pm daily 25 June-26 Aug, 11am-4pm daily rest of year), includes Norwegian visual arts from the early 19th century to the present, with emphasis on the period between 1820 and 1930. Watch for the inspired works by some of Norway's finest artists: Johan C Dahl, Christian Krogh, Edvard Munch, Axel Revold and Erik Werenskiold.

Kulturhuset Banken
Kulturhuset Banken (☎ 61 26 68 10, Bankgata; admission free; open variable hours) is a century-old bank restored as a cultural centre. The interior, richly decorated with period and contemporary art, is worth a quick look.

Norsk Vegmuseum
The worthwhile Museum of Road History (☎ 61 28 52 50, Hunderfossen; admission free; open 10am-6pm daily 18 May-31 Aug), sponsored by Statens Vegvesen (Norwegian Highway Department), is 15km north of Lillehammer. You'll get a rundown of the struggle to construct roads, bridges and tunnels through Norway's challenging terrain.

Special Events
For two weeks around the Christmas and New Year holidays, Lillehammer puts on its Christmas Festival. This event features sleigh rides, ski tours, Christmas tree felling, Christmas parties, Santa visits and especially appealing winter lighting along the pedestrian shopping street.

There's also a four-day jazz festival in mid-October and a large women-only ski race in March.

Places to Stay
Lillehammer Camping (☎ 61 25 33 33, fax 61 25 33 65, Dampsagveien 47) Tent/caravan sites from Nkr80/140, 2-bed cabins Nkr300-550. Open year-round. Camping is available here on the lakeshore, a typical urban site with cooking and laundry facilities, sports facilities, water-sports equipment, children's play areas and cable TV.

Gjeste Bu (☎/fax 61 25 43 21, Gamleveien 110) Dorm beds from Nkr100, singles/doubles with shared bath from Nkr200/300. Reception open 9am-11pm. A good-value budget option is this friendly guesthouse. There's a group kitchen, free coffee and a TV room. Breakfast costs extra.

Lillehammer Vandrerhjem (☎ 61 24 87 00, fax 61 26 25 77, Jernbanetorget 2) Dorm beds Nkr175, singles/doubles Nkr350/460. The hostel, upstairs at the bus/train terminal, has 27 two- or four-bed rooms with shower and toilet and includes breakfast.

There's also a host of more expensive options.

Birkebeineren (☎ 61 26 47 00, fax 61 26 47 50, Birkebeinerveien 24) Motel/hotel-style rooms with breakfast from Nkr315/430, self-catering apartments for up to 6 people from Nkr890. Birkebeineren offers good value in the Olympic Park.

Gjestehuset Ersgaard (☎ 61 25 06 84, fax 61 25 31 09, Nordseterveien 201) Singles with or without bathroom Nkr390-550, doubles Nkr550-750. Good mid-range accommodation is available at this old farm near the ski jump.

Comfort Home Hotel Hammer (☎ 61 26 35 00, fax 61 26 37 30, Storgata 108) Singles/doubles with half-board from

Nkr745/940. This hotel is rather charming and offers high-standard rooms.

First Hotel Breiseth (☎ *61 24 77 77, fax 61 26 95 05, Jernbanegate 1-5)* Singles/doubles from Nkr899/999. Opposite the train station, this stylish hotel offers top-quality rooms and service.

Places to Eat
Despite its size, Lillehammer offers the same culinary variety as Oslo, which isn't saying much, but most places are relatively good value.

Blå Mann (☎ *61 26 22 03, Lilletorvet 1)* Dishes Nkr58-285. The recommended Blå Mann has a trendy menu offering baguette sandwiches for Nkr58, nachos, burritos and tacos (Nkr124 to Nkr145) and a range of pasta, beef and fish dishes. You can also order reindeer (Nkr285) and ostrich (Nkr234).

Nikkers (☎ *61 27 05 56, Elvegata 18)* Lunches around Nkr59, dinner specials Nkr89, mains Nkr98-179. Open for lunch 11am-3pm, dinner 3pm-9.30pm. Nikkers, the place where a moose has apparently walked through the wall, serves international cuisine, including burgers, nachos, fajitas, chicken salads and other solid fare.

Vertshuset Solveig (☎ *61 26 27 87, Storgata 68B)* Light meals Nkr69-89, dinner specials Nkr85 (Nkr98 on Sun), mains Nkr110-163. This unpretentious restaurant does omelettes, salads and other fast stuff. Main courses include beef and fish dishes.

Øverlie Kiosken (☎ *61 25 03 61, Storgata 50)* Meals from Nkr41. The best place for filling, inexpensive meals is friendly Øverlie Kiosken which has traditional meatballs and mashed potatoes (Nkr41), kebabs (Nkr46), burgers from Nkr44 and pizza starting at Nkr42.

Peppe's Pizza (☎ *61 26 47 15, Storgaten 69)* Buffets Nkr93 (11am-3pm Mon-Fri). Peppe's Pizza offers a la carte and buffet pizza and salad.

Smuget Gatekjøkken (☎ *61 25 92 12, Storgata 83)* Cheeseburgers Nkr49-69. Smuget Gatekjøkken dishes up a variety of fast food; try the kebab, chips and salad for Nkr69.

At *Mæhlum's Bakery* (☎ *61 25 02 06, Storgata 73)*, you'll find not only the nor-mal range of bread and pastries but also fine Italian ciabatta (Nkr35). Near the highway there's a *McDonald's*, but it's aimed at motorists. There's also a *Spar supermarket (Storgata 46)*.

Entertainment
Bars and night spots are an integral part of the Lillehammer experience, especially during the ski season. Most places are clustered around the western end of Storgata and along the river Mesnaelva.

Nikkers (☎ *61 27 05 56, Elvegata 18)*. Open to 2am daily. The place with the moose and his droppings is one of the most popular bars in town.

Brenneriet/Bryggeriet (☎ *61 27 06 60, Elvegata 19)* This pub, nightclub and disco appeals to a mixed clientele aged between 20 and 40.

Zipper (☎ *61 22 22 81, Nymosvingen 2)* This student hang-out appeals to the 18 to 30 set with a pub, disco and club evenings.

Shopping
Lillehammer Kunstglass (☎ *61 25 79 80, Elvegata 17)* You can watch the glassblowers at work at this glass outlet and buy the beautiful results (from Nkr100).

Getting There & Away
Lillehammer Skysstasjon (☎ 177) is the main transport terminal for buses, trains and taxis. Nor-Way Bussekspress services to/from Oslo (Nkr240, 3½ hours) run three or four times daily. To/from the Western Fjords, buses pass through Lillehammer several times daily. There's also one daily run to/from Bergen (Nkr515, 9¼ hours). Rail services run 11 to 17 times daily between Lillehammer and Oslo (Nkr255, 2¼ hours) and four to six times daily to/from Trondheim (Nkr460, 4¼ hours).

For details of the *Skibladner* paddle steamer, see Getting There & Away under Hamar earlier in this chapter.

ELVERUM
pop 11,505
Set amid the vast timberlands of southern Hedmark county, the town of Elverum

presents a landscape more typical of Sweden or Finland than the classic image of Norway. It boasts dense populations of moose, beaver and other wildlife. For Norwegians, the area provides abundant timber resources and clear streams brimming with grayling, pike, trout and whitefish.

When Nazi forces invaded Norway in April 1940, King Håkon and the Norwegian government fled northwards from Oslo and halted in Elverum. On 9 April the parliament met at the folk high school and issued the Elverum Mandate, giving the exiled government the authority to protect Norway's interests until the parliament could reconvene. When a German messenger arrived to impose the Nazi's version of 'protection' in the form of a new puppet government in Oslo, the king issued a pithy 'no' response before heading into exile. Two days later, Elverum became the first Norwegian town to suffer massive bombing by the Nazis and most of the town's old wooden buildings were levelled.

Information

The Elverum Tourist Information office (☎ 62 41 31 16, fax 62 41 00 20) is on the main drag at Storgata 24.

Norsk Skogbruksmuseum

One of Norway's finest museums is the Norwegian Forestry Museum (☎ 62 40 90 00; adult/child, including Glomdal Museum entry Nkr70/35; open 10am-6pm daily 1 July-7 Aug, to 4pm rest of year), on Rv20, 1km south of central Elverum. This extensive place deals with Norwegian forests, including hunting, trapping, logging and freshwater fishing from ancient times to the present day. There's a nature information centre, geological and meteorological exhibits, wood carvings, an aquarium, nature dioramas with all manner of stuffed native wildlife (including a mammoth) and a 20,000-volume reference library.

Outdoor exhibits in the museum grounds and across the bridge on the island of Prestøya feature a large arboretum with 80 Nordic tree species, a couple of historic sawmills, an old bog iron plant and riverside freshwater fish ponds.

Glomdal Museum

The large open-air Glomdal Museum (☎ 62 41 91 00; adult/child, including Forestry Museum entry Nkr70/35; open 10am-4pm daily 27 May-2 Sept, to 6pm daily 1 July-12 Aug) is a collection of 90 historic buildings from along the Glomma valley, including an old apothecary and doctor's surgery. The farm animals are fed at 11am and 4pm. At the period-style restaurant you can sample traditional Østerdalen fare. The museum is accessible from the bridge from the forestry museum.

Places to Stay & Eat

Elverum Camping (☎ 62 41 67 16, fax 62 41 68 17, PC Asbjørnsensveg) Tent sites Nkr100, 4-bed cabins Nkr450. Elverum Camping is in a green setting immediately south of the Norwegian Forestry Museum. Head 2km south of central Elverum on Rv20, past the museum, and take the first right turn.

Elverum Vandrerhjem & Apartments (☎ 62 41 55 67, fax 62 41 56 00, Meieirigata 28) Dorm beds Nkr130, singles/doubles Nkr250/350, self-catering flats from Nkr500. Open mid-June–mid-Aug. This modern hostel is located 300m west of the town centre, near the train station; breakfast is Nkr40 extra.

Glommen Pensjonat (☎ 62 41 12 67, Vestheimsgata 2) Singles/doubles from Nkr300/350. The simple Glommen Pensjonat is 500m west of the centre.

Hotel Central (☎ 62 41 01 55, fax 62 41 59 56, Storgata 22) Singles/doubles from Nkr660/790. As its name would suggest, this hotel is right in the heart of town, but it's pretty drab.

Forstmann (☎ 62 41 69 10) Mains from around Nkr100. Open summer. Forstmann, the fish and game restaurant at the Forestry Museum, is a nice leafy place to enjoy lunch or dinner.

Oasen kiosk (*Borgengata*) This friendly spot, 200m north of the tourist office, serves up relatively good, inexpensive hot dogs.

The *Vinmonopolet* is just uphill from the tourist office.

Entertainment

The most popular youth hang-out is the *Triangelen pub* (☎ 62 41 17 55, *Lundsbakken)*, which often stages live concerts. For dancing, try the *Alexis disco* (☎ 62 41 01 55, Storgata 22) at Hotel Central.

Getting There & Away

Elverum makes an easy day trip by bus or train from Oslo. The Nor-Way Bussekspress 'Trysil Ekspressen' runs between Oslo (Nkr165, 2½ hours) and Trysil (Nkr85, 1¼ hours) via Elverum seven times daily. To get from Oslo to Elverum by train (Nkr220, two to 2½ hours, one to five daily), you'll have to connect at Hamar.

TRYSIL
pop 2200

The alpine resort town of Trysil sits amid the broad swathe of forest that dominates the Norwegian-Swedish border area. In summer it seems quiet and rather neglected but come winter its mazes of pistes, more than 24 chairlifts and around 1000 ski chalets hum with the bustle of one of Norway's most popular winter resorts.

The town is in two sections: the town centre, in the valley, and Trysilfjell Turistsenteret, about 2km up the hill. For tourist information, contact Trysil Turistkontor (☎ 62 45 10 00, fax 62 45 11 65, ⓦ www .trysil.com), in the valley. During the ski season, lift passes cost Nkr260/460/1180 for one/two/seven days. Ski equipment can be hired for Nkr195/280/555 and snowboard equipment for Nkr270/435/755.

Hikers may want to attempt the 240km-long Finnskogleden hiking track, which begins at Flishøgda, near Osen (south of Trysil), and winds through hills and forests along the border to Morokulien, south-east of Kongsvinger. The entire hike, part of the historic pilgrimage route between Sweden and Nidaros (Trondheim), takes two to three weeks. For information, contact Finnskog Info Center (☎ 62 94 53 44, fax 62 94 53 80), N-2260 Kirkenær.

Places to Stay & Eat

In winter, the tourist office can organise accommodation in hundreds of huts, apartments and chalets by the day or week for reasonable prices.

Klara Camping (☎/fax 62 45 13 63) Tent sites Nkr70, cabins Nkr200-500. Situated about 1km south of town, Klara Camping has reasonable facilities and hires out boats and canoes.

Trysil Hyttegrend (☎ 62 45 12 62, Øråneset) 2–6-bed cabins Nkr400-870. Trysil Hyttegrend has fairly luxurious cabins.

Norlandia Trysil Hotel (☎ 62 45 08 33, fax 62 45 12 90, Storveien 24) Singles/ doubles Nkr795/995. This pleasant hotel, right in town, is noted for its good but unusual restaurant, where steaks get cooked on blocks of soapstone at 380°C.

Husets Café (☎ 62 45 44 15) On sunny days, this is a great place for a light meal (such as filled baguettes) or fast food.

Getting There & Away

The Nor-Way Bussekspress Trysil Ekspressen runs seven times daily to/from Oslo (Nkr270, 3½ hours) via Elverum (Nkr97, 1¼ hours).

RØROS
pop 2592

Røros is a gem. Formerly called Bergstad (mountain city), this historic copper-mining town manages to preserve its past while retaining a welcoming community atmosphere. Set in a small hollow of stunted forests amid bleak and treeless fells, it also presents a different face of Norway from what most visitors expect. In 1984, Unesco added the town to its World Heritage List. Although the town lies within Sør Trøndelag county, it definitely belongs to Central Norway.

History

The Røros area has been inhabited since the Stone Age, with ruins dating back to 8000 BC. There are signs of small-scale smelting of bog iron, as well as seasonal farming, hunting, trapping and herding. When Olav Haraldsson was declared a saint after his

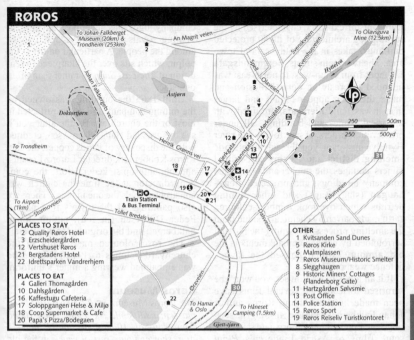

RØROS

PLACES TO STAY
2 Quality Røros Hotel
3 Erzscheidergården
12 Vertshuset Røros
21 Bergstadens Hotel
22 Idrettsparken Vandrerhjem

PLACES TO EAT
4 Galleri Thomagården
10 Dahlsgården
16 Kaffestugu Cafeteria
17 Soloppgangen Helse & Miljø
18 Coop Supermarket & Cafe
20 Papa's Pizza/Bodegaen

OTHER
1 Kvitsanden Sand Dunes
5 Røros Kirke
6 Malmplassen
7 Røros Museum/Historic Smelter
8 Slegghaugen
9 Historic Miners' Cottages
(Flanderborg Gate)
11 Hartzgården Sølvsmie
13 Post Office
14 Police Station
15 Røros Sport
19 Røros Reiseliv Turistkontoret

martyrdom at Stiklestad in 1030, hundreds of pilgrims from Sweden passed through the area.

In 1644, Hans Olsen Aasen shot a reindeer at Storvola (Storwartz) and the enraged creature leapt about and pawed up the ground to reveal the first glint of copper ore. The same year, Røros Kobberverk was established and in 1646 a royal charter granted it exclusive rights to all minerals, forest products and waterways within a 40km radius of the original discovery.

The location of the mining company headquarters at Røros was largely determined by the availability of wood and the rapids along the river Hyttelva, which provided power for the machinery used in the smelting process. However, the surrounding forests were cut down, since fire was the miners' main tool for breaking up the rock in the mines. Wood was also used to heat the ore in preparation for smelting and for the charcoal used in the smelting furnaces.

Røros first burnt to the ground during the Gyldenløve conflict with the Swedes between 1678 and 1679, and the smelter was damaged by fire in 1953. Smelting continued in Sweden but in 1977, after 333 years of operation, the company went bankrupt. Fortunately, Røros was no longer a one-industry town and managed to continue despite the initial economic hardship.

Information

The helpful Røros Reiseliv Turistkontoret (☎ 72 41 11 65, fax 72 41 02 08, **e** post@ rorosinfo.com), Peder Hiortsgata 2, is in a historic building just a block from the train station. Staff can provide all the information you'll need to explore Røros and neighbouring places (such as Tolga, Os, Vingelen and Holtålen) or set off on a hiking, biking or skiing trip. It's open year-round, 9am to 3.30pm weekdays and 10.30am to 12.30pm Saturday (9am to 6pm Monday to Saturday and 10am to 4pm Sunday from 25 June to 19 August).

Historic District

Røros' historic district, characterised by the striking log architecture of its 80 protected buildings, takes in the entire central town area. The two main streets, **Bergmannsgata** (its taper from south-west to north-east was intended to create an optical illusion and make the town appear longer and larger than it was!) and **Kjerkgata**, are lined with historical homes and buildings, all under preservation orders. If you follow the river Hyttelva upstream, you'll reach the **historic smelting district** and its tiny turf-roofed miners' cottages, the smelter and other mine company buildings, and protected **slegghaugan** (slag heaps) and other mining detritus which overlook rainbow-coloured earth made barren by chemical residue from the smelting process. Crowning the hill and surrounded by earthen embankments is the **old armoury**, which housed the town's defence weaponry.

If it all looks like a film set, you won't be surprised to learn that several films have been made here, including Røros author Johan Falkberget's classic *An-Magrit*, starring Jane Fonda. Flanderborg gate starred in some films of Astrid Lindgren's *Pippi Longstocking* classics and the district even stood in for Siberia in the film of Solzhenitsyn's *A Day in the Life of Ivan Denisovich*. In summer, guided walking tours of the historical district are conducted several times daily (the rest of the year on Saturday only) and cost Nkr45/free per adult/child.

Røros Kirke

Røros' first church *(Kjerkgata; tours adult/child Nkr25/free; tours 10am-5pm Mon-Sat, 2pm-4pm Sun 21 June-15 Aug, from 1 to 6 days per week rest of year)* was constructed on upper Kjerkgata in 1650 but by the mid-18th century it had fallen into disrepair. From 1780 to 1784 a new baroque-style church was built just behind the original at a cost of 23,000 *riksdaler* (the old currency; one riksdaler is the equivalent of Nkr4, and at the time miners earned about 50 riksdaler per year). The church is one of Norway's largest with a seating capacity of 1640. The posh King's Gallery at the back,

identified by the both royal and mining company logos, has never hosted a king, as visiting royals have always opted to sit among the people. A particular oddity is the pulpit, which sits over the altarpiece (a rendition of *The Last Supper*) rather than off to one side.

Until 1865 the building was owned by the mining company and this is reflected in most of the church art. By the altar you'll see the grizzled Hans Olsen Åsen, credited with the discovery of Røros copper; the first Røros Kobberverk director Lorenz Lossius; and philanthropist Peder Hiort, the company director at the time the church was constructed (he's the one in blue). There are also paintings of the town's first pastor, Peder Ditlevsen (in red); author Johan Falkberget; and the original 1650 church.

The rose-coloured mausoleum in the churchyard belongs to Peder Hiort, who was embalmed wearing a miner's uniform.

Røros Museum

The Røros Museum *(☎ 72 40 61 70, Malmplassen; adult/child Nkr60/30; open 10am-7pm Mon-Sat, 10am-4pm Sun 21 June-15 Aug, shorter hours rest of year)*, in the old smelting works, is a town highlight. The first smelter in Røros opened in 1646 and operations continued until a fire in 1953. However, the building was reconstructed in 1988 according to the original plan. The geological and conservation displays in the upper hall are written in the Røros dialect, without translations.

Downstairs you'll find a large balance used for weighing ore, some well-illustrated early mining statistics, and a series of brilliant working models of the mines and the water and horse-powered smelting processes. There's also a 19th-century costume exhibit. Outside the museum entrance spreads the large open area known as the Malmplassen (Ore Place), where loads of ore were dumped and weighed on the large wooden scale.

Olavsgruva Mine

Don't miss the Olavsgruva mine *(☎ 72 41 11 65, Kojedalen; mine tours adult/child*

Nkr60/30; tours 1-6 times daily 1 June-10 Sept, Sat only 11 Sept-31 Dec), 13km from Røros (head north-east from the centre of town). The mine tour first passes through the historic Nyberget mine, which dates from the 1650s and invites comparison with the modern Olavsgruva (named for Crown Prince Olav) beyond it, which was begun in 1936 and closed in the 1970s. The ground can get muddy and the year-round temperature in the mine is a steady 5°C, so bring a jacket and good footwear. To get to the mine, use your own wheels or take a taxi (Nkr400 return).

Johan Falkberget Museum

Røros' favourite son, author Johan Falkberget (1879–1967), grew up at Trondalen farm in the nearby Rugel valley. His works (now translated into 19 languages) cover 300 years of the region's mining history. His most famous work, *An-Magrit*, tells the story of a peasant girl who transported copper ore in the Røros mining district. The museum *(☎ 72 41 46 27, Ratvolden; tours adult/child Nkr45/25; tours noon, 1pm & 2pm daily 1 July-5 Aug, noon daily 6 Aug-12 Aug)* is beside the nearby lake Rugelsjø. To get there, take a local train to Rugeldalen station, 20km north of Røros, where a small walking track leads to the museum.

Activities

Hiking (and, in winter, **nordic skiing**) possibilities around the semi-forested Røros plateau are endless. Numerous tracks head out through the hills and valleys and you can walk for anything from an hour to a week; ask the tourist office for details. Note, however, that many areas remain snow-covered well into the summer and on the higher fells skiing is possible until July. Hummelfjellet, 16km south of Røros, is the largest downhill area, with two lifts and six slopes.

A short but rewarding walk from Røros will take you to the striking white sand dunes of **Kvitsanden**, the largest in Scandinavia, which lie 1km north-west of town at the end of a 30km-long esker. They were scoured, transported and deposited there by water flowing under an ancient glacier.

Another kilometre to the west lies Skårhåmmårdalen, a shallow gorge with sand-lined pools which offers **swimming** on hot days and appears as if it might harbour trolls. You'll find more inviting summer swimming at the Gjett-tjørn pond, at the edge of town.

The tourist office has details of **cycling trips**, including one-day options and a longer five-day trip. It can also organise canoe hire and advise on the best places for **canoeing**, **kayaking** and **angling** and **ice-fishing** for trout.

You can hire **horses** for Nkr100 per hour from Røros Hestesportsenter (☎ 72 41 29 83, Sundet), about 6km north of town. Both guided and unguided tours are available.

Organised Tours

In winter, the tourist office organises ski tours and excursions by dog-sled (Nkr600 to Nkr800 for two to five hours) or horse-drawn sleigh (Nkr600 per hour for four people). You can also join a winter day trip to the Southern Sami tent camp at Pinsti-tjønna, 3km from town and 1km off the road, where you'll dine on reindeer and learn such unique skills as ice-fishing and axe-throwing. The three-hour tour costs around Nkr500 per person (minimum 10 people).

Special Events

The biggest winter event is Rørosmartnan (Røros Market), which began in 1644 as a rendezvous for hunters and trappers who ventured into town to sell their products to miners and buy supplies. Thanks to a royal decree issued in 1853 stipulating that a grand market be held annually from the penultimate Tuesday of February to the following Friday, it continues today. Nowadays, it's celebrated with cultural programs, street markets and live entertainment.

The four-day Vinterfestspill i Bergstaden classical music festival in mid-March features young Scandinavian musicians.

From early to mid-August every year, Røros stages a nightly three-hour rock opera in Swedish entitled *Det Brinner en Eld*, or 'Fiery Call for Peace'. It recounts the invasion of Trøndelag by Swedish soldiers under Lieutenant-General de la Barre in 1718. This pointless struggle is followed through the lives and loves of the various players, the eventual occupation of Røros and the subsequent death of thousands of soldiers on their frozen trek homewards to Sweden. The opera was written in 1980 by Arnfinn Strømmevold and Bertil Reithaug and it's enacted on the slag heaps in the upper part of town. If you can manage to get there, don't miss it.

Places to Stay

Håneset Camping (☎ 72 41 06 00, fax 72 41 06 01, Osloveien) Cabins Nkr250-360. Cabins are available at this excellent site, with cooking and laundry facilities, a common room and TV. It's about 2km south of town.

Idrettsparken Vandrerhjem (☎ 72 41 10 89, fax 72 41 23 77, Øra 25) Tent sites Nkr60, dorm beds with breakfast Nkr190, hostel singles/doubles Nkr350/400, cabins Nkr380-600, hotel singles/doubles from Nkr590/830. Idrettsparken Vandrerhjem, only 500m from the train station, serves a good breakfast and the rooms are acceptable (showers cost Nkr10 extra).

Ertzscheidergården (☎ 72 41 11 94, fax 72 41 19 60, Spell Olaveien 6) Singles/doubles with breakfast from Nkr590/790. This 16-room guesthouse lies just a stone's throw from the church and mining museum.

Vertshuset Røros (☎ 72 41 24 11, fax 72 41 03 64, Kjerkgata 34) Singles/doubles from Nkr730/850, 2-person self-catering units from Nkr650. The cosiest and perhaps best-value choice is in this centrally located historic building.

There are also a couple of business-class hotels. Both places feature nightclubs, discos and occasional live music with dancing.

Bergstadens Hotel (☎ 72 40 60 80, fax 72 40 60 81, Osloveien 2) Singles/doubles from Nkr760/960. The cosy and down-to-earth Bergstadens Hotel, near the train station, offers well-appointed rooms.

Quality Røros Hotel (☎ 72 40 80 00, fax 72 40 80 01, An Magrit veien 10) Singles/doubles from Nkr995/1050. The Quality Røros Hotel has a commanding view from its hill-top site.

Henningsgården Turiststasjon (☎ 72 41 31 46, Brekken) Huts Nkr170, singles/doubles Nkr160/320. There are atmospheric log cabins here, in Brekken village, about 30km east of Røros. Buses run from Røros twice daily except weekends.

Vingelsgård Gjestgiveri (☎ 62 49 45 43, Vingelen) Singles/doubles Nkr260/460. At the small and appealing mountain community of Vingelen, about 40km south-west of Røros, you'll find this guesthouse.

The tourist office keeps a list of summer cabins, some within walking distance of town, from around Nkr2300 to Nkr4000 per week in the high season. All have self-catering facilities and are economical for groups, but book well in advance. The tourist office can also book rural guesthouses and cabins by the night. These include **Nordpå Fjellstue** (singles/doubles Nkr365/590) about 50km north-west of Røros; and **Langen Gjestegård** (see Femundsmarka Nasjonalpark later in this section).

Places to Eat

Vertshuset Røros (☎ 72 41 24 11, Kjerkgata 34) Pizzas from Nkr85, mains Nkr99-215. For formal dining, the finest option is probably Vertshuset Røros, with a good menu ranging from beef and freshwater fish to elk and local reindeer.

Papa's Pizza/Bodegaen (☎ 72 40 60 20, Bergmannsgata 1) Pizzas Nkr88-145, mains Nkr78-198. Open to midnight daily. Papa's serves pizza, burgers, beef, fish and chicken dishes, as well as beer and wine.

Kafestuggu cafeteria (☎ 72 41 10 33, Bergmannsgata 18) Light meals Nkr49-55, mains Nkr70-150. Open to 5pm daily. This informal cafeteria offers a good range of coffee, pastries, cold snacks and light meals. The unusual decor in the various rooms is especially interesting.

There are also many small coffee shops (some attached to crafts and souvenir shops), such as **Dahlsgården** (☎ 72 41 19 89, Mørkstugata 5) and **Galleri Thomasgården** (☎ 72 41 24 70, Kjerkgata 48), where you can enjoy a quick cuppa and a pastry or slice of pie (typically from Nkr14 to Nkr45). Within a block of the tourist office, you'll also find a couple of bakeries and a *Coop supermarket (P Hiortsgata 7)*, with an inexpensive cafeteria. *Soloppgangen Helse & Miljø (☎ 72 41 29 55, Kjerkgata 6)* sells health foods.

Shopping

Given its unaffected ambience, it isn't surprising that Røros has attracted over 40 artists and artisans. The town also has a glassblower, a copper shop and several general handicraft shops.

Hartzgården Sølvsmie (☎ 72 41 05 50, Kjerkgata) Of special interest is this silversmith's shop, where you'll find locally hand-crafted silver jewellery with an emphasis on Viking themes, as well as a small historic jewellery exhibit.

Galleri Thomasgården (☎ 72 41 24 70, Kjerkgata 48) At the worthwhile Galleri Thomasgården, potter Torgeir Henriksen creates rustic stoneware and porcelain. You'll also find the wonderful nature-inspired wood carvings of Henry Solli. The player piano is one of only two in Norway and dates back to 1929.

Getting There & Away

Røros has one Widerøe flight to/from Oslo daily except Saturday. There's a daily overnight bus from Oslo which arrives at 4.25am, then continues to Trondheim. The return bus leaves Trondheim at 9.50pm, passes Røros at 12.30am and arrives in Oslo at 7am. There are also several other daily services to/from Trondheim. Røros lies on the eastern railway line between Oslo (Nkr500, five hours) and Trondheim (Nkr188, 2½ hours).

Getting Around

Parking can be difficult in summer when the main street is (fortunately) open only to pedestrians. If you have a car, leave it at the edge of town and walk in. For a taxi, phone ☎ 72 41 12 58.

In winter, you can opt for a *spark*, a locally popular kick-sled that resembles a dog-sled without the dogs. For summer cycling excursions, you can rent a mountain bike from Røros Sport (☎ 72 41 12 18) on Bergmannsgata.

FEMUNDSMARKA NASJONALPARK

The national park which surrounds Femunden, Norway's second-largest lake, was formed in 1971 to protect the lake and the forests stretching eastwards to Sweden. This has long been a source of falcons for use in the European and Oriental sport of falconry and several places in the park are known as Falkfangerhøgda, or 'falcon hunters' height'. You may also see wild reindeer grazing in the heights and, in summer, a herd of around 30 musk oxen roams the area along the Røa and Mugga rivers (in winter they migrate to the Funäsdalen area). It's thought that this group split off from an older herd in the Dovrefjell area.

Places to Stay

Johnsgård Turistsenter (☎ 62 45 99 25, fax 62 45 99 55, Sømådalen) Tent sites Nkr85, 4–8-bed cabins Nkr150-500. Johnsgård Turistsenter offers good camping prospects, 9km west of Buvika.

Langen Gjestegård (☎ 72 41 37 18, Synnervika) Singles/doubles with breakfast Nkr305/430. Langen Gjestegård is a cosy turf-roofed farmhouse near the lake.

Getting There & Away

The ferry M/S *Fæmund II* was launched under steam power in 1905 and was converted to diesel in 1958. Daily between 10 June and 26 August, it sails between Synnervika (also spelt Søndervika), on the northern shore of lake Femunden, to Elgå (continuing to Buvika Wednesday and Sunday, early July to early August). On Wednesday from mid-July to early August, it continues all the way to Femundsenden, at the lake's southern tip.

From 10 June to 26 August, buses run between Røros and Synnervika once or twice daily. The 8.15am departure from Røros allows you to cruise around Femunden on *Fæmund II* and return to Røros on the same day. You can reach the southern end of Femunden on the Trysil Expressen bus which runs seven times daily from Hamar to Trysil, via Elverum, then change to buses for Engerdal/Drevsjø.

CENTRAL NORWAY

Northern Central Norway

OPPDAL

pop 3500

Oppdal makes a logical outdoor break between Oslo or Trondheim and the northern reaches of the Western Fjords. This outdoor-oriented town is an activity centre *par excellence* and there's plenty on offer, from winter skiing and snowboarding to summer river rafting, hiking, climbing, canyoning and hang-gliding. If you're on a short visit, it's worth taking the gondola (adult/child Nkr60/40) from the lower station about 600m from the centre to the Topprestaurant at the summit of Hovden (1125m), which rises 525m over the town. In winter this gondola provides access to a couple of challenging black diamond ski runs.

Information

The Oppdal Turistkontor (☎ 72 40 04 70, fax 72 40 04 80, e post@oppdal.com, w www .oppdal.com) is just a block from the train and bus stations.

Activities

White-Water Rafting The wild white Driva offers several excellent rafting runs. The outdoor adventure company Opplev Oppdal (☎ 72 40 41 80, fax 72 40 41 81, e opplevoppdal@online.no), Olav Skasliens vei 12, organises a range of worthwhile trips. The three-hour Class I family trip (adult/family Nkr330/990) is designed more as a wilderness experience than an adrenalin rush, but you can also opt for half/full-day Class III trips (Nkr450/690) which provide substantial thrills. The more daring can opt for a five-hour river surfing trip (Nkr690). The same company also offers canoe rental (Nkr235 per day), canyoning (Nkr690), river kayaking (Nkr750), rock climbing (Nkr690) and an elk photo safari (Nkr230).

Musk Ox Photo Safari Oppdal Booking (☎ 72 40 08 00) organises six- to eight-hour musk ox photo safaris daily from 20 June to 20 August (Nkr230).

Skiing & Snowboarding The three-part Oppdal Skisenter climbs the slopes from Hovden, Stølen and Vangslia, all within easy reach of town. The smaller Ådalen ski area nearby has two lifts. Vangslia is generally the easiest, with a couple of beginners' runs, while Stølen offers intermediate skiing and Hovden has three challenging advanced runs. Lift passes for one/two/three days cost Nkr240/420/580 and a morning/afternoon of skiing is Nkr160/210; three days of skiing in five costs Nkr620. The season varies, but generally runs from late November to late April.

Places to Stay & Eat

Oppdalstunet Vandrerhjem (☎ 72 42 23 11, fax 72 42 23 13, Gamle Kongsvei) Dorm beds Nkr150, singles/doubles Nkr370/450. Open May-Nov. Oppdalstunet Vandrerhjem, 1.5km north-east of central Oppdal, offers good hostel accommodation in intriguing buildings.

Throughout the year, Oppdal offers choices of basic two-bed or nicer four-bed holiday cabins for around Nkr200 to Nkr800 per night.

Vekve Hyttetun (☎/fax 72 42 13 19, Auneveien 10) 2-bed/4-bed huts with shower, toilet Nkr400/500. The fine cabins at Vekve Hyttetun are the nearest to town.

Quality Oppdal Hotel (☎ 72 40 07 00, fax 72 40 07 01, Olav Skasliens vei 8) Singles/doubles from Nkr795/845. This comfortable hotel offers fairly luxurious rooms near the bus and train stations.

Café Ludvik (☎ 72 42 01 40, Inge Krokanns vei 21) Mains Nkr65-135. The popular Café Ludvik serves a range of inexpensive light meals, including beef dishes, omelettes and pasta. It's 300m south of the centre, by the E6.

Entertainment

George Pub (☎ 72 40 07 00, Quality Oppdal Hotel, Olav Skasliens vei 8) If you're over 18, this English-style pub features tapas and Cajun food, and Kilkenny on tap.

Getting There & Away
The best access to Oppdal is via the four or five daily train services between Oslo (Nkr510, 4¾ hours) and Trondheim (Nkr175, 1½ hours). Oppdal lies on the twice-daily Nor-Way Bussekspress route between Bergen (Nkr670, 12½ hours) and Trondheim (Nkr160, two hours), with connections at Otta to/from Oslo.

TROLLHEIMEN
The relatively small Trollheimen range, with a variety of trails through gentle mountains and lake-studded upland regions, is most readily accessed from Oppdal. You can either hitch or hike the 15km from Oppdal up the Nkr30 toll road to **Osen**, which is the main entrance to the wilderness region. The best map to use is Statens Kartverk's *Turkart Trollheimen* (1:75,000), which costs Nkr120 at the tourist office in Oppdal.

A straightforward hiking destination in Trollheimen is the hut and historic farm at **Vassendsetra**. From Osen (the outlet of Gjevilvatnet), which lies 3km north of the main road to Sunndalsøra, you can take the boat *Trollheimen II* all the way to Vassendsetra (Nkr130 return). From 1 July to 20 August it leaves Osen daily at noon and from Vassendsetra at 3.30pm. Alternatively, you can drive or hike 6km along the road from Osen to the DNT hut, **Gjevilvasshytta**, and follow the lakeshore trail for 12km to Vassendsetra. About midway you'll pass several outstanding sandy beaches, with excellent summer swimming.

The popular three-day 'Trekanten' hut tour follows the Gjevilvasshytta-Trollheimshytta-Jøldalshytta-Gjevilvasshytta route.

Vassendsetra (☎ 72 42 32 20, fax 72 42 34 30) Beds for DNT members/nonmembers Nkr130/200. Breakfast Nkr65/105, dinner Nkr145/180. Open July & Aug. There's acceptable mountain lodge accommodation available here.

RINGEBU
pop 1100
Gudbrandsdalen, the narrow river valley which stretches for 200km between lake Mjøsa and Dombås, has long been a major farming area and also supports a string of small communities. The southernmost is Ringebu, where there's a lovely **stave church** (☎ 61 28 43 50; adult/child Nkr30/10; open 9am-6pm daily mid-June–mid-Aug, slightly shorter hours rest of year), 2km south on the E6, then east (up the hill). The church, dating from around 1220, was extensively restored in the 17th century when the odd red tower was attached. Inside, there's a statue of St Laurence dating from around 1250. The adjacent 1743 vicarage houses **Ringebu Samlingene** (☎ 61 28 27 00; adult/child Nkr50/20; open 11am-5pm daily June-Aug, 11am-5pm Sat & Sun May & Sept), a collection of 40 paintings by Jakob Wiedemann.

For information, contact the Ringebu Turistkontor (☎ 61 28 47 00).

Ringebu Hotel (☎ 61 28 26 10, fax 61 28 26 09, Brugata 27) Singles/doubles from Nkr650/730. The low-key Ringebu Hotel offers reasonable rooms.

Nor-Way Bussekspress bus routes between Oslo and the Western Fjords stop in Ringebu three times daily. Trains to Oslo (Nkr330, 2¾ hours) or Trondheim (Nkr410, 3½ hours) stop in Ringebu four or five times daily.

KVAM & SJOA
pop 1000
At the riverside chip-board town of Kvam, the main attraction is the **Gudbrandsdal Krigsminnesamling** (☎ 61 29 40 33, Kvam Sentrum; admission Nkr30; open 9am-5pm daily mid-June–mid-Aug, 10am-4pm daily 8 May-15 Sept), an exposé of Gudbrandsdalen conflicts beginning with the Sinclair expedition and the Battle of Kringom in 1612 and culminating with the Nazi occupation during WWII. The Heidalen area between Otta and Vinstra also boasts Norway's largest collection of protected buildings, most of which are still in use.

Sjoa, 8km west of Kvam, is synonymous with white-water rafting and has some of Norway's wildest and most popular liquid thrills. Heidal Rafting (☎ 61 23 60 37, fax 61 23 60 14, e heidalrafting@online.no, w www.heidalrafting.no) in Sjoa; Sjoa Rafting (☎ 88 00 63 90, fax 61 23 19 00,

CENTRAL NORWAY

e sjoa@online.no, W www.sjoarafting.com), a few kilometres upstream at Nedre Heidal; and, even farther upstream at Randsverk, Norwegian Wildlife & Rafting (☎ 61 23 87 27, fax 61 23 87 60, e nwr@nwr.no, W www .nwr.no) are the main players. All three offer half/full-day trips on the Sjoa's Class II to III white water, from around Nkr590/690. There are Class I to II family trips on the Otta river (Nkr490) and three-day Class III to IV runs (from Nkr1990) through the roiling waters of the Åsengjuvet canyon. These companies also organise other adventure activities, including river-boarding, rock/ice climbing, canyoning, dog-sledding, glacier expeditions and wildlife-viewing safaris.

Sjoa Vandrerhjem (☎ 61 23 62 00, fax 61 23 60 14, Sjoa) Dorm beds Nkr135-175, singles/doubles from Nkr225/280. Open May-Sept. Most rafting participants stay at Heidal Rafting's atmospheric 1747 log-farmhouse hillside hostel. Breakfast is included and dinner costs Nkr90.

Sæta Camping (☎ 61 23 51 47, Sæta) Cabins Nkr225-350. This camping ground, 5km upstream from Sjoa, is a pleasant grassy site near the river.

Nor-Way Bussekspress bus routes between Oslo and the Western Fjords stop in Kvam three times daily.

OTTA
pop 2500
Set deep in Gudbrandsdalen, at the junction of the rivers Otta and Lågen, scenic Otta makes a great jumping-off point for hikes in Rondane National Park. The helpful Sel-Rondane Reiselivslag tourist office (☎ 61 23 66 50, fax 61 23 09 60, e post@visitron dane.com, W www.visitrondane.com), at Otta Skysstasjon bus and train station, provides lots of local information, including details on Rondane National Park.

Kringom
At Kringom, about 3km south of Otta on the E6 and then a short distance up the hill to the east, you'll see a war memorial commemorating the 26 August 1612 victory of valley farmers over Sinclair's band of 550 Scottish mercenaries in the employ of the Swedish Kalmar aggressors.

On the opposite side of the river rises the hill **Pillarguri**, named for the woman who set the stage for the triumphant and vicious defeat of the Scots (see the boxed text 'Guri Saves the Day').

Kvitskriuprestene
The unusual 6m-high natural pillar formations of Kvitskriuprestene (white scree priests) resemble an assembly of priests and were formed by erosion of an Ice Age moraine. Although much of the moraine material has been washed away by the elements, the pillars are protected by capstones. They lie 4km east along the Nkr10 toll road from Sel towards Mysusæter, then a steep 20-minute hike uphill.

Places to Stay & Eat
Otta Camping (☎ 61 23 03 09, fax 61 23 38 19, Ottadalen) Tent or caravan sites for 2 people Nkr70, 4-bed cabins Nkr250-350, rooms Nkr300-450. The best-value budget accommodation, the convenient and popular Otta Camping, is a 1.5km walk from the train and bus stations. Cross the Otta bridge from the centre, turn right and continue about 1km upstream.

Sagatun Gjestgiveri (☎ 61 23 08 14, Ottekra 1) Singles/doubles/triples Nkr180/300/450. Open year-round. The decent hostel-style Sagatun Gjestgiveri is 600m west of the train station.

Killis Overnatting (☎ 61 23 04 92, Ola Dahlsgate 35) Singles/doubles/triples Nkr200/220/250. The acceptable Killis Overnatting has inexpensive accommodation.

Grand Gjestegård (☎ 61 23 12 00, fax 61 23 04 62, Ola Dahlsgate) Singles/doubles from Nkr490/640. A bit more plush than Killis Overnatting and just as convenient is Grand Gjestegård, just behind the bus and train stations. The attached cafeteria produces pleasant sit-down meals.

Norlandia Otta Hotell (☎ 61 23 00 33, fax 61 23 15 24, Ola Dahlsgate 7) Singles/doubles from Nkr580/790. The finest in-town choice is the rather nondescript Norlandia Otta Hotell. There's a lively disco on

Guri Saves the Day

The legend of Pillarguri – 'Guri' for short – was inspired by the Battle of Kringom, fought just south of Otta on 26 August 1612. During the Kalmar War between Sweden and Denmark, when Norway was united with Denmark, 550 Scottish mercenaries arrived in Norway to aid the Swedish cause and, along their route, they had to pass through Gudbrandsdalen.

Having heard of the approach of the mercenaries, the peasants armed themselves with axes, scythes and other farming implements; they stacked up rocks and branches across the track to block the route and, to set up a diversion, placed several older men across the river to fire their rifles at the column, using blanks.

As the Scots approached a narrow section of path between the river and a steep hillside at Høgkringom, south of Otta, the heroic Guri dashed up the hill to announce their arrival by sounding her shepherd's birch bark horn. This was the signal for the old farmers to fire; the Scots, confident they'd meet with little resistance, fired back across the river, then responded to Guri's music by waving their hats and playing their bagpipes, unaware of the trap.

As Guri sounded her horn again, more rocks and branches were tumbled across the trail behind the column, blocking any hope of retreat. At this stage, the farmers attacked with more rocks, logs and their crude weapons, savagely defeating the trapped contingent and making the river flow red with blood.

Only six farmers were killed in the battle and the victors intended to take the 134 surviving Scots as prisoners to Akershus Fortress. However, during the victory celebrations at Kvam, the farmers, who had to get on with their harvest and couldn't be bothered with a march to Oslo, executed the prisoners one by one. Thus a raggle-taggle band of 450 untrained farmers soundly defeated a larger band of professional mercenaries.

The bravery and ingenuity of the peasant 'army' is still remembered in Otta, where the local *bunad* (national costume) is a distinctly un-Norwegian tartan and there's a statue of Pillarguri near the train station.

Friday (free) and Saturday (cover charge Nkr50) which appeals to the 18 to 35 crowd.

Pizzerina Restaurant (☎ 61 23 08 77, Mostugugata 10) Pizzas from Nkr72, other mains Nkr60-138. The licensed Pizzerina Restaurant serves fairly good pizzas and a reasonable range of other dishes.

Pillarguri Kafé (☎ 61 23 01 04, Storgata 7) Lunches Nkr55-155, dinner mains Nkr85-185. This restaurant specialises in Norwegian fare, including reindeer.

Otta Kafé (☎ 61 23 03 24, Johan Nygårds-gate 10) Daily specials around Nkr100, mains Nkr65-139. Unpretentious options are on offer here, including omelettes, steak, chicken and meatballs.

Peking Garden (☎ 61 23 15 50, Storgata 16) Mains Nkr65-140. One block south of Otta Kafé, the Chinese niche is filled by Peking Garden, which offers a typical range of meals, most under Nkr100.

Self-caterers should visit the *Kiwi super-market* on Storgata.

Getting There & Away

Local buses to and from Vågå (Nkr41, 30 minutes) and Lom (Nkr69, one hour) leave two to four times daily. On Nor-Way Bussekspress, there are at least two buses to/from Lillehammer daily (Nkr125, 1¼ hours) and three daily buses between Måløy (Nkr350, 5½ hours) and Oslo (Nkr330, five hours); there are also twice-daily runs between Bergen and Trondheim (Nkr545, 9¾ hours). The town also lies on the Dovre rail line between Oslo (Nkr410, 3¼ hours) and Trondheim (Nkr350, three hours), with at least four services daily.

RONDANE NASJONALPARK

The 572-sq-km Rondane National Park, which Henrik Ibsen described as 'palace piled upon palace', was created in 1962 as Norway's first national park to protect the fabulous Rondane massif, which many regard as the finest alpine hiking country in Norway. Ancient reindeer trapping sites and burial mounds provide evidence that the area has been inhabited for thousands of years. Much of the park's glaciated landscape lies above 1400m and 10 rough and stony peaks rise to over 2000m, including the highest, **Rondslottet** (2178m), and **Storronden** (2138m). Rondane's range of wildlife includes 28 mammal species – from lemmings to reindeer – and 124 bird species.

For hikers, Rondane provides ample opportunities for high country exploration and the relatively dry climate is an added bonus. The most accessible route into the park is from the Spranghaugen car park, near Mysusæter. From there, it's an easy 6km hike to Rondvassbu and then a five-hour return climb to the summit of Storronden. Alternatively, head for the spectacular view from the more difficult summit of Vinjeronden (2044m), then tackle the narrow ridge leading to the neighbouring peak, Rondslottet; this takes about six hours return from Rondvassbu. There are also dozens of other less popular routes.

The best maps to use are Statens Kartverk's *Rondane* (1:100,000; Nkr99) and *Rondane Sør* (1:50,000). Camping is permitted anywhere in the national park except at Rondvassbu, where you're limited to the designated area.

Mysusæter

The easiest Rondane access for hikers is probably via Mysusæter, 13km uphill along a good road from Otta. About 4km beyond Mysusæter (toll Nkr10 per car), the road ends at the Spranghaugen car park near the national park border. A straightforward 1½-hour hike will bring you to the popular staffed DNT hut *Rondvassbu*; there are also other DNT huts in the park.

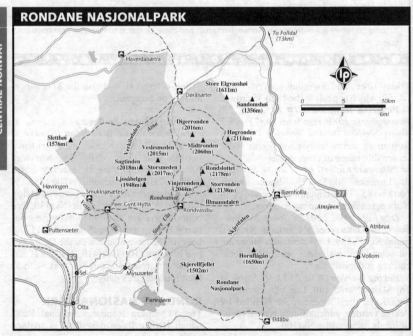

Just down the hill from the 'Bom' (toll post) gate is a small shop selling staple provisions.

Mysusæter Fjellstue (☎ 61 23 39 25) Dorm beds Nkr180, doubles without/with bathroom Nkr510/620. Mysusæter Fjellstue provides a basic roof over your head.

Rondane Spa Høyfjellshotell (☎ 61 23 39 33, fax 61 23 39 52) Beds with full board per person from Nkr740. This comfortable upmarket option has good spa facilities, including pedicures for worn-out hikers' feet.

Getting There & Away
Buses run twice daily between Otta and Mysusæter (Nkr21, 45 minutes).

From Rondvassbu, the ferry *Rondegubben* crosses the lake Rondvatnet to Nordvika (Nkr40, 30 minutes) three times daily from early July to late August.

DOMBÅS
pop 1500
Dombås, a popular adventure and winter sports centre, makes a convenient break for travellers between the highland national parks and the Western Fjords. The Dombås Turistkontor (☎ 61 24 14 44, fax 61 24 11 90, e touristoffice@dovrenett.no) is in a car park in the centre of town.

Dovrefjell-Rondane Nasjonalparksenter
The new visitor centre (☎ 61 24 14 44, Sentralplassen; admission free; open 9am-8pm daily mid-June–mid-Aug, shorter hours rest of year) at the tourist office has interesting displays on all Norway's national parks, prehistoric hunting techniques, a 3D map, stuffed wildlife and DNT information.

Dovregubbens Rike Trollpark
The children-oriented Trollpark (☎ 61 24 12 90, Sentralplassen; adult/child Nkr30/15; open 10am-8pm daily summer, shorter hours rest of year) describes the legendary Norwegian trolls and the 'Realm of the Mountain King' (the Dovre massif), inhabited by the friendliest and most powerful troll. There's also a film explaining a bit of

the local natural history and various stuffed animal displays.

Fokstumyra Naturreservat
As early as 1816, ornithologists were marvelling over the number and diversity of bird life in the Fokstumyra marshes, west of the E6 and straddling the railway line, 11km north of Dombås. Now the area is considered to have some of the best bird-watching in Norway and there's a 5km-long marked trail near the Dombås end of the reserve.

Approximately 75 species nest in the area and up to 40 others are occasionally observed. Among the more unusual species breeding near the water are the ruff, the great snipe, Temminck's stint, whimbrel, great northern diver (loon), lapwing, lesser white-fronted goose and hen harrier. Species which breed in the surrounding hills and forests include the snow bunting, ring ouzel, field fare, purple sandpiper, great grey shrike, dipper, brambling, peregrine falcon, dotterel, short-eared owl, raven and shore lark.

Transport is only available with the Dovrefjell Activitetssenter and Dombås Eventyr guided tours (see the following section). Alternatively, you can rent a bike from the tourist office for Nkr130 or take a taxi for around Nkr150 each way. A 27km portion of the Nidaros Pilgrims' Way provides an easy nature hike between Fokstumyra and the bleak settlement of Hjerkinn, farther north on the E6.

Organised Tours
A good range of adventure tours are offered by the Dovrefjell Activitetssenter (☎ 61 24 15 55, fax 61 24 15 70), Sentralplassen. See Fokstumyra Naturreservat on its canoe moose-viewing safari (Nkr220), where you'll also see myriad bird species. Just the bird-watching, with a guide, costs Nkr200. Six-hour musk ox safaris in Dovrefjell are Nkr180, technical climbing trips, with instruction, are Nkr550 per day, rafting trips cost from Nkr320 to Nkr600, glacier and ice-climbing in Jotunheimen is Nkr560 to Nkr600, and canyoning is Nkr580 to Nkr600. Book either directly or through the tourist office.

Dombås Eventyr (☎/fax 61 24 01 59) offers a three-hour elk safari for Nkr200 and a five- to six-hour musk ox safari for Nkr200 to Nkr220.

Places to Stay & Eat

Midtskog Camping, Hytter & Caravan (☎ 61 24 10 21) Tent sites Nkr60, 2-bed/4-bed cabins Nkr250/350. The central camping ground is about 800m down the E136 road towards Åndalsnes from the centre complex.

Bjørkhol Camping (☎ 61 24 13 31, Bjørkhol) Tent sites Nkr50-60, 4-bed/5-bed cabins from Nkr160/275, 4-bed cabins with shower & toilet Nkr400-600. Bjørkhol Camping, Norway's best-value and probably friendliest camping ground is 7km south of Dombås. A bus runs several times daily from Dombås.

Dombås Vandrerhjem Trolltun (☎ 61 24 09 60, fax 61 24 13 30) Dorm beds Nkr175, singles/doubles Nkr350/480, hotel-standard rooms Nkr540/760. This excellent place, about 1.5km off the sinuous E6 from the town centre, includes breakfast and offers dinner for Nkr95.

Dombås Hotell (☎ 61 24 10 01, fax 61 24 14 61, Sentralplassen) Singles Nkr480-825, doubles Nkr580-995. For a plush night's sleep, try this rich-looking hotel near the tourist office.

Jegerkroa (☎ 61 24 12 17) Mains Nkr90-150. The local Chinese restaurant, by the E6 towards Otta, is oddly named the 'hunters' inn'; you'll get a substantial meal here.

The main commercial complex in the centre includes both the popular *Frich's Cafeteria (☎ 61 24 10 23, Sentralplassen)* and the *Senter-Grillen (☎ 61 24 18 33, Sentralplassen)* gatekjøkken and pub, which also serves pizza.

Getting There & Away

Dombås lies on the railway line between Oslo (Nkr430, 3¾ hours) and Trondheim (Nkr290, 2½ hours). It is also the cut-off point for the spectacular Raumabanen line down Romsdalen to Åndalsnes (Nkr160, 1¼ hours), which runs two or three times daily. Åndalsnes (Nkr140, two hours) and Ålesund (Nkr280, 4¼ hours) are served

nightly by bus. Nor-Way Bussekspress buses between Bergen (Nkr595, 11¼ hours) and Trondheim (Nkr255, 3¼ hours) call in twice daily in either direction.

To get to Oslo, you'll normally change buses at Otta.

DOVREFJELL NASJONALPARK

The tiny 256-sq-km Dovrefjell National Park, established in 1974, exists mainly to protect the dramatic highlands around the 2286m-high Snøhetta and to provide a suitably bleak habitat for Arctic foxes, reindeer, wolverines and musk oxen (see the boxed text 'Musk Ox'). Snøhetta can be ascended by hikers from Snøheim (allow six hours). The Knutshøene massif (1690m) occupies a separate section of the park east of the E6 and protects Europe's most diverse intact alpine ecosystem.

Although only a small part of the Dovrefjell highlands lies within the park, the vast expanse of wilderness country to the south, west and north provides ample space for hiking in spectacular terrain that's well known only in European climbing circles. There are plans to protect this extended region in a new Skrymtheimen National Park.

Hikers will fare best with the Statens Kartverk map *Dovrefjell* (1:100,000). However, it doesn't include the Knutshø section; for that, you need Statens Kartverk's *Einunna 1519-I* and *Folldal 1519-II* topographic sheets.

Places to Stay & Eat

In 1959, the DNT Snøheim hut (formerly called Reinheim) was judged to be too near the army's Hjerkinn firing range and was replaced by the new self-service *Reinheim hut*, 5km north and at 1341m, in Stroplsjødalen. DNT also maintains several other self-service huts in the adjacent Skrymtheimen region; keys are available from Dombås tourist office.

Kongsvold Fjeldstue (☎ 72 40 43 40, fax 72 40 43 41, Kongsvold) Doubles from Nkr495 per person (DNT discount available). Open year-round. Park information, maps, meals and accommodation are available at this charming and historic place,

CENTRAL NORWAY

13km north of Hjerkinn on the E6. Intriguing early-18th-century timber buildings huddle deep in Drivdalen, 500m from tiny Kongsvoll station (trains stop only on request). Breakfast, lunch and dinner (possibly including musk ox steaks) are available in the attached cafeteria.

Hjerkinn Fjellstue (☎ *61 24 29 27, fax 61 24 29 49, Hjerkinn)* Singles/doubles Nkr685/915. This cosy inn, dating from 1992, is about 1.5km east of Hjerkinn on Rv29. It's the latest in a series of inns on the site, the first of which appeared around

1100. There's also a restaurant and camping is available.

Getting There & Away

There's no public transport into the park, although tours from Dombås offer musk ox safaris (see Dombås). The road to Snøheim crosses the Hjerkinn firing range and public access requires permission from the army, which is readily given at the gate unless they're conducting exercises. The only public transport between Dombås and Hjerkinn is by train (Nkr62, 23 minutes).

Musk Ox

Although a member of the *Bovidae* family, the musk ox *(Ovibos moschatus)* bears little resemblance to its nearest relations (sheep, goats and cattle) or indeed to any other animal. During the last Ice Age, it was distributed throughout much of the northern hemisphere's glaciated areas but its range is now much more restricted. Wild herds can be found in parts of Greenland, Canada, Alaska, and the Dovrefjell and Femundsmarka national parks in Norway.

The musk ox, weighing between 225kg and 445kg, has incredibly high shoulders and an enormous low-slung head with two broad, flat horns that cross the forehead, curving outwards and downwards before twisting upwards and forwards. Its incredibly thick and shaggy coat, with a matted fleece of soft hair underneath, covers the whole body and hangs down like a skirt to almost reach the ground. Below this hair only the bottom part of the legs protrude, giving the animal a solid, stocky appearance reminiscent of a medieval horse dressed for a joust. This analogy is especially appropriate because, during the rutting season, when the males gather their harems, they repeatedly charge each other, butting their heads together with a crash that's often heard for miles around. This heated battle continues until one animal admits defeat and lumbers off.

Traditionally, the musk ox's main predator has been wolves; their primary defence is to form a circle with the males on the outside and females and calves inside, trusting in the force of their collective horns to rip open attackers. This defence has proven useless against human hunters, especially the Greenlandic Inuit, and numbers have been seriously depleted. Only with restocking have they been able to thrive again.

In 1931, 10 animals were reintroduced to Dovrefjell from Greenland. Musk oxen all but vanished during WWII, but 23 were transplanted from Greenland between 1947 and 1953. The herd has now grown to around 80 animals and some have shifted eastwards into Femundsmarka National Park to form a new herd.

Musk oxen aren't inherently aggressive toward humans, but an animal that feels threatened can charge at speeds of up to 60km/h and woe betide anything that gets in its way. Hikers should stay at least 200m away; if an animal seems agitated or paws at the ground don't run, but back off slowly until it again seems relaxed.

VÅGÅ
pop 1500

Vågå surprises passers-by with its wealth of old log and timber buildings. The original wooden stave church was constructed around 1150 with a single nave and stood 300m west of the present cruciform **church** *(Vågå Sentrum; adult/child Nkr20/free; open 10am-7pm Mon-Sat 11am-7pm Sun June-Aug, closes 8pm July)*, which was reconstructed between 1625 and 1630. On the wall at the entrance, you'll see carved wooden panels from the ancient church, which mostly represent animal subjects. The baptismal font also dates from the original church, and the early Gothic crucifix is from the 13th century.

For tourist information, contact Vågå Turistkontor (☎ 61 23 78 80), open daily mid-June to mid-August.

LOM
pop 700

Lom, straddling the river Bøvra at the Prestfossen waterfall, manages to remain picturesque despite coach loads of tourists. In addition to a couple of fine attractions, there are several hiking trails with excellent views of Ottadalen and Bøverdalen. A popular route is the 3km return loop up Lomseggi to the century-old stone cottage called Smithbue, occupied by a 19th-century German artist.

The friendly Jotunheimen Reiseliv tourist office (☎ 61 21 29 90, fax 61 21 29 95, W www.visitlom.com), in the Norsk Fjellmuseum, is open 9am to 4pm or 6pm weekdays (until 9pm mid-June to mid-August) and 10am to 5pm weekends (until 8pm mid-June to mid-August). Visitors can purchase a *Fellesbillet* (adult/child Nkr80/free), which includes admission to the stave church, the Presthaugen Bygdemuseum and the Norsk Fjellmuseum.

If you're around for a while, pick up the *Nature and Culture Guide for Lom* by Torgeir Garmo, which contains an exhaustive rundown on local trails and attractions. It's sold at the Fossheim Steinsenter. Hiking maps are sold at the Lom Bokhandel and the tourist office. Internet access is available at the library and the tourist office (Nkr10 for five minutes).

Lom Stavkyrkje

This lovely 12th-century Norman-style stave church *(mobile ☎ 97 07 53 97, Lom; adult/child Nkr30/free; open 9am-9pm daily 15 June-15 Aug)*, in the centre of town, is still the local church. It was constructed in 1170, extended in 1634 and given its current cruciform shape with the addition of two naves in 1667. Guided tours explain the interior paintings (from around 1700) and Jakop Sæterdalen's chancel arch and pulpit (from 1793). Take the Rv15 towards Stryn.

Fossheim Steinsenter

The best attraction in Lom is also one of the most memorable exhibitions in the country. The Fossheim Steinsenter *(☎ 61 21 14 60, fax 61 21 11 01, Lom; admission free; open 9am-8pm Mon-Sat 9am-7pm Sun mid-June–mid-Aug, 10am-3pm Mon-Fri at other times)* combines Europe's largest selection of rare and beautiful rocks, minerals, fossils, gems and jewellery for sale, but it also includes a large museum of Norwegian and foreign geological specimens. Don't miss the humorous exhibit on compulsive collectors.

The knowledgeable owners of the centre, both avid rock collectors, travel the world in search of specimens but they're especially proud of the Norwegian national stone, Thulite. It was discovered in 1820 and is now quarried in Lom; the reddish colour is derived from traces of manganese.

Norsk Fjellmuseum

The Norwegian Mountain Museum *(☎ 61 21 16 00, Lom; adult/child Nkr60/30; open 9am-9pm Mon-Fri, 10am-5pm Sat & Sun mid-June–mid-Aug, 9am-4pm or 6pm Mon-Fri, 10am-5pm Sat & Sun at other times)* is the visitors centre for Jotunheimen National Park and contains mountaineering memorabilia (including a WC Slingsby exhibit), as well as exhibits on natural history and cultural and industrial activity in the Norwegian mountains. There's also an excellent 10-minute mountain slide show and a discussion of tourism and its impact on wilderness.

Presthaugen Bygdemuseum

Behind the Norsk Fjellmuseum, the Presthaugen Open Air Museum (☎ 61 21 29 90, Lom; adult/child Nkr20/free; open 1pm-5pm daily July) is a collection of 19th-century farm buildings, several *stabbur* (elevated storehouses), an old hut (it's claimed that St Olav slept here) and an example of a summer mountain dairy. The most interesting feature is the exhibition on early irrigation methods in highland Norway. Arrange guided tours or special openings with the tourist office.

Places to Stay & Eat

Unfortunately, Lom lacks inexpensive hostel accommodation; for that you'll have to head up-valley to Bøverdalen (see under Jotunheimen Nasjonalpark later in this chapter).

Nordal Turistsenter (☎ 61 21 93 00, fax 61 21 93 01, Lom) Basic 4-bed hut Nkr280, fully equipped 8-bed cabin Nkr990. Nordal Turistsenter, in the heart of town, offers a wide range of cabins.

Fossheim Steinsenter (☎ 61 21 14 60, Lom) 6–8-bed apartments from Nkr1100/4800 per night/week. These excellent flats, featuring modern design in a former barn, are the last word in luxury and offer great views across town too.

Fossheim Turisthotell (☎ 61 21 95 00, fax 61 21 95 01, Lom) Singles/doubles Nkr745/980. Lunch buffet Nkr195, 3-course dinner from Nkr270. At the eastern end of town is this pleasant cosy and traditional style hotel. Don't miss the traditional Norwegian meals prepared by renowned chef Arne Brimi, including wild trout, reindeer, elk and ptarmigan. The lunch buffet is also highly recommended.

Kræmarhuset (☎ 61 21 15 60, Lom) Mains Nkr85-150. Open 10am-11pm or midnight daily summer. Centrally located Kræmarhuset specialises in traditional Norwegian mountain fare.

The Nordal Turistsenter has a popular *gatekjøkken* (fish and chips is only Nkr29), which is a hang-out for local youth. The affiliated *Nordalsfjoset Pub* (☎ 61 21 93 08, Lom), in an old two-storey barn, serves up pizza from Nkr130 and the usual range of alcoholic beverages. The central *Lom Coop* sells groceries and camping supplies.

Getting There & Away

The thrice daily Nor-Way Bussekspress service between Oslo (Nkr410, 6½ hours) and Måløy (Nkr280, 4½ hours) passes through Lom. It's also on Ottadalen Billag's summer route between Otta (Nkr70, one hour) and Sogndal (Nkr185, 3½ hours), which serves the Sognefjellet road.

JOTUNHEIMEN NASJONALPARK

Lots of locals and foreigners are attracted to the high peaks and glaciers that make up Jotunheimen National Park, Norway's best-loved wilderness destination. Jotunheimen has been a popular climbing area since the celebrated first ascents by English mountaineer William Cecil Slingsby in the late 19th century.

While a handful of really popular hiking routes may at times resemble motorways, the park is so vast that it's still not that difficult to find a bit of elbow room. The range of hiking routes lead from ravine-like valleys and past deep lakes, plunging waterfalls and 60 glaciers to the tops of all the peaks in Norway over 2300m, including Galdhøpiggen (the highest peak in northern Europe at 2469m), Glittertind (2452m) and Store Skagastølstind (2405m). DNT maintains staffed huts along most of the wilderness routes and there's also a choice of private lodges by the main roads.

For park information, contact Lom tourist office (☎ 61 21 29 90).

Sognefjellet Road

The high and scenic Sognefjellet road connects Lustrafjorden with Lom and provides easy access to the northern reaches of Jotunheimen National Park. It was constructed in 1939 by unemployed youth and reaches 1434m, making it the highest mountain road in northern Europe.

The mountain views can be spectacular, but the snow doesn't normally melt until at least early July, and at higher elevations drivers should prepare for new snow at any time of year.

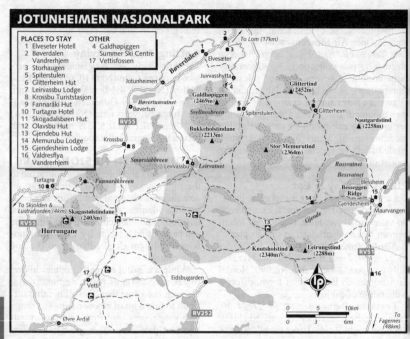

JOTUNHEIMEN NASJONALPARK

PLACES TO STAY
1 Elveseter Hotell
2 Bøverdalen Vandrerhjem
3 Storhaugen
4 Spiterstulen
6 Glitterheim Hut
7 Leirvassbu Lodge
8 Krossbu Turiststasjon
9 Fannaråki Hut
10 Turtagrø Hotel
11 Skogadalsbøen Hut
12 Olavsbu Hut
13 Gjendebu Hut
14 Memurubu Lodge
15 Gjendesheim Lodge
16 Valdresflya Vandrerhjem

OTHER
4 Galdhøpiggen Summer Ski Centre
17 Vettisfossen

From mid-June to late August, Ottadalen Billag runs two daily buses between Otta and Sogndal via Sognefjellet.

Spiterstulen *Spiterstulen* (☎ *61 21 14 80, fax 61 21 19 72, Spiterstulen)* Tent sites Nkr50 per person, singles/doubles with shared bathroom Nkr300/400. The private Spiterstulen lodge, at an old *sæter* (summer dairy), is convenient for access to Galdhøpiggen.

The poorly maintained toll road to Spiterstulen costs Nkr60 per vehicle. On foot, you can approach on the five-hour marked route from Leirvassbu hut, farther west.

Galdhøpiggen, with its tangle of dramatic cirques, arêtes and glaciers, is a fairly tough eight-hour day hike from Spiterstulen, with 1470m of ascent. Although the trail is well marked, you'll need a map and compass.

Juvvashytta Juvvashytta hut serves as the gateway to the **Galdhøpiggen Summer Ski Centre** (☎ *61 21 17 50, fax 61 21 21 72)*, at 1850m on the icy heights of Norway's highest mountain. From Galdesand on the Rv55, follow the Galdhøpiggen road (Nkr70 toll) to its end at 1841m. The season runs from June to mid-November.

Bøverdalen Beautiful Bøverdalen, the valley of the Bøvra river, descends from Sognefjell and mostly follows the main road into Lom (although the Sognefjellet road makes a 10km detour into Leirdalen). This scenic and easily accessible area adjoins Jotunheimen and is occupied mainly by a scattering of farms and tourist lodges.

Bøverdalen Vandrerhjem (☎/fax 61 21 20 64, Bøverdalen)* Dorm beds Nkr90, singles/doubles from Nkr190/230, 4-bed cabins Nkr350-450. Open June-Sept. This fine riverside hostel and community centre has a stage backed with a huge painting from 1899.

Storhaugen (☎/fax 61 21 20 69, Bøverdalen)* Self-catering traditional house from Nkr525, cabins Nkr300-1200. A highly recommended upmarket alternative is this friendly farm run by Marit and Magner Slettede. It's a traditional-style timber farm with views of both the Jotunheimen heights and Bøverdalen. At Galdesand, turn south on the Galdhøpiggen road and continue 1.5km to the signposted right turn-off for Storhaugen.

Elveseter Hotell (☎ 61 21 20 00, Bøverdalen) Singles/doubles Nkr550/750, dinner Nkr195. One of Norway's most unusual accommodation options was built up around the Sagasøyla. This 32m-high carved wooden pillar is a commemorative monument tracing Norwegian history from unification in 872 to the 1814 constitution. When the Nazis invaded Norway in 1940, the column was still only partially completed and the project went into hibernation. This white elephant deteriorated for 20 more years until Åmund Elveseter obtained it and set it up here. The lodge/hotel, a bizarre historic theme park, surpasses the column as an oddity and is particularly popular with tourists who appreciate kitsch.

Leirvassbu *Leirvassbu Lodge (☎ 61 21 29 32, fax 61 21 29 21, Bøverdalen)* Dorm bunks Nkr120/130 for DNT members/nonmembers. Singles/doubles with en suite Nkr310/540. Leirvassbu, a typical mountain lodge at 1400m and beside lake Leirvatnet, is a good base for hiking or trekking in Jotunheimen. Despite its large capacity, it can get crowded, especially in high season. Eight-hour guided glacier walks over Smørstabbreen cost Nkr450. The toll on the access road costs Nkr40 per car.

Krossbu Krossbu, near the head of Bøverdalen, lies at the outset of a tangle of hiking routes, including a short day trip to the Smørstabbreen glacier.

Krossbu Turiststasjon (☎ 61 21 29 22, fax 61 21 26 80, Bøverdalen) Doubles Nkr360, larger rooms Nkr520. At this roadside lodge, the larger rooms have attached bath and dinner is available. Guided glacier hikes and courses cost Nkr250 (four to six hours).

Turtagrø *Turtagrø Hotel (☎ 57 68 61 16, fax 57 68 61 15, e post@turtagro.no, Turtag-*

rø) Beds in 4-bed/2-bed bunk rooms in annexe Nkr200/240, singles/doubles including breakfast Nkr830/1100. Breakfast Nkr95, 3-course dinner Nkr350. This historic hiking and mountaineering centre is a friendly and laid-back base for exploring Jotunheimen/Hurrungane. The main building was completely destroyed by fire in 2001, but a new building with discreet modern design has arisen in its place.

The hotel, originally built in 1888, has been run by four generations of mountaineers in the Drægni family, who know how to create an ideal environment for outdoor enthusiasts. They also conduct weeklong climbing courses, guided day trips (hiking, climbing and skiing) and have laid out new hiking routes. There's also a great bar full of historic Norwegian mountaineering photos. The dining room serves excellent hearty meals (daily special Nkr80, available until late afternoon), and the library has Internet access.

Øvre Årdal

The toll mountain road between Turtagrø and the industrial town of Øvre Årdal (population 3500) is one of Norway's most scenic short drives. It's open late May to October and leads across high, wild and treeless country. From late June to late August, the route is served by bus once daily (Nkr100, one hour). The vehicle toll of Nkr50 is collected at the pass. For tourist information, contact Årdal Reiselivslag (☎ 57 66 11 77).

From Øvre Årdal you may want to head 12km north-east up the Utladalen valley to the farm Vetti, from where hiking tracks lead to Vettisfossen (275m), usually described as Norway's highest free-falling waterfall, and also to the little visited, unstaffed hut at Stølsmaradalen. This is also an alternative access route, via upper Utladalen, to longer hikes in Jotunheimen.

Nor-Way Bussekspress runs once daily between Lillehammer (Nkr280, four hours) and Bergen (Nkr300, 4¾ hours) via Øvre Årdal. Local and express buses also run six to nine times daily to/from Sogndal (Nkr101, 1½ hours) and every hour or two to/from Lærdal (Nkr67, one hour). Express buses to/from Oslo (Nkr410, six hours) run two or three times daily.

Gjendesheim & Valdresflya

Between Randen and Fagernes, Rv51 climbs through the hilly and forested Sjodalen country onto a vast wild upland with far-ranging views of peaks and glaciers. It's one of Norway's most scenic mountain routes and is used by thousands of hikers heading for Jotunheimen's eastern reaches.

The first DNT hut at Gjendesheim was constructed in 1878, but most of the current building dates from 1935 to 1937. It's the launching point for the popular day hike along the Besseggen ridge. Drivers not staying at the hut get ripped off Nkr30 per day for parking at the pier.

Gjendesheim Lodge (☎ 61 23 89 10, fax 61 23 89 65, Gjendesheim) Beds members Nkr85-170, nonmembers Nkr145-220. There are 175 beds in this popular DNT lodge.

Valdresflya Vandrerhjem (mobile ☎ 94 10 70 21, Valdresflya) Dorm beds Nkr115, singles/doubles Nkr200/260. About 15 minutes' drive south from Gjendesheim is this quiet, well-run hostel, which prides itself on being the highest hostel in northern Europe at 1389m. There's no guest kitchen but breakfast/dinner costs Nkr60/105 and there's a daytime cafe serving excellent waffles to passers-by.

Between 23 June and 2 September, there are two daily buses between Otta and Gol, via Vågå, Randen, Gjendesheim, Valdresflya and Fagernes. You'll have to change buses at Gjendesheim. From Otta, the trip to Gjendesheim takes two hours and costs Nkr81. Valdresflya is just 15 minutes farther.

Hiking

Jotunheimen's hiking possibilities are practically endless and all are spectacular. The best maps by far are Statens Kartverk's *Jotunheimen Aust* and *Jotunheimen Vest* (1:50,000; Nkr95 each).

The Hurrungane The fabulous Hurrungane massif rises darkly above the westernmost end of the park. Most experienced mountaineers will be able to pick their way

to some of these prominent peaks – with several even accessible to skilled scramblers.

For an amenable hiking experience, however, most people would prefer to head eastwards from Turtagrø. From the hotel, a four-hour hike will take you to Norway's highest DNT hut, Fannaråki, on the summit of Fannaråken (2069m), with fabulous views. To get started, walk about 500m up the road and follow the track up Helgedalen. At Ekrehytta hut, a narrow track starts a steep 800m climb to the top.

You can either return the way you came or descend the eastern slope along the well-marked track to Keisarpasset and thence back to Ekrehytta. To launch into a multiday trip, you can also descend Gjertvassdalen to Skogadalsbøen hut and, once there, choose from one of many routes eastwards through Jotunheimen.

Besseggen No discussion of hiking in Jotunheimen would be complete without a mention of Besseggen ridge, the most popular hike in Norway. Indeed, it could even be described as over-attended, with at least 30,000 hikers in the three months a year that it's passable. If you want to avoid the crowds, choose another route, but if you don't mind sacrificing solitude for one of Norway's most spectacular trips, you probably won't regret it. Henrik Ibsen wrote of Besseggen:

'It cuts along with an edge like a scythe for miles and miles... And scars and glaciers sheer down the precipice to the glassy lakes, 1600 feet below on either side.'

So daunting did it appear to him, that one of Peer Gynt's mishaps was a plunge down to the lake on the back of a reindeer.

Warning

When scrambling, travelling cross-country or hiking through any exposed area, be prepared for sudden inclement weather and stay aware of potential avalanche dangers, which are rife in Jotunheimen. Also, never venture onto glacial ice without the proper equipment and experience.

The day hike between Gjendesheim and Memurubu takes about six hours and climbs to a high point of 1743m. From Gjendesheim hut, follow the DNT-marked track towards Glitterheim for about 30 minutes, where a left fork strikes off up the Veltløyfti gorge, which leads upward onto the level Veslefjellet plateau.

After a short descent from the plateau, the track conducts you onto the Besseggen ridge, which slices between the deep blue lake Bessvatnet and the 18km long glacier-green lake Gjende, coloured by the 20,000 tonnes of glacial silt which are dumped into it each year by the Memuru river.

Although there's a lot of hype about its exposed nature, Besseggen is never less than 10m wide and only from a distance does it look precarious. After passing the head of Bessvatnet, the route passes a small plateau lake, Bjørnbøltjørn, and shortly thereafter begins its descent to the modern chalet-style Memurubu lodge.

Once there, you can decide whether to take the boat M/S *Gjende* back to Gjendesheim (Nkr60, 20 to 35 minutes), continue west to Gjendebu hut, either on foot or on the boat (Nkr60, 20 to 35 minutes), or hike north to Glitterheim.

Hardangervidda

The high Hardangervidda plateau has long served as a trade and travel route between eastern and western Norway. It remains on the main railway and road routes between Norway's two major cities, Oslo and Bergen.

Old snow lingers until early August and new snow is a possibility at any time of year, but the region is best known for its hiking opportunities and altitude-stretched cross-country ski season.

In 1981, the 3430-sq-km Hardangervidda National Park was established to protect the tundra landscape and Norway's largest herd of wild reindeer (caribou). Hikers and skiers will find that the Statens Kartverk maps *Hardangervidda Øst* and *Hardangervidda Vest*, both at a scale of 1:100,000, will be essential.

GEILO
pop 2500
At Geilo (pronounced **Yei**-lo), midway between Oslo and Bergen, you can practically step off the train onto a ski lift. In summer, there's plenty of fine hiking in the area. A popular nearby destination is the expansive plateau-like mountain called Hallingskarvet, frosted with several small glaciers.

For tourist information, contact Geilo Turistinformasjon (☎ 32 09 59 00, fax 32 09 59 01, e turistinfo@geilo.no). The office is open year-round, with its longest hours from 9am to 9pm Monday to Friday (to 5pm weekends) between 1 July and mid-August.

Organised Tours
Geilo Aktiv (☎ 32 09 59 30) offers Glacier trekking on Hardangerjøkulen (1860m) on Monday, Wednesday and Friday from 1 July to 15 September. The standard 10-hour tour (including train to/from Finse) costs Nkr520 per person. The company also offers a variety of rafting tours (Nkr650 to Nkr750), riverboarding (Nkr650 to Nkr750) and a two-hour moose safari (Nkr350) on Thursday evening, all from 1 July to 15 September.

Places to Stay & Eat
For its size, Geilo has a boggling choice of accommodation, most of which is geared towards the outdoor activity crowds. The tourist office has full details.

Øen Turistsenter & Geilo Vandrerhjem (☎ 32 08 70 60, fax 32 09 13 36, Lienvegen 137) Dorm beds Nkr120-150, doubles Nkr360-450. About 2km east of the train station, the hostel offers reasonable and inexpensive accommodation. Breakfast costs Nkr60 extra.

Haugen Hotell (☎ 32 09 06 44, fax 32 09 03 87, Gamleveien 16) Singles/doubles from Nkr460/720. One of the best-value summer hotels, this is 500m from the centre.

Ro Hotell & Kro (☎ 32 09 08 99, fax 32 09 07 85, Geilovegen 55) Singles/doubles Nkr470/640 summer. Dinner mains Nkr79-85. This commercial place, near the station, serves reasonable and good-value meals.

There's a *Rimi supermarket* between the tourist office and the main road through town.

Getting There & Around

The only long-distance bus service connects Geilo with Kongsberg (Nkr216, 3¼ hours) once or twice daily. Many visitors arrive on the train between Oslo (Nkr375, 3½ hours) and Bergen (Nkr340, three hours). If you wish to cycle the Rallarvegen, cycles can be hired for an astronomical Nkr190 for one day, Nkr300 for two days (Nkr490 for a weekend); to return the bike by train costs Nkr40.

FINSE

Heading west from Geilo, the railway line climbs 600m through a tundra-like landscape of lakes and snowy peaks to Finse, lying at 1222m near the Hardangerjøkulen icecap. This bleak region offers nordic skiing in winter and hiking in summer, including the popular four-hour trek to the Blåisen glacier snout of Hardangerjøkulen. The great three- or four-day Finse-Aurland trek follows scenic Aurlandsdalen down to Aurlandsfjorden and has a series of DNT and private mountain huts a day's walk apart. The nearest is Finsehytta, 200m from Finse station. For more on this route, see Aurland in the Western Fjords chapter.

Rallarmuseet Finse

The Finse Navvies Museum (☎ 56 52 69 66; adult/child Nkr30/15; open 10am-8pm daily 7 July-late Sept), east of Finse station, reveals the history of the Oslo-Bergen railway and the 15,000 people who engineered and built this hard-won line in 2.5 million worker days.

Rallarvegen

The Rallarvegen, or Navvies' Road, was constructed as a supply route for Oslo-Bergen railway workers (the railway opened on 27 November 1909). Nowadays, this 80km route of asphalt and gravel extends from Haugastøl through Finse, Hallingskeid and Vatnahalsen to Flåm, with a 43km branch from the Upsete end of the Gravhals tunnel and down the Raundal valley to Voss. The section from Storurdivatn to Myrdal via Finse passes through some lovely highland plateau country and is open only to bicycles and foot traffic, while sections down the

Flåm and Raundal valleys are also open to vehicle traffic. The popular stretch between Vatnahalsen and Flåm descends 865m in 29km, with an initial series of hairpin bends.

Cyclists and hikers will find optimum conditions between mid-July and mid-September, after the snow has melted. Most people do the route from east to west due to the significant altitude loss. Bicycles can be hired at the hotel Finse 1222.

Places to Stay & Eat

Finsehytta (☎ 56 52 67 32) Beds members Nkr85-170, nonmembers Nkr145-220. Most budget travellers stay at the staffed DNT hut.

Finse 1222 (☎ 56 52 71 00, fax 56 52 67 17, e booking@finse1222.no) Full board per person Nkr790-1000, single supplement Nkr175. The friendly Finse 1222 hotel offers comfortable rooms in sight of the glacier, and a good three-course dinner.

Accommodation is available in **huts** and **hostels** at Haugastøl, Hallingskeid (unstaffed) and Mjølfjell.

Getting There & Away

Five daily trains run between Oslo (Nkr410, 4½ hours) and Bergen (Nkr245, 2¼ hours).

MYRDAL

Myrdal, west of Finse, is the junction of the Oslo-Bergen railway and the spectacularly steep Flåmbanen railway, and a famous stop on the 'Norway in a Nutshell' tour. The dramatic Flåmbanen line twists its way 20km down to Flåm on Aurlandsfjorden, an arm of Sognefjorden. Many people make the descent to Flåm, have lunch and then return to Myrdal to catch the next Oslo-Bergen train. A better option is to transfer to the ferry from Flåm to Gudvangen, via lovely Nærøyfjorden, from where a connecting bus follows the dramatically scenic road to Voss. From there, trains to Bergen run almost hourly. For more information, see Flåm and Gudvangen & Nærøyfjorden in the Western Fjords chapter.

Vatnahalsen Høyfjellshotell (☎ 57 63 37 22, fax 57 63 37 67, Myrdal) Singles/doubles with view Nkr595/920. This quiet and comfortable place, 820m above Flåm, is accessible only by train or on foot.

Bergen & the South-Western Fjords

The southernmost of Norway's fjords, with their relative greenery and amenable landscapes for farming and larger cities and towns, contrast sharply with their more rugged counterparts farther north. Here you'll find not only charming Bergen and the sparkling oil city of Stavanger, but also some of Norway's most interesting landscapes, from the rock-studded farmlands of the south and the bright orchards of Hardangerfjord to the ethereal vertical cliffs around spectacular Lysefjord.

Bergen

pop 230,829

Bergen still manages to retain a pleasantly slow pace of life despite being Norway's second largest city. As a university town and cultural centre, it boasts oodles of museums as well as several theatres and a renowned philharmonic orchestra. Although you can reliably expect rain or showers on at least 275 days of the year, all this precipitation keeps the place clean, green and flowery, lending it a sense of cheeriness on even the dullest of days.

History

During the 12th and 13th centuries, Bergen served as Norway's capital and, despite the fact that 70% of the population was wiped out by the Black Death in 1349, by the early 17th century it served as the trading hub of Scandinavia and had also become the country's most populous city, with 15,000 people.

Set on a peninsula surrounded by seven mountains, Bergen's history is closely tied to the sea. It became one of the central ports of the Hanseatic League, which dominated northern European trade during the late Middle Ages, and its influences are still evident in Bryggen, the line-up of warehouses that provides modern Bergen with its picturesque waterfront (see the boxed text 'Bryggen & the Hanseatic League', following).

Highlights

- Visiting the homes and haunts of Edvard Grieg and Ole Bull, Norway's favourite classical musicians and composers
- Strolling through the charming, historic streets of Bergen and buying fish at the renowned Torget market
- Exploring the historic Bryggen trading district in Bergen – now a Unesco World Heritage Site
- Climbing to Preikestolen or Kjeragbolten, or driving the precarious descent into Lysebotn, to be inspired by the haunting light along Lysefjord
- Perusing the superb Rogaland Art Museum in Stavanger
- Ambling through the historic timber houses of Old Stavanger

Orientation

Hilly greater Bergen has suburbs radiating out onto outlying peninsulas and islands, but the central area remains pleasantly compact and easily manageable on foot. The

BERGEN

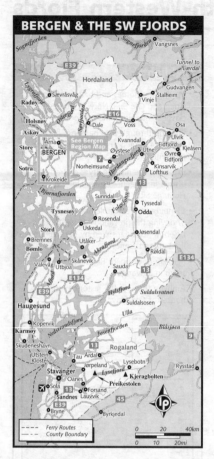

interest. It's in the hall of the old Den Norske Bank (1862) and is open 8.30am to 10pm daily June to August, 9am to 8pm daily in May and September, otherwise 9am to 4pm Monday to Saturday. While you're there, take a look at the three frescoed walls, which were painted by Axel Revold between 1921 and 1923; they portray fishing in northern Norway, trade activities in Bergen, and human commerce since the industrial revolution.

There's also the Fjord Expo information office on the 5th floor of the Galleriet shopping centre, with multimedia presentations about fjord Norway. It's open 9am to 8pm weekdays and 9am to 6pm Saturday mid-May to late August.

Bergen Card The Bergen Card covers transport on local buses, municipal parking, funicular rides and admission to most museums and historic sites both in the central area (excluding the Hanseatic Museum and Schøtstuene from June to August) and farther afield (Gamle Bergen, Ole Bull's Lysøen, Damsgård Manor and Harald Sæverud's Siljustøl). The card is sold at tourist offices, some hotels and camping grounds, and the bus terminal, and costs Nkr150/230 per 24/48 hours.

An alternative option is BergensPakken, which starts at Nkr465 per day and includes a Bergen Card and a bed in a hotel room for one night (numbers are very limited).

Money You can change money at the Kreditkassen bank on Allehelgensgaten or the nearby post office. There are plenty of other banks and ATMs nearby. The tourist office changes money at 3% less than the bank rates.

Post The main post office, on Småstrandgaten, is open 8am to 6pm weekdays and 9am to 3pm on Saturday.

Email & Internet Access You can pick up email and access the Internet for free at the library (☎ 55 56 85 00), Strømgaten 6, or pay for the privilege at Cyberhouse (☎ 55 36 66 16), Vetrlidsalmenning 13.

bus and train stations lie only a block apart on Strømgaten, a 10-minute walk from the ferry terminals, and most of the restaurants, hotels, museums, tourist sites and picturesque streets and passages cluster around Vågen, the inner harbour.

Information
Tourist Office The Bergen Reiselivslag tourist office (☎ 55 32 14 80, fax 55 32 14 64, W www.visitBergen.com), Vågsallmenningen 1, distributes a free *Bergen Guide* booklet containing a useful city centre map and basic information on tours and sites of

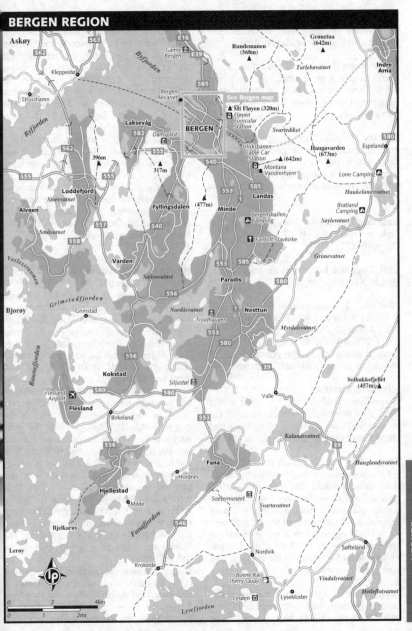

BERGEN REGION

Askøy

562
563

E16
E39

Kleppestø

Strusshamn

Byfjorden

Gamle Bergen

585

Rundemanen
(568m)

Grønetua
(642m)

Tarlebøvatnet

Indre
Arna

580

Byfjorden

Bergen
Akvariet

Laksevåg

Damsgård

582

BERGEN

See Bergen map

Mt Fløyen (320m)
Fløyen
Funicular
Station

Svartediket

Espeland

562

396m

555

317m

555

555

540

Ulriksbanen
Cable Car
Station

Montana
Vandrerhjem

642m

Haugavarden
(673m)

Lone Camping

Loddefjord

Størevatnet

Alvøen

557

558

Småvatnet

Fyllingsdalen

540

(477m)

553

585

Landas

Minde

1

Bergenshallen
Camping

Haukelandsvatnet

Bratland
Camping

Søylevatnet

Vatlestraumen

Varden

Sælenvatnet

Fantoft Stavkirke

Grimevatnet

Bjorøy

Grimstadfjorden

Grimstad

556

Nordåsvatnet

Troldhaugen

553

Paradis

553

585

580

Nesttun

1

Myrdalsvatnet

Raunefjorden

Kokstad

Siljustøl

556

580

39

Solbakkefjellet
(457m)

Flesland
Airport

Flesland

580

Birkeland

Valle

Kalandsvatnet

556

Fana

553

Hordnes

Hauglandsvatnet

Hjellestad

546

Milde

Soøtermuseet

Svartavatnet

39

Bjelkarøy

Lerøy

Fanafjorden

Krokeide

Buene Kai
(Ferry Quay)

Nordvik

Søfteland

Vindalsvatnet

Lysøen

Lysekloster

Lyseøen

Lysefjorden

Hetleflotvatnet

0   2   4km
0   1   2mi

BERGEN

Travel Agencies Kilroy Travel (☎ 02633), Vaskerelven 16, specialises in student tickets but also handles regular bookings.

Bookshops If you're after literature, travel books or just a good read, you can't beat Norli, Torgalmenningen 4, in the Galleriet Shopping Centre, which has a huge selection of books.

Library The public library, between the bus and train stations, has a good selection of foreign newspapers. It's open to 8pm on weekdays (to 4.30pm on Friday) and 2pm on Saturday, with shorter hours in July and August.

Laundry Laundry facilities are available at Jarlens Vaskoteque (☎ 55 32 55 04), Lille Øvregaten 17.

Left Luggage Lockers at the train station start at Nkr10 per day.

Medical & Emergency Services Dial ☎ 112 for police and ☎ 113 for an ambulance. The 24-hour Legevakten medical clinic (☎ 55 32 11 20), at Vestre Strømkaien 19, handles medical emergencies. The pharmacy at the bus station is open daily until midnight.

Historic District

Bergen has lots of quaint cobblestone streets lined with timber-clad houses; some of the most picturesque are the winding lanes and alleys above the Fløibanen funicular station.

Torget The waterfront fish market at Torget is a good place to begin exploring. Here, fishy odours assault the olfactory senses, spilt effluent turns the quay into a slippery mess, and you'll find a range of tasty seafood snacks at excellent prices. Adjacent Zachariasbryggen offers a range of indoor and outdoor restaurants/bars with excellent views – ideal for watching the comings and goings in the harbour.

Bryggen In the 13th century, the Hanseatic League dominated trade between 200 European towns and cities, with major centres in Rostock, London, Bruges, Riga, Novgorod and Bergen. Nowadays, the historic Bryggen waterfront is on the Unesco World Heritage List and the fascinating timber buildings shelter museums, restaurants and arty shops. The narrow alleys offer a glimpse of the stacked-stone foundations and reconstructed rough-plank construction of centuries past. See the boxed text 'Bryggen & the Hanseatic League'.

The notable tilt of the structures in Bryggen was caused in 1944, when a Dutch munitions ship exploded in the harbour, blowing off the roofs and shifting the pilings. After a fire destroyed the warehouses in 1955, archaeologists took the opportunity to excavate the area and found over one million artefacts, foundations of earlier buildings, and evidence of the big fires of 1170 and 1198.

Hanseatic Museum The worthwhile Hanseatic Museum (☎ 55 31 41 89, Finnegårdsgaten 1a; adult/child Nkr40/free May-Sept (Bergen Card not valid Jun-Aug), Nkr25/free Oct-Apr, also valid for Schøtstuene & including guided tours, 3 daily Jun-Aug; open 9am-5pm daily 1 June-31 Aug, 11am-2pm daily), in a rough-timber building from 1704, retains its period character and furnishings and offers a glimpse of the austere living and working conditions of Hanseatic merchant sailors and apprentices and the contrasting lifestyles of the management. Highlights include the manager's office and quarters, as well as his private liquor cabinet and summer bedroom; the wooden bird used for shooting competitions, whose beak was the main target; the apprentices' quarters where beds were shared by two young men for spatial rather than sensual reasons; the fish storage room, which pressed and processed over a million pounds of fish a month; and the fiskeskrue, or fish press, which pressed the fish into barrels.

The 1½-hour Nkr70/free Bryggen tour (10% discount with the Bergen Card) is conducted in English at 11am and 1pm from 1 June to 31 August. Tickets allow re-admission to the museum on the same day.

Bryggen & the Hanseatic League

By the 13th century, Bergen had developed into a major centre for European trade, as well as the episcopal seat of the Christian Diocese of Western Norway and the capital of the Norwegian monarchy. The oldest part of the town and the commercial centre lay on the eastern shore of Vågen harbour, between the king's residence at Bergenhus, Holmen, and Vågsbotn (or Torget). Here, long parallel rows of buildings run back from gabled fronts facing the wharf, where cargo ships and trading vessels moored and carried on their trade. These ships exported dried fish, butter, skins and hides, and imported mostly grain, but also luxury items such as wine, honey, textiles and pottery. In the early 14th century, there were about 30 wooden buildings on Bryggen, each of which was usually shared by several *stuer* (trading firms). They rose two or three storeys above the wharf and combined business premises with living quarters and warehouses. Each building had a crane for loading and unloading ships, as well as a large assembly room, or *schøtstue*, where employees met and ate. The greatest concern among Bryggen residents was fire; fireplaces were forbidden, barrels of water hung over the stairways, and cooks had to follow strict kitchen regulations. Despite the precautions, the buildings were destroyed by fire at least seven times.

From the mid-11th century in Germany, population growth, land pressure and greater mobility had accelerated the growth of cities. Some were considered 'imperial' and were granted autonomy by crown charter, while the 'free' cities had shaken off their clerical rulers. Both types had their own administrations and generally more liberal laws than the countryside and, as a result, peasants flocked to the urban areas. In order to protect these cities' economic interests, trading leagues were formed. The most significant was the Hanseatic League, which was amalgamated in 1358 from a collection of German urban trading areas, centred on Lübeck. At its zenith, the league had over 150 member cities and was northern Europe's most powerful economic entity.

The German Hanseatic *Kontor* at Bergen, established around 1360, was one of the league's four major offices abroad. For over 400 years, Bryggen was dominated by German merchants and, at one stage, it was home to about 2000 mostly German resident traders. These traders formed a tight-knit sub-community who busied themselves with the import of grain and export of dried fish, among other products, and weren't permitted to mix with, marry or have families with local Norwegians.

By the 15th century, the influence of the Hanseatic League began to decline, due to competition from Dutch and English shipping companies, internal disputes and, especially, the Black Death that killed a third of Europe's population. (However, Hamburg, Bremen and Lübeck are still known as Hanseatic cities and, in fact, Hamburg and Bremen remain separate independent German city-states.) As the League continued its decline through the 17th and 18th centuries, many Hanseatic traders opted to take Norwegian nationality and join the local community. Although the Hanseatic League lasted until the mid-18th century, Bryggen continued as an important maritime trade centre until 1899, when the Bergen Kontor (successor to the Norwegian Kontor, which was in turn the successor of the German Kontor) finally closed down. In 1979, 58 of the wooden structures along the Bryggen waterfront were added to Unesco's World Heritage List.

Bryggens Museum The archaeological Bryggens Museum (☎ 55 58 80 10, *Dregsalmenning 3; adult/child Nkr30/free; open 10am-5pm daily May-Aug, 11am-3pm Mon-Fri, noon-3pm Sat, noon-4pm Sun Sept-Apr)* was built on the site of Bergen's first settlement, and the 800-year-old foundations unearthed during the construction have been incorporated into the exhibits, which include excavated medieval tools, pottery, skulls and runes. Folk music and dance concerts are held at 9pm on Tuesday and Thursday from early June to mid-August; for information, call Bergen Folklore (☎ 55 31 95 50). Admission to the performances costs Nkr95 (Nkr85.50 with the Bergen Card).

BERGEN

Schøtstuene Schøtstuene (☎ 55 31 60 20, Øvregaten 50; adult/child Nkr40/free; open 10am-5pm daily Jun-Aug, 11am-2pm daily May & Sept, 11am-2pm Sun Oct-Apr) is a reconstruction of one of the original assembly halls where the fraternity of Hanseatic merchants once met for their business meetings and beer guzzling. Don't miss the interesting downstairs kitchen. Admission is also valid for the Hanseatic Museum.

Theta Museum This excellent one-room reconstruction of a clandestine Resistance headquarters, uncovered by the Nazis in 1942, is now Norway's tiniest museum (Enhjørningsgården; adult/child Nkr20/5; open 2pm-4pm Tues, Sat & Sun mid-May–mid-Sept). Appropriately enough, finding it is still a challenge – it's at the back of the Bryggen building with the unicorn figurehead; pass through the alley and up the stairs to the 3rd floor.

Mariakirken The stone Mariakirken church (☎ 55 31 59 60, Dreggen; adult/child Nkr10/free in summer, free rest of year; open 11am-4pm Mon-Fri mid-May–mid-Sept, noon-1.30pm Tues-Fri rest of year), with its Romanesque entrance and twin towers, dates from the early 12th century and is Bergen's oldest building. The interior features 15th-century frescoes and a splendid baroque pulpit donated by Hanseatic merchants in 1676.

Rosenkrantztårnet Rosenkrantz Tower (☎ 55 31 43 80, Bergenhus; admission Nkr15; open 10am-4pm daily mid-May–31 Aug, noon-3pm Sun Sept–mid-May) was built in the 1560s by Bergen governor Erik Rosenkrantz as a residence and defence post, but incorporates parts of the keep of King Magnus the Lawmender, which was completed in 1273, and the 1520s fortress of Jørgen Hansson. You can climb spiral staircases past halls and sentry posts to a nice harbour view from the lookout on top.

Håkonshallen This large ceremonial hall (☎ 55 31 60 67, Bergenhus; adult/child Nkr20/10; open 10am-4pm daily mid-May–31 Aug, noon-3pm Fri-Wed, 3pm-6pm

Thur Sept–mid-May), adjacent to the Rosenkrantz Tower, was constructed by King Håkon Håkonsson from 1247–61 and completed for his son's wedding and coronation. The roof was blown off in 1944 thanks to the explosion of a Dutch munitions boat, but extensive restoration has been carried out.

Fløibanen
For an unbeatable city view, ride the 26° Fløibanen funicular to the top of Mt Fløyen (320m), where well-marked hiking tracks lead into the forest; the possibilities are mapped out on the free Gledeskartet or Turløyper På Byfjellene Nord/Øst (Nkr10) maps, which are available at the tourist office. Track 2 makes a 1.6km loop near lake Skomakerdiket and Track 1 offers a 5km loop over hills, through forests and past several lakes. For a delightful 40-minute walk back to the city from Fløyen, follow Track 4 clockwise and connect with Track 6, which switchbacks down to the harbour through neighbourhoods of old timber houses. The funicular runs at least twice hourly from 7.30am to 11pm (until midnight May to August) and costs Nkr50/25 adult/child return.

Bergen Kunstmuseum
The three-part Bergen Art Museum (☎ 55 56 80 00, Rasmus Meyers Allé 3 & 7, Lars Hilles gate 10; adult/child Nkr50/free; open 11am-5pm daily mid-May–mid-Sept, shorter winter hours) is housed in three buildings beside the lovely lake Lille Lungegårdsvann. It exhibits a superb collection of 18th- and 19th-century international and Norwegian art, including works by Munch and JC Dahl, as well as contemporary European works by Miró, Picasso, Kandinsky, Paul Klee and others.

Vestlandske Kunstindustrimuseum
The West Norwegian Museum of Decorative Arts (☎ 55 33 66 33, Permanenten building, Nordahl Bruns gate 9; adult/child Nkr30/free; open 11am-4pm Tues-Sun mid-May–mid-Sept, shorter hours mid-Sept–mid-May), attracts a range of visiting art and craft exhibits, and there's also a fine

permanent collection of European handicrafts and design and Chinese art, including rare Buddhist temple sculptures.

Bergen Akvariet

The Bergen Aquarium (*☎ 55 55 71 71, Nordnesbakken; adult/child Nkr80/50; open 9am-8pm daily May-Sept, 10am-6pm daily Oct-Apr*), at the end of the Nordnes peninsula, has a big outdoor tank with seals and penguins as well as 70 indoor tanks. You'll never forget the loveable steinbit, the hideous anglerfish or the school of herring which seems to function as a single entity. There are seal and penguin feedings at 11am, 3pm and 6pm from May to September; noon and 3pm from October to April. The public park just beyond the aquarium has pleasant shaded lawns and an outdoor heated pool.

On foot, you can get there from the Torget in 20 minutes; alternatively, take bus No 11, marked Nordnes, or the Vågen ferry that runs between the fish market and the aquarium every 20 minutes from 10am to 6pm, May to September.

University Museums

The university, at the end of Christies gate, has the Naturhistorisk Samlinger (*Natural History Collection; ☎ 55 58 29 20, Muséplass 3; adult/child Nkr30/free, includes Cultural History Collection; open 10am-3pm Tues-Sat, 11am-4pm Sun 15 May-31 Aug, shorter hours rest of year*) full of stuffed creatures and mineral displays; and, of greater interest, the Kulturhistorisk Samlinger (*Cultural History Collection; ☎ 55 58 31 40, Haakon Sheteligs plass 10*) with Viking weaponry, medieval altars, folk art and period furnishings. There are also sections dedicated to Native American cultures, including Inuit and Aleut.

Sjøfartsmuseet

Sjøfartsmuseet (*Maritime Museum; ☎ 55 54 96 00, Haakon Sheteligs plass 15; adult/child Nkr30/free; open 11am-3pm daily June-Aug, 11am-2pm Sun-Fri Sept-May*) features models of ships from Viking times to the present, and exhibits tracing Norway's maritime history.

Gamle Bergen

The open-air museum, Gamle Bergen (*☎ 55 39 43 04, Elesro, Sandviken; Bus: Nos 20-23; adult/child Nkr50/25; open for hourly tours 10am-5pm daily 20 May-2 Sept*), is 4km north of the city centre. It consists of a collection of 35 structures from the 18th and 19th centuries, including a number of historic commercial enterprises. It lies just within walking distance of Torget (about 30 minutes), but the traffic makes it a hectic walk and most people opt for buses. Entrance to the grounds is free and is available all year.

Lepramuseet

For something a bit different, visit the unusual Leprosy Museum (*☎ 55 32 57 80, St George's Hospital, Kong Oscars gate 59; adult/child Nkr30/15; open 11am-3pm daily 20 May-31 Aug*). Although most of the buildings at St George's date from the 19th century, in medieval times the site served as a leprosarium which specialised in housing leprosy victims. Exhibits detail Norway's contributions to leprosy research, including the work of Dr Armauer Hansen, who gave his name to Hansen's disease, the modern name for leprosy.

Fantoft Stavkirke

The Fantoft stave church (*☎ 55 28 07 10, Paradis; adult/child Nkr30/5, including tour in English; open 10.30am-2pm & 2.30pm-6pm daily 15 May-15 Sept*), in a lovely leafy setting south of Bergen, was built in Sognefjord around 1150 and moved to the southern outskirts of Bergen in 1883. It was burned down by a Satanist in 1992, but it has since been painstakingly reconstructed. The adjacent **cross**, originally from Sola in Rogaland, dates from 1050. From Bergen take any bus leaving from platforms 19 to 21, get off at the Fantoft stop on Birkelundsbakken and walk uphill through the park for about five minutes.

Troldhaugen

The two-storey home Troldhaugen (*☎ 55 92 29 92, Hop; adult/child Nkr50/free, Nkr20 with Bergen Card; open 9am-6pm daily May-Sept, shorter hours Oct-Apr*),

BERGEN

designed by architect Schak Bull and constructed in 1885, occupies an undeniably lovely setting on a lush and scenic peninsula by the coastal lake Nordåsvatnet. Here composer Edvard Grieg and his wife Nina Hagerup spent every summer from 1885 until Grieg's death in 1907. Today the house and grounds are open to the public, a permanent multimedia Grieg exhibition has been opened and a 200-seat concert hall constructed. Of particular interest are the Composer's Hut, where Edvard mustered his musical inspiration; the Steinway piano, which was a gift to celebrate Edvard and Nina's 50th wedding anniversary in 1892; and the couple's tombs, which are embedded in a rock face overlooking Nordåsvatnet.

Grieg fans will best appreciate this well-conceived presentation, and anyone who's seen *Song of Norway*, the insipid film version of Grieg's life, will probably recognise a few things. In summer, concerts are held on Wednesday, Saturday and Sunday (tickets are Nkr130-200, from the tourist office). Take any bus from platforms 19 to 21 to the Hopsbroen stop (or from the stop for the stave church). From there, follow the signs to Troldhaugen; it's a 20-minute walk.

Siljustøl Museum

Another well-known Norwegian composer's home lies in a rural area only 3km south of Troldhaugen. Harald and Marie Sæverud lived in Siljustøl (☎ 55 92 29 92, Siljustøl; Bus: No 555 from platform 20; adult/child Nkr50/free; open 11am-4pm Wed-Fri & Sun 18 June-5 Aug), a simple timber home. It was constructed in the 1930s of natural stone and untreated wood in an attempt to create unity with the environment. Harald Sæverud was born in Nordnes on 17 April 1897 but moved with his parents to the city at an early age. His first symphony, completed in 1920, launched his career as a composer. During WWII, he wrote protest music against the Nazi occupation. In 1986, he was made official composer of the Bergen International Music Festival, a position he honoured by creating a symphonic suite to the Ibsen play *Kjeser og Galilæer*. When he died in March

1992, he was given a state funeral and buried at Siljustøl, as he'd requested.

Damsgård

The 1770 Damsgård manor (☎ 55 32 51 08, Laksevåg; Bus: Nos 60, 70 or 71; adult/child Nkr30/free; open for hourly tours 11am-4pm Tues-Sun 20 May-31 Aug), 3km west of town, may well be Norway's finest example of 18th-century rococo timber architecture. The building's superb (some may say over-the-top) highlight is the baroque garden, which includes sculptures, ponds and plant specimens which were in common use 200 years ago.

Ulriksbanen

The Ulriksbanen cable car (☎ 55 20 20 20; adult/child return Nkr70/35; operates 9am-10pm daily May-Sept, 10am-5pm Oct-Apr), which climbs to the radio tower and cafe atop Mt Ulriken (642m), offers a panoramic view of the city and surrounding fjords and mountains. The 'Bergen in a Nutshell' ticket (Nkr120/60) includes the cable car and a return bus from the tourist office. Otherwise, it's a 45-minute walk from the centre or a few minutes' ride on bus Nos 2 or 31 from the post office or bus No 50 from Bryggen.

A popular excursion is to ride up on the cable car and walk three hours north along a well-beaten track to the top of the Fløibanen funicular railway. For other route suggestions, pick up a copy of the free map *Turløper På Byfjellene Nord/Øst* (Nkr10), from the tourist office.

Lysøen

The beautiful Lysøen estate (☎ 56 30 90 77, Lysøen; adult/child including guided tour Nkr25/10; open noon-4pm Mon-Sat, 11am-5pm Sun 18 May-30 Aug, noon-4pm Sun Sept), on the island of the same name, was constructed in 1873 as the summer residence of Norwegian violinist Ole Bull (see the boxed text 'Ole Bull'). This rather quirky and exceptionally talented character had a great deal of influence on other musicians, who visited frequently and used Lysøen as a retreat. The grounds are crisscrossed with 13km of leisurely walks and there's a small cafe serving light refreshments. From the bus station, take the Lysefjorden bus (Nos 566 and 567) from platform 19 or 20 to Buene Kai, where there's a passenger ferry to Lysøen.

Activities

Contact the Bergen Turlag DNT office (☎ 55 32 22 30, fax 55 32 81 15, Tverrgaten 4) for maps and information on wilderness hiking and hut accommodation throughout

Edvard Grieg

Norway's best known and most universally loved composer, Edvard Grieg, was born in Bergen on 15 June 1843. Encouraged by Ole Bull, at the age of 15 he travelled to Germany to study music at the Leipzig Conservatory. After four years of intensive study, he graduated as a fully-fledged musician and composer. Until 1866, he lived and worked in Copenhagen, where Niels W Gade encouraged him to compose a symphony, but the result didn't measure up to Grieg's satisfaction and he scrawled across the score that it must never be performed. His wishes were ignored, however, and he refused to acknowledge it as his own creation!

Grieg's early style strongly reflected his German romantic training but instinctively he realised that it would be his lot to create national music for his homeland, Norway. While in Copenhagen, he met Rikard Nordraak (whose own dedication to Norway resulted in his crowning composition, the Norwegian national anthem). After returning to Christiania (Oslo) in 1866, Greig became increasingly influenced by Norway's folk music and melodies but he soon realised that the written music represented only a small portion of the effect created by traditional folk musicians.

Through the 1860s, Grieg remained in Oslo and struggled to support his family, working not only as a performer, but also as a choral leader, a conductor and a music teacher, often travelling to Germany, Italy and France to garner inspiration. He only indulged himself in composition during the slower summer months and in 1868, he'd completed his first great work, *Piano Concerto in A minor*, which has since come to represent Norway as no other work before or since.

In 1869, Grieg travelled to Italy, where he encountered Franz Liszt and found a new sense of enthusiasm. The following year, back in Christiania, he cooperated with author Bjørnstjerne Bjørnson, who had been awaiting a Norwegian composer to set his poetry and writing to music. Their efforts, *Before a Southern Convent, Bergliot* and *Sigurd Jorsalfar*, established Grieg as the musical voice of Norway, but their attempt to create a national opera based on the life of Olaf Tryggvason proved too ambitious and never came to fruition. These efforts, however, led Grieg to meet with Henrik Ibsen, who sought a composer for his fantastic novel *Peer Gynt*. Although he struggled with this project, the score found international acclaim and became his – and Norway's – best remembered classical work.

In 1874, a government grant allowed Grieg to return to Bergen and set his creative juices flowing; the result was his *Ballad in G minor, The Mountain Thrall*, the *Norwegian Dances for Piano* and *The Holberg Suite*. Between 1880 and 1882, he conducted an orchestra in Bergen, but resigned in order to return to his preferred work of composing. In 1885, he and his wife Nina moved into the coastal home Troldhaugen, from which he set off on numerous concert tours of Europe. At Troldhaugen he created the *Sonata for Violin and Piano in C minor*, the *Haugtussa Songs*, the *Norwegian Peasant Dances and Tunes*, and the *Four Psalms*, his last major work, based on a series of Norwegian religious melodies.

On 4 September 1907, he died in hospital at Bergen. In the early 20th century, Grieg's music became well known throughout Europe, and although it was somewhat trivialised by its 'coffee house' popularity, modern musicians are again recognising it as a serious force in classical music and a universal voice for the Norwegian nation. In fact, as early as the 1880s, his first biographer, Aimer Grøvald, noted that it was impossible to listen to Grieg without sensing a light, fresh breeze from the blue waters, a glimpse of grand glaciers and a recollection of the mountains of Western Norway's fjords.

BERGEN

the region, It's open from 10am to 4pm Monday to Friday (until 6pm on Thursday).

Organised Tours

A worthwhile tour is the 1½-hour guided stroll around Bryggen, which includes entertaining and informative descriptions of life during Bergen's trading heyday. The ticket (Nkr70/free adult/child) also includes admission to Bryggens Museum, Schøtstuene and the Hanseatic Museum (and allows you to re-visit these museums later on the same day). Tours in English begin at the Bryggens Museum entrance at 11am and 1pm daily, June to August.

The worthwhile three-hour Troldhaugen bus tour runs once or twice daily from May to September and includes either Gamle Bergen or Fantoft. Tickets (Nkr240/155)are available on the bus and tours commence just across the street from the tourist office.

Bergen Fjord Sightseeing (☎ 55 25 90 00) operates fjord cruises past Bergen's port and suburban islands, and through several scenic waterways. The four-hour (Nkr290/145) option leaves once or twice daily between 1 May and 30 September: There are also harbour tours (Nkr90/45) from 1 May to 26 August. Tours depart from the fish market.

The popular 'Norway in a Nutshell' tour also runs from Bergen. The day ticket (Nkr580/290) combines a morning train from Bergen to Flåm, a ferry up the spectacular Nærøyfjord to Gudvangen, a bus to Voss and a train back to Bergen in time for a late dinner (or you can continue on to Oslo to arrive around 10pm).

From early June to early September, another popular excursion is the Sunday tour by veteran steam train between Garnes and Midtun. It begins at 9am on the historic ferry M/S *Bruvik* from the Bryggen to the railway museum at Garnes (☎ 55 24 91 00) and from there the 18km steam journey to Midtun. From Midtun back to Bergen, the tour uses a historic bus. The whole trip takes four hours (Nkr195/95/495 adult/child/family). The train trip alone costs Nkr100 return.

Bergen Reiselivslag tourist office can organised any of these tours.

Ole Bull

Born in Bergen in 1810, Ole Bull was a child prodigy with an affinity for the violin. He joined the Bergen Philharmonic Orchestra when only eight years old and by age 25 had already accomplished solo performances with the Paris opera. Bull travelled and performed all over the Western world (including the USA) for 45 years, bringing Norwegian folk music to a prominence it had never before enjoyed.

After the death of Ole Bull's French-born wife, Felicité Villeminot, Bull purchased the 70-hectare Lysøen island, and between 1872 and 1873, he and architect Conrad Fredrik von der Lippe constructed the fantasy villa 'Lysøen'. This 'Little Alhambra' took much of its inspiration from the architecture of Moorish Granada and integrated not only intricate frets and trellises but also onion domes, romantic garden paths and a high-ceilinged music hall of Norwegian pine.

When Bull died at Lysøen in August 1880, tens of thousands of mourners accompanied the funeral procession to the Assistentkirkegården near Bergen's old City Gate. Through the following years, his American-born second wife Sara Thorp, daughter of a senator from Wisconsin, and their daughter Olea Vaughan spent their summer holidays at Lysøen. In 1973, Bull's grandchild, Sylvea Bull Curtis, donated the entire property to the Foreningen til Norske Fortidsminnesmerkers Bevaring (the Norwegian Society for Historical Preservation) and, since 1984, the site has been a museum dedicated to Norway's best-loved violinist. You'll also see a statue and fountain dedicated to the virtuoso on Ole Bulls plass, in the heart of Bergen.

Special Events

For a current list of events, see the Web site **W** www.visitBergen.com.

The Bergen International Festival (☎ 55 36 55 66, **W** www.fib.no), held for 12 days at the end of May, is the big cultural festival of the year, with dance, music and folklore presentations, and other events throughout the city.

On the last Sunday in May, there's the Seven Peaks Hike, where all the peaks must be visited on foot. It's an arduous 30km, with 2200m of ascent, but the record time is only 4½ hours!

Places to Stay

Camping *Lone Camping* (☎ 55 39 29 60, fax 55 39 29 79, Hardangerveien 697, Haukeland) Tent sites Nkr95 plus Nkr15/ person, cabins/rooms Nkr340-715. Open year-round. The lakeside Lone Camping is about 20km from town, at a petrol station between Espeland and Haukeland. It's overpriced for what's on offer (the cheaper cabins are fairly basic), but it's readily accessible by public transport. Bus No 900 runs to/from town (Nkr35, 30 min) approximately every half-hour during the day.

Bratland Camping (☎ 55 10 13 38, fax 55 10 53 60, Bratlandsveien 6, Haukeland) Bus: No 900. Tent sites Nkr60 plus Nkr15/person, simple cabins Nkr290, self-contained cabins Nkr620, basic rooms Nkr220. Open 20 May-10 Sept. This well-equipped site is 4km south of Lone.

Hostels *Bergen Vandrerhjem YMCA* (☎ 55 60 60 55, fax 55 60 60 51, e ymca@online.no, Nedre Korskirkealmenning 4) Dorm beds Nkr100. Check-in 3.30pm-midnight; open May–mid-Sept. This friendly 175-bed HI hostel is a good central place to crash. There are same-sex or mixed dorms, kitchen facilities are available and there's a supermarket and a bakery nearby. Best of all, it's only a 10-minute walk from the train station. Breakfast/dinner are Nkr40/75.

Intermission (☎ 55 31 32 75, Kalfarveien 8) Dorm beds Nkr100. Open mid-June–mid-Aug. The hospitable Christian Student Fellowship provides dorm space and use of the kitchen in a period home near the old town gate. The basic breakfast costs a bargain Nkr20.

Montana Vandrerhjem (☎ 55 20 80 70, fax 55 20 80 75, Johan Blyttsvei 30) Dorm beds Nkr120-180, doubles with bath Nkr500-550. Open 3 Jan-20 Dec. The fine 332-bed Montana HI hostel is 5km from the centre near the Ulriksbanen cable car.

Take bus No 31 from city centre. Breakfast is included.

Marken Gjestehus (☎ 55 31 44 04, fax 55 31 60 22, Kong Oscars gate 45) Beds in 4-bed/6-bed dorms Nkr185/160, doubles Nkr205/person. Open year-round. Marken Gjestehus, in the town centre, has breakfast for Nkr50.

Private Rooms, Pensions & Apartments

The tourist office books single/double rooms in private homes (without breakfast) starting at Nkr210/320, plus a booking fee of Nkr20.

Skansen Pensjonat (☎ 55 31 90 80, fax 55 31 15 27, Vetrlidsalmenning 29) Singles/doubles with shared bath from Nkr300/550, doubles with bath Nkr650. The centrally located, friendly and recommended Skansen Pensjonat has 14 clean, simple rooms. Breakfast is included.

Crowded House (☎ 55 23 13 10, fax 55 23 13 30, Håkonsgaten 27) Singles/doubles with shared bath Nkr390/590. Crowded House presents evidence of the fine line between travellers and tourists. It has large clean rooms, a coffee shop/pub and both cooking and laundry facilities.

Kjellersmauet Gjestehus (☎/fax 55 96 26 08, Kjellersmauet 22) Apartments Nkr250-1200. Kjellersmauet offers well-equipped apartments with bathroom and kitchen.

Nygård Apartment (☎ 55 32 72 53, fax 55 31 60 22, Nygårdsgaten 31) Singles Nkr320-375, doubles Nkr470-580. Open June–mid-Aug. The 60-bed Nygård Apartment offers small student rooms, some with private bathroom. Cooking facilities are available.

Hotels *Steens Hotell* (☎ 55 31 40 50, fax 55 32 61 22, Parkveien 22) Singles/doubles from Nkr490/720. Steens Hotell is a relatively inexpensive 19th-century-style choice. The en suite rooms all have phone and TV.

Hotel Park Pension (☎ 55 54 44 00, fax 55 54 44 44, Harald Hårfagresgate 35) Singles/doubles from Nkr550/750. For a family-owned hotel with 19th-century atmosphere and lots of antiques, try the Hotel Park Pension.

BERGEN

1

Bergenhus
2

To Bergen
Aquarium
(100m)

3

585

Vågen

5

6
7
8

9
10
11
13
14

12

Bryggen

15

Nye Sandviksveien

Nye Helgesenset

Henrik Wergelands gate

Øvre Blekeveien

Øvregaten

Rosenkrantz

Vetrlidsalmenning

Fløyfjellet

Fjellveien

Fjellveien

Fløyveien

585

Skansebakken

Skansen

Fløyfjellet

E16
E39

Fløyfjelstunnelen

16 17

18
20
19

21

Lille
Øvregaten

Bispengsgaten

Skansemyren

Fjellveien

Brattlien

Skivebakken

C Sundts gate

Strandgaten

Haugeveien Strangehagen

Verftsgaten

Holbergsalm

Klostergaten

O Muralm

C Sundts gate

Strandgaten

23

24

Strandkaien

Strandgaten

25

22

Torget

26

27
28
29

30
31
36
34
35
32
33

V Muralm

Jonsvollgaten

Engen

Smørs gate

Valkendorfsgaten

Michens

Markeveien

40
41

37

38
39

43

Domkirkeg gate

Alleheilgensg

Kong Oscars gate

44
45

46

47

Heggebk

Skivebakken

Kong Oscars gate

Grennevollen

Puddefjorden

Nøstegaten

Teatergaten

Baneveien

Engen

Engen

49

50

51

53
54
55
56

57
58
59
60
61

48

Ole Bulls
plass

N Brun gate

Vetre gate

Olav

52

Sydnes

555

Håkons

Magnus Barfots gate

Rosenberggaten

Øisteinsgaten

Lars

Kaigaten

Festplassen

*Lille
Lungegårdsvann*

63
64 65

66

72

Hilles

Strømgaten

Nygårdsgaten

Christies gate

Kyrres

Fortunegaten

Nygaten

62

Langes gt

Ivar Aasensgaten

Fosswinckelsgata

Nygårdsgaten

74

75

76
78

77

80
79

Møhlenpris

Wellhavens gate

Prof Hansteens gate

Dokkeveien

Jektevik

Jekteviksbk

Prof Keysers gate

Håkon Foss gt

Fredrik Meltzers gate

Allégaten

Parkveien

Olaf Ryes vei

Wellhavens gate

Konsul

Børs gate

Selmer

Thormøhlensgate

Zetlitz

Wolffsgate

Thormøhlensgate

Nygårdsparken

Fosswinckels gate

Lyder Sagens

Hans Tanks gt

Jonas Reins

73

Hans Tanks gate

Allégaten

81

82

Lars Hilles gate

Strømmen

Strømgaten

Vestre

Gate

Lungegårdskaien

Nye Nygårdsbroen

E16
E39

**Train
Station**

68 69

70

585

To Montana
Vandrehjem
(3km) &
Ulriksbanen
Cable Car (3km)

67

71

Puddefjorden

Wellhavens gate

Damsgårdsgaten

Iverrveien

Carl Konows gate

Frydenbø

Frydenbøveien

Damsgårdsfjelltunnelen

Damsgårdstunnelen

555

Michael Krohns gate

Gyldenpris

Gyldenprisveien

Puddefjordsbroen

Møhlenpris

Nygårdsbroen

To
Flesland
Airport
(19km) &
Tröldhaugen
(12km)

Nye Nygårdsbroen

0   150   300m
0   150   300yd

BERGEN

PLACES TO STAY		
8	Radisson SAS Royal Hotel	
17	Skansen Pensjonat	
23	Clarion Hotel Admiral	
28	Bergen Vandrerhjem YMCA	
32	Neptun Hotell	
33	Kjellersmauet Gjestehus	
44	Marken Gjestehus	
56	Radisson SAS Hotel Norge; Ole Bull	
60	Crowded House	
68	Grand Hotel Terminus	
70	Intermission	
73	Nygård Apartment	
79	Steens Hotell	
80	Hotel Park Pension	

PLACES TO EAT		
4	Sparmarket	
10	Bryggen Tracteursted	
13	Enhjørningen	
14	Bryggeloftet & Stuene	
18	Tapas Tapas Bar; Cyberhouse	
20	Mr Bean Coffee Shop	
21	Sol Brød	
22	Zachariasbryggen; Baker Brun; Pasta Basta; Fiskekrogen; Peppe's Pizza	
27	Godt Brød	
29	Louisiana Créole Restaurant	
30	Lido	
31	Burger King	
47	Ma-Ma Thai	
48	McDonald's	
50	Café Opera	

53	Pars	
54	Wesselstuen	
55	Dickens	
58	Michelangelo	
62	Kinsarvik Frukt	
65	Rimi Supermarket	
74	På Høyden	
81	Pasta Sentral	

ENTERTAINMENT		
9	Engelen Nightclub	
26	Scruffy Murphy	
35	Champions	
37	Banco Rotto & Blue Velvet Bar	
49	Rick's & Finnegan's	
51	Bergen Kino	
59	Fotballpuben	
61	Kvarteret	
64	Garage	
72	Grieghallen	

MUSEUMS		
7	Bryggens Museum; Bergen Folklore Entertainment Show	
12	Theta Museum	
15	Hanseatic Museum	
46	Lepramuseet	
63	Vestlandske Kunstindustrimuseum	
66	Bergen Kunstmuseum Complex	
75	Natural History Museum	
76	Maritime Museum	
78	Cultural History Museum	

OTHER		
1	Skoltegrunnskaien (International Ferries)	
2	Håkonshallen	
3	Rosenkrantztårnet	
5	Mariakirken	
6	Schøtstuene	
11	Bryggen Warehouses	
16	Fløibanen Funicular Station	
19	Jarlens Vaskoteque	
24	Strandkaiterminal (Express Ferries)	
25	Torget Fish Market	
34	Vinmonopolet	
36	Bergen Reiselivslag Tourist Office	
38	Sykkelbutikken	
39	Kreditkassen	
40	Husfliden	
41	Galleriet Shopping Centre; Norli Bookshop; Augustus Café; Fjord Expo	
42	Post Office	
43	Police Station	
45	DNT Office	
52	Sydnes Parking Area	
57	Kilroy Travel	
67	Library	
69	Old Town Gate	
71	Bus Terminal; Vinmonopolet; Pharmacy	
77	Frieleneskaien (Hurtigruten Terminal)	
82	Legevakten Medical Clinic	

Grand Hotel Terminus (☎ 55 21 25 00, fax 55 21 25 01, Zander Kaaesgate 6) En suite singles Nkr690-1260, doubles Nkr990-1560. Opposite the train station, the Grand Hotel Terminus has historically been the hotel of choice for the city's well-heeled visitors. Never mind that the rooms are cramped by anyone's standards – the decor more than compensates.

Neptun Hotell (☎ 55 30 68 00, fax 55 30 68 50, Valkendorfsgate 8) Singles/doubles from Nkr780/920. The Neptun Hotell is another good choice; the well-appointed rooms are decorated with original artwork.

Radisson SAS Hotel Norge (☎ 55 57 30 00, fax 55 57 30 01, Ole Bulls plass 4) Singles Nkr895-1695, doubles Nkr1094-1894. This is one of the most elegant hotels in Bergen and has a residents' bar with a library.

Radisson SAS Royal Hotel (☎ 55 54 30 00, fax 55 32 48 08, Bryggen) Singles Nkr895-1695, doubles Nkr1094-1894. If you prefer the heart of things on Bryggen, try this comfortable and modern business-class hotel.

Clarion Hotel Admiral (☎ 55 23 64 00, fax 55 23 64 64, C Sundtsgate 9-13) Singles Nkr750-1375, doubles Nkr950-1575. Okay, so you want a view of Bryggen? Not just with luxurious rooms, this plush place has its own cruise boat and a cigar and cognac salon.

Places to Eat

Every Thursday from September to May, many Bergen restaurants serve *raspeballer*,

BERGEN

a powerful traditional meal with salted meat, potatoes and mashed turnip.

Places to Eat – Budget *Augustus Café* *(☎ 55 32 35 25, Galleriet, Torgallmenningen 8)* Specials Nkr92, mains Nkr80-120. The recommended Augustus Café serves both hot and cold dishes.

Café Opera (☎ 55 23 03 15, Engen 18) Dishes Nkr57-118. Trendy Café Opera attracts artists and students with good, reasonably priced meals such as pastas, salads and grilled salmon.

Lido (☎ 55 32 59 12, Torgallmenningen 1) Specials & mains around Nkr105. Lido is another inexpensive cafeteria with good traditional grub, but the toilets cost Nkr5!

Pasta Sentral (☎ 55 96 00 37, Vestre Strømkaien 6) Pasta dishes Nkr59, pizzas Nkr65-80, desserts Nkr28-43. The unassuming Pasta Sentral (not all that central) has great pizza, pasta and desserts. There's a good range of vegetarian choices.

Mr Bean Coffee Shop (☎ 55 56 03 12, Kong Oscars gate 12) Coffee from Nkr23. Open from noon daily. This place brews up enormous cups of coffee but, unfortunately, only late sleepers can use it as a morning kick-start.

Storsenter, at the bus station, harbours a host of cheap stalls serving inexpensive sandwiches, a bakery, a burger outlet, *Vinmonopolet* and a *Rimi* supermarket.

The Zachariasbryggen quay, at the inner harbour, houses a popular *Baker Brun* konditori, with pastries (including Bergen's own *shillingsboller* buns) and sandwiches. There's also an ice cream shop, several pubs and various restaurants:

The central *Godt Brød (Nedre Korskirkealmenningen 12)* has delicious organic breads and pastries. It has cafe tables but closes at 6pm. Many other bakeries in the centre offer reasonably priced sandwiches. *Sol Brød*, on the corner of Vetrlidsalmenning and Kong Oscars gate, has recommended bread, and excellent pastries from Nkr10.50.

In the *fish market* at Torget you'll find a choice of fresh fruit and seafood snacks, including tasty open-faced salmon rolls for Nkr15 or a 500g sack of fresh shrimp or crab legs for Nkr55 to Nkr75. It's open from around 7am to 3pm or 4pm Monday to Saturday (7pm on Thursday). *McDonald's* and *Burger King* are also represented around town and present quick options for inexpensive snacks.

Supermarkets abound in Bergen. The *Rimi* chain, which has a branch on Nygårdsgaten, has longer hours than most; it's open 9am to 11pm daily (from 11am on Sunday). The *Sparmarket (Nye Sandviksveien)* has an astonishing takeaway deli with whole grilled chickens for only Nkr30. *Kinsarvik Frukt (Olav Kyrres gate 38)* is a food shop with a health-food section.

Places to Eat – Mid-Range *Pasta Basta* *(☎ 55 55 96 55, Zachariasbryggen)* Mains Nkr125-186, pizzas Nkr114. Pasta Basta is a mid-range Italian-style restaurant.

Peppe's Pizza (☎ 55 96 41 99, Zachariasbryggen) Pizza from Nkr130. The ubiquitous Peppe's offers the usual pizza and pasta menu.

There are lots of other places around town:

Michelangelo (☎ 55 90 08 25, Neumannsgate 25) Mains Nkr99-245. This dinner restaurant has authentic Italian food at moderate prices.

Pars (☎ 55 56 37 22, Sigurdsgate 5) Mains Nkr65-179. The kitschy atmosphere at the Pars Persian restaurant belies the excellent cuisine, including inexpensive vegetarian choices (Nkr65 to Nkr89).

Tapas Tapas Bar (☎ 55 96 22 10, Vetrlidsalmenning 15) Vegetarian dishes Nkr35-74, other mains Nkr130-290. Near the Fløibanen terminal, Tapas Tapas Bar offers, you've guessed it, tapas, including seven vegetarian choices.

Ma-Ma Thai (☎ 55 31 38 70, Kaigaten 20) Lunches Nkr55-63, dinner mains Nkr98-158. Ma-Ma Thai is a cosy and authentic Oriental place that attracts university students with its good value specials, including a selection of 'lunches' that are served until midnight.

Places to Eat – Top End *Enhjørningen* *(☎ 55 32 79 19, Bryggen)* 3-course dinner Nkr395, mains Nkr220-275. The popular and upmarket Enhjørningen offers fish and seafood from beginning to end. The name means 'unicorn', and above the door it appears that such a beast, clearly in a state of sexual arousal, is attempting an escape!

Bryggen Tracteursted (☎ 55 31 40 46, *Bryggen*) Mains around Nkr200. Open June-Aug. This cosy restaurant is housed in a 300-year-old Bryggen tavern. It's fairly expensive and mainly caters to tourists and the expense account brigade, but it offers a good dose of Norwegian cuisine and old-style ambience.

På Høyden (☎ 55 32 34 32, *Fosswinckelsgata 18*) Lunch Nkr55-150, dinner Nkr150-240. Open lunch & dinner Mon-Sat. The leafy and airy atmosphere in this modern and friendly bistro-style place makes it ideal to enjoy meat, wok and fish dishes, vegetarian courses, Indian dishes, salads and desserts.

Dickens (☎ 55 36 31 30, *Kong Olav Vs plass 4*) Lunch Nkr105-139, dinner mains Nkr175-230. Popular Dickens, with a sunny dining room overlooking Kong Olav Vs plass, offers lunches such as salads and other light meals, but dinners are large and filling. The bar is quite a lively night spot.

Wesselstuen (☎ 55 55 49 49, *Ole Bulls plass 6*) Light meals Nkr99-149, dinner mains Nkr169-209. The richly decorated Wesselstuen offers excellent value and is especially popular with post-graduate students, philosophers and intellectuals in the local 30- to 40-year-old crowd. In the evening, they use heat lamps in the outdoor area to keep it comfortably toasty.

Ole Bull (☎ 55 57 30 00, *Ole Bulls plass 5*) Lunch Nkr195 (noon-4pm), dinner Nkr225 (6pm-9pm). For a splurge, the Ole Bull restaurant in Hotel Norge has a pleasant 2nd floor park view and a tempting buffet that includes cold salmon and shrimp, several hot dishes, salads and sweets.

Louisiana Créole Restaurant (☎ 55 54 66 60, *Vågsalmenning 6*) Mains Nkr199-259. This is an unusual dining experience in Norway but it makes a laudable attempt at Cajun cuisine (including steak and alligator) and serves as a very pleasant top-end choice.

Bryggeloftet & Stuene (☎ 55 31 06 30, *Bryggen 11*) Daily specials Nkr89, mains Nkr95-275. In the middle of the historic

district, this place serves traditional Norwegian fare (including reindeer, venison, bacalao and catfish) in a pleasant atmosphere.

Fiskekrogen (☎ 55 55 96 55, *Zachariasbryggen*) Lunch from Nkr72, dinner mains Nkr245-295. The expensive Fiskekrogen offers gourmet game and seafood dishes.

Entertainment
Pubs, Clubs & Discos
Fotballpuben (☎ 55 90 05 79, *Vestre Torggate 9*) This is among Norway's best-value sports bars, where 500mL of lager for only Nkr30.

Kvarteret (☎ 55 30 28 50, *Olav Kyrres gate 49*) Kvarteret is another inexpensive pub, which caters to students.

Garage (☎ 55 32 02 10, *Christies gate 14*) Bergen's top rock music venue serves both local and Irish beer.

Rick's (☎ 55 55 31 31, *Veiten 3*) Fri & Sat cover charge Nkr70. This complex of pubs and discos includes a rock disco with DJ, a music bar with English staff, a varied live music and dancing venue, a disco for over-25s, and the adjacent **Finnegan's** Irish-style pub. The complex has a pithy Web site ☒ www.sodoff-werebusy.com.

Banco Rotto (☎ 55 32 75 20, *Vågsalmenning 16*) Cover charge Nkr80, free with Bergen Card. Banco Rotto attracts everyone from the ages of 30 to 60 with its weekend live music shows (contemporary/chart hits), while the attached **Blue Velvet Bar** puts on live jazz performances on weekdays.

Engelen (☎ 55 54 31 50, *Bryggen*) Cover Nkr70. Open Wed-Sat. Engelen caters to patrons in their early 20s with a disco, including a special 1950s to 1970s pop music theme on Wednesday. Thursday is 'cheap shots' night, with inexpensive booze.

Sports-oriented bars include the Irish-style **Scruffy Murphy** (☎ 55 31 34 96, *Torget 15*) and **Champions** (☎ 55 90 15 18, *Strandgaten 6*).

Other
Bergen Kino (☎ 82 05 00 05, ☒ *www.filmweb.no, Neumannsgate 3*) Movies Nkr65. First-run movies are shown at the 13-screen Bergen Kino.

Fana Folklore (☎ 55 91 52 40, *Fana church/Ramsbergstunet*) Tickets Nkr250.

The tourist-oriented Fana Folklore show presents a taste of traditional Norwegian music and dancing on Monday, Tuesday, Thursday and Friday between early June and late August. Tickets include bus transport from Festplassen, returning at 10.30pm.

Bergen Folklore (☎ 55 31 95 50) Tickets adult/child Nkr95/free. Another group performs at Bryggens Museum at 9pm on Tuesday and Thursday from 14 June to 16 August.

For details and schedules of entertainment events, contact the tourist office. Tickets to performances are sold by Billett Service *(☎ 81 03 31 33)*. In summer, classical concerts, performances and recitals are held at the ***Troldhaugen***, ***Lysøen*** and ***Siljustøl*** estates; tickets are around Nkr200.

Grieghallen (☎ 81 53 31 33, Edvard Griegs plass) Tickets Nkr95-200. The Bergen Philharmonic Orchestra stages classical concerts here.

Atop Mt Fløyen, classical concerts are held nightly at 8pm from mid-June to mid-August (Nkr160).

Shopping

The broadest selection of handicrafts, wooden toys and traditional clothing is found at ***Husfliden (☎ 55 31 78 70, Vågsalmenning 3)***.

The ***Galleriet shopping centre***, northwest of the post office, has boutiques, a grocery store and a good bookshop, Norli. The bus station holds another large shopping complex.

Getting There & Away

Bergen is a main staging point for journeys into the Western Fjords, and numerous buses, trains, passenger ferries and express boats set off daily.

Air Bergen's airport (☎ 55 99 81 55) is at Flesland, about 19km south-west of the centre. Braathens (☎ 55 23 55 23) and SAS (☎ 55 99 76 00), both at the airport, connect Oslo and Bergen many times daily. There are also direct flights to Trondheim, Kristiansand, Stavanger and Ålesund, as well as to Copenhagen, Stockholm, London, Newcastle and Aberdeen. Widerøe (☎ 55 91 78

60), also at the airport, flies to a couple of smaller airports in the Western Fjords.

Bus Nor-Way Bussekspress runs to Odda (Nkr237, 3¾ hours, one to three daily), Stryn (Nkr380, 6½ hours, three daily), Ålesund (Nkr544, 10½ hours, once or twice daily) and Trondheim (Nkr745, 14¼ hours, twice daily). Buses to/from Stavanger (Nkr370, 5¾ hours) run via Haugesund roughly every two hours. Buses to/from Oslo (Nkr610, 11 hours), via Odda, leave one to three times daily, but most travellers find the train more convenient.

Train The train line between Bergen and Oslo is deservedly billed as one of the world's most spectacular routes, climbing from the lush forested coast at Bergen to the high and lonesome Hardangervidda plateau before dropping slowly past lakes and through increasingly green hills to the capital city. The trip (Nkr570, 6½ to 7¾ hours) departs five times daily, including a convenient overnight train with 2nd-class sleepers for Nkr150. Extra local trains run between Bergen and Voss (Nkr130, 1¼ hours) roughly every hour or two; four of these trains run to/from Myrdal (Nkr185, 2¼ hours). Seat reservations are required on all Inter City rail trips.

Car & Motorcycle The main highway into Bergen is the E16. There's a toll of Nkr10 for vehicles entering the city on weekdays from 6am to 10pm.

Boat Daily Fylkesbåtane (☎ 55 90 70 70, e fsf@fylkesb.no) express boats connect Bergen with Balestrand (Nkr355, four hours) and Flåm (Nkr490, 5½ hours), in Sognefjord. To/from Måløy (Nkr530, 4½ hours) and Selje (Nkr570, five hours), near the mouth of Nordfjord, boats also sail daily. HSD/Flaggruten (☎ 55 23 87 80) has daily runs to/from Stavanger (Nkr590, 4½ hours), via Haugesund (Nkr370, three hours). In Bergen, all these boats use the Strandkaiterminal.

The Hurtigruten coastal steamer leaves from the Frieleneskaien, south of the university, at 8pm daily. See the Getting

Around chapter for details. International ferries between Bergen and Britain (Newcastle and Lerwick), the Faroes, Iceland and Denmark dock at Skoltegrunnskaien, north of the Rosenkrantz tower. See the Getting There & Away chapter for more details.

Getting Around

To/From The Airport The airport is in Flesland, 19km by road south-west of central Bergen. Flybussen (Nkr55, 45 minutes) runs at least twice hourly between the airport, the Radisson SAS Royal Hotel, the Radisson SAS Hotel Norge and the main bus terminal. Local bus No 523 also runs between the bus terminal and Flesland airport (Nkr35, one hour), with departures more or less hourly.

Bus City buses cost Nkr15, while fares beyond the centre are based on the distance travelled. Route information is available on ☎ 177. Free bus No 100 runs between the main post office and the bus terminal.

Car & Motorcycle As in most Norwegian towns, it's best to park your car and explore the city centre on foot. Except where there are parking meters, street parking is reserved for residents with special zone-parking stickers; 'P' parking signs accompanied by the word 'sone' indicate a reserved area. In busy areas, metered parking is limited to 30 minutes or two hours, but the parking areas at Sydnes allow up to nine hours (free at night). Less restricted are the indoor car parks; the largest is the 24-hour Bygarasjen at the bus terminal.

Taxi Taxis (☎ 07000) queue up on Ole Bulls plass.

Bicycle You can hire cycles from Sykkelbutikken (☎ 55 32 06 20) at Østre Skostredet 5.

Boat From 1 May to 15 September, the Vågen (☎ 55 56 04 00) harbour ferry runs between the Torget fish market and Tollbodhopen at Nordnes (near the aquarium) approximately every 15 minutes during business hours.

Hardangerfjord

VOSS
pop 6000

The inland town of Voss is the de facto capital of the Hardangerfjord region and most travellers pass through, especially on the popular 'Norway in a Nutshell' excursion between Oslo and Bergen. For Norwegians, it's also well-known as a winter sports venue.

From medieval times, the town served as an agricultural centre and a focus of trade between eastern and western Norway. In 1023, King Olav Haraldson den Heilige (St Olav) stopped by to erect a cross in honour of Voss' conversion to Christianity. The town centre was devastated by German bombers in 1940, but was reconstructed after WWII as a commercial, industrial and educational centre.

Information

The active and helpful Voss Tourist Information office (☎ 56 52 08 00, fax 56 52 08 01), Uttrågata, is open 9am to 7pm Monday to Saturday and 2pm to 7pm Sunday, June to August (otherwise, shorter hours on weekdays only).

Vangskyrkja

In a field south of the current stone church (☎ 56 51 94 00, Uttrågata; adult/child Nkr15/free; open 10am-4pm daily June-Sept) in Voss, which occupies the site of an ancient pagan temple, St Olav erected a stone cross in 1023 to commemorate the local conversion to Christianity. The first wooden church on the site was replaced with a Gothic-style stone church in the mid-13th century, as evidenced by a congratulatory letter from King Magnus Lagabøte in 1271. In 1277, the church was consecrated in honour of St Michael. Although the original stone altar and the unique wooden spire remain, the Lutheran Reformation of 1536 brought about the removal of many original features. Elias Fiigenschoug's altarpiece, representing the Crucifixion, is done in colour with the exception of Christ on the cross, who appears in black and white. On the ceiling, painted in the late

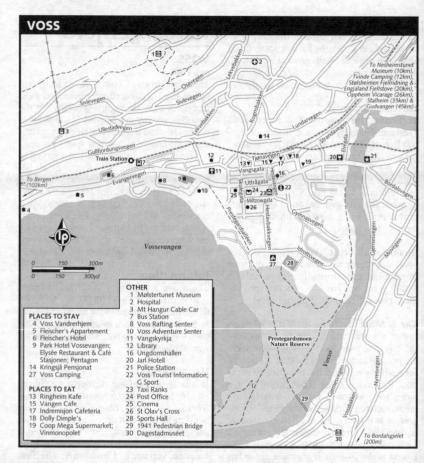

VOSS

To Nesheimstunet Museum (10km), Tvinde Camping (12km), Stølsheimen Fjellridning & Engjaland Fjellstove (20km), Oppheim Vicarage (26km), Stalheim (35km) & Gudvangen (45km)

To Bergen (102km)

Vossevangen

0   150   300m
0   150   300yd

Prestegardsmoen Nature Reserve

Vosso

To Bordalsgjelet (200m)

OTHER
1 Mølstertunet Museum
2 Hospital
3 Mt Hangur Cable Car
7 Bus Station
8 Voss Rafting Senter
10 Voss Adventure Senter
11 Vangskyrkja
12 Library
16 Ungdomshallen
20 Jarl Hotell
21 Police Station
22 Voss Tourist Information; G Sport
23 Taxi Ranks
24 Post Office
25 Cinema
26 St Olav's Cross
28 Sports Hall
29 1941 Pedestrian Bridge
30 Dagestadmuséet

PLACES TO STAY
4 Voss Vandrerhjem
5 Fleischer's Appartement
6 Fleischer's Hotel
9 Park Hotel Vossevangen; Elysée Restaurant & Café Stasjonen; Pentagon
14 Kringsjå Pensjonat
27 Voss Camping

PLACES TO EAT
13 Ringheim Kafe
15 Vangen Cafe
17 Indremisjon Cafeteria
18 Dolly Dimple's
19 Coop Mega Supermarket; Vinmonopolet

17th century, a flock of angels flit through a backdrop of sky.

Since the mid-19th century, the structure and its interior have undergone several restorations, and the 1923 stained glass work commemorates the 900th anniversary of Christianity in Voss. Miraculously, the building avoided destruction during the intense German bombing in 1940. Services are held at 11am on Sunday.

Prestegardsmoen

The Prestegardsmoen Council recreational and nature reserve, which extends southward from Voss Camping, offers a series of hiking tracks and the chance to observe 140 species of plants and 124 bird species, including waterbirds. It also contains the municipal swimming pool and sports hall.

Voss Folkemuseum

The main portion of the Voss Folk Museum is the Mølstertunet Museum (☎ 56 51 15 11, Mølstervegen 143; adult/child Nkr35/free; open 10am-5pm daily May-Sept, shorter hours Oct-Apr), which lies at the farm Mølster, on the hillside above town. This collection of historic farm buildings, which date from the mid-17th to mid-19th centuries, displays various facets of life in earlier times.

The other two portions of the museum, the Nesheimstunet Museum and the old wooden Oppheim vicarage, lie 10km and 26km from Voss respectively, along the Gudvangen road (E16). They're open by appointment only.

Dagestadmuséet & Bordalsgjelet

This museum (☎ 56 51 12 53, Helgavangen 52; adult/child Nkr25/free; open 11am-3pm Tues-Sun 1-30 June & 1-15 Aug, 11am-5pm Tues-Sun July) was opened in 1950 by local woodcarver Magnus Dagestad (1865–1957) and features his lifetime of carvings, drawings and traditional wooden furniture creations, as well as works by his wife, Helena Dagestad. It's an unusual and worthwhile exhibit. It lies about 1.5km from the town centre. On foot, use the 1941 pedestrian bridge from the Prestegardsmoen nature reserve; while you're at it, you may also want to ramble up to the scenic river potholes in Bordalsgjelet gorge, which lie about 20 minutes walk south of the museum. Look for the black and white *fossekallen* (water dipper), Norway's national bird.

Activities

The ski season in Voss runs from early December until April, depending on snow conditions. The winter action focuses on the cable-car route up Mt Hangur, which lies within easy walking distance of town. Those with vehicles can opt for Bavallen, 5km due north of the centre, which has two chairlifts and is used for international downhill competitions. Lift tickets and equipment hire are available at either slope (in summer, the Hangur cable-car whisks you to the view every 15 minutes from 11am to 5pm for Nkr50) and there's a ski school at Hangur. On the plateau and up the Raundalen valley at Mjølfjell, you'll also find excellent cross-country skiing. For weather and snow conditions, phone ☎ 56 51 94 88.

Summer visitors can opt for white-water rafting (Nkr590), canyoning (Nkr620-670), waterfall abseiling (Nkr490) and riverboarding (Nkr650) with Voss Rafting Senter

(☎ 56 51 05 25, e voss.rafting@online.no, w www.vossrafting.no), where the motto is the rather ambiguous 'We guarantee to wet your pants'. Rafters and riverboarders can choose between three very different rivers: the Stranda (Class III to IV), Raundalen (Class III to V) and Vosso (Class II).

For details on horse riding in Stølsheimen (Nkr250/330 for two/three hours), contact the English-run Stølsheimen Fjellridning/Engjaland Fjellstove (☎ 56 51 91 66, fax 56 51 11 35, w www.engjaland.no, Engjaland), 20km north of Voss. In the high season, B&B accommodation in this simple lodge costs Nkr250 to Nkr300. It's also a good base for hut-to-hut hiking in the spectacular Stølsheimen mountains. For information, contact the Bergen Turlag DNT office (☎ 55 32 22 30, fax 55 32 81 15, Tverrgaten 4, Bergen).

For details of other activities, including paragliding, skydiving and lake or river fishing, contact the tourist office.

Special Events

In late June, Voss hosts Extremesport Week, which attracts adrenalin junkies with a range of activities and competitions. Most events are open to public participation, but few mere mortals will want to take part.

The late September Sheep's Head food festival involves exploring the culinary delights of, you've guessed it, sheep heads.

Organised Tours

The famous 'Norway in a Nutshell' tour, normally done between Oslo and Bergen, also works as a day tour from Voss. It involves rail trips from Voss to Myrdal and Flåm, the boat to Gudvangen and the bus back to Voss (adult/child Nkr380/190, 6½ to 8½ hours). Book through the tourist office, any travel agency, or directly through NSB at the train station.

Places to Stay

Voss Camping (☎ 56 51 15 97, fax 56 51 66 75, Prestegardsalléen 40) Tent sites Nkr80, simple cabins Nkr300-350. The lakeside and centrally located Voss Camping has reasonable facilities.

Tvinde Camping (☎ 56 51 69 19, fax 56 51 69 19, Tvinde) Tent sites from Nkr80/person, cabins Nkr300-390. This scenic alternative lies beside a waterfall about 12km north of town. Without a car, access is on the Voss-Gudvangen bus (Nkr25, 20 minutes).

Voss Vandrerhjem (☎ 56 51 20 17, fax 56 51 08 37, e voss-hostel@voss.online.no, Evangervegen 68) Dorm beds from Nkr175, singles/doubles Nkr441/522. Dinner Nkr70-90. Open year-round. The modern Voss hostel offers en suite rooms and fine lake views; ask for a top floor room at the back. Bicycles, rowing boats, canoes and kayaks can be hired and there's a free sauna. Breakfast is included.

Kringsjå Pensjonat (☎ 56 51 16 27, fax 56 51 63 30, Strengjarhaugen) B&B from Nkr280/person. Kringsjå Pensjonat is a step up in price, atmosphere and elevation. It's run by the Ole Bull music academy for its classes and concerts, but rooms are also rented to travellers.

Fleischer's Hotel (☎ 56 52 05 00, fax 56 52 05 01, Evangervegen) Singles/doubles from Nkr625/850. Lunch/dinner buffet Nkr195/325. For historic character, the wealthy can check out the enormous but beautiful Fleischer's Hotel, opened in 1888.

Fleischer's Appartement (☎ 56 52 05 00, fax 56 52 05 01, Evangervegen) Units per person Nkr325-425. Small self-catering units by the lake are offered here.

Park Hotel Vossevangen (☎ 56 51 13 22, fax 56 51 00 39, Uttrågata 1) Singles/doubles from Nkr525/650. This upmarket option offers comfortable rooms overlooking the lake Vossevangen.

Places to Eat

Elysée (☎ 56 51 13 22, Park Hotel Vossevangen, Uttrågata 1) Mains Nkr185-255. The finest restaurant option in Voss specialises in French and international cuisine and has a particularly extensive wine list. In the same hotel is the popular train-theme *Café Stasjonen*, with snacks, soup, pasta and main courses for Nkr30 to Nkr125.

Dolly Dimple's (☎ 56 51 00 40, Vangsgata 52) Pizza from Nkr103. Dolly Dimple's serves good but rather large pizzas.

Try *Vangen Cafe* (☎ 56 51 12 05, Vangsgata 42) for cakes and snacks for Nkr19 to Nkr28 and mains for Nkr84 to Nkr92. Traditional Norwegian food is served at *Indremisjonskaféen* (☎ 51 56 14 08, Vangsgata 46) for Nkr72 to Nkr95. At the *Ringheim Kafe* (☎ 56 51 13 65, Vangsgata 32), a wider range of dishes costs Nkr84 to Nkr195.

The *Coop Mega* supermarket and *Vinmonopolet* are both in the same block on Strandavegen.

Entertainment

Park Hotel Vossevangen (☎ 56 51 13 22, Uttrågata 1) has a piano bar and the popular *Pentagon* weekend disco. The pub in the *Jarl Hotell* (☎ 56 51 19 33, Elvegata 9) has a cellar disco which attracts the 18 to 25 crowd with house and techno.

There's also a *cinema* (☎ 56 51 94 80, Uttrågata), which screens a different film every week.

More refined tastes will enjoy the concerts by pianist Åge Kristoffersen, held at 9.30pm on Monday and Wednesday from May to September, in Fleischer's Hotel. Admission costs Nkr80.

Folk dancing and folklore evenings are held in Ungdomshallen every Friday evening from June to August; contact the tourist office for details and tickets (Nkr80).

Getting There & Away

Buses stop at the train station, west of the centre. Frequent bus services connect Voss with Bergen (Nkr135, two hours) and Aurland (Nkr105, 1½ hours), via Gudvangen and Flåm, but only three to seven daily between Voss and Norheimsund (Nkr111, two hours).

NSB rail services (☎ 56 52 80 00) on the renowned Bergensbanen to/from Bergen (Nkr130, one hour, hourly) and Oslo (Nkr480, 5½ to six hours, five daily) connect at Myrdal (Nkr74, 50 minutes) with the scenic line down to Flåm.

Getting Around

Bicycle hire is available for Nkr150 per day from Voss Adventure Senter (☎ 56 51 36 30), beside Park Hotel Vossevangen.

For a taxi, phone ☎ 56 51 13 40.

MJØLFJELL
pop 20

Mjølfjell is fine hiking, skiing, fishing, riding and cycling country.

Mjølfjell Vandrerhjem (☎ *56 52 31 50, fax 56 52 31 51, Mjølfjell)* Dorm beds Nkr185, singles/doubles Nkr285/470. By the railway line between Voss and Myrdal, this is a handsome and popular overnight stop, complete with heated outdoor swimming pool; rail travellers should disembark at Ørneberget station (request stop). By car, it's accessible only on the Raundalen road from Voss.

STALHEIM

Between 1647 and 1909, travellers on the Royal Mail route between Copenhagen, Christiania (Oslo) and Bergen stopped at Stalheim to rest and change horses. The route climbed up the valley and through the Stalheimskleiva gorge, flanked by the Stalheim and Sivle waterfalls.

Stalheim Hotel (☎ *56 52 01 22, fax 56 52 00 56, Stalheim)* Singles/doubles from Nkr865/1200. Open mid-May–late Sept. An inn opened at Stalheim in the late 17th century, but the current hotel, the fourth on the site, was constructed in 1960. It offers an incredible view down Nærøydalen and the popular restaurant serves a lunch buffet for Nkr220. The attached shop has a particularly good range of crafts and souvenirs.

The **Stalheim Folkemuseum** (☎ *56 52 01 22, Stalheim; adult/child Nkr40/free; open at all times, buildings open on request)*, near the hotel, includes folk exhibits and 30 log buildings laid out as a traditional farm.

To reach Stalheim from Voss (Nkr56, one hour, four to 11 daily), take any bus towards Gudvangen/Aurland.

DALE
pop 1200

In the small and scenic town of Dale, between Voss and Bergen, you can visit Dale Kraftverk's unusual **Energisenteret** (☎ *56 59 65 48, by E16, Dale; tours per person/family Nkr40/95; tours hourly 11am-4.30pm late June–mid-Aug)*, which takes you 400m inside a mountain for a lesson on hydroelectric power. A variety of videos and exhibits

contrasts early-20th-century hydroelectric power generation with modern methods. All buses using the E16 from Bergen (Nkr85, 50 minutes, three to eight daily) to Voss pass through to Dale.

NORHEIMSUND & ØYSTESE
pop 6000

Norheimsund is a terminal for ferries to inner Hardangerfjord. Many visitors join the four-hour scenic cruise on Fyksesund (adult/child Nkr180/90), offered by Fyksund Fjordruter (☎ *56 55 57 44)* at 11am on Tuesday, Wednesday and Thursday; they depart from the quay.

At the excellent **Steinsdalsfossen waterfall**, 1km west of town on Rv7, you can walk behind the water. You'll see old wooden boats, restoration procedures, rope making and an exhibition at the unusual **Hardanger Fartøyvernsenter** (☎ *56 55 33 50, Norheimsund; adult/child Nkr50/25; open 11am-5pm daily 27 May-9 Sept)*.

Laupsa Hyttetun (☎ *56 55 51 80, fax 56 55 51 84, Hardangerfjordvegen 800, Øystese)* Cabins Nkr300-400. The en suite cabins at Laupsa Hyttetun are recommended.

Sandven Hotel (☎ *56 55 20 88, fax 56 55 26 88, Norheimsund Sentrum)* Singles/doubles from Nkr590/830. The atmospheric Sandven Hotel dates from 1857 and offers fine accommodation.

Three to seven daily buses run between Voss and Norheimsund (Nkr111, two hours) via Øystese. Six to 12 daily buses run from Øystese to Bergen (Nkr118, 1¼ hours) via Norheimsund. See the following Ulvik, Utne, Lofthus and Kinsarvik sections for details of boats around upper Hardangerfjorden.

ULVIK & OSA
pop 1202

Ulvik lies in the heart of a lovely apple-growing region and is home to Hjeltnes, Norway's oldest horticultural college (established in 1901). Visitors can stroll around the rose gardens and surrounding Ulvikpollen wetlands, which harbours 80 bird species.

At the **Stream Nest complex** (☎ *56 52 68 44, Osa; adult/child Nkr25/free; open at least 10am-4pm daily May-Aug)*, 10km east

SOUTH-WESTERN FJORDS

of Ulvik, check out the ecological herb garden and several artworks including Allan Christensen's *Rambukk* (pile driver) and the odd eponymous log sculpture, *Stream Nest*, originally conceived by Japanese artist Takamasa Kuniyasu for the 1994 Winter Olympics in Lillehammer. The sculpture resounds with the tuba music of Geir Løvold, just as it did during the Games. Nearby, the **Hjadlane Galleri** (☎ *56 52 68 21, Osa; adult/child Nkr25/ free; open 11am-6pm daily mid-Apr–mid-Sept)* features powerful local modern art.

For information, visit Ulvik Turistkontor (☎ *56 52 63 60, fax 56 52 66 23,* **W** *www .ulvik.org/ulvikinfo)*, open 8.30am to 5pm Monday to Saturday and 1pm to 5pm Sunday, mid-May to mid-September. The tourist office also hires bicycles for Nkr35/ 150 per hour/day, and organise **fruit farm** visits (Nkr125 including coffee and cake) on Tuesday and Thursday.

Places to Stay & Eat
Ulvik Fjordcamping (☎ *56 52 61 70, fax 56 52 61 60, Ulvik)* Tent sites Nkr50. This convenient place is 500m from the centre of town.

Uppheim Gård (☎*/fax 56 52 62 93, Ulvik)* Singles/doubles Nkr550/650. This excellent old farmhouse, 2km uphill and north of the village, has lovely accommodation and great views.

Rica Brakanes Hotel (☎ *56 52 61 05, fax 56 52 64 10, Ulvik)* Singles/doubles from Nkr795/950. Buffet dinner Nkr295, mains from Nkr130. You'll get wonderful balcony views from many of the fine rooms at this flash place. The hotel organises 25-minute seaplane flights (Nkr475 per person).

Getting There & Around
Between Voss and Ulvik (Nkr64, 1¼ hours), buses run two to six times daily. The HSD (☎ 56 52 69 80) ferry between Ulvik and Norheimsund (Nkr170, 1½ hours) sails at least once daily between mid-May and mid-September and connects with buses to Bergen.

Cycle between Ulvik and Osa, or take the 11am daily Ulvik tourist office tour (Nkr210,

including admission to Stream Nest), which connects with ferries to/from Norheimsund.

ODDA
pop 7890
Industrial, iron-smelting Odda is frequently cited as Norway's ugliest town, and while that's not exactly true – there are some pretty dire places in Finnmark – it isn't especially attractive. Despite its appearance, residents have a front-row view of one of Norway's finest landscapes, including the uttermost reaches of Hardangerfjord, a blue-green lake which spills into it through a riotous waterfall and the icy heights of the fabulous Folgefonn glacier.

Information
For information, stop by the Odda Næringsråd tourist office (☎ 53 64 12 97, fax 53 67 35 99), near the Sørfjorden shore, which is open 9am to 6pm weekdays, 9am to 5pm Saturday and 11am to 6pm Sunday from 21 June to 31 August. The rest of the year, it's open 8.30am to 4pm weekdays.

Folgefonn
Folgefonn, mainland Norway's third largest icefield, offers summer skiing, snowboarding and sledding from mid-June to October. Short tours to the ski centre leave from Jondal quay at 10.30am from mid-June to mid-August and return at 3.30pm, connecting with ferries and buses to/from Norheimsund. From Odda, weekend glacier trips run to Odda Turlag's Holmaskjær mountain hut; contact the Odda tourist office for details.

Anyone in good physical condition with warm clothing and sturdy footwear can take a guided one-hour hike up the lovely Buer valley followed by a glacier walk on the Buer arm of Folgefonn (minimum three persons, Nkr300/person, including crampons and ice axes). Transport to the starting point, at Buer, 9km west of Odda, isn't included. You can also walk to the glacier face on your own (24km return from Odda).

Tyssedal
Tyssedal boasts an impressive 1908 hydroelectric power plant, one of the largest of its

time and seemingly inspired by Lhasa's Potala Palace. Inside, the **Norsk Vasskraft-og Industristadmuseum** (☎ 53 65 00 50, Tyssedal; adult/child Nkr50/free; open 10am-5pm daily mid-May–Aug, 10am-3pm Tues-Fri Sept–mid-May) relates the plant's history.

The reputedly haunted **Tyssedal Hotel** (☎ 53 64 69 07, Tyssedal; admission free; always open) houses an extraordinary gallery of fantastic fairy tale and Hardangerfjord landscape paintings by Eidfjord artist Nils Bergslien (1853–1928); his renowned work Tysso & Tyssen features two Hardanger caricatures surveying the Tyssedal hydroelectric plant.

About 5km east, in Skjeggedal, the impressive **Mågelibanen Funicular** runs on Wednesday and Friday for Nkr100/50 adult/child return. Hikers can head for the top of the **Tyssestrengene** waterfall (646m) and the outrageous **Trolltunga** rock feature, from either Skjeggedal (eight to 10 hours return) or the upper funicular station (six to eight hours return). Phone the tourist office for further details.

Local buses between Tyssedal and Odda (Nkr17, 10 minutes) run hourly on weekdays and six times on Saturday.

Places to Stay & Eat

Odda Camping (☎ 53 64 34 10, Odda) Tent/caravan sites for 2 people with vehicle Nkr100/120. Open 15 May-5 Sept. The most convenient camping is on the shores of lake Sandvinvatnet, a 20-minute walk southwards and uphill from the town centre.

Hardanger Hotel (☎ 53 65 14 00, fax 53 65 14 09, Eitrheimsveien 17) Singles/doubles Nkr895/1095. Lunch Nkr52-135, dinner mains Nkr195-245, specials Nkr80-100. The upmarket Hardanger Hotel offers comfortable rooms with modern facilities and a reasonable restaurant/cafeteria.

Tyssedal Hotel (☎ 53 64 69 07, fax 53 64 69 55, Tyssedal) Singles/doubles from Nkr840/945. 3-course Hardanger menu Nkr295, mains Nkr85-289. The recommended Icelandic-run Tyssedal Hotel has great en suite rooms and an Icelandic chef, who rustles up delicacies like skyr (Icelandic yoghurt) and fruit (Nkr79).

Getting There & Away

Between Odda and Jondal (Nkr118, 2½ hours), local buses operate one to three times daily. One to three daily Nor-Way Bussekspress buses run to/from Bergen (Nkr235, 3¾ hours) and Oslo (Nkr425, 7¼ hours), with connections at Haukeligrend for Skien, Haugesund and Kristiansand.

ROSENDAL & AROUND
pop 1000

Just west of Folgefonn, Rosendal can now be reached by an 11km-long road tunnel (Nkr55/car, open 6am-10pm daily) under the icefield from Odda. The tourist office (☎ 53 48 42 80), by Rosendal quay, opens daily from May to September.

About 10km west of the tunnel, you'll see the **Furubergsfossen waterfall**. At Sunndal, 4km west of the tunnel, take the road up the Sunndal valley (driveable for 1km), then walk 2km on a good track to lake Bondhusvatnet, where there's a wonderful view of the glacier **Bondhusbreen**. In Uskedalen, 14km west of Rosendal, there's an extraordinary rock-slab mountain, Ulvenåso (1247m), reputedly giving some of the best **rock climbing** in Norway.

The 1665 **Baroniet Rosendal** (☎ 53 48 29 99, Rosendal; adult/child Nkr75/10; hourly guided tours, variable hours daily May-Aug), Norway's only baronial mansion, features period interiors, a Renaissance rose garden, concerts and art exhibitions.

In Sunndal, *Sundal Camping* (☎ 53 48 41 86, fax 53 48 18 20, Sunndal) charges Nkr45 per tent plus Nkr15 per person, and cabins are Nkr270 to Nkr470. The nearby *Mauranger Kro & Vertshus* (☎ 53 48 41 57, fax 53 48 41 81, Sunndal) offers singles/doubles from Nkr295/590 and the restaurant serves meals for Nkr60 to Nkr150.

Rosendal Gjestgiveri (☎/fax 53 47 36 66, Skålagato 17, Rosendal) B&B singles/doubles Nkr500/700. Mains Nkr75-155. The ornate Rosendal Gjestgiveri dates from 1887 and offers atmospheric B&B in rooms with shared bathrooms. The restaurant serves beef and chicken dishes, pizzas and salads; there's a decent pub in the basement.

SOUTH-WESTERN FJORDS

Buses run three to seven times daily between Rosendal and Odda via Sunndal. There are also up to seven daily runs between the Løfallstrand ferry quay (4km north of Rosendal) and Uskedalen, via Rosendal, and two daily connections to Bergen via Løfallstrand.

UTNE, LOFTHUS & KINSARVIK
combined pop 3600

At the picturesque fruit-growing village of Utne, you'll find the open-air **Hardanger Folk Museum** (☎ *53 66 69 00, Utne; adult/child Nkr40/free; open 10am-3pm Mon-Fri, 10am-4pm Sat, noon-4pm Sun May-June, 10am-6pm Mon-Sat, noon-4pm Sun July-Aug)*, which comprises a collection of historic homes, boats, shops, outhouses and a school, plus exhibitions on Hardanger women, weddings, fiddle-making, fishing, music and dance, orchard crops and the woodcarvings of local artist Lars Kinsarvik.

At Kinsarvik, a ferry ride across Sørfjorden (Nkr22/60 per person/vehicle, 30 minutes), you'll see one of Norway's first stone churches *(Kinsarvik; admission free; open 10am-7pm May-Aug)*. According to legend, it was built in Roman style by Scots in 1160, restored in 1880 and 1961, and during medieval times sails and masts were stored in the attic. Chalk paintings on the walls depict the weighing of souls by Michael the Archangel.

Kinsarvik offers an appealing access trail past the **Husedalen waterfalls** and onto the network of tracks through the wild Hardangervidda National Park. Nearby Lofthus has **Grieg's Hut** *(Lofthus; admission free; always open)* in the garden of Hotel Ullensvang.

Places to Stay

Hardanger Gjestegård (☎ *53 66 67 10, fax 53 66 66 66, Alsåker)* Singles/doubles Nkr550/600, apartments from Nkr350. This guesthouse, 10km west of Utne on Fv550, is in a charming 1898 building with atmospheric rooms.

Utne Hotel (☎ *53 66 10 88, fax 53 66 69 50, Utne)* Singles/doubles without bathroom from Nkr300/500, with en suite Nkr725/1170. The historic wooden Utne Hotel was built in 1722 after the Great Nordic War, when Peder Larsson Børsem applied to the king and received permission to set up a guesthouse; it has been in business ever since. The hotel's fabulous decor makes it worth a look even if you're not staying.

Getting There & Away

Nor-Way Bussekspress buses run between Bergen (Nkr182, 2½ hours), and Oslo (Nkr465, 8¼ to nine hours) via Odda (Nkr67, one hour), and pass through Utne once or twice daily.

Ferries from Norheimsund to Utne (45 minutes, Nkr97), Kinsarvik (one hour, Nkr120), Ulvik and Eidfjord sail two or three times daily.

EIDFJORD & AROUND
pop 950

At the innermost reaches of Hardangerfjord you'll find sheer mountains, huge waterfalls, spiral tunnels and farms perched on mountain ledges. For details of all accommodation options in the area, contact the Eidfjord tourist office (☎ 53 67 34 00), open daily mid-June to August (otherwise, open weekdays only).

Kjeåsen Farm, 6km north-east of Eidfjord, is one of Norway's top scenic locations. It's possible to climb up on foot (three hours return), but it's not easy. The road goes through a one-way tunnel – driving up on the hour, down on the half-hour. Equally impressive is the 145m-high **Vøringfoss waterfall**, by Rv7 and 18km south-east of Eidfjord.

The fine **Hardangervidda Natursenter** (☎ *53 66 59 00, Øvre Eidfjord; adult/child Nkr70/35; open 10am-6pm daily Apr-Oct, 9am-8pm daily June-Aug)* has a must-see 19-minute movie, interactive displays and interesting natural history and geology exhibits.

Sæbø Camping (☎ *53 66 59 27, Øvre Eidfjord)* Tent sites Nkr60, cabins Nkr200-500. This nicely located site has good facilities.

Eidfjord Hotel (☎ *53 66 52 64, fax 53 66 52 12, Eidfjord)* Singles/doubles Nkr650/850. You'll find comfortable en suite rooms here and the restaurant serves good filling dinners.

Buses run between Geilo and Odda via Vøringfoss, Øvre Eidfjord and Eidfjord once or twice daily, plus several extra runs daily except Sunday between Øvre Eidfjord, Eidfjord and Odda. Ferries between Eidfjord and Norheimsund/Utne (Nkr160/97, three/1¼ hours) or Ulvik (Nkr59, 30 minutes) sail two or three times daily.

Stavanger

pop 106,000

Around 1900, Stavanger, Norway's fourth largest city, was a bustling fishing centre with more than 70 sardine canneries. By the 1960s, depleted fish stocks finished off the industry, but the discovery of North Sea oil spared Stavanger from obscurity. As a haunt of oil-related business visitors from around the world, it's nearly as cosmopolitan as Oslo and is one of the tidiest cities in Norway.

Stavanger's historic harbour, medieval cathedral, timber architecture, lovely parks, and several good museums will easily absorb a day of strolling and sightseeing, and Lysefjord and Preikestolen (see the Haugelandet & Ryfylke section) make essential day trips.

Orientation

The adjacent bus and train stations lie beside the pond Breiavann, about 10 minutes on foot from the harbour. Most sites of interest lie within easy walking distance of the harbour.

Information

Tourist Office The Destinasjon Stavanger tourist office (☎ 51 85 92 00, fax 51 85 92 02, e info@visitstavanger.com, w www .visitstavanger.com), Rosenkildetorget 1, is open 9am to 8pm, June to August (shorter hours and closed Sunday from September to May). Information on hiking and mountain huts is available from Stavanger Turistforening DNT (☎ 51 84 02 00), in the pedestrian tunnel south of the train station. The travel agent Kilroy Travel (☎ 51 89 52 25) is at Breigata 11.

Money Most major banks are represented along Olav V's gate and Håkon VII's gate.

Den Norske Bank and the adjacent post office offer competitive rates.

Laundry At Fisketorget laundry services, washing and drying cost Nkr25 each plus Nkr5 door charge (the tourist office sells door tokens). It's open 24 hours.

Gamle Stavanger

A rewarding amble will lead you through Gamle (Old) Stavanger, immediately west of the harbour, where cobblestone walkways pass between rows of well-preserved early 18th-century whitewashed wooden houses. It's now home to all sorts of artists' studios selling paintings, ceramics, weavings, handcrafted jewellery and other items.

Norwegian Emigration Centre

The Norwegian Emigration Centre (☎ 51 53 88 60, Strandkaien 31) helps foreigners of Norwegian descent trace their roots. In mid-June it stages a popular Emigration Festival.

Stavanger Domkirke

The partly Gothic, partly Anglo-Norman-style Stavanger Cathedral (Haakon VIIs gate; admission free; open 11am-6pm Mon-Tue, 10am-6pm Wed-Sat, 1pm-6pm Sun 15 May-15 Sept, shorter hours at other times) is an impressive medieval stone cathedral dating from approximately 1125, but it was extensively renovated following a fire in 1272. As with the famed Winchester Cathedral in England, this church is dedicated to St Swithun and, in fact, one of the good saint's arms was brought from Winchester by Stavanger's first bishop, Reinhald. After the Reformation, however, the arm, the original altar and many other icons and relics went missing.

An atmospheric time to visit is during the organ recital at 11.15am on Thursday.

Norsk Oljemuseum

The Norwegian Petroleum Museum (☎ 51 93 93 00, Kjeringholmen; adult/child Nkr75/35; open 10am-7pm daily June-Aug, 10am-4pm Mon-Sat & 10am-6pm Sun Sept-May) traces the history of oil formation and exploration in the North Sea from discovery in 1969 until

STAVANGER

PLACES TO STAY
4 Skagen Hostel & Gjestehus
7 Commandør Hotel
8 Havly Hotel
11 Skagen Brygge Hotel & Bryggeriet Pub
33 Comfort Hotel Grand
48 Det Lille Huset
53 Stavanger B&B

PLACES TO EAT
5 India Tandoori
9 Café Sting
14 NB Sørensen's Damskipsexpedisjon
16 Craigs Kjøkken
17 China House; Kilroy Travel

19 Mikado
22 Sjøhuset Skagen
28 Mexico
29 Dickens
30 McDonald's
31 Finns Konditori
34 Rimi Supermarket
35 Burger King
42 Students House-Folken
49 Frelsersarméen Café

MUSEUMS
1 Grafisk Museet
3 Hermetikkmuseet
6 Norsk Oljemuseum; Bølgen & Moi
10 Valbergtårnet & Vektermuseet

25 Stavanger Sjøfartsmuseet
43 Ledaal
44 Breidablikk
45 Norsk Telemuseum
52 Stavanger Museum
55 Brannmuseet
56 Archeologisk Museum

OTHER
2 Strandkaien Quay
12 Clipper Fjord Sightseeing; FjordTours
13 New York
20 The Irishman
21 Kulturhus; Library; Kino Z Cinema
23 Newsman

24 Norwegian Emigration Centre
26 Taket
27 Torget Fish Market
32 Vinmonopolet
36 Destinasjon Stavanger Tourist Office
37 Fisketorget Laundry Services
38 Post Office
39 Den Norske Bank
40 Stavanger Domkirke
41 Sykkelhuset
46 Vinmonopolet
47 Train Station & Café Caroline
50 Bus Terminal
51 Stavanger Turistforening DNT Office
54 Police Station

To Utstein Kloster (20km)

To UK

To Haugesund & Bergen

To Tau

Byfjorden

Gamle Stavanger

Vågen

Nedre Holmegate
Øvre Holmegate

Tastagata
Øvre Strandgate
Nedre Strandgate
Strandkaien
Valbergata
Skagenkaien
Kirkegata
Breigata
Salvågergata
Østervåg

Stokkaveien
Løkkeveien
Møllegata
Lars Hertervigs gate
Skagen
Søregata
Laugmandsgata
Klubbgata

Steingate
Løvdahls gate
Rosenkildetorget
Haakon VIIs gate
Berglandsgata
Våisenhusgaten
Langgata
Pedersgata

Klinkenberggata
Niels Juels gate
Eiganesveien
Olavskleiv
Engelsk gate
Løkkeveien
Kongsgata
Hetlandsgata
Kirkebakken
Nytorget

Breiavatnet
Breibakken

Jernbanevn
Stiftelsgata

Prinsens gate
Dronningens gate
Maalaveien
Kannikgata
Peder Klows gate
Storgata
Saudgata
Verksdalgata
Lagårdsveien
Breikunds gate

Train Station

To Mosvangen Vandrerhjem & Camping Ground (2km), Mosvangen Park (2km) & Rogaland Kunstmuseum (2km)

To Ullandhaug Farm Reconstruction (4km), Sola Strand Hotel (14km) & Airport

0 200 400m
0 200 400yd

SOUTH-WESTERN FJORDS

the present. It's a clever modern presentation, using high-tech interactive displays, gigantic models and authentic reconstructions. Particularly impressive exhibits include the 3D video covering the history of Earth, the extraordinary model of 'Ekofisk city' and the avant-garde 'petrodome' movie feature.

Valbergtårnet & Vektermuseet

The historic tower Valbergtårnet, which was constructed as a guards' lookout from 1850 to 1853, offers a good view of the city and the harbour from . Inside is the interesting Vektermuseet, the Guards' Museum (☎ 90 72 63 94, Valbergjet 2; Nkr20/free over/under 5 years; open 10am-4pm Mon-Fri, 10am-6pm Thur, 10am-2pm Sat).

Stavanger Museum

The five-part Stavanger Museum (☎ 51 84 27 00; admission to all 5 sections on same day adult/family Nkr40/90; open 11am-4pm daily 15 June-15 Aug, 11am-4pm Sun only rest of year; Seafaring & Canning museums also 11am-3pm Tues-Fri 1–14 June & 16 Aug–1 Sept), with bits scattered around town, is good for the greater part of a sightseeing day.

Stavanger Museum The main museum (Muségata 16) reveals nearly 900 years of Stavanger's history, 'From Ancient Landscape to Oil Town'. Features include evidence of Stone Age habitation, the medieval bishopric, the herring years and the development of the city into a modern oil capital. The Stavanger of the 1880s is described in a series of tableaux focusing on local author Alexander Kielland. In another wing is a pretty standard collection of stuffed birds and wildlife, with exhibits on the migratory patterns of North Atlantic birds.

Hermetikkmuseet A canning museum (Øvre Strandgata 88A)... sounds boring, you say? Well, in fact, this appealing place, housed in an old cannery, may well be Stavanger's most worthwhile attraction (see the boxed text 'The Lowly Sardine & the Cult of Iddis'). Here you'll get the lowdown on Stavanger's main industry from the 1890s to 1960 – canning brisling and fish

balls. You can also see a couple of restored workers' cottages. On the first Sunday of every month (and Tuesday and Thursday between 15 June and 15 August), the fires are lit and you can sample smoked sardines straight from the ovens.

Ledaal The recently restored empire-style Ledaal (Eiganesveien 45) was constructed between 1799 and 1803 for wealthy merchant ship owner Gabriel Schanche Kielland, and now serves as the local royal residence and summer home. You'll see the king's 250-year-old four-poster bed, unusual antique furniture and a pendulum clock from 1680.

Breidablikk The excellent Breidablikk manor (Eiganesveien 40A) was also constructed for a merchant ship owner, Lars Berentsen. It dates from 1881 and displays old farming implements, books and knickknacks. This one lets you in on the opulent lifestyles of the rich and famous in late 19th-century Norway.

Stavanger Sjøfartsmuseet The extensive Stavanger Maritime Museum (Nedre Strandgata 17–19) outlines 200 years of Stavanger's maritime history in two warehouses dating from around 1800. There's also a large collection of model boats, sailing vessels, a noisy wind-up foghorn, a reconstruction of a late 19th-century sailmaker's workshop, a shipowner's office and an excellent general store, as well as the merchant's living quarters. The museum also owns two historic sailing vessels, the 1848 Anna of Sand and the 1896 Wyvern.

Archeologisk Museum

The well-presented Archaeological Museum (☎ 51 84 60 00, Peder Klows gate 30A; adult/child Nkr20/10; open 11am-5pm Tues-Sun in summer, shorter hours at other times), traces 11,000 years of human history including the Viking Age. Exhibits include skeletons, tools and a runestone and there's also a description of the symbiosis between prehistoric humans and their environment.

SOUTH-WESTERN FJORDS

The Lowly Sardine & the Cult of Iddis

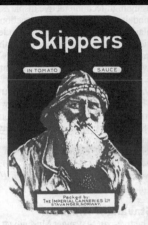

Around Stavanger the word *iddis*, derived from the local pronunciation of *etikett* (label), has come to apply to the colourfully artistic labels which appear on Norwegian sardine tins measuring precisely 75mm by 105mm. The first of Stavanger's original canneries, Stavanger Preserving, appeared in 1873 and initially produced tinned meat; by the turn of the century, however, the company's attentions had turned to brisling sardines, which had become a mainstay of the local economy. As Stavanger grew into Norway's sardine canning centre, more enterprises took interest and, by 1922, the city boasted 70 sardine canneries providing 50% of the town's employment. Each cannery had its own label, ranging from depictions of royalty, wild animals, polar explorers and seafaring scenes to architectural features, zeppelins, sports events and leisure activities. Whatever the theme, however, special care was given to achieving a warming and life-giving quality. No one knows exactly how many designs were actually used, but some estimates place the figure at up to 40,000.

These sardine tin labels created a stir in the local community, which recognised their artistry and collectability. Workers had access to the labels but other collectors had to await a *sjeining*, in which bundles of labels were cast to the wind to be gathered up by the general populace. In fact, these iddis became a form of currency for children, and were traded much the same as pokemon cards are today.

Perhaps the most popular and sought-after designs are the Christian Bjelland & Co *Man with a fish* by Kittelsen, and the Skippers' Sea captain, which depicts Scotsman William Duncan Anderson dressed in oilskins. The latter was designed by the Scottish artist Angus Watson, who came up with the name 'Skippers'. He purchased the copyright on a photo of Anderson, which he'd selected as the iddis for his brand, and commissioned an artist to come up with a likeness for the label. Unfortunately for poor William Duncan Anderson, the label turned him into a laughing stock and made it impossible for him to secure serious work with any fishing fleet. As a result, he was placed on the Skippers payroll for the rest of his days, and continued to work as an artists' model.

Today, the best of these well-appreciated labels can be seen at Hermetikkmuseet in Stavanger.

Ullandhaug Farm Reconstruction

The reconstruction of a 1500-year-old Iron Age farm (☎ 51 84 60 71, Ullandhaug; adult/child Nkr30/10; open 11am-4pm Mon-Sat noon-4pm Sun 15 June-15 Aug, otherwise noon-4pm Sun only), south of Mosvangen, features various activities, staff in period dress and food preparation on Sunday. Take bus No 25 or 26 towards Sandnes to Ullandhaug (Nkr20, 15 min).

Rogaland Kunstmuseum

The Rogaland Art Museum (☎ 51 53 09 00, Tjensvoll 6; adult/child Nkr50/free; open 11am-4pm Tues-Sun) displays Norwegian art from the 18th century to the present, including the haunting *Gamle Furutrær* and other landscapes by Stavanger's own Lars Hertervig (1830–1902). A nine-sided hall houses the Halvdan Hafsten Collection, the largest assemblage of mid-20th-century Norwegian art, including work by Harald Dal, Kai Fjell, Arne Ekeland and others.

Other Museums

If you're into phones and other forms of electronic communication, don't miss the **Norsk Telemuseum** (☎ 51 76 32 49, Dronningens

DEANNA SWANEY

Fannaråki Hut, on the summit of Fannaråken in Jotunheimen National Park

ANDERS BLOMQVIST

These boats were made for walking, Rondane National Park

ANDERS BLOMQVIST

This rock was made for…enjoying the serene view of Lake Gjende, Jotunheimen National Park

ANDERS BLOMQVIST.

The main streets of Røros are lined with brightly painted, historic houses

ANDERS BLOMQVIST

A church tower rises above Røros

ANDERS BLOMQVIST

Gudbrandsdalen valley, north of Lillehammer

*gate 12; admission free; open noon-4pm
Wed-Sun mid-June–mid-Aug, 11am-4pm Sun
mid-Aug–mid-June).*

Both pyromaniacs and firefighters will
enjoy **Brannmuseet** (☎ *51 50 88 60, Lag-
årdsvei 32; admission free; open by appointment only),* in the fire station, which is
dedicated to fires and firefighting in Norway.

Mosvangen

The large forest park at Mosvangen is a
popular destination for local recreation, but
it's also a remarkable wildlife refuge. The
lake and its small attached lagoon, which
are encircled by footpaths, attract large
numbers of nesting and breeding ducks,
geese, and sea birds, as well as songbirds.
It's a pleasant 3km walk from the centre or
10 minutes on bus No 130 (Nkr20).

Utstein Kloster

The unusually-designed stone-built Utstein
monastery (☎ *51 72 47 05, Mosterøy; adult/
child Nkr35/10; open 10am-4pm Tue-Sat &
noon-5pm Sun May–mid-Sept, also 10am-
4pm Mon July)* dates from 1257 and is reputedly haunted by the 'White Lady'. The
church hosts cultural events, including exhibitions and concerts – and it's noted for its
extraordinary acoustics. Admission includes a guided tour but events cost extra.
Take bus No 170, then No 177 to Fjøløy
(Nkr45). Motorists pay the Nkr90 one-way
toll on the undersea tunnel to Mosterøy.

Organised Tours

Stavanger's version of 'Norway in a Nutshell' is actually a self-guided triangle route
by rail to Oslo, then to Bergen and back to
Stavanger by express boat. The entire route
costs Nkr1440/720 adult/child and, for an
additional Nkr345, you can include Flåm
and Gudvangen en route between Oslo and
Bergen. Book at the train station.

See the later Lysefjord section for details
of Clipper Fjord Sightseeing and Fjordtours
tours to Lysefjord.

Places to Stay

Accommodation in Stavanger is snapped up
well in advance all year round; book as far

ahead as possible. Ask the tourist office for
the 'Bed & Breakfast Circle' leaflet. For the
hostel or camping ground, take bus No 78
or 79 (Nkr17) from opposite the cathedral
to Ullandhaugveien.

Mosvangen Vandrerhjem (☎ *51 87 29 00,
fax 51 87 06 30, Henrik Ibsensgate 21)* Dorm
beds Nkr145, doubles Nkr290. Open mid-
May–mid-Sept. The pleasant and well-
equipped lakeside hostel, 3km south-west of
the city centre, charges Nkr60 for breakfast.

Mosvangen Camping (☎ *51 53 29 71, fax
51 87 20 55, Tjensvoll 1b)* Basic 2-person/
4-person huts Nkr260/350, tent sites with-
out/with car Nkr70/105, with caravan or
camper Nkr110, extra person Nkr10. Open
mid-May–mid-Sept. During nesting season
around Mosvangen lake, campers are treated
to almost incessant birdsong.

Det Lille Huset (☎ *51 89 40 89, Vaisen-
husgaten 40)* Singles/doubles Nkr300/500.
At this recommended inexpensive place,
dating from 1869, the owner Grethe allows
access to kitchen facilities.

Stavanger B&B (☎ *51 56 25 00, fax 51
56 25 01, Vikedalsgata 1a)* Singles/doubles
Nkr450/590. This decent centrally located
guesthouse is a comfortable B&B.

Skagen Hotel & Gjestehus (☎ *51 93 85
00, fax 51 93 85 01, Nedre Holmegate 2)*
Singles/doubles summer & weekends
Nkr475/575, otherwise Nkr525/625. This
centrally located place, by the old Customs
House, offers newly renovated en suite
rooms.

Commandør Hotel (☎ *51 89 53 00, fax 51
89 53 01, Valberggata 9)* Singles Nkr400-
895, doubles Nkr550-995. The Commandør
has comfortable rooms with bath.

Skagen Brygge Hotel (☎ *51 85 00 00, fax
51 85 00 01, Skagenkaien 30)* Singles
Nkr695-1295, doubles Nkr795-1395. This
large and opulent hotel offers good weekend value.

Comfort Hotel Grand (☎ *51 89 58 00,
fax 51 89 57 10, Klubbgata 3)* Singles
Nkr695-1095, doubles Nkr895-1350. This
modern upmarket choice has friendly staff
and attractive summer rates.

Sola Strand Hotel (☎ *51 94 30 00, fax 51
94 31 99, Sola)* Singles Nkr615-995, doubles

Nkr770-1450. The recommended historic Sola Strand Hotel has large rooms and a great breakfast. It's located by a quiet sandy beach 14km south-west of Stavanger and contains an entire lounge from a former cruise ship.

Places to Eat

As you'd expect of an oil capital, Stavanger has a plethora of eating establishments offering a range of international menus, but some places charge astronomical prices.

NB Sørensen's Damskipsexpedisjon (☎ 51 84 38 20, Skagen 26) Specials Nkr99-115, mains Nkr119-255. *The* recommended seafood spot serves gourmet-quality food in a cosy setting.

Sjøhuset Skagen (☎ 51 89 51 80, Skagenkaien 16) Mains Nkr91-235. An even more atmospheric place for fish dishes, located in a restored warehouse on the wharf.

Bølgen & Moi (☎ 51 93 93 51, Norsk Oljemuseum, Kjerringholmen) Mains Nkr110-295. The imaginative menus in this stylish restaurant include monkfish, lamb and veal. The desserts are highly recommended.

Craig's Kjøkken (☎ 51 93 95 90, Breitorget) Mains Nkr195-245. The 'creative American cuisine' here includes pasta and pizza dishes. Lunchtime sandwiches are better value.

Storyteller (☎ 51 89 44 11, Skagen 27) Specials Nkr99, mains Nkr193-259. This place specialises in Cajun fare for all those homesick oil workers from around the Gulf of Mexico.

Mexico Restaurant (☎ 51 89 15 55, Skagenkaien 12) Mains Nkr145-295. Filling high-quality Mexican specialities are the forte here.

China House (☎ 51 89 18 38, Salvågergata 3) Mains Nkr119-198. China House serves decent Asian food and the all-you-can-eat Mongolian grill buffet (Nkr135) is good value.

India Tandoori Restaurant (☎ 51 89 39 35, Valberggata 14) Mains Nkr109-209. Authentic Indian dishes are on the extensive menu here.

Mikado (☎ 51 89 33 88, Østervåg 9) Lunch Nkr48-79, dinner mains Nkr83-165.

The Chinese/Japanese-oriented Mikado serves a good range of far-eastern dishes.

Dickens (☎ 51 89 59 70, Skagenkaien 6) Pizza buffet Nkr76, mains Nkr59-176. Dickens has a rustic pub atmosphere and, from 11am to midnight, you can chow down on all the pizza you can eat for a bargain Nkr76.

Café Caroline (☎ 51 52 87 47, Jernbaneveien 3) Meal and drink Nkr99. Café Caroline, at the train station, serves breakfast from 7.30am, and hot dogs, snacks and pasta dishes.

Students House-Folken (☎ 51 56 44 44, Olavskleiv 16) Snacks around Nkr50. This students' cultural hangout has an inexpensive bar serving coffee, beer and basic snacks.

Frelsersarméen Café (☎ 51 52 05 56, Kongsgata 50) Mains around Nkr50. For simple traditional food, check out this place run by the Salvation Army.

For tasty pastries, sandwiches and ice cream, try *Finns Konditori* at Arneageren.

Not surprisingly, American cuisine, such as it is, features prominently in Stavanger's petroleum circles, and both *McDonald's* and *Burger King* are represented. The bus terminal also has a fast food outlet.

Fresh fish is sold at the *Torget fish market* and you'll find wine and liquor at the Vinmonopolet outlets on Olav V's gate and Nytorget. The central *Rimi* supermarket is near the head of the harbour.

Entertainment

Bryggeriet Pub (☎ 51 85 00 00, Skagen 28) Admission free or Nkr20. You'll get good jazz here at weekends.

The Irishman (☎ 51 89 41 81, Hølebergsgata 9) Stavanger's Irish pub features live folk music five nights weekly.

New York (☎ 51 89 95 50, Skagenkaien 24) On weekends, New York provides youth-oriented fun and dancing.

Taket (☎ 51 84 37 20, Nedre Strandgate 15) Patrons over 22 may prefer the Taket nightclub.

Newsman (☎ 51 84 38 80, Skagen 14) If you're desperate for international news coverage without depth, this bar features constant CNN broadcasts. Alternatively, read newspapers at library-style reading tables while munching on nachos or sandwiches.

Café Sting (☎ *51 89 38 78, Valbergjet 3*) Café Sting offers a range of options: meals (Nkr98 to Nkr159), a pub, a bar and occasional live performances with an emphasis on jazz.

For cinema features, try the eight-screen *Kino Z* (☎ *82 05 11 00*) in the Kulturhus.

Getting There & Away

Air The international airport is at Sola, 14km south of the city centre. SAS or Braathens fly between Stavanger and Oslo, Bergen and Kristiansand at least once daily, and Widerøe offers good value to/from Bergen. Stavanger is also served by SAS to/from London, Braathens to/from Newcastle and SAS, Braathens and Widerøe to/from Aberdeen, in Scotland, several times daily.

Bus The daily Nor-Way Bussekspress between Stavanger and Oslo (Nkr620, 10¼ hours) leaves Stavanger at 9.15am. To/from Bergen (5¾ hours, Nkr370) via Haugesund (Nkr170, 2¼ hours), buses leave every two hours. Between Stavanger and Kristiansand (Nkr310, 4½ hours), buses run one to four times daily.

Train Rail services to/from Egersund (Nkr115, one hour) run numerous times daily. Direct trains to Oslo (Nkr670, eight hours), via Kristiansand (Nkr320, three hours), run one to three times daily, including an overnight service. Two extra runs require changing at Kristiansand and two services connect to Arendal at Nelaug. All Oslo trains require seat reservations.

Car & Motorcycle The E39, Norway's main west coast highway, passes through Stavanger. From the south, it becomes a motorway (motorveien) near the city. To reach the city centre, follow Madlaveien.

Boat From Fiskepiren, Flaggruten's (☎ 51 86 87 80) express catamaran to Bergen (Nkr590, 4¼ hours) via Haugesund (Nkr210, 1½ hours) leaves two or three times daily. Ferries to Tau (Nkr87/29 car/person, 40 minutes) also sail from Fiskespiren. For Lysefjord ferries from Fiskespiren, see Lysefjord, later in this chap-ter. For information on ferries between Sta-vanger's Strandkaien quay and England, see the Getting There & Away chapter.

Getting Around

To/From the Airport Between early morn-ing and mid to late evening, Flybussen airport buses (☎ 51 52 26 00) run one to four times hourly between the city centre and the airport at Sola (Nkr45, 30 minutes). Alternatively, take city bus No 143 (Nkr30, 30 minutes), which runs approximately every half-hour between early morning and midnight.

A taxi from the city centre to the airport costs roughly Nkr170 to Nkr200, and be-tween the airport and the Mosvangen Van-drerhjem and camping ground, you'll pay around Nkr160.

Bus Local buses run frequently between the centre and the outskirts, including Sola and Sandnes. Fares start at Nkr10 within the city centre.

Car & Motorcycle The city centre is a combination of narrow streets and pedes-trian walkways that are best explored on foot. Drivers will find a host of high-rise parking garages around the post office and bus terminal. Illuminated signs reveal the number of places available *(ledig)*.

Bicycle You can hire mountain bikes at Sykkelhuset (☎ 51 53 99 10), Løkkeveien 33, for Nkr60/250 per day/week. For cycle tours around the scenic Rogaland landscape, the tourist office distributes copies of Fjord Nor-way's *Sykkelkart* cycling map, which outlines three multi-day routes and 30 day-trips.

Haugelandet & Ryfylke

North and east of Stavanger lies a region of mountains, extensive fjords and relatively flat coastal islands. The coastal strip and the islands support a fair-sized population. For information about Ryfylke, see the In-ternet at Ⓦ www.ryfylke.com.

HAUGESUND
pop 28,000
Interesting Haugesund lies well off the
beaten routes and is rarely visited by travellers, but the popular jazz and film festivals
are drawing more visitors. The Haugelandet
region grew up around the early 20th-century
herring fishery and still relies to some extent
on fishing, as well as shipping, oil and gas.

Information
The Haugesund tourist office (☎ 52 72 50
55, e posthbu@hbu.no, w www.haugesund
.net), Smedasundet 77, opens 10am to 6pm
weekdays and 10am to 4pm Saturday, June
to August (otherwise 8am to 3.30pm weekdays only).

Things to See
There's a number of architecturally interesting buildings in Haugesund, including
the rådhus (town hall). Haraldshaugen, the
burial site of Viking King Harald Hårfagre,
who died of plague at Avaldsnes on nearby
Karmøy, is 1.5km north of Haugesund. The
obelisk, erected in 1872, commemorates the
decisive Hafrsfjord naval battle in 872 and
the subsequent formation of Norway as a
single realm. About 75m south is the
Krosshaugen mound and stone cross,
erected in celebration of Christian gatherings around 1000.

About 5km south of central Haugesund,
King Håkon Håkonsson's huge stone
church (☎ 52 83 84 00, Avaldsnes; admission free; open daily June-Aug) was dedicated to St Olav in 1250. The adjacent 6.5m
spire, known as the Virgin Mary's Needle,
leans towards the church wall and legend
suggests that when it actually falls against
the wall, the Day of Judgement is at hand.
Near the church, at the reconstructed Viking
farm (☎ 52 83 84 00, Avaldsnes; adult/child
Nkr30/10; open 10am-3pm Mon-Fri noon-
6pm Sun mid-June–mid-Aug), you'll be
guided by staff in period dress.

The Vigsnes copper mine (☎ 52 83 84 00,
Visnes; adult/child Nkr30/10; open 11am-
5pm Mon-Fri mid-May–mid-Aug & noon-
6pm Sun Easter-Oct), 4km west of
Avaldsnes, includes old buildings, a mine

reconstruction, lots of mining equipment and
a heather centre. The mine supplied the copper for the Statue of Liberty in New York.

Wonderful Skudeneshavn, 37km south of
Haugesund (on Karmøy), has many traditional wooden buildings and an extensive
museum, Mælandsgården (☎ 52 82 91 39,
Skudeneshavn; adult/child Nkr30/10; open
11am-5pm Mon-Fri & 1pm-6pm Sun June-
Aug) with excellent collections of household
articles, rooms with period furnishings, and
agricultural and nautical exhibits.

Haugesund also claims to be the ancestral
home of legendary actress Marilyn Monroe,
whose father, a local baker, emigrated to the
USA. A monument on the quay commemorates the 30th anniversary of her death.

Places to Stay & Eat
Haraldshaugen Camping (☎ 52 72 80 77,
fax 52 86 69 32, Gard) Tent or caravan sites
Nkr100, cabins Nkr140-530. Open June-
Aug. This recommended campground is
near the Haraldshaugen monument, 1.5km
north of town.

Strandgaten Gjestgiveri (☎ 52 71 52 55,
fax 52 71 54 35, Strandgate 81) Singles/
doubles Nkr450/600. At Strandgaten Gjestgiveri, you'll get basic rooms year-round.

Hotel Neptun (☎ 52 86 59 00, fax 52 59
01, Haraldsgata 207) Singles/doubles from
Nkr595/700. The well-appointed Hotel Neptun offers cosy accommodation.

Norneshuset (☎ 52 82 72 62, Nordnes 7,
Skudeneshavn) Singles/doubles from Nkr390/
550. One of the most atmospheric and
friendly B&Bs in Norway, Norneshuset is located in a former warehouse that was shipped
from Riga, Latvia, in the 1830s.

Lothers (☎ 52 71 22 01, Skippergata 4)
Snacks from Nkr47, specials Nkr149.
Lothers is possibly the smartest and trend-
iest restaurant in Haugesund.

Getting There & Away
The easiest approach with the Flaggruten
ferry between Bergen (Nkr370, three hours)
and Stavanger (Nkr210, 1½ hours). Nor-
Way Bussekspress buses connect Haugesund with Oslo (Nkr515, 8½ hours) daily
and there are also buses every two hours

to/from Stavanger (Nkr170, two hours) and Bergen (Nkr240, 3½ hours). SAS has five daily flights to/from Oslo and the Fjord Line ferry (☎ 52 70 93 30) between Bergen and Newcastle (England) also calls in.

LYSEFJORD

At the 42km-long Lysefjord (light fjord) the granite rock seems to glow with an ethereal – almost ambient – light, even on dull days, and the mist seems luminous. Many people consider it the most unique and beautiful fjord in the country and, whether you cruise from Stavanger, hike to Preikestolen or drive the treacherous road down to Lysebotn, it's a highlight of Ryfylke and any trip to Norway.

Lysefjordsenteret

Lysefjordsenteret (☎ 51 70 31 23, Oanes; adult/child Nkr50/25; open 11am-8pm daily June-Aug, 11am-5pm daily Sept-May), in a fabulous setting north of the ferry terminal at Oanes, provides tourist information and presents the wonders of Lysefjord in audio-visual programs, including an artificial balloon flight. There are also geological and folk history exhibits.

Landa Centre

Forsand, just across the Lysefjord suspension bridge from Oanes, has the excellent Landa Centre (☎ 51 70 39 59, Forsand; adult/child Nkr40/25; open 11am-4pm daily mid-June–mid-Aug). There are five reconstructed houses from the Bronze Age, Iron Age and Migration Period, plus reconstructions of tools and household items, and staff in period costume. If you're lucky, you might get a plate of traditionally cooked lamb for around Nkr100 to Nkr200.

Preikestolen

The two-hour trail to the granite block known as Preikestolen, or 'Pulpit Rock', leaves from Preikestolhytta Vandrerhjem. It begins along a steep but perfectly manicured route, then climbs past a series of alternating steep and boggy sections to the final climb across granite slabs and along some very windy and exposed cliffs to Preikestolen itself.

Preikestolen, with overhanging cliffs on three sides, appears about to plunge 600m into the fjord below – but that probably won't happen for thousands of years, despite the alarming crack. While looking down can be a bit daunting (and not for anyone who suffers from vertigo), you won't regret the magical view directly up Lysefjord.

The area also offers several other fabulous walks – the Vatnerindane ridge circuit (two hours), Ulvaskog (three hours), the Refsvatnet circuit (three hours) and summit of Moslifjellet (three hours) – all of which are accessible from the Preikestolhytta car park (Nkr50).

Organised Tours If you'd prefer to see Preikestolen from below (far less impressive than from above), the *Clipper* sightseeing boat (☎ 51 89 52 70) has daily cruises (Nkr280 to Nkr400) from Stavanger. Fjord-Tours (☎ 51 53 73 40) runs a 1½-hour cruise daily from 12 April to 9 September for adult/child Nkr180/90 adult/child. Book in advance at the Stavanger tourist office. Alternatively, you'll also have a view on the Lysebotn cruise (see later in this section).

Places to Stay & Eat *Preikestolhytta Vandrerhjem* (☎ 51 84 02 00, fax 51 74 91 11, Jørpeland) Dorm beds Nkr145, doubles from Nkr350. The fine turf-roofed hostel lies near the start of the Preikestolen walking track. Breakfast is Nkr60 and dinner is Nkr90 to Nkr150.

Preikestolen Camping (☎ 51 74 97 25, Jørpeland) Tent sites Nkr110, plus Nkr20/person. Open May-Sept. The overpriced camping ground, about 2km from Rv13, is cashing in on the tourist trade. Kitchen facilities are available, but you can also eat at the attached shop/restaurant.

Lysefjord Hyttegrend (☎/fax 51 70 38 74, Oanes) 4-6 person cabins Nkr385-550. There are excellent en suite chalets at Lysefjord Hyttegrend.

Lysefjordsenteret (☎ 51 70 31 23, Oanes) Mains Nkr55-120, Sunday buffet Nkr165. You'll get a good reasonably priced traditional meal here.

Getting There & Away From Stavanger take the 8.20am ferry to Tau (Nkr29, 40 minutes), from where a connecting bus (Nkr45) takes you to the trailhead (late June to early September only), then returns at 4.15pm.

If you're driving from Stavanger, the Lauvvik-Oanes ferry (accessed on Route 13 via Sandnes) is considerably shorter and cheaper (Nkr41, 10 minutes) than the route between Stavanger and Tau (Nkr87, 40 minutes). Either way, the trip between Stavanger and Preikestolen takes around 1½ hours.

Lysebotn

A four-hour ferry ride from Stavanger takes you to the fjord head at Lysebotn, where a narrow and frequently photographed road corkscrews 1000m up towards Sirdal in 27 hairpin bends. The road was opened in 1984 to service the local hydroelectric project.

Kjeragbolten After Preikestolen, the most popular Lysefjord walk leads to Kjeragbolten, an enormous oval-shaped boulder, or 'chockstone', lodged between two rock faces about 2m apart. The 10km return hike involves a strenuous 700m ascent from the Øygardsstølen Café car park (parking Nkr30), near the highest hairpin bend above Lysebotn.

The route trudges up and over three ridges and, in places, steep muddy slopes make the going quite rough. Once you're at Kjeragbolten, actually reaching the boulder requires some tricky manoeuvring, including traversing an exposed ledge on a 1000m-high vertical cliff! From there, you can step (or crawl) directly onto the boulder for one of Norway's most astonishing views, and the photo of you perched on the rock is sure to impress your friends.

Places to Stay & Eat *Lysebotn Turistsenter (☎ 51 70 34 90, fax 51 70 34 03, Lysebotn)* Tent/caravan sites Nkr100/120 Nkr10/person, caravan hire or apartments Nkr300-700. Lysebotn Turistsenter occupies an incredible setting at the head of the fjord.

Øygardsstølen Café (☎ 38 37 11 22, Lysebotn) Snacks Nkr45-70, specials Nkr98-110.

For views, you can't beat the 'eagle's nest', perched atop the cliff overlooking the hairpin twists down to Lysebotn.

Getting There & Away From Stavanger, access to Lysebotn is either by ferry or by a boat-and-bus tour combination. The sightseeing boat and return bus (Nkr400, seven hours) run only on Wednesday and Saturday in July and August, and Sunday in June; for bookings call ☎ 51 89 52 70.

Between 11 June and 19 August, Rogaland Trafikkselskap's M/F *Lysefjord* (☎ 51 86 87 90) runs once daily in each direction between Stavanger and Lysebotn. The four-hour trip leaves at 8.30am and costs Nkr266 for a car and driver, plus Nkr117 for additional passengers and pedestrians. If you wish to transport a vehicle, be sure to book in advance.

AROUND RYFYLKE

The road through the wild and lightly populated country north of Lysefjord, Rv13, has been proposed as a national scenic road. It's definitely the slow route between Stavanger and Bergen, but it's worth several days if you have time.

The finest scenery is around **Årdal**, **Jøsenfjorden**, **Suldalsosen** and **Suldalsvatnet**. The industrial town of **Sauda** (pop 3000), on Fv520 at the head of Saudafjorden, has a tourist office (☎ 52 78 39 88) which books tours of the **zinc mines** *(adult/child Nkr60/30; 2pm daily 23 June-12 August)*, 9km east of Sauda.

Sauda Turistsenter (☎ 52 78 59 00, fax 52 78 59 01, Saudasjøen) Tent sites with car Nkr110. Cabins Nkr300-575. This campground, 3km west of the town centre, has a fast food outlet, a supermarket and decent facilities.

Sauda Fjord Hotel (☎ 52 78 12 11, fax 52 78 15 58, Saudasjøen) Singles/doubles from Nkr525/730. Mains Nkr75-225. This grand old hotel offers fine accommodation and good meals at reasonable prices.

The best public transport is the ferry between Stavanger and Sauda (Nkr251, 2¼ hours, two or three daily). Rv13 is best followed by private car.

The Western Fjords

For most visitors and armchair travellers, the Western Fjords are Norway's signature landscapes. Amazingly, these formidable, sea-drowned glacial valleys, flanked by almost impossibly rugged terrain, haven't deterred Norwegians from settling and farming their slopes and heights for thousands of years. It goes without saying that this region presents some of the most breathtaking scenery in Europe. In addition, there's a confounding number of things to see and do in this part of Norway, and the topography is so convoluted that just sorting out an itinerary will prove challenging.

Highlights

- Cruising between Geiranger and Hellesylt past the daunting cliffs of Geirangerfjord
- Riding the famous and dramatic Flåm railway between the wild Hardangervidda and the lovely Aurlandsfjorden
- Driving or taking the bus between Åndalsnes and Valldal over the spectacular Trollstigen route
- Visiting a fishing village on a tiny offshore island, such as Ona or Grip
- Photographing, hiking and exploring around the vast Jostedalsbreen icecap
- Re-visiting Art Nouveau in the charming town of Ålesund
- Jazzing it up at the Molde Jazz Festival

Sognefjorden

Sognefjorden, Norway's longest (204km) and deepest (1308m) fjord, cuts a deep slash across the map of western Norway. Sheer lofty walls rise more than 1000m above the water in some places, while in others, a gentler shoreline supports farms, orchards and small towns. The broad main waterway is impressive but by cruising into its narrower arms, such as the deep and lovely Nærøyfjord to Gudvangen, you'll have idyllic views of sheer cliff faces and cascading waterfalls.

For information, contact Sognefjorden (☎ 57 67 30 83, fax 57 67 28 06, e info@sognefjorden.no, W www.sognefjorden.no), Postboks 222, N-6852 Sogndal. Details on major tourist sites, activities and accommodation are found on the Web site and in the series of *Sognefjorden* brochures, which are distributed free at most tourist offices, train stations and bus terminals. In addition, each district in the region has an exhaustive number of publications detailing accommodation, sites of interest and mind-boggling numbers of hiking possibilities in their respective areas.

Getting There & Away

From mid-May to mid-September, Fylkesbåtane (☎ 55 90 70 70, fax 55 90 70 71,

e fsf@fylkesb.no) operates a daily express boat between Bergen and Flåm, near the head of the Sognefjord, stopping at 11 small towns along the way. It leaves Bergen at 8am daily and arrives in Flåm (Nkr490, 5½ hours) at 1.25pm. Stops en route include Balestrand (Nkr355, four hours), Vangsnes

WESTERN FJORDS

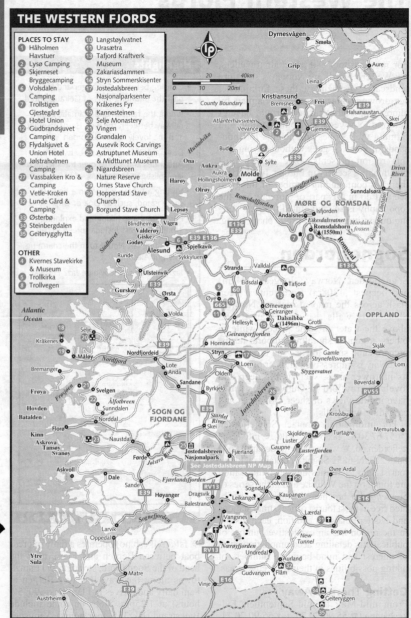

THE WESTERN FJORDS

PLACES TO STAY
1. Håholmen Havstuer
2. Lysø Camping
3. Skjerneset Bryggecamping
6. Volsdalen Camping
7. Trollstigen Gjestegård
9. Hotel Union
12. Gudbrandsjuvet Camping
16. Flydalsjuvet & Union Hotel
24. Jølstraholmen Camping
27. Vassbakken Kro & Camping
28. Vetle-Kroken
32. Lunde Gård & Camping
33. Østerbø
34. Steinbergdalen
35. Geiterygghytta

10. Langstøylvatnet
11. Urasætra
13. Tafjord Kraftverk Museum
15. Zakariasdammen
16. Stryn Sommerskisenter
17. Jostedalsbreen Nasjonalparksenter
18. Kråkenes Fyr
19. Kannesteinen
20. Selje Monastery
21. Vingen
22. Grøndalen
23. Ausevik Rock Carvings
25. Astruptunet Museum & Midttunet Museum
26. Nigardsbreen Nature Reserve
29. Urnes Stave Church
30. Hopperstad Stave Church
31. Borgund Stave Church

OTHER
4. Kvernes Stavekirke & Museum
5. Trollkirka
8. Trollvegen

(Nkr355, 4¼ hours) and Aurland (Nkr485, 5¼ hours). The return boat leaves Flåm at 3.30pm, arriving in Bergen at 8.40pm. Students and InterRail pass holders get a 50% discount. Numerous local ferries also link Sognefjord towns, and there's an extensive (if infrequent) bus network.

Getting Around
To traverse the fjord region from Flåm to Stryn/Ålesund (Nkr344/430 including ferries, seven/10½ hours), take the Nor-Way Bussekspress (direction Lillehammer) at noon, change to the Sogndal bus at the north end of Lærdalstunnelen at 12.40pm and arrive in Sogndal at 1.35pm. Buses run directly from Sogndal to Ålesund (departing 4.20pm, daily except Saturday) and Stryn (departing 4.20pm daily, with a possible change at Skei).

FLÅM
pop 400
Tiny Flåm, at the head of Aurlandsfjord, occupies a spectacular setting and, as a stop on the popular 'Norway in a Nutshell' tour, it probably sees more foreign tourists than any other village of its size in Norway. The tourist office (☎ 57 63 21 06), at the train station, opens 8.30am to 8pm daily June to August (shorter hours in May and September). The post office and an ATM are nearby.

Organised Tours
Although most visitors do 'Norway in a Nutshell' from either Oslo or Bergen (see Organised Tours in the Getting Around chapter), you can also do a mini version from Flåm. The circle route by boat to Gudvangen, bus to Voss and rail back to Myrdal and Flåm costs Nkr380/190 per adult/child. Alternatively, you can travel by boat and bus to the glaciers and museum in Fjærland daily except Sunday, mid-May to mid-August (Nkr585). Either can be booked at the tourist office.

Places to Stay & Eat
Flåm Camping og Vandrerhjem (☎ 57 63 21 21, fax 57 63 23 80) Tent sites Nkr75-100, dorm beds Nkr105, singles/doubles from Nkr200/300, cabins Nkr375-650. Open 1 May-1 Oct. This friendly camping ground and hostel has good facilities and is only a few minutes' walk from the station.

Heimly Pensjonat (☎ 57 63 23 00, fax 57 63 23 40) Singles/doubles from Nkr350/690. At Heimly Pensjonat, you'll get straightforward rooms but a great fjord view. Breakfast is included.

Fretheim Hotel (☎ 57 63 63 00, fax 57 63 64 00) Singles/doubles from Nkr640/960. The recently renovated Fretheim Hotel has en suite rooms and a restaurant.

Furukroa (☎ 57 63 23 25) Mains Nkr78-100, pizza Nkr150-180. The rustic-looking place at the ferry dock serves all culinary levels from snacks to full meals, including fish and chips and lasagne.

Togrestauranten (☎ 57 63 21 55) Mains Nkr85-115. Near the station, this novel restaurant is housed in several wooden rail cars. Some traditional Norwegian dishes and vegetarian choices are served.

Self-caterers will find a *Coop* supermarket behind Togrestauranten.

Getting There & Away
Bus Daily buses connect Flåm, Gudvangen (Nkr30, 20 minutes), Aurland (Nkr23, 10 minutes) and Lærdal (Nkr60, 50 minutes), some commencing at Undredal, but you won't see much of the spectacular scenery. Most of these routes are inside particularly long tunnels.

Train Flåm is the only Sognefjorden village with a rail link, and for many visitors, the 20.2km Flåmbanen railway is a highlight. This engineering wonder descends 865m at a gradient of 1:18 from Myrdal on the bleak and treeless Hardangervidda plateau, past thundering waterfalls (there's a photo stop at awesome Kjosfossen), to the relatively lush and tranquil Aurlandsfjord. It runs up to 10 times daily in summer (Nkr120/200 single/return, one hour), with connections to Oslo-Bergen services at Myrdal and to the Gudvangen ferry and the Sognefjorden ferries from Flåm. For information, phone Flåm station (☎ 57 63 21 00) or NSB in Myrdal (☎ 57 63 27 00).

Boat From Flåm, boats head out to towns around Sognefjorden. The most scenic trip from Flåm is the ferry up Nærøyfjorden to Gudvangen (Nkr160/200 one-way/return), which leaves at 3pm daily year-round and also at 9am, 11am and 1.15pm mid-June to mid-August. At Gudvangen, a connecting bus takes you on to Voss. All ferry tickets and the ferry-bus combination from Flåm to Voss (Nkr230) are sold at the tourist office (this is part of the popular 'Norway in a Nutshell' tour).

In addition to the at least once daily Sognefjorden express boat between Flåm and Bergen (Nkr490, 5½ hours), Vangsnes (Nkr145, 1¾ hours) and Balestrand (Nkr170, 1½ to two hours), the Flåmekspressen boat runs once daily except weekends between Flåm, Aurland (Nkr50, 10 minutes), Undredal (Nkr48, 25 minutes, advance booking required) and Sogndal (Nkr145, 1½ hours).

Getting Around
The tourist office rents bikes (Nkr30/175 per hour/day) and boats. The docks are just beyond the train station.

UNDREDAL
pop 130
If you're driving, the small goat-cheese producing village of Undredal, midway between Flåm and Gudvangen, makes an interesting short stop. The tiny **village church** (☎ 57 63 33 13, Undredal; admission Nkr15; open variable hours mid-May–mid-Sept), originally built as a stave church in 1147, is the smallest still-operational house of worship in mainland Scandinavia. For Nkr59, you can buy the Undredalskortet (Undredal Card), which provides a guided tour of the church, goat-cheese tasting at Underdalsbui and coffee and waffles at Undredal Brygge.

Also of interest is the farm **Stigen** (☎ 94 48 17 58 to arrange a visit), dating from 1603; the access path is so steep that a ladder was required to reach it (the ladder was conveniently removed whenever tax collectors were about). Hikers can follow the steep, one-day route from Langhuso to the DNT mountain hut at Grindafletene, where

other walking routes lead to Stalheim, Mjølfjell, Uppsete and Flåm.

Avoid the crowds in Flåm by camping in Undredal or staying at **Undredal Brygge** (☎/fax 57 63 17 45, Undredal), where a cabin or apartment costs Nkr700. The attached **cafeteria** serves snacks, lunches and dinners for Nkr80 to Nkr140.

GUDVANGEN & NÆRØYFJORDEN
pop 100
Nærøyfjorden lies west of Flåm and provides a vision of archetypal Norway: a deep blue fjord (as narrow as 500m in places), towering 1200m-high cliffs, isolated farms, and waterfalls plummeting from the heights above. It can be easily visited as a day excursion from Flåm.

Kjelsfossen waterfall, the fourth or tenth highest in the world depending on criteria (840m or 561m respectively, but the greatest vertical drop is only 149m), descends from the southern wall of Nærøydalen valley and is easily seen from Gudvangen village. Also look out for the **avalanche protection scheme** above Gudvangen. The powerful avalanches here typically provide a force of 12 tonnes per sq metre, move at 50m per second and have been known to blow a herd of goats across the fjord!

Kayak hire (Nkr275 per day) and kayak tours (from Nkr890 per day) are available from Nordic Ventures (☎ 56 51 00 17).

Gudvangen Fjordtell (☎ 57 63 39 29, fax 57 63 39 80, Gudvangen) Singles/doubles from Nkr570/790. Cafeteria menu Nkr82-94, 3-course dinner Nkr189. The highly recommended modern Viking-themed Gudvangen Fjordtell has good rates and an impressive glassed-in restaurant offering some of the best food and views in Norway.

Ferries between Gudvangen and Flåm (Nkr160/200 one-way/return) via Aurland leave daily at 11.30am, 12.35pm and 4pm from June to August (also at 5.10pm in May and September). The car ferry to/from Kaupanger costs Nkr150/370 per adult/car. Buses run to Flåm (Nkr30, 20 minutes), Aurland (Nkr45, 30 minutes) and Voss (Nkr70, 50 minutes).

AURLAND
pop 1000

Aurland is best known as the end of the popular and scenic Aurlandsdalen hiking route. The world's longest road tunnel (24.5km) connects Aurland and Lærdal. It provides a fast alternative to the scenic but sinuous **Snøvegen** (Snow Road; open 1 June to mid-October), which climbs and twists precipitously to the high plateau (1309m) that separates the two towns, with incredible views all the way.

Between Flåm and Aurland, the early-17th-century farm **Otternes** *(adult/child Nkr30/free; open 10am-6pm daily mid-June–mid-August)*, has 27 restored buildings.

The Aurland og Lærdal Reiselivslag (☎ 57 53 33 13, **W** www.alr.no) dispenses tourist information year-round and is open daily June to August.

Hiking

The famous route down Aurlandsdalen from Geiteryggen to Aurland follows one of the oldest trading routes between eastern and western Norway. In summer, you can start this four-day walk in Finse, on the Oslo-Bergen rail line, with overnight stops at Geiterygghytta, Steinbergdalen and Østerbø. But many people walk only the most scenic section, from Østerbø to Vassbygdi, which can easily be done as a day hike and cuts out a lamentably disagreeable trip down the Aurlandsdalen road past tangles of power lines.

From the rambling Østerbø complex, the route heads down-valley to Tirtesva, where it splits. The best option (a short cut of sorts) climbs to Bjørnstigen, at 1000m, and continues briefly to the route's signature view down the valley before it begins to descend steeply. An hour later, however, the descent grows more gentle and heads for the river far below; from there to the Vassbygdi power station, the track follows the river, passing waterfalls and sections blasted from sheer rock.

The lower sections of this route are open roughly between early June and late September. From Vassbygdi (Nkr23, 15 minutes) and Østerbø (Nkr49, one hour), buses run to Aurland three times daily.

Places to Stay & Eat

Lunde Gard & Camping *(☎ 57 63 34 12, fax 57 63 31 65)* Tent/caravan sites Nkr60/80 plus Nkr15 per adult, cabins Nkr300-600. Campers should head for this acceptable riverside place 1.4km up the valley.

Aurland Fjordhotell *(☎ 57 63 35 05, fax 57 63 36 22)* Singles/doubles from Nkr580/790. Mains Nkr135-225, 4-course dinner Nkr325. The comfortable and modern Aurland Fjordhotell has en suite rooms with fjord views.

Vangsgaarden *(☎ 57 63 35 80, fax 57 63 35 95)* Singles/doubles from Nkr260/360, breakfast Nkr70. This complex consists of the 1772 Vangen Motel, the mid-18th-century Aabelheim Inn, five sea cottages and the *Duehuset (Dovecot) Café & Pub*.

Getting There & Away

Buses run two to 11 times daily (fewer at weekends) between Aurland and Flåm (Nkr23, 10 minutes) and one to three times daily between Aurland and Lærdal (Nkr52, 30 minutes). Buses to/from Bergen (Nkr220, 3¼ hours) run two to eight times daily.

Drivers should note that there are speed cameras in Lærdalstunnelen.

LÆRDAL & BORGUND
pop 2200

Since the opening of Lærdalstunnelen, visitor numbers have increased, with more people than ever heading for the Borgund stave church, about 30km up the valley from Lærdal. Lærdalsøyri, at the fjord-end of town, makes for pleasant strolling through the collection of intact 18th- and 19th-century timber homes. The tourist office (☎ 57 66 65 09), Øyraplassen 7, is open 8.30am to 7.30pm Monday to Saturday, noon to 7.30pm Sunday from mid-June to mid-August, with shorter hours the rest of the year.

Norsk Villakssenter

The museum-like Wild Salmon Centre *(☎ 57 66 67 71, fax 57 66 66 82, Lærdal; adult/child Nkr70/35; open 10am-7pm daily June-Aug, shorter hours May & Sept)* reveals all you'd ever want to know about

WESTERN FJORDS

Tunnels in Norway

Visitors to Norway are usually impressed by the civil engineering wonders that dominate road transport around the country, particularly in the Western Fjords, Nordland and the Far North. The most extraordinary road tunnels include ones that spiral upwards through mountains, pass deep under the sea to reach offshore islands or bore through mountains which are buried underneath glaciers.

In November 2000, after nearly six years of construction, the world's longest road tunnel, from Lærdal to Aurland (24.51km long, 7.59km longer than the St Gotthard tunnel in Switzerland), was completed at a total cost of Nkr1082 million. There are no tolls to use the tunnel since it was paid for entirely by the national government. The two-lane tunnel, part of the vital E16 road connecting Oslo and Bergen, reduces the difficulties of winter driving and replaces the lengthy Gudvangen-Lærdal ferry route. It was drilled through very hard pre-Cambrian gneiss, with over 1400m of overhead rock at one point. There's a treatment plant for dust and nitrogen dioxide in the tunnel, 34 gigantic ventilation fans, emergency telephones every 500m and three bizarre 'galleries' with blue lighting to 'liven up' the 20-minute trip.

Motorists should tune into NRK radio P1 when driving through the tunnel (yes, there are transmitters inside!) in case of emergency.

Other long road tunnels in Norway include: Gudvangentunnelen in Sogn og Fjordane (11.428km, also on the E16); Folgefonntunnelen in Hardanger (11.15km, on Rv551 and passing beneath the Folgefonn icecap); Steigentunnelen in Nordland (8.062km, Rv835); and Svartisentunnelen in Nordland (7.614km, on Rv17 and passing beneath the Svartisen icecap).

Interesting undersea tunnels, which typically bore around 40m below the sea bed, include: Oslofjordtunnelen (7.2km, on Rv23, south of Oslo); Nordkapptunnelen (6.875km, on the E69 and connecting Magerøya island to the mainland); Byfjordtunnelen (5.86km, on the E39 just north of Stavanger); and Nappstraumen tunnel (1.78km, on the E10 and linking Vestvågøy and Flakstadøy in Lofoten).

the Atlantic salmon and its peculiar migration and breeding habits. You can watch wild salmon in the river through viewing windows, see a film about the salmon's lifecycle and learn to tie flies to attract the fish to the angler's hook.

Borgund Stave Church

Most visitors come to see the 12th-century Borgund stave church (☎ 57 67 88 40, *Borgund; adult/child Nkr50/25; open 8am-8pm daily June–mid-Aug, 10am-5pm May & mid-Aug–Sept)*, built beside one of the major trade routes between eastern and western Norway and dedicated to St Andrew. Not only is it one of the best-known and most-photographed of Norway's stave churches, it's also the best-preserved. Inside, there's a late 16th-century pulpit and an early 17th-century altar painting.

A recommended two-hour circular hike on ancient paths and tracks, via Sverrestigen and Vindhella, starts at the church.

Buses run around five times daily between Lærdal, Borgund and Borlaug.

Places to Stay & Eat

Offerdal Hotel (☎ 57 66 61 01, *fax 57 66 62 25, Øyraplassen 9, Lærdal)* Singles/doubles Nkr625/750. This hotel is ordinary but adequate.

Borlaug Vandrerhjem (☎ 57 66 87 80, *fax 57 66 87 44, Borlaug)* Dorm beds Nkr110, singles/doubles Nkr180/270. Breakfast Nkr50, 2-course dinner Nkr85. This friendly roadside hostel is 10km east of Borgund. It serves good meals and is frequented by hikers.

Bjøraker Camping (☎ 57 66 87 20, *Borlaug)* Tent & caravan sites Nkr50 plus Nkr10 per person, cabins Nkr200-250. This is a good grassy camping site with 15 cabins.

Potter's Kafé & Konditori (☎ 57 66 68 01, *Øyragata 15)* Most mains Nkr50-100. Potter's serves good chicken dishes, pies, pizzas, omelettes and burgers.

Getting There & Away

Many people enjoy driving the 45km-long Snøvegen between Aurland and Lærdal, which climbs from sea level to 1309m. Buses to/from Bergen (Nkr260, 3¾ hours) and Stryn (Nkr230, four hours) run one to four times daily. See also the Aurland section earlier.

VANGSNES

pop 200

The farming community of Vangsnes, across the fjord from Balestrand, is probably best known for the 12m-high hilltop statue of saga hero Fridtjof the Intrepid, erected in 1913 by Kaiser Wilhelm of Germany. The statue – and a pretty good view of Sognefjord – lie 1.5km uphill along the road from the ferry landing. Legend has it that Fridtjof is buried nearby.

A few minutes inland from the ferry quay, *Solvang Camping* (☎ 57 69 66 20, fax 57 69 67 55) offers tent sites for Nkr40/60 without/with car, while cabins and rooms are Nkr300 to Nkr600. *Sognefjord Gjestehus* (☎ 57 69 67 22, fax 57 69 62 75) has a B&B for Nkr260 to Nkr340 per person and there's an attached supermarket and cafe/pub. Otherwise, for meals you're limited to the ferry terminal snack bar, where pizzas start at Nkr69.

Ferries frequently shuttle to/from Hella (Nkr19, 15 minutes) and Dragsvik (Nkr21, 30 minutes).

VIK

pop 1300

The factory village of Vik boasts the splendid **Hopperstad stave church** (☎ 56 67 88 40, Hopperstad; adult/child Nkr40/free; open 10am-5pm daily mid-May–mid-Sept, 9am-7pm mid-June–mid-Aug), about 1km south of the centre. It was built in 1130 and barely escaped demolition in the late 19th century; it's now one of the country's finest examples of this medieval design. For an additional Nkr10, you can use the same ticket for the Hove stone church, 1km away, which dates from 1170.

Tourist information can be obtained from Vik & Vangsnes Reiselivslag (☎ 57 69 56 86), 150m from the express boat terminal in central Vik. There's a collection of boats and boat engines here.

Frequent local buses run to and from Vangsnes (Nkr23, 15 minutes). Buses also run once or twice daily to Sogndal (Nkr67, 1½ hours) and Bergen (Nkr220, 3¼ hours).

BALESTRAND

pop 1000

Balestrand, the main Sognefjorden resort destination, enjoys a mountain backdrop and a genteel but low-key atmosphere. For information and Internet access (Nkr20 for 15 minutes), contact Balestrand tourist office (☎ 57 69 12 55), by the ferry quay. It's open 8.30am to 9pm daily late June to mid-August, otherwise shorter hours.

Things to See

The road running south along the fjord, lined with apple orchards and ornate older homes and gardens, sees little vehicular traffic and is conducive to quiet strolling. In the town centre, the intriguing **Church of St Olav** *(closed to public)* was constructed in 1897 by English expatriate Margaret Green, of Leeds, who married Norwegian mountaineer and hotel-owner Knut Kvikne. She insisted that it be built to resemble a medieval stave church.

Less than 1km south along the fjord, excavation of two **Viking-age burial mounds** revealed remnants of a boat, two skeletons, jewellery and several weapons. One mound is topped by a statue of legendary **King Bele**, erected by Germany's Kaiser Wilhelm II, who was obsessed with Nordic mythology and regularly spent his holidays here prior to WWI (a similar monument honouring Fridtjof, the lover of King Bele's daughter, rises across the fjord in Vangsnes). A 2km-long cultural trail follows the coast past these sites.

For those after a longer hike, take the small ferry (Nkr10) across Esefjord to the Dragsvik side, where an abandoned country road forms the first leg of an 8km walk back to Balestrand. There's also the 1km **Granlia forest nature trail**, located just above the Rv55 tunnel.

Near the ferry dock is the **Sognefjord Akvarium** (☎ 57 69 13 03; admission Nkr25, including a free hour of canoe or rowing boat hire; open 10am-4pm daily mid-Apr–May & mid-Aug–Oct, 9.30am-6pm daily mid-June–mid-Aug), which features a saltwater fish exhibit. An audiovisual presentation, accompanied by local folk music, reveals the history of upper Sognefjorden.

Places to Stay & Eat

Sjøtun Camping (☎ 57 69 12 23) Tent without/with car Nkr30/40, 4-bunk cabin Nkr200. At Sjøtun Camping, a 15-minute walk south along the fjord, you can pitch a tent amid apple trees or rent a rustic cabin.

Balestrand Vandrerhjem Kringsjå (☎ 57 69 13 03, fax 57 69 16 70) Dorm beds Nkr180, doubles Nkr520. Dinner Nkr110. Open 26 June-18 Aug. This fine lodge-style place offers hostel accommodation and a variety of meals, including soup and meat and fish dishes. Breakfast is included.

Midtnes Pensjonat (☎ 57 69 11 33, fax 57 69 15 84) Singles/doubles from Nkr525/650. Beside the English Church of St Olav, this place is popular with returning British holiday-makers. Breakfast is included.

Balestrand Pensjonat (☎ 57 69 11 38, fax 57 69 17 11) Singles/doubles Nkr520/650. Near the church, Balestrand Pensjonat is a comfortable, modern place.

Kvikne's Hotel (☎ 57 69 42 00, fax 57 69 42 01) Singles Nkr670-1185, doubles Nkr880-1910, extra Nkr75/150 per person for fjord view in the annexe/main building. If money is no object, the pale yellow timber-built Kvikne's Hotel, right on the point near the ferry landing, provides a taste of mid-19th-century retro luxury. Guests have use of the jacuzzi, billiards room, fitness room and sauna, as well as a boat and fishing gear.

Balholm Bar og Bistro (☎ 57 69 42 00, Kvikne's Hotel) Snacks & light meals Nkr35-155, dinner mains Nkr215-295, buffet Nkr345. Snacks, sandwiches, pasta dishes, steaks and vegetarian choices are available in the hotel's upmarket dining room.

The **Joker** supermarket is opposite the ferry dock; behind it, a **cafe** serves soup

and a roll for Nkr39, burgers, chips and salad for Nkr68 and larger main courses from Nkr79 to Nkr119.

Getting There & Away

Buses travel between Balestrand and Sogndal (Nkr83, 1¼ hours) and Bergen (Nkr205, four hours). The latter departs from Vik, reached by boat (Nkr48, 15 minutes), departing Balestrand 7.55am Monday to Saturday.

Express boats to/from Bergen (Nkr355, four hours) sail twice daily except Sunday, and to/from Sogndal (Nkr105, 45 minutes) once or twice daily. A popular local ferry runs twice daily, from 25 May to 9 September, up the narrow Fjærlandsfjorden to Fjærland (Nkr130/170 one-way/return, 1¼ hours), which is the gateway to the glacial wonderlands of Jostedalsbreen. For Nkr345, you'll get a return on the ferry, bus to the glacier museum, museum admission and bus to the glacier.

Motorists can drive the scenic Gaularfjellsvegen (Rv13) to Førde, on Førdefjord, negotiating hairpin bends and skirting Norway's greatest concentration of roadside waterfalls.

Getting Around

The tourist office hires out bicycles for Nkr75/125 per half/full day.

SOGNDAL
pop 3000

The modern regional centre of Sogndal is a good base for various attractions in the area. The tourist office (☎ 57 67 30 83), a five-minute walk east of the bus station, books cabins, chalets and rooms in private homes from Nkr150 per person. Ask for the list of 16 local hillwalks and details of seaplane flights over the glaciers.

At the extensive **Sogn Folkmuseum** (☎ 57 67 82 06, Vestreim; adult/child Nkr50/25, including guiding in English; open 10am-6pm daily June-Aug, shorter hours May & Sept) there are 40 buildings covering 600 years of local history and an interesting exhibition. Constructed in 1184, **Kaupanger stave church** (☎ 57 67 88 40, Kaupanger;

adult/child Nkr30/free; open 9.30am-5.30pm daily June–mid-Aug) reveals a wonderfully ornate interior shaped like an upturned Viking ship. The wall paintings featuring music notes and the Irish-style chancel arch are quite extraordinary.

Sogndal Vandrerhjem *(☎ 57 67 20 33, fax 57 67 31 45)* Dorm beds Nkr100, singles/doubles Nkr165/230. Open mid-June–mid-Aug. This modern and well-equipped hostel, a 15-minute walk east of the bus terminal, charges Nkr50 extra for breakfast.

Vesterland Feriepark *(☎ 57 62 71 00, fax 57 62 72 00, Kaupanger)* Chalets Nkr670-995. Located 10km east of town on Rv5, this excellent and highly organised holiday park offers luxurious cabins, a pleasant restaurant, and free Internet facilities for guests.

Compagniet *(☎ 57 62 77 00, Hotel Sogndal, Gravensteinsgaten 5)* Buffet Nkr220. The hotel restaurant has great evening buffets, but there's also a cheaper section with some meals under Nkr100.

There's a cheap cafeteria in the ***Domus*** supermarket on Gravensteinsgaten.

Sogndal has Sognefjord's only airport. Local buses run between Sogndal, Kaupanger (Nkr23, 10 minutes, hourly), Fjærland (Nkr78, 45 minutes, two to six daily) and Balestrand (Nkr98, 1¼ hours, six to nine daily) and twice daily buses (17 June to 26 August) also head north-east past Jotunheimen National Park to Lom (Nkr185, 3½ hours) and Otta (Nkr255, 4½ hours). Boats connect Sogndal, Balestrand (Nkr105, 45 minutes, once or twice daily) and Bergen (Nkr430, 4½ hours, once daily).

SKJOLDEN
pop 600
Skjolden, on Lustrafjorden at the inner end of Sognefjorden, presents a surprisingly pleasant atmosphere. In Fjordstova, you'll find most things under one roof: the tourist office (☎ 57 68 67 50, fax 57 68 67 88), open 11am to 7pm daily, 25 June to 10 August (shorter hours other times); the post office; a cafe; souvenir shop; library (Internet access costs Nkr25 per half-hour); swimming pool (Nkr30 per session); and believe it or not, a climbing wall (Nkr40 per day,

Nkr40 for equipment and Nkr100 per hour of instruction). The bit of industrial-looking junk on display outside is a turbine from the Norsk Hydro power station.

About 2km east of Skjolden is the lovely turquoise glacial lake **Eidsvatnet**. The valley **Mørkridsdalen**, which runs north of the village is good for hiking.

Skjolden Vandrerhjem *(☎ 57 68 66 15, fax 57 68 12 14)* Dorm beds Nkr90, singles/doubles Nkr170/230. Open mid-June–Aug. The hostel partly occupies an old bakery, conveniently located 100m from the Fjordstova complex.

Vassbakken Kro & Camping *(☎ 57 68 61 88, fax 57 68 61 85)* Tent/caravan with car sites Nkr100, 2-bed cabins with basic cooking facilities without/with en suite Nkr320/550. Farther up the valley towards Fortun, this place has very nice sites. Meals are also available (mains Nkr80 to Nkr120).

Fjordstova Café *(☎ 57 68 67 50, Fjordstova complex)* Snacks & meals under Nkr75. This place grills up pretty good burgers or soup and bread for just Nkr40.

Bus No 155 connects Skjolden with Sogndal (Nkr78, 1¼ hours) and Fortun (Nkr20, 10 minutes) up to six times daily. Skjolden is also on the twice-daily summer bus route between Otta and Sogndal (see the earlier Sogndal section).

Note that the petrol stations are the last petrol supplies for 77km on Rv55 north.

URNES
pop 40
Norwegian poet Paal-Helge Hauge wrote of Urnes stave church: 'Someone came here, shouldering a man's load of visions, spread them out over the walls and pillars, gaping beasts angels' wings, dragons out under the knife the hand the brush, tendrils of ochre, red, grey, white, a sinuous short way from paradise to damnation…' For its unique and elaborate wooden ornamentation, well described by Hauge, the **stave church** *(☎ 57 68 39 45; adult/family Nkr40/80; open 10.30am-5.30pm daily 10 June-28 Aug)* at Urnes has been named one of Norway's four sites on Unesco's World Heritage List. This lovely structure overlooking Lusterfjord

was probably built between 1130 and 1150, making it one of the oldest stave churches in Norway. However, there have been several

Stave Churches

Most of Norway's 31 stave churches date from the 12th and 13th centuries, but two are modern reconstructions. Among the oldest, Urnes in Sogn og Fjordane, is reckoned to date from around 1130 to 1150.

Construction began by laying down horizontal sills above ground level on a raised stone foundation, on which the vertical plank walls rested. At each corner is an upright stave post – hence the name of the style – which ties together the sill below and a wall plate above.

Most stave church interiors include little more than a small nave and a narrow chancel although, in some, the nave and chancel are combined into a single rectangular space, divided only by a chancel screen. The most elaborate stave church still standing, at Borgund, includes not only a nave and chancel, but also a semi-circular apse at the eastern end. The roof of the nave is supported by freestanding posts spaced about 2m apart and standing about 1m from the walls, although smaller churches had just one central post. All remaining stave churches are surrounded by outer walls, creating external galleries or passageways. Their longevity is due to the galleries protecting the walls and the use of tar on the roofs as a preservative.

Interior walls are often painted in elaborate designs, including *rosemaling*, or traditional rose paintings, and the complex roof lines are frequently enhanced by scalloped wooden shingles and Viking-age dragon head finials, which are surprisingly reminiscent of Thai wats. Perhaps the most renowned and intricate enhancements, however, are the wooden carvings on the support posts, door frames and outer walls (especially at Urnes), which represent tendrils of stems, vines and leaves entwined with serpents, dragons and other fantasy creatures. For its creators, this artistry not only promoted an inspired effect, but also successfully meshed Norway's proud pagan past with its new Christian directions.

alterations through the ages and it's likely that the unique and elaborate carvings that cover its gables, pillars, doorframes and several strips on the outer wall were transferred from an 11th-century building that once stood here.

Vetle-Kroken (☎ 57 68 37 50, e info-sg@vetle-kroken.com, Kroken) Bunkhouse with use of kitchen facilities Nkr400-600. Vetle-Kroken, 8km north-east of the stave church, offers self-catering *stabbur* bunkhouse accommodation. The main activity here is sea kayaking, and kayak tours (Nkr190 for a sampling; Nkr390 for half-day trips; and Nkr3750 for four-day tours) are available. You can also rent kayaks from Nkr200/1350 per day/week.

The best public transport access is on the M/F *Urnes* car ferry between Solvorn and Urnes (Nkr22/60 passenger/car, 20 minutes). The Solvorn ferry terminal is reached on bus No 155, which calls in at Solvorn on its frequent runs between Sogndal (Nkr30, 25 minutes) and Skjolden (Nkr56, 1¼ hours). From the Urnes ferry landing, it's a 1km uphill walk to the stave church.

Jostedalsbreen

With a total area of 487 sq km, the many-tongued Jostedalsbreen dominates the highlands of Sogn og Fjordane county and is mainland Norway's largest icecap. In places, the ice is 400m thick and reaches 1950m above sea level. In 1991, the main icecap and several nearby outliers were set aside for protection as the Jostedalsbreen National Park. For national park information, contact Statens naturoppsyn (☎ 57 87 72 00), N-6799 Oppstryn.

The best hiking map for the region is Statens Kartverk's *Jostedalsbreen Turkart*, at a scale of 1:100,000 (Nkr110). You'll also get help at local tourist offices, as well as Norsk Bremuseum in Fjærland; Jostedal Breheimsenteret in Jostedalen; and Jostedalsbreen Nasjonalparksenter near Stryn.

For more details on the gateway towns of Skei, Olden, Loen and Stryn, see the Sognefjord to Nordfjord section later in this chapter.

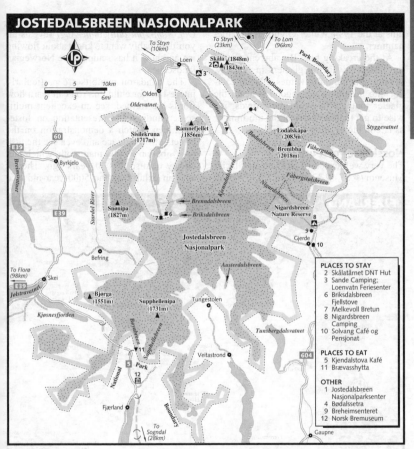

JOSTEDALSBREEN NASJONALPARK

PLACES TO STAY
2 Skålatårnet DNT Hut
3 Sande Camping;
   Loenvatn Feriesenter
6 Briksdalsbreen
   Fjellstove
7 Melkevoll Bretun
8 Nigardsbreen
   Camping
10 Solvang Café og
   Pensjonat

PLACES TO EAT
5 Kjendalstova Kafé
11 Brævasshytta

OTHER
1 Jostedalsbreen
   Nasjonalparksenter
4 Bødalssetra
9 Breheimsenteret
12 Norsk Bremuseum

FJÆRLAND
pop 300

The farming village of Fjærland, at the head of scenic Fjærlandsfjorden, lies near two particularly accessible glacial tongues, Supphellebreen and Bøyabreen. For that reason, it's one of Norway's best-attended sites, attracting upwards of 100,000 visitors a year. In 1996, however, hoping to diversify its tourist appeal, Fjærland declared itself the 'Book Town' of Norway. Now this tiny place boasts around 14 shops selling a wide range of used books mostly in Norwegian but also in English, French, German and other lan-

guages. An annual book fair is held on the Saturday nearest 23 June. If you're after something specific, contact Den Norske Bokbyen (☎ 57 69 22 10, e post@bokbyen.no).

Information

The Fjærland Info (☎ 57 69 32 33, fax 57 69 32 11) tourist office, which doubles as a bookshop, is on the main street in Mundal. It's open daily June to August.

Supphellebreen & Bøyabreen

You can drive to within 500m of Supphellebreen and walk right up and touch the ice. Ice blocks from here were used as podiums at the 1994 Winter Olympics in Lillehammer.

At the creaking blue Bøyabreen, one of the fastest advancing glaciers in Norway, it's not uncommon to witness glacial calving into the meltwater lagoon beneath the glacier tongue. To avoid the crowds, it's wise to get there as early in the morning or as late in the evening as possible.

Norsk Bremuseum
The very well executed Norwegian Glacier Museum (☎ 57 69 32 88; adult/child Nkr75/ 35; open 10am-4pm daily Apr-May & Sept-Oct, 9am-7pm daily June-Aug) reveals all you'd probably want to know about flowing ice and how it has sculpted the Norwegian landscape.

The hands-on exhibits are particularly interesting for children. You can learn how fjords are formed, see an excellent multi-screen audiovisual presentation on Jostedalsbreen, watch a demonstration on the effects of flowing ice and even see the tusk of a Siberian woolly mammoth, which met an icy demise 30,000 years ago. There's also an exhibit on the 5000-year-old 'Ice

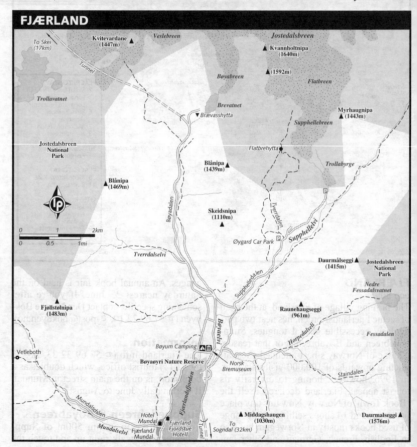

Man' corpse, which was found on the Austrian-Italian border in 1991.

Hiking
The essential map of the region, complete with descriptions of 11 major hiking routes, is *Turkart Fjærland*, at a scale of 1:50,000 (Nkr60). After you complete four of these 11 tours, the local sports association will register your achievement and issue a diploma!

Organised Tours
From Balestrand, ferries leave for Fjærland at 8.15am. There, a bus runs to the glacier (Nkr110 return), stopping en route at the Norsk Bremuseum and visiting both glacier tongues before returning to the ferry. Alternatively, a taxi from the Fjærland dock to the glacier, with waiting time, costs about Nkr350 return.

From 1 July to 10 August, guided glacier trips (☎ 57 69 32 92) on Supphellebreen start from the Øygard car park, north-east of the Bremuseum, at 9am on weekdays, but at least five persons are required. These trips, including climbs up to Kvanneholtnipa (1640m), are more difficult hikes than you'll find at other Jostedalsbreen glacier tongues. A number of other glacier routes and climbs can also be arranged through the same outfit.

Places to Stay & Eat
Bøyum Camping (☎ 57 69 32 52, fax 57 69 29 57) Dorm mattresses Nkr100, tent camping Nkr95, doubles Nkr250-300, 6-bed cabins Nkr530-630. Hostel-style accommodation, camping and cabins are available near the Norsk Bremuseum.

Ms Haugen's rooms (☎ 57 69 32 43, Mundal) Doubles Nkr300. Behind the 1861 church, Ms Alma Haugen rents rooms.

Fjærland Fjordstue Hotell (☎ 57 69 32 00, fax 57 69 31 61, Mundal) Singles/doubles from Nkr650/800. This hotel offers fine rooms with great views. Three-course dinners cost Nkr250.

Hotel Mundal (☎ 57 69 31 01, fax 57 69 31 79, ℮ hotelmundal@fjordinfo.no, Mundal) Singles/doubles from Nkr780/1190. Open mid-May–mid-Sept. This excellent

upmarket option, built in 1891 and run by the same family ever since, features a lovely round tower and a welcoming lounge. The dining room, which sports an evocative 1898 map of Sognefjorden, serves laudable traditional four-course Norwegian dinners for Nkr310 to Nkr360 (bookings necessary for non-residents).

The *Brævasshytta* (☎ 57 69 32 96, Bøyabreen) tourist cafeteria opens daily from May to September and serves filled rolls (Nkr16 to Nkr36), light meals (Nkr40 to Nkr87) and dinners (Nkr92 to Nkr130). You'll also find a good *cafeteria* at the glacier museum.

Getting There & Away
Three to seven daily buses connect Fjærland and Sogndal (Nkr78, 45 minutes). There are also daily buses to/from Stryn (Nkr175, two hours), including a 4.50pm bus (Sunday to Friday) to Hellesylt (Nkr205, three hours), with boat connections to Geiranger. Ferries run between Balestrand and Fjærland (Nkr130/170 one-way/return, 1¼ hours, twice daily) from 25 May to 9 September.

If you're driving, prepare for a road toll blow-out to visit Fjærland. The big tunnels on either side of the town cost Nkr400 million to build and there's a punitive toll of Nkr145 to travel to/from Sogndal. However, the tunnel on the Skei road is free.

Getting Around
For bike hire, contact the tourist office (Nkr25/125 per hour/day) or Bøyum Camping (Nkr20/100).

NIGARDSBREEN
Among the Jostedalsbreen glacier tongues which are visible from below, Nigardsbreen is probably the most dramatic and easily visited, so it's a very popular visitor destination. If you find it all too touristy and have a vehicle, you can always nip farther up the road past the braided glacial streams at Fåbergstølsgrandane to the dam that creates the big glacial lake Styggevatnet. Along the way you'll find several scenic glacial tongues and valleys offering excellent wild hiking.

Jostedal Breheimsenteret

For some odd reason, the incongruous looking Breheimsenteret (☎ 57 68 32 50, Jostedal; adult/child Nkr50/20; open 10am-5pm daily May-20 June & 22 Aug-Sept, 9am-7pm daily 21 June-21 Aug), designed in the form of two ice peaks separated by a crevasse, is also called the 'Glacier Cathedral'. Although there's little religion here, the displays inside do tell the story of the formation and movement of glaciers and how they sculpt the landscape. There's also a new 20-minute film on the area and an exhibit on the girl Jostedalsrypa, the only survivor of the Black Death in Jostedal.

Organised Tours

Jostedalen Breførarlag (☎ 57 68 31 11, fax 57 68 31 65, e josbre@jostedalen-breforarlag.no), at Breheimsenteret, conducts several guided glacier tours. Family walks (minimum age five years) to the glacier snout, include the boat trip across the Nigardsvatnet and a short walk along the glacier tongue (one to 1½ hours, Nkr100). Two-hour walks on the ice (Nkr225) run at 11.30am daily in summer, with an additional departure at 2.30pm on weekdays from 22 June to 10 August.

Hardy four-hour guided blue-ice walks on the glacier cost Nkr300, including instruction and use of technical equipment. Departures from the lagoon car park are at 1pm daily, 22 May to 10 September, with an additional departure at 10.30am daily from 3 July to 10 August.

More challenging is the six- to seven-hour trip to Bergsetbreen, starting at 9.30am every Saturday from 7 July to 18 August (Nkr500).

Places to Stay & Eat

Nigardsbreen Camping (☎ 57 68 31 35, Jostedal) Tent/caravan camping Nkr75/85 including 2 persons & car. Cabins Nkr275. Camping and cabins are available by the entrance to the toll road 400m from Breheimsenteret.

Solvang Kafé og Pensjonat (☎ 57 68 31 19, fax 57 68 31 57, Jostedal) Singles/doubles from Nkr300/490. Five kilometres down the road from Breheimsenteret, in Gjerde village, you'll find this homely place with simple no-frills accommodation. Breakfast is included.

Gjerde Camping (☎ 57 68 31 54, fax 57 68 31 57, Gjerde) Cabins Nkr160-190. Camp sites and basic cabins are available at this place.

The Breheimsenteret has a small and rather expensive *cafe* with a view.

Getting There & Away

From 14 June to 30 August, bus No 159 connects Sogndal and Jostedal Breheimsenteret (Nkr90, 1¼ hours) four times daily on weekdays, three times on Sunday and once on Saturday. For much of the way from the Rv55 at Gaupne, the road to the glacier follows the brilliant turquoise blue Jostedalselva. Watch also for the brilliant red lichen which is splashed across the rocks along the route.

From Breheimsenteret, a 6km-long toll road (Nkr20 per vehicle) or a pleasant hike, lead to the car park at Nigardsvatnet, the lagoon at the glacial snout. From there, you can take the M/S *Jostedalsrypa* (☎ 94 50 61 67) over the lagoon to the glacier face. From mid-June to early September, it runs frequently between 10am and 6pm and costs Nkr15/20 one-way/return.

BRIKSDALSBREEN

From the small town of Olden on Nordfjord, a scenic road leads 24km up Oldedalen to the twin glacial tongues of Brenndalsbreen and Briksdalsbreen. The more easily accessible, Briksdalsbreen, attracts hordes of tour buses and has been photographed countless times in conjunction with tourist pony carts crossing the strategically placed bridge over the river flowing from beneath the ice. Briksdalsbreen advanced over 300m in the 1990s, but has recently retreated by 50m.

Organised Tours

Briksdal Breføring (☎ 57 87 68 00, fax 57 87 68 01), Briksdalsbre Fjellstove, and Olden Activ (☎ 57 87 38 88, fax 57 87 59 61), Melkevoll Bretun, organise a good range of glacier hikes and climbs, and no previous experience is necessary. All rates include use of technical equipment.

Casual visitors can choose between a three-hour trip (Nkr230) with an hour on the ice; or a four-hour trip (Nkr280 to Nkr320) with two hours on the ice. These depart from either Briksdalsbre Fjellstove or Melkevoll Bretun at 10am, 11am, 1pm, 2pm and 4pm daily in summer.

By arrangement, more challenging trips are available year-round (minimum three persons). Olden Activ provides introductions to mountaineering and rock climbing on request. They also advise and offer training for 'kiting' (glacier wind surfing on skis!) and offer four hours of ice-climbing instruction and practice for Nkr380.

If you're not up to the mostly straightforward 6km-return walk to the glacier face, Oldedalen Skysslag (☎ 57 87 68 05) run pony cart rides (adult/child Nkr230/115), but you'll still have a 15-minute hike on a rough path to see the ice. Advance booking is required.

Places to Stay & Eat

Briksdalsbre Fjellstove (☎ 57 87 68 00, fax 57 87 68 01, **e** post@briksdalsbre.no, Briksdalsbre) Singles/doubles with shared facilities from Nkr300/400, with en suite from Nkr400/550. Briksdalsbre Fjellstove has comfortable rooms and a cafe/restaurant (mains Nkr99 to Nkr164, including trout and reindeer dishes), as well as a souvenir shop and stables.

Melkevoll Bretun (☎ 57 87 38 64, fax 57 87 38 90, **e** post@melkevoll.no, Briksdalsbre) Basic cabins Nkr200-370, fully equipped 6-bed cabins Nkr450-690. Melkevoll Bretun has a nice green camping ground with cooking facilities, basic camping cabins and holiday chalets.

Getting There & Away

The public bus leaves Stryn (Nkr56, one hour) at 10am and Olden (Nkr38, 45 minutes) at 10.15am daily from mid-June to mid-August, arriving at Briksdalsbre Fjellstove at 11am (for Melkevoll Bretun, get off 10 minutes earlier). The return bus leaves

Briksdal at 2pm. There's also a second departure at 3.45pm on weekdays from Stryn to Melkevoll Bretun and 7.45am weekdays from Briksdalsbre Fjellstove (from Melkevoll Bretun mid-August to mid-June).

Appropriately, the locals 'milk' tourists for car parking, but a free sauna is thrown in after your hike if you park at Melkevoll Bretun (Nkr40).

KJENNDALSBREEN & BØDALSBREEN

Lovely Kjenndalsbreen lies 17km by road along a glacial lake (Lovatnet) from the Nordfjord village of Loen. It's probably the least visited of the four best-known glacial tongues, and vies with Nigardsbreen as the most beautiful to approach. Bødalsbreen, in a nearby side valley, provides good hiking possibilities.

Organised Tours

Stryn Fjell og Breførarlag (☎ 57 87 68 00, **W** www.strynglaciertours.no) guides six-hour glacier walks on Bødalsbreen for Nkr350 and more serious 12-hour Saturday trips to the 2083m-high nunatak Lodalskåpa for Nkr550. These trips begin from Bødalseter, 5km up the Bødalen toll road (Nkr20) from the head of Lovatnet.

Places to Stay

Sande Camping (☎ 57 87 45 90, fax 57 87 45 91, Loen) Tent without/with car Nkr40/80 plus Nkr15 per person, cabins Nkr180-800. Popular Sande Camping, near the northern end of Lovatnet, offers scenic lakeside tent and caravan camping, as well as an exhaustive range of cabins.

Loenvatn Feriesenter (☎ 57 87 76 75, fax 57 87 77 10, Loen) Cabins Nkr250-700. This holiday park with fully equipped lakeside and woodland cabins is fine.

Getting There & Away

Without a vehicle, access is on the M/B Kjendal that chugs up Lovatnet from Sande (Nkr140/free per adult/child under 10 return), including a return bus between Kjendalstova Café, at the end of the lake, and the glacier car park. From here, it's a 2km walk to the glacier face. From 1 June to 1 September, the boat leaves Sande at 10.30am and from Kjendalstova at 1.30pm. Buses leave Stryn at 10am to connect with this boat, continue to Bødalseter, and pass Sande on the return journey at 2.15pm.

While you're sailing along, reflect on the huge blocks of stone that dislodged from Ramnefjell and crashed down into the lake in 1905, 1936 and 1950. The first wave killed 63 people and deposited the lake steamer 400m inland. The second wave killed 72, while the third just left a bigger scar on the mountain. You can book the boat trip through the Hotel Alexandra (☎ 57 87 50 50) in Loen.

If you're driving, note that the toll road (Nkr30) above Lovatnet narrows to a single track.

STRYN SOMMERSKISENTER

The Stryn Sommerskisenter (Summer Ski Centre; ☎ 92 25 83 33, W www.stryn-somm erski.no, Videdalen; open 10am-4pm daily June-Aug), which is in fact nowhere near the town of Stryn, lies on the Tystigen outlier of Jostedalsbreen. It provides Norway's most extensive and best known summer skiing, and most of those ubiquitous photos of bikini-clad skiers were taken here.

The longest alpine run here extends for 2100m with a drop of 518m. The centre also offers 10km of cross-country ski tracks. Lift tickets for one/two/seven days cost Nkr240/455/1100. Ski rental is available – phone for details. There's also a *cafeteria*.

Folven Camping (☎ 57 87 53 40, fax 57 87 53 00, Oppstryn) Doubles Nkr200-240/ person, chalets Nkr400-1050. From the ski centre, the nearest accommodation is 15km west, by Rv15. In addition to camp sites, there's a selection of fully equipped chalet accommodation. Typical snacks and light meals are available at the cafeteria.

A ski bus runs from Stryn (Nkr65, one hour) at 9am and from the ski centre at 4pm from 9 June to 29 July. Drivers will enjoy the scenic Gamle Strynefjellsvegen, the old road that connects Grotli with Videsæter, now a national tourist route. Pick up a free leaflet at Stryn tourist office.

Sognefjorden to Nordfjord

For most travellers the 100km-long Nordfjord is but a stepping stone between Sognefjorden and Geirangerfjorden. These two popular fjords are linked by a road that winds around the head of Nordfjord past the villages of Byrkjelo, Olden and Loen to the larger town of Stryn.

SKEI
pop 524

The inland village of Skei lies near the head of lake Jølstravatnet. The worthwhile **Astruptunet museum** (☎ 57 72 67 82; adult/child Nkr50/25; open 11am-4pm daily 23 May-30 Sept), 15km west of the village on the south side of the lake, is the former home of artist Nicolai Astrup (1880–1928). It includes a gallery and open-air exhibits. The affiliated Midttunet museum, 2km down the road, protects a 17th-century west Norwegian farm (view exterior only).

White-water rafting on the Class II to III Stardal and Class III to V Jølstra rivers is offered by Jølster Rafting (☎ 90 06 70 70, fax 57 72 70 71, ejol-raf@online.no, W www .jolster-rafting.no). Day trips range from Nkr450 to Nkr950 and two-day excursions are also Nkr950.

Jølstraholmen Camping (☎ 57 72 89 02, fax 57 72 75 05, Vassenden) Tent/caravan sites from Nkr55/130, cabins Nkr175-700. Located at the western end of Jølstravatnet, 20km west of Skei, Jølstraholmen Camping offers grassy tent pitches and a good range of cabins.

Skei Hotel (☎ 57 72 81 01, fax 57 72 84 23) Singles/doubles from Nkr875/990. Lunch mains Nkr95-118, dinner mains Nkr159-186. Near the junction of Rv5 and the E39, this hotel features a swimming pool, sauna, solarium and even a tennis court. The dining room does solid mid-range fare, including beef and fish dishes.

Audhild Vikens Vevstove (☎ 57 72 81 25) Mains Nkr89-95. For good value dinners, try the good-value cafeteria in Norway's largest tax-free shop. Christmas products are sold all year at this friendly place.

Many long-distance buses connect at Skei, including services to Fjærland (Nkr41, 30 minutes, three to seven daily), Sogndal (Nkr86, one hour, three to seven daily), Stryn (Nkr110, 1½ hours, three or four daily), Ålesund (Nkr288, from 4¼ hours, once or twice daily), Florø (Nkr140, 2¼ hours, one to three daily) and Bergen (Nkr290, 4½ hours, four or five daily).

STRYN
pop 1500

The small town of Stryn is the de facto capital of upper Nordfjord and, because it lies on several long-distance transport routes, many visitors break their journeys here. The helpful Stryn & Nordfjord Reisemål (☎ 57 87 40 40, [e] mail@nordfjord.no, [w] www.no rdfjord.no) tourist office arranges accommodation and charges Nkr1 per minute for Internet access. Hiking trips are described in its free booklet *Guide for Stryn* and cycling routes are outlined in *På Sykkel i Stryn* (free). It also rents mountain bikes for Nkr50/190 per hour/day. It opens 8.30am to 8pm daily in July, to 6pm in June and August and to 3.30pm weekdays only September to May.

Jostedalsbreen Nasjonalparksenter

The Jostedalsbreen National Park Centre (☎ 57 87 72 00, *Oppstryn; adult/child Nkr55/30; open 10.30am-5.30pm daily 18 May-2 Sept*), 15km east of Stryn, contains glacier-oriented exhibits on natural and cultural history, an unusual garden of 325 species of endemic vegetation and a decent audiovisual presentation. It also covers avalanches, local minerals and meteorites, and describes local sites of natural, historical and cultural interest. Look out for the 3D models and an interesting new exhibit on the Lovatnet disasters (see the earlier Kjenndalsbreen and Bødalsbreen section).

Places to Stay & Eat

Stryn Camping (☎ 57 87 11 36, fax 57 87 20 25, Bøavegen) Tent camping without/with

car Nkr100/120, cabins Nkr300-1100. There are good facilities at Stryn Camping, just two blocks uphill from the main drag at the eastern end of town.

Stryn Vandrerhjem (☎/fax 57 87 11 06) Dorm beds Nkr170, singles/doubles Nkr250/400. Open June-Aug. This excellent and friendly hostel, on the hillside overlooking the town, was formerly a military barracks. Prices include breakfast.

Stryn Hotel (☎ 57 87 07 00, fax 57 87 07 01, Visnesvegen) Singles/doubles Nkr845/1050. You'll find the best upmarket accommodation at this modern hotel just over the bridge from the centre.

Isehaug Kafeteria & Johans Pub (☎ 57 87 17 40, Perhusvegen 20) Pizza from Nkr108, mains Nkr73-129. The popular pub is open for meals by day and serves pasta, beef, chicken and reindeer dishes; the daily special is Nkr85. It's open for drinks until at least 1am.

Restaurant Bacchus (☎ 57 87 13 22, Tonningsgata 33) Open evenings only. Pizzas around Nkr100. On the main street, Restaurant Bacchus serves pizza and a few other dishes.

Mett & Go (☎ 57 87 22 11, Tonningsgata 7) Burger meals from Nkr62. This fast-food joint specialises in burgers and light snacks.

The *Rema 1000* supermarket is situated by the fjord.

Entertainment

Base Camp (☎ 57 87 23 83, Tonningsgata 31) Base Camp is a popular bar and disco.

Scala disco (☎ 57 87 07 00, Stryn Hotel, Visnesvegen) Cover Nkr60. Open to 2.30am Wed & Fri-Sun. Rock bands and other live music features here, mainly for the 18- to 21-year-old set.

Getting There & Away

Stryn lies on the Nor-Way Bussekspress routes between Oslo (Nkr525, 8½ hours, three daily) and Måløy (Nkr135, two hours); Ålesund (Nkr203, 3½ hours, one to four daily) and Bergen (Nkr380, six hours, three to five daily); and Bergen and Trondheim (Nkr485, 7½ hours, twice daily). From Bergen, the latter two buses call in at

Olden (Nkr30, 20 minutes) and Loen (Nkr22, 15 minutes). The Ålesund route passes Hellesylt (Nkr74, 50 minutes), with boat connections to Geiranger.

Self-drivers will probably enjoy the beautiful 27km Gamle Strynefjellsvegen (Rv258) back road to Grotli, which climbs past glacier tongues and stunning views to an altitude of 1139m. It normally opens around 1 June. Bus access along this route to the Stryn Sommerskisenter is described in the Jostedalsbreen section, earlier in this chapter.

OLDEN
pop 800
For visitors, Olden is a staging point for trips to Briksdalsbreen glacier but the incredible colour of the glacial river flowing from Oldedalen is an attraction in itself. The main site of interest is **Singersamlinga** (☎ 57 87 31 06, Olden; adult/child Nkr20/10; open by appointment), which displays the artworks of William Henry Singer of Pittsburgh, Pennsylvania, USA. From 1913 to his death in 1943, he and his wife, Anna Spencer, spent their summers in Olden. His generally impressionist work reflects a touch of pointillism and reveals his affinity for the landscapes of western Norway. For information, contact the Olden Tourist Info Office (☎ 57 87 31 26), open 10am to 6pm daily 10 June to 15 August.

Places to Stay & Eat
There are around 10 camping grounds in the area, most of which lie along the route to Briksdalsbreen.

Alda Camping (☎/fax 57 87 31 38) Tent sites without/with car Nkr40/50, 4-bed huts Nkr190-290. Open June-Aug. This no-frills camping ground is by the river in the heart of Olden.

Olden Krotell B&B (☎ 57 87 34 55, fax 57 87 30 20) Singles/doubles Nkr400/600. Open mid-June-mid-Aug. You'll get an en suite room, including breakfast, at this roadside inn.

Yris Kafé (☎ 57 87 32 45, Cnr Rv60 & Oldedalen road) Mains Nkr70-120. At the good-value Yris Kafé, chicken, pork, steak, chips and pizza are on the menu.

Olden Fjordhotel (☎ 57 87 34 00, fax 57 87 33 81, e post@olden-hotel.no) Singles/doubles from Nkr965/1180. The modern first-class Olden Fjordhotel offers plush en suite rooms and meals.

Getting There & Away
See the earlier Stryn section for details.

LOEN
pop 400
As with nearby Olden, Loen, at the mouth of dramatic Lodalen, serves as a Jostedalsbreen gateway. The village itself is touristy and unmemorable, but it does provide bus and boat connections along Lovatnet to the Bødalen and Kjenndalen glacial tongues.

A great, but strenuous, five- to six-hour hike from Loen leads to the Skålatårnet tower (now a self-service DNT hut), near the 1848m-high summit of Skåla. The route begins near Tjugen farm, north of the river and immediately east of Loen. For information on other excursions from Loen, see Kjenndalsbreen & Bødalsbreen under Jostedalsbreen, earlier in this chapter.

Places to Stay & Eat
Lo-Vik Camping (☎ 57 87 76 19, fax 57 87 78 11) Tent sites without/with car Nkr50/75 plus Nkr15/person, basic 4-bed cabins Nkr325, with en suite Nkr375-600. Open mid-May–mid-Sept. Lo-Vik Camping, west of the river, offers a good range of clean accommodation.

Hotel Alexandra (☎ 57 87 50 00, fax 57 87 50 51, e alex@alexandra.no) Singles/doubles from Nkr885/1330 (discounted Sept-May), luxury double suite Nkr2780. Loen's undisputed centre of action dominates tourism in the valley with its inflated walk-in rates, restaurants, bars, nightclub, swimming pool, fitness centre, mini-golf, marina, and boat and bicycle hire. Although it has been run as a family hotel since 1884, its current architecture approaches the eyesore level. The hotel is also the place to book the Lovatnet boat and other Jostedalsbreen excursions.

Getting There & Away
See the earlier Stryn section for details.

FLORØ
pop 8000

Florø is not only the westernmost town in Norway, but also one of the most pleasant and surprising. It was founded on 'fishy silver' in 1860 as a herring port, but is now sustained by fish farming, ship building and the 'black gold' of the oil industry. As one of the southernmost ports on the Hurtigruten coastal ferry route, it sees lots of short-term visitors but its gentle seaward ambience probably merits at least a day of exploring and relaxing. For a scenic overview, it's an easy 10-minute climb up the Storåsen hill from the Florø Ungdomsskule on Havrenesveien.

Information

The tourist authority for Florø and around is Vestkysten Reiseliv A/S (☎ 57 74 75 05, fax 57 74 77 16, e vestkysten@enitel.no), Strandgata 30. It's open 8am to 7pm on weekdays, 10am to 5pm Saturday and 3pm to 7pm Sunday, mid-June to mid-August (otherwise 8am to 3.30pm weekdays only). For Nkr25 per day (May to September), it rents out one-speed 'Bysykkels' for pedalling around the relatively flat town. The booklets *Cycling in Flora* and *On Foot in Flora* are also on sale and Internet is available for Nkr15/25 per 15/30 minutes.

Coin-operated laundry services are available at the Guest Harbour, in the centre.

Sogn og Fjordane Kystmuseet

At the Sogn og Fjordane Coastal Museum (☎ 57 74 22 33, Brendøyvegen; Nkr35/15 adult/child; open 11am-6pm Mon-Fri, noon-4pm Sat & Sun, mid-June–mid-Aug, shorter hours mid-Aug–mid-June), the two main buildings are chock-full of exhibits on coastal resources, particularly fishing, as well as a model 1900 fishing family's home and a collection of model boats. There are also several old warehouse buildings moved from Florø and Måløy, and the Bataldebua, which was used on the island of Batalden for salting herrings and now contains an exhibit on the herring fishery.

The highlight, however, is probably the Snorreankeret oil platform, which is dedicated to displaying the history, exploration and exploitation of the North Sea oil and gas fields.

Offshore Islands

The enigmatic island of Kinn is home to a beautifully restored 12th-century church, believed to have been built by British Celts sheltering from religious persecution. In late June, it's the site of the Kinnespelet pageant (☎ 57 75 25 30), which celebrates the church history on the island. Climbers and hikers also enjoy the dramatic landscapes, particularly the Kinnaklova cleft.

Boats between Florø and Kinn (Nkr44) run at 10am (mid-June to mid-August) and 2.30pm and return at 3.45pm, but on weekdays only.

Ferries also connect the mainland to Svanøy, Batalden, Askrova and Tansøy from Fugleskjærskaia quay. On Svanøy, you can hike, visit the **deer centre** (☎ 57 75 21 80, Svanøy; admission free; always open) or go **horse riding** (☎ 57 74 70 10). On Batalden, you can visit the 3500-year-old rock carvings or check out the gallery at the pleasant *Batalden Havbu fishing cottages* (☎/fax 57 74 54 22, Batalden). The fine restored cottages are highly recommended at Nkr450/600 per singles/doubles.

Askrova has a prehistoric Troll Cave and adjoining Tansøy rises to 233m and affords views over the surrounding archipelago.

For information on island accommodation, pick up the Florø tourist office brochure *Hytteferie på Kysten*.

Organised Tours

At 10am on Friday (mid-June to mid-August), the tourist office runs a fabulous day tour by boat to the offshore lighthouses at Stabben, Kvanhovden and the remote Ytterøyane (no landing at Ytterøyane). This worthwhile trip costs Nkr295 (including lunch) and is extremely popular, so advance bookings are advised.

Other good options are the Tuesday and Thursday tours to the islands of Kinn and Svanøy, respectively. On Kinn, a two-hour walk around the major sites of interest is included (Nkr185, five hours). On Svanøy,

WESTERN FJORDS

FLORØ

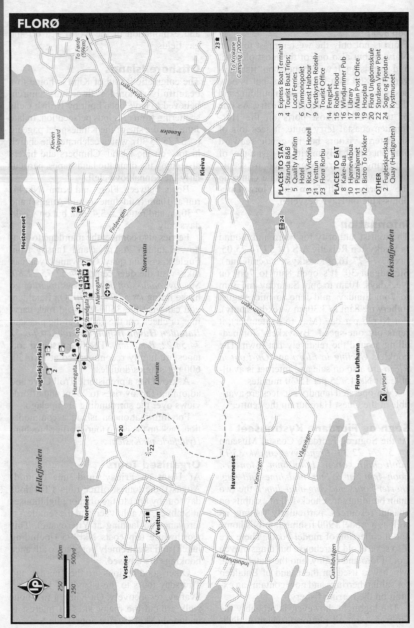

To Førde
(59km)

To Krokane
Camping (200m)

Bulnavegen

Kanalen

Kleven
Shipyard

Hesteneset

Storevatn

Fridavegen

Kleiva

Rekstafjorden

Markegata

Kinnvegen

Florø Lufthamn

Airport

Brandgata

Hammegata

Fuglskjærskaia

Littevatn

Nordnes

Vestnes

Havreneset

Kinnvegen

Vågavegen

Kinnvegen

Gunhildvågen

Industrivegen

Vesttun

Hellefjorden

PLACES TO STAY
1 Stranda B&B
5 Quality Maritim
   Hotel
13 Rica Victoria Hotell
21 Vesttun
23 Florø Rorbu

PLACES TO EAT
8 Kake-Bua
10 Hjørnevikbua
11 Pizzahjørnet
12 Bistro To Kokker

OTHER
2 Fuglskjærskaia
   Quay (Hurtigruten)
3 Express Boat Terminal
4 Tourist Boat Trips;
   Local Ferries
6 Vinmonopolet
7 Guest Harbour
9 Vestkysten Reiseliv
   Tourist Office
14 Fengslet
15 Robin Hood
16 Windjammer Pub
17 Library
18 Main Post Office
19 Hospital
20 Florø Ungdomsskule
22 Storåsen View Point
24 Sogn og Fjordane
   Kystmuseet

0   250   500m
0   250   500yd

you'll visit a 17th-century manor farm and tour the deer centre (Nkr280, five hours). Bring your own lunch.

Places to Stay

The tourist office can book holiday cabins in secluded seaside or fjordside locations.

Krokane Camping (☎ 57 75 22 50, fax 57 75 22 60) Tent/caravan sites Nkr50/100 plus Nkr10/person, 2–9-bed cabins Nkr300-850. Friendly Krokane Camping is on a peninsula 2km east of town. From the centre, buses run at least hourly from Monday to Saturday; get off at Solheim.

Stranda B&B (☎ 57 74 06 23, fax 57 74 06 61, Strandaveien) Singles/doubles Nkr350/550. This small B&B is a homely place.

Vesttun (☎ 90 69 77 04, Vestnesveien 34) Huts Nkr450-650. Vesttun has turf-roofed Russian-style huts.

Florø Rorbu (☎ 57 74 81 00, fax 57 74 32 90, Krokaveien 13A) Flats Nkr400-700. These excellent shorefront flats each sleep two people.

Rica Victoria Hotell (☎ 57 74 10 00, fax 57 74 19 80, Markegata 43) Singles/doubles from Nkr705/845. One upmarket option is this hotel, with en suite rooms and a good restaurant.

Quality Maritim Hotel (☎ 57 75 75 75, fax 57 75 75 10, Hamnegata 7) Singles Nkr595-Nkr1045, doubles Nkr795-1245. Mains Nkr185-245. The recommended Quality Maritim Hotel, on the waterfront, has two rooms with 'boat beds' and a fine restaurant serving meat and fish dinners.

Places to Eat

Hjørnevikbua (☎ 57 74 01 22, Strandgata 23) Lunch Nkr65-125. The 2nd floor of the Hjørnevikbua pub and restaurant, with its ship-like interior, serves lunches, fish soup (Nkr80 to Nkr84), and fish and meat dishes. Outdoor seating is available on a barge in the harbour.

Pizzahjornet (☎ 57 42 23 18, Strandgata 25) 30cm pizzas Nkr100-123, 40cm pizzas Nkr130-160. Pizzahjornet serves acceptable fast food and pizza.

Kake-Bua (☎ 57 74 22 42, Strandgata 21) Lunch specials Nkr89. Kake-Bua combines a pastry shop, pub, cafe and a rustic and wonderful 'museum' of nautical artefacts.

Bistro To Kokker (☎ 57 75 22 33, Strandgata 33) Dishes Nkr40-120. For light lunches, fast food and seafood dinners, this place 50m east of the tourist office does squid, salmon, monkfish and other seafood. For more pedestrian tastes, it has fish and chips for Nkr43 and burgers ranging from Nkr40 to Nkr70.

Vinmonopolet is in the same block as the *Coop Prix* supermarket, next to the bus station.

Entertainment

Fru Olsen's (☎ 57 74 10 00, Markegata 43) The pub at the Rica Victoria Hotell provides a quiet drinking spot. The *Morilden* disco, also in the hotel, attracts everyone in town between 20 to 60 years old. The cover charge is Nkr50 after 11pm.

Windjammer Pub (☎ 57 74 29 88, Strandgata 58) On weekends, this place is divided into an atmospheric pub which features live music (Thursday to Saturday), and a disco for patrons aged 18 to 22. The rest of the week, it's just a drinking den.

Fengslet (2nd Floor, Strandgata 56) The 'Prison' bar attracts a rougher and younger crowd than does the Windjammer.

Robin Hood (☎ 57 74 38 70, 2nd Floor, Strandgata 56) This calm place is popular with patrons over 20.

Getting There & Away

Coast Air flies at least daily between Oslo and Florø and daily between Bergen and Florø.

Florø lies at the end of the Nor-Way Bussekspress route from Oslo (Nkr640, 10½ hours, two to three times daily). Express boats run twice daily between Bergen (Nkr430, 3½ hours) and Måløy (Nkr145, one hour), stopping in Florø en route. The town is also a stop on the Hurtigruten coastal steamer between Bergen (Nkr437, 6¼ hours) and Kirkenes. Northbound, it calls in at 4.45am (2.15am in summer) and southbound at 8.15am. Stops farther north include Måløy (Nkr139, 2¼ hours), Ålesund (Nkr407, 6½ hours) and Trondheim (Nkr989, 30 hours).

The fastest and most scenic way to Måløy by road is via Bremanger island.

AROUND FLORØ
Vingen Petroglyphs

The 1500 incredible early Stone Age petroglyphs at Vingen, facing the sea from the slopes of Vingenfjellet, constitute the largest field of petroglyphs in northern Europe. They're thought to be the work of early Stone Age hunters and date back to between 6000 and 4000 BC. There's no road to the paintings and the only way to reach them is by the boat organised by the Florø tourist office. Departures are from Florø and Kjelkenes on Wednesday and Saturday between 1 July and 15 September (Nkr150/75 adult/child), with a minimum of five persons required.

Ausevik Rock Carvings

These excellent rock carvings are more accessible and only a five-minute walk from Fv611 (about 40 minutes drive south of Florø) and feature deer and other carvings from around 1000 BC.

Grøndalen

A large region north and east of Florø and west of the Ålfotbreen glacier presents a quite different face of Norway than surrounding areas. Here the geology consists of a predominantly pinkish sandstone formation, and the landscape is characterised by bare and rocky peaks with superb hiking potential. One of the loveliest spots is the hidden Shangri-la valley of Grøndalen, east of Norddalsfjord, which is known as the rainiest spot in Norway. The road here comes to a dead end in a magical spot, where you can leave your car and strike off up the hill. It's a rather steep 2km walk up to the private Grøndalsstølen hut, and three hours to Blåbrebu DNT hut, where there's easy access to the Ålfotbreen ice. In summer, buses run between Florø and Sunndalen (Nkr60, 1¾ hours), about 4km from the road's end, at 1.20pm on Wednesday and 3.15pm on schooldays from Florø and 7.30am on schooldays and 9.30am on Wednesday from Sunndalen.

MÅLØY
pop 2700

The dramatically located fishing town of Måløy, at the mouth of Nordfjord, lies on Vågsøy island beneath twin hills and is connected to the mainland by its landmark, the graceful S-curve Måløybrua bridge.

There's little of major interest in the town itself but the island is laced with sea-view hiking routes (you can pick up a photocopied map at the tourist office) and boasts two worthwhile destinations, the Kråkenes Fyr lighthouse and the bizarre seaside rock, Kannesteinen. The tourist office (☎ 57 85 08 50), on Sjøgata, is open 10am to 6pm Monday to Saturday between mid-June and mid-August (10am to 6pm daily in July).

Kannesteinen

The extraordinary rock Kannesteinen, which rises from the sea like a stone mushroom, makes a great destination for a day trip. It may not exactly live up to expectations – it's actually fairly small. From Måløy, take the Oppedal bus to the end of the line (Nkr23, 15 minutes). It runs two to five times daily except Sunday.

Kråkenes Fyr

Kråkenes lighthouse (☎/fax 57 85 55 27), perched precariously on a rock shoulder above a potentially wicked sea, was first opened in 1906 and automated in 1986. Even on a sunny day, it fulfils most romantics' expectations, but this German-run operation is also open for overnight guests (see Places to Stay) and the very lucky will be able to hole up there on enigmatically stormy nights. Day visitors are also welcome – there's a cafeteria on site.

Buses run from Måløy as far as Kvalheim (Nkr38, 50 minutes), about 10km away, one to three times daily except Sunday.

Places to Stay & Eat

Steinvik Camping (☎ 57 85 10 70, fax 57 85 20 63, Deknepollen) Tent sites with car Nkr100, caravans Nkr120, 4–7-bed en suite cabins Nkr400-700, 2–4-bed self-catering flats Nkr400-600. The nearest camping ground is Gerd and Oddbjørn Nygård's friendly and recommended place east of the bridge. From town, take any bus east over the bridge to the signposted turn-off and walk the 1.2km to the camping ground. Campers have use of the kitchen and free hot showers.

Kråkenes lighthouse (☎/fax 57 85 55 27, Kråkenes) Beds Nkr300. Breakfast Nkr50. The unusual accommodation at the light-house has shared facilities but includes use of the kitchen.

Norlandia Måløy Hotel (☎ 57 85 18 00, fax 57 85 05 89, Gate 1 No 25) Singles/doubles from Nkr580/790. The large glass-fronted hotel is the centre of most tourist ac-tivity in town, and shares the building with the recommended *Aquarius* dining room, where set lunches cost Nkr135 and three-course dinners are Nkr220.

Galeåsen pub (☎ 57 85 22 40, Sjøgata) Mains Nkr70-150, buffets Nkr98. Meals 3pm-8pm, pizzas after 8pm. The covered pub at the harbour opposite the hotel lays on a taco buffet on Tuesday evening for Nkr98. There's also dancing here on weekend evenings.

Bon Appetit (☎ 57 85 20 21, Gate 1 No 48) Dishes Nkr40-90. For something faster, try Bon Appetit, which serves burgers, chicken, chips, baguettes and wraps.

Mama Rosa (☎ 57 85 21 50, Gate 1 No 22) Dishes from Nkr40. Open 2pm-11pm daily. Mama Rosa specialises in pizza but also serves burgers and kebabs.

Getting There & Away

Måløy is reached on three daily Nor-Way Bussekspress buses from Oslo (Nkr685, 10½ hours) via Stryn (Nkr136, two hours), with several additional runs between Stryn and Måløy by Nordfjord og Sunnmøre Bil-lag. The express boat from Bergen to Selje goes via Florø and Måløy (Nkr530, 4½ hours, from Bergen), and the northbound Hurti-gruten coastal steamer passes daily at 4.30am (7.30am in winter); southbound at 5.45am.

SELJE
pop 1500

Few visitors traipse all the way out to Selje, which is one of the northernmost outposts

of Sogn og Fjordane county on the western edge of Norway, but those who do find a very pleasant small town and one of the finest beaches in the country. You may also want to make the trek out to Vestkapp, 32km by road from Selje, which isn't Nor-way's westernmost point but still provides superb sea views.

Many travellers to the area want to visit the lovely ruins of **Selje monastery** and the **church of St Sunniva** on Selja island, which date from the 11th and 12th centuries, re-spectively. You can climb the tower and ring the bell – quite an eerie experience. From 25 June to 5 August, ferries (☎ 91 80 74 14) leave the mainland at 10.15am, 1pm and 3.30pm, and there are one or two daily departures at other times between 25 May and 25 August. Pick up tickets (Nkr110/50 adult/child return) from the tourist office (☎ 57 85 66 06) at the harbour, which opens 8am to 3pm weekdays April to September (10am to 4pm or 6pm June and August, 10am to 8pm in July).

Places to Stay & Eat
The tourist office keeps lists of cabins and apartments in the area.

Selja Camping & Hytter (☎ 57 85 62 43) Tent sites 2 people with car Nkr70, cabins Nkr500-600. The only viable camping place is about 2km east of town.

Selje Hotel (☎ 57 85 88 80, fax 57 85 88 81, ⓔ post@seljehotel.no) Singles Nkr790-890, doubles Nkr1110-1610. 2-course lunch Nkr165, dinner mains Nkr169-239. This comfortable and well-heeled hotel is nicely located by the beach. Meals are pricey, but the Sunday seafood buffet (Nkr210) is worth a shot.

Kafé Nabben (☎ 57 85 65 40) Burgers & light meals Nkr50-60, mains Nkr80-125. The cafe upstairs at the tourist office serves meat and fish dishes, pizza and snacks.

The *Frimannsbua Kro (☎ 57 85 88 80)* pub, near the tourist office, mostly serves beer but may be able to rustle up a pizza.

Getting There & Away
Buses run between Måløy and Selje (Nkr67, one hour) three times daily on weekdays.

It's also the end of the once or twice daily Nordfjord express-boat route from Bergen (Nkr570, five hours).

The Northern Fjords

InterRail, Eurail and ScanRail pass holders get a 50% discount on all buses, ferries and express boats in Møre og Romsdal county. For tourist information, see the Internet at W www.visitmr.com.

ÅNDALSNES
pop 3500
Most people approach Åndalsnes via the spectacularly scenic Raumabanen, the rail route from Dombås, which follows a deeply cut glacial valley flanked by sheer walls and plummeting waterfalls. During WWII, the Norwegian royal family was evacuated to here before they were spirited out of the country. Shortly thereafter, however, the Germans got wise and bombed the place to the ground before setting up a major base. As a result, the modern town is rather nondescript, but the surrounding landscapes remain top notch.

Information
The useful Åndalsnes og Romsdal Reiselivslag tourist office (☎ 71 22 16 22, e andalsnes@goldenroute.com), at the train station, opens 9am to 7pm Monday to Saturday and 1pm to 7pm Sunday, June to August (shorter hours the rest of the year). Free Internet access is available at the library, on Parkvegen 22.

Trollveggen
Approaching from Dombås, the road and rail lines follow the dramatic 1800m-high Trollveggen, or Troll Wall, whose ragged and often cloud-shrouded summit is considered the ultimate challenge among mountaineers.

It was first climbed in 1965 by a joint Norwegian and English team. Since 1980, when a Finnish man leaped off it with a parachute, Trollveggen has also been a venue for now-illegal base jumping.

Trollstigen
The Trollstigen (Troll's Path), south of Åndalsnes, is a thriller of a road with 11 hairpin bends, a 1:12 gradient and, to add a daredevil element, it's one lane practically all the way. On request, bus passengers get a photo stop at the thundering 180m-high Stigfossen waterfall, and a quick halt at the top for a dizzy view down the valley. If you have a car, however, you'll probably also want to pause for photos of the dramatic 1500m- to 1600m-high peaks of Karitind, Dronningen, Kongen and Bispen, as well as Norway's only 'Troll Crossing' road sign. You may also enjoy the **Vegmuseum** (☎ 71 22 14 65, Trollstigen; admission Nkr15; open 11am-3.30pm daily late June–mid-Aug), at the pass, which tells the engineering history of this awesome road.

Activities
Hiking The tourist office has 14 leaflets (Nkr5 each) describing a range of excellent hiking tracks and routes around the Romsdalen Alps, but the best map for extensive exploration is *Romsdals-alpene* 1:80,000, which it sells for Nkr79. An excellent day hike begins in town, 50m north of the roundabout, and climbs to the summit of Nesaksla (715m), the prominent peak that rises above Åndalsnes. Although the path is quite steep, at the top you'll be rewarded with a terrific view of the surrounding fjords and mountains. In fine weather, the view extends down Romsdalsfjord, up Romsdalen and into Isterdalen (to Trollstigen), easily rivalling any in Norway.

From the shelter at the top, it's a straightforward climb to the summit of Høgnosa (991m) and beyond to Åkesfjellet (1215m). In summer, the ascent can be hot in the midday sun, so get an early start and carry water. Alternatively, you can traverse along the marked route 5km eastward and descend to Isfjorden village, at the head of the Isfjord.

Climbing The best local climbs are the 1500m-long rock route on Trollveggen and the 1550m-high Romsdalshorn, but there are lots more. Serious climbers should contact the tourist office for a copy of *Klatring i Romsdal* (Nkr280), which includes rock and ice climbing info in both Norwegian and English. Otherwise, copies may be obtained by ordering from **e** bjartebo@post.com.

Mountaineers may enjoy **Norsk Tinde-museum** (☎ 71 22 12 74, *Åndalsnes; adult/child Nkr30/15; open 1pm-5pm daily 20 June-20 Aug, or by appointment)*, 1.5km from town on the road to Åndalsnes Camping, with exhibits on the expeditions of renowned mountaineer Arne Randers Heen.

Fishing Four-hour fishing tours on Romsdalsfjorden are available through the tourist office for Nkr250 per person; they run three times daily in summer. Rod hire costs Nkr50. A local licence for the river Rauma costs Nkr150 but you must disinfect your equipment (Nkr100).

Places to Stay

The tourist office keeps a list of three to five private homes offering accommodation from Nkr250 to Nkr350 for a single or double, with linen. Breakfast may also be available.

Åndalsnes Camping (☎ 71 22 16 29, fax 71 22 62 16) Tent/caravan sites Nkr55/85 plus Nkr15/person, heated cabins Nkr160-650. This place, less than 2km from town at the mouth of Romsdalen, enjoys a dramatic riverside setting. Canoes and mountain bikes can be hired for Nkr50/200 and Nkr40/100 per hour/day, respectively.

Trollstigen Hytteutleie (☎ 71 22 68 99) Tents/caravans Nkr55/85, huts Nkr500-600. This well-organised camping ground is in a scenic location.

Trollstigen Gjestegård (☎ 92 49 84 62, fax 71 22 22 48) Rooms from Nkr185 per person, 5-bed cabins with cooking facilities Nkr300-550. This is a good place with high-standard facilities.

Åndalsnes Vandrerhjem Setnes (☎ 71 22 13 82, fax 71 22 68 35, **e** andalsnes.vandrerhjem@c2i.net) Dorm beds Nkr180, singles/doubles Nkr300/450, including breakfast. Bed only Nkr130 11 Sept-19 May. A good choice for budget travellers is the pleasant

sod-roofed hostel, 2km from the train station on the E136. It's worth staying here for the hostel's famous hotel-standard pancakes-and-pickled-herring breakfast alone. Most people walk here from town, but you can hop on the Ålesund bus which meets the train and passes right by the hostel (Nkr15).

Alpe Hotel (☎ 71 22 21 00, fax 71 22 21 01) Dorm beds from Nkr150. If the hostel is full – and it often is – try this 'hotel' with plain dormitories, located just 50m from the train station.

Romsdal Gjestegård (☎ 71 22 13 83, fax 71 22 84 15, Veblungsnes) 2-bedroom en suite cabins with kitchen Nkr600-700. These rustic cabins are highly recommended.

Grand Hotel Bellevue (☎ 71 22 75 00, fax 71 22 60 38, Åndalgata 5) Singles Nkr645-915, doubles Nkr970-1060. This hotel caps a hillock in the centre of town and it's the choice of most tour groups. It offers adequate rooms, most with fine views. For the best views and least traffic noise, ask for a room at the back, and as high up as possible.

Rauma Hotel (☎ 71 22 32 70, fax 71 22 32 71, Vollan 16) Singles/doubles with shared bathroom Nkr450/600, with en suite Nkr795/950. The smaller centrally located Rauma Hotel also offers fine rooms and a restaurant.

Places to Eat

Grand Hotel Bellevue (☎ 71 22 75 00, Åndalgata 5) Mains Nkr170-204. The most formal and expensive dining is available in this hotel restaurant, but lighter meals are only Nkr95 to Nkr98.

Vertshuset Rauma (☎ 71 22 11 20, Øran Vest) Mains around Nkr85-140. The nearest cafeteria to the hostel is on the E136 on the north bank of the river.

Buona Sera (☎ 71 22 60 75, Romsdalsveien 6) Dishes from around Nkr80. The central Italian-oriented Buona Sera predictably specialises in pizza and pasta.

For sandwiches and sweet treats, locals like the *Måndalen Bakeri* (Havnegate 5), on the waterfront near the train station. The train station *shop* sells fruit and sandwiches and there are a couple of supermarkets and cafeterias in the central area.

Getting There & Away

Trains to/from Dombås run one to three times daily (Nkr160, 1½ hours), in synchronisation with Oslo-Trondheim trains. The Oslo-Dombås-Åndalsnes route is also served overnight by bus. Trains also connect in Åndalsnes with Togbuss services to Ålesund (Nkr162, 2¼ hours, one to three daily) and Molde (Nkr78, 1½ hours, five to seven daily).

Buses along the 'Golden Route' to Geiranger (Nkr137, three hours), via Trollstigen, the Linge-Eidsdal ferry and the scenic Ørnevegen, operate from 15 June to 31 August. The Trollstigen pass is cleared and open by at least 1 June, and early in the season it's an impressive trip through a popular cross-country ski field, between high walls of snow. Buses leave Åndalsnes at 8.30am and 5.30pm daily, and from Geiranger at 1pm and 6.10pm.

Getting Around

Those who just want to spin up to Trollstigen or along the Trollvegen can rent a car for Nkr550 per day at either Åndalsnes Camping, Avis (☎ 71 22 46 80), or Hertz (☎ 71 22 14 24) at the Hydro/Texaco station. By taxi, you'll pay around Nkr450 for the return trip to the Trollstigen pass.

VALLDAL & TAFJORD
combined pop 1300

Lots of visitors pass through the 'strawberry town' of Valldal, over the famous Trollstigen pass from Åndalsnes, but few linger. There are, however, several sites of interest in the region, not to mention an annual Strawberry Festival on the last weekend in July. For details contact the Norddal Reiselivslag tourist office (☎ 70 25 77 67, fax 70 25 70 44, e norddalr@online.no), which is open from 9am to 9pm daily from 10 July to 10 August, with shorter hours the rest of the year. Bike hire (Nkr100 per day) and fishing licences are available.

Tafjord

At 3am on 7 April 1934, an enormous chunk of rock 400m high and 22m long – a total eight million cubic metres – broke loose from the hillside and crashed into Korsnæsfjord, creating a 64m tidal wave that washed 700m inland and claimed 40 people in Fjørra and Tafjord. The disaster is commemorated in the Tafjord Geosenter (not yet open to the public); it's expected to include geological exhibits on the two-billion-year-old gneiss and granite formations dominating the region.

The **Tafjord Kraftverk Museum** (☎ 70 17 56 00, Tafjord village; admission free; open noon-5pm daily 20 June-20 Aug) reveals the history and purposes of the Tafjord hydroelectric schemes and the 96m-high Zakariasdammen dam, which dates from 1967. It's housed in a now-defunct power station that operated from 1923 to 1989. The road that climbs from the village up to the Zakarias reservoir passes through a bizarre corkscrew tunnel and, a couple of kilometres higher up, a short walking route leads down to the decrepit bridge at the narrow base of the dam, where at close range you can imagine what sort of stresses the structure tolerates.

Stordal

If you're travelling between Valldal and Ålesund, be sure to stop at the amazing **Rose-Kyrkja** (Rose Church; ☎ 70 27 81 40, Stordal; adult/child Nkr25/10; open 11am-4pm daily 15 June-15 Aug). This unassuming building, constructed in 1789 on the site of an earlier stave church, contains perhaps the most incredible baroque interior of any church in Norway, thanks to the 1799 efforts of Andreas Reinholt and Vebjørn Halling, who were in the employ of local parishioners. Some elements, including the baptismal font, the pulpit base and the crucifix, came from the original stave church.

Activities

A good reason to halt in Valldal is to join a four-hour white-water rush down the Valldøla river (Nkr440). Contact Valldal Naturopplevingar (☎ 70 25 77 67, W www.valldal.no).

Places to Stay & Eat

Gudbrandsjuvet Camping (☎ 70 25 86 31, fax 70 25 70 44, Valldal) Tent sites Nkr60,

Cyclists enjoy the birds-eye view of Bergen from Mt Fløyen

Traditional timber house, Bergen

Bryggen's gabled timber buildings, Bergen

The Bryggen warehouses on the waterfront once stored dried fish, butter, skins and wines for export

Looking over Ålesund to the sea from Aksla

Map of 'Bokbyen' (Book Town)

Briksdalsbreen iceflow, Jostedalsbreen National Park

Climbers on the Berset iceflow in Jostedalsbreen National Park

cabins Nkr260-300. For a real treat, stop at this camping ground 15km up the valley from Valldal. It sits beside the hellbound river just upstream from the canyon and several of the cabins have great watery views. The adjoining kiosk offers cheap pizza and burgers.

Solbjørg Berli (☎ 70 25 77 45, fax 70 25 70 44, Valldal) Beds Nkr175. Just 300m from the tourist office, Solbjørg Berli offers beds and cooking facilities, but breakfast isn't available.

Fjellro Turisthotell (☎ 70 25 75 13, fax 70 25 75 45, Valldal) Singles/doubles Nkr585/ 800. This simple, compact and rather charming hotel has an attached restaurant where beef or seafood dishes cost between Nkr75 and Nkr120.

Tafjord Gjestegård (☎ 70 25 80 48, fax 70 25 81 33, Tafjord village) Singles/doubles Nkr450/650, 4–6-bed en suite cabins Nkr500-650. Tafjord Gjestegård, right at the head of the fjord, offers a variety of comfortable options.

Severinhuset (☎ 70 25 86 95, Valldal) Mains around Nkr60-120. This pub and restaurant, in a historic home, specialises in fish and beef dishes.

Muritunet/Lupinen Café (☎ 70 25 84 10, Valldal) Mains around Nkr90. Open daily. This cafe serves pizza, beef and fish dishes. On Sunday from noon to 6pm, it puts on an inexpensive buffet (Nkr145).

Jordbærstova (☎ 70 25 76 58, Valldal) Mains Nkr60-140. About 6km up the valley (towards Åndalsnes), Jordbærstova honours the valley's mighty strawberry. Stop in for a slice of strawberry cheesecake or the local pancake speciality known as *svele*, served with strawberries and cream. Light meals and dinner are also available.

Getting There & Away

Valldal lies on the 'Golden Route' bus service between Åndalsnes (Nkr78, 1¾ hours) and Geiranger (Nkr65, 1¼ hours). Don't miss the spectacular Rv63 approach via the Trollstigen pass. If you're driving, you may want to pause at Gudbrandsjuvet, 15km up the valley from Valldal, where the river slots through a 5m-wide, 20m-deep canyon.

Buses between Valldal and Tafjord (Nkr29, 20 minutes) run twice daily on schooldays.

GERANGER
pop 270

The towering walls of twisting, 20km-long Geirangerfjord are lined with scattered cliffside farms, some abandoned, and a lineup of breathtaking waterfalls with names such as De Syv Søstre (Seven Sisters), Friaren (Friar), the Suitor and Brudesløret (Bridal Veil). Touristy Geiranger, with fabulous views at the head of the fjord, attracts hordes of visitors on frantically rushed sightseeing trips. In the evening, however, after the cruise ships and tour buses have moved on, things get more appropriately serene.

The tourist office (☎ 70 26 30 99, fax 70 26 57 20), in the post office complex near the pier, opens variable hours daily mid-May to early September.

Flydalsjuvet

After even a few days in Norway, you're sure to see photos of the overhanging rock Flydalsjuvet, which invariably feature a figure gazing down at a cruise ship in Geirangerfjord. The car park signposted Flydalsjuvet, about 5km uphill from Geiranger on the Stryn road, overlooks a great view of the fjord and the green river valley, but doesn't provide the postcard view. For that, you'll have to trot about 150m down the hill, then descend a slippery and rather indistinct track to the edge. Your photo subject will have to very carefully scramble down to the overhang from about 50m farther along.

Ørnevegen

The Ørnevegen route into Geiranger from Åndalsnes and Valldal, constructed in 1954, twists down the almost sheer slope in 11 hairpin bends and affords incredible views along the narrow fjord. The vistas take in the Preikestolen rock outcrop and the lovely De Syv Søstre waterfall.

Hiking

All around Geiranger you'll find great hiking routes to abandoned farmsteads, waterfalls and vista points. The tourist office distributes maps featuring 12 short hikes from the village.

The most popular longer hike begins on the fjord sightseeing boat (see Organised Tours). On the way back, the boat stops (on request) at the start of the walking route. Climb from the landing for 45 minutes to the precariously perched hillside farm known as Skageflå. From there, it's a gradual 2¼-hour hike back to Geiranger. Another recommended hike follows a normally muddy path to the Storseter waterfall, where the track actually passes behind the cascading water. This one takes about 45 minutes each way.

Organised Tours

Geiranger Fjordservice's (☎ 70 26 30 99, fax 70 26 31 41) 1½-hour sightseeing boat tours are organised at the tourist office for Nkr75 per person. From 1 June to 31 August, they run five times daily, with an extra evening departure daily from 25 June to 1 August. Geiranger Fjordservice is also recommended for the popular Skageflå hike.

Places to Stay

Around the village, you'll find plenty of *Rom* signs, indicating private rooms for rent for around Nkr200/300 for singles/doubles. The tourist office can book for you. Hotels in Geiranger are often booked out by package tours, but a dozen or so camping possibilities skirt the fjord and hillsides.

Geiranger Camping (☎/fax 70 26 31 20) Camp sites without/with car Nkr60/90, plus Nkr10/person. Central Geiranger Camping, at the head of the fjord, offers acceptable facilities.

Fjorden Camping (☎/fax 70 26 30 77) 4-bed cabins Nkr150-600. Fjorden Camping, 2km from town on the west side of the fjord, has cabins with hotplates.

Grande Fjordhytter & Camping (☎ 70 26 14 00, fax 70 26 19 99) Tents Nkr70-90 plus Nkr15/person, en suite cabins Nkr250-820. This is an excellent site with an unbeatable location, 2km north-west of Geiranger.

Vinjebakken Hostel (☎ 70 26 32 05) Dorm beds Nkr130 with own sleeping bag,

Nkr180 with sheets. Open July–mid-Aug. The enterprising local woman Ms Liv-Ida Bjørnstad has turned her spacious but cosy home, with a convenient location and super views, into a hostel. Breakfast is available for Nkr50. Head up the hill to the octagonal church, look to the left and you'll see it there on the hill.

Hotel Geiranger (☎ 70 26 30 05, fax 70 26 31 70) Singles/doubles from Nkr640/800, rooms with view Nkr780/1080. This incongruous imposition at the head of the fjord is actually where many big tours stay.

Union Hotel (☎ 70 26 30 00, fax 70 26 31 61) Singles/doubles from Nkr645/970 in summer. The charming and spectacularly situated Union Hotel is high on the hill above town.

Grande Fjord Hotell (☎ 70 26 30 90, fax 70 26 31 77) Hotel & motel-style singles/doubles from Nkr700/800. This hotel, 2km north-west of the village (direction Ørnevegen), offers fine buffet breakfasts and dinners (Nkr170 to Nkr250) and rooms with great beds and excellent fjord views.

Places to Eat

Naustkroa (☎ 70 26 32 30) Mains Nkr85-178. Naustkroa, near the pier in the centre, serves inexpensive fare, including fish soup (Nkr46), pizza (from Nkr100), and beef, chicken and fish dishes. The attached *gatekjøkken* manages takeaway hot dogs, burgers and chips.

Olebuda Café-Pub (☎ 70 26 31 60) Mains Nkr55-154. Olebuda offers sandwiches, burgers, sausages, salmon, steaks and even tacos for Nkr98.

Friaren Pizza Pub (☎ 70 26 30 05) Pizza around Nkr90-170. The fairly ordinary Friaren Pizza Pub is below Hotel Geiranger.

Union Hotel (☎ 70 26 30 00) Buffet Nkr295-320. If you're feeling really hungry, head uphill to the Union Hotel for a blowout evening buffet.

You can pick up groceries at the central *Joker* supermarket, by the fjord. It's one of the only supermarkets in Norway that's open on Sunday and it serves takeaway waffles with jam, cream and a coffee for only Nkr25.

Getting There & Away
In summer, daily buses to Åndalsnes leave Geiranger (Nkr137, three hours) at 1pm and 6.10pm. The morning bus from Åndalsnes and Valldal continues from Geiranger to Langvatn and, en route back to Geiranger (Nkr60, two hours from Langvatn), does a 10km return tourist run to the 1500m summit of Dalsnibba and stops at Flydalsjuvet; from Geiranger, the return trip is Nkr100. If you're driving, the toll road up Dalsnibba costs Nkr50 per car.

For Molde, you'll have to change buses in Åndalsnes; for Ålesund, change at Linge.

The popular Møre og Romsdal Fylkesbåtar ferry between Geiranger and Hellesylt (Nkr34/107 for passengers/cars, Nkr17 with rail passes, one hour), probably represents the most spectacular scheduled ferry route in Norway, shuttles up and down the fjord four to 10 times a day from 1 May to 24 September. The latest schedules are available from MRF (☎ 71 21 95 00).

From 1 April to 30 September, the Hurtigruten coastal steamer sails into Geiranger on its north-bound run only.

HELLESYLT
pop 500
The old Viking port of Hellesylt may be calmer and less breathtaking than Geiranger, but it's still spectacular, and is lulled by a roaring waterfall that cascades through the centre.

The tourist office (☎ 70 26 50 52) dispenses information and also rents rowing boats and fishing rods. It's open from 9am to 5pm daily, mid-June to mid-August. An attached museum of local wood carvings was due to open in 2002.

Places to Stay & Eat
Hellesylt Vandrerhjem (☎/fax 70 26 51 28) Dorm beds Nkr120, single/double cabins with fjord view Nkr220/300. The fine hostel, perched on the hillside overlooking Hellsylt, is on the road towards Stranda, about 200m from the junction.

Hellesylt Camping (☎ 70 26 51 88) Tent sites with/without vehicle Nkr40/70, caravans Nkr80, plus Nkr12/person. The conve-

nient but rather exposed Hellesylt Camping is right in the centre.

Grand Hotel (☎ 70 26 51 00, fax 70 26 52 22) Singles/doubles from Nkr560/760. The rustic old 1875 Grand Hotel has fjord-view rooms and its dining room is the most formal restaurant in the village. Soup costs Nkr42 and main courses, including fish, chicken and beef, are Nkr109 to Nkr185.

Ocals Pizzabar (☎ 70 26 51 04) Pizza from Nkr70. The pizzas here are OK, but you may want to avoid the other offerings.

For quicker and cheaper meals, there's the centrally located *Burgerhjørnet*, with burgers for Nkr35 to Nkr75.

Getting There & Away
The spectacular MRF ferry ride to/from Geiranger (Nkr34/107 for passengers/cars, Nkr17 with rail passes, one hour) runs four to 10 times daily in summer. Some of these services connect with buses to/from Stryn (Nkr74, 50 minutes) and Ålesund (Nkr138, 2¼ hours). The once or twice daily Nor-Way Bussekspress buses between Bergen (Nkr420, 8¼ hours) and Ålesund also pass through Hellesylt.

NORANGSDALEN
pop 100
One of the most inspiring, yet little visited, parts of the Northern Fjords is Norangsdalen, the hidden valley that connects Hellesylt with the Leknes-Sæbø ferry, on the scenic Hjørundfjorden, via the village of Øye. If you have a car, it's not to be missed, but the partially untarred Rv665 is also served by bus.

As the scenery unfolds past towering snowy peaks, ruined old farmsteads and haunting mountain lakes, you may experience a sense of passing through some alternative reality. In the upper part of the valley at Urasætra, beside a dark mountain lake, you can see the ruins of several stone crofters' huts. Farther on, you can still see the foundations of ruined farmhouses beneath the surface of the pea-green lake Langstøylvatnet, which was created in 1908 when a rockslide crashed down the slopes of Keipen.

Hikers and climbers will find plenty of scope in the dramatic peaks of the adjacent Sunnmørsalpane, including the incredibly steep scrambling ascent of Slogen (1564m) from Øye and the superb Råna (1586m), which is a long, tough scramble from Urke.

For information on hiking, climbing and mountain huts in this majestic region, contact the local DNT organisation, Ålesund-Sunnmøre Turistforening (☎ 70 12 58 04, fax 70 12 95 60), Kaiser Wilhelmsgata 22, N-6003 Ålesund. In Øye, there's a monument to CW Patchell, the English mountaineer who lost his heart to the valley.

Places to Stay & Eat

Saksa Feriehytter (☎/fax 70 06 20 82, Urke) 6-person en suite chalets from Nkr360. Superb chalets are available at this place.

Urke Fjordhytter (☎ 70 06 20 54, Urke) 6–8-person en suite chalets Nkr400-500. At Urke Fjordhytter, there are excellent great-value chalets with all mod cons.

The atmospheric hotel in Norangsdalen is a wonderful place, but its stratospheric pricing policy doesn't match up to the service and the food has been criticised.

Hotel Union (☎ 70 06 21 00, fax 70 06 21 16, Øye) Singles/doubles Nkr890/1340. Lunch mains Nkr175-195, 4-course dinner Nkr425. Open May-Sept. The historic 1891 Hotel Union has attracted mountaineers, writers, artists and royalty for over a century. Although the period artwork, wooden panelling and original furnishings might be considered excessive, there's little to suggest that you're inhabiting the present day, and you can choose from rooms named for celebrities who have occupied them: Sir Arthur Conan Doyle, Karen Blixen, Kaiser Wilhelm, Edvard Grieg, Roald Amundsen, Henrik Ibsen, a host of kings and queens, and even Coco Chanel.

Getting There & Away

From 17 June to 18 August, bus No 533 runs through Norangsdalen between Hellesylt and Leknes (Nkr48, 45 minutes) once daily on weekdays. There are also five weekday services and one Sunday service between Øye and Leknes (Nkr20, 20 minutes).

RUNDE
pop 160

The island of Runde (W www.runde.no), 67km south-west of Ålesund, plays host to half a million sea birds of 230 to 240 species, including 100,000 pairs of migrating puffins that arrive in May and stay until late July. You'll also see colonies of kittiwakes, gannets, fulmars, storm petrels, razor-billed auks, shags, guillemots and other sea birds, and 70 other species that nest here. The best bird-watching sites – as well as offshore seal colonies – are accessed on 2½-hour boat tours from Runde harbour, departing at 11am, 1pm and 4pm daily from May to August (Nkr100 per person, minimum four people). Call ☎ 70 08 59 16 for bookings.

Alternatively, a four-hour tour around Runde on the yacht *Charming Ruth* (☎ 70 01 30 00) departs from Ulsteinvik harbour, on the neighbouring island of Hareid, at 3pm on Wednesday, 9.30am on Saturday and 11.30am on Sunday, between 22 June and 19 August. The tour costs Nkr195.

For tourist information, contact Runde Reiselivslag (☎ 70 01 37 90, fax 70 01 37 91) in Ulsteinvik.

Places to Stay & Eat

Runde Camping & Vandrerhjem (☎ 70 08 59 16, fax 70 08 58 70) Tent & car sites Nkr60 plus Nkr15/person, dorm beds Nkr110, single/double cabins Nkr220/270. This harbourside hostel provides clean and comfortable accommodation.

The *Runde Café (☎ 70 08 59 15)*, about 300m from the hostel, opens May to August.

Getting There & Away

Runde is connected by bridge to the mainland. A catamaran-bus combination day trip runs from Ålesund's Skateflukaien quay (Nkr144 one way, 2½ hours) on weekdays from 17 June to 22 September. The catamaran sails from Ålesund to Hareid (Nkr54, 30 minutes) at 8.30am, connecting with a bus to Fosnavåg (Nkr60, one hour), where another connection takes you to Runde (Nkr30, 35 minutes). To return to Ålesund on the same day, you'll have to leave Runde on the 5.05pm bus. For cruises on the

Charming Ruth, you need to get off the Hareid-Fosnavåg bus at Ulsteinvik.

ÅLESUND
pop 24,323
The agreeable coastal town of Ålesund, crowded onto a narrow fishhook-shaped peninsula in the sea, is considered by many to be even more beautiful than Bergen, and it's far less touristy.

After the sweeping fire of 23 January 1904, which left 10,000 residents homeless, the German emperor Kaiser Wilhelm II sent shiploads of provisions and building materials and Ålesund was rebuilt in characteristic Art Nouveau style (Jugendstil). Buildings adorned with turrets, spires and gargoyles can be seen throughout town, with the best examples along Apotekergata, Kirkegata, Øwregata, Løvenvoldgata and especially Kongensgata

So tightly packed is the town centre that expansion would be impossible, and today most of the town's people live scattered across surrounding islands and peninsulas.

Information
The Ålesund Reiselivslag tourist office (☎ 70 15 76 00, fax 70 15 76 01, W www .visitalesund.com) is in the town hall, diagonally opposite the bus station. It's open 8.30am to 7pm weekdays, 9am to 5pm Saturday and 11am to 5pm Sunday from June to August. The rest of the year, it's open weekdays from 8.30am to 4pm. Ask for the free booklet *On Foot in Ålesund*, detailing the town's architectural highlights in a walking tour.

Internet access is available at the library in the town hall, or try the RCG Netcafe (☎ 70 1 06 12), Tollbugata 8, which charges Nkr1 per minute.

You can do laundry downstairs in the Guest Harbour service building near the head of Brosundet.

Aalesunds Museum
The town museum (☎ 70 12 31 70, *Rasmus Rønnebergs gate 16; adult/child Nkr30/10; open 11am-4pm Mon-Fri, noon-3pm Sat-Sun 15 June-15 Aug, shorter hours Sun-Fri*

16 Aug-14 June) concentrates on the history of sealing, fishing, shipping and industry in the Sunnmøre region, the fire of 1904, the German occupation from 1940 to 1945 and the town's distinctive Jugendstil architecture. You'll also see a collection of boats and ships, including the *Uræd* lifeboat (piloted across the Atlantic in 1904 by Ole Brude), and an 1812 barn which has been converted into an old-time grocery.

The affiliated **Ålesund Fiskerimuseet** *(Fishery Museum; ☎ 70 10 00 84, Molovegen 10; adult/child Nkr20/10; open variable hours Wed-Sun July–mid-Aug)*, in the 1860 Holmbua warehouse, contains exhibits on fishing through the ages and a special exhibit on drying stockfish and the processing of cod liver oil.

Sunnmøre Museum
Ålesund's celebrated Sunnmøre Museum *(☎ 70 17 40 00, Borgundgavlen; admission to both sections adult/child Nkr50/15; open 10am-5pm Mon-Sat 24 June-31 Aug, noon-5pm Sun, shorter hours rest of year)* is housed at the site of the old Borgundkaupangen trading centre, 4km east of the centre. The main open-air exhibit consists of 55 old buildings, visiting displays on traditional crafts and textiles, and a collection of 30 historic boats, including replicas of Viking-era ships and a commercial trading vessel from around AD 1000.

There's also a **Medieval Age Museum** *(☎ 70 17 40 00, Borgundgavlen; admission to both sections adult/child Nkr50/15; open noon-3pm Tues, Thur & Sun 20 June-15 Aug)*, with archaeological excavations and an on-site reproduction of the 10th-century town of Borgundkaupangen. These exhibitions reveal the history, trade, art, industry and religion of the west Norwegian coastal folk and their hunting and fishing cultures in medieval times.

Aksla
The 418 steps up Aksla lead to the splendid Kniven overlook over Ålesund and the surrounding mountains and islands. Follow Lihauggata from the pedestrian shopping street Kongensgata to the start of the

WESTERN FJORDS

20-minute puff to the top of the hill. There's also a road to the top; take Røysegata east from the centre, then follow the Fjellstua signposts up the hill.

The *Fjellstua Kafé (☎ 70 10 74 00, Aksla)* at the overlook serves steak and bacalao, snacks and light meals (Nkr47 to Nkr85) and mains (Nkr120 to Nkr155). There is also a souvenir shop. It's open 10am to 8pm daily mid-May to August.

Atlanterhavsparken

The recommended Atlantic Ocean Park *(☎ 70 10 70 60, Tueneset; adult/child Nkr85/*55; open 10am-7pm Sun-Fri & 10am-4pm Sat mid-June–mid-Aug, shorter hours mid-Aug–mid-June),* 3km from the centre at the western extreme of the fishhook peninsula, introduces visitors to the North Atlantic's undersea world with glimpses of the astonishing submarine life around ferry harbours and piers, in main ocean currents, around offshore islands, and deep in the fjords. The most interesting feature is an enormous four-million-litre aquarium where human divers and the largest ocean fish are integrated into the underwater scene at 1pm, during feeding.

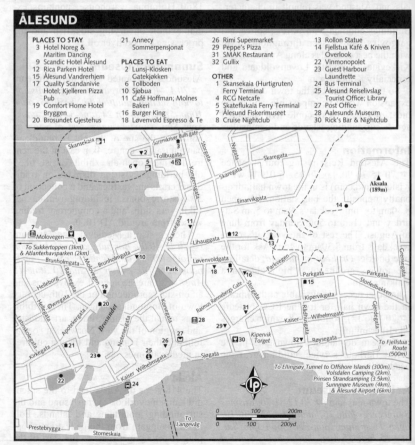

ÅLESUND

PLACES TO STAY
3 Hotel Noreg & Maritim Dancing
9 Scandic Hotel Ålesund
12 Rica Parken Hotel
15 Ålesund Vandrerhjem
17 Quality Scandanivie Hotel; Kjelleren Pizza Pub
19 Comfort Home Hotel Bryggen
20 Brosundet Gjestehus

21 Annecy Sommerpensjonat

PLACES TO EAT
2 Lunsj-Kiosken Gatekjøkken
6 Tollboden
10 Sjøbua
11 Café Hoffman; Molnes Bakeri
16 Burger King
18 Løvenvold Espresso & Te

26 Rimi Supermarket
29 Peppe's Pizza
31 SMAK Restaurant
32 Gullix

OTHER
1 Skansekaia (Hurtigruten) Ferry Terminal
4 RCG Netcafe
5 Skateflukaia Ferry Terminal
7 Ålesund Fiskerimuseet
8 Cruise Nightclub

13 Rollon Statue
14 Fjellstua Kafé & Kniven Overlook
22 Vinmonopolet
23 Guest Harbour Laundrette
24 Bus Terminal
25 Ålesund Reiselivslag Tourist Office; Library
27 Post Office
28 Aalesunds Museum
30 Rick's Bar & Nightclub

There's also a sanctuary for orphaned seals and a souvenir shop. The grounds offer superb coastal scenery, bathing beaches and hiking trails.

Sukkertoppen

A more challenging hike for an even wider ranging view leads to the summit of Sukkertoppen (314m). It begins on the street Sukkertoppvegen, on the 'hook' of Ålesund's fishhook peninsula. The track follows the easiest route, right up the east-pointing ridgeline. Take bus No 13 from town.

Offshore Islands

The offshore islands of Valderøy, Vigra, Giske and Godøy make nice day trips from Ålesund. Ytterland on Valderøy (Nkr36, 20 minutes) and Vigra (Nkr40, 30 minutes) are reached on bus No 62, and Giske (Nkr40, 30 minutes) and Godøy (Nkr44, 45 minutes) are accessed on bus No 64.

Giske is best known as the historic seat of the Viking-age ruling family, Arnungane, which ruled feudally from 990 to 1582. The island was also the home of Gange-Rolv (known as Rollon in France; he's also claimed by Vigra), the Viking warrior who besieged Paris, subsequently founded the Duchy of Normandy in 911 and was an ancestor of England's William the Conqueror. In 1911, when Normandy celebrated its millennium, a copy of the Rollon statue in Rouen was presented to Ålesund, where it now stands in Byparken.

Worthwhile sites on the islands include the Skjonghellaren caves on north-western Valderøy and the Blindheimssanden (also called Blimsand) white sand beach on north-western Vigra. Giske's 12th-century **marble church** (☎ 70 18 80 00, Giske; admission Nkr15; open 10am-5pm Mon-Sat 1pm-7pm Sun 1 June-20 Aug) was restored in 1756. The Makkevika marshes, also on Giske, offer fine bird-watching. The picturesque 1936 **Alnes lighthouse** (☎ 70 18 50 90, Alnes; admission free; open noon-6pm daily June-Aug) and fishing station, at the northern tip of Godøy, has a cafe, craft shop and art exhibit. Valderøy and Godøy also offer some excellent short mountain hikes.

On Godøy and Vigra, there are several fully equipped fishing cottages where you can stay for Nkr400 to Nkr700. Contact the tourist office in Ålesund for details.

Organised Tours

On weekdays from 17 June to 22 September, you can do a day trip to Runde island (Nkr288, 11¾ hours). Boat tours around the bird cliffs are available daily from Runde and three days a week from Ulsteinvik. For details see the Runde section, earlier in this chapter.

In summer, daily except Saturday, you can make scenic bus-ferry day trips (Nkr327) that include a cruise down the Geirangerfjord, up to 3½ hours in Geiranger and a return to Ålesund via Ørnevegen. This complicated route involves a lot of connections: a bus from Ålesund to Magerholm (weekdays at 8.50am and 11.10am, and Sunday at 11.10am), ferry to Ørsneset, bus to Hellsylt, ferry to Geiranger, bus to Eidsdal, ferry to Linge and bus back to Ålesund.

A simpler, but much more expensive, alternative is the Ålesund-Geiranger-Ålesund cruise (daily April to September) with Hurtigruten (Nkr596-656, 9¼ hours).

A Monday, Wednesday or Friday day tour to Hjørundfjord (Nkr229) on public transport begins with a bus from Ålesund to Ørsta at 10.50am; a bus from Ørsta to Sæbo; a ferry from Sæbo to Standal; a bus from Standal to Standal; and a ferry from Festøy back to Ålesund. Unfortunately, it misses out on Norangsdalen. Current bus/ferry times are given when you buy a ticket; phone ☎ 70 01 30 00 for details.

On Wednesday, mid-June to August, a Viking trading ship leaves Sunnmøre Museum (☎ 70 17 40 00) for a recommended one-hour cruise (adult/child Nkr50/free).

For details on the 1½-hour guided town walk (adult/child Nkr60/free), which runs at 1pm daily mid-June to mid-August, contact the tourist office.

Places to Stay

The tourist office keeps lists of private rooms that start at around Nkr200 per person. It also keeps a list of *rorbu* (fishing hut) accommodation, some of which is quite plush, on the offshore islands.

Volsdalen Camping (☎/fax 70 12 14 94, Volsdalsberga) Bus: No 13, 14, 18 & 24. Tent sites from Nkr50, simple 2–6-person cabins Nkr240-650. Open 1 May–mid-Sept. Above the shore about 2km east of the centre, this is the friendliest camping option and also the nearest to town.

Prinsen Strandcamping (☎ 70 15 52 04, fax 70 15 49 96, Gåseid) Tent sites Nkr50-150, rooms Nkr220-400, cabins Nkr250-900. If you want a luxurious cabin, you can try 4km east of town, but it's overpriced and the ambience seems almost comically sour.

Ålesund Vandrerhjem (☎ 70 11 58 30, fax 70 11 58 59, Parkgata 14) Dorm beds Nkr180, with breakfast, singles/doubles with breakfast Nkr370/470. Open May-Sept. The centrally located hostel offers clean rooms and cooking facilities.

Annecy Sommerpensjonat (☎ 70 12 96 30, Kirkegata 1) Singles/doubles Nkr320/420. Open mid-June–mid-Aug. The simple Annecy Sommerpensjonat lets out self-contained student rooms in summer; linen costs Nkr40 extra.

Brosundet Gjestehus (☎ 70 12 10 00, fax 70 12 12 95, Apotekergata 5) Singles/doubles Nkr570/770. You'll find a formal guesthouse atmosphere here, but the large hotel-standard rooms have great harbour views.

Hotel Noreg (☎ 70 12 29 38, fax 70 12 66 60, Kongensgata 27) Singles Nkr585-875, doubles Nkr790-1080. The fine Hotel Noreg offers comfortable en suite rooms and a good breakfast.

Comfort Home Hotel Bryggen (☎ 70 12 64 00, fax 70 12 11 80, Apotekergata 1-3) Singles/doubles from Nkr645/895. This wonderful waterfront option includes a cold evening buffet in the price.

Quality Scandinavie Hotel (☎ 70 15 78 00, fax 70 15 78 01, Løvenvoldgata 8) Singles/doubles from Nkr605/790. There's excellent Art Nouveau-style decor and real character here.

Rica Parken Hotel (☎ 70 12 50 50, fax 70 12 21 64, Storgata 16) Singles/doubles from Nkr695/895. Some of the pleasant, modern rooms here have views of the town park.

Scandic Hotel Ålesund (☎ 21 61 45 00, fax 21 61 45 11, Molovegen 6) Singles/doubles from Nkr645/845. This is a modern harbourside hotel with high standards.

Places to Eat

Sjøbua (☎ 70 12 71 00, Brunholmgata 1) Mains Nkr242-346. You'll get a gourmet meal at the rustic and stylish Sjøbua, where fish is the house speciality.

Tollboden (☎ 70 12 81 16, Tollbugata 2) Pasta dishes Nkr95-125, other mains Nkr180-206. Tollboden, a solid upper-range place with a great harbourside location near the Hurtigruten quay, has an adventurous menu and is noted for its fish soup (Nkr82).

Gullix (☎ 70 12 05 48, Rådstugata 5B) Mains Nkr98-269, 3-course fish dinner around Nkr400. With a pleasant rustic atmosphere, Gullix is good for fish, pasta, traditional Norwegian *husmannskost* (Nkr98 to Nkr122), and Mexican and Spanish dishes.

Café Løvenvold (☎ 70 15 78 13, Løvenvoldsgata 8) Mains Nkr120-230. This restaurant, in the Quality Scandinavie Hotel, serves fine Mediterranean dishes.

SMAK Restaurant (☎ 70 12 62 62, Kipervikgata 5) Lunch under Nkr100, evening mains Nkr89-182. The minimalist-style SMAK Restaurant is a cafeteria by day, but turns into a restaurant and noisy pub by night.

Peppe's Pizza (☎ 70 12 82 22, Kaiser Wilhelmsgata 25) Lunch buffet Nkr79-93. The all-you-can-eat pizza and salad lunch buffet at Peppe's operates from 11am to 3pm on weekdays.

Café Hoffmann (☎ 70 12 37 97, Kongensgate 11) Mains Nkr78-125. Open to 6pm (4pm Sat, 5pm Sun). This cafe has a fine harbour view and also serves simple meals, such as soup special with bread (Nkr40).

Løvenvold Espresso & Te (☎ 70 12 54 00, Løvenvoldgata 2) Coffee from around Nkr20. Open 8am-9pm Mon-Fri, 10am-7pm Sat. This cosy coffee shop is particularly recommended.

Lunsj-Kiosken Gatekjøkken (☎ 70 12 31 83, Tollbugata 1) Snacks & meals from Nkr20. The Lunsj-Kiosken Gatekjøkken offers what are probably the best deals in town on decent quick and light meals. Hot dogs start at Nkr20, burgers cost Nkr40 to Nkr55 and chicken and chips goes for Nkr79.

More familiar fast food is grilled up at the *Burger King (Storgata 10)*. *Molnes Bakeri (☎ 70 12 19 95, Kongensgate 11)* does the usual line of bread and pastry. The *Rimi* supermarket is downstairs in Kremmergården, behind the tourist office. At Brosundet, you can buy the catch of the day directly from the fishing vessels.

Entertainment

Cruise Nightclub (☎ 70 12 84 80, Molovegen) Immediately west of the centre, this club has a weekend disco as well as an Irish-style pub.

Rick's Bar & Nightclub (☎ 70 12 57 00, Kiperviktorget) This popular nightspot appeals mainly to the 18 to 20 gang.

Maritim Dancing (☎ 70 12 29 38, Hotel Noreg, Kongensgata 27) Maritim Dancing attracts a slightly older crowd and features a DJ at weekends.

Kjelleren Pizza Pub (☎ 70 15 78 15, Quality Scandinavie Hotel, Løvenvoldgata 8) This rough but entertaining pub has a dart board and pool table, and sometimes hosts live bands. The pizzas are recommended as the best in town.

Getting There & Away

Air Ålesund is served by Braathens (☎ 70 11 49 00), with flights to/from Bergen, Trondheim, Stavanger and Oslo, and SAS (☎ 70 10 49 00), with flights to/from Oslo.

Bus You'll find the main bus terminal on Kaiser Wilhelmsgata, diagonally opposite the tourist office. Nor-Way Bussekspress buses run to/from Hellesylt (Nkr138, 2¾ hours, one to four daily), Stryn (Nkr203, 3½ hours, one to four daily) and Bergen (Nkr523, 10¾ hours, once daily). Ålesund Bilruter Togbuss services run to/from Åndalsnes (Nkr162, 2½ hours, one to three daily). The Nor-Way Bussekspress Mørelinjen runs once or twice daily between Ålesund, Molde (Nkr123, 2¼ hours) and Trondheim (Nkr458, 7¼ hours). There's also a direct overnight run daily except Saturday between Ålesund and Oslo (Nkr610, 9¾ hours).

Boat The MRF express boat M/S *Fjørtoft* links Ålesund with Molde (Nkr162, 2½ hours) from Skateflukaia ferry terminal twice daily on weekdays in July only. Hurtigruten coastal steamers arrive/depart at 8.45am/6.45pm northbound and at 11.45pm/12.45am southbound; on its northbound run, there's a popular detour via Geiranger (hence the large gap between arrival and departure times).

Getting Around

The Ålesund airport is on Vigra island, which is connected to the town by the undersea tunnels to Ellingsøy (3.6km) and Valderøy (4.2km). Flybuss bus services (☎ 70 13 68 00) depart from Skateflukaia and the bus station in town one hour before the departure of domestic flights (Nkr67, 25 minutes).

Drivers to the airport and the offshore islands pay tunnel tolls totalling Nkr55 each way for a car and driver plus Nkr17 per additional passenger. This significantly reduces tourism in the area.

Contact the tourist office for details on bicycle hire.

MOLDE
pop 17,760

Molde, scenically situated beside the sea at the wide mouth of Romsdalsfjorden, calls itself the 'Town of Roses' but is best known for its annual jazz festival in July. In April 1940, Molde suffered almost complete destruction at the hands of the Nazis. The Luftwaffe had heard that King Håkon was holed up in a red house, and set about destroying every red building. In fact, the king personally witnessed the bombing from beneath a birch tree now called Kongebjørka, at Glomstua; the last thing he saw of the town before heading for exile in Britain was the collapsing spire of the burning church. On a happy note, one local hero saved the old altarpiece painting, Axel Ender's *Resurrection*, by ripping it out with a knife as the bombs fell, and the Norwegian resistance managed to smuggle out 36 tonnes of royal gold on the HMS *Glasgow*.

As a result of the wartime destruction, modern Molde is dominated by post-war

WESTERN FJORDS

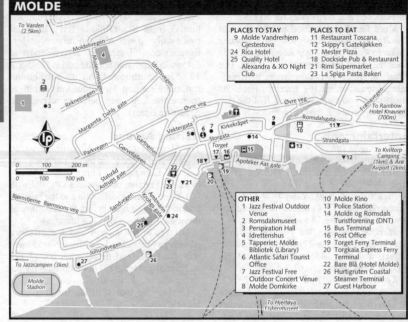

MOLDE

PLACES TO STAY
9 Molde Vandrerhjem
  Gjestestova
24 Rica Hotel
25 Quality Hotel
  Alexandra & XO Night
  Club

PLACES TO EAT
11 Restaurant Toscana
12 Skippy's Gatekjøkken
17 Mester Pizza
18 Dockside Pub & Restaurant
21 Rimi Supermarket
23 La Spiga Pasta Bakeri

OTHER
1 Jazz Festival Outdoor
  Venue
2 Romsdalsmuseet
3 Perspiration Hall
4 Idrettshus
5 Tapperiet; Molde
  Bibliotek (Library)
6 Atlantic Safari Tourist
  Office
7 Jazz Festival Free
  Outdoor Concert Venue
8 Molde Domkirke
10 Molde Kino
13 Police Station
14 Molde og Romsdals
  Turistforening (DNT)
15 Bus Terminal
16 Post Office
19 Torget Ferry Terminal
20 Torgkaia Express Ferry
  Terminal
22 Bare Blå (Hotel Molde)
26 Hurtigruten Coastal
  Steamer Terminal
27 Guest Harbour

architecture. It's a friendly and pleasantly compact little place and the unique coastal landscapes more resemble New Zealand or Seattle's Puget Sound than the rest of Norway.

For a fine overview, drive or trek up to the Varden overlook, 400m above the town.

Information

The friendly Atlantic Safari tourist office (☎ 71 25 71 33, W www.visitmolde.com), Storgata 31, opens 9am to 6pm weekdays, 9am to 4pm Saturday and 10am to 3pm Sunday from 15 June to 15 August. The rest of the year, it opens 8.30am to 3.30pm on weekdays.

For hiking and mountain hut information, visit Molde og Romsdals Turistforening (DNT; ☎ 71 25 18 66), Storgata 56.

Internet connections are available at Molde Bibliotek (library), Kirkebakken 1–3. You can do laundry at the Guest Harbour, near the western end of town.

Romsdalsmuseet

Sprawling across a large open area northwest of the centre is Romsdalen Folk Museum (☎ 71 20 24 60, Per Amdamsveg 4; adult/child Nkr40/20 including Fiskerimuseet; open 11am-6pm Mon-Sat, noon-6pm Sun 25 June-12 Aug, closing 3pm other times 9-24 June & 13 Aug), founded in 1912. It includes 40 homes that have been shifted to this spot from around the Romsdal region, 'Bygata' (an early-20th-century town street) and an intriguing 'composite church' made from bits of now-demolished local stave churches. As much as possible, original furnishings have been left intact, and the museum reveals aspects of local life from the 14th to 20th centuries. Tickets are valid for two days and include guiding in English on request.

Fiskerimuseet

A short ferry ride from the Torget terminal is the Fishery Museum (☎ 93 42 54 06,

Hjertøya; 2-day admission adult/child Nkr40/20 (also includes Romsdalsmuseet); open noon-5pm daily 16 June-19 Aug). This open-air museum brings to life the coastal fishing cultures around the mouth of Romsdalfjorden from the mid-19th-century to the present day. During the same period, ferries (☎ 93 42 54 06) run daily from Molde at noon, 2pm and 4pm and from Hjertøya at 1.45pm, 3.45pm and 5.45pm.

Special Events

Undoubtedly the pre-eminent event is the renowned Molde Jazz Festival, which is held from Monday to Saturday in the 29th week of the year, around mid-July. It attracts both Norwegian and international names, as well as at least 60,000 fans, who pay from Nkr100 to Nkr260 for the big events. Traditional jazz concerts take place in Perspiration Hall, the big concerts are held outdoors near the Romsdalsmuseet, indoor concerts take place at the Idrettenshus (sports hall) and free events (including a daily street parade) are held from noon in front of the Rådhus. For information, contact the Molde International Jazz Festival (☎ 71 20 31 50, fax 71 20 31 51, e moldeja zz@moldejazz.no, w www.moldejazz.no). Credit-card ticket sales are available for a Nkr10 surcharge through BillettService (☎ 81 53 31 33).

Molde's other festival is Bjørnsonfestivalen (w www.bjørnsonfestivalen.no), the Norwegian Festival of International Literature, which is held in Molde and Nesset (5km east of Eidsvåg) from early to mid-August to honour home-grown author Bjørnstjerne Bjørnson. It attracts literary and theatrical figures from around the world.

Places to Stay

Private homes open to visitors may be booked through the tourist office. Most have kitchen facilities and cost from Nkr150 to Nkr200 per person. During the Molde Jazz Festival, many local households also offer private accommodation, and a large temporary camping ground, *Jazzcampen*, is set up 3km west of the centre and costs Nkr60 to Nkr100 per person.

Kviltorp Camping (☎ 71 21 17 42, fax 71 21 10 19, Fannestrandveien 142) Bus: No 20 from centre. Tent sites Nkr110 with car & 2 people, 2-bed cabins Nkr350, 4-bed cabins with shower & TV Nkr600. This place occupies a rather noisy spot at the end of the airport runway but fortunately, there's little air traffic. Cabins are available year-round.

Molde Vandrerhjem Gjestestova (☎ 71 21 61 80, fax 71 24 23 09, Romsdalsgata 5) Dorm beds Nkr100, singles/doubles from Nkr150/300. Open mid-June–mid-Aug. In this centrally located hostel most rooms include a mini-kitchen with a fridge and hotplate but guests may also use the communal kitchen.

Rainbow Hotel Knausen (☎ 71 19 11 00, fax 71 19 11 10, Knausen) Singles/doubles Nkr525/790, motel doubles Nkr500. This hotel offers acceptable rooms at the eastern end of town, towards the airport. Sheets and breakfast cost extra.

Rica Hotel (☎ 71 20 35 00, fax 71 20 35 01, Storgata 8) Singles/doubles from Nkr685/830. High-standard en suite rooms and a good breakfast await travellers who stay at the Rica Hotel.

Quality Hotel Alexandra (☎ 71 20 37 50, fax 71 20 37 87, Storgata 1–7) Singles Nkr795-1095, doubles Nkr895-1295. This luxurious establishment has excellent facilities, including an indoor swimming pool.

Places to Eat

Mester Pizza (Torget) Pizza from Nkr69. Open to 1am Mon-Fri, 3am Sat & Sun. Takeaway pizzas are available from this gatekjøkken on the town square.

Skippy's Gatekjøkken (☎ 71 25 22 30, Fergeterminalen) Meals under Nkr100. Open 9am-midnight daily. The recommended Skippy's doubles as a cafe and serves fast meals such as burgers (Nkr36 to Nkr69), fish and chips (Nkr72), schnitzel (Nkr69) and the odd Hawaiian pork special (Nkr92).

Dockside Pub & Restaurant (☎ 71 21 50 33, Torget) Soup Nkr31, mains Nkr89-149. At this ordinary restaurant, reasonable pizzas range from Nkr99 to Nkr134, salads from Nkr64 to Nkr69 and beef dishes from Nkr139 to Nkr149.

La Spiga Pasta Bakeri (Gørvellplassen) Pasta dishes Nkr68-75, small pizzas Nkr39. Fast-food Italian specialities are available at the small and clean La Spiga bakery.

Restaurant Toscana (☎ 71 25 64 11, Romsdalsgata 20) Daily specials Nkr129, mains Nkr79-240. More formal Italian cuisine, including pizza, pasta, salads, meat and fish dishes, are also the speciality in the cheery Restaurant Toscana.

Quality Hotel Alexandra (☎ 71 20 37 50, Storgata 1-7) Mains Nkr85-209. The charming pub-style dining room at the flash Quality Hotel Alexandra serves fish, beef, lamb, pasta and salads.

The inexpensive *Rimi supermarket (Storgata 24)* is found right in the centre of Molde.

Entertainment

For cultural and entertainment information, check out the kommune Web site W www.visitmr.com.

Bare Blå (☎ 71 21 58 88, Storgata 19) Open to 1.30am Fri & Sat. This popular pub is in Hotel Molde.

XO Nightclub (☎ 71 20 37 50, Quality Hotel Alexandra, Storgata 1-7) Cover charge around Nkr80. This place has live music and DJs at weekends and appeals mainly to those over 30.

Dockside Pub (☎ 71 21 50 33, Torget) The disco here puts on live performances every second week or so and attracts the over 20 crowd.

Tapperiet (☎ 71 24 13 50, Kirkebakken 1-3) The 18 to 25-year-old student set will probably enjoy Tapperiet, run by the student association. Cover charges apply only when there's live music.

Molde Kino (☎ 82 00 00 90, Gotfred Lies Plass 1) This three-screen cinema shows films daily.

Getting There & Away

Molde's Årø airport lies on the shore just 4km east of the city centre; it's accessed on bus No 252 (Nkr23, 10 minutes) or the Flybuss (Nkr40, 10 minutes). Braathens (☎ 71 21 97 00) has three to five flights daily to/from Oslo.

Buses run four to nine times daily between Molde and Kristiansund (Nkr101 to Nkr128, 1¾ to 2¼ hours) and Ålesund (Nkr118, two hours). Most buses to Ålesund first require taking the ferry from Molde to Vestnes.

The express ferry *Fjørtoft* between Ålesund and Molde's Torgkaia terminal (Nkr162, 2½ hours) sails twice daily on weekdays in July only. Northbound, the Hurtigruten coastal steamer leaves Storkaia in Molde at 10pm (6.30pm from October to March) and southbound, at 9.30pm.

If you're driving towards Åndalsnes, a car and driver pays Nkr55 to pass through the Fannefjorden tunnel, plus Nkr20 per passenger. The Tussentunnelen shortcut, on the northbound Rv64, will save you 15 minutes (and cost you Nkr15), but it can easily be circumvented by following the main road via Skaret.

AROUND MOLDE
Ona

The beautiful outer island of Ona, with its bare rocky landscapes and picturesque lighthouse, represents the epitome of an offshore fishing community. Gazing out to sea, you can probably imagine the enormous tidal wave that washed over it in 1670. It makes a popular day or overnight trip from Molde. En route, WWII buffs may want to stop off at **Gossen Krigsminnesamling *(☎ 71 17 15 77, Gossen; adult/child Nkr30/15; open noon-5pm Tues-Sun 23 June-6 Aug)*** on the low island of Gossen, which is an exhibit on the Nazi wartime airstrip built by Russian POWs.

Ona Sjøhus (☎ 71 27 60 74, fax 71 27 60 95) Huts Nkr150 per person. The simple but atmospheric huts at Ona Sjøhus are recommended.

If you'd rather visit Ona on a day trip, take the 8.15am bus from Molde to Hollingsholmen (25 minutes), which connects with a ferry to Aukra (15 minutes), then a bus to Småge (35 minutes); it costs Nkr57. Ferry No 32 sails to Ona (Nkr30, 1¾ hours), via Finnøy and Sandøy. It arrives in Ona at 11.25am. You can then begin the return route at either noon or 3.35pm. On Saturday from 23 June to 11 August, ferries also run between Harøysund (near Bud) and Ona (Nkr160 return, 2½ hours), via Bjørnsund (Nkr60, 30 minutes). They leave at 11am from Harøysund and 3.30pm from Ona, but there's no connecting bus back to Ona. En route, you may want to visit the abandoned summer-house village of Bjørnsund, where a cafe and shop operate in summer only.

Mardalsfossen

If you have a car, it's about a two-hour drive up Langfjorden and past the dramatic lake, Eikesdalsvatnet, to Mardalsfossen – once the fifth highest waterfall in the world. How could it have lost this status, you might ask? Well, in the 1970s, this two-level 655m waterfall (the greatest single drop is 297m) was extinguished by a hydroelectric project. Although environmentalists chained themselves together to prevent the construction, it went ahead and Mardalsfossen now flows only during the tourist season, between 20 June and 20 August.

Also recommended is the exciting single-track mountain road **Aursjøvegen** (Nkr50 toll), which is open late June to September and provides a link between Mardalsfossen and Sunndalsøra.

Bud

Along the coastal route between Molde and Kristiansund lies the rustic little fishing village of Bud, which huddles around a compact little harbour. In the 16th and 17th centuries, it was the greatest trading centre between Bergen and Trondheim but is better known for its role in more recent history.

Ergan Kystfort (*Ergan Coastal Fort;* ☎ 71 26 15 18; *adult/child Nkr40/30; open 10am-6pm daily 1 June-27 Aug)*, which serves as a WWII museum and memorial, was hastily erected by Nazi forces in May 1940 and dismantled between May and November 1945. Various armaments and a network of bunkers and soldiers' quarters are dispersed around the hill. Guided tours are available at 1pm and 3pm.

Bud Camping (☎ 71 26 10 23, *fax 71 26 11 47)* Tent sites with car Nkr120, 4-bed/8-bed huts Nkr300/750. Bud Camping offers good facilities and cabins for campers.

Sjøbua Mat og Vinhus (☎ 71 26 14 00, *Vikaveien)* Main courses Nkr125-129. This rustic old fish restaurant serves up the local catch in a harbourfront warehouse with wooden floorboards and a boat in the middle of the room. Fish soup costs Nkr54 and main courses include whale.

For supplies and fast food, there's an **ICA** supermarket and a **gatekjøkken** just inland from the harbour.

On weekdays, bus No 253 runs between Molde and Bud (Nkr63, 50 minutes) one to four times daily except Sunday.

Trollkirka

If you're heading towards Bud and Atlanterhavsveien, it's worth making a short side trip to the mystical cave Trollkirka, the 'Trolls' Church'. This series of three white marble grottoes is connected by subterranean streams, and one contains a fabulous 14m waterfall. The entrance is an uphill walk from the road (2.5km, one hour) – you'll need a torch and good boots to explore it fully. From Molde, bus No 241 runs two to seven times daily past the Trollkirka car park.

Atlanterhavsveien & Averøya

The eight storm-lashed bridges of Atlanterhavsveien between Vevang and the island of Averøya connect 17 islands. On calm days, you may wonder what the big deal is, but in a storm, you'll experience nature's wrath at its most dramatic.

You'll find a small tourist office and souvenir shop by the road at Vevang. North of the main road, there's the frightfully exposed **Hestskjæret Fyr** lighthouse. Look out for whales and seals offshore along the route. Rock fans can check out the rather odd Steinbiten stone exhibition, at the Statoil petrol station in Bremsnes.

Worth a detour is the stave church **Kvernes stavkirke** (☎ 71 51 42 63, *Kvernes; adult/child Nkr30/free; open 10am-5pm daily mid-June–mid-August & 10am-5pm Sun mid-May–mid-Sept)* on Averøya, which dates from around 1300 but was rebuilt in 1633. Look out for the large 300-year-old votive ship and the Catholic-Lutheran hybrid altar screen from 1475 (reconstructed 1695). There's also an open-air museum and a gallery/handicrafts outlet nearby.

Håholmen Havstuer (☎ *71 51 72 50, fax 71 51 72 51, Håholmen*) Singles/doubles Nkr650/980. For accommodation, try this novel place on an offshore islet north of the middle of the route, which is run by explorer Ragnar Thorseth and his wife, Kari. The on-site 'Saga Siglar' exhibit, which concentrates on Viking voyages, is open daily in summer. Access from the main road is by Viking ship (or at least a decent replica); it leaves hourly from 11am to 9pm, late June to mid-August.

Skjerneset Bryggecamping (☎ *71 51 18 94, fax 71 51 18 15, Skeggevika*) Traditional rorbuer Nkr350-550. This appealing little sea-oriented place is in a warehouse at Skeggevika on Ekkilsøya, west of Bremsnes.

Lysø Camping (☎ *71 51 21 13, fax 71 51 24 09, Lysø, Averøya*) Car & tent sites Nkr110, cabins Nkr530-850. The clean and comfortable modern-style cabins here are recommended.

Buses run between Molde and Bremsnes (Nkr110, 1¾ hours) four times daily on weekdays and two or three times daily on weekends. Buses run from Bremsnes to Kvernes (Nkr26, 15 minutes) three to seven times daily except Sunday. From Bremsnes, there are frequent ferry connections to Kristiansund (Nkr19, 20 minutes).

KRISTIANSUND
pop 16,945
Built on a series of hills across three islands, the historic cod-fishing and drying centre of Kristiansund has friendly ambience which makes it a pleasant stop for a day or two, and both the new church and the offshore island of Grip are unforgettable.

Information
Kristiansund Reiselivslag (☎ 71 58 54 54, fax 71 58 54 55, **W** www.visitkristiansund .no), Kongens Plass 1, is open 9am to 7pm weekdays and 11am to 4pm on weekends from mid-June to mid-August, and 8.30am to 3.30pm weekdays the rest of the year. The Kristiansund og Nordmøre DNT office (☎ 71 67 69 37) is found at Storgata 8/10.

For books and maps, visit Ark Bokhandel bookshop (☎ 71 57 09 60), on the corner of Kaibakken and Nedre Enggate. Laundry facilities are available at the Guest Harbour.

Things to See
Kristiansund's **Gamle Byen**, or old town, occupies part of Innlandet island, where you'll find clapboard buildings dating from as early as the 17th century. The opulent **Lossiusgården**, at the eastern end of the historic district, is the distinguished home of an 18th-century merchant. The atmospheric 300-year-old **Dødeladen Café** hosts cultural and musical events, including a festival in early July (contact the tourist office for details). The best access from the centre is on the Sundbåt ferry (five minutes, Nkr10) from Piren.

Interesting structures in the town centre include the 1786 Christiegården house; the monumental 1914 Art Nouveau-style Festiviteten, which is used for theatrical and opera productions; and the *Klippfiskkjerringa* statue by Tore Bjørn Skjøsvik, which represents a fishwife carrying cod to the drying racks.

Mellemværftet, which to many resembles a nautical junkyard, includes the remnants of Kristiansund's 1867 shipyard, an 1872 forge and workshop, and an 1887 workers' quarters. You can stroll through at any time but from 8am to 3pm on weekdays, call ☎ 71 67 71 95 for a guided tour.

Museums
Nordmøre Museum The worthwhile Nordmøre Museum (☎ *71 67 15 78, Dalaveien; adult/child Nkr20/10; open 10am-2pm Tues-Fri, noon-3pm Sun*) includes regional archaeological artefacts from as early as 7000 BC, as well as an old *stabbur* (raised storehouse), a historic smokehouse and an early waterwheel.

Handelshuset At Handelshuset (☎ *71 67 15 78, Freiveien; admission free; open noon-8pm Tues-Sun 22 June-31 Aug, otherwise shorter hours*) you can learn about Kristiansund's commercial history and see Norway's oldest operational coffee roaster.

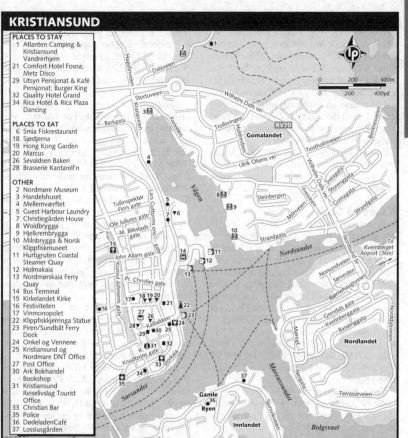

KRISTIANSUND

PLACES TO STAY
1 Atlanten Camping &
  Kristiansund
  Vandrerhjem
21 Comfort Hotel Fosna;
  Metz Disco
29 Utsyn Pensjonat & Kafé
  Pensjonat; Burger King
32 Quality Hotel Grand
34 Rica Hotel & Rica Plaza
  Dancing

PLACES TO EAT
6 Smia Fiskrestaurant
18 Sjøstjerna
19 Hong Kong Garden
20 Marcus
26 Sevaldsen Bakeri
28 Brasserie Kantarell'n

OTHER
2 Nordmøre Museum
3 Handelshuset
4 Mellemværftet
5 Guest Harbour Laundry
7 Christiegården House
8 Woldbrygga
9 Hjelkrembrygga
10 Milnbrygga & Norsk
  Klippfiskmuseet
11 Hurtigruten Coastal
  Steamer Quay
12 Holmakaia
13 Nordmørskaia Ferry
  Quay
14 Bus Terminal
15 Kirkelandet Kirke
16 Festiviteten
17 Vinmonopolet
22 Klippfiskkjerringa Statue
23 Piren/Sundbåt Ferry
  Dock
24 Onkel og Vennene
25 Kristiansund og
  Nordmare DNT Office
27 Post Office
30 Ark Bokhandel
  Bookshop
31 Kristiansund
  Reiselivslag Tourist
  Office
33 Christian Bar
35 Police
36 DødeladenCafé
37 Lossiusgården

Milnbrygga & Norsk Klippfiskmuseum

The Norwegian Klippfish museum (☎ 71 67 15 78, Strandgata; adult/child Nkr30/10; open noon-5pm Mon-Sat, 1pm-4pm Sun 18 June-20 Aug), in the 1749 Milnbrygga warehouse on the Gomalandet peninsula, presents the 300-year history of the dried-cod export industry in Kristiansund, and the setting is as interesting as the subject matter (it's all very fishy). Guided tours run every 30 minutes until 4pm. The easiest access from the centre is on the Sundbåt ferry (Nkr15, 15 minutes) – ask to be dropped at the museum.

Hjelkrembrygga & Woldbrygga This lovely old klippfish warehouse, dating from 1835, is now a tin smith's workshop (☎ 71 67 15 78, Dikselveien 16; adult/child Nkr20/10; open 1pm-4pm Sun 17 June-19 Aug). The neighbouring Woldbrygga (☎ 71 67 15 78, Dikselveien; open by appointment) displays a collection of wooden boats and rope-manufacturing equipment in an old 1875 barrel factory.

Kirkelandet Kirke

One Kristiansund building that can't be ignored is architect Odd Østby's Kirkelandet

Church (Langveien; admission free; open 10am-7pm May-Aug, 10am-2pm Sept-Apr), which was built in 1964 to replace the one bombed by the Nazis in 1940. The exterior, which was intended to expand on the theme 'Rock Crystal among Roses', is somewhat bizarre but the 320 panes of stained glass inside create an inspiring effect. Moving upward from the earthy colours at the base, they lighten and, at the top, attempt to admit the 'celestial light of heaven'.

Behind the church lies the large Vanndammene Park area, with plenty of greenery, walking tracks and the fine Varden watchtower viewpoint.

Places to Stay

Accommodation between 20 June and 31 July should be booked well in advance.

Atlanten Camping (☎ 71 67 11 04, fax 71 67 24 05, Dalaveien 22) Tent/caravan sites Nkr60/80 plus Nkr10/person, cabins Nkr330-540. This recommended camping ground lies within reasonable walking distance of the centre. Best of all, the rates include hot showers and the use of kitchen facilities.

Kristiansund Vandrerhjem (☎ 71 67 11 04, fax 71 67 24 05, Dalaveien 22) Dorm beds Nkr160, singles/doubles Nkr250/350. The well-equipped kitchen at the Kristiansund hostel contains 19 fridges!

Utsyn Pensjonat (☎ 71 56 69 70, fax 71 56 69 90, Kongens Plass 4) Singles/doubles Nkr385/495. The basic rooms here are the cheapest recommended deal.

Quality Hotel Grand (☎ 71 57 13 00, fax 71 57 13 01, Bernstorffstredet 1) Singles Nkr645-745, doubles Nkr795-845. This is the largest hotel in Kristiansund and probably also the best choice.

Comfort Hotel Fosna (☎ 71 67 40 11, fax 71 67 76 59, Hauggata 16) Singles & doubles Nkr845. Prices at this centrally located place include a light supper.

Rica Hotel (☎ 71 67 64 11, fax 71 67 79 12, Storgata 41) Singles/doubles from Nkr700/880. This hotel is fairly standard.

Places to Eat

Smia Fiskerestaurant (☎ 71 67 11 70, Fosnagata 30) Mains Nkr105-220. The atmospheric Smia fish restaurant, in an old waterfront boathouse, predictably specialises in seafood. Its famous fish soups cost Nkr75 to Nkr105, assorted fish dishes cost Nkr105 to Nkr220, and landlubbers' steak and lamb dishes cost between Nkr165 and Nkr195.

Sjøstjerna (☎ 71 67 87 78, Skolegata 8) Fish mains Nkr138-198. For seafood, you can also try Sjøstjerna, with outdoor seating right in the shopping district. It serves Gravat laks (marinated salmon) and pita (Nkr65), paella (Nkr158) and also pasta dishes, lamb and steak for mid-range prices.

Brasserie Kantarell'n (☎ 71 67 66 88, Kongens Plass 6) Lunch Nkr50-150. This is a popular and stylish place that has been around for decades and is known for its agreeable outdoor seating.

Marcus (☎ 71 58 99 50, Skolegata 2) Pizza & pasta Nkr79-100, other mains Nkr114-205. Marcus offers a wide range of meals including fish, beef, Italian and Mexican dishes.

Hong Kong Garden (☎ 71 67 55 60, Skolegata 8) Lunch Nkr69, most dinner mains around Nkr100. Chinese specialities are the forte at Hong Kong Garden, one floor above Sjøstjerna.

Local youth and families frequent the *Burger King*. Upstairs, *Kafé Pensjonat* is a popular hang-out for local seniors and it serves good cheap food (Nkr65 to Nkr98).

For a quick breakfast of coffee and pastry, visit *Sevaldsen Bakeri* (Nedre Enggata). *Vinmonopolet* is on the corner of Langveien and Helsingsgata.

Entertainment

Onkel og Vennene (☎ 71 67 58 10, Kaibakken 1) This pub/cafe has a pleasant atmosphere and is a good place for a beer in the evening.

Christian Bar (☎ 71 57 03 00, Storgata 17) The Christian Bar is a particularly decent pub for over-25s.

Metz (☎ 71 67 40 11, Hauggata 16) The Metz disco appeals to patrons aged 23 to 35.

Rica Plaza Dancing (☎ 71 67 64 11, Storgata 41) Rica Plaza Dancing is aimed at everyone over 35.

Getting There & Away

Air The Kvernberget airport is on Nordlandet island. Braathens has at least five flights daily to/from Oslo, as well as direct flights to/from Bergen, Ålesund and Molde.

Bus The main bus terminal lies immediately north of Nordmørskaia ferry quay. Buses run four to nine times daily between Kristiansund and Molde (Nkr101 to Nkr128, 1¾ to 2¼ hours). HOB runs two to five daily services between Kristiansund and Oppdal (Nkr238, 3¾ hours) via Sunndalsøra (Nkr155, 2¼ hours), which connect with trains to/from Oslo and Trondheim. The same company also has one to three daily (except Saturday) buses to/from Trondheim (Nkr346, five hours).

Car & Motorcycle For drivers on the E39, the Krifast toll tunnel between Gjemnes and the island of Frei costs Nkr60 per car and driver plus Nkr20 per passenger.

Boat For day trips to the eastern end of the Atlanterhavsveien and the Kvernes stave church, take the roughly hourly Bremsnes ferry (Nkr19, 20 minutes) from Holmakaia quay. Express boats connect Kristiansund with Trondheim (Nkr405, 3½ hours) two or three times daily from Nordmørskaia and the Hurtigruten coastal steamer also calls in daily at Holmakaia. The southbound ferry departs at 5pm, northbound at 11pm (1.45am, April to September).

Getting Around

Town buses cost Nkr15 per ride, and there are frequent weekday (few on weekends) Flybuss services to Kvernberget airport (Nkr30, 20 minutes). The Sundbåt ferry circulates from the town centre to the islands of Innlandet and Nordlandet, and the peninsula, Gomalandet. It runs constantly from 6.45am to 4.35pm Monday to Friday, and from 8.40am to 1.30pm on Saturday. The full circuit takes 20 minutes and any single journey costs Nkr15.

AROUND KRISTIANSUND
Grip

Crowded onto a tiny rocky island, the colourful village of Grip sits amid an archipelago of 80 islets and skerries, and makes a wonderful day trip from Kristiansund. In the period between 1780 and 1820, a drop in the cod fishery and two powerful storms (1796 and 1804) left the village crushed and practically abandoned. Although it eventually bounced back to become Norway's smallest municipality, in 1964 it was appended to Kristiansund.

The stave church on the island was originally constructed in the 14th century (opening hours correspond with the arrival of the ferry) and, on an offshore skerry, rises the lovely 47m Bratthårskollen lighthouse, built in 1888.

From 15 May to 30 August, the ferry M/S *Gripskyss* (☎ 71 58 54 54) plies the 14km between Kristiansund and Grip (Nkr140 return, 30 minutes) two to three times daily.

SUNNDALSØRA
pop 5000

The industrial town of Sunndalsøra enjoys a spectacular location beneath the towering cliffs of immense peaks, including Store Kalken (1884m). The recommended Aursjøvegen mountain road, via spectacular Lilledalen, heads south from the town (see the earlier Mardalsfossen section).

Sunndalsøra Vandrerhjem (☎ 71 69 13 01, fax 71 69 05 55, Trædal) Dorm beds Nkr100, singles/doubles Nkr175/240. You may want to stop at this charming traditional hostel, 3km south of town in Lilledalen.

Buses run two to five times daily to/from Kristiansund (Nkr155, 2¼ hours) and Oppdal (Nkr92, 1¼ hours), connecting with trains to/from Oslo and Trondheim.

Trøndelag

TRONDHEIM

pop 136,562

The lively, agreeable university town of Trondheim is Norway's third-largest city and first capital. It has a rich medieval history, and the centre is easily explored on foot.

History

In 997, the Christian King Olav Tryggvason selected a broad sandbank at the river Nid estuary to moor his longboat. The natural harbour and strategic position made Nidaros, as the settlement was then called, especially useful for defence against the warlike pagan chiefs of Lade, who were a perceived threat to Christianity – and to stability – in the region. It is believed that Leifur Eiríksson visited the king's farm two years later and was converted to Christianity before setting sail for Iceland and Greenland and, in turn, becoming the first European to set foot in North America.

In 1030 another, now more famous, King Olav (Haraldsson) was martyred in battle at Stiklestad about 90km to the north-east and canonised the following year (see Stiklestad later in this chapter). Nidaros became a centre for pilgrims from all over Europe. When Norway became a bishopric in 1153, Nidaros emerged as the ecumenical centre for Norway, Orkney, the Isle of Man, the Faroe Islands, Iceland and Greenland. Nidaros served as the capital of Norway until 1217, ruling an empire that extended from what is now western Russia to the shores of Newfoundland. The cult of St Olav continued until the Reformation in 1537, when Norway was placed under the Lutheran bishopric of Denmark.

After a fire razed most of the city in 1681, Trondheim was redesigned with wide streets and a Renaissance flair by General Caspar de Cicignon. Today, the Nidaros Cathedral spire remains the highest point in town.

Trondheim's location became key once again in WWII, when German naval forces made it their base for northern Norway. The

Highlights

- Touring Nidaros Cathedral, Norway's most sacred building
- Visiting the medieval battlefield at Stiklestad, where St Olav met his untimely fate
- Widening your musical horizons at Ringve Museum of Music History, and exploring local history at Trøndelag Folkemuseum, both in Trondheim
- Being able to honestly claim that you've been to Hell and back
- Hiking in the wilderness of Bymarka, right in the city's backyard
- Sailing to the charmingly preserved fishing island of Sør-Gjæslingan, near Rørvik

U-boat Tirpitz used to hide deep in its fjord, but the city avoided major damage.

Orientation & Information

Central Trondheim occupies a triangular peninsula bordered by the river Nidelva to the south and east, and Trondheimsfjorden to the

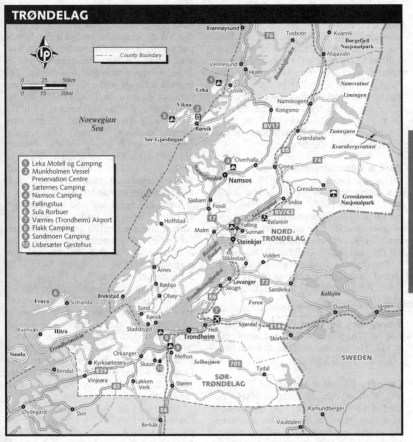

TRØNDELAG

Norwegian Sea

County Boundary

0   25   50km
0   15   30mi

1 Leka Motell og Camping
2 Munkholmen Vessel Preservation Centre
3 Sæternes Camping
4 Namsos Camping
5 Føllingstua
6 Sula Rorbuer
7 Værnes (Trondheim) Airport
8 Flakk Camping
9 Sandmoen Camping
10 Lisbesæter Gjestehus

NORD-TRØNDELAG

SØR-TRØNDELAG

SWEDEN

Brønnøysund, Tosbotn, Kvannli, Børgefjell Nasjonalpark, Majavatn, Vennesund, Holm, Leka, Gutvik, Vikna, Namskogen, Kongsmo, Namsvatnet, Liminga, Rørvik, Sór-Gjæslingan, Overhalla, Grong, Tunnsjøen, Grøndalselv, Kvarnbergsvattnet, Namsos, Gressåmoen, Gressåmoen Nasjonalpark, Sjøsen, Fossli, Snåsa, Hoffstad, Følling, Bølarein, Malm, Sunnan, Steinkjer, Stiklestad, Volden, Årnes, Levanger, Skogn, Sandvika, Kallsjön, Rødsjo, Olsøy, Feren, Duved, Järpen, Brekstad, Sund, Rørvik, Stadsbygd, Hell, Stjørdal, Trondheim, Storlien, Frøya, Sistranda, Kvenvær, Hitra, Orkanger, Melhus, Selbusjøen, Tydal, Smøla, Kyrksæterøra, Skaun, Rendal, Vinjeøra, Løkken Verk, Støren, Nesjøen, Øydegard, Skei, Berkåk, Ramundberger, Vauldalen

---

north. The train station/bus terminal (Trondheim Sentralstasjon) and boat quays are over the canal immediately north of the centre.

In town, activity focuses on the Torvet (central square, also spelt 'Torget'), with a bustling market, well-framed views of Nidaros Cathedral, a **statue of King Olav Tryggvason** atop a column, and the 13th-century stone church, Vår Frue Kirke (Church of Our Lady; ☎ 73 53 84 80) on the corner of Kongensgata and Nordregate; open 11am to 2pm Wednesday.

Just east of the centre, across the Gamle Bybro (Old Town Bridge), is the Bakklandet neighbourhood where warehouses dating back centuries have recently been renovated and house some of the city's most colourful cafes and restaurants. Bakklandet is the gateway to hilly neighbourhoods to the east.

Maps The map in the tourist office's free Trondheim Guide usually suffices for most visitors, but there's also a more detailed public transport map available free from the Sentralstasjon.

Tourist Office Trondheim Aktivum tourist office (☎ 73 80 76 60, fax 73 80 76 70,

e touristinfo@taas.no, w www.trondheim
.com), Postboks 2102, N-7411 Trondheim,
is located on the Torvet The staff are cheerful and accommodating, and it's open
8.30am to 10pm on weekdays and 10am to
8pm on weekends from late June to early
August. It opens until 8pm on weekdays
and 6pm on weekend for most of May, June
and August. The rest of the year it's open
from 9am to 4pm weekdays. The ticket
counter at the bus station provides comprehensive transit information.

Post & Communications The main post
office is at Dronningens gate 10. Schedule
free Internet access for the public library
(☎ 72 54 75 00) at Petter Egges Plass 1 just
off Kongens gate, which also maintains a list
of Internet cafes. The most central of these
is Café Dot Com at Kongens gate 19 (enter
off Prinsens gate; Nkr20 for 30 minutes).

Trondheim's best-known bookshop of
record (and historic meeting place) is Ark
Bruns Bokhandel (☎ 73 51 00 22), Kongens
gate 10.

Emergency Services For fire emergency
ring ☎ 110, police ☎ 112 and ambulance
☎ 113. The hospital emergency room number is ☎ 73 52 25 00.

Laundry Elefanten Vaskeri (☎ 73 51 29
89), Mellomveien 20, charges Nkr45 per
load of washing and Nkr15 per quarter-hour
of drying, provides free coffee and assistance with machines, *and* sells jewellery.
It's open 10am to 6pm weekdays and 11am
to 4pm Saturday. If you're headed north,
enjoy it – it's Norway's northernmost.

Nidaros Domkirke & Erkebispegården

Trondheim's most dominant landmark and
Scandinavia's largest medieval building,
constructed in 1070, is the grand Nidaros
Cathedral (*☎ 73 53 91 60, Kongsgårdsgata;
adult/child Nkr35/20, includes Erkebispegården; open 9am-6pm Mon-Fri mid-
June–mid-Aug, 9am-3pm 1 May–mid-June
& 17 Aug-14 Sept, noon-2.30pm rest of
year; 9am-2pm Sat year round & 1pm-4pm*

Sun, to 3pm mid-Sept–Apr). The altar was
placed over the original grave of St Olav,
the Viking king who replaced the Nordic
pagan religion with Christianity. When Norway became a separate archbishopric in
1153, a larger cathedral was begun. The
current transept and chapter house were
constructed between 1130 to 1180 and reveal Anglo-Norman influences, while the
Gothic-style nave, choir and octagon were
completed around the early 14th century.
Especially worth noting are the vibrantly
coloured modern stained-glass work and the
ornately embellished exterior west wall,
which is lined with statues of biblical characters and Norwegian bishops and kings.

Tours in English are held at 11am, 2pm
and 4pm Monday to Friday, 20 June to 20
August. Mass in English is held on the third
Sunday of every month at 6pm. For information on special cathedral musical programs call ☎ 73 94 52 69, or ☎ 73 53 84 88
for cathedral concerts.

The blessing/inauguration of the Norwegian king takes place here, and visitors can
view the crown jewels from 9am to
12.30pm daily except Friday and Sunday
and 1pm to 4pm on Sunday (June to mid-
August). The rest of the year they can be
seen on Friday only from noon to 2pm.
From mid-June to mid-August, you can
climb the cathedral tower for a view over
the city (Nkr5).

Admission to the cathedral also includes the adjacent 12th-century **Erkebispegården** *(Archbishop's Palace; ☎ 73 53
91 60, Kongsgårdsgata; adult/child
Nkr35/20, includes cathedral; open 10am-
5pm Mon-Sat & noon-5pm Sun in summer, 11am-3pm Tues-Sat & noon-4pm Sun
rest of year).* It was commissioned around
1160, making it the oldest secular building
in Scandinavia. The new wings, rebuilt
after a fire in 1983, house a museum with
displays on the history of the cathedral including an audiovisual program and carvings from the original building. In the
basement are excavations from the original palace, including a 15th-century drinking horn, the tile floor of the original
armoury, and early coinage.

The adjoining **Rustkammeret** *(National Military Museum;* ☎ *73 99 58 31, Kongsgårdsgata; admission free; open 9am-3pm Mon-Fri, 11am-4pm Sat & Sun June-Aug, 11am-4pm Sat & Sun only Feb-May & Sept-Nov; closed Nov-Feb)* is full of antique swords, armour and cannons and recounts the days from 1700 to 1900, when the Archbishop's Palace served as a Danish military installation. On the top floor is the **Hjemmesfront** (homefront) museum,

which tells of Trondheim's role in the WWII resistance.

Stiftsgården

Scandinavia's largest wooden palace, the late baroque Stiftsgården *(*☎ *73 84 28 80, Munkegata; adult/concession/child/family Nkr40/30/20/100; open 10am-3pm Mon-Sat 1 June-19 June, 10am-5pm Mon-Sat rest of year, noon-5pm Sun, June-20 Aug, closed during royal visits)* was constructed between

TRØNDELAG

Along the Pilgrims' Way

Nidaros Cathedral was built on the site of the grave of St Olav, who was canonised and declared a martyr after his death at the battle of Stiklestad on 29 July 1030. Since then, the cult of St Olav has grown in popularity and 340 churches have been dedicated to St Olav in Scandinavia, Britain, Russia, the Baltic States, Poland, Germany and the Netherlands. Pilgrims from all over Europe have journeyed to his grave at Nidaros, making it the most popular pilgrimage site in northern Europe. Historically, both rich and poor journeyed from Oslo for up to 25 days, while others braved longer sea voyages from Iceland, Greenland, Orkney and the Faroe Islands. St Olav's grave became the northern compass point for European pilgrims; the other spiritual cornerstones were Rome in the south, Jerusalem in the east, and Santiago de Compostela in the west.

As pilgrims travelled from church to church and village to village, their routes became arteries for the spread of the cult of St Olav. During medieval times, the journey itself was considered an exercise in unity with God, and early routes, with wild mountains, forests and rivers to cross, provided the pilgrims with time to reflect, and insights into the hardships of life's journey into eternity. Most pilgrims thus chose to travel on foot, while the better off journeyed on horseback. Those without means were forced to rely on local hospitality along the way; in Norway, travelling pilgrims were held in high esteem and openly welcomed.

In 1994, the Pilgrims' Way project of the Norwegian Ministry of Environment revived the ancient pilgrimage route between Oslo and Trondheim. The rugged way, which consists mainly of mountain tracks and gravelled roads, has been marked and St Olav devotees are officially encouraged to follow the ancient pilgrimage routes for religious purposes, outdoor enjoyment and participation in Norwegian history and cultural awareness. The present Pilgrims' Way, which follows ancient, documented trails, provides modern wanderers with the opportunity to relive the experiences of the historic pilgrims. The path is marked with place names and monuments linked to the life and works of St Olav, as well as a number of ancient burial mounds and other historic monuments.

For further information, contact the Pilegrimskontoret (Pilgrim Office; ☎ 22 11 19 05), Kristian IVs gate 15, N-0164 Oslo. The office also sells the best English-language publication about the route, *On the Pilgrim Way to Trondheim*.

TRØNDELAG

TRONDHEIM

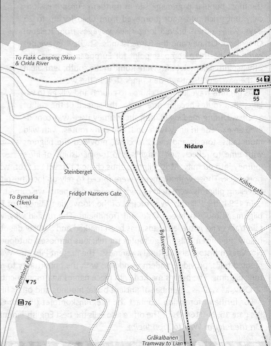

MUSEUMS
- 6 Trondheims Sjøfartsmuseum
- 30 Stiftsgården
- 42 Vitensenteret
- 47 Nordenfjeldske Kunstindustrimuseum
- 56 Vitenskapsmuseet NTNU
- 63 Trondheim Kunstmuseum
- 64 Trondhjems Kunstforening & Café Ni Muser
- 66 Synagogue & Jewish Museum
- 68 Ruskammeret & Hjemmesfront Museum
- 69 Erkebispegården
- 76 Sverresborg Trøndelag Folkemuseum

OTHER
- 1 Hurtigruten Coastal Steamer Quay
- 2 Pirterminalen Quay; Express Boats to Kristiansund
- 3 Elefanten Vaskeri
- 4 Rutebilstasjon
- 15 Ferries to Munkholmen
- 16 Ravnkloa Fish Market & Trondheim Turistforening Dnt Office
- 26 Post Office
- 28 City Bus Terminal
- 33 Sparebanken & Gregorius Kirke Ruins
- 34 Ark Bruns Bokhandel
- 35 Vinmonopolet
- 36 Cafe Dot Com
- 39 King Olav Tryggvason
- 40 Trondheim Aktivum Tourist Office
- 41 Vår Frue Kirke
- 43 Library & Olavskirken Ruins
- 50 Flybuss Terminal
- 54 Hospitalkirken
- 55 Police Station
- 60 Kristiansten Festning
- 70 Nidaros Domkirke
- 74 Hospital

PLACES TO STAY
- 5 Trondheim Vandrerhjem Rosenborg
- 7 Clarion Hotel Grand Olav & Olavshallen
- 10 Chesterfield Hotel
- 12 Rainbow Gildevangen Hotel
- 22 Radisson SAS Royal Garden Hotel
- 32 Britannia Hotel
- 37 Rainbow Trondheim Hotell
- 48 Gammeldagshuset
- 53 Munken Hotel
- 71 Singsaker Sommerhotel
- 72 Trondheim InterRail Centre; Edgar Café & Studentersamfundet
- 73 Elgeseter Hotell

PLACES TO EAT
- 8 Grønn Pepper
- 9 Akropolis
- 14 Credo
- 17 Big Horn Steakhouse
- 18 East
- 19 Szechuan
- 21 Bakeri Teatret
- 25 Egon
- 29 Abelone Mat & Vinkjeller
- 31 Café Erichsen
- 38 Rema 1000 Supermarket
- 44 Peppe's Pizza
- 45 Benitos/Zia Teresa
- 46 Havfruen
- 57 Dalat
- 58 Bryggen Restaurant
- 59 Dromedar
- 61 Bakklandet Skydsstasjon
- 62 Café Gåsa
- 67 Grenaderen
- 75 Vertshuset Tavern

ENTERTAINMENT
- 11 Macbeth
- 13 Rio
- 20 Café 3-B
- 23 Nova Kino
- 24 Replikken Kafé
- 27 Frakken
- 49 Trøndelag Teater
- 51 Smoke
- 65 Prinsen Kino

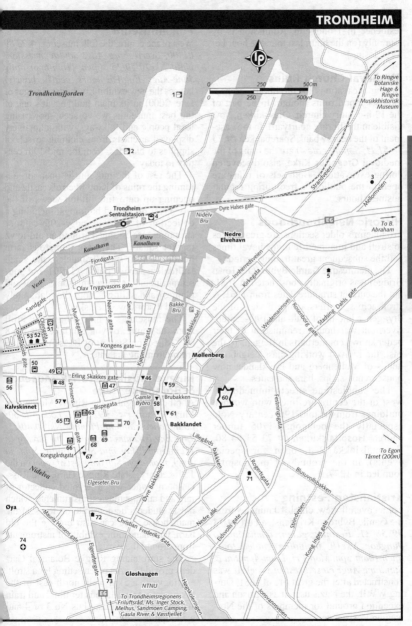

TRØNDELAG

1774 and 1778. It is now the official royal residence in Trondheim. Admission is by tour only (on the hour, last tour one hour before closing).

Medieval Church Ruins

During excavations for the library, archaeologists found ruins thought to be part of the 12th-century church, **Olavskirken**, now visible in the library courtyard. In the basement of the nearby bank Sparebanken (☎ 73 58 51 11, Søndre gate 4) are the ruins of the medieval **Gregorius Kirke**, also discovered during excavations. Both sets of ruins are open to the public for free during regular business hours.

Historic Neighbourhoods

Trondheim's older sections are great places to stroll and imagine life in medieval times and the subsequent great trading periods.

The picturesque **Gamle Bybro** (Old Town Bridge) was originally constructed in 1681, but the current structure dates from 1861. A stroll across it offers a superb view of the **Bryggen**, a line-up of 18th- and 19th-century riverfront warehouses reminiscent of their better known counterparts in Bergen. To the east, the revived working-class neighbourhoods of Møllenberg and Bakklandet now house trendy shops, bars and cafes.

The cobblestone streets immediately west of the centre are lined with wooden buildings from the mid-19th century. Note especially the octagonal 1705 timber church, **Hospitalskirken** (☎ 73 53 84 80, Hospitalsløkka 2–4, open for special events), in the grounds of the hospital founded in 1277.

Kristiansten Festning

For an overall view, climb 10 minutes from the Gamle Bybro to Kristiansten Fort (☎ 73 99 58 31, Festningsgaten; admission to dungeon Nkr10, including guided tour; open 10am-3pm Mon-Fri, 11am-4pm Sat & Sun June-Aug; closed rest of year). It was constructed after the great fire of 1681. During WWII, the Nazis used it as a prison and execution ground for members of the Norwegian Resistance.

Sverresborg Trøndelag Folkemuseum

West of the centre, the folk museum (☎ 73 89 01 00, Sverresborg Allé; adult/concession/child Nkr70/50/25; open 11am-6pm daily June-Aug; English tours nearly hourly) houses the new exhibit Livsbilder (Images of Life, 2000) in its main building. It's one of the best museums we've seen showcasing local people and folkways, with attractively displayed artefacts from clothing to school supplies to bicycles, from the mid-19th century to today.

The rest of the museum is open-air, adjoining the ruins of King Sverre's castle and opening up onto fine hilltop views of the city. Over 60 period buildings, including a collection of 18th- to early-20th-century structures, are arranged around an old-town market square. There were numerous farm buildings from rural Trøndelag, the small Haltdalen stave church (1170) and museums including telecom (some great old phones) and skiing – note the elaborately carved historic wooden skis.

The museum's a nice 40-minute stroll from the centre, or you can take bus No 8 or 9 (direction Stavset or Byåsen Heimdal) from Dronningens gate.

Ringve Musikkhistorisk Museum & Botaniske Hage

Another highlight is the Ringve Museum of Music History (☎ 73 92 24 11, Lade Allé 60; adult/concession/child/family Nkr70/40/25/140; English tours throughout the day; open 11am-3pm May–mid-Sept (until 5pm in July), 11am-3pm Sun only rest of year) on the 18th-century estate Ringve Gård. The Russian-born owner was a devoted collector of rare and antique musical instruments, which music students demonstrate on tours of the main house. You can also browse the old barn, with handsome exhibits of instruments from around the world.

The surrounding Ringve Botanical Gardens provide a quiet green setting for a stroll.

Ringve is a 3km walk north-east of the town centre from the bus terminal and train station, or you can take bus No 3 or 4 and walk uphill.

Vitenskapsmuseet NTNU

The Museum of Natural History & Archaeology (☎ 73 59 21 45, Erling Skakkes gate 47; adult/child/family Nkr25/10/50; open 9am-4pm Mon-Fri, 11am-4pm Sat & Sun May–mid-Sept, 9am-2pm Tues-Fri and noon-4pm rest of year), belongs to NTNU, the Norwegian University of Science & Technology. There's a hotch-potch of exhibits on the natural and human history of the Trondheim area: streetscapes and homes, ecclesiastical history, archaeological excavations and Southern Sami culture.

Nordenfjeldske Kunstindustrimuseum

The eclectic National Museum of Decorative Arts (☎ 73 80 89 50, Munkegata 5; adult/child/family Nkr40/20/100; open 10am-5pm Mon-Sat & noon-5pm Sun 20 June-20 Aug, 11am-5pm rest of year, closed Mon), exhibits a fine collection of contemporary arts and crafts ranging from pottery by Japan's Shoji Hamada to tapestries by Norway's highly acclaimed tapestry artist, Hannah Ryggen.

Trondheim Kunstmuseum

The Trondheim Art Museum (☎ 73 53 81 80, Bispegata 7b; adult/concession/family Nkr30/20/90; open 10am-5pm daily 1 June-early Sept, 11am-5pm Tue-Sun rest of year), houses a collection of modern Norwegian and Danish arts from 1800 on, including a hallway of Munch lithographs.

Trondhjems Kunstforening

This museum of contemporary art (☎ 73 52 66 71, Bispegata 9a; adult/concession Nkr25/15; open 10am-4pm Tues-Fri, noon-4pm Sat & Sun) houses temporary exhibits and a popular summer courtyard cafe.

Trondheims Sjøfartsmuseum

The cosy Trondheim Maritime Museum (☎ 73 89 01 00, Fjordgata 6A; adult/concession Nkr25/15; open 10am-4pm daily, June-Aug), housed in an old prison, is an appealing little place full of relics from 18th-century whaling ships and frigates; navigational instruments; and models, paintings and photos of historic sailing ships.

Special Interest Sites

Trondheim's **Synagogue** (☎ 73 52 20 30, Arkitekt Christies gate 1B) claims to be the world's nothernmost. It was restored in 2001 and contains a small museum of the history of the local Jewish community (halved by the Holocaust). Ring for hours and admission.

Children will probably enjoy the hands-on experiments at the **Vitensenteret** (Science Centre; ☎ 73 59 61 23, Kongens gate 1; adult/concession/family Nkr50/30/100; open 10am-5pm Tues-Fri, 11am-5pm Sat & Sun mid-June–mid-Aug, until 4pm rest of year).

Munkholmen

At the time Trondheim was founded, the islet of Munkholmen – the Monks' Island – was the town execution ground. That distinction

Trond-*what?*

Listen to Trondheimers talk about their city, and you may wonder whether they're all referring to the same place.

Since the late Middle Ages, the city was called Trondhjem, pronounced 'Trond-yem' and meaning, roughly, 'home of the good life'. But, in the early 20th century, the fledgling national government was bent on making Norwegian city names more historically Norwegian; just as Christiania reverted to its ancient name of Oslo, on 1 January 1930 Trondhjem was changed back to Nidaros.

Some 20,000 locals, perhaps upset at losing the good life without even moving, took to the streets in protest, and by 6 March the government relented – sort of. The compromise was 'Trondheim,' the etymologically Danish 'hj' having been duly exorcised.

Nowadays, the official pronunciation is 'Trond-haym,' but many locals still say 'Trond-yem.' Thanks to the vagaries of the local dialect, still others call it 'Trond-yahm.' Typical of this tolerant city, any of these pronunciations is acceptable, as is the 'Trondhime' used by most English speakers.

TRØNDELAG

notwithstanding, in the early 11th century it became the site of a Benedictine monastery, which stood until the mid-17th century when the island began a series of stints as a prison, a fort and a customs house. Today, it's a popular picnicking and sunbathing venue. From late May to late August, ferries (Nkr45 return) leave at least hourly between 10am and 6pm from the harbour east of the Ravnkloa fish market. Guided tours of the island are available (Nkr25; 30 minutes).

Activities

For information on outdoor activities, contact the Trondheimsregionens Friluftsråd (☎ 72 54 65 79, e trondheimsregionens-friluftsrad .postuttak@trondheim.komune.no, Holtermannsveien 1). It also distributes the free *Friluftsliv i Trondheimsregionen* (Outdoor Life in the Trondheim Region) map showing all nearby outdoor recreation areas. The map is also available from the tourist office.

Hiking West of Trondheim spreads the Bymarka, a green woodland area laced with wilderness footpaths and ski trails. The easiest access is by bus No 11, 75 or 76 west towards Trolla, bus No 10 to the Gråkallen Skistua, or the Gråkalbanen train from St Olavsgata station to Lian, which has excellent views over the city and a good swimming lake, Kyvannet.

Skiing The Vassfjellet mountains, 20km due south of town, are the place to go for cross-country skiing. Take a bus or train to Melhus and walk 2km east to Løvset, where a well-maintained trail heads into the hills. On weekends in the ski season, a ski bus runs directly from the Trondheim terminal to the Vassfjellet Skisenter. The Bymarka also offers excellent cross-country skiing, as does the Trondheim Skisenter Granåsen, with the world's largest plastic-surfaced ski jump.

Fishing The Gaula and Orkla rivers offer good salmon fishing within an hour's drive of town. Guided sea-fishing trips are available from Trondheim Aktivum (☎ 73 92 93 94), on the Torvet.

Organised Tours

Trondheim Aktivum (☎ 73 92 93 94) runs two-hour guided city tours (Nkr160), taking in the Trøndelag Folkemuseum, the cathedral and Archbishop's Palace, the Kristiansten Fort and the university. Tours depart daily at noon from 20 June to 15 August.

Special Events

Olavsfestdagene, a cultural festival in celebration of St Olav, takes place during the week around 29 July and includes a working medieval market.

Days Out in Trondheim

The following recommendations were provided by a reader who has lived in Trondheim for several years:

Boats run between Trondheim (Pirterminalen) and Kristiansund, as well as the islands of Hitra, Frøya, Ulvøya and Fjellværøya. A few days of biking and camping on these outer islands can be a great experience if the weather is fine. However, bicycles are necessary to get around on the islands, as buses run infrequently.

Begin at Fjellværøya (take your bike on the boat) and cycle or catch the local bus out to Ulvøya, where you can rent a *hytte* (cabin), or just put up a tent somewhere near the water (the *allemannsretten* dictates that you must be more than 150m from a structure). The little fishing community of Ulvøya is a pearl, and you can buy inexpensive cod from the docks where the fishing boats moor, on the Fjellværøya side of the bridge. Alternatively, you can hire a motorboat and catch the fish yourself. At the same place you'll also find a convenience store where you can weigh the fish you've caught or chosen to buy.

From Ulvøya and Fjellværøya you can bike to Hitra, where you're sure to see deer, as the island is crowded with them. The tourist office in Trondheim can provide advice about places to stay.

Tone Dragland

Every second year, Trondheim's 25,000 university students stage the three-week ISFiT UKA (the week) celebration, Norway's largest cultural festival. It's a continuous party with concerts, plays, and other festivities based at the round, red Studentersamfundet (student centre) on Elgeseter gate. It will be held in the spring of 2003 and 2005.

Places to Stay

Camping *Sandmoen Camping* (☎ 72 88 61 35, fax 72 59 61 51, **e** tras@online.no, Sandmoen) Tent sites without/with car Nkr100/130, caravan sites Nkr150, cabins Nkr450-900. The nearest camping ground to town, 10km south of the city along the E6, has an affiliated motel about 1km away. Take bus No 44 or the Klæbu bus to Sandmoen Camping stop.

Flakk Camping (☎ 72 84 39 00, Flakk; Open 1 May-1 Sept) Tent/caravan Nkr90/125, 4-person/5-person cabins (no water) Nkr350/500. Reach this beachside campsite, 10km west of town, via bus No 75 or 76.

Hostels *Trondheim InterRail Centre* (☎ 73 89 95 38, **e** tirc@stud.ntnu.no, Elgesetergate 1). Beds Nkr115 with breakfast. From late June to mid-August, the Studentersamfundet (university student centre) operates this convenient, friendly and good-value place, with free Internet access *and* no curfews. The attached *Edgar Café* serves inexpensive meals and beer. If you hear strange noises after the nightly partying subsides, it's just the ghost of S Møller, a student who mysteriously disappeared in the 1930s. The hostel is five minutes' walk south of the cathedral.

Trondheim Vandrerhjem Rosenborg (☎ 73 87 44 50, fax 73 87 44 55, **e** tr-vanas@online.no, Weidemannsvei 41) Dorm beds for members/non-members Nkr195/220. Closed mid-Dec–early Jan. On a hillside 2km east of the train station, this hostel offers various options from simple dorms to a luxurious suite for four (Nkr 2200). In the new building, rooms have nice wood paneling, and some have fjord views. Breakfast is included; take bus No 63.

Pensjonat Jarlen (☎ 73 51 32 18, fax 73 52 80 80, **e** p-jarlen@frisurf.no, Kongens gate 40) Singles/doubles Nkr400/500. There's nothing fancy about this central spot, but the rooms have TV, shower and kitchenette.

Singsaker Sommerhotel (☎ 73 89 31 00, fax 73 89 32 00, Rogertsgata 1) Beds in large/small dorm Nkr125/155, singles/doubles Nkr345/550. This good-value lodging near the Kristiansten Fort opens early June to mid-August. Breakfast is included.

B&Bs *Gammeldagshuset* (☎/fax 73 51 55 68, Hvedingsveita 8) Rooms Nkr420/person. Open summer only. This rustic old house is near the centre.

B Abraham (☎/fax 73 91 29 90, Sildedråpsveien 4D, Angelltrøa) Rooms from Nkr250/person. About 4km north-east of town you'll find simple accommodation in a residential neighbourhood. Take bus No 24.

Ms Inger Stock (☎/fax 72 88 83 19, Porsmyra 18, Tiller) Singles/doubles Nkr300/380. Kitchen facilities are also available for guest use in this wooded, quiet location about 10km south of the centre. Take bus No 46 to Tonstadgrenda.

Hotels *Rainbow Trondheim Hotell* (☎ 73 50 50 50, fax 73 51 60 58, **e** trondheim.hotell@online.no, Kongens gate 15) Singles/doubles from Nkr450/690. Pleasant, up-to-date accommodation and complementary light meals at night are offered in this central Rainbow.

Rainbow Gildevangen Hotell (☎ 73 87 01 30, fax 73 52 38 98, **e** gildevangen@online.no, Søndre gate 22) Singles/doubles from Nkr450/690. This other Rainbow has the same amenities a couple minutes' walk from the train station.

Munken Hotel (☎ 73 53 45 40, fax 73 53 42 60, **e** munken.hotell@munken.no, Kongens gate 44) Singles/doubles with bath Nkr595/750, without bath Nkr450/570. Request a room with kitchen for no extra charge at this simple, central, friendly place.

Elgeseter Hotell (☎ 73 82 03 30, fax 73 82 03 31, **e** elgeseter.hotell@munken.no, Tromods gate 3) Singles/doubles from

Nkr595/750. You'll find smallish rooms off a quiet courtyard south of the centre.

Chesterfield Hotel *(☎ 73 50 37 50, fax 73 50 37 55,* e *hotel@online.no, Søndre gate 26)* Singles/doubles from Nkr500/745. This quirky, personal lodging has commodious rooms with private bath. Rooms on the 7th floor have huge skylights and broad city views. Discounts are offered to ScanRail pass holders.

Clarion Hotel Grand Olav *(☎ 73 80 80 80, fax 73 80 80 81,* e *booking.trondheim@ clarion.choicehotels.no, Kjøpmannsgata 48)* Singles/doubles from Nkr630/845. The Clarion offers sleek luxury over an airy shopping complex and the Olavshallen concert hall.

Britannia Hotel *(☎ 73 80 08 00, fax 73 80 08 01,* e *brittania@brittania.no, Dronningens gate 5)* Singles/doubles from Nkr690/850. This huge hotel is Trondheim's most historic (1897). You'll get British-style attention to detail and breakfast in a palm-filled hall.

Radisson SAS Royal Garden Hotel *(☎ 73 80 30 00, fax 73 80 30 50,* W *www .radissonsas.com, Kjøpmannsgaten 73)* Singles/doubles from Nkr890/990. This first-class, contemporary riverside hotel (you can fish from your window) has a pool and fitness room.

Out-of-town Lodgings *Lisbesæter Gjestehus (☎ 72 86 42 10, fax 72 50 47 00,* W *www.lisbetseter.no, Skaun)* Singles/ doubles Nkr900/1400. Open mid-May–early Oct. In the mid-19th century, Dr Eyvind Kraft became personal physician to the king of Hawaii, but when one of the princesses fell in love with him the king paid Kraft a large sum to go home. In 1890, Kraft used the windfall to build a sanatorium and hydrotherapy spa on a medieval mountain dairy farm, 45km south of Trondheim, and now it's open to guests. Breakfast is included.

To really get away from it all, take a 3½-hour ferry ride to the self-catering *Sula Rorbuer (☎ 74 01 32 90, fax 73 82 96 01,* e *firmapost@sularorbuer.no, Sula)*, fishing cabins on the remote archipelago of Sula (200 people, two cars). Three-bedroom apartments cost Nkr5000 per week from April to October

(Nkr7000, mid-May to mid-August). The ferry departs from the Piterminalen quay.

Places to Eat

Cafes Trondheim has a number of lovely cafes for coffee and cakes. Some stay open at night and double as pubs.

Café ni Museer *(☎ 73 53 25 50, Bispegata 9)* Snacks & cakes Nkr37-88. For inexpensive light meals and an arty crowd, go to Trondhjems Kunstforening. On sunny afternoons, the outdoor terrace turns into a beer garden.

Café Erichsen *(☎ 73 87 45 50, Nørdre gate 8)* Pastries from Nkr10, light meals to Nkr108. Trondheim's 'establishment' cafe attracts a clientele of all ages.

Kafé Gåsa *(☎ 73 51 58 36, Øvre Bakklandet 58)* Cakes Nkr24-40; dishes Nkr40-110. In Bakklandet, this supremely lovely cafe occupies an old house and riverside garden.

Dromedar *(☎ 73 50 25 02, Nedre Bakklandet 3)*. Cakes around Nkr35. This is another longstanding local favourite.

Baklandet Skydsstation *(☎ 73 92 10 44, Øvre Bakklandet 33)* Cakes around Nkr35, mains Nkr100-200. You'll find several cosy rooms, a heated patio and famous *bacalau*.

Restaurants *Peppe's Pizza (☎ 73 50 34 41, Kjøpmannsgata 25)* Pizzas Nkr130-224. Get the pizza and salad lunch buffet (Nkr79) in this historic waterfront building.

Grønn Pepper *(☎ 73 53 26 30, Fjordgata 7)* Mains Nkr99-195. This colourful, windowed room goes well with Mexican food. Monday's special is four tacos with rice and salad for Nkr75.

Egon *(☎ 73 51 79 75, Thomas Angellsgata 8)* Mains Nkr69-222. Trondheim's most visited restaurant is a huge complex on several floors and has a menu with something for everyone.

Egon Tårnet *(☎ 73 87 35 00, Otto Nielsens veg 4)* Mains Nkr69-222. Egon's sister restaurant serves the same menu while rotating 74m up a landmark telecommunications tower east of town. Take bus No 20 or 60 from the centre.

Benitos/Zia Teresa *(☎ 73 52 64 22, Vår Frue gate 4)* Mains from Nkr75. At these two restaurants – fancy Italian *boite* and informal pizza and pasta joint – the gregarious owner bears a striking resemblance to Luciano Pavarotti and often provides operatic accompaniment.

Akropolis (☎ 73 51 67 51, Fjordgata 19) Mains Nkr108-215. This Greek place has reasonable combination plates and an intimate setting.

Dalat (73 52 33 75, Prinsens gate 4b) Mains Nkr79-135. This Vietnamese shop serves noodles, spring rolls and grills.

East (73 52 10 20, Munkegata 39) Mains Nkr50-198. Sleek East serves sushi and Japanese noodles.

Szechuan (73 52 28 67, Olav Tryggvasons gate 20) Mains Nkr84-141. One of many Chinese places, Szechuan has lunch specials for Nkr69.

Vertshuset (☎ 73 87 80 70, Sverresborg Allé 11) Meals Nkr99-235. Locals flock here to this historic (1739) spot for rotating specials of traditional Norwegian fare, or just coffee and waffles.

Grenaderen (☎ 73 51 66 80, Kongsgårda 1) Mains Nkr198-235. Another historic place (1790) near the Archbishop's Palace, has local cuisine, outdoor seating and a summer lunchtime salad buffet (Nkr85).

Abelone Mat & Vinkjeller (☎ 73 53 24 70, Dronningens gate 15) Mains Nkr96-224. This cosy cellar from 1842 specialises in steaks.

Big Horn Steakhouse (☎ 73 50 94 90, Munkegata 41) Mains Nkr146-408. This American-style place is near Ravnkloa.

Credo (73 53 03 88, Ørjaveita 4) 3/5 course menus Nkr380/470. There's no need for a menu at this adventurous Spanish-influenced world cuisine spot – the chef chooses the day's best items and serves them in fine style. There's also a trendy bar upstairs.

Havfruen (☎ 73 87 40 70, Kjøpmannsgata 7) Mains Nkr175-242.This posh riverside spot serves oysters, lobsters and fresh fish.

Bryggen (☎ 73 87 42 42, Bakklandet 66) Mains Nkr235-270. This thoroughly elegant place is just over the Gamle Bybro. Bryggen's five-course menu (Nkr650) is Trondheim's real splurge.

Rema 1000 on the Torvet is your most central supermarket, and you can purchase lovely produce from vendors outside. *Bakeri Teatret (Olavskvartalet cultural centre)* has hearty sandwiches and pizza slices from Nkr25, or you can munch on inexpensive fish cakes from the *Ravnkloa fish market*.

Entertainment

Nightlife As a student town, Trondheim offers heaps of nightlife, though venues change frequently. The free papers, *Natt & Dag* and *Plan B*, and the *DetSkjer* pamphlet have listings (mostly in Norwegian).

The *Studentersamfundet (student centre, ☎ 73 89 95 38, Elgesetergate 1)* features a lively pub, cinema and alternative music performances. During the school year the main party night is Friday, but in summer it's mostly a travellers' crash pad (see Trondheim InterRail Centre in Places to Stay).

Homesick Scots will feel at home at *Macbeth (☎ 73 50 35 63, Søndregate 22b)*. The rest of us can watch football.

Replikken Kafé (☎ 73 53 00 11, Olav Tryggvasons gate 5) has live jazz, cheap beer and a happy hour (5pm-midnight). The smoky *Café 3-B (☎ 73 53 15 50, Brattørgata 3b)* plays loud music for rockers, people in black and self-professed alternative types.

Smoke (☎ 73 50 27 05, Prinsens gate 32), full of Scandinavian design touches, hosts the city's movie premiere parties and has live jazz on weekends.

Frakken (☎ 73 52 24 42, Dronningens gate 12) is a multi-storey nightclub and piano bar featuring both Norwegian and foreign musicians. *Rio (☎ 73 52 70 20, Nordregate 23)* is the current 'it' dance club; it's almost too crowded on weekends.

Trondheim's longstanding gay club had closed as we went to press, but Trondheimers were abuzz with anticipation of a resurfacing. Check at the tourist office or W www.gaytrondheim.com.

Cultural Events & Cinema The main concert hall, *Olavshallen (☎ 73 99 40 50, Kjøpmanns gate 44)*, at the Olavskvartalet cultural centre, hosts performers from the Trondheim Symphony Orchestra to international rock

TRØNDELAG

and jazz musicians, mostly between September and May.

The handsomely refurbished *Trøndelag Teater* (☎ 73 80 51 00, Prinsens gate) stages large-scale dance and musical performances.

There are also two *cinemas*, Nova Kino (☎ 82 05 43 33, Olav Tryggvasons gate 5) and Prinsen Kino (☎ 82 05 43 33 Prinsens gate 2b).

Getting There & Away

Air The Værnes airport, 32km east of Trondheim, is connected by both SAS and Braathens to all major Norwegian cities, as well as Copenhagen. Widerøe flies between Værnes and Sandefjord (near Oslo), Namsos, Rørvik, Brønnøysund and all of northern Norway. These smaller aircraft provide the most scenic flights in the country.

Bus The city bus terminal (Rutebilstasjon) adjoins the Trondheim Sentralstasjon (train station, also known as Trondheim S).

As the main link between southern and northern Norway, Trondheim is a bus transport crossroads. Nor-Way Bussekspress services run at least daily to Oslo (Nkr590, 9½ hours), Bergen (Nkr745, 14¼ hours), Ålesund (Nkr458, 7¼ hours) and Namsos (Nkr265, 3¾ hours). For bus access to Narvik and points north you first need to travel by train to Fauske or Bodø.

Train For train information, phone ☎ 81 50 08 88. There are half a dozen daily trains to Oslo (Nkr650, 6½ to eight hours) and two to Fauske (Nkr795, nine hours) and Bodø (Nkr740, 10 hours). You can also train it to Røros (Nkr188, 2½ hours)

Car & Motorcycle The E6 passes through the heart of the city. Between 6am and 6pm Monday to Friday, drivers entering the city must pay a toll of Nkr15 (the motorway toll into town also covers the city toll, so keep your receipt). If your car is not equipped for automatic payment, you must use the 'Manuell' lanes or risk steep fines.

For car hire, Avis (☎ 73 82 17 90) is at Kjøpmannsgata 34, Budget (☎ 73 94 10 25) at Elgesetergate 21 and (☎ 73 82 88 59)

Kjøpmannsgata 73, and Europcar at Thonning Owesens gate 36 (☎ 73 82 88 50).

Boat The Hurtigruten coastal steamer stops in Trondheim, and Fosen Trafikklag's Kystekspressen boats (☎ 72 57 20 20) between Trondheim and Kristiansund (Nkr405, 3½ hours) depart from the Pirterminalen quay.

Getting Around

To/From the Airport Flybussen (airport buses, ☎ 73 82 25 00, Nkr54), leave from the Flybuss terminal on Erling Skakkes gate behind the Trøndelag Teater, from 5am to 9pm daily, every 15 minutes weekdays (less frequently on weekends). The journey takes about 40 minutes and stops en route at the train station and the Britannia Hotel.

Taxis (☎ 73 50 50 73 or ☎ 74 83 75 00) to the airport cost around Nkr480 from the centre, but you can request a shared taxi for Nkr250 per person. Also, trains run many times daily between Trondheim Sentralstasjon and the Værnes airport station (Nkr54, 35 minutes).

Bus The centre of Trondheim is easily explored on foot, but to reach some attractions (eg, the Trøndelag Folkemuseum or Ringve Museum) most people prefer the bus. The city bus service, Team Trafikk (☎ 73 50 28 70), has its central transit point on the corner of Munkegata and Dronningens gate; all lines stop here. Bus and tram fare costs Nkr22 per ride (Nkr55 for a 24-hour ticket). Exact change is required.

Tram Trondheim's tram line, the Gråkalbanen, runs west from St Olavsgata to Lian, in the heart of the Bymarka. Antique trolleys run along this route on Saturdays in summer. Transfers are available from city buses.

Car & Motorcycle Metered parking zones are marked *P Mot avgift* or *P Avgift*. Green meters cost Nkr3 per hour, while red meters are Nkr5 for 15 minutes, with a 30-minute maximum. Garages throughout town offer better rates and greater convenience.

Bicycle Trondheim has around 200 green bicycles available free of charge (locals use them mainly as shopping trolleys). You'll find them locked in bicycle racks around the city centre. To release one, insert a Nkr20 coin, which will be returned when you re-lock the bike.

Cyclists heading from the Gamle Bybro up the Brubakken hill to Kristiansten Fort can avail themselves of Trampe, the world's only bike lift. Lift cards are available for a Nkr100 deposit at the tourist office or Dromedar Café in Bakklandet.

The Route North

HELL
Home of the Hell Senteret shopping complex (look for the devilishly red shopping-bag sign), the Rica Hell Hotel (which serves as Trondheim's Værnes airport hotel), Hell Bil auto sales (you can buy the car from Hell) and a railway stop, Hell has little to offer but its name, which roughly translates as 'prosperity' in Norwegian.

Still, lots of travellers stop here for a cheap chuckle or at least to snap a photo of the sign at the train station. And forever after, whenever someone suggests you go here, you can honestly say you've already been and it wasn't all that bad.

STIKLESTAD
On 29 July 1030, an army of around 100 men led by the Christian King Olav Haraldsson was defeated in Stiklestad by the larger and better equipped forces under the command of local feudal chieftains. King Olav, a descendant of King Harald Harfågre, had been forced from the Norwegian throne by King Knut of Denmark and England. He briefly escaped to Sweden but, on his return, was met with resistance by locals who'd apparently taken exception to his tendency to destroy pagan shrines and execute anyone who persisted with heathen practices.

The Battle of Stiklestad is considered Norway's passage between the Viking and medieval periods, between pre-history and modern times. And although Olav was de-

feated, the battle is generally lauded as a victory for Christianity in Norway, as the slain hero has since been remembered as a martyr and, eventually, a saint. St Olav developed a following all over northern Europe, and his grave in Trondheim's Nidaros Cathedral became a destination of pilgrims from across the continent. The battlefield at Stiklestad continues to attract pilgrims and Norwegian holiday makers and is now one of Trøndelag's most visited attractions.

Stiklestad Kulturhus
The Stiklestad Cultural Centre (☎ 74 04 42 00, **W** www.stiklestad.no, **W** www.snk.no, Stiklestad; adult/child Nkr80/40 summer, Nkr60/30 rest of year; open 9am-8pm daily mid-June–mid-Aug, until 10pm 22-29 July, 9am-4pm Mon-Fri, 11am-5pm Sat & Sun rest of year) is laid out like a sprawling theme park, including exhibits on the Battle of Stiklestad, an outdoor folk museum and the 12th-century Stiklestad church.

The main visitors centre contains a well-executed exhibit about St Olav and the rather haunting (and over-the-top) walk-through 'Stiklestad 1030' exhibit, an imperative for Norwegians in search of their own history. It certainly evokes some strong emotions, but foreigners will probably need more background to fully appreciate its significance to locals. A good source is the English translation of the booklet St Olav – King of Norway, by Father Olav Müller, sold at the centre for a reasonable Nkr35. More general pamphlets are free.

The folk museum on site reveals aspects of life in the region from the 17th century and, over the road, you can visit the lovely Stiklestad church (built 1150 to 1180), over the stone where St Olav is said to have leaned before he died. The original stone reportedly had healing powers, but it was removed during the Reformation and hasn't been seen since. The only original item which remains is the soapstone baptismal font.

Special Events
Every year during the week leading up to St Olavs Day (29 July) Stiklestad hosts an outdoor pageant recreating the original battle

scene. The text by Olav Gullvåt and music by Paul Okkenhaug conjure up the past conflicts between King Olav den Hellige (St Olav, or Olav the Holy) and the local farmers and chieftains.

Places to Stay

Stiklestad Camping (☎/fax 74 04 12 94, E757) Tent/caravan sites Nkr60/100, plus Nkr10/person, cabins from Nkr530. Open 1 June-31 Aug. About 3km from the cultural centre, this place has fairly well-appointed cabins.

Getting There & Away

The nearest train to Stiklestad stops at Verdal (Nkr140, 1¾ hours), which is 6km away. From there any Vuku bus passes within 2km of the site (Nkr22, 15 minutes).

STEINKJER & NORTH

pop 10,136

Steinkjer was mentioned in medieval sagas as a major trading centre, and it continues to be a crossroads. The generic downtown quickly gives way to hills (including some Viking sites) and the fabulous Kystriksveien coastal route (Rv17) to Bodø. For tourist information, see Steinkjer Tourist Information (☎ 74 16 36 17, fax 74 16 10 88, e turistkontor@rv17.no, w www.rv17.no), Namdalsvegen 11, which also doubles at the Kystriksveien Info-Center. You can also choose to continue north on the E6 (Arctic Highway).

Things to See & Do

Steinkjer's main attraction is the hilltop **Egge Museum** (☎ 74 16 31 10; Fylkesmannsgården, adult/child Nkr40/free; open 10am-3.30pm Tues-Fri & noon-6pm Sun summer, 8am-4pm Tues-Fri rest of year), although the most interesting part is the Viking burial mounds outdoors.

North of Steinkjer, the E6 follows the north shore of the 45km-long, needle-thin lake **Snåsavatnet**, lined with majestic evergreen forests. However, you may want to take the Rv763 along the quieter southern shore to see the **Bølarein**, a 5000 to 6000 year-old rock carving of a reindeer and

several other images, with more still being discovered – the most recent (a man in a boat) in July 2001!

To see real antlered creatures, Beistad Utmarkslag (☎ 74 14 77 19, mobile ☎ 93 22 35 00) offers a four-hour **elk safari** daily in high season (adult/child Nkr250/150), including elk-meat snacks.

The boat *Bonden II* (☎ 74 14 46 64, mobile ☎ 90 99 27 16; Nkr195 return, including meal) sails up and down the lake between the ports of Sunnan and Snåsa, daily in summer.

The forests and uplands of Gressåmoen National Park lie east of the lake.

Places to Stay

Guldbergaunet Sommerhotel & Camping (☎ 74 16 20 45, fax 74 16 47 35, e guldsho@ online.no, Elvenget 34, Steinkjer) Tent/caravan sites Nkr110/120, singles/doubles Nkr370/850, cabins Nkr300-400. This is the major camping ground in the area.

Tingvold Park Hotel (☎ 74 16 11 00, fax 74 16 11 17, Gamle Kongeveien 47, e tingvold.hotel@nt.telia.no, Steinkjer) Singles/doubles from Nkr545/790. Amid Viking-era ruins overlooking Steinkjer is this good-value, upmarket choice.

Føllingstua (☎/fax 71 14 71 90, e post@ follingstua.com; E6, Følling) Tent/caravan Nkr75/110, cabins Nkr350-600. Heading north, near the lake's south-west end is this simply lovely, welcoming camping ground.

Snåsa Hotell (☎ 74 15 10 57, fax 74 15 16 15, e snasa.hotell@c2i.net, Snåsa) Hostel accommodation Nkr155-310, hotel doubles from Nkr715, cabins from Nkr325. This sprawling facility with a summer hostel is at the north-east end of the lake.

You can ring Statskog Trøndelag/Møre (☎ 74 14 49 92, Høvdingveien 10, Steinkjer) for information on accommodation at the six-bed *Seisjø Jaktstue* at Gressåmoen (Nkr370 for two people).

NAMSOS

pop 7000

Namsos, the first scenic port town on the northbound coastal route between Trondheim and Bodø, makes a pleasant overnight stop and has a couple of interesting diversions.

For information, contact the Namsos Turistkontor (☎ 74 21 73 13, fax 74 21 73 01, W www.namsosinfo.no), in the Kulturhuset at Stasjonsgata 3. It's open 11am to 7pm Monday to Friday and 2pm-6pm Sat & Sun, late June-late Aug, shorter hours rest of year). Ner'i Gata Internett Kafé, a block from the harbour, has Internet access.

Things to See & Do

A scenic and easy 20-minute walk up Kirkegata from the centre will take you to the lookout atop the prominent loaf-shaped rock Bjørumsklumpen (114m), which affords a view over the town and its environs as well as Namsfjorden. About a third of the way up, a sign identifies a track leading to some impressive WWII-era German bunkers hewn from solid rock. Inside, placards (in Norwegian only) describe the history.

If you're interested in wood chopping and chipping, check out the Norsk Sagbruksmuseum (☎ 74 27 13 00, Spillumsvika; admission Nkr30; open 9am-5pm Tues-Sat, May-Aug; tours at 10am, noon, 2pm and 4pm), over the bridge 4km east of town, which commemorates Norway's first steam-powered sawmill (1853). The more culturally-oriented Namdalsmuseet (☎ 74 27 40 72, Kjærlighetstien 1; adult/child Nkr20/10; open 11am-3pm Tue-Sun late June-late Aug), features antique hospital equipment and displays on local history.

For a break, drop by the novel Oasen swimming hall (☎ 74 21 90 40, Jarle Hildrums veg; adult/family Nkr50/125; open 9.30am-8pm daily summer, shorter hours rest of year). It has three pools (28°C) and a 37m water slide built deep inside a mountain about 1km east of town.

The Namsos Lysstøperi (☎ 74 21 29 00, Lokstallen) makes and sells amazingly lifelike sculptural candles (eg, tropical flowers and – incongruously – ice), in a former train shed.

Places to Stay & Eat

Namsos Camping (☎ 74 27 53 44, fax 74 27 53 93, e namscamp@online.no, Høknes) Tent/caravan Nkr85/140, cabins Nkr300-770.

This basic place is in a field east of town, next to the airport.

Borstad Gjestgiveri (☎ 74 27 21 31, fax 74 27 14 48, Carl Gulbransons gate 19) Singles/doubles from Nkr550/790. Bright and friendly Borstad has large sunny rooms and a pleasant outdoor garden.

Tino's Hotell (74 21 80 00, Verftsgata 5) Singles/doubles from Nkr650/850. Some rooms were renovated in 2001 at this clean, contemporary hotel.

Namsos Bistro (☎ 74 27 00 40, Havnegate 21) Dishes Nkr38-145. It can get smoky at this popular spot for coffees and light meals.

Numero Uno (☎ 74 27 52 66, Sverres gate 17) Pizzas Nkr55-145. Numero Uno redefines thin crust pizzas, or you can opt for pasta or salad.

Big Buffalo (☎ 74 27 22 40, Verftsgate 24) Mains Nkr79-219. This waterfront Argentinian steakhouse also serves ribs and fish and has an Irish pub downstairs.

Getting There & Away

Between Namsos and Trondheim (Nkr265, 3¾ hours), the Nor-Way Bussekspress Inherredsekspressen bus runs twice daily. Buses also run between Namsos and Brønnøysund (Nkr251, six hours), farther up the Kystriksveien.

RØRVIK

Although it's too far off the beaten track for most visitors, tiny Rørvik buzzes when the northbound and southbound Hurtigruten coastal steamers call in each day at the same time. Arrivals receive proud tours of the 1870s trading house of Woxengs Samlinger museum (☎ 74 39 04 41, Betzy Bergs gate; adult/child Nkr20/10; open 10am-3.30pm Mon-Fri, 10am-5pm Sat July, 10am-2pm Sat June & Aug, closed weekends rest of year; always open when Hurtigruten calls).

The museum also operates the Munkholmen Vessel Preservation Centre, on the islet of Munkholmen 1km from town, and the Sør-Gjæslingan fishing village on an island 35 minutes away by ferry. A ferry runs to Sør-Gjæslingan from Namsos (Nkr79, 3¾ hours) and Rørvik (Nkr38, 35 minutes)

TRØNDELAG

322 The Route North – Leka

several times per week; day trips to this interesting site are available on Saturday from Namsos and Sunday from Rørvik.

Places to Stay & Eat

Sæternes Camping *(☎/fax 74 39 38 14, Austafjord)* Tent/caravan Nkr80/120, cabins Nkr400. About 30km west of town and 100m from a fjord are camping sites and cabins without private facilities.

Kysthotellet Rørvik *(☎ 74 39 01 00, fax 74 39 02 50, Storgata 20)* Singles/doubles from Nkr550/690. Rørvik's only hotel is drab and overpriced but has a good restaurant.

If you're in no hurry, Woxengs Samlinger museum offers more interesting accommodation on Sør-Gjæslingan island with its historic **rorbuer** *(☎ 74 39 04 41, fax 74 39 22 72, Sør-Gjæslingan)* fishing huts, which cost Nkr250 plus Nkr90 per person, but you'll need to coordinate your stay around the ferry schedule. It's open 15 May to 1 September.

Brygga Fire Stuer *(☎ 74 39 10 71, Strandgata 15)* Mains Nkr25-145. The cosy confines here prove that you don't need to slum it to enjoy pub food.

Vertshuset Galeåsen *(☎ 74 39 00 88, Strandgata 26)* serves more sophisticated meals, particularly seafood (open high season only).

Getting There & Away

Buses between Rørvik and Namsos (Nkr176, three hours) run several times daily. You can get to/from Namsos via express passenger boats (Nkr129, 1¾ hours) several times weekly, or via frequent daily car ferries between the ports of Hafles and Lund (Nkr68, 30 minutes).

LEKA

You won't regret a short side-trip to the wild and beautiful red serpentine island of Leka; for hikers, the desert-like Wild West landscape is particularly enchanting. This prime habitat for the white-tailed sea eagle also has several Viking Age burial mounds and Stone Age rock paintings. For tourist information, contact the Leka Turistkontor (☎ 74 39 96 90) in Leka village or Kytsriksveien tourist office in Steinkjer. Bed down at the well-regarded **Leka Motell og Camping** *(☎ 74 39 98 23, fax 74 39 98 99, Leka)* with tent/caravan sites from Nkr80, and cabins Nkr300-650.

Leka is accessed by ferry from Gutvik (Nkr20/53 per person/car and driver, 20 minutes), which lies about 20 minutes off the Rv17 coast road. Buses run from Rørvik to Gutvik (Nkr91, 2¾ hours) on weekdays.

Nordland

As one moves northward through this long, narrow county, fields give way to lakes and forests, vistas open up, peaks sharpen and the tree line descends ever lower on the mountainsides. In summer, this is where northbound travellers get their first taste of the midnight sun, and visitors can't fail to be impressed by the razor-sharp peaks and fabulous Caribbean-coloured seas of the Lofoten islands. Whether you choose the inland Arctic Highway or the Kystriksveien Coastal Route, a trip through Nordland is hard to forget.

This chapter includes not only Nordland county but also the north-eastern section of Vesterålen, which belongs to the county of Troms. For general travel info for the region, contact Nordland Reiseliv in Bodø (☎ 75 54 52 00, fax 75 54 52 10, e nordland@nordlandreiseliv.no, w www.nordlandreiseliv.no).

GETTING AROUND
Travel through Nordland is extremely rewarding, but the maze of schedules and operators of buses, trains and, particularly, Coastal Route ferries can be daunting. Still, any challenges are eminently surmountable with a little planning (and some pocket change for ferries).

Local tourist offices are best at navigating the region, and the *Kystriksveien* (Coastal Route) booklet by the Kystriksveien Info-Center in Steinkjer, Trøndelag (☎ 74 16 36 17, fax 74 16 10 88, e post@rv17.no, w www.rv17.no) is a wonderful resource. The new Nordland travel information line (☎ 177) is also helpful, though it tends to be sketchy on smaller locales.

The Arctic Highway

MOSJØEN
pop 9652
Arriving in Mosjøen along the E6, you may be put off by the industrial face of this aluminium-producing town. Don't be. About

Highlights

- Experiencing the majestic beauty of the Arctic Highway or the Kystriksveien coastal route
- Learning fishing history at the Å Museums or Viking history at the Lofotr Museum, both in Lofoten, or aviation history at the Norwegian Aviation Museum in Bodø
- Exploring the restored fishing village of Nyksund, or hiking the Queen's Route to Stø, in Vesterålen
- Taking the Ofotbanen mountain train to the Swedish border (and hiking part of the way back to Narvik)
- Strolling Mosjøen's historic Sjøgata, with its galleries and cafes
- Visiting a glacier from land or sea or seeing the caves they carved near Mo i Rana (see Saltfjellet-Svartisen National Park)

1km west, along the lake-like Vefsnfjorden, is the Sjøgata district, a charming place to spend a few hours. The Indre Helgeland Reiseliv tourist office (☎ 75 11 12 40, fax 75 11 13 11,

NORDLAND

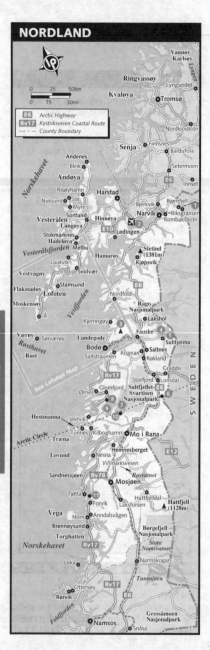

NORDLAND

1 Rallarveien (Hiking Route)
2 Evenes Airport
3 Steigtind
4 Blåmannisen (Icefield)
5 Sulitjelmaisen (Icefield)
6 Artic Circle Centre (Polarsirkelsenteret)
7 Ostisen (Icefield)
8 Svartisen Turistsenter & Engebreen (Glacier Tongue)
9 Vestisen (Icefield)
10 Pikhaugsvatnet
11 The Skier of Røøya

e info@ihr.no) is at Sjøgata's southern end. If you want to stay longer, they can also suggest several worthwhile hiking routes, including a trip to Kvannligrotta, (a 900m-deep cave, 93km from town, which can only be accessed with an underwater dive with mandatory guides), or fishing on the river Vefsna.

Things to See & Do

Sjøgata The obligatory stroll through Sjøgata takes you past galleries, coffee shops, restaurants and private homes in **historic warehouses and boatsheds**.

At Wenche's Ceramics Workshop (☎ 75 17 18 81), visitors can glaze cups which will be fired overnight and available for collection the following day (open from May to August only).

Vefsn Dolstad Museum This museum (☎ 75 17 23 95, Austerbrygdveien 2; admission Nkr20; open 10am-3.30pm Mon-Fri, 11am-3pm Sun) is in two parts. North-east of the centre, the **building collection** features 12 structures from the 18th and 19th centuries. Adjacent is the octagonal cruciform **Dolstad Kirke** (☎ 75 17 20 01, Austerbrygdveien; open 8am-3.30pm Mon-Fri summer), which dates from 1735, on the site of a medieval church dedicated to St Michael.

In Sjøgata, the **Jakobsensbrygga** warehouse houses the museum annexe (Sjøgata 31B; open 10am-3.30pm Mon-Fri, 10am-2pm Sat), which recounts the history of Mosjøen from the early 19th century up to the present.

Laksforsen About 30km south of Mosjøen, the roaring 17m Laksforsen **waterfall** is best known for its leaping salmon and the fishing possibilities in the broad river pool below it.

At the *Laksforsen Turist-Café (☎ 75 18 21 82, Laksforsen)*, you can stay dry and munch on meatballs, salmon and steaks (mains Nkr82 to Nkr120) while viewing the impressive chute.

Places to Stay & Eat
Mosjøen Camping (☎ 75 17 79 00, fax 75 17 79 01, e mosjoencamping@sensewave.com, Mathias Bruuns gata 24) Tent/caravan sites Nkr80/120, cabins Nkr300-750. At this camping ground off the E6, about 500m south-east of the centre, cabins range from basic to considerably more plush, and there's a bowling alley.

Mosjøen Hotell (☎ 75 17 11 55, fax 75 14 49 93, Vollanveien 35) Singles/doubles from Nkr490/690, less without private bath. About 100m north of the train station you'll find cosy, informal rooms at this hotel.

Fru Haugans Hotel (☎ 75 11 41 00, fax 75 11 41 01, e res@fruhaugans.no, Strandgata 39) Singles/doubles from Nkr595/790. These are Mosjøen's poshest digs, adjacent to Sjøgata and the tourist office. Sections date back to 1794.

Heimebakeriet (☎ 75 17 20 90, Cnr Jurgensens gate & CM Havings gate) This historic bakery (1842), in Sjøgata, has coffee, cakes for around Nkr25 and light dishes for under Nkr100.

Andreasbrygga (☎ 75 17 49 00, Sjøgata 1B) Mains Nkr58-163. In this lovingly renovated warehouse (1870), you'll find steaks and a pub menu. Upstairs is a disco and club.

Oksen Ferdinand (☎ 75 11 99 91, Sjøgata 23) Mains Nkr139-239. This charming steakhouse in a historic building also does nice fish dishes.

Getting There & Away
Mosjøen lies on the rail line between Trondheim (Nkr480, 5½ hours) and Fauske (Nkr365, 3¾ hours).

Buses run once or twice daily except Saturday between Mosjøen and Brønnøysund

(Nkr188, 3¼ hours); there are also connections via Sandnessjøen (Nkr94, 1½ hours). For drivers, a lovely detour follows the wild and scenic Villmarksveien route, which runs parallel to the E6 east of Mosjøen and approaches the bizarre 1128m *moberg* peak, Hatten (or Hattfjell); from the road's end, the hike to the top takes about two hours. However, taking this route does cut out Mosjøen itself.

MO I RANA
pop 17,510
Said to be Norway's friendliest town, Mo i Rana is the third largest city in the north and gateway to the spruce forests, caves and glaciers of the Arctic Circle region, one of Europe's largest wilderness areas. Its friendly reputation is often attributed to its rapid expansion due to the construction of a steel plant. Nearly everyone here knows how it feels to be a stranger, and treats visitors accordingly!

Although Mo's predominant architectural style is boxy, its heavy industry is giving way to a tech economy.

Information
The exceptionally active Polarsirkelen Reiseliv (☎ 75 13 92 00, fax 75 13 92 09, e infomo@arctic-circle.no), Ole Tobias Olsensgate 3, occupies an unassuming building near the Sørlandsveien roundabout. No question or problem is too great for the staff here, whether on the town or the region. It's open 9am to 8pm on weekdays, 9am to 4pm on Saturday and 1pm to 7pm on Sunday from mid-June to early August. During the rest of the year it's open from 10am to 3pm on weekdays.

Things to See & Do
Rana Museum of Natural History West of the rail line, this district museum *(☎ 75 14 61 80, Moholmen 15; admission Nkr10; open 9am-3pm & 7pm-10pm Mon-Fri 15 June-15 Aug, 9am-3pm Mon-Fri rest of year)* concentrates on the geology, ecology, flora and wildlife of the Arctic Circle region, and features several hands-on exhibits which will appeal to children.

NORDLAND

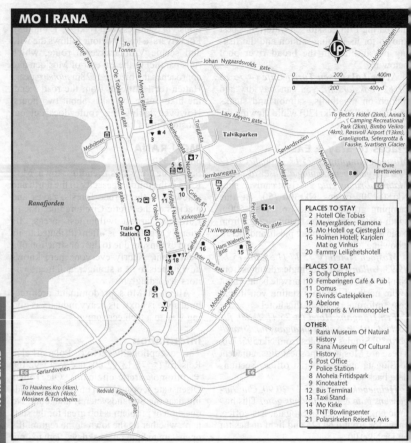

MO I RANA

PLACES TO STAY
2 Hotell Ole Tobias
4 Meyergården; Ramona
15 Mo Hotell og Gjestegård
16 Holmen Hotell; Karjolen
    Mat og Vinhus
20 Fammy Leilighetshotell

PLACES TO EAT
3 Dolly Dimples
10 Fembøringen Café & Pub
11 Domus
17 Eivinds Gatekjøkken
19 Abelone
22 Bunnpris & Vinmonopolet

OTHER
1 Rana Museum Of Natural
   History
5 Rana Museum Of Cultural
   History
6 Post Office
7 Police Station
8 Moheia Fritidspark
9 Kinoteatret
12 Bus Terminal
13 Taxi Stand
14 Mo Kirke
18 TNT Bowlingsenter
21 Polarsirkelen Reiseliv; Avis

Rana Museum of Cultural History At this museum (☎ 75 14 61 70, Fridtjof Nansensgata 22; admission Nkr15; open 10am-3pm & 7pm-9pm Mon-Fri, noon-3pm Sat in summer) you'll find exhibits on the local southern Sami culture and the history of Nordic settlement in southern Nordland.

Moheia Fritidspark The newest addition to the tourist scene here is an indoor water park, sometimes called Badeland (☎ 75 14 60 60, Øvre Idrettsveien 1; adult/child Nkr60/40; open noon-9pm Mon-Thur, noon-8pm Fri, noon-6pm Sat & Sun). The park

has four pools, three saunas, one steam sauna and a cafeteria.

Caves
The limestone and marble country northwest of Mo i Rana is riddled with caves and sinkholes, formed when river water dissolved marble between layers of mica schist. Thanks to mineral deposits, the glacial water that runs into ponds and rivers as you approach the caves has been known to change colour from green to grey to blue.

The most accessible cave to tour is **Grønligrotta** (☎ 75 16 23 05, Grønli; adult/child

Nkr70/35; tours hourly 10am-7pm mid-June–mid-Aug), in business for a century. There's electric lighting (the only illuminated tourist cave in Scandinavia), and the 30-minute tour takes you along an underground river, through a rock maze and past a granite block torn off by a glacier and deposited in the cave by the brute force of moving water.

About 1km closer to town, the trip through **Setergrotta** (☎ 75 16 23 50, *Røvassdalen; tours adult/child Nkr165/100; 2-hour tours 11.30am early June-late Aug, also 3pm 21 June-3 Aug)* is considerably more adventurous. Headlamps, hardhats, gumboots (Wellingtons) and coveralls are all required and provided by the operators. Highlights include a couple of extremely tight squeezes and a thrilling shuffle between rock walls while straddling a 15m gorge.

There's no public transport to the caves, some 22km out of town. If you don't have your own conveyance, the tourist office can help you organise a shared taxi or rent bikes.

Organised Tours

Mo I Rana is also the most convenient base for exploring the **fjords** to the west (though still some 110km away). From the port of Tonnes, Polarsirkel Maritime (☎ 75 09 47 90) offers visits to local fjords and a signature short raft trip to Vikingen (aka Polarsirkeløya), a small island with a globe marking the Arctic Circle (Nkr100). Hurtigruten and ferry riders only get to ride past it as the boats cross the magic line, blasting a celebratory toot. Trips to Hestmanna (horseman) island (see the special section 'Folklore & Legends in Norway') can also be arranged.

For tours to the **Svartisen glacier**, see Østisen under Saltfjellet-Svartisen Nasjonalpark.

Places to Stay

Anna's Camping (☎ 75 14 80 74, *E6, Røssvoll)* Caravan sites/cabins from Nkr60/105. About 12km out of town toward the glacier, this riverside camping ground has caravans and cabins with shared kitchen and bathroom facilities.

Grønligrotta (☎ 75 16 23 05, *fax 75 16 23 66, Røvassdalenveien)* Doubles Nkr400. The

caves' lodge has a few self-catering rooms, open late June to late August or on request.

Bech's Hotell (☎ 75 13 02 11, *fax 75 13 15 77, Hammerveien 10)* Singles/doubles Nkr490/590. Some 3km north of town is this nice, basic option. The nearly adjacent Klokkerhagen recreational park has picnic sites, sporting grounds and canoe hire.

Fammy Leilighetshotell (☎ 75 15 19 99, *fax 75 15 19 90,* e *post@fammy.no, Ole Tobias Olsens gate 4)* Singles/doubles/triples Nkr495/645/845. Flats are bright and have mini-kitchens at this casual, central spot.

Mo Hotell og Gjestgård (☎ 75 15 22 11, *fax 75 15 23 38, Hans Wølners gate 10)* Singles/doubles Nkr400/500. Uphill is this pleasant guesthouse in a quiet location.

Meyergården (☎ 75 13 40 00, *fax 75 13 40 01,* e *meyergarden@meyergarden.no, Ole Tobias Olsens gate 24)* Singles/doubles from Nkr595/845. This is Mo's Establishment hotel, with fine rooms, convention facilities and a popular nightclub.

Holmen Hotell (☎ 75 15 14 44, *fax 75 15 18 70,* e *ellinor.boyne@sensewave.com, TV Westens gate 2)* Singles/doubles from Nkr610/790. Rooms are quite plush here, despite the drab exterior.

Comfort Hotel Ole Tobias (☎ 75 15 77 77, *fax 75 15 77 78,* e *hotel@ole-tobias.no, Thora Meyersgata 2)* Singles/doubles from Nkr650/840. This railway-themed hotel is named after the local teacher and priest who convinced the government to build the Nordlandsbanen railway connecting Trondheim with Fauske and Bodø.

Places to Eat

Dolly Dimples (☎ 75 17 89 00, *Thora Meyersgate)* Pizzas Nkr103-228. This chain is a popular choice for pizza and beer.

Abelone (☎ 75 15 38 88, *Ole Tobias Olsens gata 6)* Mains Nkr85-125. More upscale than Dolly Dimples, Abelone serves everything from Greek to pizza, from steaks to venison.

Karjolen Mat og Vinhus (☎ 75 15 14 44, *TV Westens gate 2)* Mains Nkr80-225. The Holmen Hotel's high-end eatery is recommended for its traditional Norwegian cuisine and extensive wine list.

Eivinds Gatekjøkken (☎ 75 15 04 33, Fridtjof Nansensgata 1) This quick service restaurant stays open late on weekends with burgers, chips etc from Nkr57 to Nkr100.

Bimbo Veikro (☎ 75 15 10 01, Saltfjellet-veien 34) Mains Nkr42-150. North of town, this roadhouse serves sandwiches, pizzas and grills, for bimbos, himbos and the rest of us (the 'truck drivers' special' is eggs, bacon, beans and potatoes for Nkr65). 'Bimbo' refers to a nearby elephant-shaped rock formation.

Hauknes Kro (☎ 75 13 58 40, Nygata 100) Dishes Nkr59-129. About 4km towards Trondheim, this friendly shop dishes up hearty fish and beef specialities. It's busy in summer, thanks to the Hauknes bathing beach across the road.

Other seekers of quick bites will enjoy the pedestrian area in the centre of town, dominated by the *Domus* shopping centre *(☎ 75 13 98 00, Fridtjof Nansensgata)*. A *Bunnpris* supermarket and *Vinmonopolet* are opposite the tourist office.

Entertainment

Ramona (☎ 75 13 40 00, Fridtjof Nansensgata 28) Located at the Meyergården, this spot is said to be the largest nightclub in northern Norway.

Fembøringen Café & Pub (☎ 75 15 09 77, Jernbanegata 12) This venue in the centre has a casual atmosphere.

Kinoteatret (☎ 75 14 60 50, Rådhusplass 1) Mo i Rana's cinema is at the top of Jernbanegata.

TNT Bowlingsenter (☎ 75 15 78 00, Fridtjof Nansensgata 1) You can go bowling here for Nkr50 per round at peak times.

Getting There & Away

By air, Mo i Rana's Røssvoll airport, 14km from town, is served by Widerøe at least daily from Trondheim and Brønnøysund. It's a fabulous trip with excellent views of the Svartisen icecaps.

Most visitors arrive at Mo i Rana's unique octagonal train station (☎ 75 15 01 77) on the two or three daily trains from Trondheim (Nkr590, 6¾ hours) or Fauske (Nkr245, 2¼ hours). By bus, your options are fairly

limited. There are services daily except Saturday between Mo i Rana and Sandnessjøen (Nkr142, 3¼ hours). From Sunday to Friday there's at least one daily Ranaekspressen bus to and from Mosjøen (two hours, Nkr93). For journeys to/from Umeå in Sweden, see the Getting There & Away chapter.

Drivers can stop by the tourist office and pick up a free tourist parking permit. This novel idea proves that Mo i Rana is serious about promoting tourism!

Getting Around

You can hire a taxi through the central number (☎ 07550). Car hire is available through Avis (☎ 75 14 81 57, fax 75 14 83 90), next to the tourist office.

SALTFJELLET-SVARTISEN NASJONALPARK

The 2105-sq-km Saltfjellet-Svartisen National Park combines the Svartisen icecap (Norway's second largest icefield, with its rugged peaks, a combined area of 369 sq km); and the high and rolling moorlands of the Salfjellet massif near the Swedish border.

Information

Three DNT offices cover the park, which is broken into three regions. If you're heading for western Svartisen, contact the Bodø og Omegn Turistforening (☎ 75 52 14 13), Storgata 17 in Bodø. For the eastern side of Svartisen, see the Rana Turistforening (☎ 75 13 92 00), at the tourist office in Mo i Rana. For hiking and hut information on the Saltfjellet section, contact the Sulitjelma og Omegn Turistforening (☎ 75 64 04 01), at the Tourist & Course Centre in Sulitjelma. For national park information, see Statskog Helgeland in Mo i Rana (☎ 75 15 79 50) or Fauske (☎ 75 64 77 80).

The best map to use is Statens Kartverk's *Turkart Saltfjellet*, at a scale of 1:100,000.

Svartisen

The two Svartisen icecaps, which are separated by the valley Vesterdalen, straddle the Arctic Circle between Mo i Rana and the Meløy peninsula. In its heights, the icecap averages about 1500m altitude, but some of its tongues lick the lowlands to become the lowest-lying glaciers in Europe outside of Iceland and Svalbard. Svartisen can be visited from either the east or the west, but to travel between the two main access points requires a major technical expedition on foot and a one- or two-day detour in a car. Most visitors to the glacier just make a quick hop by boat, but hikers will find more joy approaching from the east.

Vestisen The estranged Vestisen icecap probably attracts more visitors than any other part of the park. Travellers along the Kystriksveien will catch glimpses of the Svartisen icecap from the Kilboghamn-Jektvik and Ågskardet-Forøy ferries, and good views from the highway along Holandsfjorden. From Holand and Brasetvik quays, the Engen Skyssbåt (☎ 94 86 55 16) ferries *Engebreen* and *Isprins* shuttle across Holandsfjorden to the snout of Engebreen glacial tongue (Nkr40, 15 minutes). From 1 June to 31 August the ferries sail 12 times between 7.20am and 8pm on weekdays and 10 times on weekends between 9.50am and 8pm. Polarsirkel Maritime (see Mo I Rana) also runs journeys to the glacier from the port of Tonnes.

A 15-minute walk from the ferry landing takes you to the Svartisen Turistsenter (☎ 75 75 00 11), which includes a cafe and shop; it's open from May to September. Guided glacier walks (☎ 75 75 00 32) from the end of Engabrevatnet lake are available for Nkr200 per hour plus Nkr100 for equipment. Independent hikers can slog up the steep route along the glacier's edge to the Tåkeheimen hut, near the summit of Helgelandsbukken (1454m).

Northbound travellers on the Hurtigruten coastal steamer may be able to visit Engebreen as an add-on to their journey. You can also visit by boat/bus combination from Bodø (check with the tourist office for schedules).

Østisen From the end of the Svartisdalen road, 20km up the valley from Røssvoll (the airport for Mo i Rana), ferries (☎ 75 16 23 79) across the Svartisvatnet (Svartisen lake; 20 minutes, adult/concession Nkr70/40)

operate between 20 June and 31 August. From 10 July to 10 August ferries run hourly from 10am to 4pm and at other times at 10am, noon, 2pm and 4pm. Alternatively, it's a tedious 4km walk along the lakeshore, plagued by rocks and stream crossings. From the ferry landing at the western end of the lake, it's a 3km hike to the snout of the Austerdalsisen glacier tongue, which has receded about 1km in the past two decades due to warming temperatures. It's hoped that increased snowfall higher up will eventually reverse that process and preserve this lovely feature. There's a kiosk and camping ground at the lake.

From the end of the road you can also trek up to the hut on the shore of the mountain lake Pikhaugsvatnet, surrounded by peaks and ice. This is an excellent base to use for day hikes up the Glomdal valley or to the Flatisen glacier. Experienced technical climbers will find excellent challenges on Nordre Kamplitinden (1532m) and Skiptinden (1591m).

Saltfjellet

The landscape along the Arctic Circle is characterised by the high broad plateaux of the Saltfjellet massif, connecting the high peaks surrounding the Svartisen icecap and the Swedish border. Dotted around this relatively inhospitable wilderness are numerous fences and sacrificial sites attributed to the Sami people; some sites date from as early as the 9th century AD, and evidence suggests reindeer-herding as early as the 16th century.

From the large and rather luxurious **Polarsirkelen Høyfjellshotel** (☎ 75 69 41 22, fax 75 69 41 27, Lønsdal), 20km north of the Arctic Circle, you can begin a high-country hike through a desolate and little known landscape. The hotel has singles/doubles from Nkr590/890, plus cabins (Nkr350 to Nkr600) and camp sites. DNT members may prefer **Lønsstua** (☎ 75 69 41 25, ring for key info).

A 15km walk to the east leads to Graddis, near the Swedish border, and the amenable **Graddis Fjellstue og Camping** (☎ 75 69 43 41, fax 75 69 43 88, Graddis), with singles/ doubles for Nkr350/620 and cabins for

Nkr350. This cosy little guesthouse has been run by the same family since its establishment in 1867; it's an excellent base to launch yourself into one of Norway's least attended hiking venues. Camping is also available. (Have a look at the 1000-year-old pine tree, which lies 200m from the hostel and has been named Methuselah.)

Or, head west over the moors to several unstaffed **DNT huts**: Saltfjellstua, Bukkhaugsstua, Bjellåvasstua and Krukkistua.

If you prefer an easier route, one of the area's best short hikes leads through the wildly twisting Junkerdalsura gorge, a rich botanical reserve. From the Saltdal Turistsenter (☎ 75 69 41 00), corner of E6 and E77, Storfjord, head east and cross the swinging bridge over the Junkerdal river. After 200m, you'll reach an information notice board. From there, a hiking path follows an old cart track for 4km up the gorge to the Junkerdalen bridge, near the village of Solvågli. The Turistsenter also has some grass-topped huts for lodging and a reader-recommended restaurant with pizzas and other cafeteria specialities (Nkr22 to Nkr139).

Getting There & Away

Rail travellers can disembark at Lønsdal en route between Fauske (Nkr60, 45 minutes) and Trondheim (Nkr630, 8½ hours), but you may have to request a stop. For drivers, access to Saltfjellet is either along the E6 or the Rv77, which follows the southern slope of the valley Junkerdalen. Bus No 3 runs between Bodø (Nkr155, 3¼ hours) and Fauske (Nkr93, 1¾ hours) daily except Saturday, and on Friday stops at the Junkerdal Turistsenter.

As an aside, on the E6 between Saltfjellet and Fauske, shoppers and browsers will appreciate **Arctic Lys & Design** (☎ 75 68 07 00, Røkland; open 10am-6pm Mon-Wed, 10am-8pm Thur, 11am-6pm Sat, 1pm-6pm Sun), where you'll find craggy rocks, lush, tropical flowers and other natural phenomena...and burn them (don't worry; they're candles).

ARCTIC CIRCLE CENTRE

Located at 66° 33' north latitude, which marks the southernmost extent of the mid-

night sun on the summer solstice and the ragged edge of the polar night on the winter solstice, is a mythic place. Along the Arctic Highway between Mo i Rana and Fauske, the bleak moors adjoining Saltfjellet-Svartisen National Park provide the appropriate polar illusion.

However, the **Polarsirkelsenteret** (☎ 75 12 96 96, E6, Rognan; adult/child/concession/family Nkr50/20/30/100, open 8am-10pm mid-June–early Aug, shorter hours May-Sept), which straddles the line, is the definition of a tourist trap. There's a collection of stuffed wildlife specimens and an audiovisual presentation on the Arctic regions, but the place exists mostly to stamp postcards with a special Arctic Circle postmark and sell certificates for visitors to authenticate actually crossing the magic line, as well as boreal kitsch from the gift shop. Perhaps the most worthwhile feature is the memorial to the forced labourers who, during WWII, constructed the Arctic Highway for the occupying German forces.

If it leaves you feeling unsatisfied, northbound travellers will feel better as they descend into a relatively lush, green environment more typical of northern Norway.

FAUSKE
pop 9632

Fauske is known mainly for marble quarrying and has contributed stone for numerous monumental structures, including the Oslo Rådhus and the UN headquarters in New York, but most travellers know it as a jumping-off point for Sulitjelma and the Rago National Park. It's also the place where northbound ScanRail passengers must forgo the rails and get on the bus to reach Lofoten or Tromsø. The knowledgeable Salten Reiseliv tourist office (☎ 75 64 33 03, fax 75 64 32 38, e salten.reiseliv@online.no), Sjøgata 86, provides information on the surrounding natural areas.

Unless you're pressed for time, it's worth making the trip the hour or so west to Bodø, the end of the Kystriksveien Coastal Route, where you'll find several interesting sites and ferry access to southern Lofoten.

Things to See
Sights in town include the marble-themed **town square**, and the park-like collection of historic buildings of the **Fauske Bygdetun museum** (☎ 75 64 46 98, Sjøgata; adult/child/family Nkr20/5/40; open 8am-6pm Mon-Fri, 1pm-3pm Sat & Sun in July & early Aug, 7.30am-3pm Mon-Fri rest of year) is a nice place for a picnic.

The **Norsk Vegmuseum** (Road Museum; ☎ 75 64 26 00, Follaveien 91; admission free; open 8am-3pm Mon-Fri) is certainly more unusual. Located 2km north of town (at the midpoint of the E6!), it's housed at the Statens Vegvesen (State Road Authority) complex and displays artefacts from the history of roads and roadbuilding in Norway. Note the collection of dishes embossed with the Vegvesen logo, once used by workers. Ask at the main counter for admission.

If you like Fauske's streaky salmon-coloured marble, visit **Ankerske Naturstein** (☎ 75 60 01 50; admission free; open 7.30am-3.30pm Mon-Thur, 7.30am-3pm Fri), 500m south of the centre, where you can buy a range of locally produced marble products. The tourist office can also arrange guided tours of local quarries.

Places to Stay
Fauske Camping og Motell (☎ 75 64 84 01, fax 75 64 84 13, e fausm@online.no, E6) Tent/caravan sites Nkr60/90, cabins Nkr200. About 4km south of the centre, this spot has spartan cabins.

Lundhøgda Camp & Café (☎ 75 64 39 66, fax 79 64 92 49, e lunghogda@c2i.net, Lundveien) Tent or caravan sites Nkr100, 4-bed cabin Nkr250-550. This place, 3km west of town, has superb views of the fjord and surrounding peaks and cabins of varying standards. From the centre, take the bus to Erikstad, though you'll still have to walk a kilometre.

Seljestua (☎ 90 73 46 96, Seljeveien 2) Singles/doubles Nkr350/400. This new student home/summer hostel is just 500m from the railway station and has family rooms with private facilities.

Fauske Hotell (☎ 75 60 20 00, fax 75 64 57 37, e firmapost@fauskehotell.no, Stor-gata 82) Singles/doubles from Nkr700/850. Your only upscale choice in town has renovated, cheerful rooms, though common areas feel a little dated.

Getting There & Away
Bus The popular Nord-Norgeekspressen between Bodø (Nkr81, 1¼ hours) and Narvik (Nkr313, 4¾ hours) passes through Fauske and on the especially scenic Narvik route allows substantial discounts for holders of ScanRail, InterRail and Eurail passes. You can also travel directly to Lofoten from Fauske on the Fauske-Lofoten Ekspressen, which operates between Fauske, Sortland (Nkr301, 5¼ hours) and Svolvær (Nkr425, 8½ hours).

To/from Harstad, on the Vesterålen island of Hinnøya, you can take the daily Togbussen (Nkr323, six hours). The Saltens Bilruter local bus between Fauske and Bodø (Nkr81, 1¼ hours) runs at least three times daily.

Train Trains ply the Nordlandsbanen between Trondheim (Nkr730, 9½ hours) and Bodø (Nkr86, 45 minutes), via Fauske, at least twice daily.

AROUND FAUSKE
Saltdal & Blood Road Museums
At Saltnes, the **Saltdal Historical Village** (☎ 75 69 06 60, Saltdal, Saltnes; admission Nkr50; open 9.30am-4pm Mon-Fri, 1pm-4pm Sat, 1pm-6pm Sun, 20 June-20 Aug, by request rest of year) consists of a collection of rural buildings on the site of the 1750 Skippergården farm. Catch any bus headed south along the E6. More interesting is the adjacent **Blood Road Museum**, which is housed in an old German barracks and reveals conditions for Allied prisoners of war between 1942 and 1945, who died building the highway between Saltnes and Saksenvik. The prisoners' cemetery (some 7000 souls) is about 3km north, in Botn.

Sulitjelma
Along the Rv830, south-east of Fauske, lies the community of Sulitjelma. In 1860, a Sami herder discovered copper ore in the forested country north of Langvatnet and

suddenly the Sulitjelma region was attracting all sorts of opportunists from Southern Norway. By 1876, large ore deposits were discovered, and the Sulitjelma Gruber mining company was founded in 1891. By 1928, the wood-fuelled smelter had taken its toll on the surrounding birch forests, as did high concentrations of CO_2 (a by-product of the smelting process), though the environment is on its way to recovery.

Things to See & Do Tours of local mines are available through **Sulitjelma Besøksgruve** *(mines, ☎ 75 64 06 95, Sulitjelma; tours adult/child Nkr100/50; 2-hour guided tour 1pm mid-June–mid-Aug or on request)* and include a rail ride through the copper tunnels.

You'll also want to peruse the **Sulitjelma Gruvemuseum** *(☎ 75 64 02 40, Sulitjelma; adult/child/family Nkr20/10/50; open 11am-3pm Mon-Fri & 6pm-8pm Tues July)*, which reveals the area's 100 years of mining history and some awesome, rusting equipment.

Saulo Design *(☎ 75 60 00 90, Sulitjelma; open 11am-3pm Mon Fri, longer hours in summer, including Sat)* manufactures gifts and art from stones mined from Sulitjelma and has a shop on the premises.

The country east and south of Sulitjelma enjoys especially scenic glacial surroundings and ample **hiking** opportunities. Hikers can choose from several routes past nine major huts – pick up DNT keys from the Sulitjelma Hotel (☎ 75 64 04 01, fax 75 64 06 54) or Sulitjelma Camping og Fritidssenter (☎/fax 75 64 04 33).

For technical climbers, favoured destinations are the **three nunataks** (mountain peaks protruding through a glacier or icecap), Vardetoppen (1722m), Stortoppen (1830m) and Sulistoppen (1930m), all in the Sulitjelmasisen icecap. The 123-sq-km **Blåmannsisen icecap** (1571m), farther north, is also popular and is associated with a famous saga (see the Folklore & Legends in Norway special section). The topo sheets to use are *Låmivatnet* (sheet 2229-III), *Sulitjelma* (sheet 2129-II) and *Balvatnet* (sheet 2128-I), all at a 1:50,000 scale.

Also see the Salten Reiseliv tourist office in Fauske for tours of the local caves system.

Places to Stay *Jakobsbakken Fjellsenter* *(☎ 75 64 02 90 fax 75 64 02 55, e jakobsb akken@c2i.net, Jakobsbakken Road)* Dorm beds Nkr100, apartments to Nkr1000. This hilltop, church-run facility at the end of the road has 180° views of the surrounding valleys. It sometimes closes for religious retreats.

Sulitjelma Camping og Fritidsenter *(☎/fax 75 64 04 33, e scamfri@online.no, Daja)* Cabins from Nkr450. In a dale by the lake, this camping ground has inexpensive camping and cabins.

Sulitjelma Hotel *(☎ 75 64 04 01, fax 75 64 06 54, e SUL-HOT@online.no, Andr Quales vei 15)* Singles/doubles from Nkr700/900. Surprisingly large for such a remote place, this hotel has a swimming pool, lovely wooded setting, and some renovated rooms.

Getting There & Away Buses between Fauske and Sulitjelma (Nkr49, one hour) run at least three times daily Monday to Saturday and once on Sunday.

Rago Nasjonalpark

The small (167 sq km), scarcely visited Rago National Park comprises an incredibly rugged chunk of forested granite mountains and moorlands, riven with deep glacial cracks and capped by great icefields. Rago, together with the large adjoining Swedish parks, Pakjelanta, Sarek and Stora Sjöfjallet, belongs to a protected area of 5500 sq km. Wildlife includes not only beavers in the deep Laksåga (aka Nordfjord) river valley, but also wolverines in the higher areas.

Rago is best known, however, for the series of foaming cascades and spectacular waterfalls in the relatively lush Storskogdalen valley; from bottom to top, they include Værivassfoss (200m), Trollfoss (43m) and Storskogsfoss (18m).

For serious hikers hoping to escape the crowds, hotel-like huts and highway-like tracks typical of some Norwegian national parks, Rago is the place to go. From the main trailhead at Lakshol, it's a three-hour, 7km walk up the valley to the free Storskogvasshytta and Ragohytta huts and then a stiff climb up and over the ridge into

Sweden to connect with the well-established trail system over the border. The maps to use for the park are the topo sheet *Sisovatnet* (sheet 2129-I), at a scale of 1:50,000, or *Sørfold*, at a scale of 1:75,000. To reach Lakshol, turn east off the E6 at the Trengsel bridge and continue about 6km to the end of the road.

Several buses per day (No 2 or 841) run from Fauske (one hour, Nkr36). Ask the driver to stop at Trengsel bru, and mention that you are going to Rago National Park.

NARVIK
pop 13,962

Narvik was established about a century ago as an ice-free port for the rich Kiruna iron mines in Swedish Lapland. Recently it's begun to capitalise on the unique sporting and sightseeing activities available in its majestic, wild and historic surroundings, including the spectacular Ofotbanen Railway to Sweden.

History

The Narvik region was inhabited as early as the Stone Age, as evidenced by the distinct rock carving of a moose found at Vassvik, north-west of the centre.

During WWII, this strategic port became an obvious target for the Nazi war machine, intent upon halting iron supplies to the Allies and usurping the bounty. In a blizzard on 9 April 1940, 10 German destroyers entered the port and sank two Norwegian battleships. The following day five British destroyers arrived to defend the port. A fierce naval battle resulted in the loss of two ships on each side and on 12 April, British aircraft-carrier-based planes attacked. By late May, British, Norwegian, French and Polish troops disembarked and took back the town in a single day – the first major Allied victory in the Norwegian campaign.

But the Germans didn't retreat. Between 28 May and 8 June, Narvik wasn't just bombed into submission; it was decimated, as evidenced by the remains of soldiers in the cemeteries and 34 ships of five nations (Norway, Britain, France, the Netherlands and Germany) in the harbour. Some ships actually sank themselves to avoid destruction by bombing, and were later refloated and/or salvaged.

Escalating conflicts in France prevented the Allies from dedicating sufficient resources to defending the port and on 8 June 1940 they surrendered Narvik to the occupying forces. Germany remained in control until 8 May 1945.

Although the town was admirably rebuilt, downtown Narvik is less than prepossessing (some would say it's ugly). Still, the surrounding fjord, forest and mountain country borders on the spectacular in all directions, and the trans-shipment facility bisecting the city still loads ore from rail cars onto ships and is fascinating in a big-machinery sort of way.

Orientation & Information

Straddling a valley that contains the huge iron ore docks, Narvik is surrounded by islands to the west and mountains in every other direction, with spectacular fjords to the north and south. The train station is at the north end of town, downhill from the Storsenter shopping mall, while the bus station is at the centre, at the AMFI shopping centre.

The Narvik Aktiv tourist office (☎ 76 94 33 09, fax 76 94 74 05, e post@narvikinfo .no), Kongens gate 26, is on the main drag diagonally across from AMFI. Staff are very helpful, as is the map guide given out along with an assortment of pamphlets and brochures. Hiking and hut information is dispensed by the Narvik og Omegns Turistforening (☎ 76 94 37 90), Postboks 615, N-8501 Narvik. DNT cabin keys are available from the Narvik Sparebank in the AMFI (☎ 76 92 26 83). The Web site ⓦ www .narvikfjell.no also dispenses excellent information on hiking and cabins.

Things to See & Do
Nordland Røde Kors Krigsminnemuseum
The Red Cross War Museum (☎ 76 94 44 26, Kongens gate; adult/child Nkr45/10; open 11am-3pm daily 1 Mar-30 Sept, 10am-10pm Mon-Sat, 11am-5pm Sun 10 June-20 Sept), on the town square, admirably illustrates the military campaigns

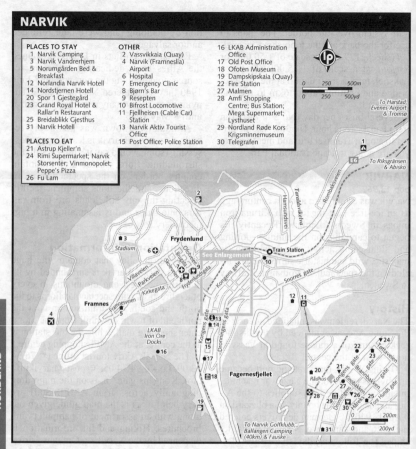

NARVIK

PLACES TO STAY
1 Narvik Camping
3 Narvik Vandrerhjem
5 Norumgården Bed & Breakfast
12 Norlandia Narvik Hotell
14 Nordstjernen Hotell
20 Spor 1 Gjestegård
23 Grand Royal Hotel & Rallar'n Restaurant
25 Breidablikk Gjesthus
31 Narvik Hotell

PLACES TO EAT
21 Astrup Kjeller'n
24 Rimi Supermarket; Narvik Storsenter; Vinmonopolet; Peppe's Pizza
26 Fu Lam

OTHER
2 Vassvikkaia (Quay)
4 Narvik (Framneslia) Airport
6 Hospital
7 Emergency Clinic
8 Bjørn's Bar
9 Resepten
10 Bifrost Locomotive
11 Fjellheisen (Cable Car) Station
13 Narvik Aktiv Tourist Office
15 Post Office; Police Station

16 LKAB Administration Office
17 Old Post Office
18 Ofoten Museum
19 Dampskipskaia (Quay)
22 Fire Station
27 Malmen
28 Amfi Shopping Centre; Bus Station; Mega Supermarket; Lysthuset
29 Nordland Røde Kors Krigsminnemuseum
30 Telegrafen

fought hereabouts in the early years of WWII. The presentation isn't flash, but you're still likely to leave feeling rather stunned.

Ofoten Museum This unique museum (☎ 76 96 00 50, Administrasjonsveien 2; adult/child Nkr25/5; open 11am-3.30pm Mon-Fri, noon-3pm Sat & Sun July, open 10.30am-3.30pm Mon-Fri rest of year) occupies a wonderfully colourful 1902 building and tells of Narvik's farming, railway building and ore trans-shipment heritage. Most interesting is the collection of historic

photos, contrasted with modern photos taken from the same angles.

In the park just up the road is the restored building which served as the post office from 1888 to 1898.

LKAB Iron Ore Docks The vast LKAB iron ore trans-shipment complex, an impressive tangle of rusty industrial machinery, conveyors, ovens, railways and heaps of iron pellets, has a strange intimidating appeal, and it says it all about Narvik's raison d'être. An average tanker-load of ore weighs in at 125,000 to 175,000 tonnes, and takes an entire day to load. The tourist office (☎ 76 94 33 09) offers one-hour tours at 1pm from mid-June to mid-August (Nkr30, minimum of eight participants), which meet at LKAB administration offices. Ask at tourist office for directions.

Fjellheisen Above the town, the Fjellheisen **cable car** (☎ 76 94 16 05, *Mårveien; return fare adult/concession/child Nkr80/ 65/45; operating 10am-1am daily 15 June-31 July, 1pm-9pm rest of June & Aug)* climbs 656m for breathtaking views over the surrounding peaks and fjords, weather permitting.

Activities

Mountaineering Extreme hiking, climbing and glacier trekking with local mountain guides are available from NordNorsk Klatreskole (☎ 76 94 30 39) and Narvik Dykk & Eventyr (☎ 99 51 22 05).

Diving Narvik Dykk & Eventyr (☎ 99 51 22 05) can also set you up with diving equipment to check out the local waters, chock-a-block with sunken ships from WWII.

Golf The fjordside journey to the Narvik Golfklubb at Skjomendalen (☎ 76 95 12 01; full round Nkr250; club rental Nkr100) is wondrous (follow the signs to Skjomdal just before the Skjomen bridge on the E6, about 18km south of town). Sheer, treacherous faces will leave you guessing how there could possibly be a golf course here. Yet nature works wonders, and there's a valley hidden amid the peaks. It's the world's northernmost 18-hole golf course (par 72), though that title is due to be usurped by Tromsø in 2003. Not a golfer? There's also hiking nearby.

Skiing From late autumn until June, Fjellheisen cable car above town will take you some 1000m up for trail and off-piste skiing (☎ 76 96 04 94, **e** ski@narvikinfo.no). The amazing views are a bonus. Skiing is also available at Riksgränsen, just across the Swedish border (see Ofotbanen Railway section later in this chapter).

Organised Tours

Sightseeing, fishing and whale-watching on the boat *Delphin Senior* can be arranged through Skipper Ivar Hågensen (☎/fax 76 95 71 51, mobile ☎ 94 86 97 62); during the herring runs between October and December you may see orcas (killer whales). In October and November, the Tysfjord Turistsenter (☎ 75 77 53 70, Storjord; **w** www .orca-tysfjord.nu), runs orca-watching cruises from Storjord, about 85km south of Narvik on the E6.

Boat tours of the fjord leave Narvik's Vassvikkaia quay to Rombaksbotn at 5pm on Saturday and Sunday from early July to mid-August, returning from Rombaksbotn at 6pm. Contact the tourist office for details (one-way adult/child/family Nkr120/60/350, return adult/child/family Nkr150/100/400).

Special Events

Each year in March, the navvies who built the railway are commemorated in the Ofotbanen festival. And on the last Saturday in June, some 2000 people take the train to various stops along the Rallarveien and hike back to a party at Rombaksbotn.

Places to Stay

Narvik Camping (☎ 76 94 58 10, fax 76 94 14 20, **e** narvik.camping@opofoten.no, Rombaksveien 75) Tent/caravan sites Nkr70/ 125, 4-bed/6-bed cabins Nkr450/650, sheets Nkr60. This camping ground, overlooking the fjord and main road, is an easily walkable 2km north-east of the centre.

Ballangen Camping (☎ 76 92 76 90, fax 76 92 76 92, **w** www.ballangen-camping .no, Ballangen) Tent or caravan sites Nkr130, 4-bed huts Nkr275, cabins Nkr375-690. Located 40km south of town, this well-organised camping ground right beside the fjord has sports facilities, a restaurant and a variety of cabins. Numerous buses run here (Nkr61, 45 minutes).

Narvik Vandrerhjem (☎ 76 96 22 00, fax 76 996 20 25, **e** ssin@ssin.no, Tiurveien 22) Dorm beds Nkr150. Open late-June–mid-Aug. Reception open 7am-noon & 6pm-8pm. Narvik's hostel is in the Jaklamyra student housing complex. Breakfast is included.

NORDLAND

Spor 1 Gjestegård (☎ 76 94 60 20, fax 76 94 38 44, e post@spor1.no, Brugata 2) Dorm beds/doubles with shared bath Nkr160/500. Made for backpackers, this brand new place has cheap but well-kept dorm rooms, enthusiastic hosts, a sauna and a nice kitchen in former rail cabins by the tracks.

Breidablikk Gjesthus (☎ 76 94 14 18, fax 76 94 57 86, e breidablikk@narviknett.no, Tore Hunds gate 41) Dorm beds Nkr185, singles/doubles Nkr400/550. This pleasant hillside pension overlooks the town.

Norumgården Bed & Breakfast (☎/fax 76 94 48 57, w norumgaarden.narviknett .no, Framnesveien 127) Singles/doubles Nkr350/500. This tiny, antique-filled place on the west side of town won Narvik's best home restoration award.

Nordstjernen Hotell (☎ 76 94 41 20, fax 76 94 75 06, e nhnarvik@online.no, Kongens gate 26) Singles/doubles Nkr550/695. Around the corner from the tourist office is Narvik's least expensive hotel with neat, basic rooms and a breakfast buffet recommended by readers.

Norlandia Narvik Hotell (☎ 76 96 48 00, fax 76 96 48 08, e service@narvik.norland ia.no, Skistuaveien 8) Singles/doubles from Nkr595/790. At the base of the cable car, you'll find a rustic atmosphere, comfy rooms and friendly staff.

Narvik Hotell (☎ 76 94 70 77, fax 76 94 67 35, e firmapost@narvikhotel.no, Kongens gate 36) Singles/doubles from Nkr700/900. The central Narvik Hotell has spacious rooms and occasionally frilly decor.

Grand Royal Hotel (☎ 76 97 70 00, fax 76 97 70 07, e grand@grandroyalhotelnarvik .no, Kongens gate 64) Singles/doubles from Nkr730/920. Narvik's top-of-the-line hotel also has some great dining options.

Places to Eat

Lysthuset (☎ 76 94 07 88, Bolagsgate 1) Mains Nkr69-168. In the AFMI centre, this piano bar serves sandwiches, steaks, salads and pizzas, but the real reason to come here may be for the city views.

Astrup Kjeller'n (☎ 76 94 04 02, Kinobakken 1) Mains Nkr83-239. Established in 1903, this place has an old-time feel and offers huge servings of pasta, steak and local specialities.

Rallar'n (☎ 76 97 70 77, Kongens gate 64). The Grand Royal's pub has pizza, pasta and other light meals, along with occasional live music.

Chinese specialities from Nkr98 to Nkr195 are served at *Fu Lam* (☎ 96 94 40 38, Dronningens gate 58), while the chain *Peppe's* (☎ 76 92 21 00, Narvik Storsenter) has its standard Nkr89 pizza and salad lunch buffet and pizzas from Nkr130 to Nkr224.

There are also large supermarkets in both the AMFI and Storsenter malls and a simple cafe at the train station. The Vinmonopolet is in the Storsenter.

Entertainment

Telegrafen (☎ 76 95 43 00, Dronningens gate 56) Open nightly. This popular local hangout attracts the 20 to 35 crowd. It shows the latest sports matches on widescreen TV and has occasional live bands (with cover charge).

Malmen (☎ 76 94 20 00, Kongens gate 44) The weekend disco here attracts mostly students from 18 to 20.

Nordlandia Narvik Hotell (☎ 76 96 48 00, Skistuaveien 8) In winter, the bar at the Nordlandia is Narvik's leading *après ski* venue.

Over the bridge from the centre are two favourite pubs: the new *Resepten* (☎ 76 94 26 38, Industriveien 5) with 60 beers and an intimate atmosphere; and the longstanding *Bjørn's Bar* (☎ 76 94 42 90, Brugata).

Getting There & Away

Air You can reach Narvik via either of two airports. Framneslia airport on the Framnes peninsula, about 3km west of the centre, is served chiefly by Widerøe to Bodø and Tromsø. Larger planes use the Evenes airport 1¼ hours away, which Narvik shares with Harstad.

Bus Several express buses between Fauske and the far north take an overnight break in Narvik. Nor-Way Bussekspress buses between Bodø and Narvik (Nkr379, 6¾ hours), via Fauske (Nkr313, 4¾ hours), run twice daily. Fares include the ferry, and holders of

ScanRail or InterRail passes get a 50% discount.

The Narvik-Lofoten Ekspressen runs daily between Narvik and Sortland (Nkr247, 3¾ hours) and Svolvær (Nkr371, 5¾ hours); fares include the ferry, with only limited weekend service.

Nord-Norgeekspressen buses between Narvik and Tromsø (Nkr305, 4¼ hours) leave at least three times daily.

Train There are at least two daily services between Narvik and Bjørnfjell (Nkr55, 45 minutes), continuing to Riksgränsen (Nkr88, 55 minutes) and Kiruna (Nkr155, three hours), in Sweden; some trains continue to Luleå and Stockholm. This route takes you up the spectacular Ofotbanen Railway and, in Sweden, past Abisko National Park, which offers excellent hiking and lovely Arctic scenery; if you're headed east, don't miss it!

Boat The M/S *Bortind* express boat (☎ 75 54 17 41) to Svolvær (Nkr286, 3½ hours) leaves the Dampskipskaia at 3pm on weekdays and noon on Sunday. The dock is on Havnegata, 1km south of the centre along Kongens gate.

Getting Around

Narvik's Framneslia airport is 3km from the centre; Flybussen buses between Narvik and Harstad's Evenes airport run six to 10 times daily (Nkr95, 1¼ hours). For a taxi, phone ☎ 07550. Hertz Car Hire (☎ 76 94 48 00) has an outlet at the Framneslia airport, and all the other majors are represented as well. Many car rental companies also handle mountain bikes.

OFOTBANEN RAILWAY & RALLARVEIEN

The incredible mountain-hugging **Ofotbanen railway** spans a range of landscapes – fjord-side cliffs, birch forests, and rocky plateaus – all within the 55 minutes between Narvik and the Swedish border. It was constructed by migrant labourers ('navvies') at the end of the 19th century to connect Narvik with the iron ore mines at Kiruna, in Sweden's far north, and was opened by King Oscar II in 1903. Currently it transports 14 to 16 million tonnes of iron ore annually. It's also a major magnet for visitors.

The train route from the Narvik train station (☎ 79 92 31 21) to Riksgränsen, the ski resort just inside Sweden (55 minutes, adult Nkr88 each way, which includes up to two children), features some 50 tunnels and snowsheds. You'll also see the impressive Norddal trestle, which was used from 1902 to 1988 when the line was shifted to the north. It was built by a German engineering firm, MAN, and during WWII, the Nazis were unable to destroy it. Toward the Narvik end of the rail line, you can also see the wreck of the German ship Georg Thiele, at the edge of the fjord.

The big summer attraction at Riksgränsen is a **exhibition** of stunning nature photographs of the region by Sven Hörnell, the Swedish photographer who made his home here *(Sweden: ☎ 46-0980 431 11, Riksgränsen; exhibit admission free, slide show Nkr60)*. There's also a slide show of his work, and although the narration is usually in Swedish, the photos and music speak for themselves.

Riksgränsen also has a big ski hotel, the *Riksgränsen Turiststation hotel (Sweden: ☎ 46-0980 400 80, fax 0980 431 25, e reservation@riksgransen.nu, Riksgränsen)*, with singles/doubles from Skr590/900. It's open mid-February to the end of September. The ski season normally runs mid-February to midsummer.

Another popular way to travel the route is on foot via the old navvy trail, the **Rallarveien**. Few people actually walk the entire way between Sweden's Abisko National Park and the sea, opting instead for all or part of the descent from Riksgränsen or Bjørnfell (in Norway) to Rombaksbotn at the head of the fjord, the location of the main camp when the railway was being built (it's since returned to nature). The E10 also runs roughly parallel.

In Sweden, several long-distance routes radiate out from the Rallarveien, including the connecting route with Øvre Dividal National Park, in the Norwegian county of Troms, and the world-renowned Kungsleden,

NORDLAND

Svartabjørn

It isn't known whether or not there actually was a cook named Svartabjørn (the 'black bear') who dished up meals for the navvies who built the railway of the Ofoten line, but her name certainly lives on in legend. In his *Malm* trilogy, published in 1914, novelist Ernst Didring recounted stories told to him by the navvies.

It's said that this dark and beautiful woman, though too young to be away from home, got on well with the rail workers and cooked their evening meals. But when she fell in love with the same man as another woman, she was beaten to death with a laundry paddle, and the navvies arranged for her burial at the Tornehamn cemetery. Today, the grave is marked *Anna Norge*, but the date of death has been changed at least three times, to fit different women who are thought to have been the real Svartabjørn.

which heads south from Abisko into the heart of Sweden.

The booklet *Hikes Along the Navvy Road* includes a good map of the route from Abisko to Rombaksbotn and costs Nkr40 from the Narvik tourist office.

Kystriksveien – The Coastal Route

At Steinkjer in Trøndelag, road travellers must choose between the Arctic Highway to Narvik, or the slower, lesser-known and more expensive – but incredibly beautiful – E17 Kystriksveien, or 'Coastal Route' which ends in Bodø. There's magic (and a photo opportunity) around every bend here, and if you have a vehicle and enough cash for the ferries – or enough time to take the buses – you won't want to miss it. Many Norwegians agree that this is the best of mainland Norway – or very close to it.

Be sure to see the note in Getting Around at the beginning of this chapter. For information on the southern Kystriksveien, see the Trøndelag chapter. Should you become confused at any point, pick up a copy of the free *Kystriksveien* booklet distributed by tourist offices and many lodgings along the way, or ring the Kystriksveien Info-Center in Steinkjer (☎ 74 16 36 17, fax 74 16 10 88, e post@rv17.no, w www.rv17.no).

BRØNNØYSUND
pop 3588
Surrounded on one side by an archipelago of islets in a tropical-looking sea, and on the other by lovely farm country, Brønnøysund is a pleasant surprise. Tourist information is provided by the friendly Torghatten Reiseliv (☎ 75 01 12 10, fax 75 01 12 19, e post@torghatten.no), named for the island peak south of town which is the region's major destination. The tourist office rents bicycles for Nkr20/80 per hour/day.

Things to See & Do
Hildur's Urterarium A collection of 400 types of herbs, 100 varieties of roses and around 1000 species of cacti make this herb farm (☎ 75 02 51 34, fax 75 02 51 07, Tilrem estate, Rv17, Tilrem; admission Nkr25; open 10am-5pm daily 15 June-15 Aug) a worthwhile stop, about 6km north of town. There are some rustic old farm buildings and an art gallery with originals by famous Norwegian artists (and many reprints), and the shop carries locally grown products. Large groups can book cultural dinners in the attached 'Viking Hall' and learn about the Viking era in the region, taste local herbal mead and sample soups and breads seasoned with locally produced herbs. Individuals may call ahead and ask to join a scheduled group (Nkr200).

Torghatten Some 15km south of Brønnøysund, this mountain on Torget island is one of the most bizarre rock formations in Norway, and a significant local landmark. The peak is pierced by a hole which measures 160m long, 35m high and 20m wide, and is accessed by a good 20-minute walking track from the base. You can reach the island via a bridge from town, but the hole is best seen from the southbound Hurtigruten coastal steamer as it rounds the island. For information on the legend of Torghatten, see the Folklore & Legends in Norway special section.

The tourist office offers a popular daily mini-cruise (adult/child Nkr250/125, 7½ hours) on the Hurtigruten. The journey from Brønnøysund, passes Torghatten to Rørvik, and returns the same day.

On Thursday and Sunday in July, the tourist office offers midnight sun cruises in the archipelago (adult/child Nkr395/265).

Places to Stay & Eat

Mosheim Camping (☎ 75 02 13 73, fax 75 02 20 12, Rv17, Mosheim) Tent/caravan sites Nkr60/80, cabins Nkr200-350. About 4km north of town, this good-value camping ground overlooks a farm.

Torghatten Camping (☎ 75 02 54 95, fax 75 02 58 89, ⓔ torghatten@bronnoy.online.no, Torghatten) Tent/caravan sites Nkr60/100, 4–6-bed cabins Nkr630. This lovely option is by a man-made lake, 15 minutes' walk from the Torghatten peak. Cabins offer private facilities; laundry, boating and diving opportunities are available.

The tourist office books private farm cabins and *rorbuer* for Nkr400 to Nkr800, for four to eight people.

Corner Motell (☎ 75 02 08 77, fax 75 02 09 41, Storgata 79) Singles/doubles from Nkr510/690. There's nothing fancy about this place except its location, opposite the piers.

Torghatten Hotell (☎ 75 00 89 00, fax 75 00 89 01, ⓔ resepsjon@torghattenhotell.no, Valveien 11) Singles/doubles from Nkr640/820. Mains Nkr158-269. Despite its dull shell, this is Brønnøysund's top lodging, with plush rooms. Its lovely restaurant, *Schrøders Stue*, serves whale, monkfish, game and more conventional fare.

Galeasen Hotell (☎ 75 02 14 44, fax 75 02 13 35, Havnegata 34–36) Singles/doubles from Nkr725/850. The Galeasen was being renovated during our visit, but has the best location, right by the docks, plus a nice restaurant.

Milano (☎ 75 02 04 40, Storgata 6) Mains Nkr70-170. Near the south edge of town, this mid-range restaurant has quite decent pizza and meat dishes.

If you stop for soft ice cream in town or anywhere in Norway, keep in mind that it contains a locally-harvested seaweed agent (also found in toothpaste!).

Getting There & Away

Widerøe (☎ 75 01 81 20) serves Brønnøysund from Bodø, Mo i Rana and Trondheim; the approach route passes right over Torghatten and azure seas.

If you're bussing the coastal route, Helgeland Trafikkselskap links Brønnøysund and Sandnessjøen (Nkr140, three hours). Brønnøysund is also a port for the Hurtigruten coastal steamer.

TRÆNA & LOVUND

If you have time for just one offshore visit along the Kystriksveien, Træna (pop 466) is a good bet. It's an archipelago of over 1000 small, flat skerries, five of which are inhabited.

Ferries from the mainland dock on the island of Husøy, which has most of Træna's population and lodgings, but the main sights are on the adjacent island of Sanna. As of this writing, locals ferry passengers from Husøy to Sanna, but there was talk that that service might end. Check with tourist offices before departing the mainland. Sanna measures just over 1km in length and features an amazing miniature mountain range culminating at the northern end in the 318m spire, Trænstaven.

Near Sanna's southern end, the cathedral-like Kirkehelleren Cave is where archaeologists discovered a cemetery and other artefacts (now at the Tromsø Museum) dating back as far as 9000 years, making it Norway's oldest fishing settlement. The little village between the north and south ends enjoys a white sand beach.

Husøy's only attraction is the jewel-box **Petter Dass Chapel** *(donation Nkr20)*, dating from 1996, with paintings by Bodø artist Karl-Erik Harr. Note the signs of the zodiac on the ceiling. The hill outside the chapel provides your best views of Sanna. Local lodgings have keys.

NORDLAND

The steep-sided island of Lovund, with 240 people, rises 623m above the sea and is home to prolific bird colonies. Every 14 April the island celebrates Lundkommerdag, the day 200,000 puffins return to the island to nest until mid-August. You need not bring a car, as the island is tiny and easily managed on foot.

Places to Stay
Træna Gjestegård (☎ 75 09 52 28, fax 75 09 52 29, Husøy) Singles/doubles Nkr450/550. This hotel's simple rooms share a bathroom.

Træna Rorbuferie (☎/fax 75 09 51 67, mobile ☎ 94 85 43 96, Husøy) 4-bed cottages Nkr500-700. Basic, harbourside self-catering cottages are available here.

Both places on Træna have restaurants and will arrange for transportation to/from the boat dock.

Lovund Rorbuhotell (☎ 75 09 45 32, fax 75 09 46 50, Lovund) Single/double rooms Nkr750/900, 4-person cabins Nkr843. This is your only option on Lovund; it's well-kept, with both hotel and cottage accommodation.

Getting There & Away
Helgelandske (☎ 75 06 41 00) runs express catamarans most days connecting Sandnessjøen and Træna (Nkr165, 2¾ hours), via Lovund (Nkr116, 2¼ hours). When available, same-day return costs adult/child/concession Nkr250/135/175. Helgelandske also operates car ferries a couple times per week: Sandnessjøen-Træna (passengers/cars Nkr85/305, 6¾ hours), and Sandnessjøen-Lovund (passengers/cars Nkr62/215, 10¾ hours). Most boats stop at smaller ports en route.

SANDNESSJØEN
pop 5327
Sandnessjøen is the main commercial centre of Nordland's southern coast, and in its backdrop rises the imposing Syv Søstre (Seven Sisters; altitude 1072m) range. All seven summits can be reached by hardy hikers without technical equipment, and every several years there's a competition taking in all the peaks. The record is three hours, 54 minutes – think you can break it? Sandnessjøen is also a nice base for 'island-hopping' in the region.

Central Sandnessjøen's backbone is the pedestrianised Torolv Kveldulvsons gate, one block off the harbour. The cheerful, informative Polarsirkelen Reiseliv tourist office (☎ 75 04 25 80, fax 75 04 64 94), by the boat docks, hires bicycles for Nkr20/80/300 per hour/day/week.

Day Trips
The tourist office can suggest walks in the Syv Søstre range, reached most conveniently via the Rv17 at Breimo, about 1km from town. From there it's a couple of kilometres' walk to the foot of the mountains.

From the port of Tjøtta (40km south of Sandnessjøen), you can catch a ferry to the island of Tro and try to make out the **Skier of Røøya** rock carving, which dates from 3000 to 4000 years ago and was the symbol of the 1994 Lillehammer Winter Olympics. Request a stop and pickup when you board. Tours can also be arranged through Mindland Boat Charters (☎ 75 04 65 67), but they're quite expensive unless you have a group.

Island-hoppers can travel the region via bike or car, ferry or speedboat, for both day trips and overnight stays. Ask at the tourist office for suggestions.

Places to Stay & Eat
Søsterhjemmet (☎ 75 04 31 49, fax 75 04 41 86, ⓔ einlu@frisurf.no, Kirkeveien 30) Singles/doubles Nkr250/400. There's no hostel in Sandnessjøen, but the brand-new and very popular renovated former nurses' residence fills that niche.

Sandnes Overnatting (☎ 75 04 10 29, Harald Hårfagres gate 35) Tent sites Nkr60, singles/doubles without sheets from Nkr150/300, with sheets Nkr300/420. This well-kept home offers travellers simple accommodation.

Rica Hotel Sandnessjøen (☎ 75 04 00 77, fax 75 04 01 86, ⓔ rica.hotel.sandnessjoen@rica.no, Torolv Kveldulvsons gate 16) Singles/doubles from 580/680. The Rica is a sophisticated choice.

Verona (☎ 75 04 40 11, Øyvind Lambes vei 4) Mains Nkr70-169. Off the Rv17 is this local favourite for pizzas, fish, barbecue and Turkish specialities.

Sjøboden (☎ 75 04 34 36, Havnegate 1) Mains Nkr90-200. This offers pizza, chicken, snacks, beer and a harbour-view terrace.

Buri's Bistro (☎ 75 04 40 40, Torolv Kveldulvsons gate 71) Mains Nkr115-232. This is a high-end, country-style option.

There's a Coop supermarket in the centre for self-catering, with a small cafeteria.

In Tjøtta, *Taraldsen Brygga (☎ 75 04 43 56, fax 75 04 43 57, Havnevegen)* offers well-equipped 3–4-person cabins for Nkr400 right by the water, plus great fjord views. Just inland, *Tjøtta Gjestegård (☎ 75 04 64 40, fax 75 04 66 28,* W *www.tjottagjestegaard.no, Tjøtta)* has a few rooms with breakfast and private bath (singles/doubles Nkr450/600) in a charming house on the grounds of a botanical institute, plus a renowned restaurant.

Getting There & Away

Buses run daily except Sunday between Sandnessjøen and Brønnøysund (Nkr140, three hours). Drivers to and from the north have to grin and bear the toll on the inordinately expensive 1073m Helgelandsbrua bridge (Nkr80 for passenger cars – though the toll is scheduled to disappear by 2004). Sandnessjøen is also a stop on the Hurtigruten coastal steamer.

ØRNES
pop 6796

Ørnes, one of the smallest ports of call for the Hurtigruten coastal steamer, is a pretty little town amid very pleasant surroundings and hiking opportunities near the Svartisen glacier (see Vestisen in the earlier Saltfjellet-Svartisen National Park section).

Ørnes Hotell (☎ 75 75 45 99, fax 75 75 47 69, Havneveien 12) Singles/doubles from Nkr600/770. This pierside hotel is a little bit blocky, but rooms are up to date.

Several times daily, buses connect Bodø with Ørnes (Nkr153, 2½ hours), and most of these continue on to the Engebreen ferry terminal at Holand (Nkr64, one hour).

BODØ
pop 31,024

Bodø, at a latitude of 67°17', is Nordland's largest town and anchors an area of diverse attractions. Founded in 1816 as a trade centre, it turned to fishing in 1860 during an especially lucrative herring boom. Because it was levelled on 27 May 1940 and completely rebuilt in the 1950s, the town centre looks rather ordinary – and in summer it can smell strongly of the fish that sustain it – but its refurbished pleasure harbour is lovely and relaxing. The city's open backdrop of distant rugged peaks and vast skies makes it one of Norway's most interestingly-positioned towns and the seas to the north feature a number of dramatic islands which support the world's densest concentration of sea eagles.

Bodø's charms are known to conference attendees, but many holiday-makers give it a miss in their rush to reach the far north. However, it's a great place to spend a day or two (it's only 63km west of Fauske on the Arctic Highway and is the northern terminus of the Nordlandsbanen railway). What's more, the hinterlands hold some top-notch attractions, and it's an easy four-hour ferry ride to the most spectacular bits of Lofoten.

Orientation

Central Bodø slopes down a gradual hill toward a channel that runs from north-east to south-west between the rail station/ferry terminal and small boat harbour, an easily walkable 10 minutes. Between them run Sjøgata and the largely pedestrianised Storgata, with the huge Glasshuset shopping mall in the centre. The tourist office, bus station and express boat terminal are a couple blocks west of the Glasshuset. Museums and churches are up the hill, and the airport is south-west of the centre.

Information

Destinasjon Bodø tourist office (☎ 75 54 80 00, fax 75 54 80 01, e destinasjon@bodoe .com, W www.bodoe.com) is at Sjøgata 3. This very active office provides local information, organises day excursions, can help get you to and around Lofoten and publishes the thorough *Bodø Guide* pamphlet. The airport also houses a small information desk.

Hiking, climbing and other outdoor information are the speciality of DNT's Bodø og Omegn Turistforening (☎ 75 52 14 13),

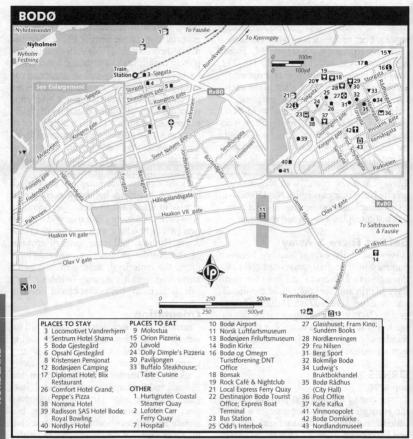

BODØ

PLACES TO STAY	PLACES TO EAT	10 Bodø Airport	27 Glasshuset; Fram Kino;
3 Locomotivet Vandrerhjem	9 Molostua	11 Norsk Luftfartsmuseum	Sundem Books
4 Sentrum Hotel Shama	15 Orion Pizzeria	13 Bodøsjøen Friluftsmuseum	28 Nordlænningen
5 Bodø Gjestegård	20 Løvold	14 Bodin Kirke	29 Fru Nilsen
6 Opsahl Gjestegård	24 Dolly Dimple's Pizzeria	16 Bodø og Omegn	31 Berg Sport
8 Kristensen Pensjonat	30 Paviljongen	Turistforening DNT	32 Bokmiljø Bodø
12 Bodøsjøen Camping	33 Buffalo Steakhouse;	Office	34 Ludwig's
17 Diplomat Hotel; Blix	Taste Cuisine	18 Bonsak	Bruktbokhandel
Restaurant		19 Rock Café & Nightclub	35 Bodø Rådhus
26 Comfort Hotel Grand;	OTHER	21 Local Express Ferry Quay	(City Hall)
Peppe's Pizza	1 Hurtigruten Coastal	22 Destinasjon Bodø Tourist	36 Post Office
38 Norrøna Hotel	Steamer Quay	Office; Express Boat	37 Kafe Kafka
39 Radisson SAS Hotel Bodø;	2 Lofoten Carr	Terminal	41 Vinmonopolet
Royal Bowling	Ferry Quay	23 Bus Station	42 Bodø Domkirke
40 Nordlys Hotel	7 Hospital	25 Odd's Interbok	43 Nordlandsmuseet

Storgata 17, open from 11am to 2.30pm Tuesday and 11am to 7pm Thursday. For cabin keys, visit Berg Sport (☎ 75 52 48 90), Torvgata 4.

For books, check out Odds Interbok at Storgata 7, Bokmiljø Bodø at Dronningens gate 13, or Sundem in the Glasshuset shopping mall. Ludvig's Bruktbokhandel at Dronningens gate 42 carries used books.

Things to See & Do
Norsk Luftfartsmuseum The Norwegian Aviation Museum (☎ 75 50 78 50, Olav V gata; adult/concession/child/family Nkr70/

50/40/170; open 10am-4pm Mon-Fri, 11am-5pm Sat & Sun Sept-May; 10am-8pm Mon-Fri & Sun, 10am-5pm Sat June-Aug) should not be missed if you have even a passing interest in flight and aviation history. Allow at least half a day to see it all.

The well-conceived exhibits begin with a technically functional control tower and proceed through an exposé of Norwegian aviation history. Other worthwhile features include hands-on demonstrations on the theory and dynamics of flight and the logistics of commercial aviation; the enormous Norwegian Air Force Museum, with examples of historic military and civilian aircraft from the Gloster Gladiator and Tiger Moth to the DeHavilland Otter and the U2; and a small, amusement park-style simulator, which, for an extra charge, allows you to 'ride along' on some pretty harrowing flights (eg, in a fighter jet).

It's less than a 2km walk from town, and if you're flying into Bodø for real note that, from above, the museum building is in the shape of an aeroplane propeller.

Nordlandmuseet The Nordland Museum (☎ 75 52 16 40, Prinsens gate 116; admission Nkr15; open 9am-3pm Mon-Fri year-round, also 10am-3pm Sat & Sun summer) has a new exhibit on the history of Bodø including a 20-minute film with English subtitles (though it may carry more meaning for locals). Our favourite treasures are the small collection of silver articles from Viking times. Other exhibits cover Sami culture, the history of women in northern Norway, regional fishing culture and natural history.

The museum has an open-air component, the Bodøsjøen Friluftsmuseum, 3km from town near Bodøsjøen Camping. Here you'll find four hectares of historic homes, farm buildings, boat sheds, WWII German bunkers and the square-rigged sloop *Anna Karoline af Hopen*. Admission to the grounds is free, but admission to the buildings is by appointment. The museum is also the start of a long-distance walking track up the river Bodøgårdselva, which eventually leads to the wild and scenic Bodømarka woods.

Bodø Domkirke The modern Gothic-style Bodø Cathedral (☎ 75 52 17 50, Torvgata 12; admission free; open 9am-2.30pm daily summer), built in 1956, sports an unusual detached spire and two stained glass windows, one a rosette and the other 12m high. The previous church on this site was destroyed during the bombings of May 1940. Contact the office for entry.

Bodin Kirke Less than 1km south-east of the Aviation Museum sits the small and quite intriguing Bodin Kirke (☎ 75 56 54 20,

Gamle riksvei 68; admission free; open 10am-7pm daily mid-June–mid-Aug), a little onion-domed stone church dating from around 1240. The Lutheran Reformation brought about substantial changes to the exterior, including the addition of a tower, and a host of lively 17th- and 18th-century baroque elements grace the interior.

Organised Tours Bodø Sightseeing (☎ 75 56 30 00, fax 75 56 30 01) conducts short informal town tours by sightseeing train for Nkr90 from the Hurtigruten pier at 1pm. The tourist office organises a midnight sun tour daily from 15 June to 12 July.

Special Events The annual Girl's Run is an informal 4.7km race for women of all ages. Its patron is Norwegian marathon champion Grete Waitz. For schedule information ring ☎ 75 52 61 55.

Places to Stay

Bodøsjøen Camping (☎ 75 56 36 80, fax 75 56 46 89, Kvernhusveien 1). Bus: No 12. Tent sites from Nkr100 plus Nkr30 per person, cabins from Nkr400. This nicely kept waterside camping ground is 3km from the centre.

Locomotivet Vandrerhjem (☎ 75 52 11 22, fax 75 52 16 35, e arnfo2@frisurf.no, Sjøgata 55) Dorm beds Nkr140, doubles Nkr280. Bodø's 25-room hostel is nothing special, but it's conveniently located upstairs at the train station.

The tourist office books private rooms from Nkr150 per person.

B&B's *Kristensen Pensjonat* (☎/fax 75 52 16 99, Rensåsgata 45) Singles/doubles without bath Nkr330/450, with bath Nkr430/550. This place offers good-value basic accommodation. Breakfast is Nkr50.

Bodø Gjestegård (☎ 75 52 04 02, fax 75 52 04 03, e johansst@online.no, Storgata 90) Singles/doubles Nkr350/550. This charmingly renovated house is at the edge of the town centre.

Opsahl Gjestegård (☎ 75 52 07 04, fax 75 52 02 28, Prinsens gate 131) Singles/doubles from Nkr350/590. The room decor here ranges from flowery to sturdy.

NORDLAND

Mid-Range Hotels *Sentrum Hotel Shama* (☎ *75 52 48 88, fax 75 52 58 90,* e *booki ng@sentrum-hotell.no, Storgata 39)* Singles/doubles from Nkr390/550. This place provides reasonable value and a restaurant serving Mongolian barbecues.

Norrøna Hotel (☎ *75 52 55 50, fax 75 52 33 88,* e *Elsa.Karlsen@RadissonSAS.com, Storgata 4)* Singles/doubles from Nkr400/500. Rooms at the Norrona are comfortable, though it can get booked with large groups.

Top-End Hotels *Comfort Hotel Grand* (☎ *75 54 61 00, fax 75 54 61 50,* e *booking .grand@comfort.choicehotels.no, Storgata 3)* Singles/doubles from Nkr495/645. The Grand has posh rooms, breakfast and light dinner buffets.

Nordlys Hotel (☎ *75 53 19 00, fax 75 53 19 99,* e *nordlys@rainbow-hotels.no, Moloveien 14)* Singles/doubles from Nkr490/690. Bodø's newest and most stylish hotel, with Scandinavian design touches throughout, is across from the small-boat harbour.

Diplomat Hotel (☎ *75 54 70 00, fax 75 54 70 55,* e *hotel@diplomat-hotel.no, Sjøgata 23)* Singles/doubles from Nkr590/790. The Diplomat offers business-class digs.

Radisson SAS Hotel Bodø (☎ *75 52 41 00, fax 75 52 74 93,* w *www.radisson.com/ bodono, Storgata 2)* Singles/doubles from Nkr595/790. This contemporary hotel has bright, windowed rooms and a panoramic top-floor bar to better view the harbour and mountains.

Places to Eat
You'd be forgiven for thinking that the entire population of Bodø has joined a pizza cult, as it seems nearly every eatery has pizza on the menu. Good-value choices include the busy, family-oriented *Orion Pizza* (☎ *75 52 73 77, Sjøgata 41)* near the train station, with mains from Nkr70 to Nkr150, and *Dolly Dimples* (☎ *75 52 53 85, Storgata 1)* with pizzas from Nkr103 to Nkr229. *Peppe's Pizza* (☎ *75 52 22 25, Storgata 3)* serves pizzas for Nkr130 to Nkr224, and its trademark pizza and salad lunch buffet for Nkr89.

Løvold's (☎ *75 52 02 61, Tollbugata 9)* Dishes Nkr23-115. This historic quayside cafeteria offers sandwiches, grills and hearty Norwegian fare.

Buffalo Steakhouse (☎ *75 52 15 40, Havnegata 1)* Mains Nkr99-340. This place is worth a visit if your tastes run to large hunks of cowboy-style beef.

Taste Cuisine (☎ *75 54 01 80, Havnegata 1)* Mains Nkr135-225. Downstairs from Buffalo you'll find highly regarded Pan-Asian specialities in an artful setting.

Paviljongen (☎ *75 52 01 11, Torget)* Mains Nkr90-130. This great outdoor spot serves coffees and light, inexpensive lunches to a bohemian crowd.

Blix (☎ *75 54 70 99, Sjøgata 23)* Mains Nkr172-206. Perhaps Bodø's most dignified restaurant, Blix serves beef, fish and has a nice wine list.

Molostua (☎ *75 52 05 30, Moloveien 9)* Mains Nkr84-209. This dockside spot specialises in fish, regional cooking, and unbeatable views.

At the docks, you can buy inexpensive fresh shrimp; the Vinmonopolet is just a couple of blocks farther west. Inside the Glasshuset shopping centre you'll find a supermarket and several quick-service choices.

Entertainment
Kafé Kafka (☎ *75 52 35 50, Sandgata 5b)* By day, this contemporary cafe serves burgers, Mexican dishes and salads (Nkr43 to Nkr128). At night it occasionally turns into a club with DJs. It's sometimes smoky, however.

Rock Café & Nightclub (☎ *75 50 46 33, Tollbugata 13b)* The town's largest disco is with concerts and dancing.

Bonsak Piano Club (☎ *75 52 29 90, Sjøgata 17)* A few doors away from Rock Café & Nightclub you get fine keyboard entertainment and a cosy intimate atmosphere for drinking and chatting.

Fru Nilsen (☎ *75 52 91 50, Geitskaret 47 Torvgata)* This is a party place for twenty-somethings.

Nordlænningen (☎ *75 52 06 00, Storgata 16)* This low-key basement pub has occasional live music.

Fram Kino (☎ *75 50 34 00, Storgata 8; admission Nkr60)* Bodø's cinema, near the

NORDLAND

entrance to the Glasshuset, has several showings daily and a downstairs pub.

You can also knock some pins down at *Royal Bowling* (☎ 75 52 28 80, Storgata 2), downstairs from the Radisson SAS Hotel.

Getting There & Away
Air Bodø's airport is just south-west of the city centre and a fairly easy walking distance of the youth hostel and hotels. The city is served by SAS, Braathens and Widerøe.

Bus Although most visitors to Bodø drive or use the train, there are still several bus services worth noting. The Nor-Way Buss-ekspress bus to and from Narvik (Nkr379, 6¾ hours), via Fauske (Nkr81, 1¼ hours), averages three services daily; ScanRail and InterRail pass holders get a 50% discount. For Sortland or Svolvær or points north by bus, change in Fauske. Along the Kystriksveien, there are one or two buses daily between Bodø and Ørnes (Nkr153, 2½ hours).

For information on buses to and from Skellefteå, in Sweden, see the Getting There & Away chapter.

Train From Bodø it's a straight shot by train to Fauske (Nkr86, 45 minutes), Mo I Rana (Nkr320, three hours) and Trondheim (Nkr740, 10 hours).

Ferry Bodø is a stop on the Hurtigruten coastal steamer. Note that the Hurtigruten quay and Lofoten car ferry docks are a five-minute walk north of the train station, while express catamaran boats dock beside the bus station.

The ferry M/S *Røst* (☎ 76 96 76 00) sails at least once daily between Bødo and Moskenes in Lofoten (Nkr420 per car and driver, three hours), and most days also calls in at the southern Lofoten islands of Røst (Nkr465) and Værøy (Nkr385), either before or after landing in Moskenes. If you're taking a car, it's extremely wise to book in advance, which costs an additional Nkr100 in summer.

Getting Around
The Sentrumsrunden bus visits most sights within the centre, at Nkr18 per ride. The

tourist office rents bikes for Nkr60/110/160 for one/two/three days, plus a deposit.

AROUND BODØ
Kjerringøy
On a sunny day, you won't regret a visit to the lovely 19th-century trading station Kjerringøy, 40km north of Bodø, on a sleepy peninsula beside luminescent turquoise seas with a backdrop of soaring granite peaks. Here, the entrepreneurial Erasmus Zahl family established an important trading post, providing local fishing families with supplies in exchange for their catches, and after making their fortune, expanded into mining, banking and steam transport concerns.

Most of the timber-built historic district has been preserved as an **open-air museum** (☎ 75 51 12 57, Kjerringøy; adult/concession Nkr40/20; open 11am-5pm daily, 11am-7pm Sun, late May-late Aug) contrasting the Spartan quarters and kitchens of the fishing families with the sumptuous decor and living standards of the merchants. The historical displays have been augmented by a cafe and audiovisual presentation. Admission to the main building is by guided tour and costs Nkr25.

Kjerringøy Prestegård (☎ 75 51 12 64, Kjerringøy; beds Nkr150, doubles in stable from Nkr500) About 1km from the historic site, basic camp sites and accommodation are available in the old rectory.

Kjerringøy Rorbusenter (☎ 75 58 50 07, fax 75 58 50 08, e post@kjerringoy-rorbu senter.no, Tårnvik) 4-person/6-person rorbus Nkr650/850. This Rorbusenter is 20km from Kjerringøy up a sometimes narrow road, but visitors agree that this seaside spot, with hot tub and restaurant, is worth it. Breakfast and sheets cost extra.

Several buses connect Bodø and Kjerringøy daily (Nkr80, 1½ hours), and in summer it's possible to do a return trip on the same day. Check at the tourist office or call ☎ 177 for schedule information.

Whether by bus or car, the trip involves the ferry (Nkr17/41 for passengers/cars, 10 minutes) between Festvåg (30 minutes by car from Bodø) and Misten (15 minutes from Kjerringøy). It runs frequently on

NORDLAND

weekdays, with shorter hours on the week-end. Along the way, take note of the distinctive profile of **Landegode** island (see the Folklore & Legends in Norway special section), the white sandy beaches at **Mjelle** (you'll need your own transport to reach them and must park some 20 minutes' walk away) and the beautiful and dramatic peak **Steigtind**, which rises a few kilometres south of Festvåg.

Saltstraumen Maelstrom

Sure, you've heard of maelstroms, but have you ever seen one? Here's your chance. At the 3km-long, 150m-wide Saltstraumen Strait, the tides cause one fjord to drain into another, creating the equivalent of a waterfall at sea. The result is a swirling, churning, 20-knot watery chaos which shifts over 400 million cubic metres of water one way and then the other every six hours. All this water action creates an ideal environment for plankton, which attracts an abundance of both fish and anglers. In the spring, you can also see the squawking colonies of gulls which nest on the midstream island of Storholmen.

This maelstrom, claimed to be the world's largest, can be readily viewed from the arching Saltstraumbrua bridge over the strait, or right at the waterside. Some people find it a wonder of nature; others go '*hunh?*'

The pricey **Saltstraumen Opplevelsessenter** (☎ 75 56 06 55, *Rv17, Knapplund; adult/concession/child/family Nkr60/50/40/175; open daily 1 May-30 Sept*) on the northern shore, presents a multimedia show and gives a surface introduction to tidal currents, as well as the local history and nature. There's also a pool with some seals, and a cafe.

From Bodø, bus No 19 travels the 33km from Bodø to Saltstraumen (Nkr44, 50 minutes) once daily on weekends, with a few trips during the week. The tourist offices in Bodø and at the Opplevelsessenter keep tide tables and can tell you exactly when to expect the best shows, and they're happy to fax or (in Bodø's case) email this information. You can also download the timetable from Destinasjon Bodø's Web site at **W** www.bodoe.com.

Lofoten

From a distance, the 'Lofoten Wall' of unearthly glacier-carved peaks appears as an unbroken mass, but once you get in closer you'll see why Lofoten is a place of incredible and, yes, intimate charm – the soul of Northern Norway.

The main islands, Austvågøy, Vestvågøy, Flakstadøy and Moskenesøy, are separated from the mainland by the Vestfjorden and boast sheltered bays, sheep pastures and picturesque villages, where the looming craggy backdrops might be mistaken for painted Hollywood film sets. This overwhelming scenery and the mystical Arctic light have long attracted artists who are represented in galleries throughout the islands.

But Lofoten is also very much a place of business. Each winter the meeting of the Gulf Stream and the icy Arctic Ocean draws spawning Arctic cod from the Barents Sea. For centuries, this in turn drew migrating north coast farmer-fishermen who found open landscapes and rich soils to complement their seafaring work. Although cod stocks have dwindled dramatically in recent years, fishing remains Lofoten's largest industry, as evidenced by the innumerable wooden drying racks which lattice every village in the region.

For independent travellers, getting around isn't too difficult, as the four main islands are linked by bridge or tunnel, and buses run the entire E10 from the Fiskebøl-Melbu ferry in the north to Å at road's end in the south-west. Note that bus fares are half-price for holders of InterRail and Scan-Rail passes between Bodø and Svolvær.

Information is available at the Web site **W** www.lofoten-tourist.no.

History

The history of Lofoten is in effect the history of its fishing industry. Numerous battles have been fought over these seas, which became exceptionally rich in spawning cod after the glaciers retreated about 10,000 years ago. In 1120, King Øystein set up the first church and built a number of *rorbuer*

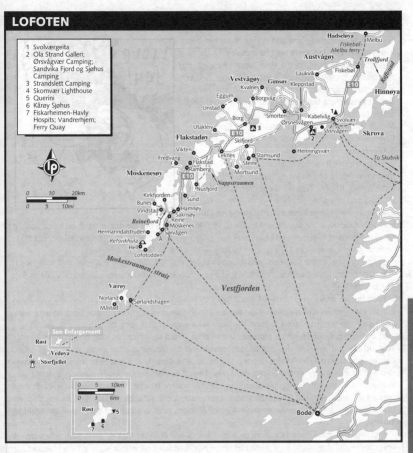

LOFOTEN

1 Svolværgeita
2 Ola Strand Galleri;
   Ørsvågvær Camping;
   Sandvika Fjord og Sjøhus
   Camping
3 Strandslett Camping
4 Skomvær Lighthouse
5 Querini
6 Kårøy Sjøhus
7 Fiskarheimen-Havly
   Hospits; Vandrerhjem;
   Ferry Quay

NORDLAND

(rowers' dwellings), 4m by 4m wooden cabins for the fishermen with a fireplace, earthen floor and small porch area. Thereby, he took control of the local economy and ensured rich tax pickings for himself.

In the 13th century, traders of the German Hanseatic League moved in and utterly usurped power, and despite an increase in exports, the general populace were left in abject poverty. By 1750, however, the trade monopoly lost its grip, locals again took control of their own economic ventures and opportunists migrated in from the south. Through the 19th century, power over the trade fell to local *nessekonger*, or 'merchant squires' who'd bought up property. These new aristocratic landlords forced the tenants of their *rorbuer* to deliver their entire catch at a price set by the landlords themselves. Fortunately, the Lofoten Act of 1857 greatly diminished the power of the *nessekonger*, but not until the Raw Fish Sales Act of 1936 did they lose the power to set prices. By the end of WWII, trade was again freed up and Lofoten fishing families could finally conduct their own trade, set prices and export their resources with a relative minimum of outside interference.

Glory Be to Cod

For centuries, catching cod and drying them has been a way of life and Lofoten's biggest industry.

MW

Although cod populations have been depleted by overfishing, the overall catch is still substantial, 50,000 tonnes annually (30,000 tonnes without the heads), reaching its height from January to April when the fish come to Vestfjorden to spawn. Around the end of March each year the unofficial World Cod Fishing Championship is held in Svolvær and can involve up to 300 entrants.

There are two methods of preserving cod. *Saltfish* requires the fish to be filleted, salted and dried for about three weeks. *Klipfish* requires the saltfish to be cleaned, resalted and dried, originally on cliffs *(klip* in Norwegian) and now in large heated plants. However, Lofoten is all about *stockfish*. In this ancient method, 15,000 tonnes of fish are decapitated each year, paired by size, then tied together and hung over huge wooden A-frames to dry. The fish lose about 80% of their weight, and most are exported to Italy, with some to Spain and Portugal.

Stockfish stays edible for years, and it's often eaten raw (a trifle chewy but goes well with beer), salted, or reconstituted with water. Note that 1kg of stockfish has the same nutritional value as 5kg of fresh fish!

Even before drying, very little of a cod goes to waste: cod tongue is a local delicacy – children extract the tongues and are paid by the piece – and the roe is salted in enormous German wine vats. The heads are sent to Nigeria to form the basis for a popular and spicy dish.

Then there is the liver, which produces the vitamin D-rich oil which has long been known to prevent rickets and assuage the depression brought on by the long, dark Arctic winters. In 1854, Lofoten pharmacist Peter Møller decided to introduce this magic-in-a-bottle to the world and constructed a cauldron for steam-boiling the livers. The oil he skimmed received honours at trade fairs in Europe and abroad. Even after skimming, the livers were steamed in large oak barrels and then pressed to yield every last (profitable) drop. Every summer, thousands of barrels of it were shipped to Europe, and the smell pervaded the village of Å; locals liked to comment that it was the scent of money.

And what of cod liver oil's notorious taste? Locals will tell you that it tastes bad only when it becomes rancid. Fresh cod liver oil can be quite nice, like salad oil with a slightly fishy bouquet.

Modern Norwegian fishing folk are vociferously protective of this asset, as evidenced by votes around 90% against EU membership in certain northern districts – if Norway joined the EU, the Spanish fishing fleet would be allowed access to Norway's inshore waters. There have even been skirmishes with Icelandic trawlers over territorial fishing rights.

Fun cod fact: one in 20,000 cod is a king cod; the distinctive lump on its forehead is said to indicate intelligence and bring good luck to the fishing family that catches it. King cod are often dried and hung on a string from the ceiling; as the string expands and contracts with humidity, the fish rotates like a barometer, hence the nickname 'weather cod'.

The latest news from the world of cod involves the fishes' mating calls; it seems that the grunts they use to attract mates are loud enough to block submarines' sonar devices, making underwater navigation almost impossible!

For more information about this piscine powerhouse, consult Mark Kurlansky's book *Cod* (1999).

Lofoten Lodging

King Øystein's legacy lives on today, as Lofoten's lodging of choice remains the *rorbu*, along with its cousin, the *sjøhus*. Whereas 'rorbu' once meant dingy, tiny red-painted fishing huts on the harbours, nowadays the name is applied to a range of structures, from historic cottages to simple holiday homes to plush, two-storey, multi-room, fully equipped self-catering units. There are few real bargain rorbus – most Norwegians are happy to pay for any semblance of nostalgia or rusticity – but some are quite atmospheric, and it's worth spending at least a night in one of the more traditional ones.

Sjøhus are normally bunkhouse-style buildings on the docks where fishery workers processed the catch, and for convenience, they also ate and slept there. While some of them retain this traditional feel, others have been converted into summer tourist lodges and apartments, which can be quite nice, though usually not luxurious. There is also a range of camping grounds and higher end hotels.

Note that while summer prices tend to be lowest in the rest of Norway, the opposite is true in Lofoten; in hotels you can expect to pay Nkr250-plus per room above the rest of the year prices; that difference is less pronounced in rorbuer and sjøhus.

AUSTVÅGØY
pop 9250

Many visitors make their acquaintance with Lofoten on Austvågøy, the northernmost island in the group and the one with the most visitor facilities. Those arriving to the modern port of Svolvær are greeted by Lofoten's finest hotels and restaurants, with most of the island's cultural attractions nearby, while if you arrive by ferry from Melbu, in Vesterålen, you'll find craggy, impossible peaks.

Svolvær

The modern port town of Svolvær is as busy as it gets on Lofoten. Svolvær once sprawled across a series of skerries, but the in-between spaces are now being filled in to create a reclaimed peninsula.

There's a choice of banks, shops, accommodation and eateries, and a bookshop, Rødsand Libris (☎ 76 07 05 33). The helpful Destination Lofoten tourist office (☎ 76 06 98 00, fax 76 07 30 01, **e** tourist@lofoten-tourist.no), just off the town square and the sightseeing quays, can provide information on the entire archipelago.

Lofoten Krigsminnemuseum The War Memorial Museum (☎ 76 07 00 49, *Fiskergata 12; adult/child Nkr40/15; open 11am-4pm daily mid-May–mid-Aug*) is one of the best such museums in Norway. It's known for its large collection of original military uniforms as well as its largely unpublished WWII-era photos and details on the 1941 commando raid on Lofoten.

Svolværgeita One of the symbols of Lofoten, the Svolvær Goat is a distinctive two-pronged peak that towers above the town. Daredevils like to scale the peak then jump from one 'horn' to the other, and although it's been listed as one of Norway's greatest adrenaline rushes, the trip is definitely for experts only. Nearly anyone can get to the base of Svolværgeita, but reaching the horns, Storhornet and Lillehornet, requires a 40m technical climb. Then there's the 1.5m jump between them – *emphatically* not recommended, but if you must, the Nord Norsk Klatreskole can set you up with a guide and equipment; see Henningsvær, later in this section.

Skrova The island of Skrova makes an amenable day visit from Svolvær, and offers a couple of short walks. The ferry from Svolvær (Nkr23, 30 minutes) runs two or three times daily in summer, then continues on to Skutvik (Nkr53, two hours), on the mainland, to connect with ferries to Bodø.

Organised Tours One of the highlights of the Hurtigruten route is the narrow Raftsund channel, which separates the Austvågøy and the Vesterålen island of Hinnøya. The short jaunt into Trollfjord, 2km long but spectacularly steep and narrow, is particularly memorable as the steamer practically

NORDLAND

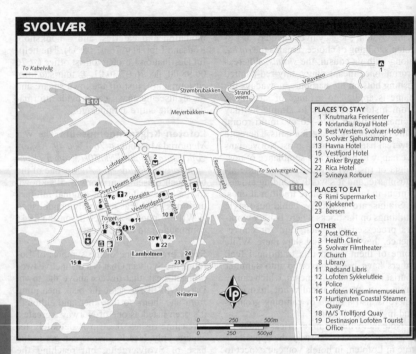

SVOLVÆR

To Kabelvåg

Villaveien

Strømbrubakken
Strandveien

Meyerbakken

E10

Lofotgata

Svolværveien

Gymnasgata

Repslagergata

To Svolværgeita

E10

Sivert Nilsens gate

Storgata

Parkgata

Vestfjordgata

Torget

Lamholmen

Svinøya

PLACES TO STAY
1 Knutmarka Feriesenter
4 Norlandia Royal Hotel
9 Best Western Svolvær Hotell
10 Svolvær Sjøhuscamping
13 Havna Hotel
15 Vestfjord Hotel
21 Anker Brygge
22 Rica Hotel
24 Svinøya Rorbuer

PLACES TO EAT
6 Rimi Supermarket
20 Kjøkkenet
23 Børsen

OTHER
2 Post Office
3 Health Clinic
5 Svolvær Filmtheater
7 Church
8 Library
11 Rødsand Libris
12 Lofoten Sykkelutleie
14 Police
16 Lofoten Krigsminnemuseum
17 Hurtigruten Coastal Steamer
   Quay
18 M/S Trollfjord Quay
19 Destinasjon Lofoten Tourist
   Office

0   250   500m
0   250   500yd

scrapes the rock walls before doing a three-point (Y) turn and heading off.

If you're not on the Hurtigruten, several smaller boats sail daily in summer from Svolvær into Trollfjord's constricted confines. Tours run five to 10 times daily between about 10 June and 20 August and cost Nkr300 per person. If you prefer to be closer to the water, informal Zodiac (inflatable raft) tours (☎ 90 79 38 47 or ☎ 90 68 92 06) to Trollfjorden and Skrova are conducted for Nkr450 per person, with a minimum of six people.

Special Events Every odd-numbered year for three weeks in June, Svolvær hosts the Lofoten Arts Festival. There's also an annual Composers' Week festival in April.

Places to Stay & Eat *Svolvær Sjøhuscamping* (☎ 76 07 03 36, fax 76 07 64 63, ⓔ noetnes@online.no, ⓦ www.svolver-sjohuscamp.no, Parkgata 12) 2-bed/4-bed rooms

from Nkr350/580. This clean, modern beachhouse over the water was undergoing renovation when we visited. Some rooms have private bath.

Knutmarka Feriesenter (☎ 76 07 21 64, fax 76 07 26 32, ⓔ knutm-fe@online.no, Leirskoleveien 10) Cabins Nkr550-1150. From mid-June to mid-August, this wooded, lakeside place 3km from town has well-appointed cabins and amenities including sauna and canoe hire.

Svinøya Rorbuer (☎ 76 06 99 30, fax 76 07 48 98, ⓔ svinoya.rorbuer@svinoya.no, Gunnar Bergs vei 2) 2-4-bed cottages Nkr700-1000. Across a bridge on the island of Svinøya, site of Svolvær's first settlement, are dozens of historic cabins. The reception is a veritable museum, in a restored *krambua* general store.

Vestfjord Hotel (☎ 76 07 08 70, fax 76 07 08 54, ⓔ service@vestfjord.norlandia.no, Fiskergata 46) Rooms Nkr545-795. This hotel on the docks is surrounded by

NORDLAND

unglamorous warehouses, but service is nice and rooms are clean and up-to-date. There's a Norwegian/Chinese restaurant.

Havna Hotel (☎ 76 07 10 55, fax 76 07 28 50, ℮ havnahotel@c2i.net, OJ Kaarbøesgata 5) Singles/doubles from Nkr595/795. This down-to-earth spot adjacent to the bus stops has large, comfortable rooms. Its *Styrhuset pub*, Svolvær's oldest, is enjoying a revival thanks to a new chef. There's also a casual cafe.

Norlandia Royal Hotel (☎ 76 07 12 00, fax 76 07 08 50, ℮ service@royal.norlandia.no, Sivert Nilsensgata 21) Singles/doubles from Nkr545/745. This hotel at the town crossroads was due to be renovated by the time you read this.

Best Western Svolvær Hotell (☎ 76 07 19 99, fax 76 07 09 09, ℮ svolho@online.no, Austnesfjordgata 12) Singles/doubles from Nkr595/690. If you like residential neighbourhoods, this place is for you. Some rooms have balconies, others kitchens.

Rica Hotel (☎ 76 07 22 22, fax 76 07 20 01, ℮ rica.hotel.svolvar@rica.no, Lamholmen) Singles/doubles from Nkr695/895. Some rooms have balconies in this over-water hotel, but room 121 has a hole in the floor so occupants can fish without leaving. The boat-shaped restaurant affords an excellent harbour views and has a chi-chi dinner buffet for Nkr235.

Anker Brygge (☎ 76 06 64 80, fax 76 06 64 70, ℮ post@anker-brygge.no, Lamholmen) Cottages Nkr1150/1600. We doubt that old Norwegian fishermen roughed it in elegant digs like these or used the lovely, rustic sauna. However, maybe they did visit the nearby (former) fish processing plant (1880).

Kjøkkenet (☎ 76 06 84 80, Lamholmen) Mains Nkr200-280. It's made up like an old-time kitchen, and the bar is a lifeboat from a WWII Polish troop ship which washed up in Svolvær in 1946. The recommended menu choice is of course fish.

Børsen (☎ 76 06 99 31, Svinøya) Mains Nkr205-235. This is an unusually atmospheric fish house whose name means 'stock exchange' for the harbourfront bench outside, where the older men of the town ruminated over the state of the world. The

dining room, with its cracked and bowed flooring, still smells of tar and cod liver oil.

There's a bakery and a couple of other eateries on the square and a *Rimi* supermarket a block inland on Torggata.

Entertainment In addition to the hotel bars, the *Svolvær Filmtheater* (☎ 75 42 00 00, Storgata 28) screens recent films nightly except – seriously, folks – Saturday.

Shopping Graphic prints at the well-regarded *Ola Strand Galleri* (☎ 76 07 74 61, Ørsnes; open 10am-9pm Mon-Fri, 10am-6pm Sat 1 June-31 Aug) reveal the nature and culture of this island. It's 10km west of town.

Getting There & Away At Svolvær's small airport you can catch flights to Bodø.

If you're heading for or coming from Vesterålen, bus No 104 between Svolvær and Sortland (Nkr124, 3¼ hours) travels the dramatic waters of the Fiskebøl-Melbu ferry (car and driver, Nkr68). Buses to Leknes (Nkr88, two hours) with connections to Å (Nkr163, 3½ hours) leave Svolvær at least four times daily. Bus fare to Bodø (Nkr292) does not include the ferry ticket (Nkr60).

Express boats ply the waters between Svolvær and Bodø (Nkr246, 3½ hours) and Narvik (Nkr286, 3½ hours) daily except Saturday.

Svolvær is also a stop on the Hurtigruten coastal steamer.

Getting Around The Svolvær area is ideal for cycling, and you can hire bikes at Lofoten Sykkelutleie (☎ 76 07 24 80, mobile ☎ 92 23 13 24) at Parkgata 8. The *Sykkelguide* booklet (Nkr100) is available around town and contains annotated routes around Lofoten.

The private Bremnes Rent-a-Car agency (☎ 95 05 35 66) has a bargain at Nkr500 per day, with unlimited mileage. All the main agencies are also represented: Hertz (☎ 76 07 07 20), Budget (☎ 76 07 00 00), Avis (☎ 76 07 11 40) and InterRent (☎ 76 06 61 40).

Kabelvåg

Quiet Kabelvåg is just 5km from Svolvær but presents a more intimate face. The town

NORDLAND

centre features a small square, a tiny harbour and a couple of nice cafes, while its Storvågen district, about 1km to the south, is home to a trio of magnet museums. A summer hostel ensures that lots of independent travellers wind up here.

Storvågan Museums Behind the old prison, a trail climbs to the statue of King Øystein, who in 1120 ordered the first rorbu to be built to house fishermen, who previously had been sleeping in their overturned rowing boats. It was more than an act of kindness, however, as the tax on the exported dried fish was the main source of the king's revenue.

Some of these original rorbuer have been excavated as part of the **Lofoten Museum** (☎ 76 07 82 23, Storvågan; adult/concession/child Nkr40/30/15; open 9am-6pm daily 15 June-15 Aug, 9am-3pm daily 16 Aug-14 June), on the site of the first town in the polar region. New artefacts are constantly being found. The museum also contrasts the lives of the commoners with those of the Lofoten squires as the town grew through the stockfish trade (it's believed that the Portuguese name for cod, bacalau, has its roots in 'Kabelvåg').

Nearby, the seafront **Lofoten Aquarium** (☎ 76 07 86 65, Storvågan; adult/concession/child Nkr70/35/25; open 10am-9pm daily 15 June-15 Aug, shorter hours rest of year) showcases some of the faces which made Lofoten great, including the heroic cod, and even some sea mammals.

The modern **Galleri Espolin** (☎ 76 07 84 05, Storvågan; adult/concession/child Nkr40/30/15; open 10am-9pm daily mid-June–mid-Aug, shorter hours rest of year) features the haunting etchings and lithographs of one of Norway's great artists, Kaare Espolin-Johnson (1907–1994). Espolin loved Lofoten and often featured its fisherfolk. His work all the more astounding given that he was nearly blind for much of his life.

Vågan Kirke (Vågan Church; ☎ 76 07 82 90, E10; admission Nkr15), built in 1898, is Norway's second-largest wooden church rises over the main road north of town. Built to minister to the influx of seasonal fisher-

folk, its seating capacity of 1200 far surpasses Kabelvåg's current population.

There is a three-museum combination ticket which sells for Nkr110 and includes entry to Lofoten Museum, Lofoten Aquarium and Galleri Espolin.

Places to Stay & Eat *Kabelvåg Vandrerhjem* (☎ 76 06 98 80, fax 76 06 98 81, e post@lofoten.fhs.no, Finnesveien 24) Dorm beds Nkr200, singles/doubles Nkr320/420. About 1km north of the centre, the institutional-looking school Vågan Folkehøgskole houses this popular hostel when school is not in session. Advance booking is essential. Breakfast is included.

Ørsvågvær Camping (☎ 76 07 81 80, fax 76 07 83 37, e booking@orsvag.no, Ørsvågvær) Tent/caravan sites Nkr70/100, huts Nkr290-890. Cabins are basic here, 3km and two inlets west of Kabelvåg, but facilities include mini golf and a sauna.

Sandvika Fjord og Sjøhuscamp (☎ 76 07 81 45, fax 76 07 90 10, Sandvika) Tent or caravan sites Nkr110, cabins-Sjøhus Nkr350-900. This beautifully located camping area, next door to Ørsvågvær Camping, has a playground and boats for rent.

Kabelvåg Hotell (☎ 76 07 88 00, fax 78 07 80 03, e kabelvag@top.no, Kong Øysteinsgate 4) Singles/doubles Nkr890/1050. In the centre of Kabelvåg, this hotel was rebuilt in 1995 in its original Art Deco style. Popular with bus tours, it's also home to the *Krambua* restaurant (mains Nkr165 to Nkr205), specialising in fish.

Nyvågar Rorbuhotell (☎ 76 07 97 00, fax 76 07 97 01, Storvåganveien 22) 4-bed rorbuer from Nkr1290 with breakfast. At Storvågan, this upmarket, seaside place is fully equipped and modern. Its acclaimed restaurant (mains Nkr175 to Nkr245) serves local specialities – and fondue!

In central Kabelvåg, the fish, sandwich and pizza pub *Præstenbrygga* (☎ 76 07 80 60, Torget) has character, history and mains from Nkr33 to Nkr149. There's often live music, and for Nkr16, you can drink coffee all day on the lively patio.

T@nte Nelly (76 07 56 60, Storgata 7) This is a new Internet cafe.

Munkholmen island once served as a Benedictine monastery, Trondheim

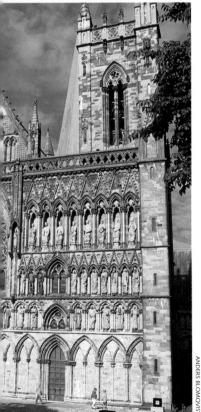

The facade of grand Nidaros Cathedral

Riding along, Trondheim

Waterfront warehouses, Bryggen, Trondheim

NED FRIARY

CRAIG PERSHOUSE

ANDERS BLOMQVIST

DEANNA SWANEY

NED FRIARY

Reine, on the Lofoten island of Moskenesøy, is 'the most scenic place in Norway'

NED FRIARY

Mmm…a hearty meal of cod tongues and fish soup

CHRISTIAN ASLUND

CRAIG PERSHOUSE

Wooden houses and jagged peaks, Lofoten islands

Azure waters surround the Vesterålen archipelago

Getting There & Away From Svolvær you can walk the 5km to Kabelvåg, or take the town bus (Nkr18, 15 minutes) which leaves (mostly) hourly. Connections are difficult on weekends.

Henningsvær

Henningsvær's nickname 'the Venice of Lofoten' may be a tad overblown, but few people would disagree that this bohemian enclave is the lightest, brightest and trendiest place in the archipelago. It's also the region's largest and most active fishing village, but these days the harbour bustles with as many pleasure craft as fishing boats. Especially on weekends, the outdoor seating at the waterside bars and restaurants is great for hours of observing the lively scene.

Things to See & Do The landmark **Lofoten Hus Gallery** *(☎ 76 07 15 73, Hjellskjæret; adult/concession/child Nkr60/50/25; open 9am-9pm daily mid-June–mid-Aug, 10am-6pm late May-early Sept, rest of year by appointment)*, in a former fish-processing house, displays a fine collection of theme paintings from around northern Norway. Admission includes an 18-minute slide show of art photos by Frank Jenssen, revealing the people and landscapes of Lofoten in all kinds of weather. It's shown mostly on the hour.

The **Nord Norsk Klatreskole** *(North Norwegian Climbing School; ☎ 76 07 49 11, fax 76 07 46 46, Misværveien 10)* offers a wide range of technical climbing, kayaking and skiing courses all around northern Norway (and overseas). If you want to tackle Svolværgeita (see Svolvær) or any other Lofoten peak, climbing with an experienced guide, including equipment, costs Nkr1500 for up to four people; book at least one day in advance. For ideas, check out the 320-page *Climbing in the Magic Islands*, by Ed Webster, which is the last word on climbing in Lofoten; it's sold at the attached mountaineering shop.

Engelskmannsbrygga *(☎ 76 07 52 85, Dreyersgate 1, admission free, open 10am-6pm late June-late Aug, shorter hours rest of year)* is the open studio of three artists: a glass blower, photographer and ceramic artist. Their original works are for sale, naturally.

Places to Stay & Eat *Den Siste Viking (☎ 76 07 49 11, fax 76 07 46 46, Misværveien 10)* Dorm beds Nkr150. Henningsvær lacks a hostel, but the climbing school's lodging crosses a Lofoten rorbu with an English pub and a Himalayan trekkers' lodge. Its *Klatrekafeen* serves up a small selection of homemade light meals (Nkr75 to Nkr130) and snacks, as well as coffee and sweets.

Johs H Giæver Sjøhus og Rorbuer (☎ 76 07 47 19, fax 76 07 49 00, Hellandsgata 790) Rorbuer Nkr400-800, sjøhus Nkr300-400. This is the least expensive of the rorbu complexes and belongs to the fish plant. In summer, the simple workers' accommodation is hired out to tourists.

Henningsvær Bryggehotel (☎ 76 07 47 50, fax 76 07 47 30, Hjellskjæret) Singles/doubles from Nkr900/1150. You'll find flash, contemprary design in the rooms and the stylish Bluefish restaurant here.

Fiskekrogen (☎ 76 07 46 52, Dreyersgate 19) Mains Nkr150-225. This dockside place is Henningsvær's culinary claim to fame. In her younger days, Queen Sonja visited on a backpacking trip and tried the fish soup (Nkr79), which remains a royal favourite. She is said to make a point of returning whenever she's in town.

Getting There & Away Bus No 510 shuttles between Svolvær (Nkr39, 35 minutes), Kabelvåg (Nkr36, 30 minutes) and Henningsvær at least four times daily.

VESTVÅGØY
pop 10,750

Vestvågøy may be known as the flattest of the Lofoten islands, but several surprises will 'peak' your interest.

Orientation and Information

The island's air and bus hub is the lacklustre town of Leknes, where you'll also find the tourist office (☎ 76 08 97 92) inside the Rådhus. Most lodgings are on the south coast, near Stamsund, a stop on the Hurtigruten and home to a popular youth hostel.

The island's only big-name attraction is the Lofotr Viking Museum.

Lofotr Viking Museum

In 1981 at Borg, near the centre of Vestvågøy, a local farmer inadvertently ploughed up the ruins of the 83m-long dwelling of a powerful Viking chieftain, which turned out to be the largest discovered in Scandinavia.

Fast forward to 1995: the Lofotr Viking Museum (☎ 76 08 49 00, W www.lofotr.no, Borg; adult/concession/child Nkr80/65/40 including guided tour; open 10am-7pm daily late May-31 Aug) opened on the site, offering a glimpse of life in Viking times. Horses graze nearby as you walk the 1.5km of trails on open hilltops from the replica of the chieftan's hall (main building, shaped like an upside-down boat) to the Viking ship replica on the water. Costumed guides conduct tours in six languages, and inside the chieftan's hall, craftspeople explain their work with leather, weaving etc.

You can row the Viking ship at 2pm daily for Nkr20.

During tourist season, visitors can try a peasants' bowl of lamb broth stew (Nkr60) or a glass of mead (Nkr45). The cafe also serves more modern specialities.

The Svolvær-Leknes bus passes the museum's entrance.

Unstad to Eggum Hike

A favourite hike connects these two tiny villages on the island's west coast. A 9km coastal track winds past several headlands, a solitary lighthouse and superb seascapes. Eggum is known for its views of the midnight sun and Vesterålen and for the ruins of a fortress by the ocean, while Unstad has the area's only accommodation, *Unstad Camping* (☎ 76 08 54 57, fax 76 08 55 18, Unstad), open May to mid-September. Tent sites are from Nkr50, caravan sites Nkr110, and there are a couple of cabins at Nkr350 to Nkr700.

Do take care after precipitation as the trail, particularly around Unstad, can be slick with mud and (pardon us, but) sheep dip. The author found out the hard way. Eggum and Unstad are both about 9km from the main road and served infrequently by buses.

Places to Stay & Eat

Storfjord Camping (☎ 76 08 68 04, e post@storfjordcamping.no, Storfjord) Caravan sites Nkr100, cabins Nkr250-600. This camping ground by a glassy lake about 8km north of Stamsund is nothing fancy, but it's perfectly serviceable.

Brustranda Sjøcamping (☎ 76 08 71 00, fax 76 08 71 44, Strandslett) Tent/caravan sites Nkr50/80 plus Nkr10 per person, cabins from Nkr200. A toneful option is this well-tended seaside place with basic cabins an art gallery and cafe.

Justad Vandrerhjem/Rorbuer (☎ 76 08 93 34, fax 76 08 97 39, Stamsund) Bunk beds Nkr90, doubles from Nkr250, 4-bed cabins Nkr400; open mid-Dec–mid-Oct. The island's hostel has a special place in our readers' hearts. They have written to describe how the unique and friendly manager, Roar Justad, takes them to see the Northern Lights, dispenses information about local hiking routes, rents old bicycles and loans out rowboats free of charge. Friendships are made for life on the dock; some visitors love it so much that they linger for weeks. Guests may use laundry and cooking facilities.

Stamsund Rorbuer (☎ 76 05 46 00, fax 76 05 46 01, e stamsund@top.no, Stamsund) 2–6-person rorbuer Nkr800-1200. This new and posh installation has early-20th-century huts. Its upscale *Skjærbrygga* restaurant, with mains from Nkr195 to Nkr245, also has a less expensive cafe menu.

Statles Rorbusenter (☎ 76 06 50 60, fax 76 08 71 11, e wenche@statles.no, Mortsund) 2–6-person cabins Nkr750-2400. The scenic hamlet of Mortsund merits a mention for this friendly facility of 40 pleasant cabins sprawling across a rocky promontory. The restaurant serves both local dishes and light meals. Bicycle and boat hire are available, as is nearby hiking. Buses run from Leknes every other day in summer, daily except Sunday during the rest of the year.

Getting There & Away

Leknes airport connects the island with Bodø. Leknes is also the island's transportation hub, with connections to Å (Nkr88, 1½ hours), Stamsund (Nkr29, 25 minutes) and Svolvær (Nkr91, two hours). Stamsund is the island's port for the Hurtigruten coastal steamer.

FLAKSTADØY
pop 1575

Most of Flakstadøy's residents live along its flat north shore, around the town of Ramberg, but the craggy south side provides the most dramatic scenery. The excellent, free *Flakstad & Moskenes Guide* is widely available.

Things to See

Nusfjord This secluded village, around a constricted little south coast harbour, makes a superb day trip or overnight stop. In addition to an excruciatingly picturesque waterfront and a lovely restored general store, you'll find a selection of rorbuer. Many artists consider it to be the essence of Lofoten and a relaxing place to hang out, but be warned: so do tour operators.

Ramberg & Flakstad Imagine an arch of tropical white sand along a sparkling blue-green bay – with a backdrop of snow-capped Arctic peaks. That pretty much describes **Ramberg**, on the north coast. If you're there on a sunny day, no-one at home will believe that your holiday snaps of this place were taken north of the Arctic Circle, but you'll know it when you stick a toe in the water.

A few kilometres away, the red onion-domed **Flakstad Kirke** (☎ 76 09 33 31, *Flakstad; admission Nkr20; open 10am-4pm summer, except during services*), was built in 1870. Most of the wood was ripped out of the ground by the Arctic-bound rivers of Siberia and washed up here as driftwood.

Glasshytta With a car, you can make a side trip to Vikten to visit the gallery (☎ 76 09 44 42, *Vikten; adult/child Nkr20/free; open 9am-7pm daily mid-June–mid-Aug, shorter hours rest of year*) of glassblower Åsvar Tangrand, famous for having designed Lofoten's seven-pronged logo, which evokes a longboat, modelled after the Lofoten Rune. Atmospheric vessels and dishes, some quite large, run from Nkr400 to Nkr3500.

Sund Fiskerimuseum This fishery museum (☎ 76 09 36 29, *Sund; adult/child Nkr35/20; open 10am-6pm daily June–mid-Aug*), near the bridge to Moskenesøy, has a collection of shacks containing displays on fishing, smithing and boat propulsion. The resident smithy has gained a reputation for his iron cormorant sculptures. While it may be interesting for those with a particular interest, the Å museums are friendlier and better organised.

Places to Stay & Eat

Nusfjord Rorbuer (☎ 76 09 30 20, fax 76 09 33 78, e *nusfjord@rica.no, Nusfjord*) Rorbuer Nkr490-960. The Rica chain operates these cabins, mostly modernised with antique touches. Its tiny **Oriana Kro** (☎ 76 09 30 90, *Nusfjord*), with mains from Nkr115 to Nkr179, serves famous fish soup and has harbourside dining.

Ramberg Gjestegård (☎ 76 09 35 00, fax 76 09 31 40, e *ramberggjest@lofoten.com; E10*) Tent/caravan sites Nkr75/100, 2-bed/5-bed cabins Nkr400/850. This friendly, well-tended and environmentally conscious guesthouse right, on the beach, hires kayaks and bicycles and has a popular Arctic menu restaurant, serving mains (Nkr130-195) and cheaper lunch specials.

Getting There & Away

Flakstadøy lies on the main bus routes between Leknes and Å, but Nusfjord, Vikten and Sund are considerable detours off the main route. For drivers, the tunnel between Flakstadøy and Vestvågøy costs Nkr65.

MOSKENESØY
pop 1350

The 34km-long glaciated island of Moskenesøy is like no place else on earth – an almost surreal world of pinnacled igneous ridges rising directly from the sea, separated by deep lakes and fjords – like an inspiration of Tolkien's. While these formations are a paradise for mountaineers, there are also a few places where non-technical hikers can reach the incredible heights of this tortured island, including the high point, Hermannsdalstind (1029m).

NORDLAND

Orientation & Information

The E10 runs along the island's south coast, past the communities of Hamnøy, Sakrisøy and Reine (voted the most scenic place in Norway) before reaching the functional village of Moskenes and its ferry terminal. The route ends at the museum-like village of Å (pop 100). Mountains occupy the rest of the island.

You'll find tourist information at the Fiskeværsferie Lofoten Turistkontoret (☎ 76 09 15 99, fax 76 09 24 25, e tour-off@lofoten-info.no, w www.lofoten-info.no), at Moskenes harbour. Hours are 10am to 7pm daily from mid-June to mid-August; at other times in June and August, it's open 10am to 5pm weekdays. It publishes the free and informative *Flakstad & Moskenes Guide*, which is excerpted on its Web site. There's an ATM at the Coop supermarket just north of Reine.

Things to See

Dagmars Dukke og Legetøy Museum

In Sakrisøy, a local woman has collected some 2500 dolls, antique teddy bears and historic toys from 1860 to 1965 into Dagmar's Museum of Dolls and Toys (☎ 76 09 21 43, Sakrisøy; adult/concession/child Nkr40/35/20; open 10am-8pm daily June-Aug, noon-5pm Sat & Sun rest of year except by appointment only Nov-Feb). This cosy building has an antique shop upstairs.

Norwegian Telecommunications Museum

In Sørvågen, south of Moskenes, the Norwegian Telecommunications Museum (☎ 76 09 14 88, E10; admission Nkr30; open 2pm-4pm daily 20 June-20 Aug) advertises itself as a study in 'cod and communications' – surely a winning combination.

Å Museums

At the tail-end of Moskenesøy, the fair village of Å (appropriately, the last letter of the Norwegian alphabet!), often referred to as Å i Lofoten, is truly a living museum – a preserved fishing village with a shoreline of red rorbuer, cod drying racks and picture-postcard scenes at almost every turn. Note that Å is a pedestrian village, and visitors arrive at a car park up the hill and must walk down.

Many of Å's 19th-century boathouses, storehouses, fishing cottages, farmhouses and commercial buildings have been compiled into the **Norsk Fiskeværs Museum** *(Norwegian Fishing Village Museum; ☎ 76 09 14 88, Å; adult/child Nkr40/30, combination ticket Nkr65/45; open 10am-6pm daily late June-late Aug, 9am-4pm Mon-Fri rest of year)*. Highlights of the guided tours (included in admission) are Europe's oldest cod-liver-oil factory, where you'll be treated to a taste of the wares; the smithy, who still makes cod-liver-oil lamps; the still-functioning bakery from 1844; the old rorbuer with period furnishings; and a couple of traditional Lofoten fishing boats.

In a former fish warehouse nearby, the **Norsk Tørrfiskmuseum** *(Stockfish Museum; ☎ 76 09 12 11, Å; adult/child Nkr35/25, combination ticket Nkr65/45; open 11am-5pm daily mid-June–mid-Aug, 11am-4pm Mon-Fri rest of June, by appointment at other times)* reveals all you ever wanted to know about Lofoten's mainstay of catching and drying cod for export, particularly to Italy. Displays take you through the production process, which begins with hauling the fish from the sea, and progresses through drying, grading, sorting and exportation. The enthusiasm of the museum's proprietor-curator may well have you considering a simpler life and a change of career!

Moskestraumen

Beyond the camping ground south of Å, you'll have an excellent hillside view of Værøy island, across the Moskenesstraumen strait. The mighty maelstroms created by tidal flows between the two islands were first described 2000 years ago by Pytheas and later appeared as fearsome adversaries on fanciful early sea charts. They also inspired tales of maritime peril by Jules Verne and Edgar Allen Poe, and are still said to be the world's most dangerous waters. This formidable expanse is exceptionally rich in fish and attracts large numbers of sea birds and marine mammals.

Hiking

Visitors won't fail to be impressed by **Reine**, which sits beside a placid lagoon

NORDLAND

Nordland Boats

No visitor to northern Norway will fail to notice the uniquely shaped Nordland boat, which takes its inspiration from early Viking ships and has served the local fishing community from the earliest days of settlement in this region. These boats have come to symbolise the earthy and self-sufficient lifestyles of the hardy northern coastal folk. Today, they remain in use from Namsos, in Nord Trøndelag, right up to the Kola Peninsula in Arctic Russia, but the greatest concentrations are found in Lofoten.

The smallest versions are known as *færing*, which measure up to 5m, while larger ones are called *hundromsfæring* (6m), *seksring* (7m), *halvfjerdeomning* (7.5m), *firroing* (8m), *halvfemterømming* (9m), *åttring* (10 to 11m) and *femboring* (11 to 13m). Traditionally, the larger the boat, the greater the status of its captain, or *høvedmann*. Whatever the size, Nordland boats are renowned as excellent for both rowing and sailing, even in rough northern seas, and historically, the fishing communities took great pride in joining sailing competitions against their neighbours. A good place to see museum-quality examples is in the harbour at Å i Lofoten.

backed by pinnacled peaks. For exceptional views of the village and the road lacing the islands in turquoise waters, climb the precipitous track to the summit of Reinebringen (670m). The track starts above the tunnel about 1.2km south of the Reine turnoff on the E10, and climbs very steeply to the ridge (448m). Experienced hikers who want to keep going can continue to the peak for spectacular views of the freshwater lake below, then steeply down a very exposed route to the col (pass) of Navaren and on to Navaren's 730m summit.

In summer, ferries run between Reine and **Vindstad** (Nkr21, 40 minutes) through the scenic Reinefjord. From Vindstad, it's a one-hour hike across the ridge to the abandoned beachside settlement of **Bunes**, where there's a camping ground in the

shadow of the amazing 610m Helvetestind rock slab. If you choose not to camp on the white sand beach, the round trip takes about five hours.

Another, more demanding, route takes you via the fjord ferry to **Forsfjord** (you must request a stop) and follows the concrete pipeline toward Tennesvatnet lake. At around 450m above sea level, follow the path to descend between Tennesvatnet and the Fjerdalsvann Lake to the DNT's Munkebu Cabin (DNT members over 25/under 25 Nkr70/50, non-members Nkr140/100; get keys at the shops Å Dagligvarer, Sørvågen Handel or Reine Handel). This should take about four hours. If you'd prefer to continue directly to Soågen near Moskenes, the moderate carried walk takes you through the Djupfjordheia moor (about five hours).

The *Flakstad & Moskenes Guide* has several other hiking suggestions.

Organised Tours

The Moskenes tourist office (☎ 76 09 15 99) can provide information on and make reservations for a variety of tours.

You can be a fisherman (or woman) for a day on tours from several Moskenesøy ports (Nkr280), with the traditional long lines and the possibility of bird and whale sightings. Options include fishing the Reinefjord, off Nusfjord or near the Maelstrom off Å.

From Reine, you can choose among several worthwhile boat tours, from June to August. The most popular is the six-hour midnight sun excursion via the Maelstrom to the cave Refsvikhula, a 115m-long and 50m-high natural rock cathedral. Around midsummer, the midnight sun shines directly into the mouth of the cave and illuminates a panel of Stone Age stick figures marching across the walls. They're thought to have been painted at least 3000 years ago. The tour costs Nkr600 (minimum eight people).

Alternatively, you can take a bird and marine mammal-watching safari into the wild and fish-rich Moskestraumen maelstrom. These five-hour tours cost Nkr490 and leave Reine twice daily Fri-Sun.

A guided tour of Å, followed by a spin in a traditional Nordland boat and a meal of

NORDLAND

traditionally prepared cod, begins at the Norsk Fiskeværsmuseum in Å at noon daily and costs Nkr350.

Adventure Rafting Lofoten (☎ 76 09 20 00) also offers bird cliff tours to Værøy (Nkr690), as well as Refsvikshula and the Mokstraumen.

Places to Stay & Eat

Moskenes & Reine *Sjøhus* signs all along the E10 indicate private rooms.

Moskenes Camping (☎ 76 09 13 44, *Moskenes*) Tent/caravan sites Nkr65/100. Despite great waterside views, this gravel-surfaced spot is pretty spartan. However, it's convenient for an early getaway from the ferry terminal 150m away. Pay at the food store by the docks.

Eliassan Rorbuer (☎ 76 09 23 05, fax 76 09 24 40, e rorbuer@online.no, Hamnøy) 2-person/4-person rorbuer Nkr550/700, linen Nkr80. The pretty little fishing island of Hamnøy doesn't have much action, but this spot is so close to the water that you think you can walk across to the towering mountains on the other side!

Hamnøy Mat og Vinbu (☎ 76 09 21 45, *Hamnøy*) Mains Nkr130-165. This new restaurant is already well regarded for local specialities including bacalao and cod tongues.

Sakrisøy Rorbuer (☎ 76 09 21 43, fax 76 09 24 88, w www.rorbu.as, Sakrisøy) Cottages Nkr450-1000. This relatively authentic complex of ochre-coloured over-water cottages is by the Doll Museum. Linen costs Nkr80 extra.

In Reine, the *Reine Rorbuer & Gammelbua Restaurant* have long been prized options, but they were undergoing a management change as of this writing. Check with tourist offices for status.

For self-catering, the fish stall *Sjømat* (☎ 90 06 15 66, Sakrisøy), across the street from the Doll Museum, is famous for smoked salmon, prawns and prepared dishes. There's also a Coop supermarket in Reine and a small food store near Moskenes' boat docks.

Around Å *Moskenesstraumen Camping* (☎ 76 09 11 48, Å) Tent sites with 1 person Nkr60, additional person Nkr10, carava

sites Nkr80, 2-bed/4-bed cabins Nkr290/490. From this simple camping ground just south of the village, you can see the mainland on clear days.

Å Vandrerhjem og Rorbuer (☎ 76 09 11 21, fax 76 09 12 82, Å) Hostel beds Nkr125, rorbus for 2-15 people Nkr450-1200. There's a variety of accommodation in some of the historic museum buildings, some furnished with antiques. This place also rents bikes (Nkr100 per day), boats (Nkr300 per hour) and cars (Nkr400 per day).

Å-Hamna Rorbuer & Hennumgården (☎ 76 09 12 11, fax 76 09 11 14, e aa-hamna@lofoten-info.no, Å) Dorm beds Nkr100, 4–8-bed rorbuer Nkr600-950. In summer you can stay here in restored fishing huts from the last century or the hostel-style Hennumgasjøhus (with free showers) from the 1860s.

Apart from the high-end over-water *Brygga restaurant* (☎ 76 09 11 21) with mains for Nkr155 to Nkr215, dining in Å is limited. Your best bet is probably to use the kitchen where you're staying. You can buy fresh fish straight off the boats and pick up other supplies at the small food shop. You can also get coffee and waffles at the Lofoten Stockfish Museum, or bread at the Fishing Village Museum bakery.

Getting There & Away

About five buses connect Leknes and Å (Nkr88, 1½ hours) daily in summer, stopping in all major villages along the E10.

Lofotens og Vesterålens Dampskibsselskab (☎ 76 96 76 00) runs car ferries between Bodø and Moskenes (Nkr420 per car & driver, three hours), with at least one daily connection to Lofoten's southern islands of Værøy (Nkr157, 1¾ hours) and Røst (Nkr310, 3¾ hours). In summer, it operates several times daily on a rather complicated schedule.

Getting Around

Buses connect Å and other island communities several times daily in summer. The Reinefjorden ferry sails between Reine and Vindstad each morning and afternoon or evening.

SOUTHERN ISLANDS

Lofoten's remote southern islands of Værøy and Røst have some of the finest bird-watching in Norway. Most people come for the clumsy little puffins but, as a result of dwindling herring stocks, their numbers have dropped by more than 50% in the past decade. Although Værøy is mainly high and rugged and Røst is flat as a pancake, both islands offer good hiking. You'll also find a rare measure of relative solitude in well-touristed Lofoten.

Værøy
pop 775

Craggy Værøy, with 775 people and 100,000 nesting sea birds – fulmars, gannets, Arctic terns, guillemots, gulls, sea eagles, puffins, kittiwakes, cormorants, eiders petrels, and a host of others – makes an unusual, laid-back getaway. But there's more; white sand beaches, soaring ridges, tiny, isolated villages, granite-gneiss bird cliffs and sparkling seas combine to make it one of Norway's finest gems. The tourist office (☎ 76 09 52 10) lies about 200m north of the ferry landing at Sørland, the main town on the east side; it's open 10am to 3pm Monday to Saturday mid-June to mid-August, as well as other times when the car ferry is in port.

Things to See & Do A great way to get around Værøy is on foot, and **hiking routes** lead to most of the larger sea-bird rookeries. The most scenic and popular hike begins at the end of the road around the north of the island, about 6km from Sørland and 300m beyond the former airstrip. It heads southward along the west coast, over the Eidet isthmus to the (mostly) abandoned fishing village of Måstad, on the east coast, where meat and eggs from the puffin colonies once supported 150 people. Note that the route is exposed in places and shouldn't be attempted in poor weather.

Really keen hikers may also want to attempt the steep climb from Måstad to the peak of Måhornet (431m), which takes about an hour each way.

Alternatively, from the quay at Sørland you can follow the road (or perhaps the more interesting ridge scramble) up to the NATO installation at Håen (438m).

Værøy's biggest celebrity, country-and-western singer Paal Arnesen offers a unique perspective with his two-hour **boat trips** (☎ 92 41 14 46). You'll get views of bird cliffs as well as Måstad and the area's white sand beaches, for Nkr150/person (minimum of three people; daily in summer).

Places to Stay & Eat *Langodden Rorbucamp og Vandrerhjem* (☎ 76 09 53 52, fax 76 09 57 01, Sørland) Dorm beds from Nkr75, rorbuer Nkr250-800, linen Nkr75. This place offers some of the most authentic rorbu accommodation in Lofoten – including occasional fish smells outside! – and a kitchen. It's about an hour's walk north of the ferry landing.

Kornelius Kro (☎ 76 09 52 99, fax 76 09 57 99, [e] korn-kro@online.no, Sørland) Rooms Nkr300-500. The island's only nightlife option has a restaurant (mains Nkr55 to Nkr150), pub and a few simple but clean cottages out back. It's known for parties around the wood-fired seawater hot tub.

Gamle Prestegård (old vicarage; ☎ 76 09 54 11, fax 76 09 54 84, [W] www.prestegaarden.no, Nordland) Singles/doubles from Nkr350/580, including breakfast. Værøy's poshest lodging and dining is on the island's north side. There's no sign, but it's the nice house left of the church.

Getting There & Away There used to be air services to Værøy, but the airstrip proved unsafe; now the only air service is by private helicopter. The rest of us must travel by ferry from Bodø (☎ 76 96 76 00, Nkr385 for car and driver, 4¼ hours) or Moskenes (Nkr157, 1¾ hours). The ferry also provides access to Røst (Nkr196, 1¾ hours). Ask the operator if return tickets are available.

Røst
pop 670

The 356 islands and skerries of Røst comprise the ragged southern edge of Lofoten. Røst stands in sharp contrast to its rugged neighbours to the north, and were it not for a small pimple in the middle, the main

NORDLAND

pond-studded island of Røstlandet would be dead flat. Thanks to its location in the heart of the Gulf Stream, this rather enchanting little place basks in one of the mildest climates in Norway and attracts 2.5 million nesting seabirds to some serious rookeries on the cliffs of the outer islands.

An unusual view of medieval life on the island is provided in the accounts of the shipwrecked merchant of Venice called Pietro Querini, who washed up on Sandøy in 1432 and eventually introduced stockfish to Italy. The tourist office distributes a sheet outlining the amusing tale.

Organised Tours The Kårøy Sjøhus arranges all-day tours for Nkr125, which cruise past several bird cliffs, hoping to also show you an orca and a seal or two. Stops include the 1887 Skomvær lighthouse, once inhabited by artist Theodor Kittelsen, and the Vedøy kittiwake colonies, where Italian sculptor Luciano Fabro placed his monument to its avian population and entitled it *The Nest*. There's a short leg-stretcher up to a fine panoramic view. Upon completion of this tour, you'll have exhausted Røst's organised activities and will be on your own until the ferry leaves.

Places to Stay & Eat The bland but friendly *Fiskarheimen-Havly Hospits* (☎/fax 76 09 61 09) was being refurbished at the time of writing. It has a cafe, as well as a sauna for guests and rowing boats for hire.

Kårøy Sjøhus (☎ 76 09 62 38) Beds Nkr100. This is a collection of three sjøhus (seamen's houses).

Querini Pub og Restaurant (☎ 76 09 64 80) Your best choice for meals is named for the patron saint of stockfish.

Røst Bryggehotel (☎ 76 05 08 00) Rooms Nkr650-950. This new spot is the island's highest-end lodging.

Getting There & Away There are scheduled flights to Røst from Bodø and Leknes on Widerøe airlines. Røst is served by the ferry to Bodø (☎ 76 96 76 00, Nkr465, 4¼ hours), Moskenes (Nkr310, 1¾ hours) and Værøy (Nkr196, 2¼ hours). Sailing times

given are for direct ferries, but note that not every service is direct.

Vesterålen

The islands of Vesterålen, the northern continuation of the archipelago which includes Lofoten, are divided between the counties of Nordland and Troms, but for convenience, the entire area is covered in this chapter. Although the landscapes here aren't as dramatic as those in Lofoten, they tend to be much wilder and the forested mountainous regions of the island of Hinnøya are a unique corner of Norway's largely treeless northern coast.

Vesterålen Reiseliv is the central tourist office (☎ 76 11 14 80), Kjøpmannsgata 2, in the main city of Sortland. Another good source of information in English is the book *An Encounter with Vesterålen – Culture, Nature & History*, which outlines the history, sites and walking routes in the region – is sold at tourist offices (Nkr117). Also, see the Web site ⓦ www.visitvesteralen.com.

HADSELØYA
pop 8325
Vesterålen's link to Lofoten is the southernmost island of Hadseløya, which is connected by ferry from the port of Melbu to Fiskebøl on Austvågøy. Melbu also has a couple of museums and a famous summer music festival. The other main town, Stokmarknes, is a quiet market community best known as the birthplace of the Hurtigruten coastal steamer.

The tourist information office, in Stokmarknes (☎ 76 16 46 60), is less than active and opens only on weekdays in summer.

Things to See & Do
Hurtigrutens Hus The Hurtigruten coastal steamer was founded in Stokmarknes in 1893 by Richard Bernhard With, with a single ship, the S/S *Vesterålen*. It called on nine ports between Trondheim and Hammerfest, carrying post, passengers and vital supplies. Now the line boasts 11 ships, serves 35 towns and villages and is a vital

link for Norway, providing transport for locals and a scenic cruise-like experience for tourists.

That innovation is commemorated with Hurtigrutens Hus Museum, a museum-hotel-cinema-conference centre complex (☎ 76 11 81 90, Markedsgata 1, Stokmarknes; museum admission adult/child Nkr60/30, M/S Finnmarken admission Nkr40/20, combined Nkr80/40; open 8am-6pm summer, noon-5pm rest of year). You can see the history of the line in all its glory, but if you haven't arrived by Hurtigruten, you may be most interested in the retired ship, M/S Finnmarken.

Melbu Museums In an abandoned herring oil factory across the harbour from the ferry pier, the **Norsk Fiskeriindustrimuseum** (Fishing Industry Museum; ☎ 76 15 98 25, Neptunveien; adult/concession/child Nkr35/30/15; open 10am-5pm Mon-Fri, 11am-5pm Sat & Sun mid-June–mid-Aug; 10am-2pm Mon-Fri rest of year) traces the life of a fish from the deep sea to the kitchen table. There's also a children's exhibition about the goings-on at the sea floor.

The **Vesterålsmuseet** (☎ 76 15 75 56, M Fredriksens alle 1; adult/concession Nkr40/20), at the northern end of town, features local culture and a home farm.

Special Events
The Summer-Melbu festival, held each July, is one of northern Norway's liveliest cultural festivals, with seminars, lectures, concerts, theatrical performances and art exhibitions.

Places to Stay
The hostel in Melbu has closed and the remaining options cannot really be recommended, but there are a few lodgings in Stokmarknes.

Turistsenter (☎ 76 15 29 99, fax 76 15 11 40, e hurtigrutenshus@hurtigrutenshus .com, Børøya, Stokmarknes) Tent/caravan sites Nkr50/120, singles/doubles from Nkr650/900. This rather ritzy camping ground has rorbuer and a hotel and conference centre.

Vesterålen Hotel (☎ 76 15 06 00, fax 76 15 11 40, e hurtigrutenshus@hurtigrutenshus .com, Markedsgata 1, Stokmarknes) Singles/doubles Nkr750/1160. Attached to Hurtigrutens Hus are ship-themed rooms and a restaurant, which give the appearance of being on board.

Rødbrygge Pub (☎ 76 15 26 66, Markedgata 6a) Mains Nkr59-185. Ahoy, this popular pub has grills, seafood and pizzas, across from Hurtigrutens Hus.

There are also supermarkets in both Melbu and Stokmarknes.

Getting There & Away
Nor-Way Bussekspress buses run between Stokmarknes and Svolvær (Nkr94, 1¾ hours), Narvik (Nkr371, six to seven hours) and Fauske (Nkr344, 6¾ hours). If you're under your own steam, the frequent Melbu-Fiskebøl ferry to Lofoten's Augustvagøy costs Nkr68 for car and driver.

And, of course, the Hurtigruten coastal steamer still stops in Stokmarknes.

Getting Around
Buses between Melbu and Stokmarknes (Nkr39, 45 minutes) run several times daily on weekdays and twice daily on weekends. You can also follow the relatively low 22km hiking route between Melbu and Trolldalen, near Stokmarknes. The Ørnheihytta hut makes a good lunch stop and offers a superb view of northern Lofoten. Strong hikers can complete the trip in about six hours.

LANGØYA
pop 9225
As the central island of Vesterålen, Langøya is well located for exploring the region and has some unique attractions, particularly the historic fishing villages to the north.

Orientation
Sortland, Vesterålen's commercial centre and transit hub, occupies a niche in the island's east coast. Although its typical architecture is large and square (they're trying to liven it up by painting the buildings in a soothing sea-blue), it has most of the island's lodgings and restaurants and is a useful base for day trips. Sortland is also where you'll find the helpful tourist office, Vesterålen

Reiseliv (see the introductory section under Vesterålen, earlier).

Langøya's only other town of any size is Myre, in the north centre, but most people bypass it en route to the more alluring north coast villages of Nyksund and Stø. The remote community of Toftenes, on the northeastern shore, has a pretty camping ground with a restaurant that's a favourite of locals.

Things to See & Do

Nyksund A highlight of the island is Nyksund, an abandoned fishing village that is now re-emerging as an artists' colony. From the crumbling and collapsing old structures to the faithfully renovated commercial buildings, it's picture-perfect, and the lively, youthful atmosphere belies the fact that Nyksund was a ghost town until only recently.

In 1874, this struggling fishing community improved its harbour and built a mole to protect ships and buildings from the open seas. A church was built in 1880, and Nyksund boasted a telegraph station, bakery, a selection of shops and a steamboat. But in 1934, a fire destroyed the harbourside; the government determined that it was too expensive to rebuild and the harbour too small for the new motorised fishing vessels.

Many residents left, but after WWII those who stayed rebuilt much of the town in stone and enlarged the harbour. In the 1960s, however, economic factors caused the closure of the bakery and post office, and nearly everyone else left in 1975 after a storm destroyed the mole. The last inhabitant, blacksmith Olav Larsen, left in 1977.

Sheep and vandals ruled the site until 1984, when an international project imported youth from around Europe to renovate Nyksund. Homes were rebuilt, electricity was installed, and prospective residents began envisioning utopia. In 1995, a cafe and guesthouse started up, along with artists' studios and relaxing hangouts. Modern Nyksund boasts a summer population of 30 to 40 people. About a half-dozen remain through the harsh winters.

Stø At the northernmost tip of Langøya clings the small, distinctive fishing village of Stø, where Whale Tours (☎ 76 13 44 99, e whaletrs@online.no) offers seven-hour whale-watching cruises for Nkr575. They're so sure you'll see sperm whales that they have a next-trip-free guarantee. They also operate seal and seabird tours, as well as fishing trips for Nkr350. Note that its name is due to change in 2002.

The Queen's Route The walk over the headland between Nyksund and Stø is fabulously scenic. Most people start out along the three-hour circular route via the 517m Sørkulen and return via the considerably easier two-hour sea level route. Its name derives from a hike taken by Queen Sonja in 1994. Free maps detailing sites of interest along the way are available in Nyksund, Stø and Sortland.

Jennestad Handelssted The lovely wooden 19th-century trading post in Jennestad, some 8km north-west of Sortland, recalls the era of heavy direct trade between the fishing grounds of Nordland and the markets of mainland Europe. The Handelssted was changing owners at the time of writing. Check with the tourist office for hours and prices.

Special Events The annual 240km Arctic Sea Kayak Race is one of the ultimate challenges in competitive sea kayaking, but lesser beings can also opt for a 150km option or an introductory course in sea kayaking, to get geared up for the race the following year. For information and dates, contact the Arctic Sea Kayak Race (☎ 76 12 12 44, fax 76 12 33 88, e karl-einar.nord ahl@tin.no), Postboks 287, N-8401 Sortland. A jazz weekend is hosted in Sortland in September.

Places to Stay & Eat

Sortland *Sortland Camping og Motell (☎ 76 12 13 77, fax 76 12 25 78, Vestmarkveien 51)* 1-person/2-person tent sites Nkr75/100, caravan sites Nkr150, cabins from Nkr400. The only camping option is 1km from the centre. It also arranges sightseeing expeditions.

Sjøhussenteret (☎ *76 12 37 40, fax 76 12 00 40,* e *sjoehus@online.no, Ånstadsjøen)* Singles/doubles with shared facilities Nkr375/ 485, 1–2-bedroom cabins Nkr800-1050. This place outside the centre has lovely water-side cabins and an Arctic menu restaurant.

Strand Hotell (☎ *76 11 00 80, fax 76 11 00 88, Strandgata 34)* Singles/doubles from Nkr795/850. Sortland's poshest lodging, the waterside Strand, has has cheery, up-scale rooms. It houses a nice restaurant and a nightclub.

Milano (☎ *76 12 28 38, Torggata 17)* Dishes Nkr49-180. This pizza-kebab house features some unusual toppings (the Sort-land pizza has kebab meat and garlic sauce).

Hong Kong (☎ *76 12 38 88, Vesteråls-gata 70)* Mains Nkr88-198. This Chinese restaurant is on the main drag.

Davida (☎ *76 12 77 00, Strandgata 9)* Mains Nkr128-238. For lamb and fish dishes, this is the town's newest and most elegant restaurant.

Nyksund *Holmvik Brygge* (☎ *76 13 47 96, fax 76 13 43 38,* e *nickel@online.no, Nyk-sund)* Singles/doubles with shared facilities Nkr175/320, sheets Nkr45. To find out what it's like to live in Nyksund full time, ask the enthusiastic German immigrant owner of this cosy, historic building.

Nyksund Brygge (☎ *76 13 44 77, Strand-flåtveien 35)* Dorm beds Nkr175, triples with shared facilities Nkr500. Across the channel, this authentically renovated guest-house also has an intimate cafe.

Stø *Stø Bobilcamp* (☎ *76 13 25 30, fax 76 13 45 91, Stø)* Tent & car/caravan sites Nkr100/110. This small, waterside facility has a windowed restaurant serving fish, whale and land-roving animals.

Whale Tours (☎ *76 13 44 99, fax 76 13 44 88,* e *whaletrs@online.no, Stø)* 2–8-person cottages Nkr350-790. You can rent *strandbo* cottages in the town centre; break-fast and linen cost extra.

Myre *Myre Hotell* (☎ *76 13 44 10, fax 76 13 41 61, Storgate 52)* Singles/doubles Nkr595/720. If you're after conventional

lodgings, this spot is plain but comfortable, with a restaurant and nightclub.

Tøftenes *Tøftenes Sjøhus-camping* (☎ *76 13 14 55, fax 76 13 34 97, Alsvåg)* Single/ double cabins or rooms Nkr400/500. About 15km east of Myre, this waterside place is based in a trading station that was moved here in 1909. It has simple, spartan cabins, tent and caravan camping and a well-regarded restaurant with a small menu of local specialities (mains Nkr110 to Nkr195).

Getting There & Away
In summer, one to four daily buses connect Sortland with Risøyhamn (Nkr70, one hour) and Andenes (Nkr124, two hours). Buses run two to four times daily between Sortland and Lødingen (Nkr67, one hour), both on the island of Andøya (see later in this section).

The express bus between Tromsø (Nkr463, 7¼ hours), and Å (Nkr284, 6¼ hours) runs Monday to Friday. Buses to and from Harstad (Nkr114, two hours) run one to four times daily. Finally, you can take the Nor-Way Bussekspress: the Narvik-Lofoten Ekspres-sen between Narvik (Nkr247, 3¾ hours) and Svolvær (Nkr124, 2½ hours) operates Sunday to Friday and the Fauske-Lofoten Ekspressen between Fauske (Nkr301, 5¼ hours) and Svolvær runs daily. Sortland is also a stop on the Hurtigruten coastal steamer.

Getting Around
You'll find buses between Sortland and Myre (Nkr56, 50 minutes) three to five times daily; some of these continue on to Stø (Nkr29, 20 minutes).

There's no public transport to Nyksund, and it's a narrow and occasionally shabby dirt road from Myre, though you can try to hitch. Otherwise, the Queen's Route from Stø is a lovely hike.

ANDØYA
pop 5750
The 1000m deep, dark and cold waters of Andøya's north-western shore attract abun-dant stocks of squid – including some very large specimens – which in turn attract squid-loving sperm whales. The result is a

NORDLAND

rather reliable whale-watching venue and a good share of the region's tourist trade, centred on the town of Andenes. On Andenes' south-east coast, the relaxing village of Risøyhamn provides an antidote for the tourist blues.

Orientation & Information

Andøya, long, narrow and flat except for mountains on its western flank, is atypical of Vesterålen. At the north end is Andenes, with a rich fishing history, whale-watching, and a charming, nostalgic jumble of wooden harbourfront boat sheds and nautical detritus.

Other nature safaris depart from the tiny ports of Bleik and Stave, about 10km and 25km south-west of Andenes.

In the south-east corner of the island, Risøyhamn is quiet and under-touristed despite being the island's only Hurtigruten stop.

Andøy Tourist Info is at Storgata 2 (☎ 76 14 18 10) in the centre of Andenes. The Andøy Museum is also housed here, though it has not opened regularly in years and nobody knows whether it will. Still, you'll find its cosy grounds and historic buildings worth a peek.

Things to See & Do

Hisnakul The Hisnakul Natural History Centre (☎ 76 14 56 66, Havnegate 1c, Andenes; adult/concession Nkr50/25; open mid-June–mid-Aug), in a restored wooden warehouse, displays the natural history of northern Norway, including seabirds, topography, marine mammals, farming, fisheries and local cultures. Not to be missed is the Northern Lights exhibit that featured at the 1994 Winter Olympics at Lillehammer. Hisnakul is also a concert venue in summer.

Whale Centre Next door to Hisnakul, the Hvalsenter (☎ 76 11 56 00, Havnegate 1; admission Nkr40; open 8am-4pm late May–mid-Sept, until 8pm mid-June–mid-Aug) provides a perspective for whale watchers, with displays on whale research, whaling and whale life cycles. Most people visit here in conjunction with a whale-watching tour (see Organised Tours).

Polar Museum This quaint Arctic-themed museum (☎ 76 14 20 88, Havnegate; adult/concession Nkr25/15; open 10am-6pm daily mid-June–mid-Aug) includes displays on local hunting and fishing traditions, with extensive coverage of Hilmar Nøis' 38 winter hunting expeditions in Svalbard.

Andenes Fyr Andenes' landmark red lighthouse opened in 1859 and has since been automated but still presents a classic form. The lighthouse was closed for repairs during our visit, but when it reopens (possibly in 2002), guided tours, which require a climb up 40m and 148 steps, will be available.

Organised Tours

Whale Safari Whale Safari's (☎ 76 11 56 00, fax 76 11 56 10, [e] booking@whalesafari .no, [w] www.whalesafari.no) popular whale-watching cruises operate from the Andenes Hvalsenter between late May and mid-September. The tour begins with a spin through the Hvalsenter, followed by a three to five-hour boat trip, with guaranteed sightings of sperm whales or your next trip is free. There's also a chance of spotting minke and pilot whales. Trips depart at least once daily (at 10.30am) and cost Nkr650. Ring to book or for information on additional sailings.

Other Nature Safaris Fjord Cruise (☎ 95 25 29 98) leaves from Bleik on 1½-hour cruises to the seabird rookeries on the pyramid-shaped island of Bleiksøya (adult/child Nkr250/150); puffins, cormorants and sea eagles are common. The company also leads two-hour deep-sea fishing trips from Bleik (Nkr350/ 175), which include a meal made from your catch.

From Stave, Seal Safari (☎ 92 68 00 18) leads tours to see seals (Nkr300/150, one hour) and gannets (Nkr400/200, two hours).

You can book these directly or with the Hvalsenter desk. Be sure to bring weather-appropriate clothing.

Places to Stay & Eat

Andenes The Norlandia hotel chain seems to have a lock on Andøya's food and lodging. It handles *Andenes Camping* (☎ 76 14

12 22, fax 76 14 19 33, Andenes) on a seaside meadow with tent/caravan sites for Nkr80/110; and the timber-built hostel **Andenes Vandrerhjem** *(☎ 76 14 28 50, fax 76 14 28 55, Havnegata 31)*, which includes the Lankanholmen Sjøhus, a great old building and a nice base for a couple of days. Dorm beds cost Nkr125, singles/doubles Nkr190/300, cabins Nkr745 to Nkr1045; it's open June to August.

Norlandia Andrikken Hotell *(☎ 76 14 12 22, fax 76 14 19 33, ⓔ andrikken@norlandia .no, Storgata 53)* Singles/doubles from Nkr715/1030. Nordlandia's house-brand lodging is boxy and overpriced, although rooms are comfortably modern.

Den Gamle Fyrmesterbolig *(☎ 76 14 10 27, Richard Withs gate 11)* Doubles Nkr400. This non-Norlandia option has rooms in the charming lighthouse keepers' cottage.

Sjøgata Gjestehus *(☎ 76 14 16 37, fax 76 14 14 53, ⓔ hansen.sjogata@nl.telia.no, Sjøgata 4)* Singles/doubles Nkr300/350. This simple house has a few rooms without private facilities.

Lysthuset *(☎ 76 14 14 99, Storgata 51)* Mains Nkr70-195. This varied restaurant has steaks, salads, local specialities and a grill cafe out front.

Aurora Borealis *(☎ 76 14 83 00, Sjøgata 19)* Mains Nkr53-184. This sparkling new spot is almost too sleek for tiny Andenes, but it has a menu to suit many tastes.

There's also an informal cafe at the Hvalsenter.

Around Andenes *Havhusene Bleik (☎ 76 14 57 40, fax 76 14 55 51, Fiskeværsveien)* Singles/doubles Nkr620/720, 2–7-person cabins Nkr880-1530. With lovely seahouses over quiet Bleik harbour, this is a nice way to rough it. Naturally, you can also book through Nordlandia.

Risøyhamn Gjestehus *(☎/fax 76 14 76 25, ⓔ risoyhamn.gesthous@c2i.net, Risøyhamn)* Singles/doubles Nkr350-650. The hosts (and chefs) have infinite enthusiasm for and knowledge of the island, making for an charming off-the-beaten-path stay. Most rooms are without private bath; breakfast is included.

Getting There & Away

The Widerøe route between Andenes and Tromsø is a contender for the world's most scenic flight, and Widerøe flights from Narvik or Bodø aren't so bad either, with spectacular aerial views of the landscapes, seas and agricultural patterns.

By bus, you can reach Andenes from Sortland (Nkr116, 2½ hours) and Risøyhamn (Nkr64, one hour) one to four times daily. As you approach the town along the Rv82, you'll cross a vast and soggy moorland that contrasts sharply with the panoramas of distant ragged peaks. Alternatively, you can travel between Risøyhamn and Andenes (Nkr74, 1½ hours) via Bleik (Nkr22, 15 minutes), twice daily on weekdays and once on Saturday.

From June to August, a special ferry link connects Andenes a few times daily with the port of Gryllefjord (Nkr80, 1¾ hours) on the island of Senja (see The Far North chapter), passing what is certainly the most incredible coastal scenery in Norway south of Svalbard. For information and bookings, contact Andøy Tourist Info (☎ 76 14 18 10).

HINNØYA

The island of Hinnøya, the largest island off mainland Norway, is divided between the counties of Troms and Nordland and consists largely of a forested green upland punctuated with bleak snow-caps and deeply indented by fjords. Off Hinnøya's west coast, Vesterålen is divided from Lofoten by the narrow Raftsund strait and its renowned offshoot, Trollfjorden.

Harstad

pop 18,364

On a nice hillside near the northern end of Hinnøya, Harstad is the largest and most active place in the Vesterålen region, even though it's technically in Troms county. This industrial and defence-oriented city is full of docks, tanks and warehouses, but it also has a certain energy and – dare we say it – sophistication.

Information At the bus station is the Harstad Turistkontor (☎ 77 01 89 89, fax 77

NORDLAND

01 89 80, e touristinfo.harstad@hoarr.no, w hoarr.no), open 7.30am to 6pm weekdays and 10am to 3pm on weekends from mid-June to mid-August.

Trondenes Most sights are on the Trondenes peninsula, north of town. Hourly buses connect Trondenes with the central bus station (Nkr19, 10 minutes).

The **Trondenes Historiske Senter** (☎ 77 01 82 30, e trondeneshs@online.no, Trondenesveien 122; adult/child/concession Nkr65/45/25; open 10am-7pm daily June–mid-Aug, 10am-6pm Sun rest of year) is a must for anyone remotely interested in Scandinavian medieval history. It tells the Viking history of Hinnøya and nearby Bjarkøy, from where chieftains controlled most of Troms and Vesterålen. It also outlines the transition between the Viking and Christian ages, and the bloody battles that marked it.

The tourist office runs guided tours of the **Trondenes Kirke** (Trondenes Church) next door. It was built by King Øystein around 1150, after Viking chieftains lost the battle against the unification of Norway under a Christian regime, and at the time it was the northernmost church in Christendom. Originally constructed as a timber building, the current – and modern-looking – stone structure replaced it around 1250 and quickly came to double as a fortification against Russian aggression. In summer, tours start at 2pm and 4pm daily except Saturdays, with additional tours according to demand (Nkr25).

The WWII relic known as the **Adolf Kanonen** is often boastfully cited as the world's largest land-based big gun, with a calibre of 40.6cm and a recoil force of 635 tonnes. Because it lies in a military area, you're obliged to take a guided tour of the site (at 11am, 1pm, 3pm and 5pm daily in summer) which cost Nkr55. Book through the tourist office. The bunker also contains a collection of artillery, military equipment and instruments used by German coastal batteries during WWII.

Groups can take fjord cruises from the Kulturhus quay, for Nkr5500 aboard the historic 36m 1868 schooner, *Anna Rogde*

(☎ 77 06 11 53, mobile ☎ 94 85 48 68, w www.annarogde.no), which may well be the oldest active sailing schooner in Norway.

By the time you read this, **Badeland**, an indoor swimming park, built into the hillside, should have opened.

Places to Stay *Harstad Camping* (☎ 77 07 36 62, fax 77 07 35 02, e hcamping@ start.no, Nesseveien 55) Tent or caravan sites Nkr125 plus Nkr18/12 per adult/child, cabins Nkr320-750. About 5km south of the centre, this plain, waterside site rents boats.

Harstad Vandrerhjem (☎ 77 07 28 00, fax 77 07 26 66, e trofo@c2i.net, Trondenesveien 110) Singles/doubles from Nkr205/290. A school most of the year, this summer hostel has captivating harbour views from Trondenes. Breakfast and sheets each cost an extra Nkr60.

Centrum Gjestehus (☎ 77 06 29 38, e seg jeste@online.no, Magnusgata 5) Singles/doubles without bath Nkr300/400, with private facilities Nkr400/500. The rooms are basic at this place but still offer a good deal.

Grand Nordic Hotel (☎ 77 00 30 00, fax 77 00 30 01, e GNH@nordic.no, Strandgata 9) Singles/doubles from Nkr640/735. This is the *grande dame* of Harstad hotels. Request one of the larger, nicer rooms in the newer section.

Viking Nordic Hotel (☎ 77 00 32 00, fax 77 00 32 01, e VNH@nordic.no, Fjordgata 2) Singles/doubles from Nkr640/735. The Grand's sister has similar rooms, but you're only a block from the harbour, as you'll see from the pool and deck on the top floor.

Quality Hotel Arcticus (☎ 77 04 08 00, fax 77 04 08 01, e arcticus@quality.choiceh otels.no, Havnegata 3) Singles/doubles Nkr715/935. Harstad's coolest hotel is full of modern design.

Places to Eat *Kaffistova* (☎ 77 06 12 57, Rikard Kaarbøsgata 6) Dishes Nkr20-115. Established in 1911, this amenable spot opens for lunch, dinner and afternoon coffee and snacks.

Havnepaviljongen (☎ 77 06 73 00, Sjøgata 8), near Kaffistova, serves all things quick and greasy for Nkr31 to Nkr130.

NORDLAND

HARSTAD

PLACES TO STAY
4 Harstad Vandrerhjem
6 Quality Hotel Arcticus
7 Centrum Gjestehus
15 Grand Nordic Hotel
23 Viking Nordic Hotel

PLACES TO EAT
8 Nordlændingen Restaurant
9 Brygga
10 Havnepaviljongen Gatekjøkken
11 Druen
13 Metzo
14 Kaffistova
17 Ming's Restaurant

OTHER
1 Adolf Kanonen
2 Trondenes Kirke
3 Trondenes Historiske Senter
5 Kulturhuskaia (Quay); Anna Røgde Schooner
12 Express Ferry Quay
16 Parking Structure
18 Bysenteret (Shopping Centre)
19 Harstad Turistkontor (Tourist Office)
20 Parabolflua (Bike Rental)
21 Bus Station
22 Hurtigruten Coastal Steamer Quay
24 Post Office
25 Hospital

Brygga (☎ 77 00 10 20, Havnegata 23B) Mains Nkr52-220. A former dockside warehouse has undergone a super-mod remodel and emerged as a cafe, with snacks to full meals, outdoor seating and weekend disco.

Metzo (☎ 77 07 58 58, Strandgata 12) Mains Nkr59-179. This popular coffee house/pub near the town crossroads serves light fare and specialities including Mexican and Cajun.

Ming (☎ 77 06 24 00, Richard Kaarbøsgata 18) Mains Nkr95-190. This local Chinese specialist sizzles up a Mongolian grill.

Nordlændingen (☎ 77 01 87 50, Strandgata 30) Mains Nkr85-200. This 1891 spot specialises in local fish and meat dishes prepared in the typical northern Norwegian manner, but those with less refined tastes can fall back on the pizza.

Druen (☎ 77 07 50 75, Strandgata 14b) Mains Nkr135-235. This handsome steak house is across from the Grand Nordic.

Getting There & Away The Harstad-Narvik airport is at Evenes, one hour east of town by bus. Harstad is served by both SAS and Braathens.

Buses to and from Sortland (Nkr114, two hours) run one to four times daily; the fare includes the ferry between Flesnes and Revsnes. The bus to/from Narvik (Nkr134, 2½ hours), via Evenes airport (Nkr58, one hour), operates two or three times daily. There is a daily service between Harstad and Fauske (Nkr323, 5¾ hours).

If you're heading for Tromsø, the easiest and most scenic option is by boat. The M/S *Fjordkongen* express ferry sails twice daily between Harstad and Tromso (Nkr365, 2¾ hours), via Finnsnes (Nkr200, 1½ hours). There are also two or three daily Fergesambandet Harstad (☎ 77 01 89 89) ferries between Harstad and Skrolsvik (Nkr200, 1½ hours), at the southern end of Senja island, where you'll find bus connections to Finnsnes and thence on to Tromsø. Directly to and from Finnsnes, Troms Fylkes Dampskipsselskap (☎ 77 64 81 00) express ferries sail once or twice daily.

Harstad is also a stop on the Hurtigruten coastal steamer.

NORDLAND

Drivers should be aware that parking in Harstad can be a nightmare; it's not only expensive, but finding a space can prove an exercise in futility. A new parking structure (opening 2002) may help. Or you may want to park well away from the centre and hoof it into town.

Getting Around Flybussen (one way/return Nkr100/150, 50 minutes) shuttles between the town centre and Evenes airport several times daily. Alternatively, you can take the regular, less frequent Narvik bus to Evenes (Nkr58, one hour). Parabolflua (☎ 77 06 50 22), Storgata 2, hires bikes for Nkr110 per day.

Lødingen

The pretty coastal village of Lødingen is a major crossroads, and while it's no tourist hotspot, it's a pleasant place to cool one's jets. Its only museum, the **Lødingen Pilots' Museum & Norwegian Telecom Museum**

(☎ 76 98 66 00, Ringveien 5; adult/child Nkr30/10; open 4pm-7pm Wed, noon-3pm Thur-Sat summer), chronicles 130 years of communications and the work of northern Norway's ship pilots.

The Lødingen Turistkontor (☎ 76 93 23 12), by the bus and taxi stand, opens mid-June to mid-August.

Centrum Overnatting (☎ 76 93 12 94, fax 76 93 15 45, Signalveien 4) Beds Nkr150, doubles Nkr400. At this friendly, immaculate guesthouse across from the water, most rooms and apartments have private bathrooms. There's also a barbecue hut outside.

The express ferry M/S *Børtind,* running between Svolvær (Nkr176, two hours) and Narvik (Nkr146, 1¼ hours), calls in daily except Saturday. Lødingen is also a stop on most of the bus routes between Narvik (Nkr176, three hours) or Fauske (Nkr229, four hours) and Harstad (Nkr97, 1¼ hours), Sortland (Nkr82, one hour) and Svolvær (Nkr201, 3¾ hours).

The Far North

Norway's northern counties of Troms and Finnmark, which arc across the top of Europe, represent the last frontier of European civilisation on the mainland, and the effort of getting there is part of the experience. From the dramatic island of Senja to the animated town of Tromsø, the tourist cul-de-sac at Nordkapp, the Sami cultures on the plateaus of Inner Finnmark and the frontierland at Kirkenes, this lovely and varied end of Norway contains some of the country's most exotic attractions and broadest horizons.

Troms

This section covers the northern two-thirds of Troms county; the Troms portion of the island of Hinnøya are included in the Nordland chapter.

TROMSØ
pop 48,159

Simply put, Tromsø parties. It's the main town of Troms county and the largest in northern Norway, filled with cultural bashes, buskers, a lively street scene, a midnight sun marathon, the hallowed Mack brewery and more pubs per capita than any other Norwegian town. A cosy backdrop of snow-topped peaks provides lush scenery, excellent hiking in summer and great skiing and dog-sledding in winter.

Many Tromsø landmarks claim northern-most titles, including the university, Protestant cathedral, brewery (not technically – but read on), botanical garden, and even the most boreal Burger King. The city lies just off the Arctic Ocean at nearly 70°N latitude – almost 400km north of the Arctic Circle – but the climate is pleasantly moderated by the Gulf Stream, and the long winter darkness is offset by round-the-clock activity through the perpetually bright days of summer.

Tromsø received its municipal charter in 1794 when the city was developing into a trading centre, but its history goes back to

Highlights

- Soaking up the street life in the lively university town of Tromsø during the midnight sun
- Viewing the ancient rock carvings at the Alta Museum, a Unesco World Heritage Site
- Heading north to dramatic Nordkapp and hiking to continental Europe's northern-most point at Knivskjelodden
- Hiking, battling mosquitoes and looking for brown bears in Øvre Pasvik National Park
- Learning about the unique Sami culture at Kautokeino and Karasjok
- Exploring the wild and grand Arctic Ocean peninsulas, fjords and islands

the 13th century, when the first local church appeared. In more recent times, the city became a launching point for polar expeditions and, thanks to that distinction, it's nicknamed 'Gateway to the Arctic' (which is probably more appropriate than 'Paris of

THE FAR NORTH

- - - County Boundary

PLACES TO STAY
1. Hamn i Senja
2. Ramfjord Camping
3. Kilpisjärven Retkeilykeskus
4. Nedrefosshytta
5. Reisevannhytta
6. Ravnastua
7. Bojobæski
8. Reinbukkelva
9. Bungaläven

OTHER
2. Tromsø Villmarkssenter
3. Altadammen
8. Sautso-Alta Canyon
12. Stabbursnes Naturreservat
13. Sletnes Fyr
14. Tanahorn
15. Varjjat Sami Musea
17. Ceavccageadge
18. Sør-Varanger Museum
19. Bjørklund Gård Farm
20. Høyden 96 Viewpoint
21. Pasvikdalen Villmarkssenter
22. Svanhovd Environmental Centre & Svanvik Chapel

Barents Sea

Barentshavet

RUSSIA

FINLAND

SWEDEN

FINNMARK

TROMS

the North', which was suggested by an apparently myopic German visitor in the early 1900s. Tromsø's great, but Paris is Paris! This tradition of explorers (and students) with money to burn keeps the pubs busy.

Orientation & Information

Tromsø's centre is on the east shore of the island of Tromsøya, separated by hills from the west shore and airport. The lively, central port area runs from the Skansen docks, past the Stortorget (main square) and Hurtigruten pier to the Mack Brewery and waterfront Polaria museum. The city also spills across a channel to Tromsdalen on the mainland, with suburbs on Kvaløya island to the west. Two arching bridges link the sections.

The Destinasjon Tromsø tourist office (☎ 77 61 00 00, fax 77 61 00 10, W www .destinasjontromso.no), Storgata 61–63, is open from 8.30am to 6pm on weekdays, 10am to 5pm on Saturday and 10.30am to 5pm on Sunday June to mid-August, with shorter hours from mid-August to May. It publishes the very thorough *Infoguide* booklet.

Long-distance hikers who plan to use DNT cabins in northern Norway can contact the Troms Turlag DNT office (☎ 77 68 51 75, fax 77 68 40 50), Grønnegata 32, where you can pay membership fees, pick up keys and buy maps and books. It's open from 10am to 2pm Tuesday, Wednesday and Friday, and 10am to 6pm Thursday.

Post & Communications The main post office (☎ 77 62 40 00) is at Strandgata 41. Internet access is available free to patrons at the Amtmandens Datter pub at Grønnegata 81. The youth-oriented computer-game place Battle Ground (☎ 77 68 68 02), Grønnegata 42a, charges Nkr1 per minute.

Bookshops The best-stocked bookshop is Centrum Libris (☎ 77 68 35 40), Sjøgata 31/33. For used books, visit Tromsø Bruktbokhandel (☎ 77 68 39 40), behind Kirkegata 6.

Film & Photography Japan Photo (☎ 77 65 71 27), Storgata 91, has the best deals.

Things to See

Tromsø Museum The Tromsø Museum (☎ 77 64 50 00, W www.imv.uit.no, Lars Thøringsvei 10; adult/concession Nkr30/15; open 9am-8pm daily June-Aug, shorter hours rest of year) near the southern end of Tromsøya, is northern Norway's largest museum, with well-presented displays on Arctic animals, Sami culture and regional history, as well as church architecture. A short, rather impressionistic film gives you a view of the Northern Lights. Catch bus No 28 from Torget or No 42 from southern Sjøgata.

Polaria Polaria, Tromsø's museum of the Arctic (☎ 77 75 01 11, W www.polaria .no, Hjalmar Johansens gate 12; adult/ concession/child/family Nkr70/55/40/160; open 10am-7pm daily summer, noon-5pm rest of year), is daringly designed and interestingly executed. A panoramic film takes you to Svalbard, the cluster of islands around 80° north latitude (tours depart from Tromsø, if you become inspired). Imaginative aquaria house Arctic fish and – the big draw – four bearded seals. Other exhibits explore nature and human habitation at both poles. Just try to leave without a polar bear mask from the gift shop.

Churches Sydney has its Opera House, and Tromsø has the **Ishavskatedralen** (Arctic Ocean Cathedral; ☎ 77 64 76 11, Hans Nilsensvei 41; admission Nkr20; open 10am-8pm June-Aug), as the Tromsdalen Kirke is informally known. Its striking design – 11 arching triangles on a hillside on the mainland – suggests glacial crevasses and auroral curtains. Sunday services are held at 11am and organ recitals have been held nightly at 11pm in June and July (check with the tourist office for current schedules).

In the city centre you'll find several period churches, including the Protestant **Tromsø Domkirke** (cathedral; ☎ 77 66 25 80; Storgata 25; admission free; open 10am-6pm Tue-Sat, 10am-2pm Sun), one of Norway's largest wooden churches, and a **Catholic church** (☎ 77 68 56 04, Storgata 94; admission free; open 9am-7.30pm daily), both built in 1861.

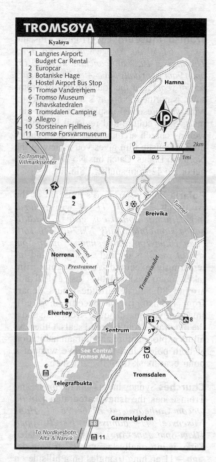

TROMSØYA

Kvaløya

1 Langnes Airport; Budget Car Rental
2 Europcar
3 Botaniske Hage
4 Hostel Airport Bus Stop
5 Tromsø Vandrerhjem
6 Tromso Museum
7 Ishavskatedralen
8 Tromsdalen Camping
9 Allegro
10 Storsteinen Fjellheis
11 Tromsø Forsvarsmuseum

Hamna

Breivika

Norrøna

Prestvannet

Elverhøy

Sentrum

See Central Tromse Map

Telegrafbukta

Tromsdalen

Gammelgården

To Tromso Villmarkssenter

To Nordkjosbotn, Alta & Narvik

Historic Buildings You'll find quite a few early 19th-century timber buildings around the centre. At Søndre Tollbugate 1, **Andreas Aagaard house**, built in 1838, was the first building in town to be electrically lit (in 1898). You'll also see a line-up of 1830s shops and merchants' homes along Sjøgata, a block south of the Stortorget (main square). At Skippergaten 11, an 1833 home adjoins Tromsø's only remaining **town garden**.

For a complete rundown of the historic buildings in Tromsø, pick up the booklet *Town Walks*, available from the tourist office (Nkr60).

Polarmuseet The harbourside Polar Museum (☎ 77 68 43 73, Søndre Tollbugata 11; adult/child/family Nkr40/10/80; open 10am-7pm daily 15 June-31 Aug, shorter hours rest of year), housed in a restored customs house near the colourful Skansen docks, focuses on polar research and exploration – and Roald Amundsen, in particularly. It also ventures into less universally agreeable issues such as the hunting and trapping of fuzzy Arctic creatures.

Nordnorsk Kunstmuseum By the time you read this, the Art Museum of Northern Norway (☎ 77 68 00 90, Sjøgata 1; admission free; expected opening hours: 11am-5pm Mon-Sat) should have opened in this new venue to display its collection of 19th to 21st-century sculpture, photography, painting and material artworks by Norwegian artists. It also features non-Norwegian artists' views of this unique part of the world.

Mack Ølbryggeri Okay, Mack Brewery (☎ 77 62 45 80, Storgata 5; open 9am-5pm Mon-Thur, 9am-6pm Fri, 9am-3pm Sat) isn't really the world's northernmost – a recently opened microbrewery in Honningsvåg near Nordkapp takes that title – but it's an institution nonetheless. Established in 1877, it now produces Macks Pilsner, Isbjørn, Haakon and several dark beers. Public tours (Nkr70, including beer stein, beer and souvenir) leave from the brewery's own **Ølhallen**, perhaps the world's only pub that closes at night, at 1pm on Tuesday and Thursday.

Tromsø Kunstforening The Tromsø location of this national contemporary art foundation (☎ 77 65 58 67, Muségata 2; adult/concession/child Nkr40/20/free) makes the most of its surprisingly old-fashioned building (1894), uphill from Polaria. There are rotating exhibits of installation and other contemporary art. The cafe serves homemade Norwegian and Italian specialties, cakes and soups.

Storsteinen Fjellheis You can get a fine view of the city and the midnight sun by taking the cable car (☎ *77 63 87 37; adult/child return trip Nkr70/30; open 10am-5pm daily 1 Apr-30 Sept, 10am-1am daily 20 May-20 Aug)* 420m up Mt Storsteinen. There's a restaurant at the top, or you can choose from a network of highland hiking routes. Take bus No 26. Combination bus/cable car tickets cost Nkr70.

Tromsø Forsvarsmuseum The southern end of Tromsø's mainland was first developed by the Germans in 1940 as a coastal artillery battery, complete with six big guns. The cannons have been restored as the basis of the **Tromsø Military Museum** (☎ *77 62 88 36, Solstrandveien; admission Nkr20; open 11am-7pm daily June-Aug, noon-5pm Sun May & Sept)*, which also includes a restored commando bunker, an old searchlight and an old ammunition dump with an exhibition on the 52,600-tonne German battleship *Tirpitz*, which was sunk by British air forces at Tromsø on 12 November 1944.

Botaniske Hage At less than two hectares, the Arctic and Alpine landscapes of Tromsø's botanical gardens (☎ *77 64 50 00, Breivika; admission free; open all day May-Sept)*, may be less than imposing, but they are the world's northernmost. Take bus No 20 or 32.

Special Events
The Midnight Sun Marathon, which features a full marathon, half marathon and mini-marathon, as well as a children's race, normally takes place on a Saturday in early July. For information and bookings, contact the organising committee (☎ *77 68 40 54, fax 77 65 56 35,* e *post@msm.no,* w *www .msm.no).* And you can just imagine what happens to Tromsø during the Øl-Festival (beer festival), in late August (the date may change, so check the tourist office Web site at w www.destinasjontromso.no).

Places to Stay
Tromsdalen Camping (☎ *77 63 80 37, fax 77 63 85 24, Tromsdalen)* Tent/ caravan sites

---

The Tromsø Palm

In and around Tromsø, you're bound to encounter the ubiquitous *Heracleum laciniatum*, which is known elsewhere by the pedestrian name of 'cow parsnip' and hereabouts by the euphemistic moniker, the 'Tromsø palm'. Although it bears a striking resemblance to edible angelica, don't mistake this poisonous beast for that tasty treat, or you're sure to regret it!

This plant, which has yellow-green flowers arranged in broad 'starburst' clusters, arrived from Asia via Britain in 1850, when it was introduced as an ornamental plant in the mining community of Kåfjord. The climate there proved too dry, however, and the seeds were transferred to Tromsø, where the plant took root, thrived and quickly spread across the island. Eventually, it took root all over northern Norway, and its enormous 2m to 3m high clusters have proven impossible to eradicate. What's more, because they're toxic, not even cows will eat them, and people who touch them may suffer an itchy rash.

Nkr100/170, cabins Nkr300-900. Most campers head for the mainland, 2km east of the Ishavskatedralen, to find leafy green sites, a slow-moving stream and a kiosk and cafeteria. Take bus No 24.

Ramfjord Camping (☎ *77 69 21 30, fax 77 69 22 60, Ramfjordbotn)* Camp sites Nkr120, cabins/caravans Nkr250-500. Those with a vehicle may prefer the nicely-situated camping ground about 25km south on the E8, with basic cabins.

Tromsø Vandrerhjem (☎ *77 68 53 19, fax 77 06 63 03,* e *hostels@online.no, Gitta Jønsonsvei 4)* Dorm beds Nkr125, singles/doubles Nkr250/300. Open late June-late Aug, reception closed 11am-5pm. The friendly hostel occupies a school dormitory 2km west of the centre. Bus No 26 takes you there, but the slog up the hill can be unpleasant if it's raining or you're carrying luggage.

The tourist office books rooms in private homes from Nkr250 per person. Most double or family rooms run around Nkr450.

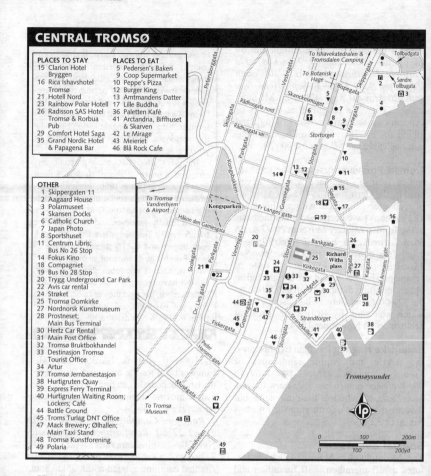

CENTRAL TROMSØ

PLACES TO STAY
15 Clarion Hotel Bryggen
16 Rica Ishavshotel Tromsø
21 Hotell Nord
23 Rainbow Polar Hotell
26 Radisson SAS Hotel Tromsø & Rorbua Pub
29 Comfort Hotel Saga
35 Grand Nordic Hotel & Papagena Bar

PLACES TO EAT
5 Pedersen's Bakeri
9 Coop Supermarket
10 Peppe's Pizza
12 Burger King
13 Amtmandens Datter
17 Lille Buddha
36 Paletten Kafé
41 Arctandria, Biffhuset & Skarven
42 Le Mirage
43 Meieriet
46 Blå Rock Cafe

OTHER
1 Skippergaten 11
2 Aagaard House
3 Polarmuseet
4 Skansen Docks
6 Catholic Church
7 Japan Photo
8 Sportshuset
11 Centrum Libris; Bus No 26 Stop
14 Fokus Kino
18 Compagniet
19 Bus No 28 Stop
20 Trygg Underground Car Park
22 Avis car rental
24 Strøket
25 Tromsø Domkirke
27 Nordnorsk Kunstmuseum
28 Prostneset; Main Bus Terminal
30 Hertz Car Rental
31 Main Post Office
32 Tromsø Bruktbokhandel
33 Destinasjon Tromsø Tourist Office
34 Artur
37 Tromsø Jernbanestasjon
38 Hurtigruten Quay
40 Hurtigruten Waiting Room; Lockers; Café
44 Battle Ground
45 Troms Turlag DNT Office
47 Mack Brewery; Ølhallen; Main Taxi Stand
48 Tromsø Kunstforening
49 Polaria

Hotell Nord (☎ 77 68 31 59, fax 77 61 35 05, e info@hotellnord.no, Parkgata 4) Singles/doubles without bath Nkr475/620, with bath Nkr620/780. This hillside spot feels like an informal guesthouse; and the staff are knowledgeable and friendly.

Rainbow Polar Hotell (☎ 77 68 64 80, fax 77 68 91 36, Grønnegata 45) Singles/doubles from Nkr615/770. This relatively simple hotel has modern rooms and a cheery breakfast room with city views.

Comfort Hotel Saga (☎ 77 68 11 80, fax 77 68 23 80, e booking@sagahotel.com, Richard Withs plass 2) Singles/doubles from

Nkr695-895. The Comfort lives up to its name with up-to-date rooms, breakfast buffet *and* a light dinner buffet.

Radisson SAS Hotel Tromsø (☎ 77 60 00 00, fax 77 65 61 10, e sales@toszh .rdsas.com, Sjøgata 7) Singles/doubles from Nkr695/895. Here you'll find professional service and a pub, the Rorbua, claiming to be Norway's most famous.

Grand Nordic Hotel (☎ 77 75 37 77, fax 77 75 37 78, e resepsjon.gnt@nordic.no, Storgata 44) Singles/doubles from Nkr750/ 890. Tromsø's old-line lodging is right in the centre.

THE FAR NORTH

Clarion Hotel Bryggen (☎ 77 75 88 00, fax 77 75 88 01, **W** *www.choicehotels.no, Sjøgata 19/21*) Singles/doubles from Nkr840/980. This waterside hotel is the city's artful choice, with odd angles, aluminium trim, images on the ceilings, and a hot tub overlooking the harbour.

Rica Ishavshotel (☎ 77 66 64 00, fax 77 66 64 44, **e** *rica.ishavshotel@rica.no, Fr Langes gate 2*) Singles/doubles from Nkr760/960. Also contemporary and lovely, the Rica has water views from most rooms.

Places to Eat

In Tromsø, the line is blurry between restaurants and pubs (see Entertainment) and many double as both.

Peppe's Pizza (☎ 77 61 11 65, *Stortorget*) Pizzas Nkr98-224. This restaurant offers good value pizzas; there's a pizza and salad lunch buffet for Nkr69.

Allegro (☎ 77 68 80 71, *Turistveien 19*) Pizzas Nkr60-240. Another pizza option is located between the Ishavskatedralen and the cable car, baking Italian-style pies in a birch-fired oven.

Paletten (☎ 77 68 05 10, *Storgata 51*) Mains Nkr45-96. This multi-level sports-bar serves everything from sandwiches to lasagnas and cakes, occasionally enhanced by live music.

Lille Buddha (☎ 77 65 65 66, *Sjøgata 25*) Mains Nkr95-170. This is a super-stylish Chinese spot near the centre of town.

Arctandria (☎ 77 60 07 25, *Strandtorget 1*) Mains Nkr125-245. By the piers, this upscale place serves filling ocean catches including some you may not want to see on a menu (eg, seal and whale).

Biffhuset (☎ 77 60 07 28, *Strandtorget 1*) Mains Nkr165-325. This place, next door to Arctandria, is a favourite steak house.

Tromsø's fast-food scene is led by kebab carts. *Pedersens Bakeri* on Storgata serves coffee and cake from a historic timber building. Supermarkets, throughout town, include Coop, on Stortoget, and you'll find fresh boiled shrimp from fishing boats at the Stortorget waterfront. If you must, there's also the world's northernmost *Burger King* (☎ 77 65 89 55, *Storgata 84*).

Entertainment

Tromsø enjoys famously thriving nightspots of which, unfortunately, we can list just a sampling. On Friday and Saturday, most nightspots stay open until 4am. Many also serve light meals.

Blå Rock Café (☎ 77 61 00 20, *Strangata 14/16*) This bustling, youthful venue is a favourite rock club, with theme evenings, 75 types of beer, live concerts and disco music on weekends.

Le Mirage (☎ 77 68 52 34, *Storgata 42*) A less rowdy crowd gathers here where you can also find sandwiches, salads, pastas and casseroles (Nkr42 to Nkr118).

Meieriet (☎ 77 61 36 39, *Grønnegata 37/39*) Mains Nkr56-136. Open from lunchtime until late. This busy cafe/pub has billiards and a menu including burgers, Mexican and Chinese dishes.

Skarven (☎ 77 60 07 43, *Strandtorget 1*) This waterfront venue offers fine bar meals (including selections from Arctandria and Biffhuset), and a hangout mainly for over-25s.

Tromsø Jernbanestasjon (☎ 77 61 23 48, *Strandgata 33*) This railway-themed pub is typical local humour – Tromsø only *wishes* it had a railway station. The over-30s here can get a little boisterous.

Rorbua (☎ 77 75 90 86, *Sjøgata 7*) The same is true at this venue located at the Radisson SAS, which bills itself as Norway's most famous pub (a TV show was shot here), with regular live music.

Amtmandens Datter (☎ 77 68 49 06, *Grønnegata 81*) This more sedate pub – the name is derived from an 1830s novel by Camille Collett – caters to a 25 to 35 crowd, and patrons may use its newspapers, books, board games, and (free!) Internet access.

Artur (☎ 77 64 79 85, *Storgata 57*) This easygoing, friendly place has been nicely renovated.

Compagniet (☎ 77 65 42 22, *Sjøgate 12*) This is a popular choice for dancing.

Tromsø's main meat market is *Strøket* (☎ 77 68 44 00, *Storgata 52*), and *Papagena* (☎ 77 75 37 77, *Storgata 44*), at the Grand Nordic, is good-naturedly referred to as a 'second-hand meat market', with a

THE FAR NORTH

crowd that starts at about age 35. There's no specific gay venue, but locals will proudly tell you that gays and lesbians are welcome everywhere.

Fokus Kino (☎ *77 75 30 95, Grønnegata 94)* Admission Nkr45-65. The main cinema is in a distinctive (if a wee bit crumbly), parabolic building.

Getting There & Away

Air Tromsø's Langnes Lufthaven is the main airport in the northern region, and is served by SAS, Braathens and Widerøe. Direct flights connect the city with Oslo, Bergen, Bodø, Trondheim, Alta, Hammerfest, Honningsvåg, Kirkenes and Longyearbyen.

Bus The bus terminal (sometimes called Prostneset) is located on Kaigata. Nor-Way Bussekspress has at least two daily express buses to and from Narvik (Nkr305, five hours) and one or two daily services to and from Alta (Nkr345, 6¾ hours). In summer, it also runs the Tromsø-Nordkapp Ekspressen bus (Nkr641, 13 hours).

Car & Motorcycle A two or four wheeled vehicle is the best way to negotiate Norway's far northern reaches. Car hire isn't cheap but it's available at Avis (☎ 77 61 58 50), Strandskillet 5; Europcar (☎ 77 67 56 00) Alkeveien 5; Hertz (☎ 77 62 44 00), Richard Withs plass 4; and Budget (☎ 77 66 19 00) at the airport.

Boat Troms Fylkes Dampskibsselskap (☎ 77 64 81 00) express ferries connect Tromsø and Harstad (Nkr405, 2½ hours), via Finnsnes (Nkr190, 1½ hours), at least twice daily in summer. Mid-week and family discounts are available. Tromsø is also a stop on the Hurtigruten Coastal Steamer.

Getting Around

To/From the Airport Tromsø's airport lies about 5km from the centre, on the western side of Tromsøy island. The Flybuss (☎ 77 67 02 33) runs between the airport and the Radisson SAS Hotel (15 minutes, Nkr35) to connect with arriving and departing flights; it also stops at the Grand Nordic Hotel and picks up or drops passengers at lodgings along the way. Alternatively, you can take the city bus for Nkr20; arriving air passengers can wait for it on the road opposite the airport entrance.

Taxis between the airport and the centre charge around Nkr75.

Bus Many sights lie outside the central area, but they're well served by local buses (Nkr20/ride or Nkr55/24-hour pass).

Car & Motorcycle Tromsø has ample parking in the centre. There's also the huge Trygg underground car park west of the harbour on Vestregata (closed to trailers and caravans).

Taxi The main taxi stand (☎ 77 60 30 00) is at Strandveien 30, outside of Ølhallen.

Bicycle You can hire bicycles from the Sportshuset (☎ 77 66 11 00) at Storgata 87.

AROUND TROMSØ
Belvik Ferry

This excellent ferry cruise will take you amid the little islands and communities to the west. The trip begins with a bus from Tromsø to Belvik (Nkr43, 45 minutes), where you board the M/F *Kjølva* ferry for the return cruise (4½ hours) and connect with a bus back to Tromsø.

Although the ferry runs every day, it's possible to do the entire trip on public transport only on Friday and Sunday from late June–mid-August. On these days, the bus leaves the Prostneset terminal in Tromsø around 4pm, and after the ferry cruise the return bus arrives in Tromsø around 10pm. Destinasjon Tromsø sells a combination bus/ferry return ticket for Nkr180.

Sommarøy

A beautiful beach that's popular with Tromsø people is on the island of Sommarøy, west of Kvaløya, where lots of locals also have holiday cottages. For a pleasant escape, *Sommarøy Kurs & Feriesenter* (☎ *77 66 40 00, fax 77 66 40 01,* **w** *www.sommaroy.no)*, Hillesøy, is a relaxing new option with both hotel and cabin accommodation. To reach Sommarøy, take the Hillesøy bus from the Prostneset terminal in Tromsø (Nkr80, 1¼ hours); it runs once or twice daily.

Sommarøy's port of Brensholmen is also a convenient gateway for Senja (see later in this chapter).

Karlsøy

The island of Karlsøy is probably one of the most interesting places in all of Troms county. After WWII, the population of this historic fishing community began to decline. By 1970 there remained only 45 people on the island, mostly elderly.

The trend switched dramatically when an emergent counterculture recognised the appeal of this remote island. Over the next decade, young people from elsewhere in Norway and abroad began moving to the island to create a sort of Arctic utopia, complete with communes, 'flower power', an artists' colony, the cultivation of soft drugs and generally anarchistic tendencies. The population eventually climbed to 80, new farmland was cultivated and a new economy emerged based on the arts, tourism and the production of goats' milk. It's still a unique community and makes an interesting visit.

For the full story on Karlsøy, see the booklet *Among Church Cottages & Goats in Alfred Eriksen's Kingdom* (Nkr50) from the tourist office in Karlsøy.

At **Karlsøy Brygge og Sjøsportell** (☎ 77 74 93 99, Karlsøy), you can camp or stay in seaside cabins from Nkr550. It also has a shop and pub and rents horses, bicycles and water sports equipment.

One or two daily buses connect the Prostneset terminal in Tromsø with the Hansnes ferry quay (Nkr85, 1¼ hours), on Ringvassøy island. From there, you can take the M/F *Fløytind* ferry to Karlsøy (Nkr29, 45 minutes) one or two times daily.

While you're in the area, you may also want to visit nearby Vannøy island, with its sandy beaches, classic staffed lighthouse and wild Arctic-looking coastlines. You can reach the port of Skåningsbukt by car ferry daily from Hansnes (Nkr29, 40 minutes)

and several times weekly from Karlsøy. Occasional buses connect the quay in Karlsøy with Torsvåg (near the lighthouse) in the north and Kristoffervalen in the east.

Lyngen Alps

Some of the most rugged alpine peaks in all of Norway form the spine of the heavily glaciated Lyngen peninsula, east of Tromsø, and you'll have the best views from the eastern shore of 150km-long Lyngenfjord. The peaks, the highest of which is Jiekkevarre (1833m), offer plenty of opportunities for mountaineers; the challenging glacial terrain is suitable only for the experienced. Tromsø Villmarkssenter (☎ 77 69 60 02) organises less challenging hikes for Nkr1100/day including transport and food.

The most accessible and popular hiking area is the Lyngsdalen valley, above the industrial village of Furuflaten. The usual route begins at the football pitch south of the bridge over the Lyngdalselva and climbs up the valley to the snout of the glacier Sydbreen, 500m above sea level (don't approach the ice as it's rotten and meltwater has created dangerous patches of quicksand).

The map to use for hiking is Statens Karverk's *M711 Storfjord*, sheet 1633IV. For information, contact the tourist offices in Furuflaten (☎ 77 71 06 92, fax 77 71 02 08), open mid-June to August or Svensby (☎/fax 77 71 22 25), open June to August.

Places to Stay *Bo-Med-Oss* (☎ 77 71 06 92, fax 77 71 02 08, e khuset@bo-med-oss .no, Hovedveien 20, Furuflaten) 3-person rooms Nkr500-750, 6-person cabins from Nkr900. The Furuflaten tourist office (and great hiking base) is in this small mountain inn with a pub serving basic meals. Guided glacier hikes are available. Signs read 'Furustua.'

Svensby Tursenter (☎ 77 71 22 25, fax 77 71 39 86, e inst@c2i.net, Svensby) Cabins from Nkr600. This place, a short jaunt from the ferry landing, can organise outdoor activities including fishing, wilderness evenings, glacier hiking, mountaineering and dog-sledding.

THE FAR NORTH

Getting There & Away The twice-daily Nor-Way Busekspress bus between Tromsø and Alta travels via Svensby (Nkr68, one hour). Bus No 3 travels between Tromsø and Furuflaten (Nkr150, two hours) at least once daily except Saturday. If you're driving, the easiest route involves a ferry from Breivikeidet (east of Tromsø) to Svensby (Nkr57, 20 minutes).

SENJA
pop 14,000

Norway's second largest island, Senja rivals Lofoten with its landscapes yet attracts a fraction of its visitors. The Innersida, the eastern coast facing the mainland, features a broad agricultural plain, while the interior is occupied by vast virgin forests. Along the western coast, the Yttersida, a convoluted series of knife-ridged peaks rises directly from the Arctic Ocean. Colourful, isolated fishing villages including Gryllefjord, Hamn, Skaland, Mefjordvær, Husøy and Botnhamn are accessible via tiny back roads, making for remote getaways. The road to Mefjordvær is particularly dramatic.

For tourist information on Senja and the region, contact the Midt i Troms tourist office in the nondescript town Finnsnes, on the mainland via a bridge from Senja (☎ 77 85 07 30, e mail@dmit.no, w www .midtitroms.no). Its helpful *Infoguide Midt i Troms* contains suggested itineraries. The office was moving to an undetermined location as of this writing.

Places to Stay

Fjordbotn Camping (☎ 77 84 93 10, fax 77 84 94 80, Botnhamn) Caravans sites from Nkr90, cabins Nkr380-700. Open Mar-Sept. This modest but friendly spot has a pretty, waterside setting on Senja's north coast.

Vertshuset Draugen (☎/fax 77 85 59 70, e post@draugen.no, Kaldfarnes) Huts Nkr1000. On the west coast, this guest house is known for its clean and well-kept huts.

Eidebrygga Rorbucamping (☎ 77 85 53 43, fax 77 65 88 81, Torsken) Huts Nkr400-500. If you can't make it to Lofoten, this camping ground offers stays in Lofoten-style fishermen's huts.

Hamn i Senja (☎ 77 85 88 50, fax 77 85 88 10, e post@hamnisenja.no, Hamn) Singles/doubles from Nkr240/480. The island's largest lodging occupies a remote corner, a combination of old and new buildings hugging the seashore.

Finnsnes Hotell Rica (☎ 77 84 08 33, fax 77 84 04 44, e firmapost@finnsness-hotell .no, Strandveien 2, Finnsnes) Singles/doubles from Nkr600/760. In Finnsnes centre you'll find business standard rooms and views from the upper floors.

Getting There & Away

Several bus companies serve Finnsnes from the central bus station (☎ 77 85 35 09), including to Tromsø (2¾ hours, Nkr179) and Narvik (3½ hours, Nkr200).

In summer, Troms Fylkes Dampskibsselskap (☎ 77 64 82 00) express ferries connect Finnsnes with Tromsø (Nkr190, 1¼ hours) and Harstad (Nkr200, 1½ hours) at least twice daily. Ferries also connect Skrolsvik, on Senja's south coast, to Harstad (Nkr250, 2¼ hours) and make convenient connections between Botnhamn on Senja's north coast and Brensholmen, west of Tromsø (Nkr110, 35 minutes).

In summer, buses connect Finnsnes and Senja villages: Skaland (Nkr36, 30 minutes), Hamn (Nkr74, one hour), Botnhamn (Nkr78, 1½ hours), Gryllefjord (Nkr93, 1½ hours), Skrolsvik (Nkr96, 1¾ hours), Torsken (Nkr96, 1¾ hours) and Mefjordvær (Nkr100, 1¾ hours). Note that Senja buses do not travel daily to every location.

Finnsnes is also a stop for the Hurtigruten coastal steamer.

BARDU

The woodsy town of Setermoen is the commercial centre for the Bardu district and a staging point for visits to Øvre Dividal National Park.

Setermoen is best known to Norwegians as a military training centre, and the local tourist office (☎ 77 18 56 50) is, fittingly, housed in the Troms Forsvarsmuseum (Defence Museum; 8am-6pm Mon-Fri, 8am-noon Sat summer, shorter hours rest of year).

Bardu Kirke

It's worth popping into Setermoen's church (☎ 77 18 52 60, E6, Setermoen; admission free; open 10am-5pm Mon-Sat, late June-early Aug), built between 1825 and 1829; the bell dates from 1698. Note the anachronistic heating system, which involves wood stoves and hot water pipes beneath the pews. Organ concerts are held at 8.30pm on Wednesday.

Polar Zoo

The Polar Zoo (☎ 77 18 66 30, Bardu; adult/child/family Nkr125/65/310; open 9am-6pm daily June-Aug, to 8pm July, by appointment rest of year) features wildlife of the boreal taiga in spacious enclosures that are virtually indistinguishable from the surrounding birch forests (OK, except for the metal fencing). Here you can watch and photograph those enigmatic, elusive faces that beam from postcards all over Norway, including moose, brown bears, deer, musk oxen, reindeer, wolves, lynx, wolverines, badgers and foxes. The zoo lies about 2km east of the E6, about 20km south of Setermoen.

Places to Stay

Most lodgings are in Setermoen.

Bardu Camping og Feriesenter (☎ 77 18 15 58, fax 77 18 15 98, off the E6) tent sites Nkr100, cabins Nkr200-600. At the foot of the mountains, this camping ground has mini-golf, a pub and river fishing.

Annekset Gjestegård (☎ 77 18 20 63, fax 77 18 24 00, Altevannsveien 20) Singles/doubles Nkr450/650. You'll find honest, comfy rooms (without phones or private facilities) and a popular restaurant at this place.

Bardu Hotell (☎ 77 18 59 40, fax 77 18 59 41, Toftakerlia 1) Singles/doubles from Nkr610/750. The lobby of this hotel has a hunting lodge look, and rooms are decorated with themes from spring to summer, and Adam to Eve.

Getting There & Away

The Setermoen bus terminal occupies a car park just east of the E6/Altevannsveien junction. The Nor-Way Bussekspress Nord-Norgeekspressen between Narvik (Nkr120, 1½ hours) and Tromsø (Nkr200, three hours) calls in one to three times daily and passes within 2km of the Polar Zoo. The bus between Narvik and Alta (Nkr470, 8½ hours) also calls in daily in summer.

ØVRE DIVIDAL NASJONALPARK

Between Setermoen and the Swedish and Finnish borders lies the wild, roadless and lake-studded Øvre Dividal National Park. While it lacks the spectacular steep-walled scenery of coastal Norway, this remote, semi-forested, 750 sq km upland wilderness still enjoys lots of alpine peaks and views.

The most popular hike is the eight-day Troms Border Trail, lacing seven unstaffed DNT huts. The route begins along the northern shore of the artificial lake, Altevatnet, about 3km east of the settlement of Innset, and twists north-eastward, passing several times into Sweden before winding up near the point where Sweden, Finland and Norway meet. At the easternmost hut, Galdahytta, the track splits and you can head for either Helligskogen in Norway or better equipped Kilpisjärvi in Finland. Many hikers also use the trail between the western end of Altevatn, in Øvre Dividal, and Abisko National Park, in northern Sweden, where you'll find the start of Sweden's world-famous Kungsleden hiking route.

The map to use for the Troms Border Trail and the Abisko Link is Statens Kartverk's *Turkart Indre Troms*, at a scale of 1:100,000. In summer, hikers cannot underestimate the mosquito nuisance in this area; use a head net and carry plenty of repellent!

Organised Tours

Winter visitors have the unique opportunity to join a dog-sled trip through Arctic Norway led by renowned and resourceful musher, Bjørn Klauer (☎/fax 77 18 45 03). In addition to tours through the national park, he runs expeditions into Finnmark, northern Sweden, Finland, and even Svalbard. With two people, seven/10/12-day tours, including

THE FAR NORTH

meals and hut or tent accommodation, cost Nkr11,600/16,800/20,400 per person.

Places to Stay

Seven unstaffed *DNT huts* run the length of the main hiking route through Øvre Dividal: Gaskashytta, Vuomahytta, Dividalshytta, Dærtahytta, Rostahytta, Gappohytta and Galdahytta. Keys and bookings are available from the Troms Turlag DNT office in Tromsø (see Information under Tromsø).

Klauerhytta (☎/fax 77 18 45 03, Innset) Nkr180/person. Dog musher Bjørn Klauer has opened this lovely and rustic hut to hikers and other travellers. A well equipped kitchen is available for guest use.

Helligskogen Fjellstua (☎/fax 77 71 54 60, E8, 30km east of Skibotn) Beds Nkr110/person. Near the eastern end of the park, this hostel is surrounded by wild open highlands. It's handy for travel between Norway and Finland, and serves hikers finishing the Troms Border Trail. Follow the 'Vandrerhjem' signs.

Kilpisjärven Retkeilykeskus (☎ 358-16 537 771, fax 16 537 702, Kilpisjärvi, Finland) 4-bed rooms Nkr400. Just over the Finnish border, this friendly, inexpensive place anchors the eastern end of the Troms Border Trail. It has simple rooms, a good value cafe and cooking facilities for guest use. You can arrange boat trips across Lake Kilpisjärvi and take a choice of scenic hikes through Finland's highest mountains.

Getting There & Away

Access to the park's main settlement, Innset, is by private vehicle, taxi (Nkr350 each way) or school bus from Setermoen. In summer, the bus runs on Thursday (one hour, Nkr50), otherwise weekdays, leaving Innset at 8am and Setermoen at 2.30pm.

Between Tromsø and the Kilpisjärven Retkeilykeskus hotel in Kilpisjärvi, Finland (Nkr245, four hours), at the eastern end of the hiking route, you can catch the Lapin Linjat bus (Finland, ☎ 358-16-3422160; W www.eskelisen-lapinlinjat .com), which runs daily from 2 June to 16 September.

Western Finnmark

Norway's northernmost mainland county, Finnmark has been inhabited for up to 12,000 years, first by the Komsa hunters of the coastal region and later by Sami fishing cultures and reindeer pastoralists, who settled on the coast and in the vast interior, respectively.

The county enjoys a distinctly dual landscape. Its wild northern coast, dotted with fishing villages, is deeply indented by grand fjords, while the relatively expansive interior is dominated by the broad Finnmarksvidda plateau, a stark wilderness with only two major settlements, Karasjok and Kautokeino.

Virtually every Finnmark town was decimated at the end of WWII by retreating Nazi troops, whose scorched-earth policy intended to delay advancing Soviets. Towns were soon rebuilt but, unfortunately, the most efficient architectural style was boxy. So in contrast to the spectacular natural surroundings, most present-day Finnmark towns are less than architecturally inspiring.

Tourist information is available from the Finnmark Tourist Board (☎ 78 44 02 00, fax 78 43 51 84, W www.visitnorthcape.com), Sorekskriverveien 13, N-9511 Alta.

ALTA
pop 17,000

Although the beautifully sheltered fishing and slate quarrying town of Alta lies at 70°N latitude, it enjoys a relatively mild climate and less precipitation than the Sahara, and outside of the centre it holds a certain frontier charm. The Alta Museum, with its ancient petroglyphs, is a 'must-see', and the lush green Sautso-Alta Canyon, a quick hop away, is simply breathtaking and houses some unique attractions (see separate Around Alta section).

The river Altaelva, which slices through the town, was once a Sami fishery and a popular haunt of sporting 19th-century English dukes and lords, but is now also one of the most contested waterways in northern Europe. In the late 1970s, despite strong local opposition, a 100m-high dam, the Altadammen, was built and this rich

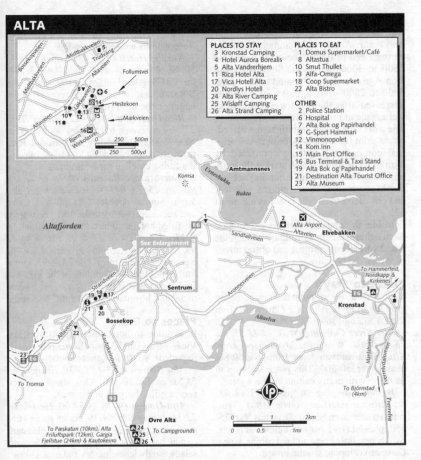

ALTA

PLACES TO STAY
3 Kronstad Camping
4 Hotel Aurora Borealis
5 Alta Vandrerhjem
11 Rica Hotel Alta
17 Vica Hotell Alta
20 Nordlys Hotell
24 Alta River Camping
25 Wisløff Camping
26 Alta Strand Camping

PLACES TO EAT
1 Domus Supermarket/Café
8 Altastua
10 Smut Thullet
13 Alfa-Omega
18 Coop Supermarket
22 Alta Bistro

OTHER
2 Police Station
6 Hospital
7 Alta Bok og Papirhandel
9 G-Sport Hammari
12 Vinmonopolet
14 Kom.Inn
15 Main Post Office
16 Bus Terminal & Taxi Stand
19 Alta Bok og Papirhandel
21 Destination Alta Tourist Office
23 Alta Museum

salmon-spawning stream was developed for hydroelectric power. Local sentiments remain vociferously opposed to the dam.

Orientation & Information

Alta has a large footprint, occupying some 15km of coastline. Its two main centres are about 2km apart: hilly Bossekop to the west, and Sentrum in – guess where – which is office-park-like, although they're trying to liven it up with a pedestrian way.

Destination Alta tourist office (☎ 78 45 77 77, fax 78 43 51 84, Sorekskriverveien 13) is in the middle of Bossekop. It's open 8am to 6pm on weekdays, 10am to 4pm on Saturday and noon to 4pm on Sunday from mid-June to mid-August, with shorter hours the rest of June and August.

There's Internet access at the tourist office (Nrk30/30 minutes), or you can use the computers for free at the church-run, youth-oriented Kom.inn coffee house (☎ 95 18 43 51), Hestekoen 18, Sentrum.

Alta Museum

Alta's big attraction is the Unesco World Heritage Site Alta Museum (☎ 78 45 63 30, Altaveien 19; admission Nkr70; open

8am-11pm daily 15 June-15 Aug, 8am-8pm rest of June & August, 9am-6pm other times May-Sept), at Hjemmeluft on the western end of town. The cliffs here hold 2500 to 3000 individual Stone-Age and Iron-Age carvings, estimated to date from 6000 to 2500 years ago. As the sea level decreased after the last Ice Age, carvings were made at progressively lower heights. The works have been highlighted with red-ochre paint (thought to have been the original colouration) and are connected by 3km of boardwalks which start at the main building. Themes include hunting scenes, fertility symbols, bears, moose, reindeer and crowded boats. One boat has a crew of 32!

Inside, the museum features exhibits on Sami culture, Finnmark military history, the Alta hydroelectric project and observations of the aurora borealis.

Places to Stay
You'll find three outstanding camping grounds in Øvre Alta, a 3.5km walk from the E6 south of town.

Alta River Camping (☎ 78 43 43 53, fax 78 43 69 02; e annjenss@online.no, Øvre Alta) Tent/caravan sites from Nkr60/80, cabins Nkr350-500. This place lives up to its name with pretty cabins by the water.

Wisløff Camping (☎/fax 78 43 43 03; e lilly@wisloeff.no, Øvre Alta) Tent/caravan sites from Nkr60/90, cabins Nkr275-350, plus Nkr10/5 per adult/child. This site, with happy little beige and red cabins, won a European camping ground award.

Alta Strand Camping (☎ 78 43 40 22, fax 78 43 42 40, Øvre Alta) Tent/caravan sites from Nkr90, cabins Nkr260-650. Just down the road, this site has mountain views.

Kronstad Camping (☎ 78 43 03 60, fax 78 43 11 55, Altaveien 375) Tent/caravan sites from Nkr50/95, cabins Nkr250-350. On the other side of Alta, the popular Kronstad has a general store.

Alta Vandrerhjem (☎/fax 78 43 44 09, e varndrehjem@trollnet.no, Midtbakken 52) Dorm beds Nkr125, singles/doubles Nkr235/270. Open 15 June-20 Aug. Reception closed noon-5pm. The youth hostel is

in a wooded residential neighbourhood, 10 minutes' walk from the Sentrum bus stop. Reservations are recommended.

Nordlys Hotell (☎ 78 43 55 66, fax 78 43 50 80; e e-post@nordlyshotell.no, Bekkefaret 3) Singles/doubles Nkr695/895. This Bossekop option has tasteful rooms that get larger on the third (top) floor.

Rica Hotel Alta (☎ 78 48 27 00, fax 78 48 27 77, Løkkeveien 61) Singles/doubles from Nkr695/865. The modern and pleasant, Rica is square and has parking lot views, making it a fitting emblem for Sentrum.

Hotel Aurora Borealis (☎ 78 45 78 00, fax 78 45 78 01; w www.ditthotell.no, Saga) Singles/doubles Nkr700/860. Cosy and secluded east of town, this renovated, art-filled hotel also has a fine restaurant.

Vica Hotell (☎ 78 43 47 11, fax 78 43 42 99, e post@vica.no, Fogdebakken 6) Singles/doubles from Nkr745/995. In a timber-built former farmhouse, the Vica has free sauna and Internet access, and commendably hospitable and helpful owners.

Places to Eat
In addition to hotel restaurants (the Rica, Vica, Nordlys and Aurora Borealis are well-regarded), you'll find these spots:

Alta Bistro (☎ 78 43 65 30, Svaneveien 7) Mains Nkr39-165. This simple choice serves grills, burgers and pizzas.

Alfa-Omega (☎ 78 44 54 00, Hestekoen 22/24) Mains Nkr79-119. As its name suggests, this place has two parts: a pleasant, casual bar and a contemporary cafe with salads, sandwiches, pastas and nice cakes.

Smut Thullet (☎ 78 44 05 11, Løkkeveien 35) Mains Nkr52-202. This popular lunch and dinner option offers pastas, salads, light fare, a pretty, contemporary setting, and a nightclub.

Altastua (☎ 78 44 55 54, Løkkeveien 2) Mains Nkr219-262. Alta's finest dining establishment serves huge portions from a rotating menu including reindeer, moose, salmon and cloudberries.

You'll also find a Coop Mega supermarket in Bossekop, a Domus Supermarket northeast of Sentrum, and the Vinmonopolet in Sentrum.

Getting There & Away

Alta's airport, four kilometres north-east of Sentrum at Elvebakken, is served by SAS, Widerøe and Arctic Air, with service including scenic flights to and from Tromsø, Hammerfest, Båtsfjord and Kirkenes.

One or two daily Nor-Way Bussekspress services from the bus terminal in Sentrum run between Tromsø and Alta (Nkr345, 6¾ hours). FFR buses run to and from Kautokeino (Nkr181, 2½ hours), Hammerfest (Nkr188, three hours), and Nordkapp (Nkr271, 5¾ hours). The Express 2000 bus (☎ 78 44 40 90) leaves Alta at noon on Monday and travels to Oslo (Nkr1850, 26½ hours), via Finland and Sweden. From Oslo, it leaves at 9am on Wednesday.

Getting Around

Fortunately, this sprawling town has a local bus to connect its dispersed ends. On weekdays, buses run more or less hourly among the major districts and airport. Services are less frequent on Saturday and don't run at all on Sunday.

Taxis (☎ 78 43 53 53) cost about Nkr80 from the airport to town, but note that there is a substantial pickup charge from hotels.

Hire bicycles from G-Sport Hammari (☎ 78 43 61 33), Løkkeveien 10 in Sentrum (Nkr100 per day).

AROUND ALTA
Sautso-Alta Canyon

The Altaelva hydroelectric project has had little effect on the most scenic stretch of river, which slides through 400m deep Sautso, northern Europe's grandest canyon. The easiest way to see this impressive forested gorge is on the four-hour tour which the tourist office organises daily in July. Tours leave from the tourist office at 4pm and cost Nkr350 per person, with a minimum of five people. In addition to views of the canyon, they also include a pass through the Alta Power Station dam and a snack of coffee, Sami máze cake and dried reindeer meat in a traditional *lavvo*.

If you have your own vehicle, you can follow the river upstream to the Gargia Fjellstue mountain lodge, 25km from town,

where a very bad road (passable to sturdy vehicles only – 4WD and high clearance are recommended) continues for 4km to end at a signpost. From this point, you'll have to walk the remaining 7km to the canyon. The route is marked in red blazes but it involves two river crossings and a bit of swamp-slogging so bring strong footwear. Most of all, don't forget your mosquito repellent!

Pæskatun Slate Quarry

Some 13km south of town, the Alta Skiferprodukter (☎ 78 43 33 45, W *www.altaskifer .no, Pæskatun; admission free; open 9am-4pm Mon-Fri*) is one of Alta's economic mainstays. Visitors are welcome to see the quarry, historical exhibits and a fine view over the canyon. It also sells a range of Finnmark minerals and souvenirs made of slate products. Guided tours must be booked in advance and cost Nkr50 per person, with a minimum of 10 participants.

Places to Stay & Eat

Nordlys Iglooen (☎ 78 43 33 78, W *www .alta-friluftspark.no, Storelvdalen*) Rooms per person with breakfast Nkr1095, with dinner & breakfast Nkr1395. This wintertime hotel, outside of town, is Norway's first lodging made entirely of snow and ice (down to the drinking glasses!). It's open January to May.

Gargia Fjellstue (☎ 78 43 33 51, fax 78 43 33 36) Rooms per person Nkr190, 4-bed cabins Nkr250, lavvos Nkr400. Package of inens, shower/sauna & breakfast Nkr125. Around 25km south of Alta, this mountain lodge offers a forest getaway and outdoor activities including the best foot access to the Sautso-Alta Canyon. There's an open-air hot tub, sauna, river excursions, horse-riding and fishing, with fishing equipment and mountain bikes for hire.

Activities

Plenty of long-distance hiking trails trace historic routes across the Finnmarksvidda plateau to the south. Among them is the five-day, 120km, post road hike between Alta and Karasjok, which begins at Bjørnstad in the Tverrelvdalen valley, climbs to 500m and passes through upland birch forests to wind up at Assebakti, on Rv92, 14km west of Karasjok. The Alta og Omegn Turlag (it doesn't have an office but the tourist office can put you in touch with the current club leaders), maintains self-service mountain huts at the Reinbukkelva river and Bojobæski, 16km apart. About 35km farther south is another hut, the Ravnastua mountain lodge (☎ 94 80 06 88), which lies just four hours from the trail's end. Note that you need a tent for the third night of the route. Maps are available in Alta at Alta Bok og Papirhandel (☎ 78 43 58 77 Parksentret, Sentrum ☎ 78 43 46 22, Altaveien 99, Bossekop).

Organised Tours

From Alta Friluftspark (☎ 78 43 33 78, fax 78 43 34 65; W alta-friluftspark.no), beside the Altaelva 16km south of town, you can choose from several riverboat rides, which last from 20 minutes to three hours and cost from Nkr115 to Nkr350 per person. They leave at 1pm and 3pm daily from June to August. From 15 July to 15 August, you can also join organised half-day and full-day sea-kayaking trips on Altafjord with AKU Finnmark (☎ 78 43 48 40, fax 78 44 04 80, e ulf@thomassen.priv.no). All of this assumes sufficient water levels.

HAMMERFEST
pop 6488

Hammerfest was inhabited as early as 1620 and made a town in 1789, and because of its strategic location and excellent harbour, it has long been an important way-station for shipping, fishing and Arctic hunting. In its heyday, Hammerfest ladies wore the finest Paris fashions, and the town had Europe's first electrical street lighting (1890). Nowadays it proudly claims to be the world's northernmost town (other Norwegian communities, while farther north, are too small to qualify as towns!).

Hammerfest has also suffered various ignominies: it was decimated in a gale in 1856, burned in 1890 and burned again by the Nazis in 1944; the only surviving prewar structure is a small chapel, and most of the other buildings don't give much clue to Hammerfest's romantic history.

If you're arriving on the Hurtigruten coastal steamer, you'll have only a couple of hours to race around, pick up an Arctic souvenir and scoff some fresh shrimp at the harbour, and for many people that will suffice. But others happily stay longer: as Bill Bryson wrote of Hammerfest in *Neither Here nor There*: 'I began to feel as if a doctor had told me to go away for a complete rest... Never had I slept so long and so well.'

Information

Hammerfest Turist (☎ 78 41 21 85, fax 78 41 19 00; W www.hammerfest-turist.no, e info@hammerfest-turist.no), inside the Reconstruction Museum, provides tourist information and books local activities. It's open 10.30am to 6pm daily in summer.

Things to See
Royal & Ancient Polar Bear Society

This renowned organisation (☎ 78 41 31 00, Rådhuset; admission Nkr20; open 7am-8pm Mon-Fri, 10am-5pm Sat & Sun), is dedicated to preserving Hammerfest culture and features exhibits on Arctic hunting and local history. The silver bears outside have posed for photos with generations of keen boreal tourists. Any visitor can become a member (Nkr150) and waive the admission fee for life, get a certificate, ID card, sticker, pin and champagne toast. The bone they use to 'knight' you – from a male walrus's most intimate of organs – will leave you either impressed or depressed.

Gjenreisningsmuseet Hammerfest's Reconstruction Museum (☎ 78 42 26 30, Kirkegate 21; adult/concession/child Nkr40/30/15; open 10.30am-6pm daily summer) commemorates the period that followed the decimation of the town after the German bombings of 1944, and reveals the hardships that the town's people endured through the following winter.

It also discusses the 'Norwegianisation' of the indigenous Sami culture in northern Norway. Note: although the exhibits are quite fine, virtually all the signage is in Norwegian; the free English audio guide does not do them justice.

Late sun reflects on Narvik's fjord

DEANNA SWANEY

Tromsø harbour experiences icy, harsh conditions in the 'dark period'

CHRISTIAN ASLUND

The midnight sun at its lowest point, Vesterålen islands

NED FRIARY

Are you sure it's Sunday?

Cruising into Hammerfest

Magdalenefjord, flanked by towering alpine peaks

The road to nowhere...or was that Nordkapp?

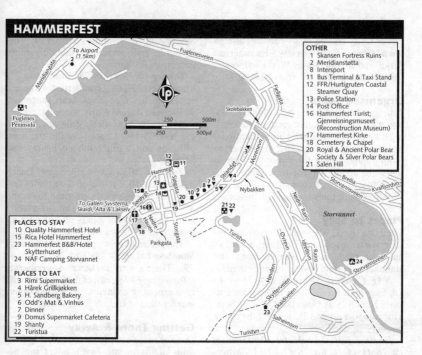

HAMMERFEST

To Airport
(1.5km)

Fuglenesveien

Fuglenes
Peninsula

To Galleri Syvsterna,
Skaidi, Alta & Lakselv

Fuglenesveien

Skolebakken

Fjellgata

Hamnegt

Strandgata

Morenevn

Nybakken

Breilia

Storvannsveien

Kvalfjordvn

Storvannet

Nedre Raivo

Øvren

Idretsvn

Raivo

Storvannsveien

Turistvn

Hårdvn

Skytterveien

Skadveien

Salheimsvn

Turistvn

Parkgata

Storgata

Nedre
Haien

Søreivg

Nedre Raivo

0   250   500m
0   250   500yd

OTHER
1 Skansen Fortress Ruins
2 Meridianstøtta
8 Intersport
11 Bus Terminal & Taxi Stand
12 FFR/Hurtigruten Coastal
   Steamer Quay
13 Police Station
14 Post Office
16 Hammerfest Turist;
   Gjenreisningsmuseet
   (Reconstruction Museum)
17 Hammerfest Kirke
18 Cemetery & Chapel
20 Royal & Ancient Polar Bear
   Society & Silver Polar Bears
21 Salen Hill

PLACES TO STAY
10 Quality Hammerfest Hotel
15 Rica Hotel Hammerfest
23 Hammerfest B&B/Hotel
   Skytterhuset
24 NAF Camping Storvannet

PLACES TO EAT
3 Rimi Supermarket
4 Hårek Grillkjøkken
5 H. Sandberg Bakery
6 Odd's Mat & Vinhus
7 Dinner
9 Domus Supermarket Cafeteria
19 Shanty
22 Turistua

Hammerfest Kirke Five minutes' walk from the harbour lies Hammerfest's contemporary church (☎ 78 42 74 70, Kirkegate 33; admission free; open 8am-3pm Mon-Fri, 11am-3pm Sat, noon-1pm Sun summer; rest of year by appointment). The main sanctuary is unusual in that it lacks an altarpiece, which has been replaced by a large stained glass window. An original altarpiece sits in a hall just to the right of the main sanctuary. Note also the friezes of town history toward the back of the sanctuary, by local woodcarver Knut Arnesen. You may find reindeer grazing in the churchyard, and the chapel (1933), across the street through the cemetery, is the only building in town to survive WWII.

Salen For panoramic views over the town, coast and mountains, climb Salen Hill (86m), topped by a restaurant/hotel and a Sami turf hut. The 10-minute trail begins at the small park uphill behind the Rådhus. For Nkr220,

the tourist office organises a Sami-style meal in the hut at 5pm each Saturday in July.

Fuglenes On the Fuglenes peninsula, across the harbour from the centre, is the **Meridianstøtta**, the marble column commemorating the first survey (1816–52) to determine the arc of the global meridian and thereby calculate the size and shape of the earth. At the end of the same peninsula lie the rather nondescript ruins of the **Skansen fortress**, which date from the Napoleonic Wars.

Galleri Syvsterna If you've ever wondered what a Nobel Peace Prize looks like, local artist Eva Arnesen has a replica of the 1997 award she designed, which went to Jody Williams and the campaign to ban land mines, at her gallery (☎ 78 41 01 60, Fjordaveien 27). Arnesen's paintings evoke the colours of the region from the Northern Lights to the bright summer palate. Don't expect her to design another Nobel, though –

THE FAR NORTH

it's a one-time honour. Her husband, wood-carver Knut, created many carvings around town (Polar Bear Society, Hammerfest Kirke) and at Walt Disney World, in Florida, USA. Works are for sale from Nkr100.

Organised Tours

Åttringen Nordlandsbåt (☎ 78 41 00 16, mobile ☎ 94 13 45 38) runs three/four hour sailing tours on Sørøysundet in a traditional Nordland boat for Nkr220/280 per person (with a minimum of three people). Fishing tours aboard the *Doffen* (three/four hour, Nkr320/450) include equipment and license. Both four-hour tours include fish dinners.

Places to Stay

The Håja Hotel, where Bill Bryson had his long winter naps (and drinking exploits), has been made into a refugee home, but Hammerfest offers several other options.

NAF Camping Storvannet (☎ 78 41 10 10, Storvannsveien) 2-person/4-person cottages Nkr320/340. Open late May-late Sept. This camping ground 2km east of the centre has cooking facilities.

Hammerfest B&B/Hotel Skytterhuset (☎ 78 41 15 11, fax 78 41 12 13, Skytterveien 24) Singles/doubles from Nkr595/795. This motel-style affair is on the other side of Salen, secluded from town.

Quality Hammerfest Hotel (☎ 78 41 96 00, fax 78 41 96 60, ℮ hammerfest@quality .choice.no, Strandgata 2) Singles/doubles from Nkr645/795. Rooms here have loads of character, eg, like ocean liner cabins, or posh mini-suites.

Rica Hotel Hammerfest (☎ 78 41 13 33, fax 78 41 13 11, ℮ oebook@rica.no, Sørøygata 15) Singles/doubles from Nkr695/890. This agreeable place is the town's business standard hotel.

Places to Eat

In addition to the restaurants at the Quality and Rica hotels, Hammerfest boasts the following eating options.

Odd's Mat & Vinhus (☎ 78 41 37 66, Strandgata 24) Mains Nkr190-325. Although rather expensive this restaurant is Hammerfest's gourmet option for meat and seafood.

Hårek Grillkjøkken (☎ 78 41 15 50, Strandgata 43) Mains Nkr36-120. This favourite grill serves considerably more pedestrian fast fare.

Dinner (☎ 78 41 38 78, Strandgata 22) Mains Nkr123-185. Hammerfest's Chinese restaurant has nice black bean sauce and well-priced *dagens* (daily specials).

Shanty (☎ 78 41 49 00, Storgata 27) Pizzas Nkr105-180. Come here for 'za, beer, billiards and a nightclub on Friday and Saturday.

Turistua (☎ 78 42 96 00, Salen) Lunch buffet Nkfr150. From atop Salen hill, Turistua offers great views over the town and an upscale lunch buffet. The off-putting name is actually for a lady named Turi, although 'turist' buses often stop here too.

The nicest place to pick up snacks is *H Sandberg bakery* (☎ 78 41 18 08, Strandgata 19). There's also a *Domus supermarket (Strandgata 14/18)*, east of the town hall with an inexpensive cafeteria, and a *Rimi supermarket (Strandgata 55)* for groceries.

Getting There & Away

Once or twice daily (four days weekly from mid-August to late June), buses run between Hammerfest and Alta (Nkr170, 2¾ hours). There's also a bus between Hammerfest and Kirkenes (Nkr682, 10 hours), via Karasjok (Nkr283, 4¾ hours) and Tana Bru (Nkr506, 6¼ hours).

The Hurtigruten coastal steamer also stops in Hammerfest for approximately two hours in either direction.

Getting Around

The Intersport shop at Strandgata 16 rents bicycles for Nkr50 per day.

NORDKAPP & MAGERØYA
pop 3517

What the Eiffel Tower is to Paris, Nordkapp is to northern Norway – the one attraction everyone seems to visit even if it is a tourist trap. Nordkapp bills itself as the northernmost point in continental Europe, and most of its island, Magerøya, seems devoted to funneling visitors there by the busload, some 200,000 each summer.

AROUND NORDKAPP

The reason is that Nordkapp sits at 71° 10' 21"N latitude, where the sun never drops below the horizon from mid-May to the end of July, and the steep cliffs and stark scenery emanate a bleak, ethereal Arctic ambience. Indeed, long before other Europeans took an interest, Nordkapp was considered a power centre and sacrifice site by the Sami people. It was named North Cape by Richard Chancellor, the English explorer who drifted here in 1553 in search of the North-East Passage, and after a much-publicised visit by King Oscar II in 1873, Nordkapp became a pilgrimage spot for Norwegians. It's also a pilgrimage for Thais, of all people, thanks to a visit by King Chulalongkorn in 1907. Today this spot is marked by Nordkapphallen, a hulking (and royally expensive) tourist centre.

Despite the fracas, Magerøya also offers some genuine treasures, but here's a secret: Nordkapp is not continental Europe's northernmost point. That award belongs to Kniv-skjelodden, a hike away, though its inaccessability by vehicle makes it clear why that fact is glossed over.

Orientation and Information

Heading clockwise around Magerøya from Nordkapp, you'll find the villages of Skarsvåg, Kamøyvær, Skipsfjord and Honningsvåg on the east coast and Gjesvær on the west, with Knivskjelodden crowning the north. There are no lodgings at Nordkapp – most are in Honningsvåg (pop 2900), the island's largest settlement.

The major tourist office is Nordkapp Reiseliv in Honningsvåg (☎ 78 47 25 99; fax 78 47 35 43; ⓔ info@northcape.no, ⓦ www.northcape.no), next to the bus station. Staff at Nordkapphallen's front desk also provide information.

Things to See & Do

Nordkapphallen Atop Nordkapp, Nord-kapphallen (☎ 78 47 68 60, fax 78 47 68 61; *adult/child/family Nkr175/50/375; open 9am-2am daily mid-June–early Aug, noon-midnight rest of Aug, noon-5pm early April-5 Oct, by appointment rest of year*) is a love/hate kind of place. It houses small exhibits about the region and its nature and history, a cafeteria, a restaurant, the striking Grotten bar, a one-room Thai museum, the trippy St Johannes chapel, a post office (for the all-important Nordkapp postmark) and souvenir shop. A five-screen, 180° theatre runs a panoramic film that's pretty, if a bit repetitious.

Mostly, though, you should go for the view, which is quite thrilling, from the cliffs. In fair weather, perched on the edge of the continent, you can gaze down at the wild surf 307m below, watch the mist roll in, pay tribute to Kinvskjelodden on a tiny spit to your left, and perhaps even dream of Svalbard, far to the north.

If you find the admission fee extortionate, rest assured that many Norwegians feel the same. It is *generously* waived if you hike from elsewhere on the island (though not from the makeshift car park 2km away – Nordkapphallen staff are said to be able to see you).

Knivskjelodden The continent's real northernmost point, Knivskjelodden, is inaccessible to vehicles, but you can hike to its lovely promontory from a marked car park about 9km south of Nordkapp. Though the 9km track is generally not difficult, it has some some ups and downs, and the lower trail is recommended toward the end, as are hiking boots – it can be mucky after precipitation. When you get to 71° 11' 08'N latitude, you can sign a guest book. The journey takes about five hours return.

Nordkapp Museum Honningsvåg's museum (☎ 78 47 28 33, Fergeveien 4, Honningsvåg; admission Nkr25; open 11am-8pm Mon-Sat, noon-8pm Sun 15 June-15 Aug) upstairs from the tourist office, concentrates on Arctic fishing culture. Many find the exhibits here superior to Nordkapphallen's, with infinitely less fray.

Honningsvåg Kirke There's also Honningsvåg's 19th-century church (☎ 78 47 68 50, Kirkegata; admission free; open 8am-10pm June-early Sept), one of just a few local structures to survive the Nazis' scorched-earth retreat in 1944.

Organised Tours Nordkapp Reiseliv tourist office can organise Fuglesafari boat tours (adult/child 12-15/child under 12 Nkr300/200/free) to the fabulous offshore **bird colony** on the island of Gjesværstappan, off the remote fishing village of Gjesvær, where you can observe seabirds including puffins, guillemots, kittiwakes, skuas, razorbills, cormorants and gannets, as well as seals on the cliffs. Simple hut accommodation is available at the Gjesvær Turistsenter (☎ 78 47 57 73, fax 78 47 57 07) for Nkr300 to Nkr600; it's open from 5pm daily.

A new tour lets you take a boat to relive the climb King Oscar and entourage made – on all fours! – to Nordkapp from the sea. Board the M/S *Thor Arild* from Skarsvåg at 11am and you'll be at the top around 2pm, with champagne and caviar waiting. The climb is not long but very steep; until 1956, this was the only way to get here (Nkr575, from June to August, book through tourist offices).

You can defy the snow-closed roads, on Magerøya in winter, with a journey by snow vehicle (contact the tourist office).

Places to Stay
Nordkapp Camping & Vandrerhjem (☎ 78 47 33 77, fax 78 47 11 77, E69, Skipsfjord) Tent/caravan sites Nk60/80, dorm beds Nkr175, doubles Nkr500, cabins from Nkr480; bungalows from Nkr840. Open 10 May-20 Sept. The stark location of this place, north of Skipsfjord, belies friendly service and a variety of lodging options.

Kirkeporten Camping (☎ 78 47 52 33, fax 78 47 52 47, Storvannaveien, Skarsvåg) Tent sites Nkr80, plus Nkr20 per person; cabins Nkr360-900. The sign out front claims 'world's northernmost' (northernmost what, it doesn't say). In fact, there are camping grounds much farther north on Svalbard, although Kirkeporten can still legitimately claim the world's northernmost camping cabins – there's quite a range of them.

Havstua (☎ 78 47 51 50, fax 78 47 51 91, e havstua@havstua.no, Kamøyvær) Singles/doubles Nkr430/650. In a former fishermen's cottage are five small rooms on the dock; the waves beneath lull you to sleep. There are no phones and no TVs. Bliss. If full, they'll rent out other rooms in the village, and there's a well-regarded Arctic restaurant.

Honningsvåg Brygge (☎ 78 47 64 64, fax 78 47 64 65, e mail@hvg.brygge.no, Vågen 1a, Honningsvåg) At this romantic former fishing warehouse, rooms (and prices) were being renovated as of this writing, but you can't beat the views of this pier location.

Rica Hotel Honningsvåg (☎ 78 47 23 33, fax 78 47 33 70, e rica.hotel.honningsvaag@rica.no, Storgata 4, Honningsvåg) Singles/doubles Nkr1095/1175. Just up the hill from the Honningsvåg tourist office, this place has a nice restaurant and a sauna.

Places to Eat
There are few dining options at Nordkapphallen; in Honningsvåg you'll find the following:

Corner (☎ 78 47 63 40, Fiskerveien 1) Mains Nkr99-160. This Arctic restaurant features a cafe, serves seafood, pizza, and has a bar and weekend disco.

Sjøhuset *(☎ 78 47 36 16, Vågen 1)* Mains Nkr164-225. On the pier is the town's most elegant establishment, with huge portions of fish and meat. It's open for dinner only.

Honningsvåg has two supermarkets: the **Rema 1000**, on the road from the ferry terminal, and the cheaper and more convenient **Rimi**.

Entertainment

Bryggerie' *(☎ 78 47 26 00, Nordkappgate 1, Honningsvåg)*. The Mack Brewery in Tromsø has been supplanted as the world's northernmost by Honningsvåg's microbrewery. A favourite brew is called 'Sårry Makk', as in 'Sorry, Mack, but actually *we're* further north.'

Nøden Pub *(☎ 78 47 27 11, Larsjorda 1, Honningsvåg)* This very Irish (and very smoky) local favourite is near the Rica hotel and has live music.

During the midnight sun, the **Grotten Bar** at Nordkapphallen is a happening place.

Getting There & Away

Although Honningsvåg airport lies only about 3km from town, there are no public bus connections.

The road approach from the E6 is via Olderfjord, where it connects with the E69. The toll for the long Nordkapptunnelen is Nkr130/450 per car and driver of four-wheeled vehicles under/over 6m. Adult/child passengers cost Nkr42/21.

The Hurtigruten coastal steamer stops at Honningsvåg. The 3¾-hour northbound stop allows a quick buzz up to Nordkapp, and the Hurtigruten offers passengers a tour (Nkr490).

From early June to mid-August a daily express bus connects Alta with Honningsvåg (Nkr241, 4½ hours) and Nordkapp (Nkr271, 5¾ hours). There's also a service between Hammerfest and Honningsvåg (Nkr230, 3¾ hours) a few times a week.

Nor-Way Bussekspress has service from Tromsø to Honningsvåg (Nkr608, 12¾ hours) and Nordkapp (Nkr641, 13 hours). Students, seniors, children and InterRail and

ScanRail pass holders receive a 50% discount. Note that passengers for Nordkapp must pay the Nkr175 admission fee, plus the tunnel passenger toll.

From mid-May to the end of August, local buses run daily at 12.15pm and 9pm between Honningsvåg and Nordkapp (one hour, Nkr66), with an additional service at 8.20pm between 2 June and 16 August and another at 10.55pm between 2 June and 9 August (when the last bus departs Nordkapp at 1.10am, allowing views of the midnight sun). If you're on a budget, avoid any ostensible 'tours', that charge considerably more for similar services.

Avis in Honningsvåg (☎ 78 47 62 62) has a special five-hour deal on car hire for Nkr725, including petrol and insurance. If that seems a bit steep, you've never hired a car or bought petrol in Norway! Taxi excursions from Honningsvåg cost Nkr850 with one hour at Nordkapp (admission extra).

If you're driving, the asphalted road to Nordkapp winds across a rocky plateau, past herds of grazing reindeer. Depending on snow conditions, it's open from April to mid-October, though it may be open only to a daily convoy in the fringe months. For current information, contact the National Road User Information Centre (☎ 175).

LAKSELV
pop 2250

The small, plain fishing village of Lakselv lies at the head of the great Porsangerfjord and is a hub for this part of Finnmark. The name means 'Salmon Stream', which reflects its main appeal to most Norwegian holiday-makers.

It has the usual stopover amenities: banks, restaurants, supermarkets, lodging and petrol. For information on the region, contact the Porsanger Arrangement tourist office (☎ 78 46 07 00, fax 78 46 07 01; **e** info@porsanger-arrangement.no), Lakselv kurssenter, Kirkeveien 26.

Bio Nordkapp

Lakselv claims to be the site of the world's northernmost winery, Bio Nordkapp *(☎ 78 46 27 20, fax 78 46 27 22, Meieriveien 11)*, which produces its own special vintages from wild Arctic berries. The winery can be toured by appointment, or you can buy the wines at the Vinmonopolet at the Torgsenteret shopping centre (☎ 78 46 35 92).

Stabbursnes Naturreservat

The Stabbursnes Nature Reserve occupies an expanse of wetlands and mudflats north of Lakselv on the Porsangerfjord's western shore. It's especially popular with birdwatchers who come to observe many species of ducks, geese, divers and sandpipers that rest in the area while migrating between the Arctic and more temperate zones. Watch for the lesser white-fronted goose, the bar-tailed godwit, the knot and the dunlin. Coastal marshes are closed to visitors during nesting season (May and June).

For the latest information, stop by the museum and visitors centre (☎ 78 46 47 65, E6; adult/concession Nkr30/25; open 9am-8pm daily mid-June–early Aug, 10am-5pm other times 1 June-31 Aug). It sells field guides and topographic maps, and the museum houses Sami exhibits and a slide show.

Stabbursdalen Nasjonalpark

Compact (98 sq km) and undervisited, Stabbursdalen National Park offers a spectacular glacial canyon and excellent hiking in the world's most northerly pine forest. Hikers are accommodated in two mountain huts, Rurkulphytta and Ivarstua, as well as a Gamma turf shelter.

Unfortunately, since the bridge over the river Stabburselva was destroyed in a flood, hikers no longer have the option of making a loop and must return the way they came. The northern track, which passes all the huts but actually lies outside the park, departs from near the Stabbursnes visitors centre. The shorter but more diverse southern track begins at the car park about 7km west of the E6. Either trail offers opportunities to venture well off the touristed track. Use the topographic maps Statens Kartverk's sheet 1935II and 2035III, in the 1:50,000 series.

From Lakselv, take the Honningsvåg bus (No 305, several days a week), and request a stop (Nkr26, 20 minutes).

Places to Stay & Eat

Solstad Pensjonat og Camping (☎ 78 46 14 04, fax 78 46 12 14, E6, Brennelv) Tent or caravan sites Nkr85, basic huts Nkr200-300, self-catering cabins from Nkr400. This convenient camping ground lies just 2km west of town.

Stabbursdalen Camp & Fritidspark (☎ 78 46 47 60, fax 78 46 47 62, e info@stabbursdalen.no, by E6) 3-person/4-person cabins Nkr410/610. Across from the nature reserve's visitors centre are these well-equipped cabins.

Porsanger Vertshus (☎ 78 46 13 77, fax 78 46 13 95, E6) Singles/doubles from Nkr695/895. This place looks institutional, but its attached **Åstedet Café & Bistro** (☎ 78 46 54 15), the town's most popular eatery, with burgers, full meals and pizzas for Nkr39 to Nkr199. There's a pub and dancing on weekends.

Lorry's (☎ 78 46 27 77, Meieriveien 1a) Dishes Nkr43-190. This roadhouse has decent snacks and grills.

Best Western Lakselv Hotell (☎ 78 46 54 00, fax 78 46 54 01, e hotell@lakselvhotellene.no, Karasjokveien) Singles/doubles from Nkr630/750. Lakselv's high-end alternative has cosy rooms, hilltop fjord views, sauna, fitness and an Arctic menu restaurant.

Bungalåven Vertshus (☎/fax 78 46 48 01, Børselv) Singles/doubles Nkr250/450, less without linen. North-east out of town toward the Nordkyn Peninsula, this lovely converted farmhouse is some 40km up the Rv98. Breakfast, with local salmon, costs Nkr75.

Getting There & Away

Lakselv's North Cape Airport is an important link for central Finnmark, served by SAS from Oslo and Tromsø, and Finnair (in summer only) from Helsinki and Rovaniemi.

Lakselv also lies on the bus route between Kirkenes (Nkr506, 7¼ hours) and Hammerfest (Nkr188, 3¼ hours). Also in summer, buses run to and from Karasjok (Nkr101, 1½ hours) and Honningsvåg (Nkr218, four hours). Buses between Nordkapp and Inari (Finland) pass two to four times daily in summer.

Eastern Finnmark

Though relatively little visited, Eastern Finnmark has a distinctly coastal feel, some charming villages and unique history including Finns, witches, explorers and Nazis. It's also the centre of the Eastern Sami culture.

NORDKYN PENINSULA
pop 2751

The church-shaped rock formation known as the **Finnkirke** marks the entrance to the village of Kjøllefjord and provides a majestic introduction to this remote corner of Finnmark, a treasure trove for collectors of 'northernmosts'.

Across the peninsula, the tiny coastal village of Gamvik (reached via a nastily potholed road on our visit), claims the world's northernmost museum, the **Latitude 71 Museum** (☎ 78 49 79 49, Strandveien 63, Gamvik; adult/concession Nkr50/25; open 9am-5pm daily mid-June–mid-Aug, by appointment rest of year), revealing the fishing cultures of these far-flung environs. Nearby, a birdwatchers' trail runs through the **Slettnes Naturreservat**, frequented by nesting and migrating ducks and wading birds (accessible only on foot or by private vehicle), and **Slettnes Fyr** is the world's northernmost mainland lighthouse.

In the centre are **Kinnarodden**, the northernmost point of mainland Europe (Knivskjelodden, near Nordkapp, is on an island) and the town of Mehamn, unremarkable except as the site of one of Norway's earliest environmental movements. In 1903, troops were brought in to subdue local fishermen, who protested that whaling was exterminating the whales which had historically made fishing easy by driving cod towards the shore.

Gamvik Gjestehus (☎ 78 49 62 12, fax 78 49 62 10, e gamvikgjesthus@gul.no, Strandveien 22, Gamvik) Singles/doubles Nkr450/550. This fishermen's cabin, preserved in its post-war state (no private bath), has a good, no-frills restaurant.

Hotel Nordkyn (☎ 78 49 81 51, fax 78 49 80 51, Strandveien, Kjøllefjord) Singles/doubles Nkr650/850. This modest hotel has sweeping views of the Y-shaped Kjøllefjord and a popular pub/restaurant.

Nordtrafikk buses connect Mehamn with Lakselv (Nkr291, 4½ hours), Gamvik (Nkr38, 30 minutes) and Kjølleford (Nkr48, 40 minutes). Kjøllefjord and Mehamn are also brief stops on the Hurtigruten coastal steamer.

BERLEVÅG
pop 1236

This pint-sized fishing village has produced one big thing, the **Berlevåg Mannsangforening**, a men's chorus that was the subject of Knut Erik Jensen's 2001 documentary Heftig og Begeistret (Cool and Crazy). The film caused a national sensation and was hailed at the Edinburgh Fringe Festival as Norway's Buena Vista Social Club. You're likely to see their CDs for sale all over the north; one cover features the bright-eyed older fellows in their trademark fishermen's caps, gazing hopefully skyward.

In town there's a **Havnemuseum** (Harbour Museum; ☎ 78 98 08 97, Havnegate; adult/concession Nkr25/10; open 10am-6pm Mon-Fri & 1pm-6pm Sat & Sun mid-June–mid-Aug, noon-3pm Mon-Fri rest of year) that contains the usual maritime displays, as well as an unusual old expedition dory, the Berlevåg II. About 12km away is a **Sami sacrificial site** atop the 269m Tanahorn, with a wonderful view over the Arctic Ocean. The 8km return walk begins 8km west of town, along the gravel road towards the equally interesting abandoned fishing village of Store Malvik (20km west of Berlevåg).

Accommodation options include:

Berlevåg Camping & Appartement (☎ 78 98 16 10, fax 78 98 08 11, Havnegate 8) Tent or caravan sites Nkr80 plus Nkr10/person, singles/doubles Nkr335/400. This friendly, well-kept complex also houses the tourist office.

Ishavshotelle (☎ 78 98 14 15, fax 78 98 16 63, Storgata 30) Singles/doubles from Nkr500/675. This unassuming place across town has a variety of rooms in two buildings, both old and new(ish).

Buses run from Tana Bru (Nkr177, 2½ hours) and Båtsfjord (Nkr120, two hours) at

THE FAR NORTH

least once daily, except Saturday. Berlevåg is also a stop on the Hurtigruten coastal steamer route.

BÅTSFJORD
pop 1434

If Berlevåg is rustic, its neighbour Båtsfjord, the largest fishing port in the Nordic countries, is dreary and industrial, although some sights to the south are worth a look. You'll find the tourist office (☎ 78 98 44 96, W www.baatsfjordnett.no), Hindberggate 15, across from the police station.

Båtsfjord Kirke

The main site in town is the church (1971; ☎ 78 98 33 33, Prestegårdsbakken; admission free; open daily summer). Its exterior is less than inspiring, but it contrasts sharply with 85 wonderful square metres of stained glass, visible from inside.

Makkaur

A 25km hike eastward along the fjord's southern shore leads to Makkaur, an **abandoned fishing village** that dates from medieval times and escaped bombing during WWII. There's all sorts of interesting junk left over, including a German POW camp from WWII. The only remaining resident is the attendant at the 1928 lighthouse.

The 113-sq-km **Makkaurhalvøya Naturreservat** immediately to the east was established in 1983 to protect the 4km-long and 200m-high Syltefjordstauren bird cliffs. In summer, it attracts around 250 breeding pairs of gannets, as well as sea eagles, cormorants, razorbills, puffins, both common and Brunnichs guillemots, and 150,000 breeding pairs of kittiwakes. Boat tours can be arranged through the Båtsfjord tourist office.

Places to Stay

Havly Fiskarheim (☎ 78 98 42 05, fax 78 98 34 81, Havnegata 31) Singles/doubles Nkr400/600. Båtsfjord's cheapest accommodation is the scruffy seamen's mission, with an attached cafeteria.

Quality Hotel Båtsfjord (☎ 78 98 31 00, fax 78 98 39 18, Valen 2) Singles/doubles

Nkr1045/1295. Though it was kind of down-at-the-heels during our visit, this large hotel is being renovated, and there's a popular restaurant.

Getting There & Away

The airport, 5km from town, is served by Widerøe from Alta and Kirkenes. These novel flights offer excellent views of the Arctic landscapes, complete with grazing reindeer.

Buses connect Båtsfjord with Berlevåg (Nkr120, two hours) and Tana Bru (Nkr143, two hours). Båtsfjord is also a stop on the Hurtigruten coastal steamer.

TANA BRU
pop 3074

Tiny Tana Bru is named for the picturesque bridge on the great Tana River, and no wonder. This is one of Europe's best salmon streams, and anglers use the odd technique of constructing barrages to obstruct the upstream progress of the fish. In fact, the natural barrage at Storfossen falls, about 30km upstream, is one of the finest fishing spots around.

Comfort Hotel Tana (☎ 78 92 81 98, fax 78 92 80 05, e admin@tana-turisthotell .no, Tana Bru) Tent/caravan sites Nkr75/100, singles/doubles from Nkr795/990. You'll find camping, comfortable rooms, a restaurant and bar *and* the tourist office here.

Polmakmoen Gjestegård (☎ 78 92 89 90, fax 78 92 84 59, e kutsi@online.no, Polmak) Singles/doubles Nkr350/400. Stay in Sami-style *gamma* (turf huts) or guesthouse rooms 20km upstream. Riverboat cruises are also conducted (Nkr75, 1½ hours).

The Nor-Way Bussekspress bus between Hammerfest (Nkr506, 7¼ hours) and Kirkenes (Nkr184, 2¼ hours) crosses the bridge at Tana Bru, and local buses run to and from Berlevåg (Nkr177, 2½ hours) and Båtsfjord (Nkr143, two hours) and to and from Vadsø (Nkr98, 1¼ hours).

If you're travelling towards Båtsfjord or Berlavåg, note the spectacular and colourful folded sedimentary layers in the Gamasfjellet cliffs, along the eastern shore of Tanafjord.

VADSØ
pop 5080

The administrative centre of Finnmark, Vadsø was the site of large-scale immigration from Finland and during the 1830s and 1840s; the town's population was 50% Kvæn (as the Finnish were known). In the centre, a 1977 monument honours this cultural heritage. Vadsø is perhaps best known to Norwegians as a site for polar exploration, several expeditions having started or ended here, including some that ended in disaster.

The cemetery on Vadsø island, a couple hundred metres by bridge from the mainland, also provides evidence of the Pomors, Russian traders and fishers from the White Sea area, who prospered here in the 17th century. There are numerous ruins of protected prehistoric turf huts. If visiting in early summer, watch for the rare Stellar's duck, which nests here. For tourist information, contact the tourist office (☎ 78 95 44 90, fax 78 94 28 99, [e] museum@vadso.kommune.no).

Things to See
The **Vadsø Museum** (*☎ 78 94 28 90; single/ combined admission Nkr20/30; open 10am- 6pm Mon-Fri, 10am-4pm Sat & Sun late June-late Aug, shorter hours rest of year*) is in three sections. The **Tuomainen-Gården** (Tuomainen estate, Slettengate 21), is a Finnish farmhouse dating from the 1840s, with the bakery and sauna still in use. It houses the tourist office in summer. **Ebensengården** (Ebensen estate, Hvistendals), a merchant house, dates from the 1850s. Part 3, the **Kjeldsen fish plant** at Ekkerøy, 15km east of town, has been painstakingly restored and has a summer cafe (open noon to 6pm Tuesday to Sunday, late June to late August).

On Vadsø island, the oil-rig shaped **Luftskipsmasta** (airship mast) was built in the mid-1920s as an anchor and launch site for airborne expeditions to the polar regions. The expedition of Roald Amundsen, Umberto Nobile and Lincoln Ellsworth, which flew via the North Pole to Alaska in the airship *Norge N-1,* first used it in April 1926. In 1928, it was used to launch Nobile's airship, *Italia,* which attempted to repeat the journey but crashed on Spitsbergen. Amundsen joined the rescue expedition and disappeared in the attempt, becoming a martyr as well as a hero. The tower is about 800 metres from the main road, and a free exhibit about it opens in summer across from the Hurtigruten pier when the ship is in port, or by request.

Vadsø's **church** (*☎ 78 95 13 96, Amtmannsgate 1B; open 9am-2pm Mon-Fri in summer*) is surely one of the most bizarre in Norway. It was built in 1958 to replace the 1861 church destroyed during WWII (and two earlier ones, constructed in 1575 and 1710). Architect Magnus Poulsson intended to recall an iceberg floating in the Arctic Ocean, but it's more reminiscent of a Jesuit mission in South America. For the Orthodox-inspired altarpiece, artist Gretha Thiis created a sort of unisex Christ figure, and Ragna Thiis Helland's stained glass work depicts the divinity of water and the seasons.

Places to Stay & Eat
Vestre Jakobselv (*☎ 78 95 60 64, fax 78 95 38 56, Lilledalsveien*) 4-bed/6-bed cabins Nkr260/300. This is the nearest camping ground, 17km west of town.

Vadsø Appartments (*78 95 44 00, Tilbergveien 3*) Singles/doubles Nkr350/450. This mid-range choice, with kitchens, is three blocks from the harbour.

Lailas Hotell (*☎ 78 95 33 35, fax 78 95 34 35, [e] epost@lailas.no, Brugata 2, Vadsøya island*) Singles/doubles from Nkr595/695. This simple place is near fishing and nature walks.

Rica Hotel Vadsø (*☎ 78 95 16 81, fax 78 95 10 02, Oscars gate 4*) Singles/doubles from Nkr675/840. Right in the centre, the Rica has nicely renovated rooms and a bar downstairs.

Boden Pub (*☎ 78 95 33 00, Havnegata 17*) is a busy and often smoky pub with pizzas from Nkr140 to Nkr195. **Xin Ya** (*☎ 78 95 43 18, Strandgata 12*) proves that Chinese food is everywhere (mains Nkr80 to Nkr230).

Getting There & Away
Vadsø is a stop on the northbound Hurtigruten coastal steamer. You can also get

Fridtjof Nansen

Anyone seeking a modern hero need look no further than Fridtjof Nansen (1861–1930), the Norwegian explorer-turned-diplomat who pushed the frontiers of human endurance and human compassion.

Nansen grew up in rural Store Frøen outside Oslo and enjoyed a privileged childhood. He was an excellent athlete, winning a dozen national Nordic skiing championships and breaking the world record for the one-mile skating course. Studies in zoology at the University of Christiania led to a voyage aboard the sealing ship *Viking* to study ocean currents, ice movements and wildlife. Here he saw tantalising glimpses of Greenland, planting the dream of journeying across the central icecap there.

That dream came true in 1888, when Nansen led a six-man expedition. Despite his young age (27), the expedition went without mishap, and Nansen stayed in Greenland through the winter, observing the Inuit peoples for his 1891 book, *Eskimo Life.*

MH

In June 1893, aboard the 400-tonne, three-layer-oak-hulled and steel-reinforced ship *Fram,* Nansen's next expedition left Christiania for the Arctic with provisions for six years. Nansen left behind his wife Eva and six-month old daughter Liv, with no idea when he'd return.

On 14 March 1895, he and Hjalmar Johansen disembarked the *Fram* for the North Pole, journeying five months and 550km on foot over the ice before holing up for nine winter months in a tiny stone hut they'd built on an island. On heading south, they encountered British explorer Frederick Jackson (for whom Nansen later named the island where they'd spent the winter), and, having given up on reaching the Pole, the three headed back to Vardø, just a week before *Fram* arrived in Skjervøy.

In 1905, a political crisis arose from Norway's bid for independence from Sweden, and Nansen, by then a national hero, was dispatched to Copenhagen and Britain to represent the Norwegian cause.

Upon independence, Nansen was offered the job of prime minister but declined in order to pursue science, exploration and an expedition to the South Pole (he's also rumoured to have turned down offers to be king or president). He did, however, accept King Håkon's offer to serve as ambassador to Britain. In 1907, after the sudden death of his wife, he permitted fellow Norwegian explorer Roald Amundsen to use the *Fram* on an expedition north of Siberia, abandoning his own South Pole dreams.

After WWI, Nansen took on large-scale humanitarian efforts: the new League of Nations; repatriating a half-million German soldiers imprisoned in the Soviet Union; and an International Red Cross program against famine and pestilence in Russia. When some two million Russians and Ukrainians became stateless after fleeing the 1917 Bolshevik revolution, 'Nansen Passports' enabled thousands of them to settle elsewhere.

Probably Nansen's greatest diplomatic achievement, however, was the resettlement of several hundred thousand Greeks and Turks who had been displaced after Turkey defeated the Greek army in 1922.

In 1922 he was awarded the Nobel Peace Prize and donated his prize money to international relief efforts. After 1925, he concentrated on disarmament and lobbying for a non-Soviet homeland for Armenian refugees. Although this project failed, he is still revered among Armenians worldwide.

On 13 May 1930, Nansen died quietly at his home in Polhøgda, near Oslo, and was buried in a garden nearby.

To learn more about this extraordinary man, look for the biography *Nansen*, by Roland Huntford, published in the UK in 1997, or EE Reynolds' book of the same title, first published in 1932.

there by bus from Tana Bru (Nkr98, 1¼ hours) or Vardø (Nkr105, 1½ hours).

VARDØ
pop 2458

Best known for its fortress and a period of witch-burning, Vardø is Norway's eastern-most town. Although this butterfly-shaped island is connected to the mainland by the 2.9km-long Ishavstunnelen (Arctic Ocean tunnel), locals are fond of pointing out that theirs is the only 'mainland' Norwegian town lying within the Arctic climatic zone (average temperature is below 10°C). Once a stronghold of trade with the Russian Pomors, it's now a major fishing port and is home to many Russian and Sri Lankan immigrants.

The Hexeria tourist office (☎ 78 98 84 04, fax 78 98 84 05, e hexeria@vardo.on-line.no), Kaigata 6, opens 10am to 7pm Monday to Saturday and noon to 6pm Sunday, May to September (otherwise 10am to 4pm weekdays). In summer, it organises short cruises to see the teeming bird cliffs on the island of Hornøya, Norway's eastern-most point, which has a picturesque lighthouse.

Things to See

The star-shaped **Vardøhus Festning** *(fortress; ☎ 78 18 85 02; Festningsgate 20; admission Nkr20; open 8am-9pm mid-Apr–mid-Sept, 10am-6pm rest of year)* – yes, it's the world's most northerly – was constructed in 1737 by King Christian VI. For a fortress, it's painted in rather fairytale colours, and on a nice day it's pleasant to stroll around its intimate, flower-covered bastions, past turf-roofed buildings and Russian cannons (which were captured by the Germans during WWII). The admission fee can be paid either at the guard office or by dropping it into the sinister-looking WWII-era sea mine that guards the entrance.

Between 1621 and 1692, 80 Vardø citizens were accused of witchcraft and burned to death; a sign and flag at Kristian IV gate 24 commemorate the site. On the 156m hill, **Domen**, about 2km south of town on the mainland, is the cave where they were supposed to have held their 'satanic' rites.

In the centre, the **Pomor Museum** *(☎ 78 98 80 25, Per Larssens gate 32; admission Nkr20; open 8am-6pm Mon-Fri, 11am-6pm Sat & Sun 15 June-15 Aug)* recaps the historic trade between Russia and Norway, which lasted until the Bolshevik Revolution in 1917. It also features the region's natural history, as well as the expeditions of Fridtjof Nansen and William Barents.

If you drop in to the 1958 **Vardø Kirke** *(☎ 78 98 70 92, Kirkegaten; admission free; open 10am-1pm & when the southbound Hurtigruten coastal steamer is in port)*, a very earnest guide may show you around.

In case you were wondering, those spheres on Vardø's hilltops contain air-traffic control and military radar.

Places to Stay & Eat

Svartnes Camping *(☎ 78 98 71 60, Svartnes)* Tent sites Nkr80, rooms from Nkr160 per person. The only budget option, is drab, unfriendly, on the mainland, and not recommended in good faith. Those with tents would probably be happier finding their own spot in the hills or along the beach.

Gjestegården *(☎ 78 98 75 29, Strandgata 72)* Singles/doubles Nkr250/300. Though cheap, this place is small, sleepy and a little run-down.

Vardø Hotell *(☎ 78 98 77 61, fax 78 98 83 97, Kaigata 8)* Singles/doubles Nkr450/550. This strictly functional place has institutional rooms, though it does overlook the harbour.

The student dorm rooms rented by the Hexeria tourist office (singles/doubles Nkr275/450) are a better bet.

Nauset *(☎ 78 98 74 74, Strandgata 8)* feels like a sports bar and has sandwiches and light meals (Nkr35 to Nkr110). The historic, wood-panelled **Nordpol Kro** *(☎ 78 98 75 01, Kaigata 21)* serves pizzas for Nkr49 to Nkr162.

Getting There & Away

Vardø is a stop on the Hurtigruten coastal steamer route, but otherwise, it's well off the beaten track for all but the most die-hard travellers. Most days buses do the scenic seaside run between Vadsø and Vardø (Nkr105, 1½ hours).

HAMNINGBERG

Tiny and utterly charming, the mostly abandoned, timber-built settlement of Hamningberg may seem like the end of the world, but locals maintain it's where Norway begins! The narrow and occasionally vertiginous road from Vardø is lined with some of the most fascinating geology in northern Norway: lichen-covered forests of eroded stone pillars, the remnants of sedimentary layers turned on end. If the lunar terrain looks familiar, you may have seen it in the James Bond film *Moonraker*.

The town's only lodging is above the only store, *Hardbakken Handel (mobile ☎ 90 86 76 83, Birger Dahlsgate 12)*, which has a few rooms with shared bath and kitchen for Nkr400.

During Vardø's Pomordagene (Pomor days) festival in early August, throngs of people set out to walk the scenic 37km from Vardø to Hamningberg, and those who make it are treated to a barbecue at the church. Visitors are welcome to join in. Otherwise, you need a private vehicle to get here.

SAMI MUSEUMS

Between Tana Bru and Vadsø are two Sami treasures, well worth visiting if you have your own transport.

At Varangerbotn, the excellent **Varjjat Sami Musea** *(Varangerbotn Sami Museum; ☎ 78 95 99 20, Varangerbotn; adult/child Nkr30/15; open 10am-6pm Mon-Fri & noon-6pm Sat & Sun mid-June–late Aug, 10am-3pm Mon-Fri late Aug–mid-June)* covers the history, religion and traditions of the coastal Sami, through a variety of media. A new installation features crafts by contemporary Sami artists.

On the E75, about 15km toward Vadsø, is an affiliated site: the **Ceavccageadge** *(fish oil stone: ☎ 78 95 99 20, Mortensnes; adult/child Nkr30/15; open noon-6pm daily mid-June–late Aug)*, where you can stroll amid remnants of 10,000 years of Sami culture. Some 8km of tracks wind up to the hills and down to the sea. At the west end, past burial sites, home ruins and a reconstructed turf hut, is the namesake ceavccageadge, a pillar standing near the water, which was

smeared with cod liver oil to ensure luck while fishing. On a hill east of the visitors centre is the Bjørnstein (bear rock), which resembles a bear and was revered by early Sami inhabitants. Tours (included in admission) run at 2pm, and there's a useful book for self-guiding (Nkr50).

See also the Savio Museum in Kirkenes.

KIRKENES
pop 3208

This is it: the end of the line for the Hurtigruten, but after the rest of coastal Finnmark, remote Kirkenes seems like the Big City. There's plenty of wartime history, and its rocky, forested surroundings are lush and welcoming, particularly the wild Pasvik River valley. It's also a popular starting point for trips into Arctic Russia, just over the border. Some tourist facilities and the camping ground are in the nearby village of Hesseng.

History

This district (Sør-Varanger) was jointly occupied by Norway and Russia until 1926, when the Russian, Finnish and Norwegian borders were set. In 1906, iron ore was discovered nearby, and Kirkenes became a major supplier of raw materials for artillery during WWI. Early in WWII, the Nazis recognised its resources and strategic position near the free Russian port of Murmansk, occupied the town and posted 100,000 troops there. As a result, Kirkenes was, after Malta, the second-most bombed place during WWII, with at least 320 devastating Soviet raids. Kirkenes was also an internment site for Norwegians from all over the country who did not cooperate with Nazi occupiers.

Kirkenes was liberated by Soviet troops in October 1944, and the retreating Nazis burned to the ground what was left. Although it was subsequently rebuilt (less than glamourously) and continued to supply iron ore to much of Europe, costs were too high to sustain the trade, and in 1996 the mines closed down.

Information
Tourist Office The helpful Grenseland Tourist Office (☎ 78 99 25 01, fax 78 99 25 25,

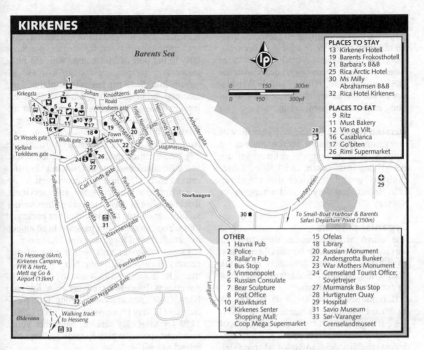

KIRKENES

Barents Sea

PLACES TO STAY
13 Kirkenes Hotell
19 Barents Frokosthotell
21 Barbara's B&B
25 Rica Arctic Hotel
30 Ms Milly
   Abrahamsen B&B
32 Rica Hotel Kirkenes

PLACES TO EAT
9 Ritz
11 Must Bakery
12 Vin og Vilt
16 Casablanca
17 Go'biten
26 Rimi Supermarket

OTHER
1 Havna Pub
2 Police
3 Rallar'n Pub
4 Bus Stop
5 Vinmonopolet
6 Russian Consulate
7 Bear Sculpture
8 Post Office
10 Pasvikturist
14 Kirkenes Senter
   Shopping Mall;
   Coop Mega Supermarket
15 Ofelas
18 Library
20 Russian Monument
22 Andersgrotta Bunker
23 War Mothers Monument
24 Grenseland Tourist Office;
   Sovjetrejser
27 Murmansk Bus Stop
28 Hurtigruten Quay
29 Hospital
31 Savio Museum
33 Sør-Varanger
   Grenselandmuseet

e grenseland@online.no), in the centre, is open from 8.30am to 6pm weekdays from 10 June to 21 August, and from 10am to 6pm on weekends. The rest of the year, it's open from 8.30am to 4pm weekdays only.

Dangers & Annoyances The Russian border is within several kilometres of Kirkenes, but don't even think about zipping across for a photo. Both Norwegian and Russian sentries are equipped with surveillance equipment, and the fine for illegal crossings, even momentary ones, starts at Nkr5000. Greeting people on the other side, tossing anything across, and using telephoto or zoom lenses all qualify as violations, and the policy states: 'any attempts at violations will be punished as if they had been carried out.'

Things to See & Do
Andersgrotta This dramatic **bunker** *(cnr Presteveien & Tellef Dahls gate; adult/child Nkr100/50; tours noon, 3pm, 6.15pm & 9pm*

daily mid-June to mid-Aug) was used as a shelter during over 1000 WWII air-raid alarms. A short video retells the tale. Take warm clothing – temperatures are consistently 1°C to 4°C! Up a short hill nearby, the **Russian Monument** is dedicated to the Red Army troops who liberated the town in 1944. You may also wish to note the **War Mothers Monument** in the centre, commemorating women's efforts for their children and homes during the war, and there's a friendly looking **bear sculpture** outside the Russian consulate.

Savio Museum The distinctive Sami-inspired woodblock prints of local artist John A Savio (1902–38) are on show at this museum *(☎ 78 99 92 12, Kongens gate 10B; admission Nkr30; open 10am-6pm daily 20 June-20 Aug)*. It's in a former library financed by teachers from all over Norway who were interned nearby for refusing to teach Nazi propaganda, in gratitude for sustenance received from local townspeople.

THE FAR NORTH

Sør-Varanger Grenselandmuseet About 1km from the centre, this well presented frontier museum (☎ 78 99 48 80, Førstevannslia; adult/concession/child Nkr30/15/ free; open 10am-6pm daily in summer), deals with the geography, culture, religion and WWII history of the border region. There are also rotating exhibits and Sami crafts.

Russian Market On the last Thursday of every month, Russian merchants set up shop around the town centre, selling everything from crafts and knitted tablecloths to binoculars. Prices aren't as cheap as in Russia, but they're still a bargain for Norway.

Organised Tours
The tourist office organises daily tours of the city and the Russian border (three hours, Nkr300) or to Grense Jakobselv or Pasvik (four hours, Nkr480). See later in this chapter for these destinations.

Barents Safari (☎ 90 19 05 94, fax 78 99 80 69, e hhatle@online.no, w www .barentssafari.no) runs a three-hour boat trip up the Pasvik River to the Russian border at the historic town of Boris Gleb (Borisoglebsk in Russian). The trip takes in the cave of Trifon the monk and includes a salmon meal in a Sami-style hut at the border, with historical commentary and nature watching along the way. There are daily departures at 3pm and 6pm (and 11.30am and 9pm on request) from Kirkenes' small-boat harbour; the cost is Nkr690 per person. In winter, similar excursions leave via reindeer sleigh or snowmobile.

If you've always dreamed of **diving** for giant crab in the Arctic Ocean, Arctic Dive (☎ 78 99 68 75, e lars.petter@arctic-dive .no, w www.arctic-dive.no) offers two dives with appropriate clothing, plus one night's accommodation in a seaside cabin, from Nkr750/day. Lars-Petter will cook your catch for free – the largest crab caught here was about 170cm across! He also offers deep-sea safari trips, in search of big waves (from Nkr450).

For adventures in the Pasvik wilderness, see the Pasvik River Valley section following.

Visiting Russia
Kirkenes' location and history make it a natural jumping-off point for Russia, particularly to the port of Murmansk, which is just exotic and inexpensive enough to make it worthwhile. *But* a trip needs to be planned in advance and in detail, or it can be expensive. It takes 12 days and an official invitation to process a visa to Russia, and without the invitation, do not expect any help from the Russian consulate in Kirkenes (☎ 78 99 37 37). Some nationalities may be issued visas at the Russian consulate in Oslo, but US citizens in particular shouldn't count on it.

Fortunately, Kirkenes has two services that specialise in Russia travel and handle invitations and visas for individuals or package tours. You can send your passport in advance by certified mail for processing and return.

Government-set visa fees are based on country of citizenship: from Nkr100 for Austrians, Icelanders and Japanese to Nkr550 for Americans. Processing fees are an additional Nkr450/400 per individual/group tour participant (12-day processing), up to Nkr1200/ 1150 for same-day service. Note that your visa must specify which Russian locales you intend to visit.

For a taste of industrial Russia, Sovjetrejser (☎ 78 99 25 01, fax 78 99 25 25, e polarscout@grenseland.no, Kongensgate 1–3), organises day/overnight trips to Nikel and Zapolyarny (Nkr780/1080 plus visa), including lunch and guide. Day/weekend trips to Murmansk cost from 1090/1290, plus visa, though at 4-plus hours each way, the day trip is a lot of driving. These tours require a minimum number of participants.

Pasvikturist (☎ 78 99 50 80, fax 78 99 50 57, e firmapost@pasvikturist.no, Dr Wessels gate 9), the other main player, specialises in adventure tours (eg, outdoor activities in the Pechenga wilderness at Nkr1500/day), a cultural history tour to Nikel, Zapolyarny and the German war cemetery at Pechenga (Nkr950) and trips to Murmansk. Visa charges are extra for non-Norwegian citizens.

Both of these offices have full service travel agencies that can also serve non-Russia needs.

Independent travellers can, with the proper visa, hop the public bus to Murmansk (Nkr350/700 one way/return, 4½ hours). It leaves Kirkenes at 2pm Monday to Friday (4pm Sunday) from the Rica Arctic Hotel and returns from the Hotel Polyarny Zory in Murmansk at 2pm and noon respectively. For further information on independent travel, see Lonely Planet's *Russia, Ukraine & Belarus*.

Places to Stay

Kirkenes Camping (☎ 78 99 80 28, fax 78 99 07 61, e ji-kla@online.no, Maggadala, Hesseng) Tent/caravan sites Nkr90/115, cabins Nkr320-600. Open early June-Aug. This kindly but slightly run-down camping ground 6km west of town is the only option for campers. The municipality has been talking about opening its own camping ground.

Kirkenes Hotell (☎/fax 78 99 88 11, Dr Wessels gate 3) Singles/doubles without sheets or towels Nkr300/400, with sheets & towels Nkr450/700. There's no hostel in the area, but this new place offers both hotel and hostel style accommodation.

Barbaras B&B (☎ 78 99 32 07, fax 78 99 30 96, e barbara@trollnet.no, Henrik Lunds gate 13) Singles/doubles (summer) Nkr300/500. There are two rooms, three friendly dogs, free Internet access, and loads of local info at Barbara's (she's also an avid motorcyclist).

Ms Milly Abrahamsen's B&B (☎ 78 99 12 48, Prestøyveien 28A) Singles/doubles Nkr250/400. Around the back of a house near the Hurtigruten pier are these three rooms and a small garden. Self-catering facilities are available.

Barents Frokosthotell (☎ 78 99 32 99, fax 78 99 30 96, e gcelius@frisurf.no, Presteveien 3) Singles/doubles without bath Nkr450/650, with bath Nkr590/700. There's warm, individual service here. Rooms with bath have been renovated.

Rica Arctic Hotel (☎ 78 99 29 29, fax 78 99 11 59, Kongensgate 1–3) Singles/doubles (summer) Nkr760/1275. This is Kirkenes' poshest lodging, with pool and sauna.

Rica Hotel Kirkenes (☎ 78 99 14 91, fax 78 99 13 56, Pasvikveien 63) Singles/doubles Nkr760/1275. This Rica feels a little older, but its location above town provides panoramic views from many rooms and the restaurant.

Places to Eat

Ritz (☎ 78 99 34 81, Dr Wessels gate 17) Mains Nkr59-203. Kirkenes' pizza place has an attached cafeteria, *Go'biten* (☎ 78 99 34 80). Friday dinner features an all-you-can-eat pizza buffet for Nkr78.

Casablanca (☎ 78 99 14 08, Dr Wessels gate 6) Mains Nkr89-175. The name's Moroccan, but dishes are from India, Mexico and Thailand.

Vin og Vilt (☎ 78 99 38 11; Dr Wessels gate 5) Mains Nkr170-360. This is your luxury option, decorated like an elegant hunting lodge and serving an Arctic menu including reindeer, grouse and fish.

The *Must Bakery* (Kirkegata 2) does breakfasts, coffees and light lunches. For self-catering, try the *Rimi* supermarket on the main square or *Coop Mega* supermarket in the Kirkenes Senter shopping mall. Near the camping ground, the *Mett og Go* cafeteria has a small food shop.

Entertainment

Ritz (☎ 78 99 34 81, Dr Wessels gate 17) This is Kirkenes' most popular hangout and has a disco and pub.

Ofelas Bar & Pub (☎ 78 99 21 68, Dr Wessels gate 3) This newly opened venue is popular for live bands.

Rallar'n (☎ 78 99 18 73, Solheimsveien 1) You can do a bit of self-entertaining with karaoke here.

Havna Pub (☎ 78 99 30 10, Johan Knudtzens gate 1) This sailors' hangout, overlooking the harbour, is a great place to play pool or darts.

Getting There & Away

SAS, Braathens and Widerøe fly into Kirkenes' airport, although savvy locals save a bundle flying in/out of Ivalo, Finland, some 250km away.

By land, buses serve Karasjok (Nkr414, five hours), Hammerfest (Nkr682, 10¼ hours) and Alta (Nkr719, 12¾ hours) and many points in between.

THE FAR NORTH

Kirkenes is the terminus of the Hurtigruten coastal steamer.

Getting Around

The airport is served by the Flybuss (25 minutes, Nkr50) which connects the hospital, bus terminal, two big hotels and Hesseng (12 minutes, Nkr23) with all arriving and departing flights. Buses run between the centre and Hesseng (15 minutes, Nkr16) every hour or two on weekdays, at least five times on Saturday and once on Sunday. There's also a pleasant walking route to Hesseng, which follows the lakeshore part of the way.

Car rental agencies include Hertz (☎ 78 99 39 73) and Avis (☎ 78 97 37 05), both in Hesseng.

PASVIK RIVER VALLEY

Even when diabolical mosquito swarms make life hell for warm-blooded creatures, the remote lakes, wet tundra bogs and Norway's largest stand of virgin taiga forest lend a strange appeal to odd little Øvre Pasvik National Park, in the far reaches of the Pasvik River valley. Some 100km from Kirkenes, this is the last corner of Norway where wolves, wolverines, lynx and brown bears still roam freely. It seems more like Finland, Siberia or Alaska than anywhere else in Norway. The park is also home to moose and a host of relatively rare birds, including the Siberian jay, pine grosbeak, cedar waxwing, black-throated diver, red-breasted merganser, capercaillie, rough-legged buzzard, spotted redshank, hawk owl, great grey owl and even osprey.

The Stone Age Komsa hunting culture left its mark here in the form of hunters' pitfall traps around the lake Ødevann and elsewhere in the region; some date from as early as 4000 BC.

Information

You'll find information at the Pasvikdalen Villmarksenter (☎ 78 99 50 01, W www .destinationkirkenes.no), inside the Svanhøvd Environmental Centre, about 40km south of Kirkenes. It has exhibits on the region's natural sites, and offers dog and reindeer sledding and bear-themed snowmobile safaris starting at Nkr350. You can also pick up the pamphlet Bears in Pasvik, which outlines hopeful directions on what to do should you encounter a testy bruin.

Things to See & Do

If you have a car, you might stop at the Strand branch of the Sør-Varanger Museum (☎ 78 99 48 80, open July–mid-Aug), which preserves Norway's oldest public boarding school and reveals the region's ethnic mix; the timber-built Svanvik chapel, dating from 1934; and the 19th-century Bjørklund Gård farm, which demonstrates the lives of early settlers in the Pasvik region.

The lookout tower Høyden 96 offers a view eastward to the Russian mining town of Nikel (tower admission Nkr20).

Hikers should douse themselves in mozzie repellent before heading off into the wilds. The most accessible route is the poor road that turns south-west 1.5km south of Vaggetem and ends 9km later at the car park near the north-eastern end of the lake Sortbrysttjørna. There, a marked track leads south-westward for 5km, passing several scenic lakes, marshes and bogs to end at the Ellenvannskoia hikers' hut, beside the large lake, Ellenvatn. To extend the hike by two days, you can walk all the way around the lake, but there are no marked tracks.

Also from the Ødevasskoia car park, it's about an 8km walk due south to Krokfjell (145m) and the Treriksrøysa, the monument marking the spot where Norway, Finland and Russia meet. Although you can approach it and take photos, you may not walk around the monument, which would amount to an illicit border crossing! Hikers may not walk around the lake Grenseparvann, which would require crossing the Finnish border.

The topographic sheet to use is Statens Kartverk's Krokfjellet 2333-I, which conveniently covers the entire park.

Places to Stay & Eat

There are several hunting and fishing huts scattered around the park but the only one that's practical for casual hikers is Ellenvannskoia, which is free. With a licence, you can also fish in the lake (which contains perch, grayling and pike).

***Øvre Pasvik Camping** (☎/fax 78 99 55 30, Vaggetem)* 1/2/4-person cabins Nkr300/ 350/400. This place rents canoes and bicycles, and provides info on local wilderness and attractions.

***Pasvikdalen Villmarksenter** (☎ 78 99 50 01, fax 78 99 53 25, [e] post@pasvikdalen.no, Svanhøvd)* Rooms with shower & kitchen Nkr430/540. Near Høyden 96 and the Svanhovd Environmental Centre, this place has some 40 rooms and its owner has endless enthusiasm for the area and its attractions.

***Pasvik Taiga restaurant** (☎ 78 99 54 44, fax 78 99 54 99, Skogfoss)* Singles/doubles Nkr1000/1800. 3-course dinners Nkr500. This highly acclaimed place presents a range of gourmet fish and game dishes. Room rates include breakfast and dinner at the attached *Skogvokter*.

Getting There & Away
Three times per week a bus leaves Kirkenes for Vaggetem (Nkr128, 2¼ hours), stopping at most sites along the way. If you plan to hike from Vaggetem, you'll have to stay the night and then hike 10.5km along the road to the park trailhead (there's little traffic, so it's wise not to rely on hitching). Most other days, buses terminate at Skogfoss (Nkr82, 1½ hours).

GRENSE JAKOBSELV
The first settlement at Grense Jakobselv probably appeared around 8000 years ago, when the sea level was 60m lower than it is today. Only a small stream separates Norway and Russia here, and along the road you can see the border obelisks on both sides. The only real attraction – apart from the chance to gaze over the magic line – is the 1869 stone church. It was constructed within sight of the sea to cement Norway's territorial claims after local people complained to the authorities that Russian fishing boats were illegally trespassing into Norwegian waters; it was thought that the intruders would respect a church and change their ways. When King Oskar II visited in 1873, he gave the church his name.

During school holidays, you can make a return trip between Kirkenes and Grense Jakobselv (Nkr172, 1½ hours) on Monday, Wednesday and Friday; the bus leaves at 9am and returns at 11.30am, allowing an hour in the village. By taxi (☎ 78 99 13 97), the return trip from Kirkenes costs Nkr800.

Inner Finnmark

Nestled against the Finnish border, Norway's 'big sky country' is a place of lush greenery and epicentre of the semi-political entity known as Sápmi, the 'land of the Sami'. The modern, desultory settlement of Kautokeino, with its decidedly non-European ambience, is the heart of the region, though Karasjok has more lively Sami institutions.

KAUTOKEINO
pop 3068
While Karasjok has made concessions to Scandinavian cultures, Kautokeino remains emphatically Sami and resembles no other town in Norway. Some 85% of the townspeople have Sami as their first language, and it's not uncommon to see (non-tourist-industry) locals dressed in traditional garb.

Settlement in the area can be traced back to the last Ice Age, 5000 years ago. From as early as 1553, during the gradual transition between nomadism and stationary lifestyles, records reveal evidence of permanent settlement at 'Guovdageainnu'. Christianity took hold early on and the first church appeared here in 1641.

Information
The Kautokeino tourist office (☎ 78 48 65 00), in the tourist kiosk on the main road, has posted hours from 9am to 4pm June to August and 9am to 8pm in July, though it has been known to close at will.

Things to See & Do
Kautokeino Museum The fascinating Guovdageainnu Gilisillju *(Kautokeino Museum; ☎ 78 48 71 00, Buaronjarga 23; adult/child Nkr20/free; open 9am-7pm Mon-Fri & noon-7pm Sat & Sun 15 June-15 Aug,*

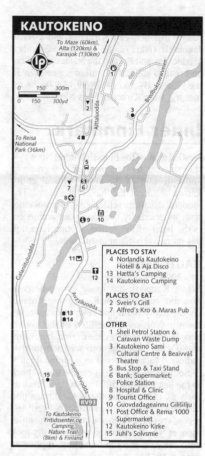

KAUTOKEINO

To Maze (60km),
Alta (120km) &
Karasjok (130km)

To Reisa
National
Park (36km)

0   150   300m
0   150   300yd

PLACES TO STAY
4 Norlandia Kautokeino
   Hotell & Aja Disco
13 Hætta's Camping
14 Kautokeino Camping

PLACES TO EAT
2 Svein's Grill
7 Alfred's Kro & Maras Pub

OTHER
1 Shell Petrol Station &
   Caravan Waste Dump
3 Kautokeino Sami
   Cultural Centre & Beaivváš
   Theatre
5 Bus Stop & Taxi Stand
6 Bank; Supermarket;
   Police Station
8 Hospital & Clinic
9 Tourist Office
10 Guovdageainnu Gilišillju
11 Post Office & Rema 1000
   Supermarket
12 Kautokeino Kirke
15 Juhl's Solvsmie

To Kautokeino
Fritidssenter og
Camping,
Nature Trail
(8km) & Finland

9am-3pm Mon-Fri rest of year) presents a traditional Sami settlement, complete with an early home, temporary dwellings, a trapping exhibit and several agricultural and pastoral outbuildings. These include a kitchen, sauna, and huts for storage of fish, potatoes and lichen (lichen, or 'reindeer moss', is considered prime reindeer fodder). The indoor museum contains Sami handicrafts, farming and reindeer herding implements, religious icons and artefacts, and winter transport gear.

Kautokeino Kirke The timbered Kautokeino church (☎ 78 48 67 70, *Suomalvodda;*

open 9am-9pm daily June–mid-Aug), which dates from 1958, is one of Norway's most used, particularly at Easter. Some fixtures were salvaged from an earlier (1701) church.

Juhl's Solvsmie In a fantastical building in the hills outside the town centre, this highly acclaimed gallery (☎ 78 48 61 89, *Galaniitoluodda; open 8.30am-9pm daily in summer)* creates traditional and modern silver and gold jewellery and handicrafts, and exhibits exotic crafts from around the world. It's all in keeping with the well-travelled owners' philosophy of humanitarian works and aiding indigenous peoples. Staff happily give tours, and you're welcome to buy of course, but unlike in similar galleries in Norway, admission is free.

Organised Tours
The main player is Cávzo Safari (☎ 78 48 75 88) in Máze village some 60km north of Kautokeino. From July to early August, it conducts five-hour riverboat trips to the Altaelva dam (aka Altadammen) for Nkr350, including a Sami-style meal. Other excursions are available from January to October.

Special Events
Easter is the big festival weekend in Kautokeino, with reindeer races and Sami and Christian cultural events.

Places to Stay & Eat
Hætta's Camping (☎ 78 48 62 60, *Suomalvodda 12)* Tent/caravan sites Nr90, cabins Nkr200-600. This camping ground between the main drag and a pond is a little run-down.

Kautokeino Camping (☎ 78 48 54 00, fax 78 48 75 05, *Suomalvodda 16)* Tent/caravan sites Nkr100, cabins Nkr280-300, motel rooms Nkr480-850. This cosier option has both fully equipped cabins and basic cabins, with access to a common kitchen. In the centre is a large Sami *lavvo,* a warm and cosy spot to relax by a wood fire.

Norlandia Kautokeino Hotell (☎ 78 48 62 05, fax 78 48 67 01, e *kautokeino@ norlandia.no, Alttaluodda)* Singles/doubles from Nkr630/890. These are Kautokeino's top lodgings.

Sami Culture & Traditions

Sami life was originally based on hunting and fishing but at sometime during the 16th century the majority of reindeer were domesticated and the hunting economy transformed into a nomadic herding economy. While reindeer still figure prominently in Sami life, only about 16% of Sami people are still directly involved in reindeer herding and transport by reindeer sledge, and only a handful of traditionalists continue to lead a truly nomadic lifestyle.

Some major identifying elements of Sami culture include the *joik* (or *yoik*), a rhythmic poem composed for a specific person to describe their innate nature and is considered to be owned by the person it describes (see Religion in the Facts about Norway chapter). Other traditional elements include the use of folk medicine, Shamanism, artistic pursuits (especially woodcarving and silversmithing) and striving for ecological harmony.

The Sami national dress is the only genuine folk dress that's still in casual use in Norway, and you'll readily see it on the streets of Kautokeino and Karasjok. Each district has its own distinct features, but all include a highly decorated and embroidered combination of red and blue felt shirts or frocks, trousers or skirts, and boots and hats. On special occasions, the women's dress is topped off with a crown of pearls and a garland of silk hair ribbons.

An informative but rather angry treatise on Sami culture is the English-language booklet *The Saami – People of the Sun & Wind,* which is published by Ájtte (Swedish Mountain and Saami Museum; ☎ 0971-17070), Kyrkogatan 3, Jokkmokk, SE-96223 Sweden. It does a good job of describing Sami traditions in all four countries of the Sápmi region, and is available at tourist shops around the area.

Svein's Grill (☎ 78 48 50 65, Cuonjalvodda) does very simple grills (Nkr45 to Nkr125), while *Alfred's Kro* (☎ 78 48 61 18, Hannoluohkka 4) gets slightly more upscale with reindeer and other choices for Nkr48 to Nkr125. Downstairs, *Maras* pub sells pizzas (Nkr65 to Nkr120). There are also a couple of supermarkets on the main drag.

Entertainment

Beaivvás (☎ 78 48 68 11, Bredbuktnesveien 50) The world's only professional Sami theatre company tours throughout the region from its base at the Kautokeino Sami Cultural Centre, which also houses the Nordic Sami Institute.

Aja Disco at the Norlandia hotel serves more pedestrian tastes Friday and Saturday nights.

Getting There & Away

Buses connect Kautokeino with Alta (Nkr181, 3½ hours). You can also travel on the Lapin Linjat bus between Kautokeino and Rovaniemi, is Finland (Nkr235, 7¼ hours).

Getting Around

Alfred's Kro hires out canoes to potter around on the river for Nkr200 per day.

REISA NASJONALPARK

Although it's technically in Troms county, Reisa National Park is most readily accessible by road from Kautokeino. For hikers, the 50km route through this remote Finnmarksvidda country is one of Norway's wildest challenges. The northern trailhead at Sarelv is accessible on the Rv865, 47km south of Storslett, and the southern end is reached on the gravel route to Reisevannhytta, 4km west of Bieddjuvaggi on the Rv896, heading north-west from Kautokeino.

Most people walk from north to south. From Bilto or Sarelv, you can either walk the track up the western side of the anomalous cleft that channels the Reisaelva river or hire a riverboat for the three-hour 27km trip upstream to Nedrefoss, where there's a DNT hut. En route, notice the 269m Mollesfossen waterfall, east of the track on the tributary stream Molleselva. From Nedrefoss, the walking route continues for 35km south to the Reisavannhytta hut on the lake Reisajävri, near the southern trailhead.

KARASJOK
pop 2901

Kautokeino may have more Sami residents, but Karasjok (Kárásjohka in Sami) is Sami Norway's indisputable capital. It's home to the Sami Parliament and Library, NRK Sami Radio, a wonderful Sami Museum and a new Sami theme park. Karasjok is also the site of Finnmark's oldest timber church, Gamlekirke, which dates from 1807 and was the only Karasjok building to survive the WWII bombings and fires.

Information

The Karasjok Opplevelser tourist office (☎ 78 46 69 00, fax 78 46 67 35, e koas@ koas.no) is in Sami Park, the theme park complex near the junction of the E6 and the Rv92. It's open from 8.30am to 7pm Monday to Saturday and 10am to 7pm on Sunday from 1 June to mid-August, with shorter hours the rest of the year.

Things to See & Do

Sami Park Sami culture is big business here, and it was only a matter of time before it was consolidated into a theme park (☎ 78 46 88 00, Porsangerveien; adult/child/family

Nkr90/60/250; open 9am-7pm daily June– mid-Aug, 9am-4pm daily rest of Aug, 9am-4pm Mon-Fri rest of year). There's a wistful, high-tech multimedia introduction to the Sami in the 'Magic Theatre', plus a Sami camp, reindeer roping, and, of course, a gift shop and cafe. It provides a good overview if you're able to visit only one Sami site, but the Sami museums in Karasjok and Kautokeino are less flash and more substance.

Sami Parliament The Sami Parliament (Sámediggi; ☎ 78 47 40 00, W www .samediggi.no, Kautokeinoveien 50; admission free) has been in existence since 1989, but in 2000 it moved into a glorious new building, encased in Siberian lark wood, with a birch, pine and oak interior. The main assembly hall is shaped like a Sami gamma tent, and the Sami library, lit with tiny lights like stars, houses over 35,000 volumes, plus other media. In summer, 30-minute tours are offered on the half-hour between 8.30am

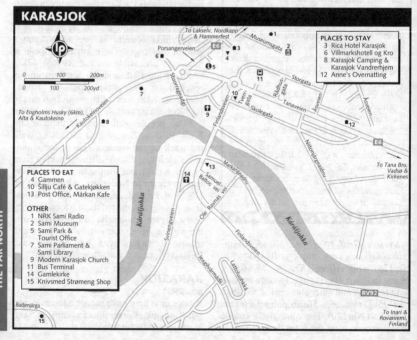

KARASJOK

0   100   200m
0   100   200yd

To Lakselv, Nordkapp & Hammerfest

Porsangerveien

To Engholms Husky (6km), Alta & Kautokeino

Kautokeinoveien

Stuorajeaggi

Finlandsveien

Tverrgata

Tanaveien

Skolegata

Storgata

Rådhusgata

Museumsgata

Nlllohalgeadnu

Åsveien

To Tana Bru, Vadsø & Kirkenes

Markangeadnu

Samuel Balto's vei

Ole Ravnas vei

Svinengveien

Kárášjohka

Kárášjohka

Jeaghilvármádii

Láttohokka

Finlandsveien

Kárášjohka

To Inari & Rovaniemi, Finland

Badjenjárga

PLACES TO STAY
3 Rica Hotel Karasjok
6 Villmarkshotell og Kro
8 Karasjok Camping & Karasjok Vandrerhjem
12 Anne's Overnatting

PLACES TO EAT
4 Gammen
10 Šillju Café & Gatekjøkken
13 Post Office, Márkan Kafe

OTHER
1 NRK Sami Radio
2 Sami Museum
5 Sami Park & Tourist Office
7 Sami Parliament & Sami Library
9 Modern Karasjok Church
11 Bus Terminal
14 Gamlekirke
15 Knivsmed Strømeng Shop

THE FAR NORTH

and 2.30pm (except 11.30am) on weekdays. The rest of the year, tours are at 1.30pm on weekdays. There are also Sami parliaments in Finland and Sweden.

Sami Museum The Sami Museum *(Sámiid Vuorká Dávvirat; ☎ 78 46 99 50, Museumsgata 1; admission Nkr25; open 9am-6pm Mon-Sat & 10am-6pm Sun 10 June-20 Aug, shorter hours rest of year)* provides a thinking-person's rundown of Sami history and culture. Rotating exhibits include reindeer sledges used in former days, displays of colourful, traditional Sami clothing, and works by contemporary Sami artists. Outdoors, a homestead reveals the simplicity of life in olden times.

Organised Tours
At Engholm's Husky (☎ 78 46 71 66, fax 78 46 71 76, **e** sven@engholm.no, **w** www .engholm.no), 6km from town on the Rv92, Sven Engholm offers winter dog-sled and cross-country skiing tours, as well as summer dog-packing tours. All-inclusive expeditions range from one-day dogsled tours (Nkr800/person) to eight-day Arctic safaris (Nkr12,700). If you just want a taste of dog mushing, 30-minute spins cost Nkr250.

Shopping *Knivsmed Strømeng (☎ 78 46 71 05, fax 78 46 64 40, Badjenjárga)* calls on four generations of local experience to create unique and original handmade **Sami knives** for everything from outdoor to kitchen use. Other worthwhile craft shops under the same roof include a silversmith. Similar wares are sold at the **Sami Park gift shop**, which can arrange a tax rebate for tourists.

Places to Stay & Eat
*Karasjok Camping (☎ 78 46 61 35, fax 78 46 66 97, **e** halonen@online.no, Kautokeinoveien)* Tent or caravan sites Nkr70, 2–7-bed cabins Nkr230-850. This hillside spot has river views and a range of cabins. It also handles the hostel, *Karasjok Vandrerhjem* (dorm beds Nkr115).

Villmarksmotell og Kro (☎ 78 46 74 14, fax 78 46 64 08, Kautokeinoveien 6) 2-person/4-person cabins Nkr360/720 (linen

and breakfast each Nkr 50), single/double rooms including breakfast Nkr500/700. Motel rooms are decently furnished and have nice views from above town.

Anne's Overnatting og Motell (☎/fax 78 46 64 32, Tanaveien 40) 2-bed/4-bed cabins Nkr320/400, with linen Nkr420/650, singles/doubles Nkr390/490. Run by a proud Sami lady, this place serves no meals, but rooms have TV and kitchen access.

Engholm's Husky (☎ 78 46 71 66, fax 78 46 71 76, Rv92) Cabins Nkr150-300, plus Nkr100 per guest. Dog lovers will enjoy the rustic, well-furnished cabins near where Sven keeps his sled dogs and pups. Most cabins have a kitchen but no bath. Linen is an extra Nkr100; breakfast/lunch/dinner cost Nkr50/200/350. Pickup from town is free for guests, as is the sauna.

Rica Hotel Karasjok (☎ 78 46 74 00, fax 78 46 68 02, Porsangerveien) Singles/doubles from Nkr760/960. Adjacent to Sami Park, this is Karasjok's premier lodging, with handsome rooms and Sami motifs throughout.

Gammen (☎ 78 46 74 00, Porsangerveien) Mains Nkr189-254. Open mid-May–mid-Aug. This rustic complex of underground Sami huts by the Rica is pricey and occasionally busy with bus tours, but it's an atmospheric and popular option for traditional Sami dishes: reindeer (stewed or with fruit) and salmon.

The shopping centre across the bridge contains a supermarket, post office, and the *Márkan Kafe (☎ 78 46 63 25, Markangeaidnu 1)*, which sells sandwiches and omelettes at bargain prices (Nkr25 to Nkr75). *Sillju Café & Gatekjøkken (☎ 78 46 68 90, Finlandsveien 2)*, also in the shopping centre, specialises in burgers and chicken (Nkr50 to Nkr119).

Getting There & Away
Buses connect Karasjok with Lakselv (Nkr101, 1¼ hours), Hammerfest (Nkr283, 4½ hours) and Kirkenes (Nkr414, 5½ hours). The Finnish Lapin Linjat buses to Ivalo (Nkr121, 35 minutes) and Rovaniemi, in Finland (Nkr310, 5½ hours), also pass through Karasjok.

THE FAR NORTH

Svalbard & Jan Mayen

The Arctic archipelago of Svalbard and the tiny mid-Atlantic island of Jan Mayen present a side of Norway that isn't present anywhere on the mainland. While the Arctic magic of Svalbard attracts increasing numbers of tours and cruise ships, storm-lashed Jan Mayen remains largely neglected.

Svalbard

Svalbard is an assault on the senses. This wondrous archipelago is the world's most readily accessible bit of the polar north and one of the most spectacular places imaginable. Vast icebergs and floes choke the seas, and icefields and glaciers frost the lonely heights, but under close scrutiny, the harsh conditions reveal tiny gems. The Arctic desert soil, however barren-looking, still produces lichens, miniature grasses and delicate little flowers, and the environment supports larger creatures: whales, seals, walruses, polar bears, Arctic foxes and Svalbard caribou (or reindeer). Add to that some of the most haunting scenery anywhere on earth, and you have a dream destination for an unforgettable holiday.

History

The first mention of Svalbard occurs in an Icelandic saga from 1194. Officially, however, the Dutch voyager Willem Barents, in search of a north-east passage to China, is credited with the first European discovery of the archipelago (1596). He named the islands Spitsbergen, or 'sharp mountains'; the Norwegian name, Svalbard, comes from the old Norse for 'cold coast'; the sagas referred to 'a land in the far north at the end of the ocean'. Today, Spitsbergen is the name of Svalbard's largest island.

At the time of Barents' discovery, the archipelago was uninhabited, as the early Inuit migrations eastward from Siberia and Alaska halted in Greenland. There's archaeological evidence of Russian overwintering

Highlights

- Cruising around ice floes in search of seals, walruses and polar bears
- Spending a sunny morning surrounded by the brilliant glaciers and turquoise waters of Magdalenefjord
- Searching for plant fossils around Longyearbreen
- Taking a Russian cultural lesson at Barentsburg or Pyramiden
- Running the Arctic tern gauntlet to appreciate Ny Ålesund's hauntingly beautiful backdrop
- Trekking through some of the most intense wilderness on earth

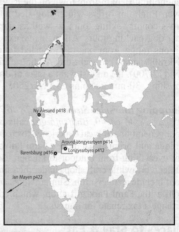

Ny Ålesund p418

Around Longyearbyen p414
Barentsburg p416 · Longyearbyen p412

Jan Mayen p422

around the beginning of the 17th century, but the first confirmed European activities in Svalbard didn't begin until a decade later. From 1612 to 1720, English, Dutch, French, Norwegian and Danish ships engaged in whaling off the western coast of Spitsbergen Island; it's estimated that the Dutch alone took 60,000 whales.

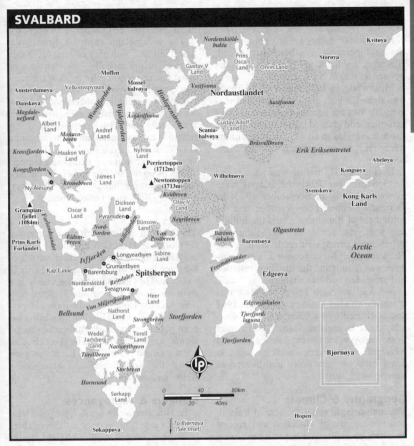

SVALBARD

The first known overwintering took place at Bellsund in 1630 by an English group, which was followed by a Dutch group at Smeerenburg in 1633; the following winter, however, scurvy took its toll and the entire settlement perished. From the early 18th century, Russian Pomor hunters and traders focused their attentions on Svalbard and began hunting walrus, caribou, seals and belugas, and from 1795, Norwegians took notice of the islands' wildlife resources and began hunting both polar bears and Arctic foxes.

In the late 19th and early 20th centuries, a series of explorers attempted to reach the North Pole using hydrogen balloons, and most met with failure. Although Roald Amundsen and Umberto Nobile were successful in 1926, Nobile disappeared two years later while making a solo attempt, as did Amundsen on an attempted rescue.

Perhaps as early as 1612, whalers had discovered coal at Ny Ålesund, but the first modern mine wasn't opened until 1906, when the Arctic Coal Company (ACC) began extracting coal from a rich seam. The settlement that grew up around this mine was named for the ACC's US owner, John Munroe Longyear. In 1916, ACC sold out to the Store Norske Spitsbergen Kull Compani (SNSK). Over the next few years, two other Norwegian companies set up operations on the archipelago's southernmost island, Bjørnøya, and the Kings Bay Kull Compani opened a mine at Ny Ålesund.

Meanwhile, in 1920 the Svalbard Treaty was signed, which granted Norwegian sovereignty over the islands, restricted military activities, and granted business and mineral extraction rights to all 42 signatories of the treaty (subject to Norwegian conservation laws).

During WWII, mining was halted, and on 3 September 1941 the islands were evacuated. Still, in September 1943 the Germans bombed Longyearbyen and the settlement of Barentsburg, and the following year, the settlement of Sveagruva. When the Germans surrendered in 1945, Norwegian civilians returned, Longyearbyen was rebuilt and the Russians resettled in Pyramiden and Barentsburg.

Ny Ålesund also re-opened, but was closed down after a mine explosion in 1962 and converted into a scientific post. Nowadays, the Sveagruva seams, 44km from Longyearbyen, are the most active mines in Svalbard, and workers – who are based in Longyearbyen – are flown into Sveagruva for one-week shifts.

Geography & Climate

The archipelago, about the size of Ireland, consists mainly of glaciated and eroded sedimentary layers laid beneath the sea up to 1.2 billion years ago. Between 300 million and 60 million years ago, Svalbard lay in the tropics, where rich layers of organic matter built up on the surface and metamorphosed under great heat and pressure into coal. The continental drift shifted it to its polar location, and most of its present-day landforms were created during the ice ages of the past two million years. Currently, the highest points are Newtontoppen (1713m) and Perriertoppen (1712m).

Svalbard's latitude ranges from 74°N at Bjørnøya in the south to over 80°N on northern Spitsbergen and Nordaustlandet. In Longyearbyen the midnight sun lasts from 19 April to 23 August, while the polar night lasts from 28 October to 14 February.

The archipelago enjoys a brisk polar desert climate, with only 200mm to 300mm of precipitation annually. Although the west coast remains ice-free for most of the summer, pack ice hovers just north of the main island year-round, and sheets and rivers of ice cover approximately 60% of the land area. Snow and frost are possible at any time of year; the mean annual temperature is -4°C, and in July, it's only 6°C. On occasion, however, you may experience temperatures of up to 20°C or higher. In January, the mean temperature is -16°C, but temperatures of -30°C aren't uncommon.

Books

The Svalbard section in this book is intended for tourists and casual independent travellers only. For more information, check out one of the three books which are dedicated only to Svalbard. The German-language *Spitsbergen Reisehandbuch*, by longtime Svalbard resident Andreas Umbreit, is the most comprehensive. An abridged English translation has been published by Bradt Publications as the *Guide to Spitsbergen*. The French tour agency Grand Nord Grand Large has published the French-language *Spitzberg – L'Archipel du Svalbard*.

Dangers & Annoyances

In real life, Svalbard's symbol, the polar bear, is not the cute fuzzy you see in the zoo. There have been several well-publicised deaths even in recent years, and anyone venturing outside the settlements is strongly advised to carry a firearm for protection. Groups are advised to carry two, in case some people need to return early. If you have your own it's best to bring it, as you're more likely to be familiar with its workings for use in an emergency. Several agencies in Longyearbyen rent them – if you rent, make sure the agency provides practice time and ammunition.

Organised Tours

It's no simple matter to arrange an independent journey to Svalbard (see "Independent Expeditions in Svalbard' boxed text), so most visitors book organised tours. Fortunately, there are numerous options from dog-sledding or snowmobiling day trips to two-week excursions to the North Pole. The tourist office's Web site, **W** www.svalbard .net, lists dozens of tours; some of the most popular are listed below. See also Organised Tours under Longyearbyen for day trips.

Svalbard Polar Travel Locally known as 'SPOT' (☎ 79 02 34 00, fax 79 02 34 01, **e** spot@svalbard-polar.no, **W** www .svalbard-polar.com), Postboks 540, N-9171 Longyearbyen, this outfit conducts the six-day Svalbard Adventure Cruise (with four days of actual cruising), twice weekly in summer, taking in many sites on the west coast. Prices per person (based on double occupancy) are from Nkr7200/12,000 without/ with private shower. Note that SPOT's prices do not include airfare from the mainland.

Another cruise, in the Realm of the Polar Bear, takes in Svalbard's north (from Nkr20,000/24,000 without/with private shower, less for triple rooms).

For hearty skiers, SPOT leads a 13-day Nordic ski trek on north-western Spitsbergen (from Nkr15,400) or 12-day trek to the North Pole (10 days on the trail), from Nkr15,000.

Spitsbergen Tours Spitsbergen Tours (☎ 79 02 10 68, fax 79 02 10 67, **e** info@ terrapolaris.com, **W** www.spitsbergen-tours .com or **W** www.terrapolaris.com), Postboks 6, N-9171 Longyearbyen, has operated since 1987 and was Svalbard's first locally based tour operator. Owner Andreas Umbreit has written a couple of books on the area.

The range of adventurous options includes an Arctic Week, based in Longyearbyen, during the long, dark polar night, in the wintry springtime, or during the summer high season, starting from Nkr8000 to Nkr13,600 per person. It includes day excursions from the settlements (eg, two days of dog-sledding, a snow machine tour, boat cruises and walks, during the applicable seasons). Week-long dog-sledding tours start at Nkr14,000. Hardy hikers can join

one of two three-week inland crossings from Nkr12,200. There are strategically placed caches of provisions, but you'll still need to carry about 22kg.

Spitsbergen Travel Spitsbergen Travel (☎ 79 02 61 00, fax 79 02 61 01, **e** spitra@ spitra.no, **W** www.spitra.no), Postboks 548, N-9171 Longyearbyen, runs week-long journeys from late June to early September, aboard the former Hurtigruten coastal steamer *Nordstjernen* and offers guided excursions along the route of Willem Barents himself. Fares include round-trip airfare from Tromsø and cost from Nkr19,425/22,255 per person (double occupancy) without/with private shower.

'Svalbard Packages' offer airfare from Tromsø and three nights accommodation at the Funken Hotel for Nkr6995 in summer (includes a boat excursion), Nkr6835 in winter (includes a dogsledding trip). Rates are per person, double-occupancy.

Svalbard Wildlife Service Svalbard Wildlife Service (☎ 79 02 10 35, fax 79 02 12 01, **e** info@wildlife.no, **W** www.wildlife .no) offers some of the usual and several unusual trips, including three days of camping, kayaking and glacial exploration (from Nkr4400), or seven days among the glaciers, seals and walruses of Prins Karls Forlandet (from Nkr9950).

LONGYEARBYEN
pop 1500
The capital and 'metropolis' of Svalbard, this very practical-looking community had its beginnings as the main export site for the rich coal seams which characterise the island.

The modern town, strewn with abandoned coal mining detritus, enjoys a superb backdrop including two glacier tongues, Longyearbreen and Lars Hjertabreen. Construction here reflects the Arctic climate – most structures are built on pilings to prevent heated buildings from melting permafrost and sinking in it! The heavily insulated plumbing pipes also run above ground.

Local decorum dictates that people remove their shoes upon entering any building

Independent Expeditions in Svalbard

The easiest way to visit Svalbard and enjoy its wilderness is with a pre-organised tour, which will take care of the logistics and provide access to the islands' finest sites with a minimum of fuss.

Virtually everything in Svalbard is controlled by the Sysselmann (Governor of Svalbard; ☎ 79 02 31 00, fax 79 02 11 66, e firmapost@sysselmannen.svalbard.no, PO Box 633, 9171 Longyearbyen), and independent travellers are not only discouraged, but they also face a host of rules and regulations aimed at protecting this fragile environment from the ravages of mass tourism (tourism operators are subject to the same regulations). Only a relatively small portion of the archipelago (mainly Nordenskiöld Land, in

MH

The polar bear (Ursus maritimus) is found only in Svalbard in Norway

the vicinity of Longyearbyen, Bünsow Land and Dickson Land) is open to independent travellers without expedition credentials, comprehensive rescue insurance and specific government approval.

Even in those open areas, logistics are complicated; travellers must carry firearms to protect themselves from polar bears, and permission and insurance may be required for mountain climbing or sea kayaking trips. Public transport is limited to boats between the Isfjord settlements and flights between Longyearbyen and Ny Ålesund, and tour operators are reluctant to sell partial passages. If you're headed for a remote area, you'll probably have to get there on foot or skis, or use private charter boats or sea kayaks.

If you're set on a remote trekking or boat trip, or wish to independently visit a national park or reserve, contact the Sysselmann's office well in advance (around six months) and post or fax a detailed description of your plans, itinerary, equipment and the experience of the participants, and

---

in town. Exceptions include most shops and eateries.

Information

Tourist Information The friendly and helpful Svalbard Tourism (☎ 79 02 55 50, fax 79 02 55 51, e info@svalbard.net, w www.svalbard.net), in the Nærings-brygget on the pedestrian street, is open from 8am to 6pm weekdays, 9am to 4pm Saturday and noon to 4pm Sunday during summer, with shorter hours the rest of the year.

Post & Communications The post office (☎ 79 02 16 04), on the main street, is open 8am to 5pm Monday to Thursday, to 4pm Friday and 10am to 1pm Saturday.

The Telenor telephone office is on the hill near the Sysselman's office.

The library, in the Lompen Senteret, opens 11am to 6pm Monday, Wednesday and Thursday and 11am to 2pm Tuesday and Saturday. The local newspaper, *Svalbardposten* (Nkr15), comes out on Friday. The Norwegian Polar Institute in the Nærings brygget sells Arctic books, maps and posters.

Money You can change cash and travellers cheques at the Sparebanken Norge (☎ 79 02 29 10), in the post office building.

Emergency Services For emergencies and medical presciptions, see the Longyearbyen Hospital (☎ 79 02 42 00).

Independent Expeditions in Svalbard

apply for permission. In most cases, the Sysselmann will then fix a maximum coverage sum required for search and rescue insurance (this may require coverage of up to Nkr300,000) or a bank guarantee, which must also amount to the recommended total to cover possible rescue costs.

Once the Sysselmann's office has received proof of this insurance or bank guarantee, the issuer may be required to sign a no-fault agreement guaranteeing payment in any case required by the Norwegian regulations for Svalbard. Norwegian insurance companies selling special comprehensive insurance for Svalbard are Europeiske Reiseforsikring (☎ 23 11 90 00, fax 23 11 90 10) and Gjensidige Forsikring (☎ 22 96 80 00, fax 22 96 92 00), both in Oslo. You may also need proof that you have the required equipment and firearms, including a rifle with a minimum calibre of 7.62mm. You can import your own weapon with a special licence or hire one in Longyearbyen. Although it's possible to organise all this at the Sysselmann's office in Skjæringa, Longyearbyen, insurance companies may not look kindly on such lack of preparation.

Note also that all cultural remains in Svalbard dating from prior to 1945 (including rubbish!) are protected by law, and other relics are protected regardless of age. Modern visitors may not leave any evidence of their own visit, nor can they pick flowers, trample vegetation, or feed, chase or otherwise disturb wildlife.

Also – and this is very important – you may only shoot a bear as a last resort, when there is a clear attack and the animal cannot be frightened away by other means – screaming, flares, sound grenades, and a number of warning shots (accordingly, you should have a rifle with a sufficient magazine capacity). A bear standing nearby or destroying non-vital equipment is no excuse for shooting it. Fines are severe.

As an aside, government, economic and scientific interests enjoy a lot more latitude than tourists and tour operators. In the interests of the environment, visitors should not only follow the rules closely, but they should also take note of any violations or unwise practices by other factions and duly report them to the Sysselmann in Longyearbyen.

For further direction, look for the pamphlets *Responsibilities & Resources, Regulations Relating to Tourism and other Travel in Svalbard, Experience Svalbard on Nature's Own Terms* and *Take the Polar Bear Danger Seriously!*, all readily available in Longyearbyen.

Svalbard Museum

Longyearbyen's little museum (☎ *79 02 13 84, Skjæringa; admission Nkr30; open 11am-7pm Mon-Fri, noon-4pm Sat, 1pm-7pm Sun summer; shorter hours rest of year*) occupies a former pig sty, one of the oldest buildings in town. Exhibits cover the history, climate, geology, wildlife and exploration of the archipelago, and include Svalbard's economic mainstay, mining – the sculpted miner illustrates how uncomfortable it is to lie in low, narrow mine shafts.

Graveyard

The haunting little graveyard on the hillside above the town dates from the early part of this century. In a few days in October 1918, seven young men in Longyearbyen were struck down by the Spanish flu, a virus which killed 40 million people in Europe, Asia and North America. Very little is known about it, but because these graves lie in permafrost, a Canadian scientist believes that the virus may remain frozen there and may yet hold enough genetic material to be cultured and studied – and that it may perhaps aid in the development of a vaccine to prevent a re-emergence. Research is ongoing.

Gallery Svalbard

The nearest thing Longyearbyen has to an art museum is Gallery Svalbard (☎ *79 02 23 40, Nybyen; admission Nkr40; contact tourist office for hours*), which features historic maps and books, the mainly Svalbard-themed works of artist Kåre Tveter and

SVALBARD & JAN MAYEN

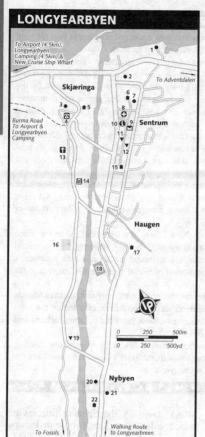

LONGYEARBYEN

PLACES TO STAY
5 Mary-Ann Riggen
6 Radisson SAS Polar Hotel, Restaurant Nansen
   & Barents Pub
15 Basecamp Spitsbergen & Kroa Pub
17 Spitsbergen Funken Hotel & Bar
22 Spitsbergen Nybyen Gjestehus

PLACES TO EAT
11 Lompen Senteret, Kafé Busen & Ferskvaren
12 Svalbardbutikken Supermarket & Nordpolet
    Off-Licence
19 Huset Restaurant, Bar, Nightclub Convenience
    Shop; Cinema

OTHER
1 Svalbard Snøscooterutleie
2 UNIS University
3 Sysselmann's Office
4 Telenor Svalbard (Telephone Office)
7 Svalbard Polar Travel
8 Longyearbyen Hospital
9 Post Office & Sparebanken Norge
10 Næringsbygget: Svalbard Tourism, Svalbard
    Wildlife Service, Norwegian Polar Institute
13 Church
14 Svalbard Museum
16 Historic Graveyard
18 Sports Hall & Swimming Pool
20 Gallery Svalbard
21 Svalbard Wildlife Service

Thomas Widerberg's short slide show on the magic of the polar light.

Organised Tours
Visitors to Longyearbyen can choose from a dizzying array of short trips and day-tours that vary with the season, including fossil hunting (Nkr300); mine tours (Nkr580); boat trips to Barentsburg and Pyramiden (Nkr900); dog-sledding (Nkr750); dog-sledding on *wheels* (Nkr400); diving trips (Nkr1200); glacial crossing (Nkr480); ice-caving (from Nkr520); kayaking (from Nkr510); mountain biking (Nkr400); horse-back riding (Nkr400); and snowmobiling (from Nkr1250). The *Svalbard* brochure lists many more and, if you don't see something you want, just ask.

For information on longer tours, see Organised Tours earlier in this chapter.

Courses
The local university, UNIS (☎ 79 02 33 00) offers courses in Arctic meteorology, geology, biology and geophysics.

Places to Stay
Longyearbyen Camping (☎ 79 02 10 68) Tents per person Nkr70. Open late June-early Sept. Near the airport, with a nice, marshy bit of turf, this is the cheapest option. Guests have use of the service building including kitchen, laundry and heated toilets. It's about an hour's walk from town. Soft drinks and basic snacks are also available on

site. Tent hire Nkr100/night; sleeping bag hire Nkr100/50 first/subsequent nights.

Mary-Ann Riggen (☎ *79 02 37 02, fax 79 02 20 97, Skjæringa*) Singles/doubles Nkr275/500. This simple guesthouse has a kitchenette and charges Nkr100 for linen and Nkr65 for breakfast.

Spitsbergen Nybyen Gjestehus (☎ *79 02 63 00, fax 79 02 63 01,* e *nybyn@spitra.no, Nybyen*) Dorm beds Nkr295, singles/doubles Nkr495/795. This is your budget choice in town.

Basecamp Spitsbergen (☎ *79 02 35 80, fax 79 02 35 81,* e *basecamp@ longyearbyen.net*) Singles/doubles from Nkr800/950. This unusual option has sealing-hut style furnishings.

Spitsbergen Funken Hotel (☎ *79 02 62 00, fax 79 02 62 01,* e *funken@spitro.no*) Singles/doubles from Nkr1195/1395. Between the centre and Nybyen, this comfortable place has valley views.

Radisson SAS Polar Hotel (☎ *79 02 34 50, fax 79 02 34 511,* e *sales@lyrzh .rdsas.com*) Singles/doubles Nkr1240/1490. Here's Longyearbyen's poshest digs.

Places to Eat

Huset (☎ *79 02 25 00*) Mains Nkr195-255. Although it's away from the centre, Huset's a popular choice for both Arctic and French-style meals. The wine cellar has over 30,000 bottles, and there's a popular pub, bar, cinema and convenience store.

Kafé Busen (☎ *79 02 36 50, Lompen Senteret*) This is the main lunchtime meeting place, with daily specials as well as typical cafeteria fare.

Restaurant Nansen (☎ *79 02 34 50, Radisson SAS Polar Hotel*) You'll find fine dining at commensurate prices. Its buffet breakfast is a real treat.

The supermarket in the *Svalbardbutikken* has a good selection of groceries, and *Ferskvaren*, in the Lompensenteret, sells groceries, takeout foods, fresh meat and fish.

Entertainment

On Friday night, the place to see and be seen is *Barents Pub* (☎ *79 02 34 50, Radisson SAS Polar Hotel*).

Meanwhile, *Huset* (☎ *79 02 25 00*) is your all-purpose nightspot, with music and a lively scene. It also houses the town cinema, screening features a couple nights a week.

The *Funken bar* at the Funken hotel also gets fairly rowdy, and there's also a pub at *Kroa* (☎ *79 02 13 00*).

For healthier activities, squash and swimming are available at the *Sports Hall*, near the school, from 6pm to 9pm on Tuesday, Thursday and Sunday.

Although alcohol is duty-free in Svalbard, it's rationed for locals, and visitors must present a valid airline ticket off the archipelago in order to buy it. The Nordpolet beer, wine and spirits outlet is at the back of Svalbardbutikken.

Getting There & Away

In clear weather, the flight between Tromsø and Longyearbyen provides otherworldly views. SAS (☎ 79 02 16 50, w www .scandinavian.net) flies this route on Monday and Friday, and Braathens (☎ 79 02 45 00, w www .braathens.no) flies almost daily. Mini-price fares start at Nkr3145.

Getting Around

Longyearbyen Buss & Taxi (☎ 79 02 13 75) charges Nkr80 to Nkr100 for a cab trip between town and the airport. The airport bus (Nkr35) serves the Spitsbergen Nybyen Gjestehus, Spitsbergen Funken Hotel, Basecamp Spitsbergen and Radisson SAS Polar Hotel, and connects with arriving and departing flights.

You can hire a car from Avis-Spitsbergen Safari (☎ 79 02 32 20) or Longyearbyen Bilutleie (☎ 78 02 11 88) – and you'll get the cheapest petrol in Norway (under Nkr5 per litre) – but there's only 45km of road and not much to see from a vehicle. Bicycles (Nkr100 to Nkr150 per day) from Spitsbergen Nybyen Gjestehus (☎ 79 02 63 00) or Spitsbergen Safari (☎ 79 02 32 20), are probably a better way to explore the area.

You need a driving licence from home in order to operate a snowmobile in Svalbard, and the area where snowmobiles can be operated will be drastically curtailed in 2003.

However, in winter, snowmobile rental agencies include Spitsbergen Safari (☎ 79 02 32 20, fax 79 02 18 10, e safari@spitra.com) and Svalbard Snøscooterutleie (☎ 79 02 16 66, fax 79 02 17 71, e info.scooterutleie@ longyearbyen.net), from Nkr600/day.

AROUND LONGYEARBYEN
Platåberget & Bjørndalen

The vast upland region overlooking Longyearbyen to the west is known as Platåberget (commonly called The Plateau), and it makes a popular day hike. You can either ascend from near the Sysselmann's office in town, which is a steep and scree-covered route, or preferably, sneak up Blomsterdalen, not far from mine No 3. You can also get onto Platåberget via Bjørndalen (yes, it means 'bear valley'), south of the airport. Once on Platåberget, you can continue to the summit of Nordenskiöldsfjellet (1050m), where a Swedish observatory operated from 1931 to 1932.

Longyearbreen

The prominent glacier tongues licking at the upper outskirts of Longyearbyen have scoured and gouged through many layers of sedimentary material, including fossil layers which were created when Svalbard enjoyed a more tropical climate. As a result, the terminal moraine is littered with unusual plant fossils – leaves and twigs that left their marks 40 to 60 million years ago. Oddly enough, there aren't yet any restrictions on collecting them, but in the interest of conservation and future visitors, it's probably best to leave them where they lie.

To get there, pass the Huset and head up the right side of the river, past the abandoned mine buildings, and onto the rough track. After the remains of a bridge (on your left), you'll approach the terminal moraine and cross a stream which flows down from your left. The track then traverses some steep slopes, crosses the river (sometimes there's a bridge) and continues upstream to

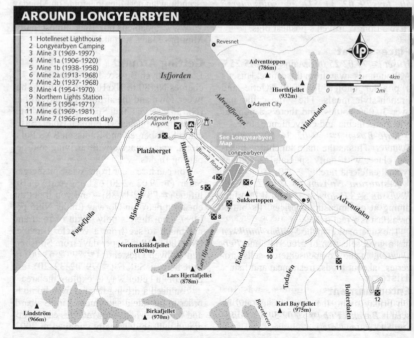

AROUND LONGYEARBYEN

1 Hotellneset Lighthouse
2 Longyearbyen Camping
3 Mine 3 (1969-1997)
4 Mine 1a (1906-1920)
5 Mine 1b (1938-1958)
6 Mine 2a (1913-1968)
7 Mine 2b (1937-1968)
8 Mine 4 (1954-1970)
9 Northern Lights Station
10 Mine 5 (1954-1971)
11 Mine 6 (1969-1981)
12 Mine 7 (1966-present day)

its end at the fossil fields. The 5km return hike from Huset takes about 1½ hours.

Burma Road

The Burma Road, which is now a walking track, follows the old coal mine Taubanen cableway to the processing plant and mine No 3, near the airport. It makes an easy half-day hike but requires a firearm.

Adventdalen

The stark and open Adventdalen beckons visitors with wild Arctic landscapes. There's pleasant hiking, but as you'll know from the polar bear crossing sign at the town end of the valley, you should carry a firearm outside the town.

After leaving town, you'll pass the pungent husky kennels; the freshwater lake, Isdammen, which provides drinking water for Longyearbyen; and a northern lights station which is linked to similar facilities in Alaska and Tromsø. Note also the mountain Operafjellet north of the valley; in 1996 a Russian Tupolev aircraft crashed into its slopes, killing 140 Russian and Ukrainian passengers and crew. With a car, you can also cruise out to the defunct coal mine Nos 5 and 6 and have a look at No 7 (the only one that still functions) in an hour or so. With a bicycle, it takes a bit longer.

BARENTSBURG
pop 950

The anachronistic village of Barentsburg, Svalbard's only remaining Russian settlement, is a fascinating place and, against all odds, continues to mine and export coal. Despite the Norwegian currency in use and the Norwegian postal icon over the post office, you may well find it difficult to believe you're still in Norway in this decaying community. If you've never visited modern Russia, you'll have a taste of it here, complete with Soviet-era relics.

History

Barentsburg, on Grønfjorden, was first identified as a coal producing area around 1900, when the Kullkompaniet Isefjord Spitsbergen started operations. A series of

other companies followed and in 1920, the town was founded by a smaller player, the Dutch company Nespico. Twelve years later it was passed to the Soviet Trust Arktikugol (☎ 79 02 18 14).

As with Longyearbyen, Barentsburg was partially destroyed by the British Royal Navy in 1941 (to prevent it falling into Nazi hands), though the German navy finished the job later anyway. In 1948, it was rebuilt by Trust Arktikugol and embarked on a period of growth, development, scientific research and Soviet social programs that lasted until the fall of the Soviet Union.

Since 1993, about 30% of Trust Arktikugol's coal shipments have gone directly to the west while the rest are shipped to Murmansk and Archangelsk but, of late, operations have been neglected and the situation continues to worsen. Paycheques are now being eaten up by Russian inflation, there are no longer flights to or from Murmansk and obsolete mining equipment is breaking down. The scientific community has now gone and the population has dwindled to some 950 people. Supplies are sparse, but Barentsburg has responded by becoming more self-sufficient. On what is certainly the world's northernmost farm, they grow greenhouse tomatoes, onions, potatoes, cabbages and other Russian staples, and raise chickens, pigs and cattle for meat and milk. For most people, conditions here are preferable to those at home in Russia (or the Ukraine, which many Barentsburg people call home) and they do what they can to remain beyond their standard initial two-year contracts.

Pomor Museum

The simple and appealing little Pomor Museum (☎ 79 02 18 14; admission Nkr30; ring for opening hours) outlines (in Russian only) the Pomor trade and Russian coal mining in Svalbard, and also has exhibits on Russian history on Svalbard. Especially worthwhile are the excellent geological exhibit and the collection of artefacts which suggests Russian activity in Svalbard even prior to its accepted European 'discovery' by Willem Barents.

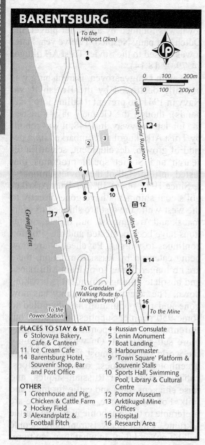

BARENTSBURG

To the
Heliopert (2km)

ulitsa Vladimir Rusanov

Grønfjorden

ulitsa Ivana

Starostina

To Grøndalen
(Walking Route to
Longyearbyen)

To the
Power Station

To the Mine

PLACES TO STAY & EAT	4	Russian Consulate
6 Stolovaya Bakery,	5	Lenin Monument
Cafe & Canteen	7	Boat Landing
11 Ice Cream Cafe	8	Harbourmaster
14 Barentsburg Hotel,	9	'Town Square' Platform &
Souvenir Shop, Bar		Souvenir Stalls
and Post Office	10	Sports Hall, Swimming
		Pool, Library & Cultural
OTHER		Centre
1 Greenhouse and Pig,	12	Pomor Museum
Chicken & Cattle Farm	13	Arktikugol Mine
2 Hockey Field		Offices
3 Alexandrplatz &	15	Hospital
Football Pitch	16	Research Area

Places to Stay & Eat

Barentsburg Hotel (☎ 79 02 10 80 or ☎ 79 02 18 14) Doubles Nkr500 or negotiated price. At the charmingly rustic Barentsburg Hotel traditional Russian meals are served, featuring such specialities as boiled pork with potatoes and Arctic sorrel, parsley and sour cream. In the bar, you can enjoy a deliciously affordable shot of Stolichnaya vodka.

In another building near the 'Town Square', there's also the **Stolovaya** bakery, cafe and workers' canteen. For meals at the cafe, visitors must pay at the hotel. A small

ice cream cafe, around the corner from the Pomor Museum, opens occasionally.

Getting There & Away

The easiest way to reach Barentsburg is on a tourist cruise, and day trips are available from Longyearbyen for Nkr960. Most longer tours also call in at Barentsburg.

In summer, strong, well-equipped hikers can walk from Longyearbyen in five days (note that huts along the way aren't open to hikers). Prepare to get wet, as there's lots of marshy ground and several substantial river crossings. The easiest and most popular route ascends Todalen (from Adventdalen), crosses Gangskardet pass into Gangdalen to the emergency hut Sørhytta. The route then crosses the river Gangselva, which can be tough, and descends into Reindalen. It then ascends the fairly level valley Semmeldalen to the small Semelbu hut before climbing past the face of the Tavlebreen glacier and crossing the pass into Grøndalen. From there, it's a fairly straightforward descent along Grøndalen to the road's end south of Barentsburg. The map to use is the Norsk Polarinstitutt map *Nordenskiöld Land*, at a scale of 1:200,000, but be sure to seek local advice (and arrange for a firearm) before you set out.

PYRAMIDEN

Pyramiden, Russia's other settlement in Svalbard, was named for the impressive Pyramiden mountain which rises nearby. In the mid-1910s, coal was discovered here and operations were set up by the same Swedish interests with holdings at Sveagruva. In 1926, it was taken over by a Soviet firm, Russkiy Grumant, which sold out to another Soviet company, Trust Arktikugol, in 1931. In the 1950s, it counted 1100 residents, and during its heyday in the early 1990s it boasted 60kms of shafts, 130 homes, agricultural enterprises similar to those in Barentsburg and the world's most northerly hotel and swimming pool.

In the late 1990s, this region ceased yielding enough coal to make the operation profitable, and Russia was no longer willing or able to subsidise the mine. Pyramiden was abandoned completely in 2001. However there's talk of bringing it back under a scheme involving tourism, science and an international community of up to 50 people.

Various Longyearbyen tour agencies take in Pyramiden.

NY ÅLESUND
pop 40

Despite its unhospitable 79°N latitude, you'd be hard pressed to find a more awesome backdrop anywhere on earth than the scientific post of Ny Ålesund, founded in 1916 by the Kings Bay Kull Compani. Ny Ålesund likes to claim that it's the world's northernmost permanently inhabited civilian community (although you could make a case for three other spots in Russia and Canada).

Through much of the 20th century, Kings Bay mined local low-altitude coalfields. As many as 300 people lived and worked here, but due to frequent explosions (one in November 1962 resulted in 21 deaths), mining activities ceased in 1963. Ny Ålesund has since emerged as a prominent scientific post with a year-round population of about 40. In summer, however, as many as 100 researchers from around the world visit to work on their own projects.

Information

Kings Bay (☎ 79 02 72 00, fax 79 02 72 01, e booking@kingsbay.no, w www.kingsbay .no) is your official tourist contact, though it operates mainly to serve the local scientific community, which has priority on flights and accommodation, and it cannot confirm tourist bookings more than five days in advance.

The scientific community doesn't seem to think very highly of tourists either. Some of the coolness is probably warranted, as careless visitors can unwittingly affect instrument readings, alter the environment or damage sensitive equipment. Best advice: stay aware, watch where you tread and make known any plans you may have to strike out into the wilds.

You'll also receive a less than friendly reception from the Arctic terns which nest in town, so it's wise to pick up a tern stick

(available free at the dock) to hold over your head and prevent a vicious pecking by a paranoid mother.

Visitors can buy a postcard at the world's northernmost gift shop and drop it off at the world's northernmost post office.

Things to See

In the early 20th century, several polar explorers set off from Ny Ålesund, including the likes of Roald Amundsen, Lincoln Ellsworth, Admiral Byrd and Umberto Nobile. The **anchor pylon** was used by Nobile and Amundsen to launch the airship *Norge* on their successful flight over the pole to Alaska in 1926 and was again used two years later, when Nobile returned to launch the *Italia* on his ill-fated repeat attempt. You'll see **memorials** around town.

Perhaps the most unusual sight is the **stranded locomotive** near the dock. In 1917, a 90cm-gauge railway was constructed to connect the coalfields with the harbour, and it remained in use until 1958. The restored locomotive is, naturally, the world's northernmost railway relic.

The town also supports a very nice little **Gruvemuseum** *(Mine Museum; donation suggested; open 24 hours)* in the old Tiedemann's Tabak (tobacco) shop, relating the coal mining history of this area.

Places to Stay & Eat

Nordpolhotellet (☎ 79 02 72 00, fax 79 02 72 01, e booking@kingsbay.no, w www .kingsbay.no) Singles/doubles Nkr1390/ 2060. Ny Ålesund's hotel opened on 3 September 1939; then WWII came along and it closed the following day. Now it's open again, with full board available.

The extremely bare-bones *camping ground* (the world's northernmost, of course, Nkr100 per site, including shower and towel) is near Nobile's airship pylon.

The *Kings Bay Cantina* offers full board for Nkr460 or breakfast/lunch/dinner for Nkr75/210/210.

Getting There & Away

As with many other places in Svalbard, most visitors arrive in Ny Ålesund on

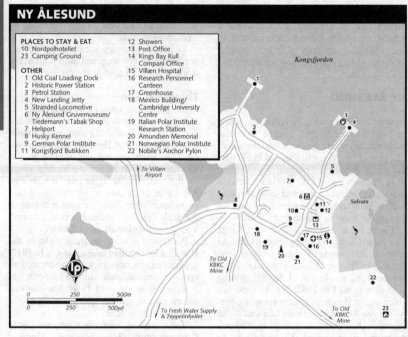

NY ÅLESUND

PLACES TO STAY & EAT
10 Nordpolhotellet
23 Camping Ground

OTHER
1 Old Coal Loading Dock
2 Historic Power Station
3 Petrol Station
4 New Landing Jetty
5 Stranded Locomotive
6 Ny Ålesund Gruvemuseum/
   Tiedemann's Tabak Shop
7 Heliport
8 Husky Kennel
9 German Polar Institute
11 Kongsfjord Butikken

12 Showers
13 Post Office
14 Kings Bay Kull
   Compani Office
15 Villæn Hospital
16 Research Personnel
   Canteen
17 Greenhouse
18 Mexico Building/
   Cambridge University
   Centre
19 Italian Polar Institute
   Research Station
20 Amundsen Memorial
21 Norwegian Polar Institute
22 Nobile's Anchor Pylon

Kongsfjorden

Solvatn

To Villæn
Airport

To Old
KBKC
Mine

To Fresh Water Supply
& Zeppelinfjellet

To Old
KBKC
Mine

0   250   500m
0   250   500yd

tourist cruises and only linger for an hour or two. Alternatively, Kings Bay (see under Information) offers air transport to/from Longyearbyen (Nkr1380 one way, 25 minutes), usually twice per week.

AROUND NY ÅLESUND

Kongsfjorden Ny Ålesund's spectacular backdrop, Kongsfjorden (the namesake for the Kings Bay Kull Compani), contrasts bleak grey-brown shores with expansive white icefields. The distinctive Tre Kroner peaks, Dana (1175m), Svea (1226m) and Nora (1226m) (named in honour of Denmark, Sweden and Norway, respectively), which rise from the ice, are among Svalbard's most recognised landmarks.

Blomstrandhalvøya Gravelly Blomstrandhalvøya was once a peninsula but, in the early 1990s, it was released from the icy grip on its northern end and it's now an island. In summer, the name Blomstrand,

or 'flower beach', would be appropriate, but it was in fact named for a Norwegian geologist. At Ny London, at the southern end of the island, Ernest Mansfield of the Northern Exploration Company attempted to quarry marble in 1911 only to discover that the stone had been rendered worthless by aeons of freezing and thawing. A couple of buildings and some decrepit machinery remain.

AROUND SPITSBERGEN

Kapp Linné

Kapp Linné consists of little more than the Isfjord Radio installation. Transport is by boat or snowmobile from Longyearbyen or Barentsburg, and independent hiking and guided day tours are available. Note, however, that much of the surrounding area is a bird reserve, off-limits for most of the summer.

Tourist accommodation is available through SPOT. Full board at *Kapp Linné*

(☎ 79 02 56 00, fax 79 02 56 01, e kapp.linne@ svalbard-polar.no, Isfjord) cost Nkr990/1580 for singles/doubles.

Sveagruva

Coal was first discovered at Sveagruva in the early 1910s. In 1917, the Swedish company,

Roald Amundsen

If Fridtjof Nansen had the biggest heart of any polar explorer, fellow Norwegian Roald Amundsen had the most determination and grit. Born in 1872 at Borge, near Sarpsborg, he dreamed of becoming a polar explorer and devoured every bit of literature he could find on the subject. Following his mother's wishes, he dutifully studied medicine, but when she died in 1893 he returned to his polar dreams and never looked back.

By 1897 he was sailing to the Antarctic as first mate on the Belgian *Belgica* expedition. That ship froze fast in the ice near Peter I's Island and became – unintentionally – the first expedition to overwinter in the Antarctic. When the captain fell ill with scurvy, Amundsen took command, displaying his ability in a crisis.

Having gained a reputation as a captain, Amundsen set his sights on the North-West Passage and study of the Magnetic North Pole. The expedition set out from Oslo in June 1903 aboard the 47-tonne sloop *Gjøa* and overwintered in a natural harbour on King William Island, which they named Gjøahavn. For two years they built observatories, took magnetic readings establishing the position of the Magnetic North Pole, studied the lives of the Inuit and learned how to drive dog teams. By August 1905 they emerged into waters that had been charted from the west, becoming the first vessel to navigate the North-West Passage. When the *Gjøa* again froze fast in the ice, Amundsen and an American companion set off by dog-sled to the telegraph station at Eagle, Alaska, over 900km away, to announce the success.

Amundsen had wanted to be the first man to reach the North Pole, but in April 1909 Robert Peary announced that he'd already been. So in 1910, Amundsen headed instead for the South Pole, only to learn that Britain's Robert Falcon Scott's *Terra Nova* expedition was setting out from New Zealand with the same goal.

Amundsen's ship dropped anchor in January 1911 at Roosevelt Island, 60km closer to the South Pole than Scott's base. With four companions and four 13-dog sleds, Amundsen reached the South Pole on 14 December 1911, and Scott arrived on 17 January 1912 to discover the Norwegian flag already there. Many historians feel that Amundsen had made the trip look too easy; Scott and four members of his expedition died of cold and starvation on the way back.

In 1925, Amundsen set about becoming the first man to fly over the North Pole. American Lincoln Ellsworth sponsored the expedition, and two planes took off from Svalbard bound for Alaska, but faulty equipment forced them to land on sea ice about 150km from the Pole. The pilot, Hjalmar Riiser-Larsen, hewed a runway with hand tools, managed to take off with all six crew members, and returned one plane to Nordaustlandet, in Svalbard, where they ditched at sea but were rescued.

Amundsen tried again the next year, aboard the airship *Norge* with Ellsworth, Riiser-Larsen and the Italian explorer Umberto Nobile. They left Spitsbergen on 11 May 1926 and, 16 hours later, dropped the Norwegian, American and Italian flags on the North Pole. On 14 May they landed triumphantly at Teller, Alaska, having flown 5456km in 72 hours – the first flight between Europe and North America. They also determined that the Arctic Ocean was all water. (Note: other expeditions claim to have been the first at the North Pole, but Amundsen's was the first with indisputable evidence of success.)

In May 1928, Nobile attempted another expedition in the airship *Italia* and, when it crashed in the Arctic, Amundsen joined the rescue. Although Nobile and his crew were rescued, Amundsen's last signals were received just three hours after take-off, and he was never seen again.

Aktiebolaget Spetsbergens Svenska Kolfält, established the first mine, which changed hands several times, passed through a fire and yielded 400,000 tonnes of coal before it was taken over by SNSK in 1934. The operations were levelled by a submarine attack in 1944, but activity snapped back after the war and by the late 1970s Sveagruva had grown into a well-appointed settlement of 300 workers and enjoyed nearly as many amenities as Longyearbyen.

Over the following years, increased production around more-accessible Longyearbyen resulted in declines at Sveagruva, and by the mid-1990s it had dwindled to just a handful of miners and administrators. But Sveagruva remains hopeful of continued coal mining in this area once other mines run out, and new buildings have been constructed to handle its anticipated resurrection.

Prins Karls Forlandet
On the west coast of Spitsbergen, the oddly shaped 86km-long island of Prins Karls Forlandet is a national park set aside to protect breeding pinnipeds. The alpine northern reaches, which rise to Grampianfjellet (1084m), are connected by Saltfjellet (430m), at the southern end, by a long flat plain called Forlandsletta.

Krossfjorden
Thanks to its grand tidewater glacier, Lillehöökbreen, and several cultural relics, Krossfjorden also attracts quite a few cruise ships. At Ebeltoftbukta, near the mouth of the fjord, you can see several whalers' graves as well as a heap of leftover junk from a 1912 German telegraph office that was shifted wholesale to Ny Ålesund in 1914 and kicked off that town's reputation as a scientific post. Opposite the entrance rise some crowded bird cliffs overlooking one of Svalbard's most verdant spots, with flowers, moss and even grasses.

Magdalenefjord
The lovely blue-green bay of Magdalenefjord, flanked by towering peaks and intimidating tidewater glaciers, is the most popular anchorage along Spitsbergen's western coast. In the 17th century, this area saw heavy Dutch whaling, and at Graveneset, near the mouth of the fjord, you can still see the remains of two stoves used to boil down the blubber. There are numerous graves of 17th- and mid-18th-century whalers, now protected as a cultural monument and marked with a 1930 memorial.

If you're there with (or at the same time as) a large cruise ship, your experience will probably be, shall we say, altered. Cruise-line crew members have been known to enhance beach barbecues by dressing up as polar bears, or even penguins, and dancing on a convenient ice floe.

Danskøya
One of the most intriguing sites in northwest Spitsbergen is Virgohamna, on the bleak and gravelly island of Danskøya, where the remains of several broken dreams now lie scattered across the lonely beach. Among them are the ruins of three blubber stoves from a 17th-century whaling station, as well as eight stone-covered graves from the same era. You'll also find the remains of a cottage built by English adventurer Arnold Pike, who took a notion to sail north in the yacht Siggen and spend a winter subsisting on polar bears and reindeer.

The next adventurer at Virgohamna was Swedish engineer Salomon August Andrée, who in the summer of 1897 set off from Virgohamna in a balloon, hoping to reach the North Pole. The fate of this expedition, which also included his colleagues Frænkel and Strindberg, wasn't known until 1930, when their crash site was discovered on the island of Kvitøya. It's thought that they survived the crash, but died of food poisoning after eating undercooked bear meat.

Then, in 1906, journalist Walter Wellman, who was sponsored by a US newspaper, attempted to reach the North Pole in a zeppelin but failed. He returned to try again the next year, when his ship was damaged in a storm. On his third attempt, in 1909, he floated to within 60km of the pole, met with technical problems and gave up for good, mainly because he'd heard that Robert Peary had already reached the pole anyway.

All of the remaining junk (including dozens of rusted 44-gallon fuel drums) is protected.

Amsterdamøya & Fairhaven
The island of Amsterdamøya was the site of the large Smeerenburg whaling station, which was co-founded in 1617 by Dutch and Danish concerns, but all that remains are seven ovens and some graves. All around the nearby sound, Fairhaven, which lies between the mainland and the four small offshore islands, are scattered numerous whalers' graves.

Moffen
Most tourist cruises attempt to approach flat and gravelly Moffen Island, known for its walrus population, but most are turned back by pack or drift ice. In any case, between mid-May and mid-September, boats can't approach within 300m of the island, lest they disturb the walruses' breeding activities.

OUTER ISLANDS
The following islands are extremely remote and accessible only via organised tour. Even then, climate and geography make them expensive and difficult to reach.

Bjørnøya
Svalbard's southernmost island, 178-sq-km Bjørnøya, is visited mainly by the curious crews of private yachts and cruise ships. There's little to see but a tiny museum, the Norwegian Bjørnøya Radio meteorological station and a couple of historic buildings. The most interesting is a former pig sty known as Hammerfesthuset, which was constructed in 1823 and is the oldest surviving building in Svalbard. The island's name is derived from an errant bear who inhabited the island when Willem Barents first landed there.

Hopen
In 1942, the narrow and lonely island of Hopen saw the wreck of the Soviet freighter *Dekabrist* (Decembrist) and only three of the 80 passengers and crew members survived the near-impossible winter conditions. The following year, the island was occupied by a German meteorological sta-tion, which was later rebuilt by the Norwegians to monitor climatic conditions and later, to study ice movements and the aurora borealis. It's now home to a handful of scientific personnel.

Nordaustlandet
Vast Nordaustlandet, Svalbard's second largest island, takes in over 14,700 sq km, about 75% of which is covered with ice. The lonely eastern coast is dominated by the vast Austfonna ice sheet, which forms the longest tidewater glacial face in the Arctic region.

Kvitøya
The 700-sq-km island of Kvitøya, or 'white island', is aptly named, as only three tiny headlands are free of ice and it's almost perpetually surrounded by either pack ice or drift ice. It's uninhabited, but there is an unstaffed radio transmitter and the odd icebreaker does call in from time to time. Its 15 minutes of fame came when the Swedish balloon expedition of Andrée, Frænkel and Strindberg crashed here (see Danskøya earlier in this chapter).

Jan Mayen

Norway's 'other' Arctic territory, the island of Jan Mayen, lies in the Norwegian Sea 600km north of Iceland, 500km east of Greenland and 1000km west of the Norwegian mainland. It sits squarely on the northern end of the mid-Atlantic ridge and at its northern end, known as Nord-Jan, rises Norway's only active volcano, Beerenberg (2277m). The island measures 54km long by up to 16km wide, and covers 380 sq km. This includes a 3.5-sq-km out-cropping called Nylandet, created by an eruption of Beerenburg in September 1970.

In 1614, English captain John Clarke stumbled upon the island and named it Isabella, but it didn't stick. Later the same year, the Dutch captain Jan Jakobs May van Schellinkhout arrived in a fog so dense that he couldn't even see the length of his own ship; the island only gave itself away

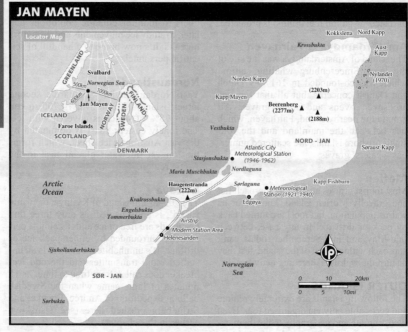

JAN MAYEN

Locator Map

GREENLAND

Svalbard

Norwegian Sea

500km

1000km

Jan Mayen

ICELAND

Faroe Islands

SCOTLAND

NORWAY

SWEDEN

FINLAND

DENMARK

Kokkssletta   Nord Kapp

Krossbukta   Aust Kapp

Nordest Kapp   Nylandet (1970)

Kapp Mayen   Beerenberg (2277m)   (2203m)

(2188m)

Vestbukta   NORD - JAN   Søraust Kapp

Atlantic City
Meteorological Station
(1946-1962)

Stasjonsbukta

Maria Muschbukta   Nordlaguna

Arctic
Ocean

Haugenstranda (222m)   Sørlaguna   Kapp Fishburn

Meteorological
Station (1921-1940)

Kvalrossbukta   Edgøya

Engelsbukta
Tommerbukta

Airstrip
Modern Station Area
Helenesanden

Sjuhollanderbukta

SØR - JAN   Norwegian
Sea

0   10   20km

0   5   10mi

Sørbukta

in the sound of the waves breaking on its barren shores. He realised he'd discovered an uncharted island, and his first mate did some mapping and named the place after the captain.

Around 1633, the Dutch began whaling in the area and sent seven sailors to overwinter and thereby establish a Dutch presence and a place to boil down the blubber, but the entire mission died of scurvy. That didn't stop the whaling, however; the Greenland right whale became nearly extinct in these waters, and commercial whaling ended in 1640.

The island was then used as a staging point for polar expeditions and a meteorological post. During WWII, it remained unoccupied by the Germans and was operated by Norwegian forces in exile. In 1943, the Americans established a radio installation called Atlantic City and, after the war, Norway and the USA set up a joint Loran (long-range navigation) station. Nowadays, all that remains is a small Norwegian meteorological post.

A dispute between Norway and Denmark regarding the fishing exclusion zone between Jan Mayen and Greenland was settled in 1988, granting the greater area of sovereignty to Denmark. Jan Mayen is now administered by the county of Nordland, from Bodø.

Visiting Jan Mayen

Independent travel to Jan Mayen is all but non-existent, and even organised visits are extremely rare, because: there's no port; safe sailing weather can never be assured; and, for each landing, ships must apply for permission from the Norwegian government, with no assurances of it being granted. Still, a handful of expeditions to or from Iceland, Greenland and Scotland list Jan Mayen in their itineraries (see Arcturus Expeditions under UK in the Organised Tours section of the getting There & Away chapter). For more information, you can check with Terra Polaris (**e** info@terrapolaris.com, **w** www.terrapolaris.com).

Language

NORWEGIAN

Norway has two official languages –
Bokmål and Nynorsk – but differences
between the two are effectively very
minor. In this language guide we have used
Bokmål – it's by far the most common language that travellers to Norway will
encounter. For a more detailed description
of these languages and their usage see
Language in the Facts about Norway
chapter. For a more comprehensive list of
Norwegian words and phrases, get a copy
of Lonely Planet's *Scandinavian Europe
phrasebook*.

The Norwegian alphabet has 29 letters:
those used in English, plus the vowels æ,
ø and å (which are listed at the end of the
alphabet). While the consonants c, q, w, x,
and z are included, they are used mainly in
foreign words. On many Norwegian place
names, the definite article 'the' – which
may be masculine (-en), feminine (-en or
-a) or neuter (-et) – is appended to the end,
eg, *Jotunheim* becomes *Jotunheimen*, and
Horningdalsvatn becomes *Horningdals-
vatnet*. Plurals are usually formed by
adding -e or -er.

Pronunciation

Norwegian pronunciation is a complex
affair for native English speakers. These
guidelines only approximate the sounds of
the language as you'll hear them in the
everyday speech of Norwegians – the best
way to improve your pronunciation is to
employ the 'listen and learn' method.

Vowels

As in English, Norwegian vowels can have
many permutations. The length of vowels is
a very important feature in the pronunciation of Norwegian. When occurring in a
stressed syllable every vowel has both a
(very) long and a (very) short counterpart.
Generally, a vowel is short when followed
by one consonant, and when followed by
two or more consonants, it's long.

a   long, as in 'father'; short, as the 'u' in 'cut'

å   long, as in the 'o' in 'lord'; short, as the 'o' in 'pot'

e, æ   long, as in posh British 'day'; short, as in 'bet'; before r, as in British 'bad'. When in unstressed syllables it's always as the 'u' in 'lettuce'.

i   very short, as the 'ea' in 'beat'; long as the 'ee' in 'seethe'

o   short, as in British 'pot'; long as in American 'zoo'; short, as the 'u' in put; long, as in 'lord'

ø   as the 'e' in 'her'

u   long, as the 'oo' in 'soon'; short, as in 'put'

y   a bit like German 'ü'; try pursing your lips and saying 'ee'

Diphthongs

ai   as the word 'eye'

ei   as the 'ay' in 'hay'

au   similar to the word 'owe'

øy   like 'er-y' in the expression 'her year', with no 'r' sound

Consonants & Semivowels

d   often silent at the end of a word, or when between two vowels

g   as in 'go' except before ei, i, j, øy and y when it's pronounced as the 'y' in 'yard'; in the combination gn it's pronounced as the 'ng' of 'sing' followed by an 'n'

h   as in 'her'; silent before v and j

j   always as the 'y' in 'yard'

k   a hard sound, as in 'kin'; before the letters or combinations ei, i, j, øy and y it's mostly pronounced as the 'ch' in 'chin'. (In many areas, these combinations are pronounced as the 'h' in 'huge', or as 'ch' in Scottish *loch*.)

l   pronounced thinly, as in 'list', except after 'ah', 'aa', 'o' and 'or' sounds, when it's like the 'll' in 'all'

ng   in most areas, as the 'ng' in 'sing'

r trilled, like Spanish 'r'; in south-west Norway the **r** has a guttural pronunciation, as in French *rien*. The combinations **rd**, **rl**, **rn**, **rt** sound a little as they do in American 'weird', 'earl', 'earn' and 'start', but with a much weaker 'r'. The combination **rs** is pronounced 'sh' as in 'fish'.

s as in 'so'; when **sk** is followed by **ei**, **i**, **j**, **øy** and **y**, it is pronounced as 'sh', eg, the Norwegian word *ski* sounds like English 'she'.

t as in 'top', except in two cases where it's silent: in the Norwegian word *det* (it, that) – roughly pronounced like British English 'dare' – and in the definite singular ending -*et* of Norwegian neutral nouns

v mostly as English 'w' but without rounding the lips

Essentials

Hello.	*Goddag.*
Goodbye.	*Morna.*
Yes/No.	*Ja/Nei.*
Please.	*Vær så snill.*
Thank you.	*Takk.*
You're welcome.	*Ingen årsak.*
Excuse me. (Sorry)	*Unnskyld.*
Do you speak English?	*Snakker du engelsk?*
How much is it?	*Hvor mye koster det?*
What's your name?	*Hva heter du?*
My name is ...	*Jeg heter ...*

Getting Around

What time does the ... leave/arrive?	*Når går/kommer ...?*
boat	*båten*
bus (city)	*bussen (bybussen)*
bus (intercity)	*bussen (linjebussen)*
tram	*trikken*
train	*toget*

I'd like a ...	*Jeg vil gjerne ha ...*
one-way ticket	*enkeltbillett*
return ticket	*tur-retur*

1st class	*første klasse*
2nd class	*annen klasse*
left luggage	*reisegods*

timetable	*ruteplan*
bus/tram stop	*buss/trikkhaldeplass*
train station	*jernbanestasjon*
ferry terminal	*ferjeleiet*

Where can I rent a car/bicycle?	*Hvor kan jeg leie en bil/sykkel?*
Where is ...?	*Hvor er ...?*
Go straight ahead.	*Det er rett fram.*
Turn left.	*Ta til venstre.*
Turn right.	*Ta til høyre.*
far/near	*langt/nær*

Around Town

bank	*banken*
chemist/pharmacy	*apotek*
embassy	*ambassade*
market	*torget*
my hotel	*hotellet mitt*
newsagency	*kiosk*
post office	*postkontoret*
telephone centre	*televerket*
tourist office	*turistinformasjon*

Accommodation

hotel	*hotell*
guesthouse	*gjestgiveri/pensjonat*
youth hostel	*vandrerhjem*
camping ground	*kamping/leirplass*

Do you have any rooms available?	*Har du ledige rom?*
Does it include breakfast?	*Inklusive frokosten?*

How much is it ...?	*Hvor mye er det ...?*
per night	*pr dag*
per person	*pr person*

Signs

Inngang	**Entrance**
Utgang	**Exit**
Opplysninger	**Information**
Åpen	**Open**
Stengt	**Closed**
Forbudt	**Prohibited**
Politistasjon	**Police Station**
Toaletter	**Toilets**
Herrer	**Men**
Damer	**Women**

I'd like a ...   Jeg vil gjerne ha ...
  single room   eit enkeltrom
  double room   eit dobbeltrom

one day   en dag
two days   to dager
one week   en uka

Food

breakfast	frokost
lunch	lunsj
dinner	middag
meat	kjøtt
beef	oksekjøtt
pork	svinekjøtt
chicken	kylling
sausage	pølse
fish	fisk
trout	ørret
salmon	laks
shrimp	reke
cod	torsk
vegetables	grønnsaker
potatoes	poteter
carrots	gulroter
peas	erter
cabbage	kål
ice cream	iskrem
chocolate	sjokolade
apple pie	eplekake
bread	brød
roll	rundstykke
jam	syltetøy
butter	smør
cheese	ost
cake	kake
biscuit	kjeks
vegetarian	vegetarisk/ vegetarianer

Drinks

water	vann
fruit juice	jus
squash	saft
fizzy drink	brus
milk	melk
coffee	kaffe
tea	te
brewery	bryggeri
beer	øl
wine	vin
vodka	aquavit
brandy	konjakk

Emergencies

Help!	Hjelp!
Call a doctor!	Ring ein lege!
Call the police!	Ring politiet!
Go away!	Forsvinn!
I'm lost.	Jeg har gått meg vill.

Time, Days & Numbers

What time is it?	Hva er klokka?
today	i dag
tomorrow	i morgen
yesterday	i går
in the morning	om formiddagen
in the afternoon	om ettermiddagen

Monday	mandag
Tuesday	tirsdag
Wednesday	onsdag
Thursday	torsdag
Friday	fredag
Saturday	lørdag
Sunday	søndag

0	null
1	en
2	to
3	tre
4	fire
5	fem
6	seks
7	sju
8	åtte
9	ni
10	ti
100	hundre
1000	tusen

one million   en million

SAMI

Although written Fell Sami includes several accented letters, it still doesn't accurately represent the spoken language – even some Sami people find the written language difficult to learn. For example, giitu (thanks) is pronounced 'GHEECH-too', but the strongly aspirated 'h' is not written.

LANGUAGE

Here are a few Sami phrases. To learn the correct pronunciation, it's probably best to ask a local to read the words aloud.

Hello.	*Buorre beaivi.*
Hello. (reply)	*Ipmel atti.*
Goodbye. (to person leaving)	*Mana dearvan.*
Goodbye. (to person staying)	*Báze dearvan.*
Thank you.	*Giitu.*
You're welcome.	*Leage buorre.*
Yes.	*De lea.*
No.	*Li.*

How are you?	*Mot manna?*
I'm fine.	*Buorre dat manna.*

1	*okta*
2	*guokte*
3	*golbma*
4	*njeallje*
5	*vihta*
6	*guhta*
7	*cieza*
8	*gávcci*
9	*ovcci*
10	*logi*

Glossary

You may encounter some of the following terms and abbreviations during your travels in Norway. See also the Language chapter and the Food section in the Facts for the Visitor chapter.

Note that the letters æ, ø and å fall at the end of the Norwegian alphabet.

allemannsretten – 'every man's right'; a tradition (now a law) allowing universal access to private property (with some restrictions), public lands and wilderness areas
apotek – pharmacy
automatisk trafikkontrol – speed camera

bacalao – fish dish using cod, common in northern coastal areas
bakke – hill
bekk – creek, stream
berg – mountain
bibliotek – library
bil – car
billett – ticket
bird cliffs – sea cliffs inhabited by colonies of nesting birds
bokhandel – bookshop
bru, bro – bridge
brygge – quay, wharf
bryggeri – brewery
bukt, bukta – bay
bunad – the Norwegian national costume; each region has its own version of this colourful affair
by – town
børsen – stock exchange
båt – boat

col – mountaineering term for a pass between peaks

dagskort – 'day card', a daily bus pass
dal – valley
DNT – *Den Norske Turistforening* (The Norwegian Mountain Touring Club)
domkirke – cathedral
drosje – taxi

elv, elva – river
etasje – floor, storey

ferje – ferry
festning – fort, fortress
fjell, fell, fjall – mountain
fjord – drowned glacial valley
fonn – glacial icefield
forening – club, association
foss – waterfall
Fv – *Fylkesvei*; county road
fylke – county
fyr, fyrtårn – lighthouse

galleriet – gallery or shopping arcade
gamma, gammen – Sami turf hut, sometimes partially underground
gamle, gamla, gammel – old
gamlebyen – the 'old town'; the historic portion of a city or town
gate, gata – street (often abbreviated to **g** or **gt**)
gatekjøkken – literally 'street kitchen'; street kiosk/stall/grill selling greasy fast food
gjestehavn – 'guest harbour', the area of a port town where visiting boats and yachts moor; washing and cooking facilities are normally available
gjestehus – guesthouse
gravlund, gravplass – cemetery
grense – border
grotta – grotto, cavern
gruve, gruva – mine
gård, gard – farm or courtyard

hage – garden
halvøya – peninsula
hamn – northern Norwegian word for harbour
hav – ocean
havn – harbour
hule, hula – cave
Hurtigruten – literally 'the Express Route'; system of coastal steamers plying the route between Bergen and Kirkenes
hus – house

husmannskost – traditional Norwegian food; home cooking
hytte – cabin, hut or chalet

iddis – colourful sardine tin label; Stavanger dialect for *'etikett'* or label
innsjø – lake
is – ice
isbjørn – polar bear
isbre – valley glacier

jernbanestasjon – train station
jul – Christmas
juvet – gorge

kai, kaia – quay
kapp – cape
kart – map
kirke, kirkja, kirkje, kerk – church
klokken – o'clock; the time
koldtbord – cold buffet or smorgasbord
kong – king
kort – card
krone – Norwegian currency unit
kunst – art
kyst – coast

lavvo, lavvu – tepee; Sami tent dwelling
legevakten – clinic
libris – books; indicates a bookshop
lompen – miners' coveralls, used in the Svalbard coal mines
lufthavn – airport

magasin – department store
mark – woods
mat – food
MOMS – Value Added Tax/sales tax
M/S – *motorskip* or motor ship, used to designate ship names
museum, museet – museum
mush – to drive a dog-sled (word of Alaskan origin)
myntvaskeri – coin laundry

nasjonalpark – national park
naturreservat – nature reserve
navvy – railway worker
nedre – lower
nord – north
nordlys – northern lights, aurora borealis

Norge – Norway
Norges Turistråd – Norwegian Tourist Board, formerly NORTRA
Norsk – Norwegian
'Norway in a Nutshell' – a range of tours which give high-speed travellers a glimpse of the best of Norway in one or two days
NSB – *Norges Statsbaner* (Norwegian State Railways)
ny – new

og – and

pensjonat – pension or guesthouse
plass – plaza, square
polarsirkelen – Arctic Circle; 66°33'N latitude
Pomor – the Russian trading and fishing community from the White Sea area, which prospered in northern Norway in the 17th century
postkontor – post office
påske – Easter

reker – shrimp
rorbuer – cabin/fishing hut
rosemaling – painted floral motifs
rutebilstasjon – bus terminal
ruteplan – transport timetable
Rv – *Riksvei*; national highway
rådhus – town hall

selskap – company
sentrum – town centre
sjø – sea, ocean
sjøhus – fishing bunkhouse on the docks; many are now available for tourist accommodation
skerries – offshore archipelago of small rocky islets
skog – forest
skål! – cheers!
slott – castle, palace
snø – snow
spark, sparky – a kicksled that's popular in winter
stabbur – raised storehouse
stasjon – station
Statens Kartverk – State Mapping Agency
stavkirke – stave church
stokkfisk – 'stock fish'; dried cod
storting – parliament

strand – beach
sund – sound, strait
Sverige – Sweden
svømmehall, svømmebad – swimming pool
sykehus – hospital
sykkel – bicycle
sør – south
søyle – column, pillar

teater – theatre
telekort – telephone card
tog – train
togbuss – bus services in Romsdalen and Nordland run by NSB to connect railheads with other popular destinations
torget, torvet – town square
torsk – cod
turistkontor – tourist office
tårn – tower

utleie – hire company, as in *bilutleie* (car hire), *sykkelutleie* (bicycle hire), *kanoutleie* (canoe hire) or *hytteutleie* (hut hire)

vandrerhjem – youth hostel
vann, vatn, vannet, vatnet – lake
vaskeri – laundry
vei, veg – road (often abbreviated to **v** or **vn**)
vest – west
vidde, vidda – plateau
vinmonopolet – 'wine monopoly shop'; government-run shop selling wine and liquor
værelse – room

Zodiac – small inflatable boat powered by outboard engine

øl – beer
ølutsalg – beer sales outlet
øst – east
øvre – upper
øy – island

Date Abbreviations
f. Kr – før Kristi fødsel – BC
e. Kr s – etter Kristi fødsel – AD

LONELY PLANET

ON THE ROAD

Travel Guides explore cities, regions and countries, and supply information on transport, restaurants and accommodation, covering all budgets. They come with reliable, easy-to-use maps, practical advice, cultural and historical facts and a rundown on attractions both on and off the beaten track. There are over 200 titles in this classic series, covering nearly every country in the world.

 Lonely Planet Upgrades extend the shelf life of existing travel guides by detailing any changes that may affect travel in a region since a book has been published. Upgrades can be downloaded for free from **www.lonelyplanet.com/upgrades**

For travellers with more time than money, **Shoestring** guides offer dependable, first-hand information with hundreds of detailed maps, plus insider tips for stretching money as far as possible. Covering entire continents in most cases, the six-volume shoestring guides are known around the world as 'backpackers bibles'.

For the discerning short-term visitor, **Condensed** guides highlight the best a destination has to offer in a full-colour, pocket-sized format designed for quick access. They include everything from top sights and walking tours to opinionated reviews of where to eat, stay, shop and have fun.

CitySync lets travellers use their Palm™ or Visor™ hand-held computers to guide them through a city with handy tips on transport, history, cultural life, major sights, and shopping and entertainment options. It can also quickly search and sort hundreds of reviews of hotels, restaurants and attractions, and pinpoint their location on scrollable street maps. CitySync can be downloaded from **www.citysync.com**

MAPS & ATLASES

Lonely Planet's **City Maps** feature downtown and metropolitan maps, as well as transit routes and walking tours. The maps come complete with an index of streets, a listing of sights and a plastic coat for extra durability.

Road Atlases are an essential navigation tool for serious travellers. Cross-referenced with the guidebooks, they also feature distance and climate charts and a complete site index.

LONELY PLANET

ESSENTIALS

Read This First books help new travellers to hit the road with confidence. These invaluable predeparture guides give step-by-step advice on preparing for a trip, budgeting, arranging a visa, planning an itinerary and staying safe while still getting off the beaten track.

Healthy Travel pocket guides offer a regional rundown on disease hot spots and practical advice on predeparture health measures, staying well on the road and what to do in emergencies. The guides come with a user-friendly design and helpful diagrams and tables.

Lonely Planet's **Phrasebooks** cover the essential words and phrases travellers need when they're strangers in a strange land. They come in a pocket-sized format with colour tabs for quick reference, extensive vocabulary lists, easy-to-follow pronunciation keys and two-way dictionaries.

Miffed by blurry photos of the Taj Mahal? Tired of the classic 'top of the head cut off' shot? **Travel Photography: A Guide to Taking Better Pictures** will help you turn ordinary holiday snaps into striking images and give you the know-how to capture every scene, from frenetic festivals to peaceful beach sunrises.

Lonely Planet's **Travel Journal** is a lightweight but sturdy travel diary for jotting down all those on-the-road observations and significant travel moments. It comes with a handy time-zone wheel, a world map and useful travel information.

Lonely Planet's eKno is an all-in-one communication service developed especially for travellers. It offers low-cost international calls and free email and voicemail so that you can keep in touch while on the road. Check it out on **www.ekno.lonelyplanet.com**

FOOD & RESTAURANT GUIDES

Lonely Planet's **Out to Eat** guides recommend the brightest and best places to eat and drink in top international cities. These gourmet companions are arranged by neighbourhood, packed with dependable maps, garnished with scene-setting photos and served with quirky features.

For people who live to eat, drink and travel, **World Food** guides explore the culinary culture of each country. Entertaining and adventurous, each guide is packed with detail on staples and specialities, regional cuisine and local markets, as well as sumptuous recipes, comprehensive culinary dictionaries and lavish photos good enough to eat.

LONELY PLANET

OUTDOOR GUIDES

For those who believe the best way to see the world is on foot,
Lonely Planet's **Walking Guides** detail everything from family strolls
to difficult treks, with 'when to go and how to do it' advice supple-
mented by reliable maps and essential travel information.

Cycling Guides map a destination's best bike tours, long and short,
in day-by-day detail. They contain all the information a cyclist needs,
including advice on bike maintenance, places to eat and stay, innovative maps with detailed cues to the rides, and elevation charts.

The **Watching Wildlife** series is perfect for travellers who want au-
thoritative information but don't want to tote a heavy field guide.
Packed with advice on where, when and how to view a region's
wildlife, each title features photos of over 300 species and contains
engaging comments on the local flora and fauna.

With underwater colour photos throughout, **Pisces Books** explore
the world's best diving and snorkelling areas. Each book contains listings of diving services and dive resorts, detailed information on
depth, visibility and difficulty of dives, and a roundup of the marine
life you're likely to see through your mask.

LONELY PLANET

OFF THE ROAD

Journeys, the travel literature series written by renowned travel authors, capture the spirit of a place or illuminate a culture with a journalist's attention to detail and a novelist's flair for words. These are tales to soak up while you're actually on the road or dip into as an at-home armchair indulgence.

The range of lavishly illustrated **Pictorial** books is just the ticket for both travellers and dreamers. Off-beat tales and vivid photographs bring the adventure of travel to your doorstep long before the journey begins and long after it is over.

Lonely Planet **Videos** encourage the same independent, tough-minded approach as the guidebooks. Currently airing throughout the world, this award-winning series features innovative footage and an original soundtrack.

Yes, we know, work is tough, so do a little bit of deskside dreaming with the spiral-bound Lonely Planet **Diary** or a Lonely Planet **Wall Calendar**, filled with great photos from around the world.

TRAVELLERS NETWORK

Lonely Planet Online. Lonely Planet's award-winning Web site has insider information on hundreds of destinations, from Amsterdam to Zimbabwe, complete with interactive maps and relevant links. The site also offers the latest travel news, recent reports from travellers on the road, guidebook upgrades, a travel links site, an online book-buying option and a lively travellers bulletin board. It can be viewed at **www.lonelyplanet.com** or AOL keyword: lp.

Planet Talk is a quarterly print newsletter, full of gossip, advice, anecdotes and author articles. It provides an antidote to the being-at-home blues and lets you plan and dream for the next trip. Contact the nearest Lonely Planet office for your free copy.

Comet, the free Lonely Planet newsletter, comes via email once a month. It's loaded with travel news, advice, dispatches from authors, travel competitions and letters from readers. To subscribe, click on the Comet subscription link on the front page of the Web site.

Lonely Planet Guides by Region

Lonely Planet is known worldwide for publishing practical, reliable and no-nonsense travel information in our guides and on our Web site. The Lonely Planet list covers just about every accessible part of the world. Currently there are 16 series: Travel guides, Shoestring guides, Condensed guides, Phrasebooks, Read This First, Healthy Travel, Walking guides, Cycling guides, Watching Wildlife guides, Pisces Diving & Snorkeling guides, City Maps, Road Atlases, Out to Eat, World Food, Journeys travel literature and Pictorials.

AFRICA Africa on a shoestring • Botswana • Cairo • Cairo City Map • Cape Town • Cape Town City Map • East Africa • Egypt • Egyptian Arabic phrasebook • Ethiopia, Eritrea & Djibouti • Ethiopian Amharic phrasebook • The Gambia & Senegal • Healthy Travel Africa • Kenya • Malawi • Morocco • Moroccan Arabic phrasebook • Mozambique • Namibia • Read This First: Africa • South Africa, Lesotho & Swaziland • Southern Africa • Southern Africa Road Atlas • Swahili phrasebook • Tanzania, Zanzibar & Pemba • Trekking in East Africa • Tunisia • Watching Wildlife East Africa • Watching Wildlife Southern Africa • West Africa • World Food Morocco • Zambia • Zimbabwe, Botswana & Namibia
Travel Literature: Mali Blues: Traveling to an African Beat • The Rainbird: A Central African Journey • Songs to an African Sunset: A Zimbabwean Story

AUSTRALIA & THE PACIFIC Aboriginal Australia & the Torres Strait Islands •Auckland • Australia • Australian phrasebook • Australia Road Atlas • Cycling Australia • Cycling New Zealand • Fiji • Fijian phrasebook • Healthy Travel Australia, NZ & the Pacific • Islands of Australia's Great Barrier Reef • Melbourne • Melbourne City Map • Micronesia • New Caledonia • New South Wales • New Zealand • Northern Territory • Outback Australia • Out to Eat – Melbourne • Out to Eat – Sydney • Papua New Guinea • Pidgin phrasebook • Queensland • Rarotonga & the Cook Islands • Samoa • Solomon Islands • South Australia • South Pacific • South Pacific phrasebook • Sydney • Sydney City Map • Sydney Condensed • Tahiti & French Polynesia • Tasmania • Tonga • Tramping in New Zealand • Vanuatu • Victoria • Walking in Australia • Watching Wildlife Australia • Western Australia
Travel Literature: Islands in the Clouds: Travels in the Highlands of New Guinea • Kiwi Tracks: A New Zealand Journey • Sean & David's Long Drive

CENTRAL AMERICA & THE CARIBBEAN Bahamas, Turks & Caicos • Baja California • Belize, Guatemala & Yucatán • Bermuda • Central America on a shoestring • Costa Rica • Costa Rica Spanish phrasebook • Cuba • Cycling Cuba • Dominican Republic & Haiti • Eastern Caribbean • Guatemala • Havana • Healthy Travel Central & South America • Jamaica • Mexico • Mexico City • Panama • Puerto Rico • Read This First: Central & South America • Virgin Islands • World Food Caribbean • World Food Mexico • Yucatán
Travel Literature: Green Dreams: Travels in Central America

EUROPE Amsterdam • Amsterdam City Map • Amsterdam Condensed • Andalucía • Athens • Austria • Baltic States phrasebook • Barcelona • Barcelona City Map • Belgium & Luxembourg • Berlin • Berlin City Map • Britain • British phrasebook • Brussels, Bruges & Antwerp • Brussels City Map • Budapest • Budapest City Map • Canary Islands • Catalunya & the Costa Brava • Central Europe • Central Europe phrasebook • Copenhagen • Corfu & the Ionians • Corsica • Crete • Crete Condensed • Croatia • Cycling Britain • Cycling France • Cyprus • Czech & Slovak Republics • Czech phrasebook • Denmark • Dublin • Dublin City Map • Dublin Condensed • Eastern Europe • Eastern Europe phrasebook • Edinburgh • Edinburgh City Map • England • Estonia, Latvia & Lithuania • Europe on a shoestring • Europe phrasebook • Finland • Florence • Florence City Map • France • Frankfurt City Map • Frankfurt Condensed • French phrasebook • Georgia, Armenia & Azerbaijan • Germany • German phrasebook • Greece • Greek Islands • Greek phrasebook • Hungary • Iceland, Greenland & the Faroe Islands • Ireland • Italian phrasebook • Italy • Kraków • Lisbon • The Loire • London • London City Map • London Condensed • Madrid • Madrid City Map • Malta • Mediterranean Europe • Milan, Turin & Genoa • Moscow • Munich • Netherlands • Normandy • Norway • Out to Eat – London • Out to Eat – Paris • Paris • Paris City Map • Paris Condensed • Poland • Polish phrasebook • Portugal • Portuguese phrasebook • Prague • Prague City Map • Provence & the Côte d'Azur • Read This First: Europe • Rhodes & the Dodecanese • Romania & Moldova • Rome • Rome City Map • Rome Condensed • Russia, Ukraine & Belarus • Russian phrasebook • Scandinavian & Baltic Europe • Scandinavian phrasebook • Scotland • Sicily • Slovenia • South-West France • Spain • Spanish phrasebook • Stockholm • St Petersburg • St Petersburg City Map • Sweden • Switzerland • Tuscany • Ukrainian phrasebook • Venice • Vienna • Wales • Walking in Britain • Walking in France • Walking in Ireland • Walking in Italy • Walking in Scotland • Walking in Spain • Walking in Switzerland • Western Europe • World Food France • World Food Greece • World Food Ireland • World Food Italy • World Food Spain **Travel Literature:** After Yugoslavia • Love and War in the Apennines • The Olive Grove: Travels in Greece • On the Shores of the Mediterranean • Round Ireland in Low Gear • A Small Place in Italy

Lonely Planet Mail Order

Lonely Planet products are distributed worldwide. They are also available by mail order from Lonely Planet, so if you have difficulty finding a title please write to us. North and South American residents should write to 150 Linden St, Oakland, CA 94607, USA; European and African residents should write to 10a Spring Place, London NW5 3BH, UK; and residents of other countries to Locked Bag 1, Footscray, Victoria 3011, Australia.

INDIAN SUBCONTINENT & THE INDIAN OCEAN Bangladesh • Bengali phrasebook • Bhutan • Delhi • Goa • Healthy Travel Asia & India • Hindi & Urdu phrasebook • India • India & Bangladesh City Map • Indian Himalaya • Karakoram Highway • Kathmandu City Map • Kerala • Madagascar • Maldives • Mauritius, Réunion & Seychelles • Mumbai (Bombay) • Nepal • Nepali phrasebook • North India • Pakistan • Rajasthan • Read This First: Asia & India • South India • Sri Lanka • Sri Lanka phrasebook • Tibet • Tibetan phrasebook • Trekking in the Indian Himalaya • Trekking in the Karakoram & Hindukush • Trekking in the Nepal Himalaya • World Food India **Travel Literature:** The Age of Kali: Indian Travels and Encounters • Hello Goodnight: A Life of Goa • In Rajasthan • Maverick in Madagascar • A Season in Heaven: True Tales from the Road to Kathmandu • Shopping for Buddhas • A Short Walk in the Hindu Kush • Slowly Down the Ganges

MIDDLE EAST & CENTRAL ASIA Bahrain, Kuwait & Qatar • Central Asia • Central Asia phrasebook • Dubai • Farsi (Persian) phrasebook • Hebrew phrasebook • Iran • Israel & the Palestinian Territories • Istanbul • Istanbul City Map • Istanbul to Cairo • Istanbul to Kathmandu • Jerusalem • Jerusalem City Map • Jordan • Lebanon • Middle East • Oman & the United Arab Emirates • Syria • Turkey • Turkish phrasebook • World Food Turkey • Yemen **Travel Literature:** Black on Black: Iran Revisited • Breaking Ranks: Turbulent Travels in the Promised Land • The Gates of Damascus • Kingdom of the Film Stars: Journey into Jordan

NORTH AMERICA Alaska • Boston • Boston City Map • Boston Condensed • British Columbia • California & Nevada • California Condensed • Canada • Chicago • Chicago City Map • Chicago Condensed • Florida • Georgia & the Carolinas • Great Lakes • Hawaii • Hiking in Alaska • Hiking in the USA • Honolulu & Oahu City Map • Las Vegas • Los Angeles • Los Angeles City Map • Louisiana & the Deep South • Miami • Miami City Map • Montreal • New England • New Orleans • New Orleans City Map • New York City • New York City City Map • New York City Condensed • New York, New Jersey & Pennsylvania • Oahu • Out to Eat – San Francisco • Pacific Northwest • Rocky Mountains • San Diego & Tijuana • San Francisco • San Francisco City Map • Seattle • Seattle City Map • Southwest • Texas • Toronto • USA • USA phrasebook • Vancouver • Vancouver City Map • Virginia & the Capital Region • Washington, DC • Washington, DC City Map • World Food New Orleans **Travel Literature:** Caught Inside: A Surfer's Year on the California Coast • Drive Thru America

NORTH-EAST ASIA Beijing • Beijing City Map • Cantonese phrasebook • China • Hiking in Japan • Hong Kong & Macau • Hong Kong City Map • Hong Kong Condensed • Japan • Japanese phrasebook • Korea • Korean phrasebook • Kyoto • Mandarin phrasebook • Mongolia • Mongolian phrasebook • Seoul • Shanghai • South-West China • Taiwan • Tokyo • Tokyo Condensed • World Food Hong Kong • World Food Japan **Travel Literature:** In Xanadu: A Quest • Lost Japan

SOUTH AMERICA Argentina, Uruguay & Paraguay • Bolivia • Brazil • Brazilian phrasebook • Buenos Aires • Buenos Aires City Map • Chile & Easter Island • Colombia • Ecuador & the Galapagos Islands • Healthy Travel Central & South America • Latin American Spanish phrasebook • Peru • Quechua phrasebook • Read This First: Central & South America • Rio de Janeiro • Rio de Janeiro City Map • Santiago de Chile • South America on a shoestring • Trekking in the Patagonian Andes • Venezuela **Travel Literature:** Full Circle: A South American Journey

SOUTH-EAST ASIA Bali & Lombok • Bangkok • Bangkok City Map • Burmese phrasebook • Cambodia • Cycling Vietnam, Laos & Cambodia • East Timor phrasebook • Hanoi • Healthy Travel Asia & India • Hill Tribes phrasebook • Ho Chi Minh City (Saigon) • Indonesia • Indonesian phrasebook • Indonesia's Eastern Islands • Java • Lao phrasebook • Laos • Malay phrasebook • Malaysia, Singapore & Brunei • Myanmar (Burma) • Philippines • Pilipino (Tagalog) phrasebook • Read This First: Asia & India • Singapore • Singapore City Map • South-East Asia on a shoestring • South-East Asia phrasebook • Thailand • Thailand's Islands & Beaches • Thailand, Vietnam, Laos & Cambodia Road Atlas • Thai phrasebook • Vietnam • Vietnamese phrasebook • World Food Indonesia • World Food Thailand • World Food Vietnam

ALSO AVAILABLE: Antarctica • The Arctic • The Blue Man: Tales of Travel, Love and Coffee • Brief Encounters: Stories of Love, Sex & Travel • Buddhist Stupas in Asia: The Shape of Perfection • Chasing Rickshaws • The Last Grain Race • Lonely Planet ... On the Edge: Adventurous Escapades from Around the World • Lonely Planet Unpacked • Lonely Planet Unpacked Again • Not the Only Planet: Science Fiction Travel Stories • Ports of Call: A Journey by Sea • Sacred India • Travel Photography: A Guide to Taking Better Pictures • Travel with Children • Tuvalu: Portrait of an Island Nation

LONELY PLANET

You already know that Lonely Planet produces more than this one guidebook, but you might not be aware of the other products we have on this region. Here is a selection of titles that you may want to check out as well:

Scandinavian & Baltic Europe
ISBN 1 86450 156 1
US$21.99 • UK£13.99

Scandinavian phrasebook
ISBN 1 86450 225 8
US$7.99 • UK£4.50

Copenhagen
ISBN 1 86450 203 7
US$14.99 • UK£8.99

Stockholm
ISBN 1 74059 011 2
US$14.99 • UK£8.99

Finland
ISBN 0 86442 649 6
US$19.95 • UK£12.99

Denmark
ISBN 1 74059 075 9
US$17.99 • UK£12.99

Sweden
ISBN 0 86442 721 2
US$17.99 • UK£11.99

Europe on a shoestring
ISBN 1 86450 150 2
US$24.99 • UK£14.99

Read This First: Europe
ISBN 1 86450 136 7
US$14.99 • UK£8.99

**Summer Light:
A Walk across Norway**
ISBN 1 86450 347 5
US$12.99 • UK£6.99

Available wherever books are sold

Index

Text

Note that the letters æ, ø and å fall at the end of the Norwegian alphabet.

Bold indicates maps.

Bold indicates maps.

Boxed Text

MAP LEGEND

CITY ROUTES

Freeway	Freeway
Highway	Primary Road
Road	Secondary Road
Street	Street
Lane	Lane
	On/Off Ramp
	Unsealed Road
	One Way Street
	Pedestrian Street
	Stepped Street
	Tunnel
	Footbridge

REGIONAL ROUTES

	Tollway, Freeway
	Primary Road
	Secondary Road
	Minor Road

BOUNDARIES

	International
	State
	Disputed
	Fortified Wall

HYDROGRAPHY

	River, Creek
	Canal
	Lake
	Dry Lake; Salt Lake
	Spring; Rapids
	Waterfalls

TRANSPORT ROUTES & STATIONS

	Train
	Underground Train
	Metro
	Tramway
	Cable Car, Chairlift
	Ferry
	Walking Trail
	Walking Tour
	Path
	Pier or Jetty

AREA FEATURES

	Building
	Park, Gardens
	Market
	Sports Ground
	Beach
	Cemetery
	Campus
	Plaza

POPULATION SYMBOLS

✪ CAPITAL	National Capital
◉ CAPITAL	State Capital
● CITY	City
● Town	Town
● Village	Village
	Urban Area

MAP SYMBOLS

▪ Place to Stay	▼ Place to Eat	● Point of Interest	
✈ Airport	▲ Camping Area	❶ Information	✚ Police Station
Archaeological Site	Castle of Fort	Internet Cafe	Post Office
Bank	Chalet, Hut	Lookout	Pub, Bar
Bird Sanctuary	Church, Cathedral	Mine	Shopping Centre
Bus Station	Cinema	Monument	Ski Field
Bus Stop	Embassy, Consulate	Museum	Telephone
Cable Car, Funicular	Hospital, Clinic	Pass	Zoo

Note: not all symbols displayed above appear in this book

LONELY PLANET OFFICES

Australia
Locked Bag 1, Footscray, Victoria 3011
☎ 03 8379 8000 fax 03 8379 8111
email: talk2us@lonelyplanet.com.au

USA
150 Linden St, Oakland, CA 94607
☎ 510 893 8555 TOLL FREE: 800 275 8555
fax 510 893 8572
email: info@lonelyplanet.com

UK
10a Spring Place, London NW5 3BH
☎ 020 7428 4800 fax 020 7428 4828
email: go@lonelyplanet.co.uk

France
1 rue du Dahomey, 75011 Paris
☎ 01 55 25 33 00 fax 01 55 25 33 01
email: bip@lonelyplanet.fr
www.lonelyplanet.fr

World Wide Web: www.lonelyplanet.com *or* AOL keyword: lp
Lonely Planet Images: lpi@lonelyplanet.com.au